Third Edition

Adapting Early Childhood Curricula for Children with Special Needs

RUTH E. COOK
Santa Clara University

ANNETTE TESSIER
California State University—Los Angeles

M. DIANE KLEIN
California State University—Los Angeles

Merrill, an imprint of
Macmillan Publishing Company
New York

Maxwell Macmillan Canada
Toronto

Maxwell Macmillan International
New York   Oxford   Singapore   Sydney

Cover photo by Larry Hamill
Editor: Ann Castel
Production Editor: Constantina Geldis
Cover Designer: Cathleen Norz
Production Buyer: Pamela D. Bennett

This book was set in Zapf International by TC Systems, Inc., and was printed and bound by R. R. Donnelley & Sons Company. The cover was printed by New England Book Components.

Macmillan Publishing Company
113 Sylvan Avenue, Englewood Cliffs, NJ 07632

Library of Congress Cataloging-in-Publication Data
Cook, Ruth E.
    Adapting early childhood curricula for children with special needs
/Ruth E. Cook, Annette Tessier, M. Diane Klein.—3rd ed.
      p. cm.
    Includes bibliographical references and index.
    ISBN 0-675-21356-8
    1. Handicapped children—Education (Preschool) 2. Handicapped
children—Education (Preschool)—Curricula. 3. Mainstreaming in
education. I. Tessier, Annette. II. Klein, M. Diane. III. Title.
LC4019.2.C66 1992
371.9'0472—dc20
                                    91-21799
                                      CIP

Printing: 5 6 7 8 9   Year: 5

We dedicate this edition to the following friends and colleagues, who have significantly touched the lives of young children with special needs and their families:

Virginia B. Armbruster, M.A., CCC-Sp
LaVonne Bergstrom, M.D.
Margaret H. Jones, M.D.
Janice M. Kyne, M.A.
Jeanne Mendoza, M.F.C.C., Ph.D.

Foreword

Four years ago, when Ruth Cook and Annette Tessier asked me to write the foreword to the 1987 edition of their book, I concluded that the field was in a transition period and that many changes were in progress. These included the increasing emphasis on early identification and services for young children with problems, the importance of integrated or mainstream experiences for children with disabilities, and the value of parent-professional collaboration.

It is gratifying to find that in 1991 many of these trends have become realities and that educational opportunities for young children with disabling conditions have improved in scope and in quality. Some of these changes have resulted from the passage of legislation at the federal level, with Public Law 99-457 a particularly noteworthy example. This legislation mandates services for children from 3 to 5 years of age who have disabilities. In addition, part H of Public Law 99-457 stimulates program development at the state level by making financial support contingent upon the provision of services for children ages birth to 3 years who have disabilities or are at risk. The legislation also makes specific the mandate for services for a broader age range of children, and it places increased emphasis on parents' input into treatment and intervention planning. Indeed, rather than an Individualized Education Program, the cornerstone of Public Law 99-457 is an Individualized Family Service Plan. Parents are viewed as integral in the planning process and in the delivery of services. Recognition of the need for early services and for services that are family, rather than individual, centered is a major step toward effective programs.

Consistent with the spirit and language of this legislation, it is also fair to say that current planning for services for children with disabilities is based on recognition of the importance of "normalization," of ensuring that individuals with disabilities—young children as well as adults—are provided opportunities to experience life in regular environments, including schools. The principle of normalization is not new, but in recent years we have seen the principle operationalized and implemented in a number of arenas, especially in education. These changes have had a major impact on the scope and the content of schooling, necessitating that we rethink *when* educational services should be provided, *what* should be the content of educational programs, and *where* and *under what conditions* educational services should be delivered.

These changes in our views of the educational needs of young children with disabilities carry powerful implications for practice, and, thus, for the preparation of professionals who work with young children and with their parents. The present edition of *Adapting Early Childhood Curricula for Children with Special Needs* directly addresses these issues. Ruth Cook and Annette Tessier made a real contribution to educational practice in their earlier version of the book, and the work has been enhanced by Diane Klein's substantive contributions to the present edition. Taken as a whole, this is an informative and useful text for teachers and other professionals who work with young children with disabilities.

The content of this edition builds upon the previous book coauthored by Cook and Tessier, but it reflects the changes that have influenced special education practices in recent years. More emphasis is placed on infancy and on the education and intervention needs of infants and their families. Problems are viewed from a developmental perspective so that generic intervention strategies appropriate for all children, as well as specific strategies for facilitating the development of children with special needs, are emphasized.

Discussion of the implications of major legislative mandates on planning and on the delivery of services frames the argument for the need for early services and opportunities for integrated experiences. Strong emphasis is placed on the role of parents and families in planning for young children with special needs. The parent-professional relationship advocated is collaborative, not just cooperative, an important distinction that implies specific skills and attitudes on the part of professionals who work with parents. These topics are discussed in detail, and practical strategies for improving collaborative efforts are provided. Indeed, the new edition as a whole is enriched by many examples or workable and effective approaches to intervention.

The content is also enriched through the increased attention given to the role of communication skills in the development of young children with disabilities and to the impact of communicative competence on children's social experiences. As with other sections of the revised volume, the discussion of communication is embedded in a broader context of personal/social development. Thus, the discussion is not limited to verbal skills, but includes consideration of nonverbal and social aspects of communication as well. Given the limitations of verbal communication so often found in young children with disabilities, these additions are especially useful.

Just as the content of the present volume has been enhanced, so the target audience has been broadened. While earlier editions were aimed primarily at early childhood special educators, the present edition will also be useful for those who work in other capacities with young children who have disabling conditions or are at risk, such as physical and occupational therapists, school administrators, speech/language specialists, psychologists, family counselors, paraprofessionals, and parents. Because the book contains a well-balanced blend of theory and practice, it should provide content of interest to practitioners who represent a variety of disciplinary perspectives.

This foreword would not be complete without a brief personal comment. I have had the good fortune to work with Ruth Cook, Annette Tessier, and Diane Klein and to know them as friends as well as colleagues. They bring a world of experience and understanding to the education and intervention needs of infants and young children at risk for developmental problems. Their insights are evident throughout the book, and are presented with the warmth and empathy that are characteristic of the authors themselves. Their perspective provides a positive direction for the development of programs for young children with special needs.

Barbara K. Keogh
Professor, Special Education,
University of California
at Los Angeles

Preface

This book is written with you, the student of early childhood special education, in mind. Whether you are studying to become a teacher of young children with special needs or are an early interventionist with a related background who wishes to develop greater versatility in your chosen field, we have designed this to be an easy-to-read, interesting, and comprehensive resource for you. It provides extensive use of examples, dialogues, practical illustrations, checksheets, and a focus on the newest and best practices in the field.

When this text was originally published in 1983, the field of early childhood special education was in its formative years. Since that time the field has expanded, and this book has successfully grown with it. Young children with special needs are now enrolled in a variety of settings and are served by professionals and paraprofessionals with diverse backgrounds. Our objective now, as it was in the first two editions, is to present a text that will play a major role in the professional development of early interventionists. The focus is on the skills necessary to assist infants, young children, and their families to meet their special challenges and develop to their fullest potential.

Distinguishing Features

This book has four main strengths that make it a compelling self-learning resource:

1. It emphasizes the importance of understanding the natures of all young children and how they learn. Adapting curricula and intervention approaches for children with special needs works effectively only when professionals build on a strong foundation of understanding of what is common to all young children. On the basis of this necessary foundation, students can begin to consider strategies for meeting the developmental and educational needs of infants and young children who have disabilities or who experience circumstances and conditions that potentially interfere with optimal growth and adjustment.

2. The approach taken in this text also stresses the absolute necessity of understanding young children within the context of the family. Every family is unique and complex, reflecting the many influences of history, culture or ethnicity, economics, and family dynamics (which may include divorce or abuse). Early childhood special educators must focus not on the detailed analysis of these many factors, but on ways of supporting families that will maximize their day-to-day fulfillment as caregivers to their young. As explained in the text, your job in part is to help parents develop a sense of competence in their own abilities to nurture their children regardless of family circumstances. Appreciation of families' roles in the development of children and respect for families' concerns and priorities are critical to effective curriculum design and program development.

3. A significant portion of the text is organized according to traditional developmental domains: social-emotional, motor, communication, and cognitive skills. As an early childhood special education professional, these are the growth areas you will seek to develop in the children entrusted to you. Thus, you must

develop a thorough understanding of each of these complex domains.

4. Finally, you must ultimately understand that all of the growth areas and individual and family background factors must be synthesized into a view of the whole child. As in any other form of synergy, the whole child is much greater than the sum of his or her parts. This holistic view relates directly to the book's emphasis on activity-based and play-based approaches to intervention. You will learn how to integrate goals and objectives for all domains into developmentally appropriate and motivating activities. Throughout, best practices are explained for home, center, or classroom application.

What is new about this third edition? The four points just mentioned suggest the framework and approach that have consistently made this book appealing to readers of two earlier editions. They have been time tested and consistently found to be helpful. However, changes have been made in both style and in substance. The third edition:

- Incorporates the spirit and expectations of Public Law 99-457.
- Takes an ecological view of the child within a family systems approach.
- Provides an interdisciplinary perspective that acknowledges the contributions of a variety of early intervention specialists.
- Demonstrates understanding and appreciation of cultural differences.
- Includes practical techniques for meeting a great variety of societal needs such as those produced by prenatal exposure to drugs, child abuse, and poverty, as well as the need for foster care.
- Broadens the coverage of child needs to include children who are at risk for delay or disability as well as those who have been recognized as having disabilities.
- Updates student-friendly annotated bibliographies, lesson plans, a glossary, descrip-

tions of assessment tools, developmental charts, and a list of early intervention competencies.

Organization

The text opens with a presentation of our philosophy of early childhood special education. It recognizes human likenesses and value differences and discusses our belief in the importance of providing services in the most normalized settings possible. Chapter 2 highlights the historical contributions of the fields of early childhood education and special education. Important features and implications of Public Laws 94-142 and 99-457 are summarized, along with alternative approaches to service delivery.

Chapter 3 presents techniques to involve families in a collaborative partnership with the variety of professionals with whom they must interface. In developing a family-focused approach, students are encouraged to view families from a systems perspective. Special attention is given to the various methods of parent involvement that can accommodate cultural diversity, language differences, and unique family situations.

Issues and methods of infant and child assessment, including both formal and informal methods, are presented in Chapter 4. Students are introduced to team approaches and the importance of ecologically valid assessments. Chapter 5 defines the components of Individualized Education Programs and Individualized Family Service Plans. Strategies for collaborative program and transition planning are outlined. Chapter 6 focuses on curriculum development within a framework of generic instructional strategies. Specific adaptations for young children with special needs provide a point of departure for facilitating integration.

Chapter 7 begins by describing the stages of psychosocial development as a precursor to understanding how to facilitate social skills through the medium of play. Considerable attention is given to helping children who experience particular emotional and behavioral challenges and working with those who have been maltreated and/or exposed prenatally to drugs. After describing typical development of motor skills, Chapter 8 examines atypical motor development. Practical intervention strategies are offered, including handling and positioning guidelines.

Chapters 9 and 10 focus on the development of communication and cognition. The importance of caregiver-child interactions and the role of play in optimal development is recognized throughout. Special attention is devoted to specific strategies for enhancing communication skills in children with severe disabilities, visual impairments, and hearing impairments, as well as children from non-English-speaking families. Unique to this edition is the section devoted to understanding the social and linguistic factors related to children's emergent literacy skills and strategies for encouraging these skills.

The final chapter prepares early childhood special educators to work effectively with paraprofessionals. The potential of paraprofessionals is beginning to receive attention in light of the shortage of trained early intervention specialists. The format and tone of this chapter are somewhat different because we believe that students must learn to be managers of the human resources available to them. If they do not, precious time and skills will be wasted.

Finally, the appendixes offer a wealth of practical information, including developmental guidelines, annotated descriptions of assessment techniques, recommended materials, periodicals, and a list of competencies that we hope will be developed by each and every reader.

Acknowledgments

We present this book with gratitude to the hundreds of children and parents who have been *our* teachers. From them we have learned to value and nurture the uniqueness of each child regardless of background, skills, or abilities. We believe we have found a way to meet children's unique needs in whatever setting they appear. It has been our purpose to convey the essence of this process to anyone interested in working with young children.

We wish to thank sincerely the many colleagues and friends who assisted and supported us in the development of the first edition and in the redevelopment of the second and third editions, including Maurine Ballard-Campbell, Sacramento State University; Linda Brekken, California State Department of Education; and Phyllis Povell of Long Island University. We are especially grateful for the conscientious efforts of those who so kindly read and commented on the prospectus and rough drafts of the present edition: Lawrence J. Johnson, University of Illinois at Urbana-Champaign; Lise Fox, Florida State University; Evelyn C. Lynch, Moorhead State University; David W. Anderson, Lock Haven University of Pennsylvania; Tandra Tyler-Wood, West Georgia College; Melanie B. Jephson, Stephen F. Austin State University; Barbara Lowenthal, Northeastern Illinois University; Maureen R. Bertolone, Bellarmine College; Helmi C. Owens, Pacific Lutheran University; and Eleanor B. Wright, University of North Carolina at Wilmington.

Special appreciation goes to Brigitte Ammons, former Coordinator and Head Teacher of Centro de Niños y Padres, who taught us a great deal by virtue of her example as one who could optimize children's development in the context of a culturally diverse, family-centered program. We also thank Brigitte for providing us with many of the photographs found throughout the text.

There are many people who enrich and enhance one's personal and professional life along the way. We are grateful to be blessed with such a wonderful mentor and friend in the person of Dr. Barbara Keogh, who watched over us in our studies at the University of California at Los Angeles. We are honored to once again include a foreword by Dr. Keogh, and we wish her well in her richly deserved retirement.

Personal appreciation is extended by Annette to some other very special people, including Lisbeth Vincent, Carole Cole, Dee and Bro Park, Ruth Westphal, Linda Laisure, Eleanor Napier, and Dottie Tison, for their continuous support and encouragement. Diane expresses her gratitude to Pat Huffman for sharing her insight into the intricacies of effectively serving families of high-risk infants. Ruth extends appreciation to Dean Jo Ann Vasquez from Santa Clara University and Peggy and Ray Ellis for their continued support and encouragement.

Throughout this project, the personal support of those with whom we live and work has been invaluable. After all, it was the close working relationship between Ruth Cook and Virginia Armbruster that brought the first edition to fruition. Virginia's deep love of children and thoughtful wisdom continue to permeate the pages of the text even though her official authorship capacity has been retired.

Deep appreciation is extended to the parents, children, and outstanding staff of Centro de Niños y Padres, the Southern Illinois University Early Childhood Center, and the Mount Saint Mary's College Child Development Center, whose inspiration is a source of strength.

Very special thanks go to Erin Klein and Christopher and Kimberly Cook, without whose own being our understandings of child growth and development would have been superficial, at best. Sincere gratitude goes to Curtis Cook and Marvin Klein, whose patience, tolerance, and editorial skills over the years made this project possible.

The editors and staff at Merrill, an imprint of Macmillan Publishing Company, have been most pleasant to work with and have managed to keep us on target. Particular praise and gratitude go to our editor, Ann Castel, whose patience and encouragement have been invaluable throughout the acquisition and development of this manuscript. Finally, we offer our thanks to Ann Mohan and Laura Cleveland for their conscientious efforts and expertise throughout production.

Ruth E. Cook
Annette Tessier
M. Diane Klein

Contents

Chapter 1

Introduction

Key Points

▶ Programs for infants and toddlers with special needs must be based on the same principles and strategies that are considered best practices for *all* young children.

▶ The effective early childhood special educator must first understand how children learn.

▶ There are compelling ethical, legal, and educational reasons for including young children with special needs in regular early education programs.

▶ The current focus in early childhood special education is not whether young children with special needs can be served in mainstreamed environments, but how integrated programs can be designed most effectively.

▶ All early intervention goals are best achieved through collaborative partnerships with parents.

Key Topics

▶ Text philosophy.

▶ Including children with special needs in regular early education programs.

▶ Programmatic arrangements that facilitate integration.

▶ Special concerns of parents.

▶ Successful inclusion of children with special needs.

From the mother of a 5-year-old child with special needs.

I have come to accept that my daughter will not be quite like everybody else when she grows up, but then who of us is? We are all unique individuals, and we should appreciate our differences rather than scorn them. We all have our strengths and weaknesses, and how many of us, even without disabilities, ever realize our full human potential?

Lora Jerugim

Helping children to realize their full human potential: This is our challenge. By recognizing the human similarities in each of us and by positively valuing differences, parents and educators together can provide each child with the opportunity to develop his or her unique strengths. For children who appear to have developmental disabilities or characteristics that interfere with normal growth and learning, the stage must be prepared more thoughtfully. Parents, educators, and other community members must work together to create a nurturing environment sensitive to, but not solicitous of, children's special needs.

Many aspects of mental and physical development seem to "just happen" to most children. They are, however, the result of interaction between innate capacities and appropriate environmental experiences. With most children, comparatively little deliberate effort has to be made to synchronize capacities and experiences. Most have a repertoire of skills and interests that motivates them to explore, experiment, and therefore learn. However, children with special needs may not be able to learn spontaneously from the play experiences they naturally encounter. Educators must carefully adapt materials, equipment, space, instructions, and expectations to provide environmental experiences conducive to learning.

Bijou (1977) concisely captured the basic aim of all early childhood education: "Such a general goal would be the maximization of development of each child in the context of his or her circumstance of living" (p. 13). It is toward this goal that the theory, lessons, and adaptations suggested in this book are focused. Guidelines for applying developmentally appropriate practices within an intervention-oriented context are offered (Safford, 1989). Suggestions are given for adapting strategies to accommodate individual styles of learning. The intent is to identify ways and means to make it possible for children with special needs to be educated appropriately in regular early childhood programs with "typical" peers. However, these same adaptations are useful to special educators in any environment.

PHILOSOPHY OF THIS TEXT

It is important to understand that the field of early childhood special education is, in many ways, in its infancy. There have been many approaches and underlying philosophies for early intervention, ranging from highly structured behavioral approaches that emphasize preparation for the next environment and academic readiness to child-centered developmental approaches that emphasize exploration and the development of self-esteem. Some have espoused more eclectic approaches without a clear theoretical framework or philosophical basis.

The philosophy of this text emphasizes that the goal of early intervention is to optimize each child's learning potential and daily well-being, as well as to increase opportunities for the child to function effectively in the community. We believe this is best accomplished by facilitating the child's underlying developmental processes by encouraging the child's active and dynamic interactions with the world around him or her, particularly the social world. Perhaps the term

that best reflects this orientation is **transactional.** It is through the child's active and successful transactions with the environment that optimal growth and development can best be achieved.

To achieve this end, early interventionists must first have a thorough understanding of how children learn. Programs for infants and young children with special needs must be based on the principles and best practices that are important for *all* children.

There are many tools and strategies available to assist the early interventionist. This text describes the basic principles of how children learn, as well as specific teaching strategies. It also demonstrates applications of these principles and strategies to meet the needs of a wide range of children within a mainstreamed environment.

WHY INCLUDE CHILDREN WITH SPECIAL NEEDS IN REGULAR EARLY EDUCATION PROGRAMS?

Educational literature is replete with convincing arguments in favor of educating children with disabilities and nondisabled children in the same environment. Even today, the most often cited reasons for the integration of early intervention programs include the three arguments advanced by Bricker (1978): social-ethical, legal-legislative, and psychological-educational.

1. Social-ethical arguments seek to discourage a negative view of children with disabilities. This demeaning view is perpetuated by isolating such children. Integration contributes to altering societal perceptions; at the same time educational resources are used more efficiently.

2. Legal-legislative arguments evolve from the recent court decisions and legislative acts that mandate that children with special needs are to be educated in the most "normal" appropriate setting.

3. Psychological-educational arguments consider the need for children to interact with a progressively more demanding environment. An integrated program is thought to be more characteristic of such an environment. Studies suggest that learning through imitation occurs when suitable models are available and activities are arranged to elicit imitative behavior. Integrated intervention programs have been successful when carefully planned and evaluated.

Is Mainstreaming Appropriate for All Children with Special Needs?

Terms such as **mainstreaming, integration,** and **least restrictive environment** are often used interchangeably and seldom are well defined. However, Odom and Speltz (1983) differentiated between the terms **mainstreamed** and **integrated.** They described mainstreamed preschools as those in which children with disabilities are placed in programs designed primarily for nondisabled children, who constitute at least 50% or more of the enrollment. Integrated early education programs are designed primarily for children with disabilities, with nondisabled children making up less than 50% of the enrollment. Nevertheless, in each situation, all the children are being educated in the same environment. Throughout this text, the terms *mainstreaming* and *integration* will both refer to the general practice of including normally developing children and children with special needs in the same environment.

The term *mainstreaming* developed as a result of legislation mandating that children be educated in the least restrictive environment, but some confusion has followed. Believing that the least restrictive environment is automatically a mainstreamed one, some educators quickly returned special education students to the regular classroom. Negative feelings arose from an apparent disregard for the unique needs of the children or for proper preparation of their environ-

ment. A major purpose of this text is to help prepare early interventionists to successfully develop the most natural or least restrictive environments for *all* children.

Least restrictive environments are not limited to public schools. They can include a variety of community settings such as Head Start centers, state and local preschools, private day care centers, and campus child care centers. However, traditional early childhood settings may not be able to serve the needs of *all* young children with special needs. Some young children with special developmental needs will require very specialized intervention early in life in order to accommodate their medical needs or maximize development of their potential. It is well understood that the amount or kind of contact with typical peers appropriate for any given child must be determined individually. Only through careful study and analysis of each child and the available educational alternatives can the most appropriate placement be determined.

The Early Years: The Best Time to Integrate Children with Special Needs

Today it is not unusual to find children with special needs enrolled in regular early education classrooms. Many teachers welcome children with special needs and try to provide worthwhile experiences even with limited resources. However, it is also not unusual to find that children with disabilities are included only through the untiring efforts of parents and other child advocates. Sometimes a mother has had to accompany her child to the preschool and serve as an aide in order for the child to be accepted. Only recently have educators begun to consider the regular preschool classroom as an appropriate placement alternative. The 1972 mandate requiring Head Start to enroll children with disabilities certainly gave the proponents of mainstreaming a chance to demonstrate the wisdom of their beliefs.

Although systematic research into the effectiveness of integrating or mainstreaming young children with special needs is still in its infancy, it is developing rapidly. Researchers tend to agree that simply placing children with disabilities in the same educational settings with nondisabled children does not accomplish all the goals of mainstreaming (Cooke, Ruskus, Apolloni, & Peck, 1981, p. 73; McLean & Hanline, 1990). However, studies suggest that it is possible to structure interactions so that children with special needs acquire more competent behaviors (Vaughn, 1985). Research also indicates that normally developing young children involved in mainstreamed programs tend to make expected developmental progress (Bricker, Bruder, & Bailey, 1982; Odom, Deklyen, & Jenkins, 1984).

Perhaps the single most significant achievement in the field of early childhood education in the decade of the 1980s has been the repeated demonstration that mainstreamed programs can be implemented effectively. . . . The contemporary issue is clearly not whether early childhood mainsteaming is feasible and should be encouraged, but rather how one can design programs to maximize its effectiveness. (Guralnick, 1990, p. 3)

The Optimal Early Years

It is easy to speculate on the factors that may interact to make the early years optimal ones for mainstreaming children with disabilities. First, most early education programs expect children to mature at varying rates during these years of enhanced growth and development. Differences in skills are expected and accommodated within the curriculum. The range of so-called "normalcy" in preschools is much broader than that usually found in elementary school classrooms.

Early children educators also tend to focus on the *process* more than the product of learning. They are busy setting up centers to allow for sensory exploration rather than grading spelling papers or preparing the next day's language test.

In addition, the methods and materials usually found in early education centers are conducive to the development of all young children. Exploration, manipulation, expression, sharing, and active involvement provide easy opportunities for educators to structure and reinforce meaningful interaction between children with disabilities and those without.

Anyone who has worked with young children is readily aware of their natural abilities to accept and even appreciate individual differences. Children respond to one another without making judgments and comparisons. Spontaneous friendships abound, with little in the way of ongoing expectations. When differences are observed, questions reflect a natural curiosity. If answered in genuine, thoughtful ways, children accommodate and accept those who are different.

The Hazards of Labels

Children with presumed developmental delays or differences traditionally have been given labels such as mentally retarded, emotionally disturbed, learning disabled, or at risk for academic failure. Advocates argue that labels lead to efficiency of "treatment" and are often required for financial reimbursement for services. But most who make recommendations for young children try to avoid attaching labels, because they realize how tenuous the diagnostic results for children are prior to school age. As Keogh and Daley (1983) stated,

It is clear that the process of early identification of children at-risk is complex. Yet, we are convinced that the goal of effective early identification is important and achievable. We suggest, however, that this goal will be reached only when we think of early identification as a part of a full program of services, not just as a test or assessment instrument. (p. 15)

Yes, educators do question the practice of early assessment and labeling of young children. Services must be based on the obvious and changing individual needs of children, not on static and narrowly defined labels. There is a valid and longstanding concern that labels may bias the behavior of others toward those who are labeled, negatively affecting self-esteem. Nor can labeling be defended as an aid to program development. Siegel and Spradlin (1978) pointed out that "the instructional tasks seem to be the same, regardless of whether the child is labeled autistic, brain damaged, retarded or congenitally aphasic" (p. 378).

Because of the obvious dangers involved in labeling, the format of this book has avoided the traditional categorical approach. Although several terms are used throughout the book (for example, *special needs*, *developmentally delayed*, *slow* and *visually*, *physically*, or *hearing impaired*), their use does not suggest that labeling should occur. These terms are used for clarity of communication, not as diagnostic labels.

EARLY INTERVENTION SPECIALISTS: THEIR ROLE IN THE INTEGRATION OF CHILDREN WITH SPECIAL NEEDS

Professionals who specialize in early childhood education and early childhood special education will play the most extensive role in the integration of young children with special needs. "The ability and attitude of the teacher appear to be *the* most important factors in the success of an integrated program" (Wynne, Ulfelder, & Dakof, 1975, p. 75). It is the teacher who must structure the environment, adapt the materials, determine the child's most profitable mode of learning, initiate the desired responses, and reinforce those that should be encouraged. Research to date suggests that systematic intervention efforts guided by the teacher are necessary in order to promote positive results when mainstreaming occurs (Madden & Slavin, 1983; Wang & Birch, 1984).

To fulfill such a multifaceted role teachers are expected to develop competencies characteristic of both the early childhood educator and the special educator. Fortunately, the skills needed are basically the same as those necessary to work with all young children. However, there are certain areas in which added emphasis or expertise is desirable. Safford (1989) and Fallen and Umansky (1985) have listed several skill areas. These areas and others often found in the literature are listed in Table 1–1. A detailed list of instructional competencies for early childhood special educators is included in Appendix D.

CO-LOCATED PROGRAMS: A PROGRAMMATIC ARRANGEMENT THAT FACILITATES INTEGRATION

To facilitate integration of children with special needs, a decision must be made as to the nature of the children the program will be serving. It is necessary not only to plan the physical environment, but also to determine what delivery system will be most effective.

One programmatic arrangement that facilitates integration of children with special needs and typical children in age-appropriate environ-

ments is known as **co-located programs.** In this arrangement, a classroom of children with special needs is located on the same site as a regular early education or child care program. This arrangement provides for a continuum of integration opportunities. It allows service provision to children with mild to severe disabilities and typical children on the same site. Children with mild disabilities may spend most of the day with groups of typical peers as part of a mainstream program and receive support services from visiting specialists or from the special class teacher during part of the day or week. Children with more severe disabilities, on the other hand, may spend most of their day in the special class and interact with nondisabled peers during outside play time or special events.

This approach also allows for **reverse mainstreaming,** when nondisbled children are integrated for part of their day or week in the special class. Finally, the arrangement makes **dual enrollment** possible. For example, a child may attend a special early intervention program during the morning and a typical child care program in the afternoon. These arrangements allow for the flexibility necessary to meet the

---

Table 1–1   Necessary competencies for early childhood special educators

1. Knowledge of normal and atypical processes and stages in children's development.
2. Ability to recognize symptoms of specific disabilities.
3. Skill in observing and recording behavior of individual children.
4. Ability to employ informal procedures in diagnosing developmental problems.
5. Ability to prepare long-term goals and short-term objectives that are developmentally appropriate and consistent with each child's style of learning and observed strengths and weaknesses.
6. Ability to read children's cues and utilize this information in structuring an environment responsive to individual needs and conducive to maximization of children's active involvement.
7. Ability to develop a trusting relationship with children through effective communication.
8. Skill in techniques that enhance positive interactions among children of varying levels of ability as well as cultural and ethnic backgrounds.
9. Ability to demonstrate knowledge of and respect for cultural differences.
10. Understanding and belief in the philosophy that underlies the curriculum model in use.
11. Ability to listen reflectively to parents and to develop a viable program of family involvement that demonstrates understanding of family systems theory.
12. Skill in recruiting, training, and working cooperatively with paraprofessionals.
13. Familiarity with and ability to work effectively as a team member with a wide variety of professionals.
14. Ability to recognize one's own limitations and to seek assistance when appropriate.

needs of individual children and allow the maximum amount of time possible within the least restrictive environment.

Co-located programs also provide for flexibility in training and placing staff. Instead of requiring that every staff member who works in any way with a child with special needs be highly trained in all aspects of early intervention, a **transdisciplinary team** approach to service provision is possible. Campbell (1987) described a transdisciplinary team as a group of professionals and family members who work together to assess, plan, and provide early intervention services to a young child and his or her family.

These team members train each other in their areas of expertise and share responsibility for implementation of the early intervention services. For example, it is not uncommon for an early education program to have a few children with language delays enrolled. Instead of isolating these children for traditional speech therapy, the specialist can instruct and model techniques that encourage and respond to the children's communication attempts during normal daily activities. Whenever more than one early interventionist is involved, communication among specialists and with parents is essential and must be well planned. Appendix D outlines some of the competencies required of all early intervention specialists, regardless of discipline.

Conditions Necessary for Effective Mainstreaming

One consistent theme runs throughout studies that have evaluated the effectiveness of efforts to teach children with special needs and normally developing children in the same classroom or center. Even though research efforts have been limited, specialists agree that just putting children together physically does not create the desired results. Or, as Rogers-Warren (1982) stated:

Enrolling handicapped and nonhandicapped children in the same classroom may be a necessary, but not entirely sufficient, method of increasing social interaction skills. Other socially based interventions may be needed to gain the maximum beneficial effects of these arrangements. Pairing children with different skills by way of teacher prompts and praise, prearranging seating placements, and setting rules that require bringing a friend to engage in attractive activities may be useful. Specific training to imitate peers or to interact with them may also be needed. (p. 23)

The following sections elaborate on some of the conditions necessary for effective mainstreaming.

Systematic Planning

Well-planned, structured practices that facilitate cross-peer interaction appear necessary to optimal development in a mainstreamed program. Directly instructing children with disabilities to imitate nondisabled peers has shown promising results (Apolloni, Cooke, & Cooke, 1977; Vaughn, 1985). Positive results occur when interventionists set up socially integrative play situations and then systematically reinforce both children with special needs and typical children for playing together cooperatively. (Techniques to facilitate cooperative behavior are discussed in Chapter 7.)

Ratio of Children with Special Needs to Typical Children. Experience has not specified a certain number of children that should be integrated into any one classroom. However, specialists find that when only one or two are included isolation is more likely to occur. Several years ago, Guralnick (1981) suggested that there be an absolute maximum of 33% children with special needs in regular classrooms. In the case of integration or reverse mainstreaming, he also suggested a minimum of 33% nondisabled children be the norm. However, more recently, Guralnick (1990) had the following to say:

We should also not be rigid about the issue of ratios of handicapped to nonhandicapped children or the absolute number of handicapped children in a program, although the availability of other handicapped children as peers and models for certain groups of children with disabilities may turn out to be advisable. Equal proportions of handicapped and nonhandicapped children do not typically occur due to the nature of community programs. However, it is the case that some excellent programs result when previously existing specialized programs for handicapped children merge with typical nursery schools, yielding programs containing approximately equivalent numbers of handicapped and nonhandicapped children. (p. 5)

Decisions regarding how many must be based on the needs of the children being integrated, characteristics of the nondisabled children, the attitudes and training of the staff, support services available, and the ratio of adults to children.

Developmental Levels Rather Than Age. Consideration should be given to integrating children with special needs with normally developing children of a lower chronological age to decrease the developmental differences (Peck, Apolloni, Cooke, & Raver, 1978; Guralnick, 1981; Strain, 1984). Children more readily imitate those who are only slightly more advanced. To group children according to developmental levels rather than ages, specialists must observe and assess individual differences carefully. (These important skills are discussed in Chapter 4.)

Individualized, Structured Learning Experiences. Tawney (1981) credited Dunn (1968) with correct identification of the key element in any program of early education: "individualized, structured learning experiences" (p. 29). Such an approach is natural to educators with a developmental orientation, allowing them to identify each child's strengths and weaknesses. Children are not expected to move as a group from level to level. Instead, a child's weakness becomes the basis for a teaching objective. The child's strengths are incorporated into instructional strategies matched to specific objectives. Progress is then determined by individual rather than group accomplishment. Within small

groups, adaptations are made in materials used, questions posed, and directions given. The same basic task can be presented with modifications for a number of children during the same lesson period. (Examples of such individualized instruction are found throughout this book.)

Partnership with Parents

Educators have moved from a position of allowing only limited parent involvement to encouraging extensive participation of parents in educational planning for their children. One of the major elements of a high-quality early childhood center is significant involvement of families. Interventionists are urged to recognize that parents are the primary advocates for their children. No one else knows their children as well or, hopefully, spends as much time with them. Parents can become extended hands of the interventionist, increasing the opportunities for individualization. (Techniques for encouraging meaningful parent involvement are discussed thoroughly in Chapter 3.)

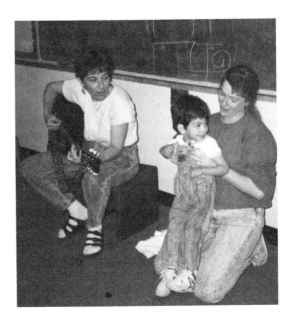

Interagency Collaboration

Educational programs that serve young children with special needs can provide all the services that children and families require only through collaboration with other programs and agencies. **Community networking** describes the efforts involved in coordinating services among agencies. Community networking can reduce fragmentation, avoid duplication, and help families gain easy access to needed services.

In order to develop efficient and effective interagency collaboration, programs must involve a variety of networking activities. Networking programs vary because of differences in resources or community needs and geographic and cultural factors. Early education specialists need to develop a clear understanding of the needs of each child and family and a thorough knowledge of the available resources. A personal evaluation of programs and personnel fosters a useful match between needs and services. Attention should be paid to the quality, breadth, and cost of services. Families will need help in complying with referral procedures and support during waiting periods. Ideally, networking efforts will result in formal or informal interagency agreements that extend services to meet the special needs of children and their families.

Collaboration also includes involvement in activities that create awareness of the early education program and its contribution to the process of networking. Open houses, personal contacts, media coverage, brochures, presentations at meetings, and participation on community advisory councils develop public awareness. Even though networking activities will change with time, they remain essential to the delivery of a successful early intervention program.

SPECIAL CONCERNS OF PARENTS

A parent of a nondisabled child might worry that the child will imitate the behavior of those with special needs. Although most imitated behavior is constructive, some children may briefly imitate delayed behavior. This imitation disappears quickly unless reinforced by adults. Some parents may need reassurance and help in ignoring such behavior so that it may naturally disappear.

Parents of children with special needs may fear that their children will be the object of rejection or ridicule. These parents are reassured when they discover the many similarities among all children and realize that children's questions come from their sense of curiosity rather than from an intent to harm. Young children also tease less about visible disabilities, and more about personal, social, or emotional issues, for a short time only. They might say, "Only girls can come in here," or, "I only want to play with Billy, not you." Such remarks probably have nothing to do with a disabling condition. Even so, children who tease must be helped to know that words do hurt people's feelings. At the same time, the child being teased must be assisted in standing up for his or her rights.

Parents with such typical concerns should be encouraged to visit the program and helped to observe carefully. There they will find that children are much more alike than they are different. They all ask direct, honest questions and expect direct, honest answers.

SUGGESTIONS FOR SUCCESSFUL INTEGRATION OF CHILDREN WITH SPECIAL NEEDS

The following suggestions are based on the belief that teachers play the central role in the development of programs to successfully integrate children with special needs. The tone of the classroom is set through the teacher's attitudes and actions. Therefore teachers are strongly encouraged to acknowledge their own fears and apprehensions before initiating a mainstreamed program. It helps to remember that every child is more like others than different from them. Understanding that all children can have adjustment problems because of their stage of development makes it possible for teachers to recognize that some deviant behavior is just plain normal. Learning something about each specific disability will alleviate many fears and make the teacher feel less helpless. The following suggestions are general and can be considered only in light of each specific situation:

1. *Meet with the child's parents before including him or her in the program.* Besides seeking vital parental support, you can explore special interests, specific problems, and solutions. Unpleasant times may be avoided through preventative advice. Some teachers find it helpful to have the child visit the classroom either as a guest for a short time during the day or after the other children have departed. Arranging such a visit before a regular day of enrollment relieves the fears of many children.

2. *After the brief visit just described, phase children in slowly.* A parent may need to be present in the beginning. Adding only one child with special needs at a time will allow you the opportunity to give as much individual attention as necessary.

3. *Be positive.* Focus on the attitudes and behaviors you wish to see in children. Be what you want to see expressed.

4. *Be realistic.* Do not expect too much or too little. Go slowly. Get to know the child well. By thoroughly understanding the child's educational strengths and weaknesses, you can be realistic.

5. *Do not be afraid to be structured.* Young children need clear, firm guidelines for behavior. Identify specific safety rules. Tell and show the children what to do from the first day when safety and cleanliness are involved.

6. *Develop guidelines for classroom behavior* with *the children whenever possible.* Keep the rules simple and few in number. Do not expect the child with special needs to understand and follow all rules immediately. Tell other children that they must help the new child learn by showing him or her how to behave.

7. *Focus on each child's strengths.* Each child does have strengths. By pointing these out, you will help children realize their own strengths as well as those of others.

8. *Avoid negative expectations.* Remember, if you think Johnny will misbehave, the chances are that he *will* misbehave.

9. *Respect each child.* Show your respect by listening thoughtfully to what each one says. Encourage the children to suggest ideas, help solve problems, and take care of the things in the room.

10. *Avoid doing for children what they can do for themselves.* Try not to be overly solicitous if help is needed. Provide what is necessary in a matter-of-fact way. Be alert to opportunities to withdraw assistance as soon as possible.

11. *Express enthusiasm and pleasure as each milestone (no matter how small) is achieved.* Be genuine. Do not exaggerate.

12. *Be honest in dealing with children's questions.* Give short, truthful answers. Avoid making a big production about introducing the child or explaining his or her differences. Remember, children are more alike than different. To the child who asks, "Why does Susie talk so funny?" you can reply, "Susie had an operation so that she can learn to talk just like you. Perhaps you will be able to help her make new words while you are playing with the puppets today."

13. *Give all parents support and encouragement.* They will need it. They especially want to be kept informed of their child's progress. Be positive and encourage them to participate as much as possible.

14. *Most of all, do not expect too much of yourself or of the situation.* Progress takes time. Innovation takes courage.

The next chapter will review the history of early childhood education and discuss models for accommodating unique needs. It will also discuss the impact of litigation and legislation on the field and will introduce the key features of Public Laws 94-142 and 99-457.

Summary

Young children with developmental lags or special needs require individualized educational experiences to promote attainment of their unique potential. Within early education programs, this involves sensitive adaptation of curriculum, materials, space, instruction, and adult expectations to stimulate a nurturing environment.

The question of how to provide learning opportunities best for young children with special needs has sparked controversy and differing philosophies among educators for generations. Currently the scales are tipped in favor of integrating young children with special needs with normally developing children within the same center. There are educational advantages that make integration or mainstreaming especially workable for most young children with special needs.

In an integrated center or classroom, children serve as role models to stimulate developmental imitation. Imitative learning is especially strengthened when three or more children with special needs are grouped with normally functioning children who may be slightly younger. Matching children by developmental levels rather than ages appears to be showing positive results.

During the early years, the educational focus is more on the processes of exploration, manipulation, expression, sharing, and active involvement than on the content or products of learning. Such processes, when modified for the child with special needs, enhance growth and development within the context of the regular preschool experience.

The early placement of children with special needs into the educational mainstream carries certain cautions and challenges that are not commonly encountered in preschools without children with disabilities. Diagnostic labels, which categorize the type of disability, may accentuate the effects of the disability (leading to self-fulfilling prophecies) rather than help the search for appropriate intervention strategies.

The ability and attitude of the educator are key factors in successful mainstreaming. Knowledge of how to individualize instruction within a regular curriculum becomes a requisite skill. The ability to individualize instruction is built on a series of skills beginning with an understanding of normal and atypical stages of child development. These skills range from recording observed behaviors to preparing appropriate developmental goals and objectives; to task analyzing and sequencing lessons; to working directly with parents, paraprofessionals, specialists, and community agencies.

Mainstreaming is not the only, and at times not the best, alternative for educating young children with special needs. The value of early integration of children with special needs and normally developing children achieved national importance with the passage of Public Law 94-142. This law mandated that children with special needs be placed in the *least restrictive environment* appropriate to their needs. Over time, the extent of federal funding of preschool special education may be questionable because of shifts in political ideologies and governmental needs. Nevertheless, even if publicly supported education of young children with special needs is severely cut, the spirit (if not the mechanism) for this integration into regular programs remains a viable educational ideal.

References

Apolloni, T., Cooke, S., & Cooke, T. (1977). Establishing a normal peer as behavior model for developmentally delayed toddlers. *Perceptual and Motor Skills, 44,* 231–241.

Bijou, S. W. (1977). Practical implications of an interaction model of child development. *Exceptional Children, 44,* 6–14.

Bricker, D. D. (1978). A rationale for the integration of

handicapped and nonhandicapped preschool children. In M. J. Guralnick (Ed.), *Early intervention and the integration of handicapped and nonhandicapped children*. Baltimore: University Park Press.

Bricker, D. D., Bruder, M. B., & Bailey, E. (1982). Developmental integration of preschool children. *Analysis and Intervention in Developmental Disabilities*, 2, 207–222.

Campbell, P. (1987). *Clarification of transdisciplinary team*. Sacramento, CA: State Department of Education.

Cooke, T., Ruskus, J., Apolloni, T., & Peck, C. (1981). Handicapped preschool children in the mainstream: Background, outcomes, and clinical suggestions. *Topics in Early Childhood Special Education*, 1, 73–83.

Dunn, L. M. (1968). Special education for the mildly retarded—Is much of it justifiable? *Exceptional Children*, 35, 371–379.

Fallen, N. H., & Umansky, W. (1985). *Young children with special needs*. Columbus, OH: Charles E. Merrill.

Guralnick, M. J. (1981). Programmatic factors affecting child-child social interactions in mainstreamed preschool programs. *Exceptional Education Quarterly*, 1(4), 71–91.

Guralnick, M. J. (1990). Early childhood mainstreaming. *Topics in Early Childhood Special Education*, 10(2), 1–17.

Jerugim, L. (1982). A personal perspective on raising a child with developmental problems. (Unpublished paper).

Keogh, B. K., & Daley, S. E. (1983). Early identification: One component of comprehensive services for at-risk children. *Topics in Early Childhood Special Education*, 3(3), 7–16.

Madden, N. A., & Slavin, R. E. (1983). Mainstreaming students with mild handicaps: Academic and social outcomes. *Review of Educational Research*, 53, 519–569.

McLean, M., & Hanline, M. F. (1990). Providing early intervention services in integrated environments: Challenges and opportunities for the future. *Topics in Early Childhood Special Education*, 10(2), 62–77.

Odom, S. L., Deklyen, M., & Jenkins, J. R. (1984). Integrating handicapped and nonhandicapped preschoolers: Developmental impact on nonhandicapped children. *Exceptional Children*, 51, 41–48.

Odom, S. L., & Speltz, M. L. (1983). Program variations in preschools for handicapped and nonhandicapped children: Mainstreamed vs. integrated special education. *Analysis and Intervention in Developmental Disabilities*, 3, 89–104.

Peck, C., Apolloni, T., Cooke, T., & Raver, S. (1978). Teaching retarded preschoolers to imitate the free play behavior of nonretarded classmates: Trained and generalized effects. *The Journal of Special Education*, 12, 195–207.

Rogers-Warren, A. K. (1982). Behavioral ecology in classrooms for young, handicapped children. *Topics in Early Childhood Special Education*, 2(1), 21–32.

Safford, P. L. (1989). *Integrated teaching in early childhood*. New York: Longman.

Siegel, G. M., & Spradlin, J. E. (1978). Programming for language and communication therapy, In R. L. Schiefelbusch (Ed.), *Language intervention strategies*, Baltimore: University Park Press.

Strain, P. S. (1984). Social behavior patterns of nonhandicapped and nonhandicapped-developmentally disabled friend pairs in mainstreamed preschools. *Analysis and Intervention in Developmental Disabilities*, 4(1) 15–28.

Tawney, J. W. (1981). A cautious view of mainstreaming in early education. *Topics in Early Childhood Special Education*, 1, 25–36.

Vaughn, S. R. (1985). Facilitating the interpersonal development of young handicapped children. *Journal of the Division for Early Childhood*, 9, 170–174.

Wang, M. C., & Birch, J. W. (1984). Effective special education in regular classes. *Exceptional Children*, 50, 391–398.

Wynne, S., Ulfelder, L., & Dakof, T. (1975). *Mainstreaming and early childhood education for handicapped children: Review and implications of research*. Washington, DC: Division of Innovation and Development, Bureau of Education for the Handicapped, United States Office of Education.

Chapter 2

Providing for Special Needs
in Early Education:
The Challenge

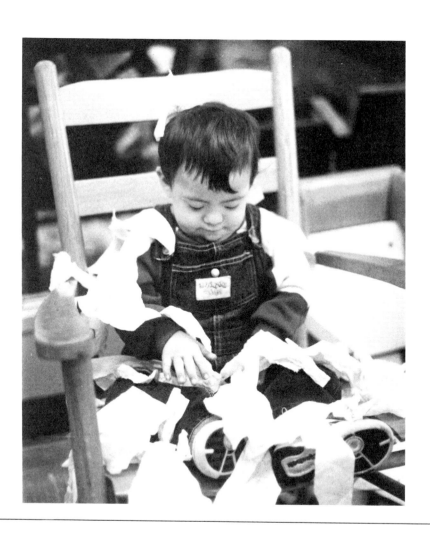

Key Points

▶ The history of early childhood special education reflects influences from both the field of early childhood education and the field of special education.

▶ A variety of theoretical approaches and program models has contributed historically to the current status of the field of early childhood special education.

▶ U.S. federal legislation, including Public Law 92-142 and Public Law 99-457, has provided an important impetus to the development of programs for infants and young children with special needs, particularly the provision of services in the least restrictive environment and family involvement.

▶ Current trends in the field include

Family focus
Interagency collaboration
Transdisciplinary service delivery
Integration with nondisabled peers
Developmentally appropriate activities in natural settings (i.e., play)

Functional-ecological approach
Social-transactional approach

▶ Best practices in early childhood special education include those identified by the National Association for the Education of Young Children (NAEYC) and are based on the following two major principles: (1) Programs must meet the individual developmental needs of each child and (2) The best medium through which to meet these needs is children's play.

▶ A child with special needs must be viewed as a child first; the special need or disability is secondary. All children are best understood within the context of their family, rather than within the context of their disability.

▶ Children's needs can be met within a variety of service delivery models and settings, including both home- and center-based programs.

Key Topics

▶ Historical perspectives on early childhood special education.

▶ Intervention programs for children with special needs: types of programs and program efficacy.

▶ Societal pressures: the impact of litigation and legislation.

▶ Historical approaches to early education programming.

▶ Current trends in early childhood special education.

▶ Best practices.

▶ Service delivery systems.

Attitudes toward young children have changed dramatically in the last 100 years. In the 19th century children were required to work on farms and in factories at a very early age. In the initial part of the 20th century, large numbers of children under age 10 worked 12 hours a day, 6 days a week, for a total wage of 75 cents a week! Going to school at all was a luxury. Children were "to be seen and not heard." In an environment that encouraged child labor, the weak, the infirm, and those with disabilities presented an intolerable burden to all but the wealthiest of families.

Imagine you are the parent of a child with a disability about 100 years ago.

You've just become a parent. You are so excited, but you look at John and he doesn't look right. Your child grows, but he is different. He doesn't walk as early as your other children or as early as your neighbor's child. He falls a lot. His speech is very difficult to understand. It is 1880. There is little you can do to help John. No one seems to care about him. As time goes on, you will be able to send him away to an institution and you will be advised to forget him.

Continue to imagine. Times have changed. You are parents halfway through the 20th century. It is 1945. People do care. Your child, Jimmy, will be tested, labeled, and put into a special program. That special program will be in a separate school. It may be far from your home. He will not bother anyone. He certainly won't get in the way of the "normal" children. You are encouraged to accept him and to take advantage of the special facilities provided. If you have means, you have the option of sending him away to a private school.

Imagine again. Now it is 1978. Experts are eager to identify your child, Mary, as soon as possible. They want to help both of you. In fact, you are even being told that she will receive part of her education in the classroom with typical children. They are going to do something for her called "mainstreaming." You will be asked to help decide what education will be the most appropriate for Mary. You have some choices, because a range of special services is available. You are excited but somewhat apprehensive.

And now we have entered the 1990s. Not only are professionals and parents around the nation collaborating to find and offer services that will help Jose function well in normal environments, but they wish to make it easier for your family to cope with the demands of parenting a child with special needs.

Being the parent of a child with special needs, one who is different, has never been easy. It is not easy today either. But times are changing, and help is more readily available than before. Parents are able to choose from a variety of placement alternatives. Specialists work with parents in choosing the placement and array of special services that are most *appropriate*. In fact, legislation passed in the form of Public Law 94-142, the Individuals with Disabilities Education Act (formerly known as the Education for All Handicapped Children Act of 1975), and Public Law 99-457, the Education of the Handicapped Amendments of 1986, require children to be educated in the *least restrictive environment*. When developing individualized program plans, schools serving young children with special needs are required to include a statement indicating the extent to which the child will be participating in the regular education environment. Such a mandate presents a continuing challenge, both legally and professionally: how to best adapt early childhood curricula for children with special needs? To meet this challenge, educators from early childhood education and special education have combined forces in creating the emerging field of early childhood special education.

HISTORICAL PERSPECTIVES ON EARLY CHILDHOOD SPECIAL EDUCATION

Bettye Caldwell reminded us just how new this field of early childhood special education really is. Speaking at the Invisible College Conference on Early Childhood Education and the Exceptional Child held in 1972 in San Antonio, Texas, she characterized the period before the 1950s as a period of "forget and hide." The next two decades were a time to "screen and segregate." The most recent decade she described as a time to "identify and help." Caldwell (1973) emphasized the rapid progress that is continuing to unfold in early childhood special education.

While the 1980s opened with concern for the rights of individuals with disabilities, the 1990s are recognizing the rights and needs of the *families* of those with special needs. Children are no longer viewed in isolation. Attention is focused on understanding the needs of the child within the context of his or her family. Early intervention services are gaining new momentum as the nation recognizes its responsibility to provide services from the moment of birth.

Historical perspectives, summarized in Figure 2–1, are included to help the reader visualize some of the achievements that have given birth to the new subfield of early childhood special education. This figure presents only highlights of the forces that have contributed to the development of this exciting field—those that combine the thinking of authorities in early childhood education and special education.

Pioneering Influences on Early Childhood Education

The field of early childhood education is relatively new. So new, in fact, that a number of states have not developed certification programs. Despite this, however, there are historical roots. As early as the late 1600s, voices cried out in search of special consideration for the individuality and innate goodness of young children. John Locke, concerned about the harsh discipline of his time, cultivated the "blank tablet" concept of the newborn's mind to overcome the popular belief that a child was born full of evil ideas. He advocated that children be given empathic understanding.

In his book *Emile*, Jean Jacques Rousseau (1762/1911) stressed the importance of beginning the child's education at birth. He believed that strong discipline and strict lessons were inappropriate conditions for optimal learning. Children should be treated with sympathy and compassion as humans in their own right.

Johann Pestalozzi's writings in the early 1800s indicated his belief in children's ability to learn through self-discovery. He felt that education should be based on the natural development of children. Mothers were believed to be the best teachers. He felt that the home served as the basic model for learning. It was the expression of humane attitudes such as these that served as the original source of an attitude of caring for the unique needs of special children.

The First Kindergartens. During the 1830s, the first kindergarten was developed in Germany. Friedrich Froebel created this kindergarten in his native homeland because of his concern for the social and emotional development of the "whole child." He sought to make the education of young children different from that of older children. Indeed, certain modern methods of preschool education such as block building, clay modeling, and painting were originally a part of the early training program developed by Froebel.

Influenced by Froebel's philosophy, Margarethe Schurz immigrated to America and established a kindergarten for German-speaking children in 1856 in Watertown, Wisconsin.

Elizabeth Palmer Peabody was so impressed with the work of Schurz that 4 years later she opened the first English-speaking American kindergarten in Boston. Peabody was instrumental in getting William Harris, then superintendent of schools in St. Louis, Missouri, to open the first public school kindergarten in the United States. And so, in 1873, early childhood education was established within the public schools to become a part of the American educational tradition.

The Beginnings of Special Education

Jean-Marc Itard undertook one of the first documented efforts to work with a child with special needs. In 1799, a child approximately 12 years old was found living in the forest near Aveyron, France. The boy, named Victor, was thought to have been raised by animals and was described as "an incurable idiot." Itard refused to accept the idea that Victor's condition was incurable

1600 —— 1700 —— 1800 —— 1850 —— 1900 →

HUMANISTIC ADVOCACY
+ John Locke's "blank tablet" (1600s)
+ Rousseau's *Emile* (1762)
+ Pestalozzi (1800s)

CONSIDERATION FOR HANDICAPPED
+ Itard (1799)
+ Seguin (1840s)
+ Montessori (1907)
+ Binet (1904)

EARLY PROGRAMS FOR YOUNG CHILDREN
+ Froebel (1830s)
+ Schurz (first U.S. kindergarten) (1856)
+ Peabody (first English-speaking kindergarten) (1860)
+ First public kindergarten (1873)

SPECIAL PROGRAMS FOR INDIVIDUALS WITH DISABILITIES
+ Gallaudet (deaf) (1817)
+ Howe (blind) (1830s)
+ NEA Division (for students with disabilities) (1897)
+ 100 plus public classes for students with disabilities (1911)
+ International Conference for Exceptional Children (1922)
+ White House Conference (1930)

Figure 2–1 (pp. 19–20) Contributions to early childhood special education.

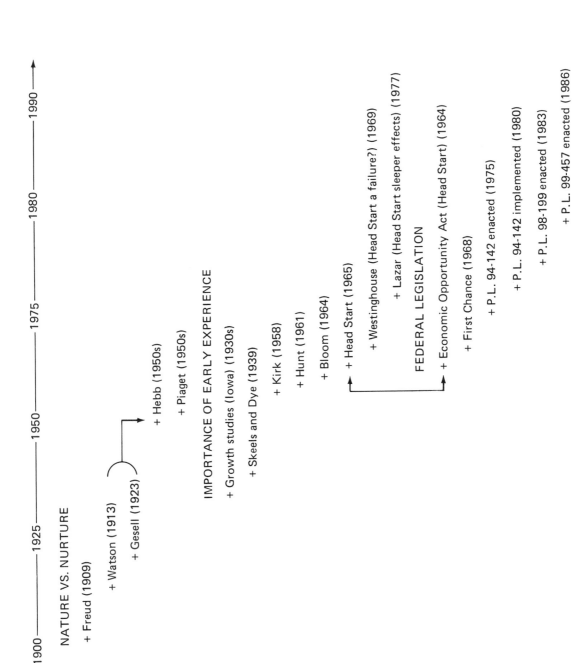

NATURE VS. NURTURE

+ Freud (1909)

+ Watson (1913)

+ Gesell (1923)

+ Hebb (1950s)

+ Piaget (1950s)

IMPORTANCE OF EARLY EXPERIENCE

+ Growth studies (Iowa) (1930s)

+ Skeels and Dye (1939)

+ Kirk (1958)

+ Hunt (1961)

+ Bloom (1964)

+ Head Start (1965)

+ Westinghouse (Head Start a failure?) (1969)

+ Lazar (Head Start sleeper effects) (1977)

FEDERAL LEGISLATION

+ Economic Opportunity Act (Head Start) (1964)

+ First Chance (1968)

+ P.L. 94-142 enacted (1975)

+ P.L. 94-142 implemented (1980)

+ P.L. 98-199 enacted (1983)

+ P.L. 99-457 enacted (1986)

+ P.L. 101-476 enacted (1990)

1900 ———— 1925 ———— 1950 ———— 1975 ———— 1980 ———— 1990 →

Figure 2–1 (continued)

and irreversible. He undertook to humanize Victor through a series of carefully planned lessons stimulating the senses.

Itard (1962) recounted his feelings of optimism, frustration, anger, hope, and despair in *The Wild Boy of Aveyron*. Teachers today who work with children who have extreme disabilities may easily recognize these feelings. Although Itard did not achieve the success he visualized, his efforts had a significant impact on the future of special education. Itard was one of the first to demonstrate and record an attempt to understand empathically the needs of a child with disabilities.

In addition, Itard developed unique teaching techniques and provided much encouragement to one of his students, Edouard Seguin. Seguin profoundly influenced international progress in the treatment of people with mental retardation. He brought his pioneering work in the systematic training of these individuals to the United States, where he is credited with founding the American Association on Mental Deficiency.

First Attempt to Identify Children in Need of Special Instruction. Public attention was given to the identification of children with disabilities as early as 1904. Alfred Binet was commissioned by France's minister of public instruction to design a test to determine which children could succeed in the public schools and which children needed special attention. It is interesting to note that the French had as a major consideration the retention of special children in regular classrooms. Just as we are concerned today with mainstreaming or integration, they wanted to keep children with disabilities together with their with nondisabled peers. They sought to create a method of identification that would avoid the problem of prejudice. Imagine the chagrin of the French commissioners if they could witness the need for legal trials to reduce the labeling of and discrimination against children with disabilities today!

Casa dei Bambini. While France was developing special public school programs for children who

were found by Binet and co-worker Theophile Simon to be in need of such services, Maria Montessori was busy in Italy creating a nursery school, Casa dei Bambini. Montessori revolutionized the notion of early education with her establishment of the "Children's House" in the Roman slums in 1907. She began her career as a physician and spent her earliest professional years working with children who had mental retardation. Because of her training, early interests, and the nature of the school she was asked to develop, Montessori stressed cleanliness, order, and housekeeping skills as well as reading, writing, and arithmetic. Aspects of both the discovery approach to learning and programmed instruction can be found in the techniques developed by Montessori. She suggested that teachers observe the natural, spontaneous behavior of children and then arrange learning experiences to encourage their development. Her nursery school included children as young as 2 1/2 years of age at a time when American educators were considering the use of her ideas in programs for 4- and 5-year-old children.

Like Edouard Seguin, Montessori believed in developing the child's natural curiosity through systematic training of the senses. Both proceeded with optimism and determination to train those who some might believe to be beyond hope. Even so, Montessori's approach was out of favor in the United States for some time. The 1960s brought a resurgence of interest in Montessori techniques. Montessori's "sensorial" materials are advocated for use with children with disabilities because they are manipulable, three-dimensional, and concrete. Advocates cite the emphasis on task analysis, sequencing, and individualization evident in the Montessori approach as worthy for use with children who have limited abilities as well as those who are gifted.

Nature vs. Nurture Controversy

With a faith in the influence of genetically predetermined patterns, Arnold Gesell established the Yale Clinic of Child Development, which was a center for research on children for over 3 decades. Historically, Gesell is the most articulate spokesman for maturation as the central concept of child development. Although Gesell acknowledged the role of the environment as the setting for growth, he simply contended that children would grow as their genes directed.

Gesell's Normative Stages. In *The Preschool Child*, Gesell (1923) emphasized the importance of the early years. He stated that the preschool period "is biologically the most important period in the development of an individual for the simple but sufficient reason that it comes first in a dynamic sequence; it inevitably influences all subsequent development" (p. 2).

Gesell's influence on early childhood special education came from his interest in abnormal children and his clinical goal—diagnosis of developmental deviance. To this end, he created the normative approach based on keen observation of children at various ages. To Gesell, age was unquestionably a convenient line along which to show the orderliness of development. However, Gesell warned that the "ages and stages" concept could be interpreted too literally. He did not feel that norms were rigid but rather were indices of types of behavior likely to occur at a particular age. Gesell's warning is still appropriate, because current preschool screening efforts often use the Gesell scales as convenient measures of what is or is not considered to be "normal" development.

Watson's Environmental Behaviorism. At the same time Gesell was continuing his work on measurement and diagnosis, John Watson sought to study behavior by more objective methods. In 1913, he made the leap from a theory that emphasized the influence of heredity in the development of children to one that emphasized the contribution of specific environmental influences.

His most lasting contribution to our knowledge of children is derived from his studies of infants and his surprising proposal that parents could make of their children what they wished. Parents were warned that the most sensible way to treat children was to be objective and kindly firm. Children were not to be coddled. Indeed, this more rigid disciplinary approach was reflected in the articles from popular women's magazines analyzed by Stendler (1950). Present-day curriculum for children with behavior disorders that stresses the use of behavior modification might be said to have its roots in the behaviorism espoused by Watson as well as such famous scientists as Ivan Pavlov and B. F. Skinner.

Freud's Affective Development. While Gesell was espousing maturation and Watson emphasized the role of classical conditioning in the development of the child, Sigmund Freud added yet another dimension to the understanding of the child. Concentrating on affective development, Freud brought back a pessimistic view of the child long forgotten. Childhood, as depicted by Freud, was ambiguous, incoherent, and filled with conflict (Freud, 1953; Kessen, 1965). He espoused a subtle form of maturationism. Permissiveness was advocated to free the child of conflict and neurosis. Present-day treatment of children with emotional disturbances that uses free expression in such therapeutic techniques as play therapy originated in Freud's psychoanalytical approach.

Hebb's Interaction Model. In the late 1950s, D. O. Hebb insisted that child development was not the result of either heredity or environment alone. The heredity versus environment/nature versus nurture controversy began to gain the perspective that is present today. Hebb proposed that behavior is produced by the interaction between genetic and environmental variables. It is this interaction model of child development that is espoused currently as the most realistic approach to the education of young children with disabilities. In fact, the keynote address given at The Council for Exceptional Children's first series of training institutes on early childhood educa-

tion (held in February, 1977) was entitled "Practical Implications of an Interaction Model of Child Development" (Bijou, 1977).

It is fortunate for children with disabilities that educators are realizing the need to consider both the developmental characteristics of children and the present as well as the predicted future characteristics of the society. Either extreme position would be to the detriment of young children with disabilities. For example, individuals who see heredity or nature as the prime determinant of development may question the need for individualized instructional techniques. After all, what can the early childhood specialist provide that will not be provided as a result of maturation anyway? The very concept of labeling implies an irrevocable condition that must be controlled internally.

On the other hand, educators who feel the environment to be the primary determiner of development may take on an unrealistic burden, leaving them defeated and feeling much the same as Itard. Even though the environmentalist position is the more optimistic of the two, extreme advocacy could lead to unrealistic rather than appropriate educational experiences for children. Educators would have to be infallible in their ability to regulate contingencies within the environment of the child with special needs.

As a result, some theorists who consider the interactional model to be too static turn to a more dynamic theory to explain developmental deviations. This theory, the *transactional model*, considers both the organism and the environment to be plastic in nature. A continual and progressive interrelationship is fostered, with the organism functioning as an active participant in its own growth. "From this position the child's response is thought to be more than a simple reaction to his environment. Instead, he is thought to be actively engaged in attempts to organize and structure his world" (Sameroff & Chandler, 1975, p. 235).

Piaget's Spontaneous Cognition. Although published in the early 1900s, it wasn't until the 1950s that Jean Piaget's elaborate descriptions of the development of children's thinking began to be accepted by American psychologists. Piaget proposed an inborn tendency toward adaptation that, in its encounter with the environment, results in categories of knowledge that are remarkably similar among all human beings. Piaget's concept of child development and his stages of cognitive development will be considered again in Chapter 10. His prolific writings and those of followers continue to remind us of the need to be aware of the unfolding internal mental capacities of children.

According to Piaget, the purpose of education is to provide opportunities that allow a child to combine experiences into coherent systems (schemes) that constitute the child's knowledge. "Knowledge" then is constructed from within rather than acquired from without (Furth, 1970). Therefore, each child's capacity to learn is thought to be uniquely experientially based. Piaget's concept of the child as an active learner stimulated by inborn curiosity has prompted the development of preschool programs designed to allow the child to become an active initiator of learning experiences. From a developmental point of view, a child's strengths, rather than deficits, receive emphasis. Most notable of the Piagetian-based programs is the Perry Preschool Project developed in the late 1950s in Ypsilanti, Michigan. An extension known as the High/Scope First Chance Preschool serves as a model program for those desiring to integrate preschoolers with disabilities into programs with nondisabled preschoolers (Banet, 1979).

INTERVENTION PROGRAMS FOR CHILDREN WITH SPECIAL NEEDS

In 1817, the first residential school for the deaf was organized in Connecticut by Thomas Hopkins Gallaudet. Using the terminology of the time, it was known as the Asylum for the Education and Instruction of the Deaf and Dumb.

Samuel Howe directed the opening of the New England Asylum for the Blind in Boston in the 1830s. Over 100 large city school systems had established special schools or special classes for students with disabilities by 1911.

Before World War II, parents were inclined to hide their children who had severe disabilities in institutions or were unwilling to admit their children needed special services. Children with mild disabilities usually received no services before placement in regular classrooms, where they were unsuccessful, frustrated, and humiliated and usually dropped out.

After World War II, the public began to feel some awareness of and guilt over the numbers of formerly healthy young men who returned in a maimed condition. Parent organizations developed and directed political pressure toward improvement of services for people with disabilities, including children. Success of the programs for individuals with sensory impairments (which had provided stimulation to children from nonstimulating, possibly overprotective environments) were certainly a boost to the efforts of advocates of special education. Between 1953 and 1958, the increase in enrollment in special classes was 260% (Love, 1972).

Project Head Start

The creation of Project Head Start is thought to have evolved as a result of a series of influences. One of the earliest attempts to demonstrate the close relationship among nurturing, environmental stimulation, and mental growth processes grew out of the Iowa growth studies in the late 1930s. Skeels and Dye (1939) transferred 12 children under 3 years of age from an orphanage to an institution for individuals with mental retardation. In the institution the children were cared for with great affection by adolescent girls who were considered to have retardation. A comparison group of children remained in the orphanage where they received no specialized attention. Follow-up testing demonstrated that those placed in the stimulating environment increased their intelligence test scores while those who remained in the orphanage decreased their intelligence test scores (Skeels, 1942). Twenty-one years later, Skeels (1966) found dramatic differences between those who had been placed in the enriching environment and those who had not. The 12 children in the experimental group were found to be self-supporting. Of the comparison group, four had been institutionalized and one had died. Educationally speaking, four of those who had been in the enriching environment completed college, and the others had a median high school education. On the other hand, the median education for the comparison group was only at the third-grade level.

Samuel Kirk (1958) also conducted experiments on the influence of early education on the development of young children with mental disabilities. In his textbook, Kirk's suggestion that an inadequate cultural environment might be a cause of mental retardation helped to convince politicians of the need for compensatory educational programs for young children. Perhaps more convincing was the conclusion reached by Benjamin Bloom (1964) that claimed that about "50% of the [intellectual] development takes place between conception and age 4, and about 30% between ages 4 and 8, and 20% between ages 8 and 17" (p. 88).

Bloom's argument was advanced by J. McVicker Hunt's popular book *Intelligence and Experience* (1961), which argued eloquently against the notion of fixed intelligence. Attempting to lay to rest the heredity versus environment controversy, Hunt supported well his contention that heredity sets the limits, whereas environment determines the extent to which the limits will be achieved. And so, under the belief that children's intelligence develops early and rapidly and that enrichment early in life can have profound influences on the child's development, federal funding for Project Head Start was provided in 1965.

A Breakthrough. The primary purpose in passing the Economic Opportunity Act of 1964 was to break the cycle of poverty by providing educational and social opportunities for children from low-income families. The result was the implementation of Head Start during the summer of 1965 with approximately 550,000 children in 2,500 child development centers. Parent involvement both within the Head Start classroom and on policy committees set a precedent. This has, no doubt, influenced legislators to require parent involvement in current decisions involving children with disabilities.

The Head Start program had a significant impact on the development of early childhood special education. It was the first major public exposure to the importance of early educational experiences. As Caldwell (1973) pointed out, "the implicit strategy of early Head Start was to devise a program that fits the children as they are found and that institutes remedial procedures to correct whatever deficiencies they have, whether they are nutritional, experiential, or medical" (p. 5).

Legislation enacted in 1972 required Head Start programs to include children with disabilities to the extent of at least 10% of their enrollment. Mainstreaming children with disabilities into classrooms with typical children has become a major activity of Head Start. In fact, the 1985 Head Start enrollment of preschoolers with disabilities exceeded 60,000.

Doubts. After the extreme optimism that accompanied the establishment of Head Start, it came as a shock to those who worked daily with the children and their parents that the program failed to produce notable gains. The Westinghouse report of 1969 cited data suggesting that measured gains made by Head Starters faded rapidly. By the end of the first grade, there often were no significant differences between the overall academic performance of children who had attended Head Start programs and those from the same kinds of homes who had not.

Doubting the validity of this investigation, influential people fought for a stay of execution (Gotts, 1973). Among them was Edward Zigler, a member of the original planning committee that conceptualized Head Start and later director of the Office of Child Development. Zigler (1978) retorted, "I ask my colleagues in the research community to forgo the temptation of delivering definitive pronouncements concerning the fade-out issue and await instead the collection and analyses of more data" (p. 73).

Efficacy of Early Intervention

Indeed, Zigler was to be rewarded for his faith. Both the quantity and quality of research on the effectiveness of early intervention programs has been improving (Farran, 1990). A powerful case for federal support of early intervention programs appears in the report of a well-designed 19-year longitudinal study of the effects of the Perry Preschool Project (Schweinhart & Weikart, 1988). Exhibit 2–1 lists some of the gains attributed to early intervention with children who are primarily at-risk and disadvantaged.

EXHIBIT 2–1

Effects of Early Intervention

Children who have participated in early education programs:

1. Are less likely to be assigned to special education classes or to be held back a grade.
2. Have more positive attitudes toward high school and are more likely to graduate.
3. Are less likely to be arrested as youth and young adults.
4. Are less likely to experience teen pregnancy.
5. Are more likely to secure gainful employment after leaving school.

Early Intervention with Children with Disabilities. Responding to the need to understand the effects of early intervention on children with disabilities, the Utah State Early Intervention Research Institute has analyzed the most comprehensive collection of early intervention research studies available. After considering the research design difficulties inherent in research with young children with special needs, these researchers have offered some tentative conclusions (personal communication, S. Barnett, July 1990; Shonkoff, Hauser-Cram, Krauss, & Upshur, 1988). It appears that (a) early intervention does produce immediate and short-run positive effects on cognitive and motor development; (b) these effects do persist at least to school entry; and (c) larger effects are produced if early intervention is begun before age 2 than if it is begun between ages 2 and 4. Too little information is available to draw conclusions regarding duration and intensity of programs. However, it appears that programs for children with special needs that include parents are more effective than those that do not.

In interpreting the findings of early intervention research, it is important to keep in mind the diversity with which this field deals. When policymakers ask, "What are the benefits of early intervention?" the response will inevitably be, "It depends." This is not because researchers cannot agree or because of the limitations of research methods, but because of the great diversity among children and families and the circumstances in which they live. There is no one best intervention for everyone all of the time. There is not even one best intervention for a very narrowly defined group such as infants with Down syndrome and their families. Even infants with Down syndrome differ so much from one another that an intervention for a group of these infants probably would not be very successful. Research does provide some pieces of this complex, highly individualized puzzle indicating that early intervention can yield important benefits. Because of the complexities involved in documenting positive effects of early intervention, professionals in the field do not know enough to put the complete picture together to produce reliable generalizations (Barnett, July 1990).

Caregiver-Focused Models of Early Intervention. Recently, attention has been drawn to a report from The Infant Health and Development Program (1990), which documents long-term effects of early intervention services for low-birthweight, premature infants who may have biological constraints that compromise their development. In this study, 985 infants were randomly assigned to receive educational intervention as well as family support and pediatric follow-up, or only pediatric follow-up. The group that received early intervention and parent support had significantly higher mean IQ scores at age 36 months and significantly fewer behavior problems. The long-term significance of these findings is being addressed in the continued follow-up project. Evidence from the Yale Family Support Project (Seitz, Rosenbaum, & Apfel, 1985), which combined day care with social services for families, also suggested significant improvement in the children as evidenced in fewer special education placements.

Given the results of these projects, the mechanism that maintains child change over time becomes obvious. The parent/caregiver appears to be the factor that assists the child in maintaining the advantage stimulated by the early intervention (Bricker, Bailey, & Bruder, 1984). Even though a great deal of research is needed to explore how specific interventions can influence parent-child relationships, research results to date suggest a cumulative-transactional model of development (Sameroff & Fiese, 1990). Part H of P. L. 99-457 recognizes the impact of the interaction between a child and his or her environment by viewing the family as a system embedded within a larger ecological network. The requirement of an Individualized Family Service Plan, to be discussed in Chapter 5, attests to this realization.

If, as speculation suggests, the mechanism that facilitates and maintains the impact of early intervention services is the caregiver, current programs will need to consider focusing more of their efforts on the caregiving environment than on the infant or child. Changes in the child may enhance parental attitudes as well as improve the interactional nature of the parent-child relationship. Conversely, changes in parent responses can reinforce and build desired responses in the child. Thus, a mutually reinforcing cycle of parent-child interactions will help to maintain the impact of early intervention services. As Meisels stated in 1985, "the primary intervention target should not be the child, but the child within the context of the family" (p. 8).

The First Chance (HCEEP) Program

In 1968, Congress recognized the need for model programs to spur the development of services for children with disabilities from birth through age 8. Legislation was enacted to establish the Handicapped Children's Early Education Program (HCEEP), better known as the First Chance program. These projects were required to include parents in their activities, run inservice training, evaluate the progress of both the children and the program, coordinate activities with public schools, and disseminate information on the project to professionals and the public. In 1980, the total number of funded projects was 177, with 111 including infants in their population (Swan, 1981). These projects serve two basic purposes: (1) to provide models of exemplary services that can be replicated for young children with disabilities and (2) to disseminate information that will encourage this replication.

Delivery Systems. The concept of delivery systems applies to how, when, and where services are delivered to children and their families. Karnes and Zehrbach (1977) summarized the unique approaches of 120 HCEEP programs. The majority of these fell under the following delivery system headings: (a) home, (b) home followed by center, (c) home and center, (d) center, and (e) technical assistance and consultative services.

Most projects that deliver only home-based services view the parents as the primary teachers of their children. Beller (1979) described these as "parent-oriented" programs. Such programs are especially useful in rural areas or where parents are reluctant to have their children leave home. For example, the Portage Project (Shearer & Shearer, 1976) developed a home-based program to meet the needs of children where geography prevented transportation. Such home-based programs have the advantage of allowing intervention within the natural setting of the home. However, these programs put added stress on the parents, who have little respite from their children and must take on more teaching responsibilities.

Many of the children originally served only at home may enter a center program around the age of 18 months. Some receive services in both a center and at home. Staff members model appropriate teaching techniques in the child's home. A number of the center-based programs are not only cross categorical but also include children who have no disabilities. According to Beller (1979), center-based programs tend to be child oriented, emphasizing direct intervention with the child. Finally, those centers that use technical assistance do so for help with diagnosis and inservice training.

Research does not indicate clearly discernible advantages from either home- or center-based service delivery systems. Therefore, professionals suggest that a combination of home-based plus center-based services may offer the best alternative, especially for very young children and infants (Garwood & Fewell, 1983). Thurman and Widerstrom (1990) and Meisels and Shonkoff (1990) have provided more details on a number of fascinating projects that vary due to population served, geographical location, theoretical basis, and delivery system.

SOCIETAL PRESSURES: THE IMPACT OF LITIGATION AND LEGISLATION

As illustrated in the historical overview, it was not until the mid-1900s that the public schools really began to make provisions for children with varying degrees of disability. Concerned citizens and active parent and professional associations have played a vital role in society's changing attitude toward children with special needs.

Development of Professional Groups

It has been said that Alexander Graham Bell, inventor of the telephone and a strong advocate of oral education of the deaf, should be given credit for organizing professional advocates of special education. He petitioned the National Education Association (NEA) to establish a division to be concerned about the needs of people with disabilities. In 1897, the NEA established such a division and named it the Department of Education of the Deaf, Blind, and the Feebleminded. As attitudes toward and knowledge of this population changed, this name was later changed to the Department of Special Education.

The formation of The International Council for Exceptional Children in 1922 provided the impetus for what some believe to be the most influential advocacy group continuing to provide national leadership on behalf of children with special needs. The 1930 White House Conference on Child Health and Protection was a milestone in marking the first time that special education had received national recognition. Today, educators turn to the Division for Early Childhood (DEC) of The Council for Exceptional Children as a continuing source of advocacy for young children with disabilities.

The Power of Private Citizens

Several factors came together after World War II that gave rise to the development of strong parent organizations in the late 1940s. Professional knowledge was expanding, the country felt responsible to aid its wounded, and prominent people such as Pearl Buck, Roy Rogers and Dale Evans, and the Kennedy family were visibly calling for better education of individuals with special needs. Parents no longer felt the need to hide their children with disabilities. Pressure groups such as the United Cerebral Palsy Association, the National Association for Retarded Citizens, and the American Foundation for the Blind began to demand alternatives other than institutionalization for the education of their children with disabilities.

Professional groups joined parent groups in capitalizing on the historic Supreme Court decision in *Brown* v. *Board of Education of Topeka* (1954). Although primarily an integration initiative, the Court ruled that state laws that permitted segregated public schools were in violation of the Fourteenth Amendment's "equal protection under the law" clause. Realizing that decisions applicable to one minority group must be applicable to another, pressure groups sought to secure legislation that would create significant educational changes on behalf of children with special needs. However, little actually occurred until after the publication of an article by Dunn (1968) that provided a blueprint for changes recognizing the rights of students with disabilities. Exhibit 2–2 summarizes some of the landmark court cases and legislative milestones in the development of free and appropriate education for all children.

Public Law 94-142—The Individuals with Disabilities Education Act

In 1975, with the passage of P.L. 94-142, the right to a free, appropriate public education was mandated for all children of school age. This law did not require states to offer services to young children with disabilities, but it did provide financial incentives for states to provide services to chil-

dren with special needs as young as 3 years of age. In addition, the National Center for Clinical Infant Programs (NCCIP) was founded in 1977 to recognize and support the needs of very young children and their families. (It should be noted that P.L. 101-476, passed in October 1990, changed the name of P.L. 94-142 from the Education for All Handicapped Children Act to the Individuals with Disabilities Education Act.)

Purpose. The purpose of P.L. 94-142 is

To insure that all handicapped children have available to them . . . a free, appropriate public education which includes special education and related services designed to meet their unique needs, to insure that the rights of handicapped children and their parents or guardians are protected, to assist States and localities to provide for the education of all handicapped children and to assess and insure the effectiveness of efforts to educate handicapped children. (Sec. 601 [c])

Appropriate Public Education. The law requires that a qualified school representative, teacher, the parents or guardian, and whenever possible the child join together in the development of an individualized education program (IEP). This written statement must include (a) a statement of the child's present level of academic functioning; (b) a declaration of annual goals complete with appropriate short-term instructional objectives; (c) a description of specific educational services to be provided to the child and the degree to which the child will participate in regular educational programs; (d) the proposed date for initiation and estimation of the required length of services; and (e) annual evaluation procedures specifying objective criteria designed to determine whether or not the short-term instructional objectives have been met (Sec. 602, 19).

Procedural Safeguards. The law requires that children with disabilities be served in the least restrictive environment appropriate to their educational needs. Children can be placed in separate classes or schools only when their disability

EXHIBIT 2–2

Significant Litigation

Litigation	Description
A. The right to free education *Pennsylvania Association for Retarded Children* v. *the Commonwealth of Pennsylvania* (1971).	The court ruled through a consent agreement that the state must provide free public education to all children with mental retardation regardless of the degree of their disability. It is interesting to note that the court also intended that placement be in the most integrated environment (Gargiulo, 1980). The PARC case established the right of parents to participate in major decisions affecting their children.
Mills v. Board of Education of the District of Columbia (1972).	The court specifically established the constitutional right of all children with exceptionalities, regardless of the degree of severity of their disability, to a public education.
B. The right to appropriate education *Diana v. State Board of Education of California* (1970).	Through a court-approved stipulation it was agreed that Mexican-American and Chinese-American children enrolled in classes for the educable mentally retarded (EMR) would be reevaluated using their primary language, test items would be revised to be suitable to the minority culture, and misplaced children would be returned to the regular programs.
Larry P. v. Riles (1972).	The court ruled that no black student could be placed in an educable mentally retarded class on the basis of criteria that rely primarily on the results of intelligence tests. It further required school officials to demonstrate the rationality of test-based classification procedures. In a subsequent ruling the court prohibited the public schools "from utilizing, permitting the use of, or approving the use of any standardized intelligence tests . . . for the identification of black E.M.R. children or their replacement into E.M.R. classes, without securing prior approval by this court" (*Larry P. v. Riles*, 1972, p. 104). This decision was based on the court's finding that standardized intelligence tests are racially and culturally biased and therefore have a discriminatory impact on black children.
Public Law 95-568 (1964) Economic Opportunity Act	Created the Office of Economic Opportunity, which developed and began administration of Project Head Start during the summer of 1965.

Public Law 89-10 (1965) Elementary and Secondary Education Act (ESEA)	Provided a $1.33 billion commitment to improve elementary and secondary education; expanded special programs.
Public Law 89-750 (1966) Education for Handicapped Children Act	Expanded P.L. 89-10, authorizing funds to initiate, improve, and expand services for individuals with disabilities; established a National Advisory Committee on Handicapped Children and created the Bureau of Education for the Handicapped (BEH).
Public Law 90-538 (1968) Handicapped Children's Early Education Assistance Act	Significant to the education of preschool children with disabilities; established experimental early education programs throughout the country.
Public Law 91-230 (1969) ESEA	Extended P.L. 89-10 by authorizing the establishment of model education centers for children with learning disabilities; included a provision for gifted and talented youth.
Public Law 92-424 (1972) Economic Opportunity Act Amendments	Established a preschool mandate that required that not less than 10% of the total number of Head Start placements be reserved for children with disabilities.
Public Law 93-380 (1974) Education Amendments	Preceded P.L. 94-142 and established a total federal commitment to the education of children with disabilities; concerns included education within the least restrictive environment, nondiscriminatory testing, and privacy rights (Title V., "Buckley Amendment").
Public Law 94-142 (1975) Education for All Handicapped Children Act	Revised and expanded P.L. 93-380; provided a free, appropriate public education with related services to all children with disabilities between ages 3 and 21.
Public Law 98-199 (1983) The Education of the Handicapped Act Amendments of 1983	Provided financial incentives for states to extend service levels down to birth.
Public Law 99-457 (1986) The Education of the Handicapped Act Amendments of 1986	Extended P.L. 94-142 to include 3- to 5-year-olds; added a new grant program to assist states in establishing a comprehensive system of early intervention services for infants and toddlers with disabilities and their families.
Public Law 101-476 (1990) Individuals with Disabilities Education Act (IDEA)	Reauthorization of P.L. 94-142 to reflect a change in philosophy away from labeling children as "handicapped children" to referring to them as *individuals* first, with "disabilities" following as a secondary description.

is so severe that regular school placement is considered inappropriate. The act also requires non-discriminatory testing and the use of multiple criteria in the determination of placement (Sec. 612, 5, C). This requirement implies the need for all teachers to become skilled in the education of children who exhibit a variety of educational needs.

P.L. 94-142 provides for the right of parents or guardians to examine all records, obtain independent evaluation, and require written notification in their native language of plans to change a child's educational program. The intent is to ensure that the child's rights are legally protected. Parents or guardians are entitled to a hearing before termination, exclusion, or classification of a student into a special program.

Public Law 99-457—The Education of the Handicapped Act Amendments of 1986

P.L. 99-457 is thought by some to be the law that has legitimized the field of early childhood spe-

cial education (Bricker, 1988). At the very least, it has created a national agenda that has federal, state, and local planners collaborating with parents in unprecedented efforts to develop new and expanded services for infants and young children who have disabilities or are at risk and their families. Title II of the law required all states to extend all of the provisions of P.L. 94-142 to children 3 to 5 years old by the 1990–1991 school year. States that did not comply were to lose federal monies they had been receiving for other preschool services.

School districts throughout the country have already developed early intervention services for preschool-aged children with severe disabilities. Amendments to P.L. 94-142 now require school districts to provide services to those with mild disabilities just as they do for older children with less intensive needs.

Part H. Part H of P.L. 99-457 established a discretionary program for states to facilitate the design and implementation of comprehensive systems of early intervention services for in-

fants and toddlers with developmental delays or disabilities. As defined by the law, early intervention services "are designed to meet a handicapped infant's or toddler's developmental needs in any one or more of the following areas: physical development; cognitive development; language and speech development; psychosocial development; or self-help skills" (Sec. 672).

Part H defines the eligible population as all children from birth through age 2 who have developmental delays, have conditions that typically result in delay, or are at risk for significant developmental delay. States must make independent decisions about the definition of developmental delay and "at risk" as well as the criteria used to make these determinations. Therefore, the populations of children eligible for services will vary from state to state. In order to design "a statewide, comprehensive, coordinated, multidisciplinary, interagency program of early intervention services for all handicapped infants and their families" (Sec. 671), each governor appointed a lead agency and established an interagency coordinating council. States are struggling through the conceptual morass and facing the political challenges that will determine the nature of early intervention services in the 1990s.

The Individualized Family Service Plan (IFSP). A major goal of P.L. 99-457 is to strengthen families as a means of promoting the development of young children with special needs. States that elect to fully implement Part H will need to establish a service delivery system encompassing a more collaborative and less hierarchical relationship between service providers and service recipients. To this end, P.L. 99-457 specifies the Individualized Family Service Plan (IFSP) to be the vehicle through which child and family services will be implemented. This written service plan is to be developed collaboratively by families and the professionals involved in assessment and service delivery. The contents and procedure for developing the IFSP are described

in Chapter 5. It is important to note that this new legislation has provided the framework for a family-focused approach to early intervention. While P.L. 94-142 clearly sought family involvement when it established the Individualized Education Program (IEP), which will also be described later, it fell short of developing the family's capabilities in relation to the needs of their child. Important components of P.L. 99-457 are included in Exhibit 2–3.

HISTORICAL APPROACHES TO EARLY EDUCATION PROGRAMMING

With the focus on public-supported preschool education created by the 1964 funding of Head

---

EXHIBIT 2–3

Major Features of P.L. 99-457

- Establishes state-level interagency councils on early intervention.
- Institutes individualized family service plans.
- Provides case management services to families.
- Maintains a public awareness program that includes a comprehensive child find system and a central early intervention resource directory.
- Establishes a single line of responsibility for general supervision and monitoring of services.
- Requires the development of a multidisciplinary, coordinated interagency model of service delivery.
- Establishes procedural safeguards.
- Acknowledges the family to be the central focus of service.
- Provides for smooth transitions as a family moves from one service or system to another.
- Facilitates development of a comprehensive system of personnel development.

Start came the need for development of model centers. Preschool education had been almost exclusively the domain of the middle and upper classes within settings that did not provide for the inclusion of children who were different in culture or ability. Programs primarily followed what has become known as the "child-development" or "normal-development" model (Anastasiow, 1978; Mayer, 1971; Thurman & Widerstrom, 1990). The concept of "readiness" has been associated with this model. Children were thought to develop at their own rate if encouraged by a warm, nurturing, and organized environment.

Educators were highly influenced by developmental age enthusiasts such as Gesell and prepared curricular experiences according to the developmental scales available. Children were seen as active learners capable of choosing activities from a variety of activity centers. Social-emotional development, large-group involvement, self-concept enhancement, and child-to-child interaction were high priorities. Teacher-oriented activities were prepared for groups of children. By all appearances these programs, which really did not have to accommodate significant differences in behavior or ability, were successful. But nothing noteworthy had been done in the way of program evaluation or the development of model programs that could be replicated readily.

Faced with a lack of program models, directors of the newly funded programs for children of low-income families began to experiment with ideas and techniques. Out of their efforts came the development of programs based on (a) behavioristic principles as purported by Watson, Skinner, and others; (b) the cognitively oriented strategies of Piaget; and (c) the resurgence of techniques developed by Montessori. These programs, in turn, served as the bases for the development of the model programs funded by the Bureau of Education for the Handicapped in the late 1960s and 1970s.

Early Childhood Education and Special Education

Programs that adapt curricula to meet the needs of children with a wide range of differences in skills, learning styles, background, and potential require deliberate integration of facets from both early childhood education and special education. Early childhood specialists promote awareness of needs of the "whole child," whereas special educators promote awareness of unique needs within the child. These unique needs are considered in relation to tasks being taught and the environment in which they are taught. Learning characteristics of the child as well as the tasks are analyzed. The focus of this book is one of combining the best of both fields.

Anastasiow (1981) challenged teacher preparation departments to recognize that children with disabilities are more like typical children than they are different. He expressed special concern with basic needs such as emotional development and creative play. Future coursework in the area of early childhood special education needs to encompass widely what is known in child development and learning theory. Anastasiow envisioned the development of early childhood programs in which "behaviorism [task analysis or applied behavioral analysis] will be used as a technology of program construction and implementation while cognitive theories will be used as the theoretical basis to account for and describe human behavior" (p. 277).

Options Within Early Childhood Education

Theoretical approaches within early childhood education have been categorized in a number of ways. For clarity, the categorical approach selected here is in keeping with the historical overview presented earlier. It should be remembered that these approaches overlap in a variety of ways and that there are almost no "pure" programs. Therefore, this description may be somewhat unlike that of others who set about to relate the same basic information.

The Child-Development, Maturationist Approach. The child-development, maturationist approach was discussed briefly earlier in this chapter, because it has been typical of traditionally oriented nursery schools or kindergartens. Curriculum experiences are organized around units and themes such as community helpers, the family, and the zoo. Unique abilities are developed within a relatively unrestrictive environment in which the teacher facilitates each child's natural rate of development. Early compensatory Head Start programs turned to this model in their quest to provide enrichment for children thought to be deprived of experiences received by children of better means. Activities are often carried on in groups using activity centers. Field trips are a highly valued part of the curriculum. Play is considered essential to both cognitive and emotional development. Gesell, of course, is regarded as the originator of this maturationist viewpoint.

Behaviorist Approach. In contrast to the compensatory programs that provided enriching theories through the somewhat nondirected approach of the child-development model, the behaviorist approach concentrates on direct teaching of skills. Whereas child developmentalists view the child as a very active participant in learning, behaviorists perceive the child as passive. Behavior is to be shaped through manipulation of environmental circumstances that produce specific responses to be rewarded. Academic skills receive high priority. Skills are analyzed, and component skills are sequenced. This sequence then directs the curriculum content. Direct Instruction Systems for Teaching Arithmetic and Reading (DISTAR), which originated with a program begun by Be-

reiter and Engelmann (1966), is considered characteristic of this approach.

The Psychoanalytical-Psychosocial Approach. The psychoanalytical-psychosocial approach originated with Freud but is recognized most easily through the writings of Erikson (1963). It emphasizes the emotional, affective nature of a child's development. The child is seen as evolving through a series of psychosexual stages, which are discussed in detail in Chapter 7. Proponent curricula focus on attitudes, values, and promotion of positive interaction with others. Children explore and actively interact with their environment under the watchful eyes of teachers who encourage autonomy and development of self-esteem. The Bank Street model (Biber, 1970) is characteristic of this approach.

Cognitive Approach. Programs within the cognitive approach envision active learners who seek interaction through which cognitive development occurs. Although different in structure, programs developed according to the teachings of both Piaget and Montessori stress this basic view. Reference is made to the cognitive curriculum developed during the course of the Perry Preschool Project by Weikart (1971). Children are encouraged to become actively involved and to engage in "discovery learning" designed to foster movement through the Piagetian stages of cognitive development. Teachers set up opportunities for experiences in classification, seriation, temporal relations, and spatial relations that are facilitated through observation and questioning.

Within a Montessori program, children learn through active discovery but rely more on highly sequenced, specialized materials. The importance of sensory-motor learning is again paramount. Children's learning can be self-directed because the materials permit self-correction. Learning is highly individualized, with little opportunity for group teaching. Specific skill development is ensured through this highly structured approach.

Contribution of Special Education

The contribution of special education is derived primarily from emphasis on the need to consider individual differences when selecting curriculum approaches and planning activities. Thus the new field of early childhood special education has developed to meet unique needs not accommodated in regular early education centers. A diagnostic-prescriptive program is often the result. Such an approach has roots in the medical model, where the individual's condition is diagnosed and treatment is prescribed. Ysseldyke and Salvia (1974) discussed two basic models within the diagnostic-prescriptive teaching approach. Descriptions follow.

Ability Training Approach. The ability training approach seeks to identify the processes or abilities that create observed interindividual and intraindividual differences (Adelman & Taylor, 1986). Profiles of an individual's strengths and weaknesses in perceptual, cognitive, psycholinguistic, and psychomotor development are constructed from information obtained from testing. Activities based on the test constructs are then prescribed. The GOAL kit developed and used by Karnes in the Precise Early Education for Children with Handicaps (PEECH) project (Karnes & Zehrbach, 1977) contains characteristic activities.

Although ability training as a total approach is under criticism (Hammill & Larsen, 1978), it has made a worthy contribution. Understanding an individual child's strengths and weaknesses, both in terms of his or her individual profile and in comparison to others of the same age, allows teachers to adapt the curriculum accordingly. For example, children who have better auditory than visual processing skills will perform better when something is explained verbally as well as demonstrated visually. This combination allows the weaker visual skills to be strengthened with the help of the stronger auditory skills.

Behavioral/Skills Approach. While the ability training approach analyzes the process or ability strengths and weaknesses within a child, the task

analysis or observable-skills approach looks at the subcomponents of a task. The ability training approach may look at the child's performance in terms of visual, auditory, and tactile performance. This approach examines the requirements of the task. What is the child expected to learn, and how is he or she expected to learn it? Terminal behaviors (skills) are broken into enroute behaviors that are sequenced from the easiest to the most difficult. This approach is critical to the development of so-called "functional" skills that are necessary to survival and to acceptance by significant others in one's environment. Chapter 6 describes this essentially behavioral approach.

The Move Toward Noncategorical Instruction. For years, special education has focused on diagnosing children and teaching them according to categories such as mental retardation, emotional disturbance, and learning disability. The detrimental effects of labels (Meisels, 1989) and the difficulty of making a differential diagnosis of young children (Lerner, Mardell-Czudnowski, & Goldenberg, 1981) strengthen the arguments for noncategorical placement. Such placement also recognizes the needs of children with multiple disabilities. However, the instructional techniques developed for use within various disabling categories should not be overlooked. These have evolved through much effort, and their use has been evaluated often. They are a contribution from the field of special education. The literature devoted to these categories serves as a rich resource from which to choose instructional strategies. Many of these have been incorporated throughout this book.

Bricker's "Developmental-Prescriptive" Approach

Notable is the extensive program developed by Bricker and Bricker (1976) that integrates a variety of theoretical bases. After careful consideration, these researchers felt that adherence to either a traditional maturational orientation or a behavioristic learning theory approach could not adequately account for the complexities of human behavior they would encounter. Therefore, they combined several key Piagetian concepts into a position they refer to as the "constructive interaction-adaptive" position. Believing that the sensorimotor period is critical to subsequent language development and that infants learn from active interaction, they insisted on beginning intervention in the first year of life.

The parent training program became an integral part of the project, because these developers believed strongly that parents and interventionists must avoid working at cross purposes. Parents were trained in the use of behavioral management techniques. A task analysis orientation, characteristic of special education and called "developmental programming" by the Brickers, was used to organize an educational curriculum covering language, sensorimotor, social, and motor development. Lessons were planned in small steps, and positive reinforcement (rewarding appropriate behavior) was used. Psycholinguistic and perceptual theory, again drawn from the field of special education, provided needed contributions to critical language training. The teachings of social learning theory were used to promote positive peer modeling.

Table 2–1 provides a brief comparison of some of the early intervention models that have been described in the literature. Because this is an effort to summarize some very involved theories, it does not do any of them justice. This interpretation is also open to question and perhaps rebuttal. We are taking the risk of including it here in hopes of generating student-instructor discussion and investigation that will lead to greater understanding of possible theoretical underpinnings. An annotated bibliography is included at the end of the chapter to facilitate such inquiry.

Table 2–1 Comparison of program models

Variables	Approaches				
	Child-Development	Behavioral	Piagetian	Montessori	Developmental-Prescriptive
View of child					
Active	X		X	X	X
Passive		X			
Stage determined					
Age determined	X		X	X	X
Focus-emphasis					
Sensorimotor			X	X	X
Language		X			X
Thought processes			X		X
Social-emotional	X				X
Self-help	X			X	X
School readiness	X	X			X
Self-concept	X				X
Approach					
Skill assessment		X		X	X
Sequenced, small steps		X		X	X
Modeling-reinforcement		X			X
Repetition-drill		X			X
Prescriptive training		X			X
Inquiry			X	X	
Play highly valued	X		X	X	
Planned language learning		X			X
Incidental language learning	X		X		
Self-correction		X	X	X	
Self-paced		X	X	X	X
Activity centers	X		X	X	
Creative activities	X		X	X	X
Direct instruction		X		X	X
Teacher as facilitator	X		X	X	X
Inquiry encouraged			X	X	X

Based on interpretations of Anastasiow, 1978; Anastasiow and Mansergh, 1975; Safford, 1978; Stevens and King, 1976.

Model Similarities. Generally all programs, perhaps with the exception of the strictest of behavioral approaches, see the child as an active explorer intrinsically involved in learning. White (1959) referred to the child's tendency toward playful exploration as *competence* or **effectance motivation.** It is this capacity to interact effectively with the environment that is thought to result in cumulative learning, paving the way to maturity.

Most programs thus emphasize the role of sensorimotor involvement in the development of curricula for young children. They recognize the importance of stimulation in the development of "typical" children. Children with disabilities may have a natural lack of stimulating opportunities by virtue of being deprived of sensory or motor experiences. Early interventionists therefore are faced with the necessity of searching continuously to find techniques or approaches that might make effectance motivation possible for children who lack the capacity to explore or investigate on their own.

Model Differences. Although most models of early childhood education would agree that instructional goals must include all aspects of development, they differ in their presentation of how one aspect of development relates to another. For example, there is disagreement as to whether social maturity is the result of cognitive development or both develop simultaneously. The strict behaviorist stresses that academic accomplishments will lead to self-esteem. On the other hand, child developmentalists see intellectual growth developing out of feelings of self-worth and social competence.

Role of the Early Interventionist

The role of the interventionist and the methods of intervention differ considerably among the models illustrated. The teacher in the traditional child development model sets up an environment conducive to activity in both small and large groups. This teacher nurtures the children's interests and waits to observe as their needs unfold. Opportunity to experiment in a stimulating environment where the teacher uses a questioning approach to guide hypothesis generation characterizes a Piagetian approach. In a Montessori school a director or directress would encourage individual involvement with concrete materials designed to achieve self-paced sequential learning with little verbal interchange. Children attending a strict behavioral program would receive considerable direct instruction planned to prompt, model, and shape observable behavior toward clearly defined academically oriented goals. Finally, a developmental-prescriptive model would promote the analysis of tasks and the assessment of individual children's strengths and weaknesses in relation to the task sequence. Instruction would then begin at each child's level of entry and proceed in development sequence. A variety of techniques might be used to proceed from step to step.

Individualization Encourages Adaptive Innovation. P.L. 94-142 requires an individualized education program developed by an interdisciplinary team for each child with identified special needs. Therefore, it is reasonable to expect a variety of approaches to be used in meeting the great diversity of needs encountered. For example, children who need help controlling aggressive tendencies may profit from the consistent, systematic approach of the behaviorists. Shaping behavior through prompting and reinforcement helps some children develop self-control. Children who need opportunities to manipulate concrete materials at their own pace with immediate feedback and repetition will benefit from the Montessori orientation. The multisensory discovery approach advocated by Piaget may be the best way to meet the needs of highly talented children as well as those who lack appropriate sensory stimulation.

Safford (1978, pp. 19–20) summed up the similarities and differences in theoretical approaches to early childhood special education by identifying two "streams." The first stream is characteristic of privately operated nursery schools, parent cooperatives, and laboratory schools that are identified with the "traditional" or "child-development" model. Spontaneity and social cooperation are highly valued. The second stream involves a high degree of structure and teacher-directed activities. The Montessori approach is used as an example. Safford further stated,

In practice, there are probably very few early childhood educators who adhere to a "pure" approach. Most are eclectic, drawing from various theories, adapting what others have found to be successful, and modifying their program on the basis of their own experience. (p. 24)

Teacher Preparation Is Critical. Yes, teachers do adapt and modify on the basis of their own experience. Therefore, any approach will be only as good as the teacher who implements it. According to a research report discussed in the seventh annual report on Head Start published by the Department of Health and Human Services, one of the primary reasons for Head Start's success in mainstreaming is in the implementation of training programs. The most important factor cited for success was the teacher's experience in working with children with special needs.

To develop and implement the IEP required by law, teachers must be able to plan programs that incorporate techniques from the variety of remediation and enrichment strategies available. They must be able to choose those most appropriate for each child. To do so, teachers should have the ability to assess the educational needs of each child, implement step-by-step programming, and evaluate the effectiveness of techniques used.

Probable Dimensions of Effective Early Intervention Programs

Even though evaluation studies have failed to determine that any one model of early childhood education is the most effective, these studies point the way to some probable dimensions of effective programs. In brief, teachers are urged to consider the following 12 elements when initiating or evaluating a program (Anastasiow, 1978; Brekken, 1986; Safford, 1989; Strain, 1986; Weikart, 1972):

1. High adult-to-child ratio (one adult to four or five children).

2. A well-defined program model and philosophy with staff commitment to the approach being implemented.

3. Extensive and cooperative planning for instruction.

4. High level of family involvement and support.

5. Facilitation of functional skills to enable children to cope with environmental expectations.

6. Interdisciplinary involvement and interagency coordination.

7. Individualized instructional objectives with continuous evaluation and revision when necessary.

8. Experimentation and evaluation of a variety of techniques to determine those most effective in meeting child- and family-focused objectives.

9. Strong emphasis on language development.

10. Provision for positive reinforcement and effective use of principles of behavior management, task analysis, and modeling.

11. Enhancement of social skills of both children with special needs and nondisabled

children by allowing them to share common experiences.

12. Ongoing program evaluation and program revision as needed.

CURRENT TRENDS IN EARLY CHILDHOOD SPECIAL EDUCATION

Figure 2–2 (Lynch, 1990) reflects the major changes and trends in the field of early childhood special education that will become increasingly important in the 1990s. These include changes in both program philosophies and program practices. Some of the current trends are discussed briefly here.

Family Focus

A genuine understanding of early intervention requires that the infant or young child be viewed within the context of his or her family. Current program philosophy can be described as more family focused and more sensitive to the diverse

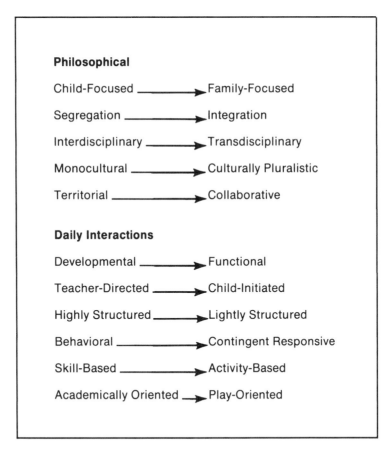

Figure 2–2   Best practice continua for children who have disabilities or are at-risk and their families. *Source:* **Eleanor Lynch, April 14, 1990**

cultural and structural differences among families than were earlier philosophies.

Interagency Collaboration and Transdisciplinary Service Delivery Models

Assessment and intervention practices are characterized by collaboration among professionals and agencies. A move toward transdisciplinary service delivery models encourages early childhood special educators to seek assistance and consultation from a team of related service professionals. Professionals from various disciplines work together cooperatively to educate one another so that one professional can provide a broader range of essential services. For example, a teacher or caregiver may, on the advice of a speech-language pathologist, redirect an informal playground activity to facilitate language development.

Integration

Program philosophy of the 1990s strongly supports opportunities for integration of children with special needs into their neighborhood schools and day care programs. Early childhood special educators must be prepared to collaborate with regular early education personnel to ensure the success of children with special needs in a variety of community settings. It is with this success that equal access to community resources will be achieved.

Developmentally Appropriate Activities in Natural Settings

Program practices emphasize teaching children within the context of play and developmentally appropriate activities. Greater value is placed on children's initiation. Program goals are functional and relevant to children's and families' lives. Highly structured approaches utilizing strategies of behavior analysis and behavior modification are seen as useful tools for refinement of specific behaviors rather than as predominant teaching methodologies.

Functional-Ecological and Social-Transactional Approaches to Curriculum Development. Two current trends in curriculum development are the functional-ecological approach and the social-transactional approach. Guess and Noonan (1982) have argued that educational goals should be selected on the basis of their functional utility for the child in his or her immediate or next environment. Murphy and Vincent (1989) have emphasized the importance of identifying goals that have meaning and relevance within the child's real-life environment of home and community. These ideas form the basis of the **functional-ecological approach** to early intervention.

The **social-transactional approach** emphasizes the role of social and communicative interactions in children's development. Research and theoretical discussions forming the basis of this approach are abundant (Sameroff & Fiese, 1990). According to Mahoney and Powell (1988), this approach suggests that the main goal of intervention is to maximize children's intrinsic motivation through effective interactions. The focus of interventions is on the *quality* of interactions between children and their caregivers. The major strategy is to provide opportunities that encourage children to increase the frequency of interactive experiences that seem appropriate to the promotion of their development. The role of the interventionist is to assist parents and other primary caregivers to function more effectively as children's interactive partners.

BEST PRACTICES IN EARLY CHILDHOOD EDUCATION

The best practices for the field of early childhood special education must be built on those well-established principles of practice which are best for *all* young children. These are perhaps best stated in the 1986 position statement offered by the National Association for the Education of Young Children (NAEYC, 1986). Two major themes have guided the development of these best practices: (1) that early education must meet the individual developmental needs of each child and (2) that the best medium through which to do this is children's play.

Several key recommendations emerge within this NAEYC framework related to curriculum, adult-child interactions, family involvement, and evaluation that are essential to high-quality early intervention programs. These are summarized below. However, it will become apparent throughout the remainder of this text that early interventionists must move beyond the criteria of NAEYC's best practices to ensure specific instructional techniques necessary to meet the unique needs of young children with disabilities and their families. The field of early childhood special education is built on best practices from the fields of both early childhood and special education. Reference to these practices is incorporated throughout this text.

Curriculum

- Educational goals are incorporated into all daily activities. Objectives are not taught in isolation, but are integrated into meaningful activities and events.

- Curriculum planning and intervention are based on the teacher's specific observations of each child in natural contexts.

- Learning is an *interactive* process. Children's interactions with adults, peers, and the physical environment are all important.

- Learning activities and materials must be concrete and *relevant* to children's lives. Teachers should make use of real-life objects and activities (e.g., make a trip to the fire station, not just read a story about fire engines).

- Programs must be able to meet a wide range of interests and abilities. Teachers are expected to *individualize* instructional programs.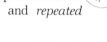

- Teachers must increase the difficulty and challenge of activities gradually and skillfully.

- Teachers must be able to facilitate *engagement* of each child by offering choices, making suggestions, asking questions, and describing events in ways that are meaningful and interesting to the child.

- Children should be given opportunities for *self-initiation*, *self-direction*, and *repeated practice.*

- Teachers must accept and appreciate cultural differences in children and families and avoid ethnic and gender stereotypes.

- Programs must provide a balance between rest and activity, and they should include outdoor activities each day.

- Outdoor activities should be *planned*, not simply opportunities to release pent-up energy.

- Programs must create careful *transitions* from one activity to the next. Children should not be rushed, and schedules should be flexible enough to take advantage of impromptu experiences.

Adult-Child Interaction

- Adults should respond quickly and directly to children's needs and attempts to communicate. Whenever possible, adults should be at eye level with children.

- Children must be provided with a variety of opportunities to communicate. Interaction is best facilitated on a one-to-one basis, or in groups of two to three children. Large-group instruction is less effective in facilitating communication.

- Professionals must be alert to signs of stress and provide sensitive, appropriate assistance to children.

- Adults must facilitate the development of self-esteem by "expressing respect, acceptance, and comfort for children, regardless of the child's behavior" (NAEYC, 1986, p. 14).

- Adults must use disciplinary techniques that enhance the development of self-control. These include setting clear, consistent limits; redirecting inappropriate behavior; valuing mistakes; listening to children's concerns and frustrations; helping children solve conflicts; and patiently reminding children of rules as needed.

- Adults must be responsible for all children at all times. Health and safety issues must be addressed constantly.

- Adults must plan for gradually increasing children's independence.

Family Involvement

- Parents have the right and the responsibility to share in decision making regarding their children's care and education. Professionals must maintain frequent contact, and parents should be encouraged to participate.

- Professionals must regularly share information and resources with parents, including information regarding stages of child development. They must also obtain and respect parents' views of individual children's behavior and development.

Evaluation

- Child evaluations should not rely on a single instrument.

- Evaluations should identify children with special needs and provide information that will lead to meaningful educational modifications.

- Evaluations must be culturally appropriate.

ADDITIONAL BEST PRACTICES FOR CHILDREN WITH SPECIAL NEEDS

In addition to the NAEYC recommendations just summarized, certain other recommendations are particularly important for young children with special needs. McDonnell and Hardman (1988) have suggested the following:

- Services for young children with disabilities should be provided in integrated settings within the local community.

- A transdisciplinary model of service delivery should be utilized; isolated therapies should be minimized.

- Artificial reinforcement and aversive control techniques should be avoided.

- Training should emphasize function rather than form of response.

- Program planning should include planned enhancement of the child's skill development within daily family routines.

- Curriculum should be developed with reference to the individual child, as well as to family, peers, and the community.

- Program evaluation and child assessment should be accomplished using a variety of outcome measures.

- Transitions from one educational setting to the next should be planned carefully.

A Cautionary Note

Students of early childhood special needs must realize that, as is the case with any new field, early childhood special education is constantly evolving. The ideas and notions that comprise today's "best practices" may be very different from those which evolve by the year 2000. Early intervention professionals must have a thirst for knowledge and a genuine desire to better understand how to meet the needs of young children with disabilities. They must also have considerable tolerance for ambiguity as the field continues to define itself and its methodologies. Finally, early interventionists must have an understanding of the potential contribution of research. Practitioners must be responsible for maintaining an important two-way dialogue with the field's researchers. They must help identify important research questions, insist on the use of research methods that are appropriate to answer those questions, and then apply the findings of that research to their own practice.

VIEWING THE CHILD WITH SPECIAL NEEDS AS A CHILD FIRST

It is impossible to overstate the point that children with special needs are children first—children who have the same characteristics and needs as so-called "typical" children. The beauty of being young and "new" is the potential for growth and change. All infants and young children, no matter how significantly challenged or disabled, will benefit from those best practices which create supportive and nurturing environments for all young children. This belief must be the foundation of early childhood special education.

For some children, additional strategies, techniques, and adaptations will be required to maximize their opportunities to experience, enjoy, and learn from the world around them. Thus, students of early childhood special education must master two sets of skills: one related to facilitating learning and healthy growth and development in all children, and another related to the very specific and special needs of children with disabilities. Appendix D provides a sample list of important competencies for professionals in early childhood special education to master.

SERVICE DELIVERY SYSTEMS

The placement options available for young children with special needs are, of course, dependent on the service delivery systems within their communities. The term *service delivery system* in early intervention refers to several components that, together, describe and define the parameters of any early intervention program. According to Peterson (1987), these include the following components:

1. *Who:* The target of service (e.g., child, mother, family).

2. *When:* The beginning point of service (e.g., birth, infancy, preschool).

3. *What:* The services that are provided (e.g., screening, diagnostic assessment, education programs, therapeutic services, family counseling, medical services, transportation, etc.).

4. *Where:* The setting of the services (e.g.,

home-based, center-based day care or pre-school, clinic, etc.).

5. *By Whom:* The primary intervention agent (e.g., parent, teacher, paraprofessional, transdisciplinary team, etc.).

6. *With Whom:* The social context of services (e.g., individual program, integrated program, segregated program).

7. *Through Whom:* The agencies providing the services (e.g., public schools, private programs, government agencies, etc.).

Several of these parameters are of special interest today as professionals plan and families select service delivery alternatives. Of particular concern to parents may be the issues of who is the focus of service, where the service will be offered, who will provide the service, and to what extent their child will be provided service alongside normal peers. Professionals are required to offer the service delivery option that is most appropriate for each child. While the term *appropriate* is not well defined, the law does, at least, require each placement team to specify the extent to which the child will participate in regular educational programs.

The following section summarizes some of the major points related to the determination of individually appropriate placement options and services to be delivered.

Home-Based and Center-Based Programs

Considerations of where early intervention takes place focus on home-based versus center-based programs. For infants and for children with severe disabilities, home-based services often are considered to be the least restrictive because they are in the most "normal" environment. In home-based programs, early intervention professionals or paraprofessionals visit the child and family in the home. The range of frequency of such visits

varies widely from weekly to once every several months.

It is "normal" for toddlers and preschool-aged children to attend center-based day care and preschool programs. These center-based programs are typically somewhat structured group settings to which families bring their children. As with home-based programs, the frequency varies. However, there is typically more frequent contact, ranging from 1 to 5 times weekly. Some service delivery models combine home- and center-based services. Children may be enrolled in a center 2 or 3 days per week while home visits continue ranging from monthly to quarterly.

Setting alone does not determine the effectiveness of an early intervention program. Because there is much variability across program types (e.g., frequency, degree of parent involvement, strategies used, etc.), it is difficult to compare the relative effectiveness of home-based versus center-based programs. While there have been few carefully conducted studies comparing the two types of approaches, Bailey and Simeonsson (1988) have suggested the following possible advantages and disadvantages of each:

1. Center-based programs may be more effective in preparing children for school environments by emphasizing such skills as focusing attention, following directions and schedules, completing tasks, and so on.

2. Home-based programs may offer more intensive one-on-one intervention, and children may spend less time waiting their turn to participate in activities.

3. Home-based programs may have a greater effect on parent-child interactions, since this is often more of an emphasis in home-based than in center-based programs. On the other hand, home-based programs that emphasize the parent's role as teacher may place stress on parents that interferes with their spontaneity and their interactions as parents and nurturers.

4. Center-based programs can provide relief from the often overwhelming caregiving responsibilities of parents of children with special needs.

5. Infectious diseases such as otitis media and diarrhea occur at higher rates among children who attend center-based programs than those who do not. However, for children from impoverished environments, center-based programs may offer opportunities to obtain nutritious meals.

6. Some studies have suggested that parents in home-based programs have more positive attitudes toward their children than parents of children in center-based programs. Moran (1985) found that mothers in home-based programs had strong relationships with the service provider and were more likely to follow through on specific suggestions.

7. Parents participating in center-based programs are more likely to develop social networks and gain support from other parents.

It should be clear that no one setting is definitely the best for all children and families. Settings must be selected by families with assistance from professionals according to the specific needs of each child and his or her family. When determining which setting is most appropriate, primary attention must focus on whether or not the services available will increase the chances that the child will be able to function more independently as he or she grows older. The setting selected will have to be culturally compatible with the values and child-rearing practices of the child's family if the child is to be in an environment that is most normal for him or her.

Child-Focused and Family-Focused Programs

Another parameter of service delivery of particular interest today is the target of intervention, that is, whether intervention is directed primarily toward the child or the caregiver. In both instances, with the passage of P.L. 99-457, the family must be the primary focal point and context within which the child is viewed. However, even within this family-centered framework, intervention may be focused more on the child or on the caregiver.

Child-Focused Approaches. Bricker and Veltman (1990) defined child-focused programs as those which have as their primary focus the enhancement of the child's development. They stated that such programs are based on two theoretical assumptions: (1) that biological problems can be overcome or ameliorated and (2) that early experience is important. Related to the latter assumption is a third assumption: that the potential to have a positive impact on children's development is greater when intervention occurs at younger ages.

Traditionally, under the influence of behavioral theories and the field of special education, child-focused programs have been more teacher directed than child directed. Such approaches have been characterized by carefully planned and highly structured programs that were controlled primarily by a teacher using behavioral analysis techniques.

Currently, child-focused programs are becoming more child directed. Child-directed programs assume that the child's development can best be facilitated through opportunities for self-initiation and exploration that are carefully mediated by responsive adults.

Child-focused programs do not ignore family needs. Family involvement is primarily in the context of enabling family members to meet the child's needs while at the same time having some of their own needs met. Parents are included as partners with professionals and as members of the child's intervention team.

Caregiver-Focused Approaches. Caregiver-focused approaches are those that concentrate primarily on the delivery of services to parents. Within this category, there are two fairly distinct kinds of programs. The first seeks to establish a clinical therapeutic relationship with the parents, usually the mother, in an effort to bring about some psychodynamic change. For example, this may include changes in the caregiver's view of herself and how she perceives and experiences her infant (Zeanah & Barton, 1989). In this approach, it is assumed that once these psycho-emotional changes are brought about, the mother's interactions and relationship with her child will automatically be positive and facilitative. Other approaches may be less focused on a therapeutic relationship, but they continue to assume that providing emotional support and guidance for the caregiver will have positive effects on the infant. Elements of both of these approaches can be found in the Yale Child Welfare Program described by Provence and Naylor (1983).

A second major category of caregiver-focused intervention programs are those which concentrate specifically on the training of caregiver-infant interaction strategies, often focusing particularly on communicative interaction. These approaches attempt to change or enhance caregivers' behaviors as they care for their infants or young children within the context of daily routines. This approach does not ask parents to be trainers, but rather to be responsive in particular ways to their infant's naturally occurring cues. (See Chapter 9 for a fuller discussion of the bases of these programs.) Examples of this type of caregiver-focused approach have been described by Klein and Briggs (1987) and MacDonald (1989).

It is readily apparent that selection of systems in which to deliver or receive services is a complex process requiring careful collaboration between parents and professionals. The more in tune professionals are with child and family needs, the more likely it is that appropriate recommendations will be made. The next chapter will address the complicated issues involved in assessing these special needs.

One of the points emphasized in this review of the best practices for early intervention services is that interventionists must view all children within the context of their families and communities. The next chapter discusses the family-focused skills that enable the development of family-professional partnerships. It also discusses how families affect and are affected by children with special needs, and it offers a variety of service options for families.

Summary

This chapter reviews the field of early childhood special education historically and theoretically. Over the past 100 years, the lot of children with special needs has shifted from "hide and forget" to "identify and help." Pioneering ventures into formal early education in the United States began with the establishment of kindergartens during the 1850s. With the testing performed by Binet soon after the turn of the century, the identification of children with disabilities progressed toward a formal societal concern.

Controversy over the influence of nature (genetics) versus nurture (environmental experiences) has spawned numerous theoretical and empirical approaches. Gesell stressed biological importance and developed normative "ages and stages" indices. Watson and Skinner emphasized the importance of environmental contingencies as forerunners to current behavior modification approaches. Between the extremes, in the late 1950s Hebb proposed that behavior is an interaction between genetic and environmental variables. Meanwhile, Piaget emphasized the role of the child as active learner with inborn tendencies toward patterned stages of cognitive development that are experientially based.

Results of several research studies led to greater acceptance by the mid-1960s of the belief that intelligence develops rapidly in the primary years of life and early stimulation can influence this development. Head Start began as a federally funded project in 1965 to provide enrichment opportunities for young children in impoverished families and was subsequently extended to include at least 10% children with disabilities. Initial research indicated that the immediate educational gains for Head Start children quickly faded, but longitudinal studies have substantiated long-term persistence of this early intervention. Children between birth and 8 years of age who have disabilities were given a boost in 1968 through legislation that created the Handicapped Childrens Early Education Program. The resulting model programs emphasized inclusion of parents in their child's educational activities.

P.L. 94-142 mandates that appropriate public education be made available to all children with disabilities as early as possible. One significant provision of this law is that each child should have a written IEP. Children with disabilities also are to be served in the least restrictive environment that meets their needs. The law mandates inclusion in a regular classroom unless the child's disabilities are too severe. In effect, the thrust is to fit the schooling to the child rather than fit the child to the school. Such an aim provides the major impetus of this book. This aim is pursued through informed selection of intervention strategies, with preparation of the interventionist as the critical foundation.

P.L. 99-457 is legitimizing the field of early childhood special education. Federal, state, and local planners are collaborating with parents in unprecedented efforts to develop new and expanded services for infants and young children who have disabilities or are at risk and their families. Part H provides incentives for states to provide comprehensive, coordinated family-focused interagency programs for children from birth through age 2. Unique to this law are the requirements for collaborative case-management services designed to implement individualized family service plans (IFSPs).

Strategies for inclusion of children with special needs into the early education curriculum have had several theoretical origins. Traditionally, nursery schools and kindergartens have been designed around the child-development or normal-development model, organizing enriching experiences around theme units and play. The behaviorist and special education approaches involve a more deliberate manipulation of the environment to reward desired behavioral responses, which typically were structured around sequences of skills. Others have drawn heavily from the affective nature of child development, as an outgrowth of Erikson's theory, or from the cognitive-interactional approach to learning through discovery, as advocated by Piaget.

Current approaches to early childhood special education continue to combine influences from both the early education and special education fields. The child development and early education literature emphasizes the importance of child-directed methods that are developmentally appropriate and utilize play and social interaction as primary vehicles for teaching and learning. Special education legislation has mandated a focus on family involvement and education within integrated, community-based settings. Researchers have pointed out the importance of functional, ecologically relevant goals appropriate to both child and family priorities and needs.

Although they are by no means clearly defined, two major curricular approaches appear to be emerging: a social-transactional approach and a functional-ecological approach. Fortunately, these two emphases are complementary. They are effectively combined in the operation of many programs. It will become evident that both approaches are also highly compatible with the philosophy of this textbook.

Finally, the field of early childhood special education is fortunate to be able to combine what researchers and practitioners have found to be the best practices of the two dynamic disciplines of early childhood education and special education. The evolving delivery systems offer a variety of opportunities to meet the unique needs of each child and his or her family.

Discussion Topics and Activities

1. Characterize the impact on an interventionist's behavior of the belief that a child's growth is determined primarily by heredity-nature or the belief that growth is determined primarily by the environment. What is your belief? How do or how will your beliefs influence your behavior as a teacher?

2. Choose at least six articles about childrearing or education that have appeared in leading popular magazines during the past year. Discuss these in light of the beliefs espoused. How can these beliefs influence behavior of parents and early interventionists? Do you see any relationship between these beliefs and historical developments? In what way might these be setting precedents?

3. Read the summary or complete report from Lazar and Darlington (1982). Discuss the full implications of the research results with class members. What aspects should be translated into classroom or center practice or program development and how?

4. Research one of the First Chance programs or any program funded through the Handicapped Children's Early Education Program. Send for literature or visit a program, if possible. Share what you have learned with classmates.

5. Discuss specific criteria an evaluator might use to determine whether or not a program encompasses the best practices of effective intervention programs listed in this chapter.

6. Obtain and study copies of guidelines explaining state and local implementation of P.L. 94-142 and P.L. 99-457.

7. Become informed of the service delivery options available in your area. Role play a transdisciplinary team meeting to determine which would be the most appropriate options for children and families with differing needs.

Annotated Bibliography

Historical Perspectives on Early Childhood
Special Education

Berrueta-Clement, J. R., Schweinhart, L. J., Barnett, W. S., Epstein, A. S., & Weikart, D. P. (1984). *Changed lives: The effects of the Perry Preschool Program on youths through age 19.* Ypsilanti, MI: High/Scope Press.

This most welcome book details the results of 20 years of study of children who attended the Perry Preschool Project in the 1960s. The positive findings should be helpful in convincing legislators, school board members, and other concerned citizens of the societal benefits derived from high-quality early educational experiences.

Bailey, D. B., Jens, K. G., & Johnson, N. (1983). Curricula for handicapped infants. In S. G. Garwood and R. R. Fewell (Eds.), *Educating handicapped infants* (pp. 387–416). Rockville, MD: Aspen.

This book discusses the practical and theoretical issues that determine the usefulness of curricula for early education. It explains the developmental milestones, Piagetian, and functional models, and compares curriculum packages on the basis of content, teaching strategies, provisions for assessment, and the availability of evaluation data.

Gray, S. W., Klaus, R. A., & Ramsey, B. K. (1982). *From three to twenty: The early training project.* Baltimore: University Park Press.

Here is the summary of a unique longitudinal study of an early intervention project initiated prior to Head Start. This book is nicely organized and well written. It is based on a study with an excellent research design. The findings of this research are suggestive of the long-range motivational impact of early intervention.

Hendrick, J. *The whole child.* (1988). Columbus, OH: Merrill.

This is a comprehensive, well-written book designed to equip beginning teachers with the attitudes and specific skills necessary to function effectively. An entire chapter is devoted to working with children with disabilities within the ordinary nursery school. Special attention is given to the teacher as a screening agent and to specific guidelines for including exceptional children in heterogeneous programs.

Jordan, J. B., Hayden, A. H., Karnes, M. B., & Wood, M. M. (Eds.). (1977). *Early childhood education for exceptional children.* Reston, VA: The Council for Exceptional Children.

This book focuses on the First Chance programs and presents exemplary practices in such areas as identification, recordkeeping, curriculum, physical environments, parent involvement, staffing patterns, and evaluation. Included is a directory of the BEH First Chance programs along with a list of standardized tests used by these programs. This is a valuable resource, because it offers insight into the legislation that established the First Chance programs as well as providing an excellent overview of the contributions of these programs.

Lazar, I., & Darlington, R. (1982). Lasting effects of education: A report from the Consortium for Longitudinal Studies. *Monographs of the Society for Research in Child Development*, 47 (Serial No. 195).

This report is the result of a collaborative effort of 12 research groups conducting longitudinal studies of low-income children who participated in experimental infant and preschool programs initiated in the 1960s. It is essential reading for anyone who doubts or wishes to secure evidence for the value of early childhood education.

Lombardo, V., & Lombardo, E. (1983). *Developing and administering early childhood programs.* Springfield, IL: Charles C. Thomas.

This comprehensive book is full of practical suggestions including sample forms; a policy handbook; and ideas for newsletters, parent handbooks, and recordkeeping. Readers are introduced to the historical background of early childhood education evolving into the variety of programs available today.

Weber, E. (1984). *Ideas influencing early childhood education: A theoretical analysis.* New York: Teachers College Press.

This volume examines the ideas that have shaped the behavior of several generations of early childhood educators. Advanced students interested in the diversity, even turbulence, existing in the theory and practice of early childhood education will appreciate this book.

Intervention Programs and Strategies for the
Inclusion of Young Children with Special Needs

Allen, K. E. (1981). Curriculum models for successful mainstreaming. *Topics in Early Childhood Special Education*, 1, 45–55.

Curriculum models described as behavioral, language-based, open-education, Piagetian cognitive,

Montessori, and developmental-interaction are analyzed according to their use as mainstreamed approaches. The role of the teacher, program structure, physical arrangements, learning through imitation, and interdisciplinary programming merit discussion as important components of a successful mainstreaming program.

Allen, K. E., & Goetz, E. M. (Eds.). (1982). *Early childhood education—Special problems, special solutions.* Rockville, MD: Aspen.

This book, appropriate for the more advanced student, is intended to "weave together the many threads of research related to a behavioral analysis of early identification and intervention of developmental problems in young handicapped, normal, and at-risk children" (p. xvii). Of particular interest is the chapter on transition from preschool to kindergarten for children with special needs. Those who wish to learn how to apply the behavioral approach to education will find this volume most intriguing.

Anastasiow, N. J. (Ed.). (1978). Strategies and models for early childhood intervention programs in integrated settings. In M. J. Guralnick (Ed.), *Early integration of handicapped and nonhandicapped children.* Baltimore: University Park Press.

This classic chapter clearly describes and analyzes four basic preschool model programs: behavioral, normal-developmental, cognitive-developmental, and cognitive learning. The author concludes that the cognitive-developmental and cognitive learning models may be the most adaptable to the environmental changes necessary to successful mainstreaming of children with disabilities. This assumption is made because these two models are thought to pay considerable attention to individual differences.

Bredekamp, S. (Ed.). (1986). *Developmentally appropriate practice.* Washington, DC: National Association for the Education of Young Children.

This book contains clear statements describing what NAEYC considers to be developmentally appropriate practices or "best practices" in early childhood programs serving children from birth through age 8. The book can be obtained from NAEYC and is a "must" for any caregiver or teacher of young children.

Hanson, M. J., & Lynch, E. W. (1989). *Early intervention: Implementing child and family services for infants and toddlers who are at-risk or disabled.* Austin, TX: PRO-ED.

A reader-friendly text with a best-practices approach to early intervention. Underlying the authors' recommendations for services is the philosophy of (a) a transactional model of child development; (b) a family-focused model; (c) a collaborative, community-based, interdisciplinary approach; (d) a continuum of services; and (e) an approach that is systematically planned and structured around achievement of specific goals.

Meisels, S. J., & Shonkoff, J. P. (Eds.). (1990). *Handbook of early childhood intervention.* New York: Cambridge University Press.

Here is a handbook designed to integrate the theory, research, and practical knowledge that guide current practice in the field of early intervention. It summarizes and synthesizes the vast knowledge base arising across the many disciplines involved in early intervention services. This is an excellent resource for serious students who wish to become familiar with the substantial literature underpinning this new field of study.

Peters, D., Neisworth, J. T., & Yawkey, T. D. (1985). *Early childhood education—From theory to practice.* Monterey, CA: Brooks/Cole.

This readable text places early childhood education within a historical and cultural context. It also provides an extensive presentation of operant behavior theory and cognitive-developmental theory, with classroom applications included for each model. This book is highly recommended for those who wish to understand just how to apply theory to daily practice.

Project Head Start. (1978). *Head Start, mainstreaming preschoolers series.* Washington, DC: U.S. Department of Health and Human Services, OHD—OCD.

This series of eight guides may be out of print, but it can be found in libraries and at Head Start centers. These are excellent resource guides. Looking for them is worth the effort. There is one for each traditional category of exceptionality. Although originally intended for teachers, parents, and volunteers who work in the Head Start program, anyone working with young children with disabilities will find this series to be extremely practical, well organized, and easy to understand.

Safford, P. L. (1989). *Integrated teaching in early childhood.* White Plains, NY: Longman.

The purpose of this text is to demonstrate a teaching philosophy that enables all teachers in public schools and preschools to respond effectively to the special needs of all children. It focuses on individualization, social interaction, working with parents, and use of resources. Also included is a section on integrating young gifted children.

Souweine, J., Crimmins, S., & Mazel, C. (1981). *Mainstreaming ideas for teaching young children.* Washington, DC: National Association for the Education of Young Children.

This is a clearly written, practical paperback book that offers valuable suggestions derived from the authors' experiences developing an integrated program in the Amherst-Pelham Public Schools in Massachusetts. It describes the philosophy, approach, strategies and sample activities used by the interdisciplinary staff. It answers many common questions and offers helpful suggestions for developing the IEP, setting up a mainstreamed classroom, planning each day involving parents, and using resources.

Thurman, S. K., & Widerstrom, A. H. (1990). *Infants and young children with special needs: A developmental and ecological approach.* Baltimore, MD: Paul H. Brookes.

Chapter 13 of this text discusses the models of early education based on delivery systems as well as the models based on philosophy. A fine array of example programs is described in sufficient detail. Readers can see how different approaches can provide necessary early educational experiences.

Widerstrom, A. H., Mowder, B. A., & Sandall, S. R. (1991). *At-risk and handicapped newborns and infants.* Englewood Cliffs, NJ: Prentice Hall.

This book addresses the major issues and trends confronting early interventionists working with very young children and their families. Especially valuable is the chapter that outlines the determinants of risk in infancy.

Winton, P. J., Turnbull, A. P., & Blacher, J. (1984). *Selecting a preschool: A guide for parents of handicapped children.* Baltimore: University Park Press.

This sensitive book is not only a boon for parents but it helps professionals be more effective in their efforts to support parents in preparation of their children for preschool, in developing the IEP, in home training, and in understanding their legal rights and responsibilities. This book is a must for any parent lending library.

Societal Pressures: The Impact of Litigation and Legislation

Cohen, S., Semmes, M., & Guralnick, M. J. (1979). Public Law 94-142 and the education of preschool handicapped children. *Exceptional Children, 45,* 279–284.

This article provides a concise historical perspective and explanation of P.L. 94-142, including its limitations in the area of education for handicapped preschoolers. The status of mandated programs within the United States is described along with the role of Head Start and continuing concerns related to the implementation of P.L. 94-142.

Gallagher, J. J., Trohanis, P. L., & Clifford, R. M. (Eds.) (1989). *Policy Implementation and PL 99-457.* Baltimore, MD: Paul H. Brookes.

This resource text offers guidelines and action plans for assisting policy makers move toward full compliance with P.L. 99-457. It is a helpful reference for those who wish to more fully understand lessons learned from P.L. 94-142 and the issues currently being considered as states move toward full implementation of P.L. 99-457.

Neisworth, J. T., & Garwood, S. G. (Eds.). (1984). Social policy and young handicapped children. *Topics in Early Childhood Special Education, 4(1).*

The entire issue of this relevant journal is devoted to examination of the factors, processes, and outcomes of social policy regarding handicapped children. It provides insight into what social policy is, pivotal litigation and legislation, a policy analysis of P.L. 94-142, trends within early childhood special education programming, and the dynamics of interaction among special education advocacy groups. Advanced students will find the issues very thought-provoking.

Roberts, J., & Hawk, B. (1980). *Legal rights primer for the handicapped: In and out of the classroom.* Navato, CA: Academic Therapy.

This valuable publication is an important tool for parents and professionals who serve the handicapped. It clarifies various issues and aspects of the law in a simple manner, avoiding much of the legal jargon. It is unique in covering life outside of formal education and addresses the legal rights surrounding schooling. The complete text of P.L. 94-142 is included.

References

Adelman, H. S., & Taylor, L. (1986). *An introduction to learning disabilities.* Glenview, IL: Scott, Foresman.

Anastasiow, N. J. (1978). Strategies and models for early childhood intervention programs in integrated settings. In M. J. Guralnick (Ed.), *Early intervention and the integration of handicapped and nonhandicapped children.* Baltimore: University Park Press.

Anastasiow, N. J. (1981). Early childhood education for the handicapped in the 1980s: Recommendations. *Exceptional Children, 47,* 276–282.

Anastasiow, N. J., & Mansergh, G. P. (1975). Teaching skills in early childhood programs. *Exceptional Children, 42,* 309–317.

Bailey, D., & Simeonsson, R. (1988). Home-based early intervention. In S. Odom & M. Karnes (Eds.), *Early intervention for infants and children with handicaps: An empirical base* (pp. 199–215). Baltimore: Paul H. Brookes.

Banet, B. A. (1979). A developmental approach for preschool children with special needs. In S. J. Meisels (Ed.), *Special education and development.* Baltimore: University Park Press.

Beller, E. K. (1979). Early intervention programs. In J. D. Osofsky (Ed.), *Handbook of infancy research.* New York: Wiley.

Bereiter, C., & Engelmann, S. (1966). *Teaching disadvantaged children in the preschool.* Englewood Cliffs, NJ: Prentice-Hall.

Biber, B. (1970). Goals and methods in a preschool program for disadvantaged children. *Children, 17,* 15–20.

Bijou, S. W. (1977). Practical implications of an interactional model of child development. *Exceptional Children, 44,* 6–14.

Bloom, B. S. (1964). *Stability and change in human characteristics.* New York: Wiley.

Brekken, L. (1986). Early intervention programs are different. *SERNews.* Sacramento, CA: Special Education Research Network.

Bricker, D. D. (1988). Commentary: The future of early childhood/special education. *Journal of the Division of Early Childhood, 12,* 276–278.

Bricker, D., Bailey, E., & Bruder, M. B. (1984). Efficacy of early intervention and the handicapped infant: A wise or wasted resource. *Advances in Developmental and Behavioral Pediatrics, 5,* 373–423.

Bricker, D., & Veltman, M. (1990). Early intervention programs: Child-focused approaches. In S. Meisels & J. Shonkoff (Eds.), *Handbook of early childhood intervention* (pp. 373–399). New York: Cambridge University Press.

Bricker, W. A., & Bricker, D. D. (1976). The infant, toddler and preschool research and intervention project. In T. D. Tjossem (Ed.), *Intervention strategies for high risk infants and young children.* Baltimore: University Park Press.

Brown v. Board of Education. 347 U.S. 483, 1954.

Caldwell, B. M. (1973). The importance of beginning early. In J. B. Jordan & R. F. Dailey (Eds.), *Not all little wagons are red: The exceptional child's early years.* Reston, VA: The Council for Exceptional Children.

Diana v. State Board of Education. Civil No. C-70-37 RFP (ND, Cal, January 7, 1970 and June 18, 1973).

Dunn, L. M. (1968). Special education for the mildly retarded—Is much of it justifiable? *Exceptional Children, 35,* 5–22.

Erikson, E. H. (1963). *Childhood and society.* New York: W. W. Norton.

Farran, D. C. (1990). Effects of intervention with disadvantaged and disabled children: A decade review. In S. J. Meisels & J. P. Shonkoff (Eds.), *Handbook of early childhood intervention* (pp. 501–539). New York: Cambridge University Press.

Freud, S. (1953). Three essays on sexuality. In *Standard edition* (Vol. 7). London: Hogarth.

Furth, H. (1970). *Piaget for teachers.* Englewood Cliffs, NJ: Prentice-Hall.

Garwood, S. G., & Fewell, R. R. (1983). *Educating handicapped infants.* Rockville, MD: Aspen.

Gesell, A. L. (1923). *The preschool child.* New York: Macmillan.

Gotts, E. E. (1973). Headstart research, development and evaluation. In J. L. Frost (Ed.), *Revisiting early childhood education.* New York: Holt, Rinehart & Winston.

Guess, D., & Noonan, M. J. (1982). Curricula and instructional procedures for severely handicapped students. *Focus on Exceptional Children, 14,* 1–12.

Hammill, D., & Larsen, S. (1978). The effectiveness of psycholinguistic training: A reaffirmation of position. *Exceptional Children, 44,* 402–414.

Hunt, J. M. (1961). *Intelligence and experience.* New York: Ronald.

The Infant Health and Development Program. (1990). Enhancing the outcomes of low-birth-weight, premature infants. *Journal of the American Medical Association, 263*(22), 3035–3042.

Itard, J. M. G. (1962). *The wild boy of Aveyron.* New York: Appleton-Century-Crofts.

Karnes, M. B., & Zehrbach, R. R. (1977). Alternative models for delivering services to young handicapped children. In J. B. Jordan, A. H. Hayden, M. B. Karnes, & M. M. Wood (Eds.), *Early childhood education for exceptional children.* Reston, VA: The Council for Exceptional Children.

Kessen, W. (1965). *The child.* New York: Wiley.

Kirk, S. (1958). *Early education of the mentally retarded.* Urbana, IL: University of Illinois Press.

Klein, M. D., & Briggs, M. (1987). Facilitating mother-infant communicative interaction in mothers of high-risk infants. *Journal of Childhood Communication Disorders*, *10*(2), 1–91.

Larry P. v. Riles, 343 F Supp 1306 (ND, Cal, 1972).

Lazar, I., & Darlington, R. (1982). Lasting effects of early education: A report from the Consortium for Longitudinal Studies. *Monographs of the Society for Research in Child Development*, *47* (Serial No. 195).

Lerner, J., Mardell-Czudnowski, C., & Goldenberg, D. (1981). *Special education for the early childhood years*. Englewood Cliffs, NJ: Prentice-Hall.

Love, H. D. (1972). *Educating exceptional children in regular classrooms*. Springfield, IL: Charles C Thomas.

Lynch, E. (1990, April 16). *Best practice continua for children who are at-risk or disabled and their families*. Paper presented at San Jose State University.

MacDonald, J. D. (1989). *Becoming partners with children*. San Antonio, TX: Special Press.

Mahoney, G., & Powell, A. (1988). Modifying parent-child interaction: Enhancing the development of handicapped children. *Journal of Special Education*, *22*(1), 82–96.

Mayer, R. S. (1971). A comparative analysis of preschool curriculum models. In R. H. Anderson & H. G. Shane (Eds.), *As the twig is bent* (pp. 286–314). Boston: Houghton Mifflin.

McDonnell, A., & Hardman, M. (1988). A synthesis of "best practice" guidelines for early childhood services. *Journal of the Division of Early Childhood*, *12*, 328–341.

Meisels, S. J. (1985). The efficacy of early intervention: Why are we still asking the question? *Topics in Early Childhood Special Education*, *5*(2), 1–11.

Meisels, S. J. (1989). Meeting the mandate of Public Law 99-457: Early childhood intervention in the nineties. *American Journal of Orthopsychiatry*, *59*, 451–460.

Meisels, S. J., & Shonkoff, J. P. (Eds.). (1990). *Handbook of early childhood intervention*. New York: Cambridge University Press.

Mills v. Board of Education of the District of Columbia, 348 F Supp 866 (D.C. 1972).

Moran, M. (1985). Families in early intervention: Effects of program variables. *Zero to Three 5*(5), 11–14.

Murphy, M., & Vincent, L. (1989). Identification of critical skills for success in day care. *Journal of Early Intervention*, *13*, 221–229.

National Association for the Education of Young Children (NAEYC). (1986). Position statements on developmentally appropriate practice in early childhood programs. *Young Children*, *41*, 3–29.

Pennsylvania Association for Retarded Children v. *Commonwealth of Pennsylvania*, 334, F Supp 1257 (ED, Pa, 1971).

Peterson, N. (1987). *Early intervention for handicapped and at-risk children*. Denver, CO: Love.

Provence, S., & Naylor, A. (1983). *Working with disadvantaged parents and their children: Scientific and practice issues*. New Haven, CT: Yale University Press.

Public Laws 85-926, 88-164, 89-10, 89-750, 90-538, 91-230, 92-424, 93-380, 94-142, 95-568, 98-199, 99-457, 101-476. Washington, DC: U.S. Government Printing Office.

Rousseau, J. J. (1911) *Emile*. (B. Foxley, trans.). London: Dent. (Originally published 1762).

Safford, P. (1978). *Teaching young children with special needs*. St. Louis: C. V. Mosby.

Safford, P. L. (1989). *Integrated teaching in early childhood*. New York: Longman Inc.

Sameroff, A., & Chandler, M. (1975). Reproductive risk and the continuum of caretaking casualty. In F. D. Horowtiz (Ed.), *Review of child development research* (Vol. 4, pp. 187–245). Chicago: University of Chicago Press.

Sameroff, A. J., & Fiese, B. H. (1990). Transactional regulation and early intervention. In S. J. Meisels & J. P. Shonkoff (Eds.), *Handbook of early childhood intervention* (pp. 119–149). New York: Cambridge University Press.

Schweinhart, L. J., & Weikart, D. B. (1988). The High/Scope Perry Preschool Program. In R. H. Price, E. L. Cowen, R. P. Lorion, & J. R. Mc-Kay, (Eds.), *14 ounces of prevention* (pp. 53–65). Washington, DC: American Psychological Association.

Seitz, V., Rosenbaum, L. K., & Apfel, N. H. (1985). Effects of family support intervention: A ten-year follow-up. *Child Development*, *56*, 376–391.

Shearer, D. E., & Shearer, M. S. (1976). The Portage Project: A model for early childhood intervention. In T. D. Tjossem (Ed.), *Intervention strategies for high risk infants and young children*. Baltimore: University Park Press.

Shonkoff, J. P., Hauser-Cram, P., Krauss, M. W., & Upshur, C. C. (1988). Early intervention efficacy research: What have we learned and where do we go from here? *Topics in Early Childhood Special Education*, *8*(1), 81–93.

Skeels, H. (1942). A study of the effects of differential stimulation on mentally retarded children: A follow-up study. *American Journal of Mental Deficiency*, *46*, 340–350.

Skeels, H. (1966). Adult status of children with contrasting early life experiences. *Monographs of the*

Society for Research in Child Development, 32(2).

Skeels, H., & Dye, H. A. (1939). A study of the effects of differential stimulation on mentally retarded children. *Proceedings of the American Association on Mental Deficiency, 44*, 114–136.

Stendler, C. (1950). Six years of child training practices. *The Journal of Pediatrics, 36*, 122–134.

Stevens, J. H., & King, E. W. (1976). *Administering early childhood education programs.* Boston: Little, Brown.

Strain, P. (1986, October). *Obtaining robust and lasting effects with early intervention.* Paper presented at the Second National Early Childhood Conference on Children with Special Needs, Louisville, KY.

Swan, W. (1981). Programs for handicapped infants and their families supported by the office of special education. *The Communicator, 7*(2), 1–15.

Thurman, S. K., & Widerstrom, A. H. (1990). *Infants and young children with special needs.* Baltimore: Paul H. Brookes.

Weikart, D. (1971). *The cognitively oriented curriculum: A framework for preschool teachers.* Washington, DC: National Association for the Education of Young Children.

Weikart, D. (1972). Relationship of curriculum, teaching, and learning in preschool education. In J. C. Stanley (Ed.), *Preschool programs for the disadvantaged: Five experimental approaches to early childhood education.* Baltimore: The Johns Hopkins University Press.

Westinghouse Learning Corporation, Ohio University. (1969). *The impact of Head Start: An evaluation of the Head Start experience on children's cognitive and affective development.* Washington, DC: Department of Health and Human Services.

White, R. (1959). Motivation reconsidered: The concept of competence. *Psychology Review, 66*, 297–333.

Ysseldyke, J. E., & Salvia, J. (1974). Diagnostic-prescriptive teaching: Two models. *Exceptional Children, 41*, 181–186.

Zeanah, C. H., & Barton, M. L. (1989). Internal representations and parent-infant relationships. *Infant Mental Health Journal, 10*(3), 135–141.

Zigler, E. (1978). The effectiveness of Head Start: Another look. *Educational Psychologist, 13*, 71–77.

Chapter 3

In Partnership with Families

Key Points

▶ A child with special needs can only be understood within the context of his or her family.

▶ Early childhood special education (ECSE) professionals must develop the skills necessary to form effective parent-professional partnerships.

▶ Families are best understood as dynamic social systems. Each is comprised of its own values, roles and functions, and life cycle.

▶ Parent involvement in early education programs will vary according to the needs and preferences of individual families.

▶ ECSE professionals must be able to use a variety of communication and involvement strategies to meet the needs of each family.

▶ Understanding the range of possible cultural differences among families and respecting those differences are essential to successful early intervention. Cultural stereotyping must be avoided.

▶ ECSE professionals must acquire strategies for working with special populations of parents, such as those who have developmental disabilities or who have a history of child maltreatment or drug abuse.

Key Topics

▶ Emotional needs of families with children with disabilities.

▶ The family as a system.

▶ Sibling and extended family needs and reactions.

▶ A continuum of parent involvement.

▶ Home-based programs.

▶ Parents in the preschool center.

▶ Parent support groups.

▶ Working with culturally diverse families.

▶ Working with parent populations with special needs.

Helping parents to understand that parent-child interaction may be the single best predictor of child outcome is clearly a responsibility of early intervention specialists. Collaboration with parents or other caregivers is essential to the development of families' awareness of the importance of their role in facilitating, guiding, and supporting their infants' development. With time and understanding, parents do become their child's best ally in interpreting his or her needs. The following parent perspective illustrates how time and professional concern helped to enable one parent to develop the coping skills needed to face the day-to-day realities of parenting a young child with special needs.

A Personal Perspective on Raising a Child with Developmental Problems*

by Lora Jerugim

My daughter Elisa is five years old. She is a developmentally delayed child whose delays range from mild to borderline and are of unknown etiology. I do not have any research findings to present. I have no statistics for you. But what I can share with you is something that I know a lot about—what it *feels* like to raise a child with developmental problems.

When Elisa was born, I was ecstatic. I had two sons, and I had dreamed about having a daughter. I had fantasies about who she would be and what we would share. Of course she would be completely articulate by the age of two, and someday I would teach her to play the piano. And when she grew older we would recommend books to each other to read, and I had images of our whole family sitting at a table assembling a thousand-piece puzzle together. So much for the fantasy.

Elisa's birth was 5–6 weeks premature, but it was normal and no one suspected that there was anything wrong with her. So I took home what I thought was a perfectly normal baby. Elisa always seemed alert and responsive, but by the time she was six months old and was not able to roll over, I sensed that something was wrong. Like so many parents, I was encouraged to believe that Elisa would catch up, and I only wish that pediatricians could be as attuned to the signs of delay as parents are so that we would not lose so much precious time in getting help for our children. By the time Elisa was a year old, she couldn't sit up and was severely hypotonic. It was clear at that point that she was not developing normally, and we were finally referred to a developmental specialist. What was once like a dream come true had turned into a living nightmare. My first reaction was one of complete shock and disbelief. I would wake up in the morning and wonder if it was all just a bad dream. Certainly disabled children are born every day, but it couldn't be happening to me . . . not my child. I felt a sense of panic and helplessness as I waited for almost two months for the test results to come back. And when I learned that the results were negative, I felt relieved and yet confused. Elisa had no diagnosis and consequently no clear prognosis. I was told that she might have a brain dysfunction, but having a label to hold onto didn't seem to help much. We don't know what caused this dysfunction, and although I feel somehow responsible, I have nowhere to place my diffused sense of guilt. In a way I feel lucky that I do not know precisely what happened, because if I did I would probably run that moment over in my mind for the rest of my life wishing that I'd done something differently.

There are times when I feel such rage that this has happened to my child and to our whole family. I am angry with a world that is intolerant of people who are different—a society that is so focused on achievement that we often forget to look into a person's soul. I feel jealous and lonely as I listen to friends discuss whether their children are highly gifted or just gifted, while I'm praying that someday my daughter will be capable of leading an independent life. I feel so much pain as I watch Elisa at nursery school struggling to do things that younger children do with ease. I am exhausted because a special child requires twice the work to get half the distance. But most of all I live in fear of the unknown, because I don't know what limitations my daughter's handicap will impose on her, and I do not know how the world will respond to her being different.

Having a young child whose development is delayed but whose disability is not visible poses a number of special problems. These children seem to be caught somewhere between the normal world and the handicapped world. Normal toddler programs are not quite appropriate, and yet early intervention programs in the area are populated with children whose disabilities are more severe and/or visible. When Elisa entered her first intervention program at 20 months, I was traumatized. I wept on and off for weeks. I had never had any exposure to handicapped children and being in their presence was a painful reminder of life's incomprehensible injustices. I also realized that I wasn't just visiting the class. I was there because my daughter was handicapped and this was her school! But it was this same environment that fostered my denial of Elisa's problems. After all, Elisa looked so "normal" compared to most of the other children.

Attending parent groups often made me feel more depressed. I felt so guilty that I experienced such despair over Elisa's condition, when other parents envied me and thought my daughter seemed like a genius compared to their children. Furthermore, most of the children had been diagnosed at birth, and not only did a diagnosis help the parents face the reality of their situations, but they'd had so much more time to come to terms with their children's disabilities, while I felt as though I was just beginning. They also had special support groups and an abundance of literature to refer to dealing with their children's specific disabilities.

I also decided to place my daughter in a normal nursery school part time where she was the only handicapped child, and although my daughter, who is very competent socially, adjusted fairly well, I felt lonely, isolated, depressed, and at times embarrassed. During my daughter's first few weeks there, when I stayed with her to ease her separation, I had to leave the room on a few occasions when I began to cry. Being around all those normal three year olds was a constant reminder of how verbal and adept little children are and how far behind Elisa was in her development.

Furthermore, when my sons were in nursery school, I became acquainted with the other parents primarily through my children playing after school with other children or being invited to birthday parties. Elisa is rarely invited to birthday parties, and she has been invited to play at another child's house twice in two years. I have made some attempts to invite children over, but I not only have to find an appropriate playmate, I also must determine if the parent is the type who would be receptive to having their child play with a child who is "slow."

There were times in the past when my feeling of isolation became so pervasive that I found myself wishing that somebody I know, whether family or friend, would give birth to a disabled child just so that someone close to me would truly understand what I was experiencing and that I would no longer feel so alone. Then, of course, just the idea that I could entertain such

a terrible thought made me feel the most unbearable guilt. For several years I felt as though I was riding a roller coaster in the dark. I could never see when the dips were coming, and when they did, I would be dropped into a depression that could last for weeks. Sometimes a stranger's question would be enough to do it, like the woman who asked me how old my daughter was and proceeded to ask me why she couldn't talk. If Elisa had been in a wheelchair, that woman would never have dared to ask me that question.

Parents of children with delays must endure many types of stress. We live with financial stress, and we worry about governmental budget cuts and changes in the laws protecting handicapped children. We are responsible for selecting schools and therapies, but when our children are receiving such a variety of services, how are we supposed to determine what's working and what's not? Often we do not know from one year to the next where our children will go to school, because we can't predict what their needs will be in a year, and we don't know what programs will be available. Even a class that is appropriate now may not be appropriate six months from now just because the population of children in the class may change so radically. We find ourselves battling with school districts and forever fighting against society's prejudicial attitudes towards the disabled. I've often wished that I could hire a full time advocate to deal with all these external stresses so that I could just focus my energies on raising my daughter.

There are constant family stresses as well, since one child requires more help and attention than the others. Resentments build up, and I find myself doing a perennial balancing act with my husband and children trying to make sure that everyone gets their fair share of me. All this is aggravated by the fact that when you have a delayed preschooler, what you really have on your hands is a child who seems to be stuck in the "terrible two's." I'm sure any of you who have raised children will remember the nightmare of the terrible two's and how grateful you were that it only lasted a year. Try to imagine the shape our nerves are in after we've endured the terrible two's for two or three years and with no end in sight. Elisa is destructive without malintent and is forever testing us. She frequently spills her drinks, and the other day she tried to pour herself a bowl of cereal and poured cereal all over the floor. I sometimes wonder if she'll ever be fully toilet trained or if she will ever sleep through the night.

Testing is another source of stress for parents of delayed youngsters. Elisa's behavior and skills vary from day to day and often from one part of the day to another, so she is difficult to assess. Her most organized time of the day is usually the evening, and evaluations are generally done in the morning. Furthermore, her fine motor and language problems make assessment even more difficult. In one testing situation, she was asked to stack one-inch cubes and was then scored in two areas: fine motor and cognitive. Her poor fine motor development prevented her from stacking more than a few blocks, so I asked the woman who was administering the test if she would try it again while steadying the tower for Elisa. Elisa then stacked all ten blocks, and her cognitive score on that item jumped by 18 months! For example, sometimes Elisa can show where a puzzle piece should go but can't maneuver it into place. I often feel that the standard tests used are designed for normal children and, consequently, are inadequate for handicapped children. They certainly fail to pick up the qualitative changes that our children's abilities undergo over time. Professionals also need to be aware that the whole concept of testing triggers a special response in well-educated parents, because for us, perhaps on a subconscious level, poor performance is equated with failure.

Perhaps one of my areas of greatest frustration, anger and despair has been the area of diagnosis. How much more difficult it is to accept your child's handicap when you don't know what it is. I have received so many conflicting opinions about who Elisa is that I've stopped

listening. I just don't care anymore about having a label for her, because the only appropriate label for my daughter is the one I gave her at birth: ELISA. One physician told me that I'd thoroughly confused Elisa's diagnosis by all the work I'd done with her. I remember thinking at the time that you can't teach a child anything they're not capable of learning. A psychologist labeled her mentally retarded, and two weeks later, I was told that according to test results from a research project, Elisa did *not* appear to be mentally retarded. I had another doctor tell me that Elisa would grow up and be able to feed herself and dress herself, while yet another doctor told me that we should have expectations of normalcy for Elisa and that she in turn would have those expectations for herself. He said that by working with disabled children for 30 years he knew by observing Elisa that she was not mentally retarded. Looking at the child seemed more important to him in his assessment than simply looking at test scores. He also told me that she would grow up and be able to lead a normal life, that she would not be a Phi Beta Kappa, but that where she would fall in between no expert could ascertain. The level she would attain would depend on many variables that could not be measured, and that the most important of them would be her own motivation to succeed.

This particular doctor deserves special mention, because he is not only a skilled physician, he is a humanist as well. He still sees Elisa regularly, and I feel that the way he has related to us over the years could well serve as an example to everyone in the helping professions. He has treated us with sensitivity and respect and has valued our input, recognizing that we, as Elisa's parents, probably know her better than anyone else in the world. He has been honest with us and has freely admitted that he doesn't have all the answers. He has always looked at Elisa as a human being and not simply as a composite of her problems. He has made us aware of her strengths, and he has acknowledged our efforts in providing Elisa with the help that she needs. He always questions us about our whole family and reminds us of the importance of keeping our lives in balance. But the most important lesson to be learned from this man is that you must not take parents' hope away. Hope is what keeps us going, even if it's only the hope that things will be a little better than they are today. Without hope, we would stop fighting for our children and working so hard to provide the services they need. I believe that parents and professionals share the same goals for our disabled children. We want them to grow up to be independent, productive, and self-actualized human beings, so we must be sure that we are working together towards these goals, rather than in opposition.

A friend of mine shared a quote with me that says, "Thank you, God, for reminding me that thorns have roses," and with that thought in mind, I want to share with you the joy and growth I've experienced in raising Elisa, and not just the pain and frustration.

Elisa has taught me more about love and patience than anyone I have ever known, and she has drastically altered my perception of what matters in life. And as I have watched her development and lived with the uncertainty of not knowing when or even *if* she will acquire certain skills, I have come to appreciate my sons' normal growth in a way that I never could before. She has shown me that a "spoken word" and a simple "step" are among life's greatest gifts and that the miracle of normal development must never be taken for granted.

I have come to accept that my daughter will not be quite like everybody else when she grows up, but then who of us is? We are all unique individuals, and we should appreciate our differences rather than scorn them. We all have our strengths and weaknesses, and how many of us, even without disabilities, ever realize our full human potential?

I have struggled to redefine the meaning of joy in my life, and I have learned to live with sorrow and to move beyond it. I have discovered that life is very precious and that none of us has any guarantee of what the future will hold. Parenting Elisa has been a challenge for me, and I have found a strength within myself that I didn't know existed.

I've also become aware of the importance of seeing myself as a human being separate from mother and wife and of nurturing my own growth. And as I nourish myself, I find that I have just that much more to give. Elisa's education is in good hands, and I no longer want to be her teacher. I just want to be her mother and to teach her the things that I know about: appreciating life and being a caring human being. At the same time, she is teaching me, because Elisa has no prejudices and doesn't let her head get in the way of establishing human relationships. Instead, she seems to have a direct line to people's hearts.

I can honestly say that I love and accept my imperfectly perfect daughter for exactly who she is rather than for who she might have been. I hope that sharing my experiences will in some way help the professional community to be more sensitive to the needs of parents of delayed children and that we will be better able to work together to serve these children.

As this parent so clearly illustrates, all children do affect and are affected by their families. Conceptual contributions such as the transactional model of child development elaborated by Sameroff (1987) have played a significant role in helping early interventionists understand the continuous dynamic interactions of the child within the context of the family. When children with special needs began to receive early intervention services, parents were usually passive bystanders watching their children "receive" therapy or infant stimulation. Then, Public Law 94-142 formalized parents' participation in the educational planning process of school-aged children. Parents were encouraged to become involved, but the nature of the involvement was not clearly delineated. Parents of young children with special needs often were trained to carry out therapeutic or instructional activities with their children. While many found their role as "teachers" to be fulfilling, others became frustrated with these teaching expectations. Their lives were too demanding to cope with one more expectation.

Today, Public Law 99-457 has officially marked a new era in the recognition of families as integral parts of the early intervention process. The recognition of the family as a legitimate client in early intervention is spelled out in the formal requirements of family assessment, family goals, and family services within the regulations of P.L. 99-457. Experiences provided for the child are not viewed as independent of the family. The family is seen as the essential component of the caregiving environment that influences and is influenced by the child over time, resulting in differential outcomes for both the child and the family (Simeonsson & Bailey, 1990). To understand the reciprocal nature of the relationship between young children with special needs and their families, the family is viewed as a system with interacting subsystems. No family member is thought to function in isolation from other family members. Therefore, after reviewing some of the needs and emotions that appear to be characteristic of families with special needs, we will explore family dynamics from a **family systems perspective** (Turnbull & Turnbull, 1990).

EMOTIONAL NEEDS OF FAMILIES WITH CHILDREN WHO HAVE SPECIAL NEEDS

The majority of new parents start out with little or no preparation to meet the unique, ongoing challenges of caring for a newborn. Even experienced parents must readjust their style of living whenever another child is added to the family. The birth of any child brings adjustments within family systems. Parents of infants with special needs must deal not only with the usual adjustments of parenthood, but also with additional stresses and concerns for which they are not likely to be prepared. Each change in their child's condition brings about new questions, concerns, and challenges.

Today there are many ways that parents can obtain help and emotional support. For example, they can join support and therapy groups composed of parents of children with special needs. Participants offer support and encouragement to one another and exchange information about useful resources. Public Law 99-457 has mandated that psychological and case management services be provided to families of children from birth to age 3 who may have developmental delays or be at risk for such delays. When emotionally supportive services are provided while children are very young, adjustments may be made within family systems more readily. However, it must be remembered that the emotional needs of families may be constantly changing and the emotional and physical demands that accompany the advent of a child with special needs should never be underestimated. The following description of basic family needs and perceived emotional responses is offered to facilitate understanding of individual family reactions.

Basic Needs

Certain needs are basic to all parents who seek professional help. First, they want to be assured that they are receiving the best and most up-to-date information possible. They want to have confidence in those who profess to know how to help their child. Second, parents want to be recognized as caring, intelligent people. They need to be viewed as individuals capable of effective parenting, and they want to know that they are seen in this way. Third, they want and urgently need guidance in what to do in the immediate *now*. Although they want positive opinions about what the future holds, they need to have useful suggestions immediately (Ehly, Conoley, & Rosenthal, 1985).

Failure to Consider Basic Needs. Many of the emotional reactions attributed to parents may be heightened by the failure of those to whom the parents have turned for help to consider their basic needs. Professional mishandling of parents' needs is a serious problem. Roos (1975) identified eight categories of mishandling, as follows:

1. *Professional ignorance.* Professionals fail to recognize a disabling condition. They tend to predict either that the child will outgrow the problem or that the child's condition is hopeless.

2. *Professional hopelessness.* Professionals generate self-fulfilling and self-limiting prophecies. They convey defeatist or negative attitudes.

3. *Referral ad infinitum.* Perhaps because of a lack of expertise, some professionals refer parents from professional to professional. Although it is true that some parents shop around hoping for more positive diagnoses, numerous occasions of unneeded referrals do occur.

4. *Veil of secrecy.* Despite the encouragement of P.L. 94-142 to include parents in making decisions involving their children, some medical and mental health professionals still attempt to withhold information necessary to effective decision making.

5. *Deaf ear syndrome.* Many parents still experience the frustration of having their requests ignored or their opinions seemingly unheard.

6. *Professional omniscience.* Whereas most parents can accept the honesty of a professional who readily admits that he or she does not have all of the answers, it is difficult for parents to cope with one who wishes to claim that he or she knows everything.

7. *Professional omnipotence.* Many parents still believe that only professionals have enough wisdom to determine what is best for a child. Adherence to the requirements of P.L. 94-142 and P.L. 99-457 will ideally stop the practice of professionals informing parents *after* they have made important decisions about a child's educational program.

8. *Parents as patients.* As some professionals still continue to see the parents as having a problem (a child with disabilities); they have the tendency to confuse a need for information with a need for "therapy."

Even if early interventionists do not mishandle the needs of parents in any of these ways, they should realize that some parents may have experienced such treatment by someone. This realization will help interventionists to sustain the patience and understanding so necessary when working with parents who are anxious, angry, or troubled.

The Need for Emotional Support. Parents need emotional support. Assuming that parents are seen as partners by all of the professionals with whom they come into contact, their ability to cope effectively with their problems will influence what they do and how well they are able to do it.

Mori (1983) discussed the following six needs as typical of families of young children with disabilities:

1. Need for self-esteem
2. Need to achieve self-confidence in parenting skills
3. Need to overcome feelings of isolation, depression, and ambivalence toward the child
4. Need to attend to their own needs and the needs of other family members
5. Need for the working mother to overcome guilt
6. Need to know what to expect from the child, the program of intervention, and the future. (pp. 211–213)

In order to assist parents in meeting these basic needs, professionals must learn to provide emotional support as well as educational programming or therapeutic intervention. Parents of young children with disabilities need to feel the warmth and caring support of people who understand.

PARENTAL REACTIONS

A number of writers, both parents and professionals, have described various phases of adjustment in parents' acceptance of their child and his or her disabling condition. Boyd (1950) discussed three levels of adapatation: the need to pull back and focus solely on one's own needs, a gradual turning toward the needs of one's immediate family, and a desire to aid others with similar problems. More recently, writers are turning to the grieving process described by Kübler-Ross (1969) for an understanding of the possible emotional reactions of some parents to the perceived "death" of a normal child (O'Hara & Levy, 1984).

Figure 3–1 illustrates the phases of emotional reactions that may be experienced by families with children who have special needs. It is important to remember, however, that parental reactions are unique. Some parents take issue with the whole concept of stages or phases of emotional adjustment (Blacher, 1984). Early interventionists must therefore apply the concept of stages cautiously, realizing that the sequence and completeness of each phase of adjustment may differ with each individual. Individual family members may differ from each other in developing an accepting attitude. Some may never fully accept their child and his or her condition.

Shock, Disbelief, and Denial

Parents and professionals alike describe the first stage of parental reaction as one of shock and disbelief upon learning of a child's disability or disfigurement. This shock and possible disbelief may be accompanied by feelings of shame, guilt, and unworthiness. As the reality of the child's condition is slowly assimilated, parents may try to deny the existing problems. Often, first attempts to find out what is wrong are really attempts to find someone who will say that nothing is wrong. For this reason, some parents go from doctor to doctor and from clinic to clinic seeking opinions. Some parents do this, however, because each professional recommends that they seek additional opinions. Diagnosis of problems in young children is far from an exact science. Rather, it is a piecing together of diverse observations, bits of information, and confusing evidence. Cause and effect interact to the point that it is difficult to decide which is which.

Some parents refuse to seek any guidance. They can be heard telling relatives and friends, "Oh, he's just like Uncle Joe. He didn't talk until he was 7," or "Aunt Susie never did learn how to do puzzles, and our Sally is just like her."

Other parents may deprive the rest of their family while working diligently to prove diagnosticians wrong. They hope that intensive instruction will eliminate whatever developmental lag exists. But their nagging suspicions continue to grow. Unless parents can and will accept available guidance, precious time is lost. Fear that is allowed to grow undermines effective solutions to the simplest of problems.

Early Interventionists Can Help. The interventionist can help if he or she suspects that a parent is feeling fearful, guilty, or anxious while experiencing shock, disbelief, or denial. The parent needs help to understand that these feelings and experiences are appropriate. It is normal and acceptable for parents temporarily to blame, reject, or even hate the child or themselves (Lepler, 1978). Professionals should listen with acceptance. Pushing parents to "face the child's limitations" will only create defensiveness (Seligman, 1979). Parents need help to focus on ways the professional and parents can work together on behalf of the child. Early interventionists can become effective "active listeners" (Gordon, 1970) through patience and practice.

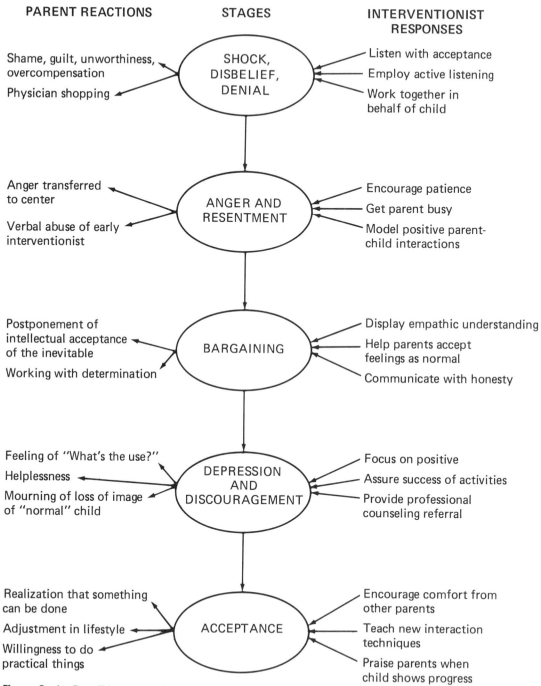

PARENT REACTIONS   STAGES   INTERVENTIONIST
                                          RESPONSES

Shame, guilt, unworthiness,   Listen with acceptance
overcompensation   SHOCK,   Employ active listening
                           DISBELIEF,
Physician shopping   DENIAL   Work together in
                                          behalf of child

Anger transferred   Encourage patience
to center   ANGER AND   Get parent busy
                           RESENTMENT
Verbal abuse of early   Model positive parent-
interventionist   child interactions

Postponement of   Display empathic understanding
intellectual acceptance   Help parents accept
of the inevitable   BARGAINING   feelings as normal
Working with determination   Communicate with honesty

Feeling of "What's the use?"   Focus on positive
Helplessness   DEPRESSION   Assure success of activities
                              AND
Mourning of loss of image DISCOURAGEMENT Provide professional
of "normal" child   counseling referral

Realization that something   Encourage comfort from
can be done   other parents
Adjustment in lifestyle   ACCEPTANCE   Teach new interaction
                                          techniques
Willingness to do   Praise parents when
practical things   child shows progress

Figure 3–1   Possible parental reactions.

Interventionists must remember that anxiety creates problems, and that lack of knowing what to do creates anxiety. This is why parent-infant programs are needed. Initial fear and grief can be minimized if parents can be taught to do constructive things from the beginning. Energy is wasted by grief and anger. Energy used to play with children in positive ways minimizes grieving time.

Anger and Resentment

When parents can no longer deny the existence of their child or his or her condition, they may feel anger, resentment, rage, or envy. Even though they may have accepted the child's problems intellectually, they may be so caught up in their emotions that they cannot focus on positive approaches to their concerns. They may even direct their anger at the very professionals who are trying to help the most. Suspicions about a professional's motives may explode in angry accusations. Other parents try to prove that the interventionist is "wrong." Verbal abuse is common. At this stage interventionists need to demonstrate true professionalism. They need to be understanding, compassionate, and gently caring.

Getting Parents Busy. The anger will pass, and it will pass more quickly if the parents are given play activities to do with their children at which they absolutely cannot fail. This is not the time to try to make rapid progress with either children or their parents. Rather, the parents need to have constant reminders that they do indeed make a difference to their children. They must discover and rediscover that they have resources within themselves that they did not know were there. They must be provided with supports that match their individual needs. All of this must be done with a kindness that refuses to blame or to react to the unreasonable demands that accompany the grief of parents.

Bargaining

Some parents may try to resolve their anger and resentment by going through what Kübler-Ross (1969) described as a process of bargaining. It resembles an attempt to postpone complete intellectual and emotional acceptance of the inevitable. During this time, parents and other family members may work with great diligence and determination. It is as if they are saying "If I do everything you tell me to do, then surely this problem will go away." If progress is not as rapid or as great as they expect, bargaining is sometimes followed by the gray-black world of depression.

Empathy Is Essential. To be helpful, interventionists must display empathic understanding by recognizing and accepting the natural feelings of the parents. Helping parents to realize that their feelings and states of mind are normal can convey an attitude of interest and caring. A simple statement reflecting active listening such as "It must be very frustrating to have the constant care of a child with special needs" can be very comforting (Lichter, 1976).

Depression and Discouragement

"What's the use?" and "Why bother?" can become the reaction of some parents to all suggestions. An oppressive weight of hopelessness can add new dimensions to the problems. For some, this very feeling of helplessness may make them more amenable to being helped. Because of feeling helpless, they may be more likely to ask for assistance. Roos (1979) contended that "the absence of such feelings [depression], particularly when realization of the child's retardation is recent, is unusual enough to raise suspicions regarding the possibility of atypical techniques of handling emotions (e.g., repression and isolation of affect)" (p. 104). A parent of a child with disabilities, Kirk (1979) described the need at this point to mourn as if to say good-bye to a disappearing image of one's missing, "normal" child. He felt that once this mourning occurs, the parent can begin to accept the child as she or he is. Parents can begin to focus on productive solutions to their problems.

Focus on the Positive. Professionals must focus on the positive and avoid adding to parents' depression by their own eagerness to get on with the task of teaching the child. During this time, activities must be planned for the parents in a way that ensures success. Interventionists must halt the growth of seeds of self-doubt about being a good parent. They should avoid all indirect and direct criticism. They must also avoid giving excessive, unwarranted praise, because parents interpret it as insincere.

Parents who continue to suffer deep depression may need professional counseling. Interventionists should not hesitate to find some tactful way to suggest this. Often the simplest way is to listen carefully to the cry of "What's the use?" and then suggest that they may find help in many ways. Some parents will want and need the counsel of psychologists and psychiatrists. Others may find great comfort from other parents who have passed through depression and have moved on to practical solutions to their problems. An informal parent support group may help some parents find comfort from one another. Many might benefit from an opportunity to look through a carefully developed file of local resources including churches, synagogues, mental health agencies, and parenting groups. All parents need to know someone cares.

Acceptance

Acceptance, the final stage in parents' emotional recognition of the need to modify their lives or their kinds of interactions with the child with disabilities, means parents have an increasing willingness to do practical, useful things. Acceptance means that today's needs are recognized,

not denied. It means they have a willingness to learn and to apply new knowledge to meet day-to-day needs. It means they have a deep conviction that each human being is unique, special, and worthy of love and affection.

Acceptance should not mean that the disabling condition is accepted as unalterable. Rather parents accept the need to learn skillful ways to alter the negative effects of the condition. True acceptance includes the conviction that much needs to be done and that what is done will make a difference.

Consider this mother's definition of acceptance:

To me acceptance means finding whatever pleasure I can in caring for Benjamin day to day. It means looking at other children without always wishing that he were like them. It means looking at the situation not in terms of what Benjamin can do for me, but what I can do to enhance his potential. (Lepler, 1978, p. 33)

Encourage Patience. Interventionists must encourage patience when parents have begun to accept their children as they are, because most can achieve realistic expectations and give appropriate help. They will quickly and often eagerly learn new interaction techniques. There will be occasions, however, when they will feel stupid and confused. They must be helped to understand that the disability they are dealing with is a new experience and they will need time to grow accustomed to it. Parents can be helped to learn to read their child's unique cues. Professionals must give the parents much praise for their child's progress and for the parents' participation. All parents feel better when they are able to see themselves as vital contributors to their child's progress. Parents who focus on positive interaction techniques will provide constructive options for mutually satisfying interactions.

A Father's Perspective

Commenting to a group of educators on his own experience as a father, Kirk (1979) stated,

If you help us to recognize the normality of our "abnormality," the appropriateness of our strange and sometimes frightening feelings, we will more quickly and smoothly graduate to acceptance. We need your nurturance and acceptance, your sharing of the commitment that has drawn you to this work. I believe that with you we can more fully realize that we can grow stronger and stand taller as a result of our pain and frustration—that we can mend our shattered egos and evolve into more sensitive, more tolerant and wiser parents. (p. 6).

Mending shattered egos may be particularly difficult for some fathers. "Fathers appear to be more affected by attributes that stigmatize the family's social and community image and are particularly affected by the birth of a handicapped son, often reacting in extremes of total involvement or total withdrawal" (Bristol & Gallagher, 1982, p. 146). Fathers (or mothers) whose daily life is oriented to the outside world may experience more stress when the child fails to conform to its norms. Such times as school entrance or soccer sign-up may create special crisis periods that can be extremely threatening to parental self-esteem.

Crisis Periods

Crisis periods can occur at any point from conception on through life. Parents often report that they "recycle" through the stages described earlier in this chapter. This is especially likely to occur at times of crisis. Some parents conceal these crises from professionals; others do not. Nevertheless, a supportive atmosphere that offers help and encourages adaptations can make a significant difference. Parents are comforted when they know someone understands their need to cry, yell, or scream.

Even though parents may have basically accepted their child and the disabling condition, adaptation may never be complete for some (Blacher, 1984). Parents report that tears come even as the child grows into adulthood. Sometimes a crisis brings out the incompleteness of a parent's adaptation. Interventionists can avoid judging or comparing parents' coping skills. The reassurance that someone who understands is available to listen may make the difference between a productive reaction to a crisis and a debilitating one. Professionals will remember that the emotional needs of families are as unique as the needs of the child. Reactions to the shattering of parental expectations and to the real concerns of daily care and worry about the future must be coped with adequately before parents can fully participate in whatever parent involvement opportunities are available.

THE FAMILY AS A SYSTEM

From a **family systems perspective,** the reciprocal nature of the relationship between young children with special needs and their families becomes clearer. No family member is seen to function in isolation from other family members. Any intervention with one family member is found to have an impact on other members and interactions in the family (Hanson & Lynch, 1989). The needs of the child and of the parents or siblings are viewed within the context of the entire family as it functions within the larger societal system. Every family system is composed of subsystems. Turnbull and Turnbull (1990) have described four such subsystems: The **marital subsystem** (parent-parent), the **parental subsystem** (parent-child), the **sibling subsystem** (child-child), and the **extrafamilial subsystem** (family-extrafamily). Of course, the actual makeup of families differs greatly. For example, single-parent families have no marital subsystem. However, a single-parent family may have more than one person exercising a parental role if extended family members are actively involved.

How a family member functions in one role in a subsystem is not predictive of how he or she will behave in another subsystem. Parents behave differently when interacting with one an-

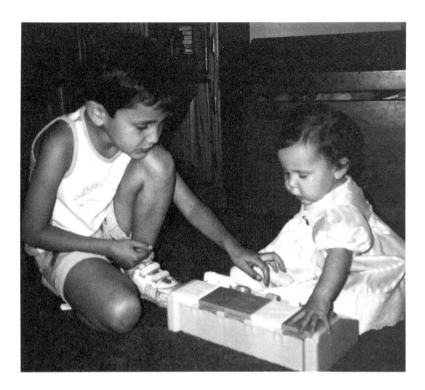

other than they do when interacting with their children. Whole families behave differently toward one another at home than they do when visiting with their neighbors. The advent of a child with disabilities has implications for all four subsystems. The special needs of the child may impose additional stress on the marital subsystem, while the extrafamilial subsystem is hardly affected. There may be no sibling subsystem if fear of giving birth to another child with special needs curtails future pregnancies. Alternatively, older siblings may be brought into the parental role to help alleviate the stress placed on either the marital or parental subsystem. Anything that happens in one subsystem has effects on all of the others.

The manner in which a child with special needs affects family members cannot be predicted or assumed, because families differ along many dimensions. While it is not the role of early interventionists to intervene in family interac-

tions, they can better understand and appreciate family dynamics by fostering an awareness of the entire family system. Professionals who look at each family in relation to its own interactional system and the manner in which these interactions are used as tools to fulfill the tasks of daily life will find it easier to provide services to meet the total needs of the family.

It is clear that the unique needs of families cannot be met by providing the same prescribed set of services for each family. When designing early intervention services, Turnbull, Summers, and Brotherson (1983) have recommended adoption of the following four assumptions:

1. Each family is unique due to the infinite variations in membership characteristics, cultural and ideological styles.
2. The family is an interactional system whose component parts have constantly shifting boundaries and varying degrees of resistance to change.
3. Families have a variety of functions to fulfill for

each member collectively and individually to aid their continued growth and development.

4. Families pass through developmental and non-developmental changes which produce varying amounts of stress affecting all members. (pp. 4–5)

Interventions planned from a family systems perspective will also carefully consider four major components described by Turnbull and Turnbull (1990). These include family resources, family interactions, family functions, and the family's life cycle. **Family resources** include the characteristics and strengths available to families to help them meet their needs. The effectiveness of early intervention may depend on the existence of productive interactions between the resources of professionals and the resources of families.

Family interactions are the processes families use to accomplish the "duties" of the family system. Families meet their needs through such processes as sharing affection, planning together, resolving conflicts, teaching new skills, and accomplishing daily tasks. **Family functions** are the outputs of the interactional system. These represent major areas of need such as economic, domestic/health care, recreation, socialization, self-identity, affection and educational/vocational (Turnbull & Turnbull, 1990). **Family life cycle** refers to the developmental and non-developmental changes that alter the family's structure and needs over time. Issues evolving at each stage in the family life cycle impact every member of the family. Barber, Turnbull, Behr, and Kerns (1988) offered possible issues encountered when the child with special needs is in the early childhood life cycle stage. These are illustrated in Table 3–1. Of course, it is not enough to support families during the early years. They must be helped to develop coping strategies that will help them avoid the burnout that can come from lifelong challenges.

SIBLING AND EXTENDED FAMILY NEEDS AND REACTIONS

As predicted from family systems theory, siblings and the extended family of the child also have needs and reactions. Grandparents grieve deeply, too. Theirs is often a double hurt because they not only experience pain for their grandchild, but they also grieve for their own children. Seeing a loved son or daughter try to cope with long-term problems is disheartening. One grandfather arrived at a diagnostic clinic with a blank check. "Just tell me what it costs," he said, "I'll find the money somehow."

Denial, blame, and anger may run rampant among grandparents. They may say "It's because

Table 3–1 Possible Issues encountered at life cycle stages

Life Cycle Stage	Parents	Siblings
Early childhood, ages 0–5	Obtaining an accurate diagnosis Informing siblings and relatives Locating services Seeking to find meaning in the exceptionality Clarifying a personal ideology to guide decision-making Addressing issues of stigma Identifying positive contributions of exceptionality	Less parental time and energy for sibling needs Feelings of jealousy over less attention Fears associated with misunderstandings of exceptionality

Source: Barber et al., p. 194.

she smoked while she was pregnant," or "His family never was any good," or "If only they hadn't. . . ." There is no doubt to whom the angry grandparents are referring.

Most grandparents and other close relatives, however, can be helped to provide needed moral, mental, and emotional support (George, 1988; Mori, 1983). Often relatives are the major source of babysitting relief for parents. All of those who spend much time caring for a child with disabilities will find it helpful to be included in conferences and planning and teaching demonstrations. Often involved grandparents feel left out and deeply confused about what they should do. Professionals must be sensitive to this, and, with the parents' approval, include these extended family members.

Chinn, Drew, and Logan (1979) discussed the needs of able-bodied siblings. Among these are (a) the need to be included in discussions about decisions concerning the child with special needs; (b) the need to have opportunities to express their feelings about the reactions of peers and to acknowledge their own feelings of guilt; (c) the need for an adequate amount of attention from parents; and (d) the need for honesty in general. Even with their own unique needs, nondisabled siblings usually adopt their parents' attitudes toward their sibling with disabilities (Lobato, 1990; Schwartz, 1984).

Parents and professionals can help siblings cope with their needs. One effective way is to provide siblings with opportunities to participate in working with their brother or sister with disabilities. Even very young children can learn to be effective teachers. In fact, young children who have just learned how to do something themselves may be superior teachers. It is imperative, however, that parents be sensitive in their requests of able-bodied siblings. Ehly, Conoley, and Rosenthal (1985) warned that siblings who assume too much responsibility for the care of their sibling with disabilities can create their own inadequate personal adjustment. Along these same lines, it is essential that parents refrain from expecting too much from siblings. Sometimes the siblings are expected to make up for what the son or daughter who has disabilities cannot do.

In his discussion of concerns and questions of siblings, Gargiulo (1985) cited the following list originally prepared by Cansler and Martin (1974):

1. Siblings wonder about the cause of their brother's or sister's handicap, and sometimes fear that something may be wrong with themselves.
2. Siblings sometimes feel that having to help take care of the handicapped child interferes with their own activities.
3. Siblings may want to talk with their parents about the handicapped child's problems but do not know how to bring up the subject.
4. Siblings may feel upset and angry when parents have to spend a lot of time with the handicapped child. Sometimes siblings try to get attention from the parents by acting like the handicapped child.
5. Some siblings feel that they have to work extra hard (in school, sports, etc.) to make up to the parent for the handicapped child's deficiencies.
6. Siblings worry about how to tell their friends that they have a retarded brother or sister and wonder if their friends will make fun of them or their family for being different.
7. Siblings wonder if they will be able to get married and have children.
8. Siblings may worry about whether they will have to take care of the handicapped child in the future; they may wonder if they will be able to take care of him or her if anything happened to their parents.
9. Siblings may want to know how they can get along better with their handicapped brother or sister—how to help him/her learn to do things, how to play with him/her, what to do when babysitting. (p. viii)

In reviewing the effects of children with disabilities on their siblings, Gallagher and Powell (1989) reported that able-bodied older siblings tended to be kinder when their younger siblings had disabilities than when younger siblings did not have special needs. Similarly, sibling interactions, in general, were rated as more positive when at least one child had disabilities.

Regardless of the age or the relationship of the extended family members, the interventionist must be tactful, open, and honest. The parents' feelings and attitudes must always be given careful consideration and top priority. Everyone in the family interacts in some way with everyone else. Insofar as the interventionist can influence these interactions in positive ways, the children will gain. Having faith that one can be a positive help to a child with special needs buoys young siblings and mature grandparents. Specific tasks at which success is guaranteed are the place to begin. Then everyone benefits.

Foster Caregivers

Foster care is increasing by staggering proportions across the United States. For example, in California, between 1985 and 1989, the number of all children in out-of-home care increased by 65% while the number of children less than 4 years of age increased by an amazing 165% (County Welfare Directors Association of California et al., 1990). These children, including both those with and without disabilities, were placed because of existing laws related to abuse, neglect, and abandonment. Prenatal substance abuse is now considered one of the leading causes of the high infant out-of-home placement.

The foster child, in addition to possibly having developmental disabilities, often has overwhelming social-emotional needs. Caregivers and early interventionists must be concerned about such issues as attachment, diminished use of adults for comfort, passivity, inappropriate emotional responses, impulsivity, and fearfulness in their efforts to provide developmentally appropriate support to the young child. Because of the complexities associated with a child's removal from his or her natural parents, a team approach to placement, care, and reunification (when possible) is critical.

The implications for early interventionists are in working with foster families and encouraging participation in home and center activities. Intervention needs of the child with a developmental disability are developed with foster parent input as well as with the natural parent (as appropriate). In addition, the foster parents are encouraged to be a part of parent groups to take advantage of ongoing emotional support, training, and educational opportunities.

CAREGIVERS AS TEAM MEMBERS

Professionals have become more aware that caregivers play an important role not only in providing an emotional support system for the developing child but also as contributing team members in educating and instructing their child in classes and at home. However, some parents of young children with special needs feel that often too much emphasis is placed on the parent as teacher. To avoid creating additional stress, professionals should try not to overwhelm the parents as they become involved in their child's education.

In helping caregivers understand the intervention needs of their children, those who evaluate children's skills and developmental levels are expected to communicate the results of their testing to caregivers meaningfully. If caregivers are to become contributing team members, they first need to understand what the professionals are talking about. This means that information must not be given in professional jargon. Professionals can translate test results and implications into layman's language. For example, telling parents that their child may have a "visual perceptual problem" is meaningless to many of them. But parents can grasp their child's problem readily when the interventionist describes tasks

using the eyes and the hands at the same time such as buttoning, eating, doing puzzles, or stacking blocks. The caregivers' role in child assessment will be discussed further in Chapter 4.

P.L. 99-457 provides a legal mandate to ensure that in all stages of planning and implementation of services, caregivers are an integral part of the early intervention team.

Children with Disabilities and Children Without: More Alike Than Different

Success in working with children with special needs often depends on the realization that children with special needs and children without are more alike than different. Early interventionists can help parents understand that all children exhibit frustrations, misbehave, and refuse to cooperate at times. Parents of a child with a mild disability often interpret every childish antic as a symptom of some serious problem. Minor infractions of parental rules are seen as major catastrophes. All children, however, behave unpredictably. Most of them learn to manipulate their parents well before they are 2 years old. This comes as a genuine surprise to most parents. Even in the presence of overwhelming evidence, it is difficult for many adults to believe that such little ones are astute observers and efficient managers of parents.

Normally developing children experience many traumas, fears, and aggravations as they learn and grow. Alert parents and professionals seek to allow reasonable challenges. They try to prevent overwhelming demands on young children whenever possible. One "exceptional" parent summed up the need to accept the challenges presented by a developing child as follows:

A handicapped child takes just the same knowledge and love that a normal child takes, but you have to learn to accept that child for what he is. And if he can't walk, then he can't walk (Hodel, 1981).

OPTIONS FOR
FAMILY INVOLVEMENT

Just as children with special needs and non-disabled children are more alike than different, so are parents of children with special needs and parents of nondisabled children more alike than different. They have needs, frustrations, hopes, fears, and dreams similar to those of any other parent, although they also have feelings that may be special to parents of children with special needs. Even so, interventionists cannot expect to use the same method of working with all families just as they cannot expect to use the same method of working with all children. According to Powell (1986), research indicates that "there is no convincing evidence that one particular program [of parent participation] is more effective than another" (p. 49). Powell went on to enumerate some of the reasons why an unstructured

discussion group can be as effective as a highly structured behavioral group or why parent support groups can be as effective as parent education groups. As stated earlier, parents may be coming from different developmental stages and different circumstances. Parents' personality factors tend to influence participation. Some parents relate more readily to staff members while others prefer to relate to other parents. Socioeconomic and ethnic background may determine response to differing program contents. Therefore, attempts must be made to match total family needs with available parent involvement opportunities (Shea & Bauer, 1985).

It is extremely important to remember that families should clearly feel that participation is, indeed, an *option*. Professionals must help families understand the continuum of services and opportunities from which they may make choices. Procedures for helping families identify their resources and needs, as well as appropriate participation, will be discussed in Chapter 5.

A Continuum of Family Involvement

Even though P.L. 99-457 sets the stage for **family-focused early intervention,** in reality family involvement will fall along a continuum. Some families may elect not to be involved in early intervention services, while others will seek the fullest possible involvement. Simeonsson and Bailey (1990) have outlined hierarchical levels of involvement ranging from electing not to be involved to active participation in decision making, program implementation, and advocacy activities. Each successive level illustrates an increase in the comprehensiveness of services and the family's desire for these services. Each higher level includes and extends services from the lower levels. Family needs, values, and lifestyles, as well as program characteristics, are likely to determine the level of family involvement. Early interventionists may be directly involved as therapists or teachers or they may only provide referral information. It is the intent of the individualized family service plan to clearly delineate the level of both family and professional involvement. *It is important for professionals to avoid implying that the degree of parent involvement is synonymous with parent concern. Parent involvement is certainly not a measure of parent concern.*

Individual needs and capabilities must be balanced with the goals of parent involvement. Some parents will have a greater need and capacity for cognitive information delivered through lectures, panel discussions, and films. Other parents may most desire and need one-to-one conversations with the professional when privacy is assured and they can feel comfortably accepted. Still other parents will thrive on being shown how to teach their child.

The remainder of this chapter focuses on the primary considerations to be thought through carefully in making each type of involvement effective. Unique needs are also discussed, along with helpful hints for the professionals who must work with these unique needs.

Home-Based Intervention Programs

Home-based intervention programs offer many advantages. Young children and parents are most natural at home. At home they do not have to develop the feeling of comfortable belonging; they do not have to be transported either by the parents or a school bus. Interventionists can take the home life into consideration when planning for the child.

Generally a teacher, nurse, therapist, or trained paraprofessional makes regularly scheduled visits (weekly or monthly) to offer educational services and sometimes social and health services. Parents are encouraged and taught how to interact with their own children using household objects or materials. Integrating intervention activities into daily living obviates the necessity for planning special times for "lessons." For

instance, the parent of a young child with cerebral palsy might integrate stretching exercises into diapering time or language activities during feeding.

At first some parents may feel uncomfortable having a professional in their homes. Tact, courtesy, and sensitivity can overcome this initial discomfort very quickly. The professional or trained paraprofessional becomes an anticipated visitor. Toys to share, ideas that work, and a sympathetic ear usually endear the home visitor to both parents and children.

The success of these visitations is highly dependent on the visitor's training and preparation. This section offers practical suggestions for effective home intervention and discusses important considerations when making home visits. Because only the most critical points are covered, readers are urged to consult the references for more in-depth consideration of home-based programs and resources available. Practical suggestions for the home visitation follow:

1. *Take time to gain information on family life and daily schedules.* This knowledge gives insight into optimal times for home visits and functional activities.

2. *Be informal, but not too casual.* You are functioning as a professional.

3. *Be prepared.* Have materials, activity plans, and backup ideas ready. To interact more freely, try to avoid filling out forms. If writing is necessary, explain what you are doing and why.

4. *Be flexible.* If what was planned is inappropriate for any reason, change it at once. Also encourage parents to vary the activities to meet their needs, as well as the child's needs. Do not plan too much for the parents to do. They have other responsibilities.

5. *Carry materials in a picnic basket.* Briefcases look too much like a doctor's medical bag. Be sure to include an appealing game to play

and a surprise that the child may keep. You might include a toy or game for siblings to use during the visit.

6. *Be ready to admire pet frogs, favorite toys, and other family treasures.* Take the time to know what the children and their parents are proud of and what they value most. Compliment the home in some way.

7. *Encourage parents to show or demonstrate how they interact with their child.* Show that their ideas are worthwhile. Express approval and admiration. Avoid direct criticism. Rather, suggest changes by saying something such as "Some of the time you will want to try _____," or "At school we notice that children seem to progress faster when _____."

8. *Do not smoke in the home unless invited to do so.* This can be very irritating to some people.

9. *Avoid confrontations.* Even if parents insist that what has been suggested won't work or is not something they can or will do, the visitor must not argue or insist that parents should conform.

10. *Begin and end your visit on time.*

11. *Before you leave, schedule and discuss the next visit.* Review with the parents what you did today and what you will do next visit. Write out any suggestions for activities for parents to follow. Schedule the next visit and write the date and time on the activity plan form left with the parents. Assure them that they can reach you by telephone if they should have any questions or comments.

12. *Maintain confidentiality.* At all times remember that you are a professional. Whatever you observe in the parents' home and any judgments you make are not to be discussed in public. Families have a right to their privacy and their choice of living style. The effectiveness of visits may depend on your ability to be mature, objective, and professional.

Important Considerations When Making Home Visits. In addition to the preceding points, home interventionists should remember the following:

1. From the beginning, avoid talking about the children and their special needs when they can possibly overhear. Even completely nonverbal children understand much more than is supposed. Even if they do not understand the words, they will understand the facial expressions, gestures, and body language of the adults. During each home visit, some opportunity for such discussion is useful. If parents are told this in advance, most can arrange for a neighbor or friend to take the child for a time. If this is impractical, an aide should go with the interventionist at least some of the time. The aide can take the child outside or to another part of the home during the time the child is being discussed by parents and professional.

2. Plan to demonstrate at least two or three activities. Even though written suggestions are provided, showing is more effective than merely telling or describing. Ask parents whether they would like to choose an activity. Activities accumulate, and by choosing among them parents' interests and time demands can be considered.

Sometimes an older child can be helpful. Teach brothers and sisters the activities. Often they can participate with the parent and the child for whom the activity was planned. Including other children serves two purposes: they are usually excellent teachers, and including them can prevent jealousy and feelings of being left out.

3. Call attention to particular intervention strategies. It will come as a surprise to many parents that children learn little by failing. It is crucial to show parents how to develop activities at which their children can succeed. At first, home interventionists must be very explicit about the need to avoid activities that result in failure for the children. Showing parents how to prompt their children and then gradually reduce and

fade the prompting is important. This strategy is basic to successful home intervention. Give the parents specific guidelines such as those noted in Exhibit 3–1.

4. Be nonjudgmental. Some parents will be embarrassed about their homes or will be afraid of criticism. It is important to be blind to the things that are not relevant to working with the children and to notice things parents are proud of, especially things that they have done for their children.

5. Refer to the child's individualized education program (IEP) or individualized family service plan (IFSP) regularly. Help parents to see how the home program relates to the goals and objectives on the IEP.

6. Help parents to develop behavior management skills. Many parents are concerned about their child's inappropriate behavior and attribute it to the disability. Usually the basis of the problem is not the disability itself, but rather not knowing how to communicate effectively with the child. If inappropriate behavior is reported at the supermarket, plan some intervention there. The interventionist's demonstration of effective controls can be immensely helpful to parents who are frightened and worried.

Directions for managing the behavior of young children should be explicit. The interventionist can give reasons for what is suggested in a manner and language that parents understand. Exhibit 3–2 shows how this is achieved. Role playing with the parent taking the part of the

---

EXHIBIT 3–1 _____

Activity Guidelines for Parents

1. *Be ready to praise.* Praise your child's efforts and successes. Use hugs, pats, smiles, and positive words readily.

2. *Correct with care.* When your child makes mistakes, do not tell him or her that he or she is wrong. Instead, gently show or tell him or her the preferred response. For example, if your child hands you a spoon instead of the requested fork, say, "You've handed me a spoon. Now hand me the fork," instead of "That's not a fork. I asked for the fork."

3. *Find an appropriate time and place.* Do not remove a child from an activity in which he or she is involved. Keep the activity short, from 5 to 15 minutes. Be certain your child is wide awake, not hungry or "keyed up." Prepare a place to work where the child is comfortable and not distracted by sound or sight.

4. *Do not use force.* Do not force your child to continue an activity. Attention spans vary with the child and with the activity. Treat your child with the same consideration you would give your friends. If your child senses that you are tense, angry, or critical, he or she will learn to dislike the activities.

5. *Be flexible.* Vary the activity and methods to fit the child's needs. If one approach does not work, try another. Some learn more quickly while being active; others prefer being more passive. Use as many senses as possible, especially if one or more of the senses is impaired.

6. *Speak clearly.* Use a normal voice when talking to your child.

7. *Be prepared.* Assemble materials and prepare the working space in advance. Do not waste the child's attention on preparation activities. Consider taking the phone off the hook during the short activity period.

8. *Be enthusiastic.* Do not under any circumstances let your child feel that you are working with him or her because "you have to." If you do not feel like working with your child, he or she will feel your tension. Reschedule your activity. By selecting a rather consistent time each day, you will find it easier to manage your time. If you find you are not enjoying your involvement, talk this over with your child's teacher or other professional. An adjustment in the activities or the approach may bring greater enjoyment.

EXHIBIT 3–2 _____

Directions to a Parent for Managing a Screamer

Scene: It is time for Ms. McLynn's second home visit. Danny's mother has asked her to help with Danny's screaming. When things don't go exactly the way he wants, he just screams. The neighbors are complaining. Several of them call their children in when Danny comes out.

Mrs. Dickson: "Hello, Ms. McLynn. I'm so glad you could come again so soon."

Ms. McLynn: "Well, I try to go to all of my parents in turn. But if one asks me, I can always return more quickly. Now, let's think about Danny's screaming together. You remember, last week I emphasized that especially with these young children we must work as a team. Unless we are consistent in the way we discipline him at home and at school, he will be even more confused."

Mrs. D.: "Oh yes, I do understand that. That's why I asked you to come back. The morning I visited the classroom he didn't scream once. Here he screams several times every hour!"

Ms. McL.: "The first few days he screamed at school, too. My aides and I have a routine when this happens. Many children try to control us by screaming. One of us picks the child up with no comment, and carries him or her to a small room that has only one chair. Then, the adult puts the child down, shuts the door, picks up a book, and sits down. No matter how loud the noise is, the adult just reads. As soon as the noise stops, the adult says matter of factly, "If you are ready, we can go back to the room." Because of Danny's hearing problem, it helps to gesture toward the room, too. Nothing more is said. Sometimes children begin to scream again, so it's back to reading the book. As soon as the child is quiet, the statement is made again."

Mrs. D.: "How long does it take?"

Ms. McL.: "Some children need to return to the room two or three times in the first week. Rarely more often."

Mrs. D.: "Do you explain to them why?"

Ms. McL.: "Only very briefly. Usually something like "We can't play if you scream in our room, so we go to our special place until you feel better.""

Mrs. D.: "That's all?"

Ms. McL.: "That's all. Talking won't do it. Our consistent responses will. Whoever takes the child to the little room remains very quiet, never appears upset, and does not scold."

Mrs. D.: "And how do I do that?"

Ms. McL.: "The first time, do it on faith. After you see it work a few times, you will fully expect it to be effective. Danny will sense this. Remember, you are not punishing him. You are simply communicating that when he screams, he has to go to a certain place alone or with you until he is quiet."

Mrs. D.: "Then, I should stay with him, too?"

Ms. McL.: "Whatever you think is best. Some parents pick the children up and isolate them in a special place, often their own room. If you feel that is safe, it serves the same purpose. But never put him into a dark or dangerous place. Remember, you want to communicate just two things: (1) When you scream, you will never get what you want, and (2) When you scream, it bothers us, so you must be away from your friends until you are quiet."

Mrs. D.: "But how will he understand if he can't understand the words?"

Ms. McL.: "He screams because in the past it got him what he wanted. Now, he just has to learn that won't work anymore."

Mrs. D.: "Ok—Please, can I call you if it doesn't work?"

Ms. McL.: "Of course. I'll check back in 3 days."

child will help parents master the needed management skills. Most important, the interventionist must explain that behavior is learned. Changing habits and behavior patterns may not be easy, and improvement may not be made overnight. Parents may be helped by talking about their problems with other parents who have successfully learned improved child management skills.

7. Never forget that parents know their children better than the professional does in some ways. Most parents are accurate observers of what their children do and do not do. But their interpretation of the observed behavior is often inappropriate. For example, a child who screams and has a trantrum when denied something that he or she wants may be described by the parents as "bad" or "just like Uncle Will." Usually children who behave in this way have been rewarded by receiving the things they want when they cry. This cause-and-effect relationship is not well understood by many parents. The professional cannot explain it in a 5-minute lecture!

Chapter 7 enumerates some of the ways early interventionists can help parents in this essential task. The goal is to assist parents in reinterpreting the behaviors they have called "bad" as something the children have learned and not something "in" them. By the interventionist's example and explanations, parents can learn to think about their children more constructively.

8. Playfulness and the expression of enjoyment are essential if children are to achieve their potential. Let the parents observe activities during which the interventionist is expressing these feelings. Be willing to play with children, enjoying the games they like. This is very effective interaction. Avoid being too serious.

9. Introduce parents to other parents who have similar interests and needs. Even if most of the intervention is done in the home, plan occasional get-togethers for parents who have similar needs and interests.

10. Communication with all caregivers is essential. In some cases, the early interventionist may plan activities in the home to supplement the child's *regular* preschool or day care center program. When this is the case, a system of reporting what is done can be very useful. Common goals and objectives are essential. Methods of communication include the following:

a. Phone calls to the child's regular early childhood teacher, usually brief, to report on what was accomplished and to suggest carryover activities.

b. Written goals and objectives, with copies given to parents and to the preschool or day care teachers.

c. A passport notebook with comments and observations made by all concerned. This passport notebook may travel with the child and be used by all who are responsible for care and teaching. An example of a page from such a passport notebook is illustrated in Figure 3–2. Shea and Bauer (1991) offered the following guidelines for writing notes in the passport:

1. Be brief. (Parents and teachers are busy.)

2. Be positive. (Parents know their child has problems and need not receive constant negative reminders.)

3. Be honest (Don't say a child is doing fine if he or she is not. However, write noncommittal comments or request a face-to-face or telephone conference in place of negative notes.)

4. Be responsive. (If the parent or teacher asks for help, respond immediately.)

5. Be informal. (All participants are equals.)

6. Be consistent. (If the passport is the communication system of choice, use it consistently and expect the same from other participants.)

7. Avoid jargon. (Parents may not understand educational jargon, and even professionals may use jargon at cross-purposes.)

8. Be careful. (No one should project personal feelings or the frustrations of a bad day onto the child, parent, or teacher.) (p. 1181)

Dec. 10, Mrs. J. (Susan's mother):

Susan wouldn't eat her breakfast this morning. She didn't seem sick, just not hungry. Could you give her an early snack, please?

Dec. 10, Ms. S. (Susan's teacher at day care):

Susan _was_ hungry when she got here. Two glasses of juice and a piece of toast disappeared right away. And then she ~~asked~~ to go "potty." We are making progress. No accidents today! Hooray.

Dec. 11, Mrs. J.:

Ms. R., Susan's home teacher, came yesterday afternoon. She suggested that we continue to work on teaching Susan the names of her clothes. I'm going to put her clothes on the bed, and then tell her to bring me each thing, one at a time. Could you help with this at school, please?

Dec. 11, Ms. S.:

We surely can. Susan brought me her boots and her tote bag when I asked her today. Progress is good.

Figure 3–2   **A passport page used by the day care teacher, parents, and the home interventionist. This page was chosen from notes written during the fourth month of school attendance. Susan is 3 years old and has been described as "developmentally delayed." She uses two-word "sentences" that are partially intelligible. She has frequent "accidents," wetting and soiling herself at home and at school.**

Parents in the Early Childhood Center

Involving parents in daily center activities can be useful in a variety of ways. The center staff is able to model preferred techniques of teaching specific skills and effective approaches to behavior management. Many parents will then be able to translate some of what they have observed into more useful interactions in the home environment. Parents with specific skills or talents such as in music or art can feel good about the contributions they can make to the center. Parents who accompany classes on field trips to such familiar places as the grocery store can observe and, ideally, generalize ways of using everyday activities to teach their child. Finally, many parents will feel that their child is more like other children than different from them. As they observe progress over time, they will feel encouraged and more hopeful. The first few times parents come to the center will be difficult for them and for their children. Some parents will feel compelled to direct and correct their own children constantly. They may be deeply distressed by every small infraction of the rules. Tears and tantrums are the outward signs of the distress of the children. Nervousness and apologizing for the child's "badness" may be the parents' reaction. With careful planning, the center staff can prevent or at least minimize most of these problems.

First Step: Parents Meet Other Parents. Before parents begin to observe or participate, they can benefit by meeting with "veteran" parents. Parents from previous years, whether or not their children are currently enrolled, can be called on to help. If these experienced parents assist with planning and presenting the program, it will be much more believable and useful to the new parents. The opportunity to talk with other parents who have been through the program is the best preparation for beginners.

Centers should plan the orientation program *with* parents, not *for* them. Parents themselves can plan the agenda, choosing items to be dis-

cussed and points to be emphasized. Both the nature of the community and the characteristics of the children will influence what needs to be done.

A letter of invitation from the parents who are planning the meeting is more effective than a letter from the center. This is especially true if the letter from the center is duplicated on a faded ditto! One parent group sent handwritten notes to each new parent one week in advance. A follow-up phone call, including an offer to pick up the new parents, resulted in nearly 100% attendance.

Although traditionally mothers have come to school, fathers can be especially helpful. Having one father call another helps to make it seem less strange. Other family members should be included whenever practical.

Evening meetings are usually more convenient for fathers. Fathers who do shift work or who work at night, however, can be encouraged to come to the center during the day. Properly welcomed, fathers have even been known to take a vacation day to attend.

The orientation meeting. For the orientation meeting, the chairperson should be a parent. If at all possible the program presenters should also be parents. Refreshments made by the children are best. Cookies are fun to make and decorate, and concentrated punch is easy to stir. A special touch is added by having the children snip the edges of construction paper or scribble pictures to make placemats.

During the first meeting, program presenters can suggest the advantages of parent participation in the center. This includes observation visits, conferences, meetings, and regular volunteer work in the center. Parents who are genuine believers in the value of their classroom participation communicate this effectively. A sign-up sheet for classroom involvement should be placed in a conspicuous place. First visits should be short—30 minutes to 1 hour is sufficient. It will surprise most parents that coming to the center as often as once a week is desirable. This may not be possible for some, but all parents should be encouraged to come at least once a month.

The center may present specific participation guidelines. An example of a letter used for this purpose is found in Exhibit 3–3. Some parent groups prefer to have a roundtable discussion, talking about each item of the guidelines. Other groups prefer films or videotapes.

Relaxing and getting acquainted. After the planned meeting, a social time provides the opportunity for the center staff to introduce parents to each other. Name tags, including the name of the child who attends the center, are helpful. Although staff members will want to greet each parent individually, they will also want to encourage parents to talk to each other. Professionals will need to be wise in sharing their time equally among parents. This is not the time for in-depth parent conferences. An announcement to this effect just before the social time begins may prevent problem discussions.

Follow-up. The day after the meeting a letter from the center thanking the parents who participated and pointing out how much was accomplished is necessary. If these are handwritten and mailed, instead of sent with the children, the effect is much greater. In addition to the notes, a summary of what happened should go home with each child. This summary should be sent to each family, whether or not they attended the meeting. The guidelines distributed at the meeting can also be sent home at this time. If at all possible, parents who attended the meeting should contact those who did not come. Knowing they were missed is important to many parents.

Parents as Observers. All parents will feel unsure at first, even if they hide their feelings well. They will wonder what their children will do, and will expect the worst. Often their children will oblige.

Center staff must strive to make parents feel comfortable and welcome, giving their children specific things to do to keep them from seeking attention in undesirable ways.

Interacting with their own child. The center should encourage parents to greet their own child and allow their own child to show them around. These social skills must be taught to many children. Initial awkwardness can yield quickly to confidence and security if the center staff sets the stage and does a bit of managing. Cues such as "Show Dad where we keep our big blocks. I'll bet he can build a tall tower," or "Show Mother where we keep the easel and the markers. I wonder if she knows how well you can draw," may be effective. Naturalness, friendliness, and a comfortable feeling for all should be the goal.

If the parents indicate that they would enjoy it, encourage them to play a game with their own child and one or two others. A demonstration by a center staff member starts the game, but then the professional should be busy with others to allow the parent the opportunity to develop his or her own style. The intent is to set the stage for parents and children to have a good time and feel at ease.

Keeping the visit short. The time schedule should be understood by everyone before the visit begins. Parents should be encouraged to vary the time of day they visit to create a more complete understanding of their child's involvement in the program.

Providing observation guidelines. Staff can help parents become astute observers by telling them what to look for. A short list of focus points might be helpful. For example, Ms. McLynn may wish Danny's mother to observe his reaction to sound in the classroom. She could prepare the following short list:

1. What does Danny do when someone calls his name?

EXHIBIT 3–3

Sample Center Participation Guidelines

Dear Parents,

As you know, it is very important for you to come to our center regularly to help us in the classroom, and to learn more about working with your children at home. But some of you have told me that you felt a little uncomfortable—that you really were not sure what to do sometimes. So I asked one of our "experienced mothers," Laura, to jot down some guidelines that will help you feel more at ease. Laura and I talked about these guidelines and she helped me to understand how you feel. Both Laura and I hope you will suggest other things that will make your time at our center more useful and enjoyable. These suggestions are just a beginning. Here they are:

Guidelines for mothers (fathers, grandparents, and aunts, too)

1. Don't panic. The children are allowed to do *some* things at the center that they cannot do at home, or that they do not normally do at home (using scissors, putting things into the refrigerator, or helping another child).

2. *Don't get "up tight."* If your child "shows off" because you are there, that is perfectly normal, and nobody will blame you.

3. *Don't talk in front of the children (either at home or at school).* Even if you do not think they will understand, never talk about them when they can overhear.

4. *Take time. Try what the teacher suggests.* It might seem the teacher's way makes matters worse, and sometimes it will, at first. But time (lots of it) will make a difference. Ms. McLynn says that with our children we are not just working for this minute. We want them to learn how to use self-control and good judgment. And this takes experience with "logical consequences" of things they do.

5. *Learn the class rules.* Find out what is a "no-no" and what's all right. For example, Hot Wheels—no riding inside, but the balance toys are okay. Moving the kitchen stuff around is okay, just like we change the room arrangement at home sometimes. Yelling is a "no-no." (That is an "outside voice.") Putting stuff away after you use it is also a rule. But some of them have not learned that yet.

6. *Ask.* If you are not sure what to do, ask. If you do not know why the teacher does things her way, ask. And do not be afraid to say how you feel. She will listen. Sometimes she misses something that happens, and it helps if you clue her in. (Remember, do not let the children overhear.) If you have a problem with your child, ask to talk about it with the teacher. She will find a way to talk to you so your child will not overhear. It is also important to tell the teacher if you do not agree with what is happening. Find out why it is happening. The reason wil probably make it feel better.

7. *Talk.* Talk to the teacher and the children in the regular way. Ms. McLynn wants you to have "conversations" with the children except during "circle time." These conversations help the children learn. Those words on the bulletin board behind her desk are the cues for words they are working on. Try to use them often while you are talking to the children. Don't try to make them say things "the right way." Conversations should be fun. They help to teach language. Speech lessons are at a separate time, unless Ms. McLynn says otherwise, because trying to make a child correct a speech sound can make things worse. The child may just stop talking to you.

8. *Play with your child and other children at playtime.* You will learn, just as they will. Remember, someone else will be playing with your child. It averages out.

9. *Don't feel silly or useless.* It is really important to be there. Cutting stuff, helping clean up, or just listening are all important. Lots of things are important for the children to learn before kindergarten.

10. *Have an open mind when the teachers correct your child.*

Courtesy Laura Bridgeman

2. Does Danny act differently when I stand directly in front of him and speak to him than when he cannot see my face?

3. Does Danny respond to noises made behind him or anywhere out of sight?

Such a list of focus points makes it easier to discuss the observations with everyone focusing on the child's behavior rather than on more subjective aspects of the child such as personality. Mr. Curtis might prepare the following list to help Vicky's parent understand his or her concerns:

1. What was the first thing Vicky did? What was the second?

2. Approximately how long did Vicky stay with each activity?

3. Which activity held Vicky's attention the longest?

A sample of a parent observation form that helps to focus the parent's attention is presented in Exhibit 3–4.

Conducting miniconferences. Parents should not expect a parent conference per se when they observe or participate. However, occasional miniconferences (5 to 10 minutes long) following an observation are helpful if they can be arranged. This should not take place where the children can overhear. The professional will want to call attention to the positive aspects of the visit. Noting a child's progress is always a good idea. The observation guidelines provide a mutual point of discussion. Parents should be encouraged to ask questions and make comments. They will feel like partners only if their opinions are obviously valued.

If a miniconference is not possible, the visit may be followed up by a telephone conversation. Parents can also be encouraged to leave written comments or questions in a designated place if there is no time for discussion.

Parents as Participants. In some centers, parents are encouraged or expected to participate as aides. Chapter 11 is designed to assist professionals in making effective use of parent volunteers. When parents are able to work only occasionally, the interest checklist also found in Chapter 10 may be helpful in motivating their involvement. Some parents will be willing to assist the professional in individual center activities. Such experiences provide excellent opportunities for the professional to model desired strategies for working with young children.

It is often helpful to ask parents to play a game or teach a lesson that has been done before with the children in the center. Children love repetition. If they have experienced the activity before, it will be easier for the parent to conduct the lesson. The activity should be one that is useful for the parent's own child. Suggestions such as the following can be put in a parent handout and can be posted or distributed when parents choose to participate:

1. Plan for success for both the parents and the children.

2. Choose an activity that can be demonstrated easily. Provide a brief written description of the objective and procedures of the activity.

3. Keep the group small (two or three children).

4. Explain the purpose of the lesson or game. Be specific.

5. Emphasize that learning should be fun even if it is also hard work.

6. Do not emphasize "winning." Little children just like to play. Winning and losing are artificial concepts and interfere with learning.

7. Select a game or activity parents can use at home. Most commercial games or lessons can be duplicated with things found in most homes. Whenever possible, choose an activity that will benefit the child and interest his or her parent.

EXHIBIT 3–4 _____

Parent Observation Report

Date:_____

Who was involved in this experience?_____

What happened first?

Then what did the child do?

What did you do, or what did another adult caregiver do?

What were the results?

Do you think you or the other adult caregiver might have done something better? Why or why not?

---

8. Specifically explain how to manage children's errors and misbehaviors. Demonstrate and talk about various techniques. A mistake or "failure" is merely a clue to try another way.

Conferences with Parents

Individual conferences with parents can and should be one of the most effective methods of parent involvement. Inherent in this approach is flexibility. Either the parent or the professional can request the conference. It can be held at the center or at home at any convenient time as long as parents feel the comfort of privacy and confidentiality. The content varies with the needs of the parents, the child, and the professional. The professional can individualize the specific suggestions made and the level of language used. With conferences, parents who cannot read or understand written comments do not miss important information about their child's progress.

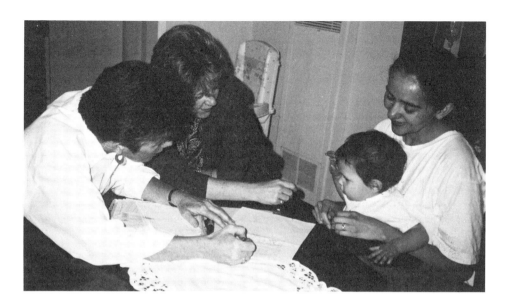

Stephens (1979) discussed four sets of behaviors needed by professionals to conduct effective parent conferences: (1) skills in rapport
building; (2) obtaining information from parents; (3) providing parents with helpful information; and (4) summarizing, identifying new
objectives, and making recommendations. Developing these skills takes preparation, practice,
time, and patience. By being aware of the need to
develop competence in these four important behaviors, professionals who are new to the field
can focus on developing habits conducive to successful conferencing.

Preparing for the Conference. The objectives for
conferences should be planned with situational
needs in mind. For some the objectives will be
general, such as merely becoming acquainted
and helping to assure the parents that their child
is well cared for and progressing. Another conference may be requested by the parent or the
professional because of a specific concern. For
example, Mr. Curtis may need to know whether
Vicky is as inattentive and active at home as she
is in the center. If he understands her parents'
attitudes and reactions, he may be able to work

with her family in developing consistency between school and home. Mr. Curtis realizes,
however, that his objectives will have to be flexible enough to accommodate the parents' needs
as well.

The professional should be prepared to
provide parents with adequate information.
Consider the information gathered through the
various observation techniques discussed in
Chapter 4. Samples of the child's work, anecdotal records, tape recordings, logs, and assessment data should be readily available on request. Special care must be taken to discuss this
information in layman's terms.

When conferences are initiated by professionals, personal invitations should be extended
by telephone or through letters. A mimeographed note is not very personal. Whenever possible, parents should be given a choice of date
and time. A quiet, uninterrupted setting must be
prepared with comfortable adult-sized chairs.
The professional should not be seated behind a
desk because this puts a distance between him or
her and the parent, who may already be tense.
Offering a beverage can make the parent feel
more relaxed. Babysitting may need to be ar-

ranged because the presence of children distracts the conversation and destroys the confidentiality necessary. Scouts and aides can help out by taking the child and siblings to the playground or to another room.

Beginning the Conference. Often the initial few minutes of a conference are the most uncomfortable and are perhaps the most critical in building the necessary rapport. Initial impressions can create defensiveness that gets in the way of objective thinking and the creation of a productive relationship. Greetings, a handshake, and thanking the parent for coming help the parent to see that the professional appreciates his or her effort to come. To help the parent feel at ease, it is helpful to begin with nonemotional topics, although these must be brief because the parent is usually anxious to get to the purpose of the meeting.

A time limit for the conference should be made clear so that the parent will not feel rejected when it is necessary to close the conversation. A statement such as the following can establish the time limit of a conference and clarify the purpose of the meeting: "I am so happy, Ms. Jones, that you are able to share the next 15 minutes with me today. I have so much to tell you about Jamie's progress, and I want to hear how you feel about it."

If the parent has initiated the conference, the professional might say: "I am so glad, Ms. Dickson, that you felt free to request this conference. I will be free until 4:00 and am eager to know where you would like to begin." If the parent hesitates, the professional should try not to become tense. If the silence or apparent reluctance of the parent to speak seems to go on too long, the professional should then make a facilitating comment such as "It is sometimes hard to express what we are thinking or feeling." All the while the professional should try to show by body language that he or she cares, is ready to listen, and is not pushy.

Conducting the Conference. Once the purpose of the conference is clarified, the parent should be encouraged to talk if he or she has said very little. The professional can make a facilitating comment such as "I thought you might share some of your observations and concerns about Mary so that we might plan a way to work together to help her progress." The professional should then listen very carefully to whatever the parent says. Parents usually express their primary concerns at this time. The professional is also given a glimpse of the sophistication level of the parent and can gear his or her language to that level.

Listening carefully. Listening carefully is absolutely critical in the development of productive relationships with parents. Attentive listening not only encourages parents to express themselves, but it demonstrates the professional's acceptance and concern. Valand (1975) discussed the following four attending skills as basic to effective listening: (1) minimal encouragers to talk, (2) reflection, (3) paraphrasing and summarization, and (4) clarification.

Minimal encouragers to talk are expressions and nonverbal cues that let the speaker know you want to hear more of what he or she has to say. Gordon (1970) referred to these as *door-openers.* Typical of these are such comments as "un-huh," "yes," "that's interesting," and "hmmm." These can be useful in getting parents to continue talking, but they should not become overused or be used stereotypically. The professional should be certain not to interrupt the parent with these or other comments. Leaning somewhat forward is usually a sign of listening and trying to focus on what is being said.

Reflection involves comments that let the parent know the professional has heard and understood what the parent is saying. It helps to focus the parent's comments by recognizing a specific comment. It is a cue to parents to elaborate on that specific idea, concept, or question. If the reflection also includes the feeling that is perceived, then the professional will be demonstrating the active listening encouraged by Gordon (1970). Consider the following example of a partial reflection and a reflection involving feeling necessary to active listening (Valand, 1975):

Parent: "I had thought that when he began speech therapy, his talking would improve."
Teacher: "Would improve?" or "You're feeling pretty discouraged."

Lichter (1976) spelled out the advantages of active listening for the professional working with a parent of a child with disabilities. In his work with the parents of children with moderate retardation, he has found "active listening" to be "a profound way to communicate a willingness to hear, to understand, and to have empathy with someone who is isolated and struggling to be heard" (p. 68). Considering the emotional needs of parents of children with disabilities, it is well worth the time to invest the energy necessary to become a good active listener.

Paraphrasing and summarizing occur when the professional attempts to repeat to the parent in revised form what he or she has said. This demonstrates that what the speaker said has been heard and gives the speaker the chance to clarify any misunderstanding the professional may have. Finally, *clarification* completes the process of active listening. It is necessary to clarify what the parent is saying whenever there are any doubts. If it cannot be done through active listening, then it can be done directly by asking, "Are you saying . . . ?" or "Do you mean . . . ?" Exhibit 3–5, which depicts a home conference, illustrates the skills involved in reflection, paraphrasing, summarization, and clarification.

Questioning. Morgan (1977, p. 4) suggested using questions for only two purposes: (1) to obtain specifically needed information or clarification, and (2) to direct the parent's conversation when it runs astray. Questions such as "Can you tell me exactly what Susie did that bothered you so much?" help to focus the conversation and provide additional information. Such an open-ended question, which cannot be answered with a "yes" or "no," encourages a reluctant parent. On the other hand, a closed question, which can be answered with a "yes" or "no," helps to narrow the focus of a disorganized parent. Since professionals need to avoid interrogation, they should practice becoming skilled in using productive questions.

Recognizing parents' concerns. This chapter has been emphasizing the importance of a warm, caring attitude that conveys understanding. Of course, this attitude and the skills to convey it are absolutely essential for an effective parent conference. Professionals must expect parents to be reluctant at first. They must be given time to learn that the professional cares. Reflective listening is one way to let parents know that their concerns have been heard and understood. Another is by being prepared and honest. If parents ask a question and the professional does not know the answer, he or she should kindly say so. The early childhood interventionist is not a medical doctor or a psychotherapist and must not pretend otherwise by giving misleading information. He or she can and should be prepared to make appropriate referrals. A file or notebook listing names and telephone numbers of local agencies can be helpful. It is important not to be biased in referrals or to endorse anyone in particular. It is a good idea to obtain a list from the local special education regional office, school psychologist, social worker, nurse, or principal.

Describing childrens' progress. The professional should be organized and positive in describing children's progress, giving specific examples of a child's skills or behavior whenever possible. The professional should encourage par-

EXHIBIT 3–5 _____

Dialogue: A Home Conference Between Parent and Teacher

Scene: Matt is a four year old who has been described by his mother as "never still" and by his father as "all boy." In the last week, the mother reports that several of her favorite plants have crashed to the floor as Matt walked by. "He never does anything mean or on purpose," she said. He bumps into things and is surprised when adults complain or he breaks things.

It is time for Ms. McLynn's first home visit. Matt's mother, Ms. G., greets her at the door.

Ms. G.: "Hello. Matt has been so excited about your coming, and when he heard you knock, he hid under the bed!"

Ms. McL.: "Good to be here, Ms. G. At school Matt is so helpful. I can always count on Matt to see what needs doing and to do it. He seems to sense the other children's needs, as well as mine."

Ms. G.: "But he is so rough. And always breaking something. My neighbors say he is hyperactive."

Ms. McL.: "What does that mean to them?"

Ms. G.: "Oh, you know, never still. He just can't seem to be quiet for a minute."

Ms. McL.: "But he has been very quiet since I've been here."

Ms. G.: "He's still hiding under the bed. Oh, he can be quiet when *he* wants to be."

Ms. McL.: "So you feel he really does have control of how active he is?"

Ms. G.: "Yes, I guess so. But just tell him to sit still and he bounces all over the place."

Ms. McL.: "You feel he is too active."

Ms. G.: "Yes. And he won't listen when I tell him to sit still. That burns me up."

Ms. McL.: "His constant moving annoys you."

Ms. G.: "You bet it does. What can I do to make him behave? I've tried spanking, but he forgets right away."

Ms. McL.: "From watching at school and with what you told me, I'd like to suggest that we both try something. Let's catch him being quiet and gentle."

Ms. G.: "When? How?"

Ms. McL.: "At school I'll keep a special paper on my desk. Every time he is quiet or gentle, I'll say something like, 'Matt, I like the way you helped Missy with her coat. You were so gentle,' or 'Matt, you are doing a good job with that puzzle. You are so quiet that I can hear the birds singing outside.' Then, I'll make a quick note—for example 9:03—Quiet and gentle. Helped Missy with coat. 9:10—Worked puzzle. Quiet 3 minutes."

Ms. G.: "Well, it can't hurt."

Ms. McL.: "I'll call you in 2 days to see how it's working." And 2 days later when Ms. McLynn called, she was not surprised that Ms. G. could report more quiet and gentle times than noisy ones. So could Ms. McLynn.

ents to discuss individual points of progress and to ask questions and should not overwhelm them with information or use jargon. Evasiveness or "fortune telling" are to be avoided. The professional can only discuss what the child will be doing in the center, what the child has accomplished, and what might be expected in the immediate next step. He or she cannot predict how the child will be functioning next year or the year after.

Closing the Conference. The professional has the primary responsibility for ending the conference in conformity with the time limit. Such comments as, "Given the few minutes we have left, could you explain . . . ? or "It is about time to call it a day; do you have any additional questions?" are gentle reminders that the conference must come to an end. Arranging for future contacts ("Let's see, our next regularly scheduled meeting is . . .") and thanking parents for their time certainly helps to bring a conversation to a close. By standing or by closing the child's folder, it is easy to demonstrate that time is up. Finally, switching back to social conversation, the professional can lead the way to the door.

After the Conference. Professionals need to allow enough time between conferences to record what has occurred during the conference. This record retains vital information, documents the visit, and helps create continuity between meetings. Although occasional notes may be taken during the conference, extensive notetaking is unwise because it interferes with listening and often makes parents uncomfortable. Parents should be apprised of any notes that are taken and the purpose they will serve. Only information that can directly be used to improve the instruction of the child is worth recording.

Involving Parents in Group Meetings

In many communities, parent involvement is synonymous with group meetings. If parents are invited to attend scheduled group meetings, then the center has fulfilled its commitment to parent involvement. Little attention is given to whether or not the planned meetings meet the needs of those invited to participate. Such meetings are usually designed to provide educational information to relatively large groups of people. Professionals are invited to speak, films are shown, books are displayed, and refreshments are served. The level of vocabulary used may or may not be understood by the audience. Eager parents may be able to resolve their confusion only by taking advantage of the question-and-answer period. As a result, parents who manage to attend one meeting may not return for the next.

In a study attempting to identify factors that cause parents to avoid involvement, Stile, Cole, and Garner (1979) reported such factors as (a) meetings held at inconvenient times or in inconvenient locations, (b) parent participation in planning not encouraged, (c) programs not aimed at "social" needs of parents in addition to skill deficits of children, (d) parents not allowed to organize or run their own programs, and (e) parents threatened by professionals or by situations.

To maximize the value of group meetings, professionals will need to keep these factors in mind. They should realize that group meetings will meet the needs of some, but not all, parents. Group meetings are often welcomed by parents who wish to meet and talk with other parents who have children with similar disabilities. Other parents attend primarily to seek the knowledge of the experts in the field. Some rather shy parents may enjoy not being the focus of attention, while other shy parents may be too inhibited to come in the first place. Whereas those parents who linger on are obviously enjoying the experience, some parents may feel awkward socializing or feel pressure to hurry home. Because of the great diversity of individual needs, meetings should provide a balance between educational concerns and social involvement. Not all parents can be expected to be equally involved in all activities. Professionals must observe carefully and try to plan activities that will meet the needs of all of the parents at least some of the time.

Rationale for Parent Education Groups. If parents of children with similar problems are brought together, a supportive climate can be developed for families to learn about and share feelings concerning their children with disabilities. Parent education groups also enhance the opportunity to provide parents with knowledge in specific skill areas such as home-based teaching and child management. Alternative approaches to childrearing can be presented.

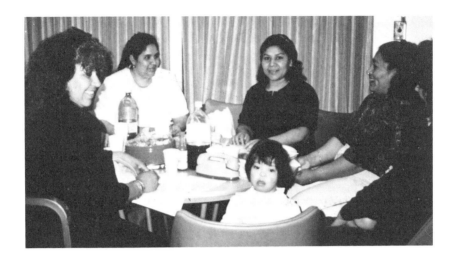

Parents can more readily become acquainted with local community resources. Finally, professionals have an opportunity to get to know parents in a setting that can be more relaxed than the parents' home or the child's classroom. Figure 3–3 provides a sample of topics typical of programs designed for parents of young children.

Guidelines for Developing Successful Group Meetings. Parents to Parents. A review of the literature indicates that parents are increasingly requesting a true partnership in all aspects of the education of their children and themselves (Turnbull & Turnbull, 1990). Parents who feel they have a voice in selecting topics, speakers, times, dates, and hours of meetings are usually more actively involved. This is why the suggestion was made earlier to involve parents in developing the orientation meeting. Parents who help plan have a tendency to recruit other parents to attend to realize the fruits of their labors. Note that Figure 3–3 not only presents possible program topics, but it also illustrates one way to assess the interests of parents.

Frequency of meetings. Because large-group meetings should be only a part of the total parent involvement program, they should not be called too frequently. Parents cannot handle more than one such meeting a month. If small-group meetings involving parents with very similar needs have been developed to offer social and emotional support, more frequent meetings may be desirable. If these meetings are being organized by the parents with the professional acting as a consultant, the parents will probably create the needed flexibility for these more informal meetings.

Notification of meetings. Large-group meetings must be advertised at least 1 month in advance. Multiple media should be used. Written flyers or notes sent home with the children, telephone calls through a calling chain, newspaper articles, and cable television and local radio announcements will be necessary for maximum participation. Follow-up notices approximately 1 week before the meetings will be helpful. Of course, small-group meetings with the responsibility for planning rotated among the interested participants will not take such elaborate notification. Usually one telephone call to each participant is sufficient.

Content of meetings. The content of meetings is where the active participation of an ad-

Dear Parents:

Listed below are a number of topics that can become the focus of one or more parent meetings. Because we would like to arrange meetings that will be helpful to you, we would appreciate your cooperation in filling out this questionnaire. Please indicate by checking the appropriate spaces below which meetings would interest you enough for you to take the time to join us. Your comments and opinions are really needed. Please complete this form today and return it with your child by Friday.

Sincerely,

Your Parent Planning Committee

	Yes	No	Maybe
1. How children grow and develop			
a. Learning to talk	[ ]	[ ]	[ ]
b. Learning to think	[ ]	[ ]	[ ]
c. Getting along with others	[ ]	[ ]	[ ]
2. Understanding my child's special needs			
a. A pediatrician's views	[ ]	[ ]	[ ]
b. A physical therapist helps	[ ]	[ ]	[ ]
c. Other: _____	[ ]	[ ]	[ ]
3. The importance of play			
a. Helping your child learn to play	[ ]	[ ]	[ ]
b. Choosing appropriate toys	[ ]	[ ]	[ ]
4. Living with your child			
a. Eating hassles	[ ]	[ ]	[ ]
b. Bedtime nuisances	[ ]	[ ]	[ ]
c. Toileting troubles	[ ]	[ ]	[ ]
d. The babysitter search	[ ]	[ ]	[ ]
e. Brothers and sisters	[ ]	[ ]	[ ]
f. Other: _____	[ ]	[ ]	[ ]
5. Nutrition	[ ]	[ ]	[ ]
6. Safety/first aid	[ ]	[ ]	[ ]
7. Community resources	[ ]	[ ]	[ ]
8. Helping my child behave	[ ]	[ ]	[ ]
9. Parent effectiveness training	[ ]	[ ]	[ ]

10. What we need the most is:

_____

_____

11. The best day(s) for meetings are:

_____ ____ A.M. ____ P.M.   _____ ____ A.M. ____ P.M.

Figure 3–3   Sample parent program topics (interest checklist).

visory group of parents is critical. Parents know what they need and should be encouraged to express their needs. Besides a written needs assessment as illustrated in Figure 3–3, professionals can be alert to needs expressed during home visitations, parent conferences, or informal conversation. Speakers need to be dynamic and able to speak on a comprehensible and assimilable level. The best recommendations usually come from the parents. Whenever possible a speaker should be heard before his or her assistance with a parent group is requested. Films or videotapes should also be previewed ahead of time.

Child involvement. Involving children's work or the children themselves can lure the parents into attending. Parents will come to see their child in a presentation, their child's work displayed, or their child on a film or a videotape. One early childhood center that had difficulty getting parents to form an advisory group planned an Easter egg hunt for the children. While the children were hunting eggs with the supervision of aides, the director offered the parents refreshments and conducted a brief but successful orientation and organizational meeting.

Variety. The need for variety is an important factor. Not every meeting should focus on a very serious topic that calls for the complete attention of the parents. Humor and fun are a necessary part of the learning of many parents who must face serious problems every day. Each meeting should involve some socializing, and some meetings should be purely social. Some groups of parents will plan and enjoy an occasional potluck dinner involving just the parents or even whole families. Workdays can be a very productive means of fostering informal communication. Some parents will feel much more comfortable in informal clothes, painting classroom furniture or making educational toys. Still other parents would gladly organize and conduct a garage sale with proceeds to benefit their children.

Child care and carpools. The need for child care and carpools is another important factor. Research has already indicated that parents of children with disabilities suffer from a lack of relief from physical demands and time constraints. It is irresponsible to expect such parents to use their limited babysitting resources to attend a parent meeting (Dunlap, 1979). The planning committee must arrange child care through local service clubs, high school students, or other volunteers. Carpools or other transportation arrangements may also increase the attendance at meetings. Such practical matters can be all important to parents who may already have more than they need in the way of problems.

Evaluation. Evaluation is of crucial importance. The atmosphere during group meetings of any size must reflect friendliness, caring, and relaxation. If staff members are tense, then parents will find themselves responding to this tension. Professional staff must be alert to activities that lessen tension, bring smiles to faces, generate questions, prompt people to lean toward action, and are talked about positively during the socializing period. Attendance itself is only one form of evaluation. Evaluation can be informal anecdotal records or logs focusing on the items just mentioned or it can be formal written reactions by the parents. Formal evaluations should be kept to a minimum.

Parent Support Through Parent Resource Centers

Professionals and parents involved in the planning phases of Public Law 99-457 are finding that parents' needs assessment survey results show a strong desire for increased emotional support and counseling. One of the most economical and effective ways to provide needed support is through the development of parent support groups. One example of an effective group is Parents Helping Parents, which is de-

EXHIBIT 3–6 _____

> ## Parents Helping Parents, Inc.
>
> In 1976, two mothers of children with Down syndrome co-founded Parents Helping Parents. With help from local agencies, PHP became incorporated and a United Way agency. Financial support is realized through individual donations, grant receipts from local foundations and corporations, memberships, and various fundraising projects. Until 1985, it was an all-volunteer agency.
>
> _PHP philosophy:_ The most important thing a child with disabilities needs is well-informed, emotionally balanced, caring, accepting, and assertive parents. Parents Helping Parents gives to kids with special needs what they need most—special parents.
>
> _PHP purpose:_ To help children with disabilities receive the care, services, education, love, hope, and acceptance they need to enable them to become all they can be, through direct services to their parents.
>
> _PHP desire:_ To collaborate with professionals committed enough to the benefits of peer support that they themselves call and make the referrals. Their devastated clients should not be left to follow through on a suggestion and/or brochure laid in their unsure hands.
>
> Like many parent support groups, PHP started because:
>
> 1. Other parents had much vital information about available resources as well as about the disability being confronted.
> 2. Peer counseling, with its immediate credibility and empathy, was paramount to working through the grief/loss process and on to recovery.
> 3. Many professionals lacked adequate knowledge about community resources and also lacked sensitivity to the financial, social, and emotional problems faced by entire families.
> 4. There was no easy way for new parents to meet experienced parents. Such meetings were too important to be left to chance.
>
> Services include visiting parents, family rap or guidance sessions, newsletters, telephone counseling, information packets, gifts to newborns with special needs, workshops for parents in the IEP process, peer counseling, a speakers bureau, symposiums, sibling fun days, and workshops for medical professionals in better ways of helping families cope with the advent of a child with special needs.
>
> Parents Helping Parents distributes manuals to assist other groups in the development of similar programs throughout the world. Family groups include any kind of physical, mental, emotional, or learning disability due to birth defects, illnesses, accidents, and developmental delays. Divisions include parents of near drownings, preemies and intensive care nursery support parents, an information and support network for individuals with learning disabilities, and help for those who have experienced neonatal death.
>
> Interested individuals may contact Florence M. Poyadue, Executive Director, Parents Helping Parents, Suite #220, 535 Race Street, San Jose, California 95126. Telephone (408)288-5010.

scribed in Exhibit 3–6. This program provides parent-run support groups for families with a variety of needs; it also has become a well-established model parent resource center. Not only should early interventionists become familiar with whatever groups may be available in their areas, but they should also be prepared to assist in the development of such groups if none is available.

WORKING WITH CULTURALLY DIVERSE FAMILIES

Maria Diaz, the early interventionist from Centro de Niños, is knocking on the door of the Ramirez family to do her weekly home visit with Elena, a 30-month-old girl with severe cerebral palsy. The family of seven (including grandmother) came to the United States from Mexico to obtain help for Elena. They are all currently living in a converted garage in a neighborhood known for gang activity, drugs, and high unemployment. As Maria waits for the door to open, she thinks of the risks in this area as well as the extensive number of concerns this family has. At this home visit Maria will help set up a corner chair for Elena to use so that she can sit on the floor and play with the other children. She will also listen to Mrs. Ramirez expressing disappointment at Elena's progress and the desire to seek services of a "curandera" (folk healer) rather than return to the hospital clinic. Mr. Ramirez is in agreement, but he is even more concerned about finding work.

Besides working with Elena at home and school, what is Maria's responsibility to this family? How do culture, values, language, and resources of the Ramirez family enter into the interactions between the family and Maria, other early intervention team members at Centro de Niños, and community agencies?

There are probably few early education programs in the United States at present that do not include families and children from diverse cultural and language groups. Over the past 15 years, thousands have arrived in the United States from Mexico and Central America, Southeast Asia, and the Mideast. Hanson, Lynch, and Wayman (1990), in their discussion of demographics, indicated that 36% of infants born in the United States in 1984 were born to ethnolinguistically diverse families. It is estimated that by the year 2000, 38% of children in the United States under age 18 will be members of nonwhite, non-Anglo-European groups. In many parts of the country the percentages are even higher. Because of economic and cultural barriers to prenatal care and environmental support, it is reasonable to assume that a number of young children from these groups will need early intervention services. Thus, the challenge for

professionals working with young children, whether in early intervention for high-risk infants or in a migrant worker's day care center, is to be responsive to individual family cultural and language difference.

All families assume the role of socializing children to become part of the larger community. An examination and understanding of the differences between "mainstream" values of communities and specific families within these communities are a critical part of the ecological approach to intervention (Vincent, Salisbury, Strain, McCormick, & Tessier, 1990). The role of early interventionists must include acknowledging different cultural perspectives and learning how to work effectively within the boundaries that are comfortable for the family, while increasing the family's understanding of and improving their ability to work within the larger mainstream culture.

Cultural Practices and Language Differences

Two areas of cultural awareness that may have important implications for early interventionists and child development specialists are related to views on childrearing and medical practices. Insights into how parents view children and their upbringing are critical in developing working relationships with families. Beliefs about such issues as adult-child interactions, feeding, toileting, sleeping, and discipline will emerge as the early interventionist gathers information about the child and family. "Regardless of the developmental and functional goals that provide the cornerstones for early intervention, the cultural preferences of the families form the primary basis for program planning" (Hanson, Lynch, & Wayman, 1990, p. 118). In fact, having inappropriate cultural expectations for a child's family could create more problems than the child's actual disability.

Differing views on medical practices may be a significant source of family and professional conflict. Families from a wide range of subcultures may hold on to traditional health practices. Faith healers, herbs, massage, animal rites, and other rituals are often a part of treatments that lead to misunderstandings. For example, some Vietnamese parents have been reported for child abuse when using the technique of "coining" to treat conditions such as colds, sore throats, and headaches. The process involves applying a medicated salve and then stroking the affected area with a hot coin. The superficial red marks raise suspicions of abuse. Such judgments often grow out of the assumption that these families are not concerned about or caring for their children. Vincent and colleagues (1990) reminded us that we often judge parents to be uncaring when they actually care *differently* for their children.

Language

Perhaps the most obvious difference among subcultures is communication, both verbal and nonverbal. The inability to communicate directly with families in their primary language creates a great deal of frustration for both parents and professionals. It is often the source of misunderstanding and an inadequate transmission of information. The need for translation in both spoken and written communication is critical in any early intervention program serving other than English-speaking families. Some suggestions for working through a translator are found in Exhibit 3–7. It is equally imperative that materials such as reports, newsletters, and home programs be prepared in parents' languages.

One way to break through the language barrier and enhance the family's involvement in a child's program is to provide support and encouragement from other parents. The Multicultural Training of Trainers program (Chan & Mahseredgian, 1989), in the Los Angeles area, recruited and trained bilingual parents of children with special needs to work with non-

EXHIBIT 3–7

Communicating Through a Translator

For the Professional:

1. Spend a few minutes with the translator, prior to the meeting, discussing topics to be covered. Make sure the translator understands the concepts.
2. Your translator should be someone you trust, especially with confidential or sensitive information.
3. In a group situation, sit next to the translator.
4. Use simple words. Talk slowly and in a few sentences at a time.
5. Look at and talk to the parent, not the translator.
6. Use nonverbal communication when talking. Observe the nonverbal communication used by the parent.
7. Allow sufficient time for the meeting.
8. After the meeting, ask the translator for his or her overall impression of the meeting.
9. In families with both English- and non-English-speaking members, be aware of the tendency to ignore members who do not speak English.
10. When young family members speak English and adults do not, if possible, avoid using children as translators.

For the Translator:

1. Develop reference materials for medical, educational, and psychological terminology.
2. Make it a point to understand the culture and beliefs of the families.
3. Ask clarifying questions if the meaning of statements is unclear.
4. If line-by-line translation is not clear, use your own words, verifying changes with the professional and the parent.
5. Be aware of both verbal and nonverbal communication.

English-speaking parents in their communities. This form of peer counseling assists other parents in understanding "the system" and community resources while offering much-needed emotional support. (See Exhibit 3–8). Special conferences such as "Fiesta Educativa" for Spanish-speaking parents and professionals has been another effective means of reaching the growing population of Hispanic and Latino families (I. Martinez, personal communication, October 17, 1990).

As Maria Diaz discovered in her home visits with the Ramirez family, the effectiveness of her work is clearly tied not only to understanding the unique values of the family but also to her own cultural biases and values. Although Maria speaks Spanish fluently, her upbringing in an upper middle class family in Spain has little relation to the experiences of the Ramirez family. Conversations have raised a number of differences in the way they view such issues as health, childrearing, and education. Maria feels that in recognizing their differences she has begun to work within the boundaries that are comfortable to the family while sharing with them information about the ways of the larger culture.

In her ongoing experiences with the Ramirez family and other parents in the intervention program, Maria and the rest of the early intervention team must continually use caution in making

EXHIBIT 3–8 _____

Suggestions for Working with Culturally Diverse Families

1. Make sure that program staffing reflects the cultures and languages of the children and families in the program.

2. Provide ongoing staff training related to family differences.

3. Encourage families to share their beliefs and traditions. Invite speakers to discuss all aspects of the culture and its relationship to disabilities, child rearing, medical practices, and so forth.

4. Network with other community resources that are meaningful to families such as churches, community advisors from subcultural groups, and the media (local television, radio, newspapers, etc.).

5. In addition to using trained interpreters for all parent interactions, provide written materials in the language of the participating families. Be sensitive to the comprehension and reading levels required. Be creative in addressing the needs of parents with limited reading ability. Bilingual curriculum materials and activities should also be an integral part of the child's program.

6. Learn at least a few words of the languages represented in the program; especially common greetings and phrases used in speaking to children.

7. Avoid stereotyping. Within cultural groups, recognize individual differences in background experiences, coping styles, interests, economic levels, and so forth. Parents from the same cultural group do not always have the same needs. Meet individual families at their own level of need and life experience. Remember that "*Families are different, not deficient*" (Mendoza & Cegelka, 1988).

---

prejudgments based on attitudes toward and stereotypes of certain subcultures. As Hanson, Lynch, and Wayman (1990) suggested,

The effectiveness of programs often will depend upon the development of ethnic competence and behavioral changes by the service providers. . . . becoming ethically competent requires early interventionists to engage in four tasks. First, they must clarify their own values and assumptions. Second, they must gather and analyze ethnographic information regarding the cultural community within which each family resides. Third, they must determine the degree to which the family operates transculturally; and finally, they must examine each family's orientation to specific childrearing issues. (p. 126)

WORKING WITH PARENTS WHO ABUSE OR NEGLECT CHILDREN

The laws on child abuse and child neglect are explicit. If early interventionists (and others responsible for working with children) notice any signs of abuse or neglect, they must report their suspicions to community or county authorities. Ideally, the procedure for dealing with abusive parents should be worked out before it is ever necessary to report abuse. Principals, directors, nurses, and social workers should meet with interventionists to plan what to do when they suspect abuse.

Guidelines for Professionals Working with Abused Children

The following guidelines can be a starting point for a discussion or for developing a policy for working with abusive parents:

1. Be alert for signs of sadness or anger, as well as bruises, burns, and cuts. Listen to what the child says. Be especially alert for changes in behavior that cannot be explained by impending illness or a "happening" at school. Begin *at once* to record specific details of your observations. Be certain to make a

written note of the date, time, and manner of observation. These may be necessary if a report must be made to authorities. Keep these confidential and under lock and key.

2. Cigarette burns are usually round. Small, round burns should always be investigated.

3. Bruises on legs and buttocks can be the result of falls. The frequency and the severity of the bruises are useful criteria. Even clumsy children stay unbruised most of the time. If the child is nearly always bruised, be suspicious.

4. Black eyes do result from bumping into things. So do bumps on heads. Again, the severity and the relative frequency of the bruises dictate the degree of teacher concern.

5. Little children usually "tell all," but even 3 year olds can be frightened into lying about how they were hurt. It is not unusual for parents to tell little ones that if they say that mommy or daddy hurt them a big bad person will come and take them away. When this happens, the children's explanations are usually and obviously "dictated." If the story changes, be suspicious.

6. After a report to the proper authorities has been made, the interventionist should seek help and guidance from the principal or the director of the center. Next steps with the parents should not be decided by the interventionist alone. Home visits should be discontinued at least for some time. This is a needed safety precaution for both the professional and the parents.

7. On subsequent visits, after conferences with persons who are competent to advise on what to do and how to do it, the interventionist should not go to the home alone. An aide should accompany him or her and should be alert to what is said. Confidential notes made after the meeting should not become part of the child's file but should be kept in the interventionist's personal posses-

sion. These can be destroyed when there is no longer any need for them.

8. Regardless of the nature or severity of the case, if the child continues to attend the center, it is the center's responsibility to continue to try to encourage the parents to participate in parent meetings and in volunteering at the center. Center staff should have the help of persons who are trained and skilled in helping abusive or neglectful parents. If the center does not offer this service, the staff should insist on receiving it from some public or private source. Skill in interaction does not imply that the professional must be all things to all people. Trying to be so can result in disaster.

Maintaining Perspective

Early interventionists need to maintain perspective on the situation. It may be particularly difficult to forgive and forget the abuse or neglect of a young child. They will find it helpful to learn about causes and effects of mental and physical abuse. Professionals from community agencies are often willing to present workshops on the subject. If this cannot be arranged easily, reading about the subject can be useful. Halperin (1979) helped to put the problem into perspective in the following statement:

Maltreating parents are adults with problems rather than inhuman monsters who delight in hurting their children. They are people who have problems that affect their ability to be good parents, rather than hopeless mental and social misfits. (p. 65)

Of particular interest is the continuing research into the child's contribution to his or her own abuse. Parke and Collmer (1975) discussed a number of ways a child plays a role in the abuse process. For example, there may be genetically determined characteristics or learned behaviors that elicit abuse. Abused children may become difficult to manage. These characteristics may in turn provoke even more of the very abuse that caused their origin.

Adults who maltreat children may have been conditioned to abuse or neglect while growing up. They may be imitating the parenting behavior they once experienced. Often they have failed to internalize the values of the general society in regard to children and childrearing; sometimes the very structure of the family unit precipitates maltreatment. The frustration of daily living frequently combines with other factors to lead parents to abuse or neglect their youngsters.

Head Start Policy

Head Start teachers are well advised to heed the policy of Head Start governing the prevention, identification, treatment, and reporting of child abuse and neglect. The policy emphasizes that:

Head Start programs will not undertake, on their own, to treat cases of child abuse or neglect. Head Start programs will, on the other hand, cooperate fully with child protective service agencies . . . and make every effort to retain in their programs children allegedly abused or neglected. (Halperin, 1979, p. 191)

Without the help of trained teachers who understand and know how to deal with the special problems of young children with disabilities, many parents of these youngsters are stressed and tempted beyond their ability to cope. This is why teachers of these children and their parents must establish a workable partnership early. It is useful for teachers to ask themselves how well they would be able to cope if the situation were reversed and they were the parents instead of the teachers.

WORKING WITH PARENT POPULATIONS WITH SPECIAL NEEDS

In addition to the challenges encountered in working with all parents, many professionals who work with young children will discover that they are working with parents who have unique needs themselves. The nature of the disabilities of these parents will vary widely. Although overt behaviors may appear to be similar, causes can be very different. It is unwise and dangerous to generalize. Each parent is an individual with unique needs. In some way, each one can be helped. Sometimes the best a teacher can do for some parents with disabilities is to find other professionals trained to help these parents directly.

Parents with Developmental Disabilities

All of the suggestions made for working out a partnership with parents are also useful in working with parents with developmental disabilities. The following guidelines may be useful:

1. *Establish priorities.* To help parents with developmental disabilities develop effective parenting skills, professionals must choose priorities carefully. The first priority may be to help parents to discontinue yelling and spanking their children for every minor offense. One parent was observed shrieking her child's name and "no" at 1-minute intervals during a 20-minute home visit. Another mother complained that her child was always "bad." When asked to explain what he was doing that was "bad," she said that he just never stopped running in the house. For this mother, the suggestion that she take him outside to play every day was a brand new idea. Within a short time the indoor running stopped.

2. *Coordinate help.* As soon as possible, discover which other agencies and persons are extending help to these parents. If there are several, get them together if possible to plan for effective communication and concerted action. (After a mother complained that everybody was telling her to do something different, the interventionist discovered that 15 different persons working for

seven agencies were in fact trying to tell her what she should do. The resulting contradictions would have baffled any parent.)

3. *Make frequent, brief contacts.* Telephone calls are better than notes, and 10 minutes with the parent in the home can pay quick dividends.

4. *Avoid lengthy explanations.* Be brief. Be explicit. Show parents what to do and how to do it. They are usually willing to try, if they understand what is wanted.

5. *Require little or no reading.* Send only one request or direction in notes, if they can read. A list of things to do will probably be ignored.

6. *Involve parents with developmental dis-abilities.* Whenever possible, include these parents in center observations, volunteer activities, parent conferences, and meetings. Answer their questions in short sentences and with simple language. Supervise their activities closely. It is helpful to remember that they are with their child far more than the professional. If their interaction skills and behavior management can be improved, both parent and child will benefit.

The next chapter will focus on strategies for identifying and assessing each child's unique needs. It will also elaborate on the role of interventionists in using assessment information in the development of appropriate program plans.

Summary

Properly trained professionals will recognize and actively work toward involving families in a partnership of responsibility for their child's development. One of the first steps in bridging a link between parents and professionals is for the professional to recognize the emotional needs of families with children with disabilities. Parents often react to the realization that their child has a disabling condition in stages similar to the emotional adjustment encountered with the loss of a loved one. The alert and informed professional can help parents work through each stage from initial feelings of shock, disbelief, and denial through anger and resentment, bargaining to make it go away, depression and discouragement, and on to acceptance. Understanding the family as a system is essential to true parent-professional collaboration.

Children and members of the extended family can be included in the process of emotional and educational adjustments. Siblings are an especially valuable ally, as children typically accept a child who has disabilities without jealousy or anxiety. Especially in early sessions with family members, it is important to avoid jargon and technical concepts. Test results should be explained in terms of common behaviors.

A variety of methods of parent involvement are surveyed, such as home-based instruction, observations, passports, and meetings. For effectiveness in home visits and instruction, teachers learn to use two-way communication, taking time to listen and observe, as well as to inform and demonstrate.

Guidelines are provided for working with parents within the center under a variety of purposes. With planning, it is possible to create a developmental approach for bringing parents into contact with other parents of children with disabilities (the more seasoned veterans), orienting them to observation and eventual participation within the center. Parent education groups and parent-teacher conferences can be viewed as requiring special teacher skills rather than simply as an opportunity to meet.

Special consideration is given to working with culturally diverse families. Understanding cultural practices and language differences is essential to successful early intervention.

Finally, professionals are reminded that

some parents of children with disabilities may have special needs themselves. These include parents who themselves have disabilities and parents who abuse or neglect their children. Throughout the chapter, sufficient details have been provided to encourage professionals to pick and choose the type and extent of involvement most appropriate for their parents, their children, and themselves.

Discussion Topics and Activities

1. Do additional reading and research into the emotional needs and feelings of parents of children with disabilities. Discuss these feelings with class members. If possible, try to empathize with these feelings.

2. Make a list of the public and private institutions in your area whose purpose is to help exceptional parents cope with their problems. Organize the list as a referral file including contact person, telephone number, and cost and type of services.

3. Assume the role of parent of a child with disabilities and do a local telephone survey. Describe your child's condition and ask for information as to where and how to obtain help. Record this information in a file and share it with classmates. Try to get some idea of how parents might feel when in this situation.

4. Review and discuss why parents may feel fearful about their meetings with center personnel. What can teachers do to help relieve these feelings?

5. Prepare and role play an orientation meeting. Try to be as convincing as possible when giving the reasons why you would like to get your children's parents involved.

6. Develop a questionnaire that you can use to determine the interests and needs of parents for parent involvement. Try it out on a few parents. Compare it to that of classmates and revise when necessary.

7. Collect magazine, newspaper, and journal articles about working with parents. Make a file of useful ideas.

8. Role play a home visit with classmates. Share constructive criticism.

9. Consider and discuss the possibility of a values collision between a home visitor and a family. How can such a collision be avoided? Have you ever been involved in such a situation?

10. As a class, discuss issues of confidentiality, privileged communication, and conversation in the teacher's lounge in relation to parent involvement.

11. Gather and discuss newsletters from local early childhood centers. Develop one that may be appropriate for a class you will teach.

12. Develop a "happygram" to be sent home to parents.

13. Spend some time walking in a variety of neighborhoods. Learn what resources are or are not available to families living there.

Annotated Bibliography

Emotional Needs of Families of Children with Disabilities

Blacher, J. (1984). Sequential stages of parental adjustments to the birth of a child with handicaps. *Mental Retardation, 22,* 55–68.

Blacher examines the literature for patterns of parental reaction to the birth of a child with special needs. Most important, he presents both sides of the question of whether parents follow a sequence of adjustment and raises practical questions to guide future research.

Blacher, J. (Ed.). (1984). *Severely handicapped young children and their families.* New York: Academic Press.

This edited text offers comprehensive, multidisciplinary reviews of literature in areas of family adjustment, dynamics, and involvement related to young children with severe disabilities. It gives new insights into the adaptation of family members following the birth of a child who may be diagnosed as autistic, severely emotionally disturbed, developmentally disabled, or severely or profoundly retarded. An important chapter on individuals with severe disabilities and child abuse discusses critical factors found in family function and dysfunction that precipitate or exacerbate child abuse.

Buscaglia, L. (1983). *The disabled and their parents: A counseling challenge.* Thorofare, NJ: Charles B. Slack.

Everyone who works with children with disabilities and their parents should read this book seriously. In a direct writing style, the author makes a demand for competent, reality-based, and sensible guidance. He offers practical, down-to-earth suggestions for improved counseling. Most of all, the author considers disabilities to be made, not born.

Kübler-Ross, E. (1969). *On death and dying.* New York: Macmillan.

With warm sensitivity, the author depicts the delicate subject of people who are terminally ill and the struggle to accept death. This remarkable book not only helps the reader to face the inevitable end of life more professionally and personally, but it also lends insight into the stages through which some parents of children with disabilities may pass.

Lobato, D. J. (1990). *Brothers, sisters, and special needs.* Baltimore: Paul H. Brookes.

This book not only describes the psychological basis for understanding needs of siblings, but also offers practical activities to assist them in coping constructively with a brother or sister who has developmental disabilities or a chronic illness.

Mori A. A. (1983). *Families of children with special needs.* Rockville, MD: Aspen.

This comprehensive source book gives extensive attention to the impact of a young child with disabilities on the family. Suggestions are made for helping families deal with practical problems; specific recommendations are given for working with families of children who are emotionally disturbed, gifted, or mentally retarded and those with sensory, physical, and learning disorders.

National Center for Clinical Infant Programs. (1985). *Equals in this partnership: Parents of disabled and at-risk infants and toddlers speak to professionals.*

The purpose of this booklet is to help voices of parents reach a wider audience. It contains direct contributions of parents of young children with special needs as well as addresses delivered at the 1984 Conference on Comprehensive Approaches to Disabled and At-Risk Infants held in Washington, DC.

Opirhory, G., & Peters, G. A. (1982). Counseling intervention strategies for families with the less than perfect newborn. *Personnel and Guidance Journal, 60,* 451–455.

This article provides a conceptual framework for understanding and dealing with the total impact of the birth of a less than perfect newborn on parents and other family members and presents a model depicting the series of emotional traumas and adjustments believed to occur following the birth of such a child. Specific techniques for early counseling intervention are discussed.

Roos, P. (1979). Psychological counseling with parents of retarded children. In L. Baruth & M. Burggraf (Eds.), *Readings in counseling parents of exceptional children* (pp. 103–107). Guilford, CT: Special Learning.

The author clearly describes typical parental reactions to their child's retardation. The author outlines a number of specific suggestions for working with these parents and emphasizes the importance of attentive listening. Consideration is given to using formal test results when working with the parents.

Seligman, M. (1979). *Strategies for helping parents of exceptional children.* New York: Free Press.

The major purpose of this excellent book is to help teachers become more knowledgeable about the exceptional parents they confer with, and to augment their heightened awareness through the improvement of their own communication abilities. One well-written chapter is devoted to understanding the dynamics of families with an exceptional child. The author offers specific strategies for working with parents, including a section on problem parents and on critical incidents for role playing and discussion.

Options for Family Participation

Anderson, P., & Fenichal, E. S. (1989). *Serving culturally diverse families of infants and toddlers with disabilities.* Washington, DC: National Center for Clinical Infant Programs.

This astute publication may serve as a guide to understanding the major cultural groups within the United States. It provides important considerations for working within our multicultural society.

Bakley, S. (1986). *But I wasn't trained for this: A manual for working with mothers who are retarded.* San Diego, CA: San Diego State University.

This manual provides insight into the characteristics of parents with developmental disabilities as well as useful techniques and suggestions to help meet their unique needs. This manual may be ordered from the San Diego State University Foundation, San Diego State University, Department of Special Education, San Diego, CA 92182.

Bristol, M. M., & Gallagher, J. J. (1982). A family focus for intervention. In C. T. Ramey & P. L. Trohanis

(Eds.). *Finding and educating high-risk and handicapped infants* (pp. 137–161). Baltimore: University Park Press.

This chapter explores the evolution of the role of parents as central to the effectiveness of early intervention. It promotes an understanding of present-day concerns such as the reciprocal nature of the parent/child interaction, the effect on the total family of a child's disability, and the need to create an environment responsive to the needs of the entire family.

Dunst, C., Trivette, C., & Deal, A. (1988). *Enabling and empowering families: Principles and guidelines for practice.* Cambridge, MA: Brookline Press.

This book is designed to assist professionals working with families in early intervention settings in carrying out the intentions of P.L. 99-457. Focus is on *enablement*, or creating opportunities or activities that strengthen family functioning and empowerment. The intent is to support families in their efforts to realize intrafamily mastery and control over important aspects of family functioning. A number of assessment forms are included in the appendixes.

Ehly, S. W., Conoley, J. C., & Rosenthal, D. (1985). *Working with parents of exceptional children.* Columbus, OH: Merrill.

This book provides an overview of activities involving parents of children with special needs in educational programs, and is intended to prepare teachers to involve parents in working with their children at school or at home. As an overview, it provides a good introduction to the area of parent involvement. References can be pursued for more in-depth understanding.

Gargiulo, R. M. (1985). *Working with parents of exceptional children.* Boston: Houghton Mifflin.

This paperback book is intended for all individuals in the helping professions. Its purpose is to promote understanding of and sensitivity toward parents of children with special needs. The first section of the book focuses on relationships among family members while the second section covers the major concepts and theories of helping. Numerous dialogues help readers see how specific helping skills are applied from different professional viewpoints.

Gollnick, D. M., & Chinn, P. C. (1990). *Multicultural education in a pluralistic society.* Columbus, OH: Merrill.

Using culture as a basis for understanding multicultural education, the descriptions of seven microcultures to which Americans belong are included in this informative text. Chapters discuss the microcultures of class, ethnicity and race, gender, exceptionality, religion, language, and age. The concept of pluralism and how to use it effectively in centers and schools is helpful.

Kroth, R. L. (1985). *Communicating with parents of exceptional children: Improving parent-teacher relationships.* Denver: Love.

This is a book of techniques designed to help teachers understand the child and his or her family, to provide parents with information, and to help parents solve problems. It is aimed at teachers who wish to go beyond individual parent-teacher conferences and report cards. The author emphasizes using appropriate reinforcers as a tool in changing children's behavior and provides case studies to assist teachers in skill development.

Lacy, A. (1981). *Project Hope—Inservice manual for home teachers.* San Diego, CA: San Diego County Superintendent of Schools.

This helpful manual should be in the library of anyone involved in working with parents in the home. It includes a parents' needs assessment procedure, step-by-step implementation procedures, self-quizzes, and "Dear Mom and Dad" letters, which are given to parents to help them understand normal child development.

Michaelis, C. T. (1980). *Home and school partnerships in exceptional education.* Rockville, MD: Aspen.

Writing from the viewpoint of a professional and a parent of a child with disabilities, the author is able to present the major communication blocks of home-school interrelationships that must be overcome. Throughout the book, practical recommendations are made to help parents and teachers work together on behalf of children with disabilities. Of particular interest is a chapter that translates technical language into common terms.

Seligman, M., & Darling, R. B. (1989). *Ordinary families, special children.* New York: Guilford.

Parents and professionals alike will profit from this systems approach to working with children with disabilities and their families. Authors include an important chapter on cultural reactions to childhood disability and subcultural variations. Practical applications are noted throughout the text.

Shea, T. M., & Bauer, A. M. (1991). *Parents and teachers of children with exceptionalities. A handbook for collaboration.* Needham Heights, MA: Allyn and Bacon.

Shea and Bauer's comprehensive text explores the potential of parents to be full participants. The first section discusses the reactions and rights of special parents ending with a model for parent-teacher collaboration. Worksheets, forms, lesson plans, examples of handouts, and personal anecdotes are included to help the reader grasp the continuum of cooperative activities for full parent participation. A full chapter is devoted to transition issues.

Stewart, J. C. (1986). *Counseling parents of exceptional students.* Columbus, OH: Merrill.

This paperback text combines coverage of the counseling process with an insightful overview of the social, personal, and economic problems encountered by parents of individuals with disabilities. For those especially interested in helping or counseling parents, the book provides an excellent conceptual framework from which to proceed. It presents a good literature review and a useful list of resources.

Tingey-Michaelis, C. (1983). *Handicapped infants and children: A handbook for parents and professionals.* Baltimore, MD: University Park Press.

This book provides parents and professionals with practical information to help them meet the needs of the child who has disabilities with the least disruption to family life. It stresses the importance of balancing extra care and attention for the child with disabilities with the child's need for usual childhood experience and helps parents organize daily routines and develop wholesome family and neighborhood interaction.

Turnbull, A. P., & Turnbull, H. R. (1990). *Families, professionals, and exceptionality: A special partnership.* Columbus, OH: Merrill.

This text is based on the family systems approach and offers ideas for individualizing relationships between individuals with exceptionalities, families, and helping professionals. Unlike most texts, this one speaks to the needs of the family throughout the lifespan of the individual with special needs.

Vincent, L. J., Salisbury, C. L., Strain, P., McCormick, C., & Tessier, A. (1990). A behavioral-ecological approach to early intervention: Focus on cultural diversity. In S. J. Meisels & J. P. Shonkoff (Eds.), *Handbook of early intervention* (pp. 173–195). New York: Cambridge University Press.

In this scholarly text, there is an effort to bring together the best in current research and practice in early intervention. This chapter speaks to the issues of an ecological approach to early intervention with an emphasis on cultural diversity. The stated implications of a wide range of family differences suggest the critical need to understand the diverse values and approaches necessary to working with families and children in today's society.

Wasik, B. H., Bryant, D. M., & Lyons, C. M. (1990). *Home visiting: Procedures for helping families.* Newbury Park, CA: Sage.

In this book, home visiting is defined as the process by which a professional or paraprofessional provides help to a family in its own home. It provides a comprehensive history and philosophy of home visiting along with discussion of the skills essential for an effective home visitor. The authors speak from practical experiences gained from involvement in two early intervention programs.

References

Barber, P. A., Turnbull, A. P., Behr, S. K., & Kerns, G. M. (1988). Family systems perspective on early childhood special education. In S. L. Odom & M. B. Karnes (Eds.), *Early intervention for infants and children with handicaps* (pp. 179–198). Baltimore: Paul H. Brookes.

Blacher, J. (1984). Sequential stages of parental adjustments to the birth of a child with handicaps. *Mental Retardation, 22,* 55–68.

Boyd, D. (1950). *The three stages.* New York: National Association for Retarded Children.

Bristol, M. M., & Gallagher, J. J. (1982). A family focus for intervention. In C. T. Ramey & P. L. Trohanis (Eds.), *Finding and educating high-risk and handicapped infants.* Baltimore: University Park Press.

Cansler, D., & Martin, G. (1974). *Working with families: A manual for developmental centers.* Reston, VA: The Council for Exceptional Children.

Chan, S., & Mahseredgian, H. (1989, May). *Cultural competence: Effectively serving ethnic minority children and families.* Workshop presented at the Infant Conference-89, Los Angeles.

Chinn, P., Drew, C., & Logan, D. (1979). *Mental retardation.* St. Louis: C. V. Mosby.

County Welfare Directors Association of California et

al. (1990). *Ten reasons to invest in the families of California.* Published by a grant from the Edna McConnell Claru Foundation.

Dunlap, W. R. (1979). How do parents of handicapped children view their needs? *Journal of the Division of Early Childhood, 1,* 1–10.

Ehly, S. W., Conoley, J. C., & Rosenthal, D. (1985) *Working with parents of exceptional children.* Columbus, OH: Merrill.

Gallagher, P. A., & Powell, P. H. (1989). Brothers and sisters: Meeting special needs. *Topics in Early Childhood Special Education, 8*(4), 24–37.

Gargiulo, R. M. (1985). *Working with parents of exceptional children.* Boston: Houghton Mifflin.

George, J. D. (1988). Therapeutic intervention for grandparents and extended family of children with developmental delays. *Mental Retardation, 26,* 369–375.

Gordon, T. (1970). *Parent effectiveness training.* New York: Peter H. Wyden.

Halperin, M. (1979). *Helping maltreated children: School and community involvement.* St. Louis: C. V. Mosby.

Hanson, M. J., & Lynch, E. W. (1989). *Early intervention.* Austin, TX: PRO.ED.

Hanson, M. J., Lynch, E. W., & Wayman, K. I. (1990). Honoring the cultural diversity of families when gathering data. *Topics in Early Childhood Special Education, 10*(1), 112–131.

Hodel, M. B. (1981, January 16). Parents learn to share with son. *The Intelligencer* (Edwardsville, IL), p. 2.

Kirk, W. (1979). A parent's perspective. *Illinois Regional Resource Center Newsletter, 2,* 5–6.

Kübler-Ross, E. (1969). *On death and dying.* New York: Macmillan.

Lepler, M. (1978). Having a handicapped child. *The American Journal of Maternal Child Nursing,* 32–34.

Lichter, R. (1976). Communicating with parents: It begins with listening. *Teaching Exceptional Children, 8,* 66–71.

Lobato, D. J. (1990). *Brothers, sisters, and special needs.* Baltimore, MD: Paul H Brookes.

Mendoza, J., & Cegelka, P. (1988). *Parents and professionals advocating for collaborative training.* San Diego, CA: San Diego State University.

Morgan, W. (1977). *Skills in working with parents* (1240). Champaign, IL: University of Illinois, Institute for Research on Exceptional Children.

Mori, A. A. (1983). *Families of children with special needs.* Rockville, MD: Aspen.

O'Hara, D. M., & Levy, S. M. (1984). Family adaptation to learning disability: A framework for understanding and treatment. *Learning Disabilities, 3*(6), 63–77.

Parke, R. D., & Collmer, C. W. (1975). Child abuse: An interdisciplinary analysis. In E. M. Hetherington (Ed.), *Review of child development research* (pp. 509–590). Chicago: University of Chicago Press.

Powell, R. (1986). Parent education and support programs. *Young Children, 41,* 47–53.

Roos, P. (1975). Parents and families of the mentally retarded. In J. M. Kauffman & J. S. Payne (Eds.), *Mental retardation: Introduction and personal perspectives.* Columbus, OH: Merrill.

Roos, P. (1979). Psychological counseling with parents of retarded children. In L. Baruth & M. Burggraf (Eds.), *Readings in counseling parents of exceptional children* (pp. 103–107). Guilford, CT: Special Learning.

Sameroff, A. J. (1987). The social context of development. In N. Eisenberg (Ed.), *Contemporary topics in developmental psychology* (pp. 273–291). New York: Wiley.

Schwartz, L. L. (1984). *Exceptional students in the mainstream.* Belmont, CA: Wadsworth.

Seligman, M. (1979). *Strategies for helping parents of exceptional children.* New York: Free Press.

Shea, T., & Bauer, A. (1991). *Parents and teachers of exceptional students: A handbook for involvement.* Rockleigh, NJ: Allyn and Bacon.

Simeonsson, R. J., & Bailey, D. B. (1990). Family dimensions in early intervention. In S. J. Meisels & J. P. Shonkoff (Eds.), *Handbook of early childhood intervention* (pp. 428–444). New York: Cambridge University Press.

Stephens, T. M. (1979). Parent/teacher conferences. *The Directive Teacher, 2,* 2.

Stewart, J. C. (1986). *Counseling parents of exceptional children* (2nd ed.). Columbus, OH: Merrill.

Stile, S. W., Cole, J. T., & Garner, A. W. (1979). Maximizing parental involvement in programs for exceptional children. *Journal of the Division of Early Childhood 1,* 68–92.

Turnbull, A. P., Summers, J. A., & Brotherson, M. J. (1983, October). *Working with families with disabled members: A family systems approach.* Lawrence: University of Kansas, Kansas University Affiliated Facility.

Turnbull, A. P., & Turnbull, H. R. (1990). *Families, professionals, and exceptionality: A special partnership.* Columbus, OH: Merrill.

Urwin, C. A. (1988). AIDS in children: A family concern. *Family Relations*, 37, 154–159.

Valand, M. C. (1975). Conducting parent-teacher conferences. (Mimeographed paper). Chapel Hill: The University of North Carolina, Chapel Hill Training-Outreach Program.

Vincent, L. J., Salisbury, C. L., Strain, P., McCormick, C., & Tessier, A. (1990). In S. J. Meisels & J. P. Shonkoff (Eds.), *Handbook in early childhood intervention* (pp. 173–195). New York: Cambridge University Press.

Chapter 4

Recognizing Special Needs: Identification and Assessment

Mr. Curtis is a third-year teacher at Happy Hours Preschool. He especially enjoys the 3 year olds. But Vicky has him worried. She is always "on the go." From the moment she arrives she flits from one toy to the other. And en route she bumps into everything and everyone! Today he has arranged for his aide and two mothers to supervise the free choice session. He plans to observe Vicky and write down what he sees. He is using a form developed to help him observe objectively.

Where: Happy Hours Day Care Center
Time: 10:00 A.M.–10:15 A.M.
Activity: Free Choice Time
Others present: 15 boys and girls, aide, and 2 mothers

Child: Vicky R.
CA: 3 yrs., 8 mos.
Day: Thursday
Week: 10
Observer: Mr. Curtis

Preceding Activity	Child's Behavior
Vicky bumped into Sara, knocking Sara flat.	Vicky kept right on going, ignoring Sara's yell.
Vicky picked up form board from shelf.	Dumped pieces of board on floor and put in two pieces. Got up and wandered away.
Vicky walked to doll corner and grabbed Tina's doll.	Vicky tugged at the doll until she got it, then ran to corner of room and sat on the doll.
Tina ran after Vicky and began to push her.	Vicky screamed and kicked until Miss J. walked over to her.
Andy painting at the easel; Vicky grabbed his brush.	Vicky painted three long strokes over Andy's picture and giggled, running away when he reached for the brush.
Four children in the kitchen individually "cooking and stirring."	Vicky ran into the kitchen, yelled "Me cook too," and grabbed a bowl, knocking the artificial vegetables to the floor. Other children just stared. Tim began to cry.

Follow-up: Contact Mr. Jones, the psychologist, to work out a plan to help Vicky control her behavior. Maybe Vicky's vision should be checked. She seems to bump into so many things.

Ms. McLynn's Observation

Ms. McLynn teaches a preschool class of 4 year olds. For several weeks she has been puzzled about Danny. He just won't pay attention. Sometimes when she calls him he comes right away. Other times he pays no attention until she raises her voice and speaks firmly. Often he acts as if he hears her call, but then he looks for her in the wrong direction. Or when she tells him to do something he does something else. Then he just gives her a blank look when she explains all over again what she wants him to do. (At first Ms. McLynn had wondered whether he had a hearing problem, but the nurse said he had passed the hearing screening.) Today she has decided to observe him carefully and take notes. Her aide, Ms. Cain, is playing a game with 4 children, while 10 others, including Danny, are playing with various toys and games. Here is what she wrote.

Danny is playing in the corner with some toy animals. Another child called him but he didn't turn, so Susan poked him. He turned, surprised. Tim said, "Danny, I want that little duck." When Danny gave him the dog, Tim said, "Not dog, you silly. I want the duck.". Danny obligingly gave him the toy truck! So Tim went over and picked up the duck.

Danny walked over to the clay table and began to pound the clay. He hit it with all his 4-year-old's vigor.

Remember to ask Danny's mother about allergies. His nose always seems to be dripping. Even though he passed our screening, he just doesn't seem to be hearing.

Key Points

▶ The purpose of initial assessment is to help identify the child's strengths, needs, and learning characteristics in order to generate an individualized program plan.

▶ Assessment must be an ongoing process, used to fine-tune educational strategies and identify new goals and objectives.

▶ The professional's best assessment strategy is careful observation of the child.

▶ Professionals must understand the usefulness and limitations of both criterion-referenced and standardized assessment measures, as well as the important role of informal measures such as observation of the child in natural settings and the use of parent interviews.

▶ Assessment must be ecologically valid (i.e., occurring within relevant and typical contexts) and must focus on describing functional needs (i.e., those behaviors needed by the child in order to participate in meaningful and purposeful activities.)

Key Topics

▶ Changing philosophies related to assessment.

▶ The process of identification.

▶ The purpose of assessment.

▶ Evaluation.

▶ The early intervention team.

▶ The teacher's role as an observer of children.

▶ Use of standardized tests.

▶ Assessment within the classroom and use of criterion-referenced techniques.

▶ Situational factors to consider during assessment.

▶ Conducting ecologically valid assessments.

▶ Problems associated with early identification, assessment, and evaluation.

▶ Future trends in assessment of young children.

Historically, young children were considered too young for formal schooling until age 5 or 6. Children who were "slow" were expected to be "late bloomers." "Don't be a worried mother; Johnny (or Susie) will outgrow it" was the advice most often received by alert and concerned parents. "Children learn at different rates; you can't hurry them" was also a frequently heard comment.

When concerned parents sought to enroll their late bloomers in kindergarten, they were often told to wait a year, because their children were immature and needed an extra year of growing time. It was not unusual for such children who repeated a grade to become "failures." Finally, by third grade, these children were considered old enough to test.

By this time, failure had convinced everyone, most of all the child, that something was wrong in the child. Testing, done by one examiner, was brief and often inappropriate. Labels such as *retarded* and *emotionally disturbed* were attached. Special education then was offered in a state or county facility, often away from children's homes. Lives of both parents and children were disrupted. Potential was ignored. The label predicted the outcome to be expected! Usually, those who predicted useless lives in care facilities were right. Failure was assured.

CHANGING PHILOSOPHIES AND PRACTICES

Practices in identification, assessment, and evaluation are changing rapidly. New systems for describing special education services and the children who need them are evolving. It should be recognized that practices in some communities may vary somewhat from those described here.

The trend is away from categorical descriptions such as *retarded* and *learning disabled*, toward descriptions that convey an understanding of the intervention needs of children. The emphasis is shifting from diagnosis of a problem to be found in the child to (a) analysis of the specific instructional needs of the child, (b) determination of services required to meet these needs, and (c) avoidance of the stigma that can accompany traditional labeling. Both the kinds of tests used and the interpretations made of resulting information are changing. Greater care is given to recognizing the effects of ethnic background, previous experiences, daily environment, and the stress placed on children during testing. For example, historically, Vicky (p. 109) would have been described as hyperactive, without consideration of previous experience and daily environment.

Perhaps most apparent is the earlier age at which testing and intervention begins. Many programs provide diagnosis and assessment from birth. In fact, P.L. 94-142 and P.L. 99-457 actually specify that birth is the point at which "child-find" should begin. Additional adaptations include the following:

1. A multidisciplinary team conducts the diagnostic study.

2. Parents and teachers are included in programmatic decisions and planning.

3. Labeling is avoided whenever possible.

4. Education is provided in the homes or at such nearby facilities as day care centers, preschools, and public school early education classes.

If early educators are to provide appropriate programs and comprehensive services for young children with special needs, there must be an interdisciplinary or team approach in identification, screening, assessment, and eventual program planning. The team approach emphasizes the collaborative and cooperative interaction of parents and professionals from such fields as medicine, allied health, social service, psychology, and education. The teacher will often take on the role of team leader and coordinate the efforts of all contributing members. The information related to such areas as prenatal history, medical diagnoses, developmental progress, parents' perceptions of the child's needs, classroom observations, and so forth must be brought together in order to present a comprehensive yet dynamic view of the child and his or her environment.

The recognition of the child's interaction with the environment has added a vital dimension to the assessment picture. Ulrey and Rogers (1982) used the term "the ecology of assessment." The **ecological approach** includes community and cultural influences as well as the complex interactions young children with disabilities have with family and others in their life space. Barnard and Kelly (1990) emphasized the need for systematically observing structured and unstructured interaction between the child and parents, siblings, teachers, or clinicians. The efforts in providing a more realistic view of the child, the family, and the environment should lead to a more meaningful intervention plan.

From Child-Find to
Program Evaluation

The very nature of early intervention requires interventionists to be primary observers of children. Therefore professionals must assume responsibility for continuous involvement in the processes of identification, diagnosis, assessment, and evaluation. The complete sequence of observational opportunities is presented in this chapter. Also outlined are the processes from the professional or parent's initial concern about a particular child to the point at which the young child begins to receive appropriate special services. NOTE: Because the terms *diagnosis*, *assessment*, and *evaluation* are used in a variety of ways in the literature, there may be disagreement with the manner in which these terms are used in this chapter. Considerable study went into the decision to separate the identification, diagnostic, assessment, and evaluation procedures as we have. It was out goal to achieve clear communication of actual practices regardless of the terms used to describe them.

WHAT IS THE PROCESS
OF IDENTIFICATION?

P.L. 94-142 and P.L. 99-457 mandate free appropriate public education for *all* children ages 3 to 21. To receive services, children with special needs must be found and identified. **Identification** involves both the child-find and screening activities that locate and identify disabling conditions in children who either are not receiving early intervention or are receiving inadequate intervention services.

Child-Find. The process of **child-find** includes finding and identifying children with disabling conditions. Educational regions within states often hire child-find teams that are usually interdisciplinary in nature. These teams are responsi-

ble for planning and conducting a public awareness campaign to inform and educate community members concerning the right to a free and appropriate education for all children. A primary goal of the public awareness campaign is to generate referrals for screening.

Screening. **Screening** is the initial step in the assessment and intervention process intended to assist children in receiving an appropriate education. "The purpose of developmental screening tests is to identify at an early stage those children who have a high probability of exhibiting delayed or abnormal development" (Meisels & Wasik, 1990, p. 612). Screening is a limited procedure. The intent is to identify those children who *might* have a problem that should be investigated thoroughly. Children with obvious or severe disabling conditions who have been located through child-find procedures should not be involved in the screening process. These children should be referred directly to the local department or agency responsible for thorough diagnosis of the disabling conditions.

Role of the Early Interventionist in the
Processes of Identification

Traditionally teachers referred children for testing and received reports of the diagnosis. Currently the role of the interventionist in the processes of child-find and screening varies with local areas and professional expertise. In some areas teachers and therapists have been asked to assist in public awareness activities and in conducting massive screening programs, sometimes called "roundups." At the very least, all educators of young children are expected to be able to recognize high risk or danger signals of disabling conditions in the children within their classes. (See Figure 4–1.)

Professionals who consent to participate in screening young children should do so realizing

REFERRAL SIGNALS CHECKLIST

AUDITORY SIGNALS Observable Signs, Symptoms, or Complaints	Some- times	Yes	No
Has fluid running from ears.	[ ]	[ ]	[ ]
Has frequent earaches.	[ ]	[ ]	[ ]
Has frequent colds or sore throats.	[ ]	[ ]	[ ]
Has recurring tonsillitis.	[ ]	[ ]	[ ]
Breathes through mouth.	[ ]	[ ]	[ ]
Complains of noises in head.	[ ]	[ ]	[ ]
Voice is too loud or too soft.	[ ]	[ ]	[ ]
Has delayed or abnormal speech, excessive articulation errors.	[ ]	[ ]	[ ]
Seems to "hear what he or she wants to hear."	[ ]	[ ]	[ ]
Seems to be daydreaming.	[ ]	[ ]	[ ]
Often looks puzzled, frowns, or strains when addressed.	[ ]	[ ]	[ ]
Appears uninterested in things others find interesting.	[ ]	[ ]	[ ]

Observable Behaviors

Turns or cocks head to hear speaker.	[ ]	[ ]	[ ]
Scans when called rather than turning to source.	[ ]	[ ]	[ ]
Does not pay attention.	[ ]	[ ]	[ ]
Is especially inattentive in large groups.	[ ]	[ ]	[ ]
Exhibits extreme shyness in speaking.	[ ]	[ ]	[ ]
Has difficulty in following oral directions (and records).	[ ]	[ ]	[ ]
Acts out; appears stubborn, shy, or withdrawn.	[ ]	[ ]	[ ]
Exhibits marked discrepancy between abilities in verbal and performance test items.	[ ]	[ ]	[ ]

Figure 4–1 (pp. 114–118)   Referral Signals Checklist. NOTE: One or two symptoms do not a problem make. Tables of normal development found in Appendix A should be checked carefully because preschoolers naturally exhibit some degree of many of these behaviors. Patterns should be noted and observation continued when there is a question. Language signals can be found in Chapter 8. Adapted from Garwood et al. (1979); Gearhart and Weishahn. (1984).

	Some-times	Yes	No
Watches classmates to see what they are doing before beginning to participate.	[ ]	[ ]	[ ]
Often does not finish work.	[ ]	[ ]	[ ]
Hears teacher only when he or she sees teacher.	[ ]	[ ]	[ ]
Hears some days but not others.	[ ]	[ ]	[ ]
Gives answers totally unrelated to question asked.	[ ]	[ ]	[ ]
Frequently requests repetition or says "Huh?"	[ ]	[ ]	[ ]

VISUAL SIGNALS
Observable Signs, Symptoms, or Complaints

	Some-times	Yes	No
Red eyelids.	[ ]	[ ]	[ ]
Pupils turned in, out, up, or down (perhaps independent of each other).	[ ]	[ ]	[ ]
Watery eyes or discharges.	[ ]	[ ]	[ ]
Crusts on lids or among the lashes.	[ ]	[ ]	[ ]
Recurring styes or swollen lids.	[ ]	[ ]	[ ]
Pupils of uneven size.	[ ]	[ ]	[ ]
Excessive movement of pupils.	[ ]	[ ]	[ ]
Drooping eyelids.	[ ]	[ ]	[ ]
Excessive rubbing of eyes (seems to brush away blurs.)	[ ]	[ ]	[ ]
Shutting or covering one eye.	[ ]	[ ]	[ ]
Tracking or focusing difficulties.	[ ]	[ ]	[ ]
Headaches or nausea after close work.	[ ]	[ ]	[ ]
Tensing up during visual tasks.	[ ]	[ ]	[ ]
Squinting, blinking, frowning, and distorting face while doing close work.	[ ]	[ ]	[ ]

Observable Behaviors

	Some-times	Yes	No
Tilts head (possibly to use one eye) or thrusts forward.	[ ]	[ ]	[ ]
Tries to avoid or complains about light.	[ ]	[ ]	[ ]
Complains of pain or ache in eyes.	[ ]	[ ]	[ ]
Holds objects close to face.	[ ]	[ ]	[ ]

Figure 4–1 (Continued)

	Some-times	Yes	No
Complains of itchy, scratchy, or stinging eyes.	[ ]	[ ]	[ ]
Avoids or is irritable when doing close work.	[ ]	[ ]	[ ]
Moves head rather than eyes to look at object.	[ ]	[ ]	[ ]
Tires easily after visual tasks.	[ ]	[ ]	[ ]
Frequently confuses similarly shaped letters, numbers, or designs.	[ ]	[ ]	[ ]
Is unusually clumsy or awkward; trips over small objects.	[ ]	[ ]	[ ]
Has poor eye-hand coordination.	[ ]	[ ]	[ ]
Cannot follow a moving target held 10 to 12 inches in front of him.	[ ]	[ ]	[ ]

HEALTH OR PHYSICAL SIGNALS
Observable Signs, Symptoms, or Complaints

	Some-times	Yes	No
Flushes easily or has slightly bluish color to cheeks, lips, or fingertips.	[ ]	[ ]	[ ]
Has excessive low-grade fevers or colds.	[ ]	[ ]	[ ]
Has frequent dry coughs or complains of chest pains after physical exertion.	[ ]	[ ]	[ ]
Is unusually breathless after exercise.	[ ]	[ ]	[ ]
Is extremely slow or sluggish.	[ ]	[ ]	[ ]
Is abnormal in size.	[ ]	[ ]	[ ]
Is excessively hungry or thirsty.	[ ]	[ ]	[ ]
Complains of pains in arms, legs, or joints.	[ ]	[ ]	[ ]
Has poor motor control or coordination.	[ ]	[ ]	[ ]
Walks awkwardly or with a limp.	[ ]	[ ]	[ ]
Shows signs of pain during exercise.	[ ]	[ ]	[ ]
Moves in a jerky or shaky manner.	[ ]	[ ]	[ ]
Walks on tiptoe; feet turn in.	[ ]	[ ]	[ ]
Has hives or rashes.	[ ]	[ ]	[ ]
Loses weight without dieting.	[ ]	[ ]	[ ]
Appears to be easily fatigued.	[ ]	[ ]	[ ]
Has excessive or frequent bruises, welts, or swelling.	[ ]	[ ]	[ ]

Figure 4–1 (Continued)

Observable Behaviors	Some-times	Yes	No
Moves extremely slowly or in a sluggish manner.	[ ]	[ ]	[ ]
Is excessively hungry or thirsty.	[ ]	[ ]	[ ]
Complains of pains in arms, legs, or joints.	[ ]	[ ]	[ ]
Is excessively restless or overactive.	[ ]	[ ]	[ ]
Is extremely inactive; avoids physical exercise.	[ ]	[ ]	[ ]
Faints easily.	[ ]	[ ]	[ ]
Is extremely inattentive.	[ ]	[ ]	[ ]
Is unable to chew and swallow well.	[ ]	[ ]	[ ]
Exhibits difficulty with motor tasks, including balance.	[ ]	[ ]	[ ]
Complains of pain or discomfort in the genital area.	[ ]	[ ]	[ ]

LEARNING SIGNALS
Observable Signs, Symptoms, or Complaints

	Some-times	Yes	No
Cries easily; is easily frustrated.	[ ]	[ ]	[ ]
Is clumsy, awkward; has visual motor difficulties (for example, unusual difficulty with coloring, puzzles, or cutting).	[ ]	[ ]	[ ]
Exhibits visual or auditory perceptual difficulties.	[ ]	[ ]	[ ]
Appears easily disturbed by loud noises.	[ ]	[ ]	[ ]
Often seems confused or unsure of self.	[ ]	[ ]	[ ]

Observable Behaviors

	Some-times	Yes	No
Works very slowly or rushes through everything.	[ ]	[ ]	[ ]
Has difficulty working independently.	[ ]	[ ]	[ ]
Is highly distractible, impulsive.	[ ]	[ ]	[ ]
Has extremely short attention span.	[ ]	[ ]	[ ]
Is unable to follow directions.	[ ]	[ ]	[ ]
Is excessively active or excessively inactive.	[ ]	[ ]	[ ]
Perseverates (repeats activity over and over)	[ ]	[ ]	[ ]
Seems to catch on quickly in some areas but not in others.	[ ]	[ ]	[ ]
Is extremely inconsistent in performance.	[ ]	[ ]	[ ]
Does not transfer what is learned in one area to another.	[ ]	[ ]	[ ]

Figure 4–1 (Continued)

	Some-times	Yes	No
Actively resists change.	[ ]	[ ]	[ ]
Constantly disrupts class.	[ ]	[ ]	[ ]
Does not remember classroom routine; has other memory problems.	[ ]	[ ]	[ ]
Has difficulty making choices.	[ ]	[ ]	[ ]
Lacks inventiveness; has interests below age level.	[ ]	[ ]	[ ]
Learns so slowly that he or she cannot participate well with others.	[ ]	[ ]	[ ]

Figure 4–1 (Continued)

the responsibilities involved in the process. Even though great efforts are usually taken to ensure that the screening process is fun for children, it is, nevertheless, a time of anxiety. Parents, especially, need support and encouragement to realize that screening is only a preliminary step and does not determine the definite existence of a disabling condition. Care must be taken to avoid labeling children. As Frankenburg (1973) stated, "It is important to explain to parents that results of a screening test do not make a diagnosis, and the results of screening should not be interpreted to parents as indicating that a child has a particular problem" (p. 33).

The selection of a screening test is an important decision. Numerous tests have entered the market in the last several years. The selection committee must consider the following factors when selecting a screening instrument:

1. Qualifications of individuals who will use the test.

2. Reliability (consistency or stability) of the test.

3. Validity of the test (extent to which the test screens what it is supposed to screen).

4. Provision of items that cover the major functional areas, including language skills, cognitive skills, fine and gross motor skills, and social-emotional development.

5. Similarity of the children used to establish the norms to those being screened.

6. Degree to which the screening instrument discriminates against minority groups or specific disabling conditions.

7. Cost and time factors.

Publications mentioned in the annotated bibliography at the end of the chapter can be used as guides to prepare professionals for involvement in the process of test selection. In addition, brief descriptions of some of the most used tests are included in Appendix E.

Regardless of the instrument or test to be used, participating professionals assume responsibility for preparedness to administer whatever section of the instrument is assigned to them. Reading the manual of directions the night before is not enough. Practice is essential. Teachers must also recognize their own limitations. They should only agree to administer those sections of a test that are within their areas of expertise. For example, only trained ears really hear and differentiate articulation errors. Teachers who do not have this skill should not give speech and language sections that require this skill.

The Goal of Diagnosis

Diagnosis is considered by Cross and Goin (1977, p. 25) to be "a process designed: (a) to confirm or disconfirm the existence of a problem, serious enough to require remediation, in those children identified in a screening effort and (b) to clarify the nature of the problem (is it organic, environmental, or both?)." The goal of diagnosis is thorough, multidisciplinary investigation yielding information comprehensive enough to generate an intelligent decision on the appropriate educational placement for the child. The process of diagnosis determines the type or kind of intervention appropriate for the child. The type of intervention can range from placement in a regular early education program, on the least restrictive side of the continuum, to placement in residential programs that represent the most restrictive placement possible.

The Role of the Early Educator. Historically teachers were not seen as active participants in decision making about children with problems. Increasingly, teachers are expected to be astute observers and communicators of their observations. Teachers are included as part of the multidisciplinary diagnostic team. This is especially true of teachers or therapists who have been asked to serve as case managers. Their careful observations are helpful in corroborating or refuting formal test results. Current practice requires that teachers understand what each specialist is saying and recommending. Teachers today must be alert to recognize conflicting advice, the failure of a specialist to use tests that take into account multiple problems, or the need to coordinate conflicting opinions and directions. It is critical that *all* information, whether derived from formal testing, parental interviews, or informal observations, be integrated and synthesized. It is often the teacher who must assume this responsibility in an effort to see that a comprehensive picture of the child's level of functioning is obtained.

EXHIBIT 4–1

Special Considerations When Testing Children with Disabilities

Before testing, examiners should try to determine what impairments the child has and how these might influence the administration of the test or the test results. Are there any special problems that might occur during testing, such as a seizure? How long and in what position can the child work effectively? Should some parts of the test be omitted? Do the directions or materials used have to be adapted? What is the child's most efficient mode of communication? Does the child respond better to auditory or to visual cues? What form of reinforcement does the child respond to? Will the child respond more optimally in the presence of a parent or at home?

During the testing, examiners must be continually alert to such factors as fatigue and frustration. Without giving the answers to a child, they should do everything possible to find out what the child's actual capabilities are. If formal tests are used, notes can be made of the adaptations needed. Examiners should be positive and encouraging.

Tests should be interpreted in light of the child's disabilities. The examiner should seek observational information from others before any conclusions are made from test results and be willing to disregard test results if observations to the contrary can be documented. The child should be given the benefit of the doubt.

Recently a child with a mild hearing problem was judged to have retardation by a psychologist who used norm-referenced IQ tests that required understanding and use of language. Because of the hearing loss, language was limited, scores were low, and an inappropriate diagnosis was made. This same child, tested by another psychologist who based decisions on performance testing (nonverbal IQ tests), was again described as having retardation. Even though the test scores were in the range of retardation, both the parents and the teacher were unconvinced that the child was indeed retarded. Fortunately, the second psychologist noted, "Vision should be checked."

A thorough visual examination revealed severe myopia (nearsightedness)! Provided with glasses and teaching adapted to both vision and hearing problems, this 3 year old began to learn. In this case if the teacher had not observed that specialists were not communicating, and if the teacher had not persisted in encouraging the parents to see that all of the team members had all of the information, the diagnosis of retardation might have been accepted. The child's precious early learning years might have been lost.

Teachers are expected to be completely familiar with the environmental aspects of their own classrooms. If asked whether or not a child would benefit from placement in their particular classrooms, teachers should be able to answer with confidence. Thus, for example, if Mr. Curtis has 20 children in his group and the IEP for Vicky notes that she will need small-group activities, he may say his classroom is inappropriate for her. If she needs to be in a group of three or four children to modify her behavior effectively, a special education class in a public school may be the preferred alternative.

Teachers can develop understanding of their own personal teaching styles and the atmospheres they develop only through willingness to be honest and to seek feedback from others who observe them. They should initiate dialogues with directors, school psychologists, speech ther-apists, and nurses to help gain as objective a picture as possible of the characteristics of the classroom in which they teach. Use of audiotapes and videotapes may help teachers (a) determine whether they seem to have greater patience with one type of disability than with another; (b) see whether they seem to reinforce children differentially by age or sex; (c) assess the degree of structure they impose in a classroom; and (d) discover their most effective techniques of child management. Just as children differ, so do teachers and parents. Honesty and objective observation will help create the learner-environment match that is increasingly being encouraged in the literature (Burstein, 1986).

The Purpose of Assessment

Historically, there has tended to be a mismatch between the information obtained from a thorough diagnosis and the information needed by early interventionists to plan and provide direct services. Originally, it was thought that information gathered during diagnosis would be useful in the development of instructional programs. However, such information is usually provided only on a very general level. Therefore, most early intervention programs require additional **assessment** upon program entry. "Although [assessment] uses and builds upon information gathered in the diagnostic assessment, its purpose is to provide a more detailed description of the child's strengths and weaknesses for day to day programming (Hanson & Lynch, 1989, p. 105). Peterson and Meier (1987) have actually suggested that in a high-quality intervention program assessment serves "as a guide for everything that happens to a child" (p. 276).

Assessment is an *ongoing* process. Initially it is necessary to use various informal and formal techniques to carry out in-depth observation in an effort to pinpoint each child's skills and deficits. What the child can or cannot do and under what circumstances, must be determined to se-

lect appropriate behavioral objectives and effective instructional strategies. As the child's program progresses, ongoing assessment data need to be collected to update individual objectives and intervention procedures.

The Role of the Early Educator. Historically, teachers followed an adopted curriculum and activity plans. Although good teachers have always individualized activities to some extent, current practice requires much more thorough initial assessment, increased ongoing assessment, and continuous adaptation of activities.

Assessment is essentially the first task of the teacher in developing the individualized instruction program required for each child with disabilities. Assessment requires frequent observation of children in a variety of situations. Observation may be done with the help of standardized (formal) or informal teacher-made

techniques of measurement. This observation helps to confirm or refute diagnostic testing results; at the same time, concerns are pinpointed and a basis for individualized planning is developed. For example, Mr. Curtis would observe Vicky regularly to determine whether or not the planned adaptations are achieving the objectives.

Program assessment procedures must be directly related to program objectives, which emanate from the program curriculum adopted. (The process of developing program objectives is discussed in Chapter 5.) As Bricker and Veltman (1990) pointed out, the major differences in assessment activities are in the types of tools and procedures used. They offer the example of Piagetian-based programs, which logically choose to use the Infant Scales of Psychological Development (Uzgiris & Hunt, 1975). Appendix E contains descriptions of some of the assessment tools available, and readers are also referred to the annotated bibliography at the end of the chapter for guidance in selecting materials for an in-depth study of assessment tools and processes.

Evaluation

"**Evaluation** differs from other purposes of testing in the sense that the educational program rather than the student is being evaluated" (Salvia & Ysseldyke, 1978, p. 16). Although the term *evaluation* is sometimes used interchangeably with *assessment* and *diagnosis*, evaluation is considered here as a separate but vital process. There are generally two purposes for evaluation: (1) to collect evaluative information that is used as the basis for ongoing program decision making and (2) to provide evaluative information for external support agencies such as the Office of Special Education and The Danforth Foundation.

Evaluative information is used in making value judgments as to whether or not an instructional program produced the desired results. Evaluators discuss two types of evaluation: formative and summative. With **formative evaluation,** data on the progress of children are collected periodically and used to make ongoing program changes. **Summative evaluation** is concerned with the overall effectiveness of a program. It is a final accounting of program success. Testing typically is done at the beginning of an instructional program and at the end to determine whether or not desirable learning changes have occurred.

The Role of the Teacher. Often teachers in early intervention programs have had little input into curriculum planning and program evaluation. Present practice, demanding teacher accountability, makes their participation in these areas a necessity. Teachers may or may not be directly involved in the process of gathering information to determine the effectivenss of a program. Some programs choose to acquire assistance from an outside agency to conduct the evaluation. These evaluations are usually summative in nature.

However, evaluation procedures must be planned at the beginning of a program to ensure ease of information gathering and to avoid the hazard of gathering data that are not relevant to the instructional program. Information gathered during the formative or ongoing assessment of a child's progress is usually appropriate in making summative program evaluations. Whenever ongoing assessment information is used to make value judgments about a program's effectiveness, teachers are most certainly involved. Therefore the more organized, objective, and thorough a teacher is when observing and recording, the easier program evaluation will be.

THE EARLY INTERVENTION TEAM

Today, the team approach is considered to be an essential component of good early intervention programs. The number and type of professional team members vary with the perception of the needs of the child and family, the approach taken, and the financial resources of the program (Widerstrom, Mowder, & Sandall, 1991). A brief description of the roles various specialists play on early intervention teams is found in Table 4–1. It must be remembered that parents or other caregivers are an essential part of the team throughout all aspects of the early intervention process. To be effective, the team approach requires participants to collaborate fully with one another. To do so, they must possess good communication skills, the ability to solve problems, and knowledge of available resources. Most of all, team members must demonstrate respect for one another.

A review of the literature reveals three primary approaches to team development. The most traditional model is the **multidisciplinary approach** in which each professional conducts his or her own assessment and intervention in isolation. While professionals may confer with one another, consultation is not necessarily systematic and planned. Team members who work

Table 4–1 Roles of specialists on intervention teams

Specialist	Description
Audiologist	Conducts screening and diagnosis of hearing problems and may recommend a hearing aid or suggest training approaches for children with hearing disabilities.
Early childhood special educator	Conducts assessments and implements individualized programs for young children with special needs; is concerned with all aspects of the child's development that impact upon learning and successful daily living.
Early interventionist	Any professional who is a primary service provider for infants and toddlers with special needs and their families.
Neurologist	Conducts screening, diagnosis, and treatment of brain and central nervous system disorders.
Nurse	Oversees the overall medical well-being of the child and family. May initiate preventive procedures as well as take responsibility for specific treatments such as management of a gastrostomy tube.
Nutritionist	Conducts an evaluation of a child's eating habits and nutritional status; provides advice about normal and therapeutic nutrition and information about special feeding equipment and techniques to increase a child's self-feeding skills.
Occupational therapist	Conducts evaluation of children who may have difficulty performing self-help or other preschool activities that use arms, head, hand, and mouth movements; suggests activities to promote self-sufficiency and independence.
Ophthalmologist	Conducts screening, diagnosis, and treatment of diseases, injuries, or birth defects that limit vision.
Orthopedist	Conducts screening, diagnosis, and treatment of diseases and injuries to muscles, joints, and bones.
Otolaryngologist	Conducts screening, diagnosis, and treatment of ear, nose, and throat disorders; is sometimes known as an ENT (ear, nose, and throat) physician.
Pediatrician	Specializes in the diseases, problems, and health care of children.
Physical therapist	Conducts an evaluation of a child's muscle tone, posture, range of motion, and locomotion abilities; plans physical therapy programs aimed at promoting self-sufficiency primarily related to gross motor skills such as walking, sitting, and shifting position; helps with special equipment such as wheelchairs, braces, and crutches.
Psychiatrist	Conducts screening, diagnosis, and treatment of psychological, emotional, developmental, or organic problems; prescribes medication; is alert to physical problems that may cause nervous disorders.
Psychologist	Conducts screening, diagnosis, and treatment of children with emotional, behavioral, or developmental problems; is primarily concerned with cognitive and emotional development.
Social worker	Provides counseling or consultative services to individuals or families who may be experiencing problems.
Speech-language pathologist	Conducts screening, diagnosis, and treatment of children with communication disorders.

Adapted from Project Head Start, *Head Start: Mainstreaming Preschoolers Series.* Washington, DC: U.S. Department of Health and Human Services, Office of Human Development Services, Administration for Children, Youth and Families, 1978.

as part of an **interdisciplinary team** often work together in the same environment. While each member carries out his or her own assessment and intervention, there is frequent communication and planning within the team.

A model that has recently received considerable emphasis is the **transdisciplinary team approach.** As discussed in Chapter 1, transdisciplinary team members share their expertise and may cross the boundaries of their professional disciplines. All team members become sensitive to understanding the professional perspectives of other team members. Transdisciplinary team members must be open to sharing their expertise with others and open to learning new skills. By doing so, they are in a position to maximize what they can offer to a child and his or her family. For example, a physical therapist may carefully instruct an infant educator in appropriate positioning techniques for a child with a particular disability. The infant educator can then use those techniques in the future with a child whose disability is similar. Of course, the educator would always consult with the physical therapist before employing techniques learned earlier.

Characteristics of Transdisciplinary Team Assessment

Administrators, specialists, and parents must meet to agree on a set of common attitudes and values regarding what makes up a good assessment. The team's philosophy will determine the goals of the assessment process and the procedures used. After clarifying priorities, team members will define their roles and responsibilities in relation to one another. Teams often choose to conduct **arena assessments,** in which active spectators observe while the parent or a specialist guides the child through prescribed activities. The observers take notes and complete assessment tools appropriate to their disciplines. On occasion, team members may interact directly with the child or request that specific

tasks by attempted. Parents are encouraged, throughout, to comment and to validate the child's performance (Widerstrom et al., 1991).

Family-Based Child Assessment

When family members participate actively on early intervention teams, family-based assessment is more likely to occur. **Family-based child assessment** involves selecting assessment questions that are important to the family. It also means choosing assessment procedures that can answer these high-priority questions and incorporating family input throughout the assessment process (Stevens Dominguez, Beam, & Thomas, 1989). Practitioners in the field of early intervention are in the process of developing procedures that will enable assessment of a family's concerns, priorities, and resources along with the child's strengths and needs without being too intrusive into the family system (Lynch, Mendoza, & English, 1990).

THE EARLY EDUCATOR'S RESPONSIBILITY AS A PRIMARY OBSERVER OF CHILDREN

Recognizing children's special needs is often the primary responsibility of the teacher. Observing children and measuring their progress in accomplishing stated objectives are two critical components of a teacher's job. Unless the teacher systematically collects and records information about children's strengths and weaknesses (what they can or cannot do), the preschool experience will not be truly individualized to meet each child's particular needs.

Professionals in programs in which children with disabilities are included have a threefold responsibility: (1) recognition of the existence of or potential for special needs that were not identified previously; (2) continuous assessment of each child's strengths and weaknesses to establish appropriate objectives and to provide developmental and/or remedial instruction; and (3) determination of the adequacy of each child's progress. *The teacher's skills in observing and hypothesis making are thus critical to the success of any program of early childhood special education.*

Knowledge of Normal Development Is Critical

Recognition of special educational needs requires that an observer be keenly aware of the behavior normally exhibited by children within the environments in which they function. This awareness makes it possible for the observer to identify unique behaviors that may signal the need for special instruction. It is important to know the ages at which specific development is expected. Developmental delays, as well as unusual behaviors, are significant warning signs that special help may be needed. For example, Vicky's constant flitting from one thing to another is not typical of children her age.

Developmental scales are included in Appendix A as an aid in becoming thoroughly familiar with normal developmental milestones. An annotated bibliography is provided to further encourage in-depth understanding of basic sequences of growth and development.

Watch for the Unusual

With the exception of those with the most serious impairments, *children with disabilities are more like their normal peers than unlike them.* Therefore, we must be ever cognizant of the basic developmental changes through which all children pass. However, deviations in cognitive, language, social, and motor skill development should alert caregivers to the possible existence of special needs.

Although these developmental domains are the traditional areas of concern, other unusual behaviors should also attract attention. Children who overreact to failure or who resist new experiences may need help. Learning styles that are ineffective, apparent lack of motivation to learn, and failure to exhibit enjoyment of problem solving are warning signals. Lack of willingness to accept direction and correction, as well as lack of age-appropriate self-discipline and social interaction, are signs that help is necessary.

Figure 4–1 represents a composite of the most obvious signs that should signal referral to specialized personnel or agencies for complete diagnosis. The teacher should not be reluctant to seek additional evaluations if observation suggests undetected or incorrectly diagnosed problems. If a problem goes unnoticed, the child's special needs cannot be met.

Making a Referral

If a problem is suspected, the observer must be able to list the specific signs or behaviors that suggest a special need. A checklist such as the one illustrated in Figure 4–1 is a convenient way to record the information needed. This information is then given to the appropriate professionals, as outlined in the center's procedures for referral. Suspected speech, language, or hearing problems are usually referred to the speech clinician, the audiologist, or a regional diagnostic facility. Physical or vision problems are reviewed by the center's nurse or a public health nurse. Probable learning or behavior problems can be referred to a counselor, psychologist, or local community agencies. Table 4–1 gives brief descriptions of the roles various specialists play in the diagnostic process.

If appropriate professionals are not available, the referral is made to the school director or directly to the parents. A list of local referral resources should be given to the parents at this time. The teacher should always seek a conference with the director to determine the established referral policy. It is important to remember that written permission to release information must be obtained from the parents or guardians before information about any child can be released to an outside agency. For example, it would be inappropriate for Mr. Curtis to discuss Vicky's behavior with others before written permission is obtained.

Guidelines for Successful Observation

Observation is the skill of deliberately listening to and watching children's behaviors. They can be observed alone or in a group, at any time of the day, and under a variety of circumstances. While observing, the teacher notes aspects of appearance or behavior. Specific behaviors to be observed are determined by the purpose of the observation. Observers differ considerably in the process of recording information. Teachers often just make mental notes of what they see or hear. But use of an organized record-keeping form results in more systematic recording procedures. If the purpose of the observation is to assess the child's progress in an individualized program, systematic recording is essential to ensure objective, comprehensive data collection. The following guidelines help prepare teachers to become systematic, objective observers.

1. *Focus on observing exactly what the child does.* Record special, detailed observations of precisely what the child *does* and *says.* Use action verbs. Note the date, time, setting, what preceded the child's action or reaction, and what followed the behavior. *Do not* record inferences or opinions. Write down what is actually seen or heard. Mr. Curtis was careful to do this.

2. *Record the observational details as soon after the observation as possible.* With practice, teachers develop the ability to participate and observe simultaneously by making mental notes. However, it is important to plan schedules so that recording of details can be done as quickly as possible. Details are important and are easily

forgotten. That is why Mr. Curtis planned ahead to make observation time available.

3. *Observe in a variety of settings and at different times during the child's school day.* Changes in time and setting will often provide clues about children's interests. For example, children who are not comfortable on the playground may seek the solitude they never seek when in the classroom. Or they may become bullies on the playground, whereas they are self-controlled within the classroom. Children may be overly active when playing with other children but not so when playing alone. There may be a certain time of day, perhaps just before lunch, when some children are especially irritable. Identifying these times and circumstances makes it possible to plan needed changes that create a smoothly run day. Watching for patterns often leads to an explanation of behavior.

4. *Be realistic in scheduling observations.* When the purpose of the observation is to determine the developmental level at which a child is functioning, it is critical to be able to observe and make notes as often and in as many situations as necessary to get a complete record of the developmental areas under concern. Observations that are haphazard or incomplete jeopardize the correctness of any resulting hypotheses. Be realistic when planning observation time. Be certain that there is a chance the observation will actually occur. On some days the only available observation time might be free-choice time.

5. *Begin by focusing on one child at a time.* Focusing on one child at a time and using checklists or rating scales will help to develop observational skills without running the risk of missing or forgetting information.

6. *Avoid being obvious.* Avoid calling attention to the child being observed or the fact that the observation is taking place. Interact as naturally as possible. Be seated in a place normal for the teacher to be during the activity that is being observed. For example, when observing play-

ground activities, teachers usually post themselves in a spot providing optimal visibility. Stand or sit in the usual position when observing any activity. Mr. Curtis made all the needed arrangements before the children were present.

7. *At all times, ensure confidentiality.* Notes must *never* be left around; a system of coding names should be developed to ensure privacy. *Never* discuss observations in front of other children or parents of other children. Read and become familiar with The Family Educational Rights and Privacy Act of 1974 (P.L. 93-380), because it is important to be aware of the parents' rights to read the records created. Never send or give data collected from observation or test scores to outside agencies or individuals without written parental permission.

8. *Choose a workable recording system.* Teachers often need to experiment with file cards, notebooks, and three-ring binders to determine exactly what process is most convenient for them. Of course, the system used depends on the purpose and method of the observation. Well-organized, easy-to-review notes will facilitate the detection of patterns of behavior that may be extremely vital to real understanding of the child. Mr. Curtis preferred using a 8½" × 11" page format whereas another teacher might choose 6" × 9" file cards.

9. *Share your observational reports with parents as appropriate.* Objective evidence of child progress is always welcome.

TYPES OF OBSERVATION TECHNIQUES

Teachers should observe children in a variety of situations with as many purposes as they have objectives for the children. The particular technique chosen should relate directly to the purpose established. The following list describes some of the more common types of observation. As the list progresses, the techniques become more standardized (formal), requiring greater systematic planning and structure from the observer.

1. *Photographs.* Photographs provide a quick, easy method of obtaining children's reactions to various lessons. They provide an automatic record of involvement. These pictures can be taken at planned intervals to demonstrate sequential development. A dual purpose is served when the snapshots are used to stimulate language development, as discussed in Chapter 8. Using photographs in bulletin board displays offers repeated chances to encourage the development of self-esteem.

2. *Videotape and cassette recordings.* With the advancement of instructional technology, more and more classrooms commonly employ videotape and cassette recorders. Teachers have the advantage of participating directly in the activities and can later review the children's responses to their unique teaching styles. However, care must be taken to prevent the presence of recording equipment from distorting the observation. Children thoroughly enjoy observing and listening to themselves. Again, such techniques provide ideal opportunities for language stimulation and allow the teacher to collect language samples. Moving pictures have often been used to provide evidence of development in such areas as motor coordination and social interaction. Local service clubs are often willing to make donations to help with film and processing costs.

3. *Collection of children's work.* Although early childhood education is usually process oriented rather than product oriented, there are opportunities to collect children's work. Collecting samples of such things as a child's paintings, tracings, cuttings, and attempts to print his or her name allows the teacher to analyze progress and to make this obvious to parents. Vicky's paintings also demonstrated a lack of coordination.

4. *Activity lists.* Programs that provide activ-

ity centers with some degree of free-choice time may post lists of children's names to be dated or checked off at each center area. By listing each child's name and the length of participation, the child's interests and level of involvement can be determined. The teacher will need to decide whether choices should be limited or children should be encouraged to broaden their participation. Mr. Curtis identified Vicky's short participation span this way.

5. *Anecdotal records, diaries, and logs.* Teachers record specific details of their observation, including exact behavior; precisely what precedes the behavior; and any reactions to the behavior, time, setting, and individuals involved. Care is taken to avoid making judgments, choosing isolated events, or overgeneralizing from atypical incidents. Systematic and regular recording allows the teacher to study patterns of behavior.

6. *Passports.* The passport (Shea & Bauer, 1991) is an ordinary spiral notebook that the child carries daily to and from home and the intervention program. An example of a passport is found in Chapter 3. All adults who work with the child are encouraged to make observational notations in the passport. Records are required to be brief, positive, honest, and consistent. The objective of the passport is to promote positive parent-teacher communication and cooperation. A passport might help Vicky by creating consistency in behavioral expectations at home and at school.

7. *Time sampling and event recording.* In time sampling the observer selects specific behaviors that are readily observable and occur often. A few behaviors are chosen and their occurrence is recorded on a prepared recording sheet during regularly scheduled, short observation periods. Unlike time sampling, event recording is not restricted to specific preplanned time intervals. A targeted behavior such as temper tantrums is recorded on occurrence. This

method is often used with infrequently occurring behaviors.

8. *Checklists and rating scales.* Checklists and rating scales help specify exactly what the observer is to be observing. Use of such instruments makes it possible to vary the observer and still maintain consistency in the behavior that is observed. Illustrations of checklists and developmental scales are included throughout this text and in most texts in the field of early childhood special education. However, teachers are encouraged to design their own to ensure that the behavior observed is related to the goals and objectives of their program. (Another teacher may have different priorities for her program than Mr. Curtis does for his.)

9. *Criterion-referenced tests.* Criterion-referenced devices or tests are designed to compare a child to a set of standards rather than to other children. Commercial tools usually establish the set of standards by selecting and sequencing items from several standardized developmental scales such as those developed by Bayley (1968) and Gesell (1940).

10. *Norm-referenced tests.* Norm-referenced tests provide the most standardized information-gathering opportunities for observation. The intent of norm-referenced measurement is to compare a child's performance to the performance of other children who are the same chronological age. Few norm-referenced instruments are useful in planning individualized programs for children. These tests tend to be less reliable with young children. "Norm-referenced tests are most useful for screening and classification, while criterion-referenced measures identify what to teach" (Smith, 1983, p. 325). However, funding agencies sometimes do require norm-referenced tests to complete program evaluations. Cautions when using such tests are discussed later in this chapter. An annotated bibliography at the end of the chapter supplies sources for brief descriptions of the tests that are

available commercially and listed selectively in Appendix E.

DETERMINING THE FOCUS OF AN OBSERVATION

As previously stated, the target, setting time, and conditions should be determined by the purpose of the observation. Informal observations help provide a more comprehensive view of the child than the observations obtained solely with the aid of structured inventories, checklists, rating scales, and tests. The focus of the observation is limited only by the imagination and time of the observer. It is important to observe a variety of situations during different times of the day. The focus should be more general when teachers are assessing the overall development of a child.

On the other hand, if teachers are trying to determine whether a child has accomplished a particular objective, they will narrow their observation to a very specific behavior under specified conditions. (Mr. Curtis looked for the number of things Vicky did as well as exactly what she did.) Most teachers will refer to a written objective to guide their observation. For example, if the IEP requires the child to learn to button a coat, the observer will watch specifically to see whether the child can button a coat, under what conditions, and with what degree of skill.

Observing How Children Perform a Task

The primary purpose of most teacher observation is to determine the strengths and weaknesses in children's learning repertoires in order to develop instructional goals and strategies. The teacher should not be concerned with etiology (investigation of causative factors) or assignment of diagnostic labels. The teacher must instead be concerned with exactly what children

can (and cannot) do and how they do it. In closely analyzing task performances the teacher observes children's processes or styles of performance, in addition to determining whether or not children can perform specific tasks.

For example, when asked to describe what is happening in a picture, does a child respond impulsively? Or does he or she give a more deliberate or reflective response, taking time to note details while carefully scanning the picture? When copying a figure does the child seem to study the picture and plan? Or does he or she start drawing with only a brief reference to the drawing presented? Research on problem-solving style indicates that differences in cognitive styles may influence individual differences in performance in a variety of school-related tasks (Keogh, 1977).

Considering Temperamental Factors

Children's performance is also greatly influenced by temperamental factors. Children who are afraid to try new tasks or take risks obviously miss out on learning opportunities and may not be able to exhibit the breadth of their capabilities. Some children appear to be highly dependent and are unable to work well alone. These children depend on assurance or reinforcement from adults or other children to give them confidence to perform. Investigators have found that, as early as first grade, children who are autonomous standard setters tend to read better than children who constantly turn to teachers or parents for feedback of whether their efforts have been good enough (Dreyer & Haupt, 1966).

Realizing Environmental Influences

Later in this chapter the importance of environmental or situational influences on task performance is discussed. Various researchers have discussed the importance of focusing on the in-

teraction of the child with the environment rather than focusing on either the child or the environment independently (Rogers-Warren, 1982). Stoneman and Gibson (1978) found the assessment performance of preschool children with developmental disabilities improved when they were tested by familiar figures and away from classroom distraction. The influence of situational factors again suggests that the teacher must vary the conditions of observation to get the most comprehensive view of a child's learning strengths and weaknesses.

Recognizing the Interrelationship of Skills

Finally, observers must be aware of and attuned to the interrelationship of skills. Children who are concentrating on the development of a motor skill may or may not exhibit what might be considered to be normal verbal or social interaction with other children during that period. On the other hand, children who are skilled in the motor activity may exhibit greater verbal fluency because of their confidence in their motor skills and lack of verbal inhibition.

Young children do not develop skills in isolation. The most obvious example of the interdependence of skills development is noted by psycholinguists in their study of language development. Chapter 9 elaborates on the importance of realizing that the potential for language development is present during every waking moment, assuming the child does not have severe impairments and is in a relatively stimulating environment. The teacher then must be aware of the child's total performance even when focusing on a single aspect of behavior.

In summary, observation is a complex, critical skill that can be developed only through systematic practice. The importance of becoming skilled in objective, systematic observation was made clear by a study conducted by the Illinois State Board of Education (1980). The study found that the most frequently used technique for child performance evaluation by teachers of young children with disabilities was observation of the child's behavior. In addition, national model programs also reported making frequent use of observational data. Therefore it is imperative that teachers strive to incorporate the following six abilities into their observational repertoire.

1. In-depth understanding of what is considered to be normal behavior.

2. Skill in recognizing high-risk behavior or danger signals.

3. Ability to follow the guidelines for responsible observation.

4. Ability to choose types of observational techniques appropriate to the purpose of the observation.

5. Awareness of the influence of performance styles, motivational factors, environmental variables, and extraneous behaviors on the judgments to be made about children's strengths and weaknesses.

6. Continuous practice of professionalism through respect for confidentiality, restraint from labeling, and attempts to counteract any tendencies toward placing stereotyped expectations on children.

USE OF STANDARDIZED TESTS WITH YOUNG CHILDREN

In recent years emphasis has been given to a shift away from the use of standardized or formal tests to assess learning strengths and weaknesses. Increasing emphasis is given to the logical match between instructional goals and assessment procedures. Standardized instruments continue to be used, however, during initial processes of screening and diagnosis. They also continue to be used for summative evaluation of learning progress. But increasingly, teacher-developed informal techniques are seen as the mainstay of assessment and evaluation.

Contributing to this move away from routine standardized testing are (a) the lack of reliability and validity of standardized tests for use with young children; (b) the need to obtain information that can easily be transformed into individualized instruction plans; (c) the cultural biases built into many standardized instruments; (d) the influence of situational factors on test performance; and (e) the increased recognition of the teacher as the individual most responsible for any child's progress.

Cautious Use of Norm-Referenced Tests

Standardized tests are instruments designed to be administered by a trained examiner following specified procedures. Depending on the purpose, standardized tests or assessments could be completed by psychologists or psychometrists; speech, language, and hearing clinicians; pediatricians; or social workers. Typically these examiners report test scores and norm-referenced information.

Norm-referenced test scores reflect comparison of the performance of the child being tested with performance of other children of the same chronological age (CA) who took the test when norms were being established. Thus a child with a mental age (MA) of 3 years and 6 months (3–6) is said to have performed on the norm-referenced tests, such as the Stanford-Binet test, in a way that most children do at CA 3 1/2. If that child were, in fact, age 2 1/2, his or her IQ would be 132. This child would be identified as superior in intellectual functioning. On the other hand, a child with a CA of 5 years with the same MA of 3–6 would have an IQ of 67 and would be considered to have mild retardation if deficits in adaptive behavior were also evident.

Instruments such as those that assess MA are of little value when assessing the performance of children with disabilities or those from a minority culture if the normative standards do not take into account the influence of the children's unique conditions or the nature of their development. *Children who have developed in a different manner by virtue of having disabilities or being bilingual or deprived cannot be compared logically to children who have been raised in what society considers to be normal circumstances.* Only when used with caution by a skilled examiner can standardized, norm-referenced tests provide information worthy of consideration for planning individualized instruction programs.

For example, norm-referenced tables typically are used by speech, language, and hearing clinicians as a comparison for a child's receptive and expressive language skills. Usually children have internalized most of the rules of grammar and syntax by age 4. Those who do not speak distinctly and in grammatically correct ways by that age are described as having delayed speech and language development. Useful information can be gained about the specific nature of a child's delay by analyzing performance on individual items of standardized, norm-referenced tests. Practitioners who are skilled in analyzing performances on individual test items will note patterns in development and behavior that can serve as the basis for instructional goals and objectives.

For example when Mr. Curtis looked closely at Vicky's Peabody Picture Vocabulary Test results (Dunn & Dunn, 1981), he noted that she consistently missed items that included verbs. Recorded observations also revealed less than average vocabulary and sentences that were immature for her age. These patterns prompted Mr. Curtis to seek advice from the speech and language clinician to plan lessons that would enrich Vicky's receptive and expressive language skills.

Awareness of specific task performance can also be helpful to the teacher who has an understanding of the thinking and acting processes involved in test items missed. Knowledge of weaknesses will allow the teacher to use informal observational techniques to observe the child doing similar tasks. This observation will create increased understanding of how or why the child missed the items. The opportunity to refute or collaborate the original test results is thus provided by observation.

When observing her student, Ms. McLynn, another teacher, had the uneasy feeling that Danny could not hear well, even though he had passed the auditory screening test. She decided to play games with Danny such as asking him to point to the source of sound when blindfolded and to repeat simple sentences. Danny had much more difficulty with these tasks than the other 4 year olds in the room. Ms. McLynn became even more convinced that Danny must have a complete audiological examination. She spoke to Danny's parents, who agreed to take Danny to the speech and hearing clinic at the nearby university.

These illustrations emphasize that it is the responsibility of the teacher to determine whether or not a child's test scores are an accurate reflection of abilities. Only observation on a day-to-day basis can confirm or refute examiner conclusions based on test performance. In this regard, Hare and Hare (1977) offered valuable advice to teachers of young children:

A critical factor for the teacher to remember is that test scores should not determine an educational program; they are contributing bits of information. All standardized tests provide only a sample of the child's behavior at a specific point in time . . . . The teacher also should be aware that traits are not immutable, and even what we call intelligence varies during the life of an individual. (p. 31)

Exhibit 4–2 details some special considerations in assessing infants and toddlers, while Exhibit 4–3 lists techniques for assessment that are culturally fair.

Considerations for Interpreting Standardized Test Results

P.L. 94-142 specifies that placement decisions cannot be based on the results of any single test. The norm-referenced or ability training approach is being criticized partly because of the tendency of some educators to make generalizations based on low performance on one process test. For example, poor performance on the repetition of digits designed to measure short-term memory does not necessarily reveal a weakness in all aspects of the auditory memory process. The skill of repeating back digits or nonsense syllables may be very different from remembering meaningful auditory directions. Yet some educators have tended to generalize from this and initiate training in all aspects of auditory memory. Summative program evaluations of such training have yielded disappointing results. This

---

EXHIBIT 4–2 _____

Special Considerations in Assessment of Infants and Toddlers

1. Although standardized instruments are available for assessment of various aspects of infant and toddler development, they *must* be accompanied by extensive use of informal measures as well.

2. Infants and toddlers must be assessed within the context of their families, ideally within their natural home environment.

3. Special considerations must be given to infant behavioral and physiological states, which may change quickly and dramatically due to factors such as hunger, fatigue, and lability. Assessment sessions need to be rescheduled several times. Also, infant state considerations will require that infants be observed on more than one occasion, at different times of the day.

4. Parents must play a key role in the assessment of infants and toddlers, in terms of both the information they can provide to the professionals and the need to observe the infant's behavior in the most optimal environment—that is, with the caregiver.

---

suggests that educators need to rethink and redesign programs that have been based on such generalizations.

Furthermore, educators need to be alert to hidden penalties that may understate test results of children who have disabilities and those who are culturally different. What amounts to impossible response requirements for some children distorts even further the inappropriateness of single-test normative samples. A recent example comes to mind. Consider the validity of a norm-referenced IQ on a child with severe visual disabilities who was given a Stanford-Binet test with no accommodations for the visual impairments. What is even more disturbing is the fact that the child's mental capacity was classified and reported according to the score received.

It is the teacher who may need to confirm or refute the face validity of test results. Do scores seem reasonable when reality tested against the teacher's observational experiences with the child? To provide assistance to teachers who will be expected to interpret the results of tests or reports filed by diagnostic specialists, *selected measurement terms* can be found in the glossary at the end of this text. An understanding of these

---

EXHIBIT 4–3 _____

Techniques to Accomplish Culturally Fair Assessment

1. Use multiple assessment techniques within naturalistic settings, involving the parents or other caregivers as significant partners in the process.

2. Examine test items to be certain they are not biased against children or families of a certain cultural background.

3. Examine test manuals to determine whether the group to which the child is being compared is culturally compatible.

4. Give directions in the child's native language.

5. Use a multidisciplinary or transdisciplinary process so that more than one professional, along with the parents, can contribute to hypotheses developed from the observations.

helps teachers to explain the results of assessment procedures to parents and/or instructional aides, just as they help in the use of test information for the development of instructional strategies.

But even before becoming involved in the assessment process, teachers should talk with the specialists involved in their children's multidisciplinary assessment. They should discuss the instruments used by these specialists and techniques for interpretation and translation of diagnosis into instructional goals. Such a discussion helps the teacher to understand the situational factors that may influence the performance of children tested by these specialists. Teachers will also be able to determine the referral information most useful to the specialists. Providing useful referral data enables teachers to establish themselves as necessary members of the team.

ASSESSMENT WITHIN THE CLASSROOM

Criterion-Referenced Techniques

Comparing a child's performance to that of other children the same age is the traditional norm-referenced assessment. By contrast, **criterion-referenced assessment** compares the child's performance to a standard or expected mastery of a skill. A few criterion-referenced instruments that provide information directly transferable to program objectives are the Carolina Developmental Profile, Boehm Test of Basic Concepts, Brigance Diagnostic Inventory of Early Development, and the Hawaii Early Learning Profile. Some others are listed in Appendix E. However, directors and teachers of preschools often choose to develop their own criterion-referenced measurement instruments. They have the advantage of being able to tie the assessment devices to the program objectives.

It should be readily apparent that criterion-referenced devices facilitate daily planning for children. Appropriate tasks are sequenced, and the child is requested to perform each item, beginning with the most difficult. Instruction begins with the first item a child cannot complete in a sequence. It is said that we assess from the top down, or the hardest to the easiest, and teach from bottom up, from the easiest to the hardest. When assessing, concern is not with how well a child did in comparison to other children but with determining the next appropriate skill for a child to master. This process is discussed thoroughly in Chapter 6.

Cross and Goin (1977) enumerated the strengths and weaknesses of criterion-referenced tools. As strengths they cited (a) the measurement of intraindividual progress; (b) the ease in developing program objectives as a result of sequentially developed devices; (c) the fact that such devices usually cover many developmental areas and often have more items than norm-referenced techniques; and (d) the greater flexibility of administration necessary for use with children who have disabilities. Weaknesses of criterion-referenced devices include (a) the tendency to design techniques for specific groups of children; (b) the inclination to test very specific skills that may not give a picture of the total child; and (c) the characteristic of measuring skills in acquisition rather than generalization. For example, there is a big developmental difference between a child who happens to place items correctly on a form board through trial and error and one who places the items correctly with obvious ease. Even considering the weaknesses of criterion-referenced tests, Salvia and Ysseldyke (1985) concluded:

When tests are administered for the purpose of assisting the classroom teacher in planning appropriate programs for children, criterion-referenced devices are recommended. When planning a program for an individual student, a teacher obviously should be more concerned with identifying the specific skills that the

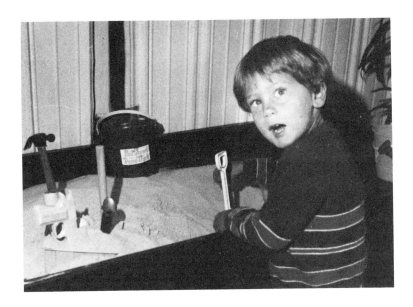

student does or does not have than with the knowing how the student compares to others. In criterion-referenced measurement that emphasis is on assessing specific and relevant behaviors that have been mastered. Criterion-referenced tests treat the student as an individual rather than simply providing numerical indexes of where the student stands on a variety of subtest continua. (p. 30)

Curriculum-Based Techniques

Curriculum-Based or -Referenced Assessments are similar to criterion-referenced techniques. Curricular objectives are used as the standard against which performance is judged. The child's performance is observed on tasks requiring skills that are targets of the curriculum. Curriculum-based assessments are popular because they provide direct linkage between assessment and the development of curriculum-related intervention goals and objectives. **Task analysis** is the procedure often used to break the curriculum-related skills into "testable" and "teachable" steps. This process is also discussed in detail in Chapter 6.

SITUATIONAL FACTORS TO CONSIDER DURING ASSESSMENT

Increasingly, attention is being given to consideration of the importance of situational factors in determining a child's performance on specified tasks (Thurman & Widerstrom, 1990). Examiners consider such variables as the setting of the assessment, the timing of the assessment, and the individuals involved in the assessment, as well as the actual techniques of measurement used when implementing any type of evaluative process. Figure 4–2 emphasizes the dynamic, interactive nature of five primary variables.

One rule of thumb to remember is that *a child is capable of doing as well as his or her performance demonstrates, but we are never certain of how much better the child might do given optimal circumstances.* Unfortunately, many school districts lock assessment into the calendar rather than into the child. That is, testing is scheduled for the first 3 days of school and is to be completed within that time. Sometimes little attention is given to establishing a rapport or to the fact that a child might be nervous in a new situation, sick, or drained by the heat of September. Federal agencies are guilty of establishing timelines for preassessment and postassessment that may not consider the critical influence of situational factors on assessment performance.

Establishing Rapport

Before beginning any type of assessment or even observation, the teacher or other examiner has the responsibility of working to establish rapport with the child. Establishing rapport involves the development of a climate or an atmosphere in which the child feels comfortable enough to perform as well as possible. Rapport is evidenced when the child does not feel anxious, threatened, sad, or angry, or experience any feeling that might lead to lack of cooperation. Preschool children often feel shy, uneasy around strangers, generally afraid, or even indifferent. To gain the child's trust and confidence, examiners may provide interesting toys and cooperative playtime before testing.

The need to establish rapport is another reason why examiners should not allow assessment procedures to be determined by the calendar.

Several days may be needed to help the child feel comfortable and secure when interacting with the examiner. Needless to say, results from some team diagnostic interviews may be suspect if examiners have not taken sufficient time and effort to establish rapport. Again, we see the need to confirm or deny conclusions from initial diagnosis through continual and ongoing assessment.

Allowing Sufficient Time

Young children with disabilities may need several days to complete what children who have no disabilities may do in one sitting. The length of time devoted must be very short to ensure the necessary on-task behavior. Young children children cannot be expected to concentrate for much longer than 10 to 20 minutes depending on how demanding the task is. Children with disabilities often fatigue more quickly than nondisabled children. Examiners should observe the child before assessment to determine how much concentration time can be expected of the child before testing begins. Informal testing, as accomplished by observing a child in play and checking a simple rating scale, often capitalizes

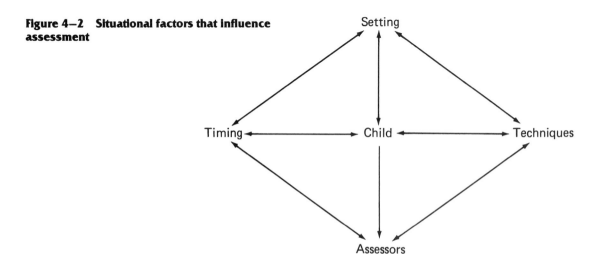

Figure 4–2   Situational factors that influence assessment

on the child's natural display of motivation and concentration. Mr. Curtis needs to do more of this kind of observation.

Conducting Ecologically Valid Assessments

When possible, young children should be observed in settings with which they are familiar. *Ecology* refers to the interrelationship of organisms to their environments. Assessments that focus on observation of children's behaviors in the context of normally occurring routines such as eating and playing are considered to be **ecologically valid.** Including parents as interacting partners will help ensure the ecological validity of the observations. If it is not possible to observe a child in his or her home, caregivers might videotape the child's behavior during naturally occurring activities. Ecologically valid assessments not only help the interventionist understand what skills are demonstrated by the child at home, but they also give clues to those behaviors that are functionally relevant to the family. Behaviors that are **functionally relevant** are those that enable the child to become more independent or to better interact with the environment.

Selecting the Most Appropriate Time

Timing, as well as length of assessment, can influence results. Some children are slow starters in the morning and may need to ease into the day's routine. Other children are eager beginners and become increasingly tired as the day wears on. Generally, young children and children with disabilities tire more easily than older or non-disabled children. Nutritional factors can influence optimal timing of assessment. Care should be taken not to remove a child from his or her favorite activity of the day.

Children who have been playing outside may need time before they can be expected to concen-

trate on a demanding quiet task. Visual or auditory concentration should be interspersed with active periods for most children. However, some children might be "set off" by activity, and a different type of relaxing approach such as closing the eyes or listening to music would be in order. An often forgotten feature of timing is toileting. Many examiners have realized too late just why a child was squirming in the seat rather than concentrating as desired. The examiner should always suggest the child get a drink of water and use the bathroom before sitting down to concentrate. In any case the individual behavioral characteristics of each child should be observed and recorded before the assessment procedure is initiated.

Considering the Appropriateness of Directions

One of the major reasons why testing of young children is often unreliable is the difficulty of the directions involved in some formal testing procedures. If an examiner chooses to use a standardized test, he or she is compelled to follow the directions explicitly. However, it is not unusual to find that the formal test must become an informal one because of the need to alter directions. Cues frequently need to be offered for a young child or a child with disabilities to understand directions. There is more to be gained from altering directions so that a child can respond than from declaring the child untestable because he or she could not comprehend the task.

If the examiner must alter procedure in any way, this should be noted and generalizations made accordingly. Again, observation ahead of time will help the examiner to know what can reasonably be expected of the child to be tested. It should be remembered that it is critical to establish eye contact and to get the child's attention before ever beginning to elicit a testing response. Sometimes gentle cues of touching or holding the child's hand are necessary to help gain attention. This would definitely hold true for Vicky. Each time a new item is presented, attention must be regained. Even if the teacher chooses to do only informal testing, time could be well spent reading standardized test manuals to acquire some of the testing skills required.

Focusing on What the Child Can Do

Examiners must be very careful observers. If a child fails an item, they must try to determine why. Did the child actually lack the knowledge or thinking ability to respond? Or is his or her performance penalized by an inability to respond as directed? For example, a child may not be able to make a cross on the Boehm Test of Basic Concepts but may be able to demonstrate understanding of the concept by touching the picture named. There is a vast difference between a child who stands limp and gazing off into space when a bean bag is thrown to him or her and one who coordinates eye and hand in reaching for, but missing, the bag. However, both responses might be counted as failures on some standardized tests. From the teacher's point of view, the process involved in the catching attempt is more important than the product of catching or not catching the object.

Young children and children who have emotional disabilities have the tendency to perseverate when being tested. They get a "set" with one task and cannot switch to the requirements of the next task. If the correct picture is in the upper right-hand corner of the Peabody Picture Vocabulary Test plate, the child might point to the upper right-hand corner time after time. The examiner then should discontinue the task until the child is able to cooperate more adequately. The same procedure would be necessary if obvious random guessing were occurring. All of these influences combine to make it extremely important that the examiner carefully observe the child. It is always better to record "test incom-

plete" on a folder than to enter results that are known to be invalid.

PROBLEMS ASSOCIATED WITH EARLY IDENTIFICATION, ASSESSMENT, AND EVALUATION

Educators continue to raise questions, discuss concerns, and encourage caution in attempts to diagnose young children or to attach labels to them. The necessity of early identification of readily apparent physical, sensory, or gross developmental problems is not questioned. However, as Keogh and Becker (1973) so convincingly argued, extreme care must be taken in hypothesizing about the potential for learning failures that have not actually occurred. Hypothesizing future learning problems may indeed create an expectancy phenomenon. Salisbury and Vincent (1990) have emphasized the need to be more concerned with what is functionally necessary for success in the present or very near future. In other words, the teacher of 3 year olds should be more concerned with acquisition of motor skills that influence the children's ability to dress themselves than with how well the children will be able to print their names.

Labels Not Suitable for Children

Another caution that has led some states to establish noncategorical preschool classrooms is a concern over the possible negative effects of labeling children. Research suggests that categorizing and labeling children, for example, those with emotional disturbances, hearing impairments, or learning disabilities may be responsible for the development of negative expectations on the part of classroom teachers and others. These negative expectations in turn may further the child's existing difficulties (Algozzine, Mercer, & Countermine, 1977; Safford, 1989). For example, if a child is described as retarded, the lowered expectations of parents and other care-givers may lead to delayed development. Failure to stimulate, reward, and expect typical mental growth may result from the labeling. This failure to nurture, rather than an innate limitation, may exaggerate the developmental delay.

Importance of Reliable and Valid Tests

Tests developed for young children usually lack rigor in terms of reliability and validity. Therefore it is difficult to use norm-referenced tests in developing educational plans with any confidence (Salvia & Ysseldyke, 1985). The term **reliability** refers to the consistency or dependability of a testing procedure. It is the degree to which a child's score is a true score. That is, little or no error in measurement is present. The reliability of a test is often determined by comparing results from repeated administrations of the test (test-retest), by giving equivalent forms of the test, by comparing the results from each half (split-half), and by noting the consistency in rating between two or more scorers (interscorer). Even though it is essential to be certain that results do not reflect considerable error, many test manuals do not report results from efforts to determine the reliability. Consistency in any performance is not characteristic of young children, but attempts must continue to be made to ensure as much reliability as possible when assessments are made.

When a test is reliable, it may not necessarily be valid. **Validity** refers to what a test measures and how well it does so (Compton, 1989). Does it measure what it is supposed to measure? For example, if a teacher wishes to determine a child's level of problem solving, then he or she must require the child to solve problems. Asking a child to identify pictures by pointing to those named and recording a resulting MA score does not tell a child's potential for solving problems. A

valid problem-solving test has not been given. Instead a valid test for assessing a child's level of receptive language and ability to associate a verbal symbol with a visual symbol has been given.

Three types of validity are usually discussed: construct validity, content validity, and predictive validity. Of the three, **construct validity,** or the ability to determine how well a test measures the conceptual idea behind its construction, is the most difficult to determine. Today many question whether or not intelligence tests actually measure the abstract quality called intelligence. **Content validity** assumes that the test has a representative sample of the behaviors it is supposed to measure. Tests of eye-motor coordination that omit eye-foot tasks do not include a truly representative sample of test items. **Predictive** or **criterion-related validity** is concerned with whether or not performance on the test items can predict actual achievement on another test that is supposed to measure related skills or future performance in related life skills.

Predictive validity is an issue of considerable concern to developers of screening or readiness tests. The very attempt to predict difficulties that have not occurred is risky (Keogh & Becker, 1973). Furthermore, ethical considerations interfere with attempts to determine validity. Children are not expendable! If we know how to help children, it is unthinkable to withhold the help.

When concerned adults learn of a child's potential learning problems through the diagnostic interpretation of testing, they feel compelled ethically to implement remedial or preventative actions as soon as possible. Therefore, the researchers are prevented from conducting long-term studies to find out whether or not the predicted problems actually did occur. That is, if the remedial program has been successful, then children suspected of having learning problems would not be expected to continue to exhibit the predicted problems. As a result, the ability of tests to predict the actual existence of future problems is questionable.

Rather than prevent children from obtaining the services they need, educators are choosing to rely less on test results and more on professional and parent observation and judgment.

FUTURE TRENDS IN ASSESSMENT OF YOUNG CHILDREN

The previous discussion points out only some of the serious issues that exist with regard to the validity and appropriateness of use of standardized assessment instruments with infants and young children with special needs. A recent position statement of the National Association for the Education of Young Children decries the use of formal standardized instruments with young children who have no disabilities (NAEYC, 1988). Such arguments are even more valid for young children with disabilities.

A more appropriate assessment model being described in the literature is dynamic assessment. **Dynamic assessment models** are concerned not with a child's current performance output, but rather with understanding learning styles and potential through careful observation of how children learn in a dynamic, interactive setting.

Also more appropriate are **authentic assessment strategies** which strive to obtain information from multiple sources (e.g., direct observation, parent report, child interviews, samples of the child's work, etc.). The argument is presented that young children cannot possibly be understood and appropriately described on the basis of a single, highly structured, performance-based test. Unfortunately, eligibility criteria in special education continue to require the use of standardized tests.

Clearly such issues will become increasingly important in the near future in the field of early childhood special education. Professionals must be prepared to assist in the transition to new models of assessment. Many assessment strategies mentioned in this chapter, including direct observation, family-based child assessment, arena assessment, and ecologically valid approaches can make major contributions to the development of new assessment models in early intervention.

Now that the factors to be considered carefully in determining children's strengths and needs have been reviewed, the next chapter will look specifically at the development of Individualized Education Programs and Individualized Family Service Plans.

Summary

Today there is a movement away from categorical descriptions of children with disabilities toward an analysis of specific instructional needs of the child. Typically a multistage process is involved that consists of (a) initial identification of children with problems, perhaps involving observational comparisons against a developmental checklist and screening for medically related problems; (b) diagnosis resulting in multidisciplinary staff development of an IEP; (c) teacher assessment, determining appropriate daily objectives and activities based on a developmental curriculum; and (d) evaluation of the child's progress on a continuous basis for the purpose of updating the child's program and periodically to review success of the overall program.

Several phases in the process of recognizing and accommodating a child's special needs require assistance of numerous specialists. But the early childhood teacher plays an instrumental role in the continuous success of the child's ef-

forts. To be successful at this, part of the teacher's role is to know what constitutes so-called "normal" behaviors. Armed with such knowledge, the teacher can then systematically observe for high-risk signals that might indicate the need for referral to specialized personnel or agencies. Guidelines and suggestions are given for how to strengthen this observational process.

Early childhood teachers should be particularly cautious when using standardized tests as part of the assessment process. Norm-referenced tests that compare a child's scores with norms established by groups of children of the same age may distort a child's capabilities if disabilities or unique needs are not considered. Criterion-referenced assessment compares a child's performance to a developmental standard or sequence of skills to be mastered. But increasingly, curriculum-based, teacher-developed techniques serve as the basis for assessment and evaluation.

This chapter emphasized that the ultimate responsibility for assessment, choice of daily objectives, and effective teaching remains with the teacher. This is a responsibility for which few teachers feel prepared. To become skilled in the techniques of observation, formal and informal testing, and programming, practice and patience are essential.

Finally, this chapter has attempted to clarify some of the ambiguities in the whole arena of evaluation, bring to light some of the critical concerns surrounding evaluative procedures, and encourage study and practice.

Discussion Topics and Activities

1. Differentiate identification, diagnosis, assessment, and evaluation. Give the purposes of each process.

2. Select or construct your own developmental rating scale. Observe at least two children. If possible,

observe a child suspected of having a disability and a child with no known deficits. Check and compare their performances according to your rating scale. Write a summary of the educational strengths and weaknesses you observed. Be certain you have parental permission, and observe all aspects of confidentiality.

3. Design a few informal assessment procedures that you can use to determine the educational strengths and weaknesses of a young child with disabilities. Note the behaviors you would look for in order for the procedure to be useful to you in writing plans for the child being assessed.

4. Differentiate norm-referenced and criterion-referenced tests, and give the advantages and disadvantages of each type of test.

5. Use the Buros *Mental Measurements Yearbook* to thoroughly research a commonly used assessment instrument such as the Peabody Picture Vocabulary Test or the Developmental Test of Visual-Motor Integration (VMI). Present a critique to your classmates. Be certain to research such important factors as reliability, validity, and the characteristics of the normative sample.

6. Role play techniques for developing rapport with a young child with disabilities.

Annotated Bibliography

Barnes, K. E. (1982). *Preschool screening: The measurement and prediction of children at-risk.* Springfield, IL: Charles C. Thomas.

This book is evenly divided between coverage of measurement issues and reviews of selected screening measures. Advanced students will appreciate the comprehensive treatment of measurement issues. The authors chose to review those screening measures that do not require professional administration, scoring, or interpretation. Rather, they focus on measures that have potential on a low-cost, large-scale basis administered by volunteers as well as professionals in the field.

Bailey, D. B., & Wolery, M. (1989). *Assessing infants and preschoolers with handicaps.* Columbus, OH: Merrill.

This comprehensive text addresses issues, considerations, and procedures in assessing infants and preschoolers with disabilities. It is intended for professionals who are responsible for designing and implementing individualized intervention programs for young children with special needs. It serves as a valuable resource for the variety of professionals who are requested to collaborate in meeting the special needs of young children and their families.

Compton, C. (1989). *A guide to 85 tests for special education.* Belmont, CA: Pitman.

This book is intended to be a resource for teachers who must interpret reports on children tested by other examiners. It describes the object, method, and meaning of each test. Reviews introduce the tests, give an overview of the format, and point out each test's basic strengths and limitations. One section focuses on preschool and kindergarten tests.

Conoley, J. C., & Kramer, J. J. (Eds.), 1990. *Tenth mental measurements yearbook.* Lincoln: University of Nebraska Press.

The purpose of these yearbooks is to present comprehensive reviews of a large variety of assessment instruments. Critical reviews from professionals both question and support claims made by test authors and publishers. Before using any instrument, these yearbooks should be consulted. Recent publications may not be included, whereas older tests may be found in previous editions of the yearbook.

Copeland, M. E., & Kimmel, J. R. (1989). *Evaluation and management of infants and young children with developmental disabilities.* Baltimore, MD: Paul H. Brookes.

This in-depth resource offers instruction to early interventionists in defining the roles they will play in developing successful interactions between children and their caregivers, teaching parents to use therapeutic techniques that will actively involve them in the treatment process, and identifying appropriate evaluation tools and management techniques for use with young learners. Students may find the specific sections on dressing, toileting, behavior management, physical transfers, and health/safety procedures to be particularly helpful.

Fallen, N. H., & Umansky, W. (1985). *Young children with special needs.* Columbus, OH: Merrill.

Of particular interest is the listing of numerous instruments ranging from those utilized in child-find programs to developmental/educational assessment. The purpose, appropriate age range, special characteristics and producer of each are detailed.

Garwood, S. G., et al. (Eds.). (1983). *Educating young handicapped children: A developmental approach*. Germantown, MD: Aspen Systems.

In addition to the provision of a strong theoretical background for the understanding of the relationship between normal developmental progress and the educational implications of disabling conditions, this book provides an annotated listing of many of the assessment measures currently in general use.

Keogh, B. K., & Daley, S. E. (1983). Early identification: One component of comprehensive services for at-risk children. *Topics in Early Childhood Special Education*, 3(3), 7–16.

This article is essential reading for anyone involved in the process of early identification. Of particular interest are the cautions surrounding screening. Six questions critical to a professional approach to early identification are posed and discussed. The argument that early identification must be viewed as a comprehensive set of services, not just a test or assessment procedure, should be uppermost in the minds of all who have at heart the interests of young children with special needs.

Lichtenstein, R., & Ireton, H. (1984). *Preschool screening*. Orlando, FL: Grune & Stratton.

This unique sourcebook covers such practical issues as program planning, personnel, screening procedures, and evaluation of screening outcomes. It also attends to screening objectives, historical trends, public policy, and an overview of relevant research. The listings and critical reviews of preschool screening instruments are most useful.

Linder, T. W. (1990). *Transdisciplinary play-based assessment: A functional approach to working with young children*. Baltimore, MD: Paul H. Brookes.

This intriguing book is intended to be a guide to a flexible new model for conducting assessment and intervention for children who are developmentally functioning between the ages of 6 months and 6 years. Intended for use by a transdisciplinary team, this book contains descriptive observation guidelines for assessing a young child's cognitive, social-emotional, communication, and sensorimotor development through child-directed play interactions. The requirement for parent participation results in a session that is less stressful for the child and less intimidating to the family.

Meisels, S. J. (1985). *Developmental screening in early childhood: A guide*. Washington, DC: National Association for the Education of Young Children.

The purpose of this book is to clarify some of the issues and practical components necessary for the design of an effective developmental screening program for young children. Critical decisions involved in planning the screening program, selecting instruments, and involving parents and the community are discussed. Included is an annotated bibliography of appropriate readings.

Paget, K. D., & Bracken, B. A. (1983). *The psychoeducational assessment of preschool children*. New York: Grune & Stratton.

Here is a book that finally recognizes preschool assessment as a separate entity, rather than an extension of school-age assessment. Preschool-aged children are treated as qualitatively different from both infants and older children. The advanced student will find this a useful reference covering all areas of development as well as special populations.

Robinson, C., & Fieber, N. (1988). Cognitive assessment of motorically impaired infants and preschoolers. In T. Wachs & R. Sheehan (Eds.), *Assessment of young developmentally disabled children*. New York: Plenum.

This chapter considers issues involved in and procedures available for the assessment of infants and preschoolers with motor impairments. Problems in the use of traditional approaches in assessment of motorically impaired young children are discussed thoroughly. The process approach is presented as an alternate assessment procedure for infants and toddlers with physical disabilities. Well-documented case studies illustrate the process.

Salvia, J., & Ysseldyke, J. E. (1985). *Assessment in special and remedial education*. Boston: Houghton Mifflin.

This text is an introduction to psychoeducational assessment in special and remedial education. It is an excellent resource for those who wish to gain a deeper understanding of testing in the broader context of assessment. Most of the major tests in use are described objectively. For each test, the general format, kinds of behaviors sampled, kinds of scores provided, nature of the standardization sample, and evidence of validity and reliability are described. Technical adequacy of various tests is evaluated.

Taylor, R. L. (1984). *Assessment of exceptional students*. Englewood Cliffs, NJ: Prentice-Hall.

This text serves as an excellent reference to what research has to say about a variety of norm-referenced instruments. The technical characteristics and conclusions from relevant research are presented for each instrument. One chapter is devoted to screening and readiness tests. Informal techniques of assessment, as well as the controversy over labeling, receive considerable attention.

Ulrey, G., & Rogers, S. J. (1982). *Psychological assessment of handicapped infants and young children.* New York: Thieme-Stratton.

"The purpose of this book is to present the information that psychologists need to evaluate young developmentally disabled children more accurately" (p. v.). However, other professionals will appreciate the wide variety of processes and techniques related to the assessment of atypical children. Those techniques most utilized by psychologists are discussed in detail. Of particular value is the focus on parent involvement and the complex and changing interactions of the child and the environment.

Assessment Within the Center or Classroom

Allen, K. E., & Marotz, L. (1989). *Developmental profiles: Birth to six.* New York: Delmar.

The purpose of this handbook is to provide a brief yet comprehensive guide to the development of young children from birth to 6 years of age. This is a nontechnical presentation intended to supplement a basic text on child development. Included are concise profiles of developmental areas, descriptions of daily activities and routines typical of children at each level, and appendixes containing growth charts, reflex schedules, and a sample health history form.

Beaty, J. J. (1990). *Observing development of the young child.* Columbus, OH: Merrill.

This attractive textbook offers students a method of observing and recording natural development of children ages 2 to 6. Its primary purpose is to teach nonspecialist observers to understand child development through the assistance of objective data gathered by observation in natural settings. Each of 12 chapters is devoted to a different aspect of development. A "Child Skills Checklist" made up of eight or nine specific items from each area systematically guides observations. Of particular value are the helpful intervention techniques given with each set of items to be observed.

Boehm, A. E., & Weinberg, R. A. (1987). *The classroom observer: Developing observation skills in early childhood settings.* NY: Teachers College Press.

This book focuses on skills that will enable early educators to make appropriate, valid inferences and to arrive at decisions based on objective observation gathered in natural learning environments and diverse educational settings.

Cohen, D. H., & Stern, V. (1983). *Observing and recording the behavior of young children* (3rd ed.) New York: Teachers College Press.

This book carefully presents and discusses the details of observing and recording while maintaining the quality of interaction. The reader is treated to a multitude of examples of what to look for and how to look for it throughout daily activities.

Lindberg, L., & Swedlow, R. (1980). *Early childhood education: A guide for observation and participation.* Boston: Allyn and Bacon.

Numerous worksheets are provided to focus attention on the specific components of an early childhood program. The content is arranged according to both the activities of a program and the curriculum areas of social studies, communication arts, mathematics, and science. Each section includes objectives, pretests, posttests, worksheets, and resource materials that give theoretical and practical background.

McCormack, J. E. (1976). The assessment tool that meets your needs: The one you construct. *Teaching Exceptional Children, 8,* 106–109.

This article presents a step-by-step process beginning with the identification of skills to be taught and ending with a pupil analysis sheet that allows the teacher to determine appropriate objectives for each child. An excellent example of an effective classroom assessment process is described and illustrated in this article.

Phinney, J. S. (1982). Observing children: Ideas for teachers. *Young Children, 37,* 16–24.

This article examines some of the most useful observational skills and suggests ways to develop these skills. The emphasis is on techniques that help teachers gain information on which to base immediate decisions on how to direct, guide, or teach young children. Strategies discussed include the running record or specimen description, time sampling, event sampling or anecdotal record, and the informal interview.

Sugai, G. (1986). Recording classroom events: Maintaining a critical incidents log. *Teaching Exceptional Children, 18,* 98–102.

This article contains a simple procedure for documenting critical classroom occurrences. The resulting log provides accurate and specific information about critical behaviors and events occurring in the classroom. It is the author's opinion that this systematic procedure can be extremely useful to professionals who may be called on to provide testimony in support of their instructional decisions.

References

Algozzine, B., Mercer, C., & Countermine, T. (1977). The effects of labels and behavior on teacher expectations. *Exceptional Children, 44*, 131–132.

Barnard, K. E., & Kelly, J. F. (1990). Assessment in parent-child interaction. In S. J. Meisels & J. P. Shonkoff (Eds.), *Handbook of early childhood intervention* (pp. 278–302). New York: Cambridge University Press.

Bayley, N. (1968). *Bayley infant scales of development.* New York: Psychological Corporation.

Bricker, D., & Veltman, M. (1990). Early intervention programs: Child-focused approaches. In S. J. Meisels & J. P. Shonkoff (Eds.), *Handbook of early childhood intervention* (pp. 373–427). New York: Cambridge University Press.

Burstein, N. D. (1986). The effects of classroom organization on mainstreamed preschool children. *Exceptional Children, 52*, 425–434.

Compton, C. (1989). *A guide to 85 tests for special education.* Belmont, CA: Pitman Learning.

Cross, L., & Goin, K. W. (Eds.). (1977). *Identifying handicapped children: A guide to casefinding, screening, diagnosis, assessment and evaluation.* New York: Walker.

Dreyer, A. S., & Haupt, D. (1966). Self-evaluation in young children. *Journal of Genetic Psychology, 2*, 185–197.

Dunn, L., & Dunn, L. (1981). *Peabody Picture Vocabulary Test—Revised.* Circle Pines, MN: American Guidance.

Frankenburg, W. (1973). Increasing the lead time for the preschool aged handicapped child. In J. B. Jordan & R. F. Dailey (Eds.), *Not all little wagons are red.* Arlington, VA: The Council for Exceptional Children..

Garwood, S. G., & Fewell, R. R. (1983). *Educating handicapped infants.* Rockville, MD: Aspen Systems.

Garwood, S. G., Alberto, P., DuBose, R. F., Hare, B. A., Hare, J. M., Kauffman, J., Kodera, T. L., Langley, M. B., & Page, D. A. (1979). *Educating young handicapped children.* Germantown, MD: Aspen Systems.

Gearheart, B. R., & Weishahn, M. W. (1984). *The exceptional student in the regular classroom.* Columbus, OH: Merrill.

Gesell, A. (1940). *The first five years of life.* New York: Harper & Row.

Hanson, M. J., & Lynch, E. W. (1989). *Early intervention: Implementing child and family services for infants and toddlers who are at-risk or disabled.* Austin, TX: Pro-Ed.

Hare, B. A., & Hare, J. M. (1977). *Teaching young handicapped children: A guide for preschool and the primary grades.* New York: Grune & Stratton.

Keogh, B. (1977). Research on cognitive styles. In R. D. Kneedler & S. G. Tarver (Eds.), *Changing perspectives in special education.* Columbus, OH: Merrill.

Keogh, B., & Becker, L. D. (1973). Early detection of learning problems: Questions, cautions, and guidelines. *Exceptional Children, 40*, 5–11.

Lynch, E., Mendoza, J., & English, K. (1990, April). *Implementing individualized family service plans in California.* Final Report, Submitted to California Department of Developmental Services.

Meisels, S. J., & Wasik, B. A. (1990). Who should be served? Identifying children in need of early intervention. In S. J. Meisels & J. P. Shonkoff (Eds.), *Handbook of early childhood intervention* (pp. 605–632). New York: Cambridge University Press.

National Association for the Education of Young Children. (1988). Position statement on standardized testing of young children 3 through 8 years of age. *Young Children, 43*, 42–47.

Paget, K. D., & Bracken, B. A. (1983). *The psychoeducational assessment of preschool children.* New York: Grune & Stratton.

Peterson, N. L., & Meier, J. L. (1987). Assessment and evaluation processes. In N. L. Peterson, (Ed.), *Early intervention for handicapped and at-risk children* (pp. 275–326). Denver: Love Publishing.

Rogers-Warren, A. K. (1982). Behavioral ecology in classrooms for young handicapped children. *Topics in Early Childhood Special Education, 2*, 21–32.

Safford, P. L. (1989). *Integrated teaching in early childhood.* White Plains, NY: Longman.

Salisbury, C., & Vincent, L. (1990). Criterion of the next environment and best practices: Mainstreaming and integration ten years later. *Topics in Early Childhood Special Education, 10*, 78–79.

Salvia, J., & Ysseldyke, J. E. (1978). *Assessment in special and remedial education.* Boston: Houghton Mifflin.

Salvia, J., & Ysseldyke, J. E. (1985). *Assessment in special and remedial education. 3rd ed.* Boston: Houghton Mifflin.

Shea, T. M., & Bauer, A. M. (1991). *Parents and teachers of children with exceptionalities: A handbook for collaboration.* Boston: Allyn and Bacon.

Smith, C. R. (1983). *Learning disabilities: The interaction of learner, task and setting.* Boston: Little, Brown.

Stevens Dominguez, M., Beam, G., & Thomas, P.

(1989). *Guide for family-centered services.* Albuquerque: University of New Mexico.

Stoneman, Z., & Gibson, S. (1978). Situational influences on assessment performance. *Exceptional Children, 45,* 166–169.

Thurman, S. K., & Widerstrom, A. H. (1990). *Infants and young children with special needs: A developmental and ecological approach* (2nd ed.). Baltimore, MD: Paul H. Brookes.

Ulrey, G., & Rogers, S. J. (1982). *Psychological assessment of handicapped infants and young children.* New York: Thieme-Stratton.

Uzgiris, I., & Hunt, J. M. (1975). *Assessment in infancy: Ordinal scales of psychological development.* Urbana: University of Illinois Press.

Widerstrom, A. H., Mowder, B. A., & Sandall, S. R. (1991). *At-risk and handicapped newborns and infants.* Englewood Cliffs, NJ: Prentice Hall.

Chapter 5

Developing Individualized Intervention Programs and Plans

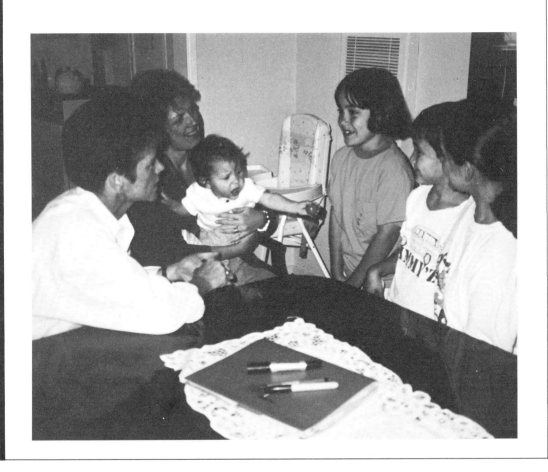

Key Points

▶ An Individualized Education Program (IEP) must be developed for each child based on assessment information gathered through a variety of processes.

▶ Program planning must be carried out by an interdisciplinary team that includes the parents as members.

▶ P.L. 99-457 requires that an Individualized Family Service Plan (IFSP) be generated for families of infants and toddlers. The IFSP differs from the IEP in that it contains family goals in addition to child goals.

▶ The IFSP document itself is not as important as the process of generating the program plan.

▶ The role of the early childhood special education professional is to determine the concerns, priorities, and resources of families, not to diagnose needs or "weaknesses."

▶ An important part of program planning for any child is careful consideration of how transition to the next educational environment will be carried out.

Key Topics

▶ Developing the Individualized Education Program (IEP).

▶ The Individualized Family Service Plan (IFSP).

▶ Transition practices.

The previous chapter introduced some of the major issues surrounding the processes of identification, diagnosis, assessment, and evaluation. Attention was given to preparing early childhood special education teachers for their primary role as astute observers of children's behavior. The options available for assessment within the classroom or center were discussed. This chapter explains and illustrates the Individualized Education Program (IEP) and Individualized Family Service Plan (IFSP) processes.

BEFORE ACTIVITY PLANNING CAN BEGIN: THE IEP

Current federal guidelines require children who will receive any special education services to be

seen for a diagnostic study by members of a multidisciplinary team before services can begin. They do not specify the professionals to be included. However, it is expected that choice of the members for a specific team will be determined by the characteristics and suspected disabling conditions of a particular child. For example, in all cases of suspected speech and/or language delays, the child should be seen by a speech-language pathologist. This pathologist should also be present at the subsequent meeting or "staffing," at which time the IEP is developed. Other people who attend this meeting include the following:

1. Any member of the school staff, other than the child's teacher, who is "qualified to provide, or supervise the provision of, specially

designed instruction to meet the unique needs of handicapped children" (P.L. 94-142, Sec. 602[19]).

2. At least one teacher, special or regular, who will implement the child's IEP.

3. One or both of the child's parents.

4. The child, when appropriate.

5. Other individuals whose expertise may be desired by the parent or school.

6. A member of the diagnostic team or a representative who is knowledgeable about the evaluation procedures used with the child and is familiar with the results of the evaluation.

For example, Danny's IEP conference members would include his preschool teacher and the speech-language pathologist who had evaluated him (pp. 151 to 159). His parents and another member of the school staff, qualified to provide or supervise needed services, would be present. If a nurse had done part of the evaluation, he or she would also be present.

The Multidisciplinary Diagnostic Team

The **multidisciplinary diagnostic team,** including the parents as valid members, considers the child's current educational needs. Priorities are chosen. **Goals** are specified and **behavioral objectives** written for each goal.

Referring Professional's Preparation. In preparation for the multidisciplinary staffing, Ms. McLynn would write observations of Danny in several different settings and circumstances. She would summarize any information gained from informal or formal classroom assessment and gather relevant samples of Danny's work. She must be prepared to give evidence of Danny's present level of classroom functioning. A copy of

the referral form she had completed earlier on Danny would be included in her preparation file. Questions based on her concerns should be prepared. These might include the following:

1. Sometimes he seems to hear us and at other times we get the feeling he doesn't want to pay attention. Does his hearing change from time to time?

2. He seems to pay more attention to a man's voice than to a woman's. Why is this?

3. It is very difficult to understand Danny. He can't be deaf. He loves to sing, and he keeps on pitch as well as the others do. But his speech is nearly unintelligible. Why is this?

4. If we show him how to do something, he is quick to learn. Why is he so slow when we tell him what to do?

Ms. McLynn would be ready to present any information she has about Danny, and she would be prepared to answer any questions other team members would have. Of course, she would have obtained a signed "release of information" from Danny's parents. She would also plan to report any intervention she has already tried with Danny, including any special materials or methods. For example, when Ms. McLynn worked with Danny alone, he seemed to do much better. She also found that Danny had difficulty following musical records with directions. He could, however, follow the same directions when she sang them.

Finally, Ms. McLynn would be prepared to state as clearly as possible exactly what she needs to know to instruct Danny appropriately. Her prepared questions will help her gain the information she needs. Having her questions and concerns written down ahead of time will help her to be certain that no important consideration is overlooked. Professionals must actively seek all the information they feel necessary for the planning and implementation of the services listed on the IEP form. The professional's responsibility in this role cannot be overemphasized.

Specialists' Preparation. Whenever possible, the specialists who evaluate young children ask to see observations made by others, including teachers and parents. Many use a questionnaire to elicit information relevant to their particular field before they begin formal testing. Often a screening test is used as a preliminary to in-depth evaluations.

Each specialist will choose test instruments judged to be relevant to the suspected problems. During the diagnosis it may become apparent that additional tests are needed. If one specialist obtains information that suggests that additional specialists need to be included in the multidisciplinary diagnostic team, it is his or her responsibility to request the necessary additional diagnosis. The chairperson of the staffing in which the IEP is developed is the person referred to in the law as the "representative of the local educational agency . . . who shall be qualified to provide, or supervise the provision of, specially designed instruction" (P.L. 94-142, Sec. 602 [19]). This person may be responsible for collecting all assessment information and being certain that no important aspect of the diagnostic process is overlooked. Specialists must be prepared to relate test results, their level of confidence in the child's performance, and recommendations for placement and services to the chairperson. They should make every possible effort to translate their findings into information directly useful to program and activity planning.

When participating in the multidisciplinary staffing, professionals should be prepared to speak in language that parents understand. They must remember that parents, as well as professionals, are to be included as active, vital members of the team.

Parents' Preparation. Parents will be expected to organize any information they have received

from previous examiners. They have the responsibility of honestly and accurately sharing information about their child's behavior and perceived strengths and concerns. Parents serve as the child's advocate.

Professionals can be very helpful in assisting parents to prepare information they wish to share as well as in developing a list of questions to be asked of specialists. Parents should be given any assistance they need to fully understand the program and services being proposed. In some cases translators or multilingual specialists will have to be included as part of the multidisciplinary team. It is especially important for professionals to understand exactly which intervention goals are important to each child's parents. A questionnaire or interview asking parents to identify those skills that they would *most* like to see their child accomplish in the coming year, behaviors that would reduce stress in the family, increase independence, and so on, is an effective way to ensure parents' *active participation* in selecting and prioritizing goals for their children. Parents' goals should take highest priority on the list of objectives to be achieved. For example, the parent may think the child's becoming independent in feeding is more important than making eye contact with the staff. It is more important that the child be accepted by significant others throughout the day than by those who work with the child at preschool. While professionals tend to feel that they know what is most important for the child to learn and achieve, the needs and desires of the parents should take precedence whenever realistically possible. Initial understanding and genuine acceptance by parents of services to be offered can save many hours of discussion or even the necessity of changes later on.

Sending home a rough draft of goals and objectives for the family to review and react to *prior* to the IEP meeting is another way to solicit active parent participation in setting priorities. This approach may also help to relieve parental anxiety.

EXHIBIT 5–1

A Child Care Center Where Children with Special Needs Are Welcomed

Until recently many public and private child care centers were reluctant to accept children with special needs. They said that they were neither trained nor equipped to help them. Other centers accepted children with disabilities but simply took care of their physical needs.

Ms. Johnson and Ms. McLynn want to provide the best possible services for the children with special needs who come to their center. They begin by listening carefully to the parents' requests and descriptions of their children. Then they observe the children in their preschool environment.

These teachers find the following sequence helpful:

1. Before a child is enrolled, parents meet with the director and the teacher. Information, parent concerns, and available services are considered. The enrollment form includes questions about previous experiences as well as a health history. The child's developmental level is discussed.

2. For the first few weeks the child is observed throughout the day. Special needs are identified. Ms. McLynn and Ms. Johnson discuss these with the parents at a second conference.

3. During this second conference recommendations are made to the parents about where and how to find special educators and other trained personnel to evaluate the child's needs, if this seems appropriate.

4. After a child has been evaluated and recommendations for intervention services and procedures have been received at an IEP conference, Ms. McLynn and Ms. Johnson incorporate the suggestions and activities into the child's daily program.

5. Regular contact with parents and others working with the children is maintained through telephone conversations, conferences, and written reports.

This child care center includes several children with disabilities during each session. If these children require a great deal of extra time and attention, an additional aide is provided. In some cases parents are required to pay for this service in addition to the tuition. Where federal and state money provide for the education of very young children, parents are not expected to pay.

Today this child care center and others accept the challenge of including children with special needs. Wise teachers refuse to merely "love and take care of children." They are aware that the most critical years for learning occur before the traditional school entrance age of 5 or 6. As a result, they cooperate with parents and involved professionals by including children with special needs in their centers. They are careful to meet individual needs appropriately.

THE CASE OF DANNY

The following narrative gives insight into the background and proceedings of one child's multidisciplinary conference.

Background Information

Danny's parents are worried. Twice they have been asked to withdraw him from child care centers. Now the private preschool that he has been attending has called them in for a conference. Both parents work, and they want the best possible placement for Danny. Several friends have told them that they know he would not be accepted in the public school kindergarten next year. He rarely talks, and when he does, it is very difficult to understand him. He is also stubborn. Many times when they tell him to do something, he acts as if he does not hear them unless they yell at him. They have heard that he would be placed in a special education class if they took him to a public school. They are frightened.

October 21, 1991. Danny has now been enrolled in a private preschool for 3 weeks. Ms. McLynn and Ms. Johnson are anxious to discuss their observations with Danny's parents, the Dicksons.

Ms. Johnson: Thank you for coming. We are enjoying Danny and hope he is enjoying us. We have observed Danny in a variety of situations and would like to discuss our observations with you.

Mrs. Dickson: We are so pleased that Danny is coming to your program. We are grateful for the help you have given Danny and are anxious to hear about how he is doing.

Ms. Johnson: Well, as you know, it is sometimes difficult for us to understand what Danny is saying, and it seems that often he doesn't understand us. When we try to tell him to do something, he just seems so confused. We can get him to pay attention by standing in front of him and talking directly to him. He also seems to have trouble with the names of things like colors and body parts.

Mrs. Dickson: We have also noticed some of the things you are talking about. His pediatrician examined him, as you suggested, and he said he is fine. He told us that many children don't learn to speak clearly until they are in school. He said that we could take him to the public school and they might give him speech therapy. However, he had heard that they don't begin therapy until second grade, because most children outgrow their baby talk.

Mr. Dickson: Our friends the Joneses have a little girl who the psychologist said is very slow. She doesn't talk clearly either, and they put her in a special class. We really don't want Danny put in a class with children who have problems or can't learn. Danny isn't dumb.

Ms. McLynn: I agree with you, Mr. Dickson. Danny isn't dumb. But something is wrong. He misunderstands us most of the time, and we can't understand him. He doesn't know the names of lots of things the others know.

Ms. Johnson: We feel that we aren't helping Danny enough. He needs special kinds of help that we aren't trained to provide. We are hoping that you will agree to have specialists test Danny to help us find the best ways to work with him. There is a new law that requires the public schools to give children special tests and to provide a free, appropriate education for any child who needs specialized help. Danny could

attend the local public school. Or, if you would like, he could also come to our program for part of the day. Transportation is provided. We will be happy to work with his teacher at the public school and with you in any way that we can. Before any decisions are made about how best to educate Danny, you will receive the test results and can ask questions. In fact, you are supposed to be totally involved in any decisions that are made. In other words, agreeing to let Danny be tested doesn't mean he will have to be in a special program. What do you think?

Mr. Dickson: I'm not sure. Are you sure that Danny needs all of this help? We can understand him.

Ms. Johnson: Yes, I believe you can understand Danny. He does the most difficult puzzles easily and builds wonderful towns with blocks. We would just like to find out what is causing Danny's problems and how we should be working with him. Why don't you think about finding out what educational possibilities are available. You can visit any classrooms that might be suitable. You will get to make any final decisions.

Mr. Dickson: Okay. Who do we call?

As Mr. and Mrs. Dickson left the preschool, they still felt somewhat frightened. Mrs. Dickson remembered that one preschool teacher had said her son had a "dull expression" and another said that he seemed "bewildered." But when they spoke to friends and relatives, they all reassured them that Danny was just a late bloomer. In spite of their fears, they did call their local public school office, and an appointment for a diagnostic interview was made. They had to sign papers to release information from the preschool and to confirm that they agreed to the testing.

January 15, 1992. A multidisciplinary team staffing conference is in progress at the Special Education Office. In addition to Danny's teacher from the private preschool and his parents, a school psychologist, nurse, social worker, speech-language pathologist, and supervisor of special education are present. The supervisor has reviewed the background information.

Supervisor: So, you see, on the basis of these tests, it appears that Danny would be eligible for placement in our early childhood special education class.

Mrs. Dickson: What kinds of children are in this special education class?

Supervisor: Well, lots of kinds. They are all between the ages of 3 and 5. One wears very thick glasses, another walks with a brace, and two don't talk very well. The little boy with the brace is already reading. Why don't you come to visit the class? I think you will be surprised at how friendly the children are and how much they are learning. Some even spend part of their day in the kindergarten.

Mr. Dickson: I am eager to hear what the psychologist has to say.

Psychologist: Danny worked very hard and seemed to want to try everything. Because Danny seemed to understand so little speech and language, and I had a hard time understanding him, I gave him two kinds of tests. Well, really three. First, I tried a vocabulary test. For that test, I show pictures and name them. All Danny had to do was point to the picture that I named. There are four pictures on each page, and only one is correct. On that test, Danny responded by naming or pointing to a few pictures correctly. He often seemed confused. He couldn't identify as many pictures as most children his age. Then, I attempted to use a standardized intelligence test that requires Danny to listen to me and answer questions and point to things, too. Again, he was unable to do most of the items that other 4 year olds can do. So, next I used a nonverbal performance test. On this test, Danny had to listen to only a few directions and did not have to talk to me. He did have to watch me carefully, and then imitate some of the things I did. And here he was more successful. He seemed to enjoy these activities. His confused expression disappeared and he looked more interested. Danny was able to match the colors very well. He could do difficult puzzles, complete copying designs, and put pattern pieces together. When he finished, he grinned at me and seemed to want to do more.

Ms. McLynn: That's the way he is at school, too. He can color and draw better than most of the other children. He is quick to learn how to make things.

Speech-Language Pathologist: When I evaluated his speech and language, I observed that he has all of the "music of speech" when he talks but few of the right speech sounds.

Mr. Dickson: What is music of speech?

Speech-Language Pathologist: One of the first things babies learn to do as they are learning to talk is to imitate the way we raise and lower our voices to signal statements or questions. At first, if you listen to babies about 9 or 10 months old, it almost sounds as if they are talking, but there are no words. You can year the rising pitch at the end of their "sentences," and it really sounds like questions some of the time. We call those pitch changes *suprasegmental aspects* or *prosodic features.*

Mr. Dickson: Now that you mention it, I've noticed that music too. But you can't understand what he's saying when he is making those sounds.

Speech-Language Pathologist: Right. By themselves, those pitch changes aren't enough. My tests indicate that Danny says most of the vowels correctly, although the short vowels as in p*i*n, p*a*n, p*e*n, and p*u*n aren't distinct. He can imitate the voiced consonants, for example, /b/, /d/, /g/, /m/, and /n/, and he uses them in some words but he often omits them on the ends of words. He says ba*w* for ba*ll* and d*aw* for d*og*, for example. When he tries to make sentences, he leaves off /s/, /t/, and /z/ at the ends of words, so he cannot "signal" past tense as in hopp*ed* and look*ed*. He doesn't use plurals, as in car*s* and truck*s*. Notice when you say "hopped," you are putting a /t/ sound on the end, even though we write the letter *d*. When you say "balls" you are using a /z/, even though we spell it with an *s*. He doesn't say /p/, /t/, or /k/ in any words, so of course it is impossible to understand him.

When I asked him to listen to me say a sentence and point to the picture that showed what I had said, he was really confused. One picture page has a little boy looking into a mirror seeing himself and another picture where he is looking at a shelf. Danny had no idea what I wanted him to do. When I said "He sees himself," he pointed to both pictures. Also, I recorded more than 50 things that he said while we played with some cars and trucks and a toy garage. He really enjoyed that. When I analyzed what he said, I found that he is using three- and four-word sentences, although the words are not clear. He tried to ask me for things, too.

Nurse: Danny responded very quickly and accurately to my vision screening test. I showed him just once what I wanted him to do. He was all business, paid close attention, and quickly demonstrated that he has good eyesight. But the hearing testing was another story! He wiggled and giggled. He said he heard the tones when the audiometer was off. At 25 decibels, the loudness level used for hearing screening, he heard 500 and 1000 Hertz in one ear, but he did not respond to the same loudness at higher frequencies. In the other ear, he did not answer correctly at all at 25 decibels. So, I referred him to our speech and hearing center for a complete hearing evaluation with more sophisticated equipment. The audiologist, a specialist in evaluating hearing and recommending needed remediation, reported that Danny exhibited a precipitous high frequency sensorineural hearing loss in one ear and a mild conductive loss in the other ear. The audiologist said that Danny's problems understanding speech and learning to talk could be explained on the basis of his hearing problems alone. He recommended that Danny be seen by an otologist, an ear specialist, to determine the causes of the hearing loss. He said that it was possible that Danny might benefit from a hearing aid. Efforts to correct the hearing loss should be made first.

Speech-Language Pathologist: Danny has problems hearing the difference between the high frequency sounds in particular. He had trouble with other auditory processing tasks, too.

Mr. Dickson: But if he can't hear, how come he can hear us when he wants to? He can be sitting in front of the TV and just pay no attention when I tell him something. But if I get angry, he jumps right away.

Speech-Language Pathologist: When you get angry, you probably speak louder, and your tone of voice changes.

Mr. Dickson: You bet it does.

Speech-Language Pathologist: He can hear those changes, because the vowels are in the lower frequencies, and he hears them almost as you and I do. He can hear the change in your tone of voice for the same reason. What he cannot hear is the consonants. All those years he must have been hearing things with the most important parts missing. For instance, with the reported hearing loss he hears "Come to supper" as "um oo u er."

Mrs. Dickson: Why, that is exactly what he says when he tells someone it is time to eat!

Speech-Language Pathologist: So, you see, he has been saying what he has been hearing.

Mrs. Dickson: But he has only had one earache, and it didn't last long. His nose "runs" a lot, but he is never sick. He does have lots of allergies, though.

Nurse: Often children don't complain about mild earaches. You will want to check with your pediatrician to be sure that his ears are okay now.

Speech-Language Pathologist: But even if his ears are perfect now, his speech won't be cleared up right away. You see, it is as if he has been looking through smeary glasses that really were not right for his eyes. Everything he has heard has been distorted and incorrect. Now, he has learned to say many things the wrong way, and he will have to learn to talk all over again in the right way.

Mr. Dickson: So what do we do now?

Ms. McLynn: Is there someone who can help us to teach him what he needs to know? We really want to help Danny.

Speech-Language Pathologist: My suggestion would be that he attend the special education class in our school each day for 2 1/2 hours. During that time I can work with him regularly. I'll give his teacher many special activities to help him to learn in spite of his hearing loss. He can learn to use his hearing better, and he can learn to supplement what he hears through lipreading.

Mrs. Dickson: But we both work. We need to have him in the right place all day.

Psychologist: Could he attend the special class in the morning and go to your preschool in the afternoon, Ms. McLynn?

Ms. McLynn: Could someone teach us, too?

Supervisor: Yes, we could arrange for you to visit the special class and talk with his teacher and the speech pathologist. They could suggest special ways of helping him while he is at your school. We can include that in his IEP if you wish.

Mrs. Dickson: That would be a great help to us. We really do think Danny can learn.

Psychologist: You are right, even though all of his test scores that include understanding or using languages are very low. The important clue is that when the tests did not require him to understand what I *said* or to talk to me, he was able to score well within the normal range.

Mr. Dickson: I'm ashamed for all of the times I've spanked him for not listening. But he always heard his brother's motorcycle when he was half a block away. And he was always the first to run outside to look for jet planes. He loves the hi-fi and sings right along with the tunes. You are telling me he can hear all that but not hear the speech sounds like /p/ and /t/?

Speech-Language Pathologist: Right. And I can teach him how to make those sounds and to recognize them when he sees them on people's lips, even if his hearing doesn't improve. Of course, we will expect that it will.

Psychologist: You may be disappointed with yourselves, but remember, very few parents discover this kind of problem themselves. That is why the federal law encourages local school districts to test *all* children by age 3.

Ms. McLynn: We've noticed he seems to hear a man's voice best. Should he be placed in a man's class?

Speech-Language Psychologist: Not necessarily. But it will be helpful if you speak more slowly and in shorter sentences. Be close to Danny, and be sure that you have his attention before you tell him something. Avoid having sources of bright light such as a window behind you when you talk to him. He will need to see your lips and mouth. Even though he is not dependent on lipreading, he will be taught to use visual as well as auditory clues. If the light is in his eyes, it is harder to see your lip movements.

Ms. McLynn: What about the singing times?

Speech-Language Pathologist: By all means include him, but if you use records, be sure you sing along with them. He needs to see your lips as well as hear the sounds.

Ms. McLynn: What should we do when we don't understand Danny?

Speech-Language Pathologist: Use all the situational cues available. Sometimes tell him to tell you again. If you still don't understand, ask him to show you. Encourage him to use gestures. When you do understand, let your face show your pleasure. Then, say what Danny was trying to say. Look expectant. Be pleased if he repeats your model, but don't insist. Make no corrections of his articulation at this time. You are striving to motivate him to talk more and to keep trying.

After the discussion, the members of the multidisciplinary team wrote the IEP that is illustrated in Figure 5–1. His parents agreed that it was an excellent plan. They were grateful for the care with which everyone had evaluated Danny. They felt that the specific suggestions met his needs very well.

Some weeks later Danny's parents were happy to report that the runny nose and the fluid in Danny's middle ear that had apparently caused much of his hearing problem had been taken care of, although the high frequency hearing loss in one ear had been described to them as a sensorineural loss. The otologist (a physician who specializes in problems with ears) and the audiologist (a specialist trained to evaluate hearing and assist with the choice of hearing aids) had explained to them that Danny would benefit from wearing a hearing aid in the ear with the high frequency loss. Mr. Jones, the audiologist, explained that unless people can hear with both ears, they cannot tell where sounds are coming from until they see the source. In addition, conversations or the teacher's voice would be distorted and difficult to understand unless Danny had his "good ear" toward the speaker. People need two ears for effective listening. This is particularly important for young children. These specialists told Danny's parents that in the past they could not have suggested amplification for a high frequency loss, but in the 1970s technical improvements in hearing aid design as well as new techniques for making ear molds made it possible to fit children like Danny with hearing aids.

The audiologist explained that Danny would not suddenly begin to speak distinctly, nor would he respond to everything that he heard. That would take time, patience, and special education. He also showed Danny's parents how to care for the hearing aid, test its functioning, and adjust it properly. Then he talked about helping Danny learn to use and enjoy his new aid. He explained that they should begin gradually, letting him wear it in quiet places and for a short time at first. Later, Mr. and Mrs. Dickson laughed as they told Ms. McLynn that once Danny had his new hearing aid, he did not want to take it off. They were grateful, because some children find the adjustment difficult.

Required Contents of the IEP

The IEP is a written plan that must contain the following elements:

1. A statement of the child's present levels of educational performance (based on results of norm-referenced and criterion-referenced tests).

2. A statement of annual goals and related short-term behavioral objectives.

3. A statement of the specific special education and related services to be provided to the child.

4. The extent to which the child will be able to participate in regular education programs.

INDIVIDUALIZED EDUCATIONAL PROGRAM

I. STUDENT INFORMATION
Date   Jan. 15, 1992

Student name   Dickson   Danny   R.   Sex   M
                         Last   First   Initial   Grade placement   M-F

Birth date   June 6, 1976   Parents   John and Mary Dickson   Phone 463-9546
                    Mo Day Yr

Address   61 Lakeside Road   Lincoln   Zip   69745
                        Street   City

District of residence   Lincoln   Receiving school/agency   Lincoln

II. MEDICAL INFORMATION

A. Vision screening _____ Nov. 5, 1991 _____ Ms. Land, R.N. _____ Passed
                              Mo   Day   Yr   Examiner   Results
B. Hearing screening _____ Nov. 5, 1991 _____ Ms. Land, R.N. _____ Failed
                              Mo   Day   Yr   Examiner   Results

Comments _____ Failed screening at 25 db. Referred to Speech & Hearing Center

III. LEVEL OF CURRENT PERFORMANCE
(Based on achievement, diagnostic, and criterion-referenced testing and teacher observation.)

A. Achievement

   Spelling level   *Pretest*   ~~Posttest~~   *Date*

   Math level   ~~Pretest~~ not appropriate   *Posttest*   *Date*

   Reading level   *Pretest*   *Posttest*   *Date*

B. Mental ability   *Test*   *Date*
   MA 3-0   IQ 65   (CA 4-6)   Stanford-Binet   Nov. 25, 1991
   Perf.   IQ 92   Wechsler Preschool and Primary Scale

C. Psychomotor   *Test*   *Date*
   VMI age 4-4   Beery-Buktenica Test of Visual Motor   Nov. 25, 1991
                                  Integration (VMI)

D. Social behavior   *Test*   *Date*
   As reported by parents, age   Teacher observation   Nov. 5, 1991
   appropriate, except for severe
   tantrums

E. Speech-language   *Test*   *Date*
   Articulation—multiple   Goldman-Fristoe Articulation   Nov. 13, 1991
   omissions and substitutions
   Language age—approximately   Environmental Language Inventory
   30 mo.

F. Other (Self-help, vocational, etc.)
   Self-help—superior for age

IV. PROGRAM ELIGIBILITY *(Check appropriate item[s].)*

[ ] A. EMH	[x] E. Speech impaired (SI)	[ ] J. Deaf-blind (DB)
[ ] B. THM	[x] F. Visually impaired (VI)	[ ] K. Physical handicap (PH)
[ ] C. BD	[ ] G. Autistic (AUT)	[ ] L. Educational handicap (EH)
[ ] D. LD	[ ] H. Deaf (D)	[ ] M. Early childhood (EC)
	[x] I. Hard of hearing (HH)	[x] N. Other (specify)

Figure 5–1 (pp. 156–159)   An example of an IEP.

Student name <u>Dickson,   Danny   R.</u>
                      Last   *First*   *Initial*

V. PROGRAM PLACEMENT *(Enter information in columns following listing.)*

	Date	Duration	Extent of participation in percentages
A. Waiting list			
B. Regular class			
C. Regular class with consulting	2/1	90 days	50% (2½ hours daily)
D. Regular class with supplementary intervention			
E. Regular class with rest room			
F. Part-time special class	2/1	90 days	50% (2½ hours daily)
G. Full-time special class			
H. Residential school			
I. Special day school			
J. Hospital school			
K. Hospital-treatment center			
L. Alternative school			
M. Homebound			

VI. SUPPORTIVE SERVICES *(Enter item[s] in columns following listing.)*

	Date	Duration	Extent of participation in percentages
A. Counseling	2/1	90 days	Weekly – 1 hour
B. Individual psychological counseling			
C. Group psychological counseling			
D. Speech therapy	2/1	90 days	Consulting and individual
E. Occupational therapy			
F. Hearing aid evaluation			
G. Adaptive physical education			
H. Regular physical education			
I. Parent-infant education			
J. Remedial reading			
K. Social work			
L. Braille-large print			
M. Orientation-mobility			
N. Adaptive equipment			
O. Barrier-free environment			
P. Diagnostics			
Q. Physical therapy			
R. Audiological therapy	2/1	90 days	Consulting – evaluation only
S. Hearing therapy	2/1	90 days	Consulting – twice weekly
T. Vision therapy			
U. Physically disabled-mentally disabled			
V. Behavior therapy			
W. Supportive materials			
X. Other (specify)			

Figure 5–1 (Continued)

p. 3

Student name   <u>Dickson,   Danny   R.</u>
                Last   First   Initial

Primary language   <u>English</u>

VII. IEP TEAM

> Mrs. L. Wilson, Supervisor
>
> Mrs. N. Hess, Speech-language pathologist
>
> Ms. A. Neff, Social worker
>
> Ms. C. Land, Nurse
>
> Mr. B. Decker, School psychologist
>
> Ms. McLynn, Preschool teacher

VIII. REVIEW SCHEDULE

> [ ] A. 30 days   [X] C. 90 days 1st review
>
> [ ] B. 60 days   [X] D. Annual

IX. ASSESSMENT CRITERIA

> Review for appropriateness of of plan after 90 days. Review again after 1 year

X. ANNUAL GOALS (CHILD)

> A. To develop attention and concentration skills.
>
> B. To improve expressive language skills.
>
> C. To develop the ability to imitate speech sounds.
>
> D. To increase vocabulary.
>
> E. To improve articulation of phonemes and syllables.
>
> F. To reduce temper tantrums.

XI. ANNUAL GOALS (FAMILY)

> A. To gain a better understanding of Danny's hearing and speech problems.
>
> B. To learn to utilize strategies for facilitating Danny's speech and receptive language skills at home.
>
> C. To learn how to deal with Danny's temper tantrums.

XII. PARENT CONSENT

> *I have been involved in the preparation of this individual plan and*
>
> [X] *I am in agreement with it.*
>
> [ ] *I disagree with its contents.*
>
> *I realize that this is an educational plan and not a binding legal contract.*
>
> *John Dickson   Mary Dickson*
> Signature of parent(s) guardian(s)

Figure 5–1   (Continued)

p. 4

Student name <u>Dickson,   Danny   R.</u>
                  Last   First   Initial

XII. SUMMARY OF SERVICES RECOMMENDED BY THE MULTIDISCIPLINARY TEAM AT THE IEP CONFERENCE, JAN. 15, 1992

Because Danny's parents both work, they need him to be cared for throughout the day. The early childhood special education class maintains a daily program for 2½ hours each day. As a result, it was decided to plan Danny's day as follows:

AM: The school bus will pick Danny up at his home at 8:50 and take him to the public school near his home for a 2½-hour session. His program will include all of the planned curriculum appropriate to his present level of performance, as well as the specific goals and objectives in his IEP. Each week he will receive two 20-minute speech and language lessons with three other children. In addition, the speech-language pathologist will plan and monitor a developmental speech and language program at both his preschool center and the special education class. This pathologist will also provide guidance to his teachers and parents with regard to his special needs as a child with mild hearing impairment.

PM: The preschool center will pick Danny up at his public school at 11:30 each day. He will be served luncheon at that center. After a nap time, he will participate in the activities at the center. The speech-language pathologist will be available for consultation with Danny's teachers there. Twice each month, Danny's special education teacher will contact the preschool center for consultation. Teachers from the preschool center will visit the special education class to observe Danny after 1 month.

XIII. INSTRUCTIONAL OBJECTIVES FOR ANNUAL GOALS INCLUDING EVALUATION CRITERIA AND DATE

A. Given a two-stage direction in one utterance, Danny will (1) attend to the speaker, (2) wait until directions are completed, and (3) do the activities in the order presented within 1 minute.

B. During a 30-minute activity period Danny will converse with the teacher or another child at least five times. He will use three- or four-word sentences. The conversation will fit the situation and be spontaneous, not directed.

C. When the teacher models a sentence for Danny, he will imitate her, using the same number of syllables (up to four syllables) and with partially intelligible articulation.

D. When shown five pictures in each of five categories—(1) clothing, (2) toys, (3) foods, (4) transportation, and (5) furniture—Danny will name them correctly, with no more than one error within each category.

E. During a structured speech lesson, Danny will imitate the teacher's production of all vowels and these consonants in isolation and syllables: /p/, /t/, /k/, /f/, /m/, /b/, /d/, and /g/.

F. During a 30-minute play period, Danny will not have any temper tantrums. During the complete school day, he will have no more than one outburst of anger.

Figure 5–1   (Continued)

5. The supporting services needed within the regular program.

6. The projected dates for initiation of services and the anticipated duration of services.

7. The appropriate objective criteria and evaluation procedures.

8. The schedules for determining whether the short-term instructional objectives are being achieved (each child's program must be evaluated at least once each year).

Although the precise written format may differ from area to area, the required content must be included. Figure 5–1 is an example of a typical IEP report form.

Purposes and Limitations of the IEP

The **annual goals** included in the IEP describe what a child with disabilities can be expected to accomplish within a specified period. Usually the allotted time is 1 school year. However, the scheduled period may be as little as a few weeks or months.

There must be a direct relationship between the child's present level of educational performance and the goals, objectives, and services to be provided. However, the IEP is *not* intended to be detailed enough to be used as a complete instructional plan. The written goals and objectives are expected to state skills that are most needed based on assessment of a child's level of achievement. They are designed to target remediation of particular developmental lags or to accelerate learning. The intent is to focus attention and teaching effort on critical areas that are listed by priority and area of need.

The IEP is intended to serve as a basis for the subsequent development of a detailed, individualized instructional program that encompasses the complete curriculum. For example, although Danny's IEP focuses on his goals and objectives in speech and language, his complete instructional program would include social development,

gross and fine motor skills, cognitive development, and school readiness activities. In all of these areas Danny would be expected to participate and learn. Adaptations to meet his needs would be made in the process of instruction.

In Vicky's case (Chapter 4) her IEP would state specific goals and objectives related to her behavior and her motor skills. Her complete instructional program would include her participation with the other children in language and cognitive development as well as readiness skills. Of course, the activities throughout the day would become one of the vehicles for nurturing her improved behavior. Behavior management techniques would be used during the complete class day.

Considerations Beyond the IEP

Interpreters of the law recognize that special education teachers have primary responsibility for implementation of the IEP. These teachers are expected to monitor each child's progress. If at any time they feel that plan is no longer appropriate, they are expected to request another meeting to review the IEP. Parents may also request a review of the individual program.

When children with special needs attend regular classes, even part time, their mainstream teachers should have copies of their IEPs. The special education teacher should explain the contents of each plan. This teacher should be available to serve as consultant to the classroom teacher. Consultations should include a mutual sharing of concerns and information, suggestions for behavior management, materials, and teaching strategies.

THE INDIVIDUALIZED FAMILY SERVICE PLAN (IFSP)

The Individualized Family Service Plan (IFSP) is the written document specified in P.L. 99-457 to guide the implementation of early intervention services for children from birth to age 3 and their families. It is to be developed through **collaborative interchanges** between families and the professionals involved in assessment and service delivery.

The purpose of the IFSP is to identify and organize formal and informal resources to facilitate families' goals for their children and themselves. The IFSP is a promise to children and families—a promise that their strengths will be recognized and built on, that their needs will be met in a way that is respectful of their beliefs and values, and that their hopes and aspirations will be encouraged and enabled. (Johnson, McGonigel, & Kaufmann, 1989, p. 1)

The written document, in and of itself, is not considered to be as significant as the *process* involved in the development of the written product. Service providers are expected to form partnerships with families built on trust and respect that are expected to be a viable part of each child's program throughout the critical first few years of the child's life. The IFSP process is intended to support the natural caregiving role of families. In keeping with the family systems dynamics outlined in Chapter 3, young children with special needs can be understood only within the context of their families. In this way, the IFSP is viewed differently from the IEP. The IFSP process is *family centered* while the IEP tends to be child centered. The IFSP approach takes into account the fact that infants and toddlers are uniquely dependent on their families for physical and emotional sustenance.

The IFSP Process

The process for developing the IFSP consists of the gathering, sharing, and exchange of information between families and staff to enable families to make informed choices about the early intervention services they want for their children and themselves. (Johnson et al., 1989, p. 11)

Families may move through the dynamic process differently according to their concerns, desires, and choices. However, several key activi-

ties are expected to occur. These include the following:

1. A phase of first contacts between a family and early intervention service providers.

2. Assessment planning.

3. Child assessment.

4. Identification of family priorities, resources, and concerns.

5. Statement of desired outcomes to meet child and family needs.

6. Designation of a resource coordinator (case manager).

Section 300.322e of the federal regulations states that a meeting to develop the initial IFSP must be conducted within 45 days of the initial referral. A review of the IFSP must be completed every 6 months or more frequently if deemed appropriate. In addition, a full evaluation of the IFSP is to be conducted on an annual basis. Meetings are to take place in settings and at times convenient for families. The family's native language is to be used, unless it is clearly not feasible to do so.

Participants in the initial and annual IFSP meetings include the following:

1. The parent or parents of the child.

2. Other family members as desired by the family.

3. An advocate or person outside the family, if the parent requests that the person participate.

4. The case manager who has been working with the family since the initial referral or who has been designated by the public agency to be responsible for the implementation of the IFSP.

5. A person or persons directly involved in the assessment process.

6. As appropriate, persons who will be providing services to the child or the family.

If any of these persons are unable to participate, arrangements are to be made to include their involvement through other means such as arranging a telephone conference call; employing the services of a knowledgeable, authorized substitute representative; or making available pertinent records.

Identifying Family Strengths, Concerns, and Priorities

Although P.L. 99-457 does require identification of family strengths and needs as related to enhancement and development of the child, professionals are increasingly wary of the use of the term *needs*, which implies that families may need to be fixed. The term *concerns* is used here in an effort to encourage the view that families are competent and able to make choices based on their concerns and priorities. It is not that families are just "needy" and we must help. It is *not* appropriate for early childhood special education professionals to decide what areas of family life should be assessed to determine family strengths and concerns (Bailey & Simeonsson, 1988).

When general problems in family functioning are suspected, it is appropriate to explore with the family the possibility of referring them to appropriate professionals for counseling or other forms of assistance. Only families can decide for themselves which aspects of their functioning are relevant to their ability to help their child develop optimally. As Vincent (1990) pointed out, we need to understand the concerns and priorities of the family from the family's point of view and then identify the concerns and priorities from the professional's point of view. Through collaboration, concerns are then prioritized before resources can be identified.

Florene Poyadue, Executive Director of Parents Helping Parents (see Chapter 3), has referred to **CPR (concerns, priorities, and resources)** as the lifeline of families who have children with special needs. Once concerns are prioritized, the responsibility of both the professional community and families is the identification of viable resources. It is important that professionals assist families in identifying and building on their own resources and strengths while at the same time helping them to link up with appropriate community resources. It must be remembered that only resources that are easily accessible to families are useful.

Considerable discussion has been generated among professionals and families as to the least intrusive way to help families identify their concerns, priorities, and resources. It is clearly acknowledged that professionals need training and experience in a more **family-centered approach to assessment** in order to balance their needs for specific information to determine eligibility and programming against families' priorities and concerns. As communities work through this planning phase of P.L. 99-457, they must be creative in designing data-collection methods that maintain the integrity of each family as primary decision makers. This means that whenever there is doubt about a family's concerns or a child's need, the opinions of the family should be sought first. Whether families complete interview forms or provide information through descriptive stories about their children, they must be given a choice in the assessment procedures used. Essential to success of the whole process is a relationship between families and professionals built on trust and respect.

Bailey (1987) listed five basic skills professionals need to develop in order to work collaboratively with families. These include the ability to (1) look at families from a systems perspective; (2) identify relevant family needs; (3) use appropriate listening and interviewing techniques; (4) negotiate thoughtfully with families to reach consensus on solutions; and (5) help families match their concerns with available resources.

Contents of the IFSP

In written form, the IFSP must contain the elements that are listed here. One important difference from the IEP includes a statement of "outcomes expected to be achieved for the infant or toddler and the family" (Section 677) rather than goals and objectives. These **outcome statements** are to reflect changes family members want to see for their child or themselves. Each outcome is to be stated functionally in terms of what is to occur (process) and what is expected as a result of these actions (product).

Even though an example form is shown in Figure 5–2, readers are cautioned to realize that final formats have yet to be decided by states that, in the next few years, will elect to fully participate in P.L. 99-457. By the time this text is printed, most states should be nearing completion of the planning phase. A telephone call to health, education, and social service agencies should be able to direct interested individuals to the right sources to determine progress of implementation of early intervention services for birth to 3 year olds and their families in local areas. Each IFSP should include the following:

1. A statement of the child's present levels of physical development (including vision, hearing, and health status), cognitive development, language and speech development, psychosocial development, and self-help skills.

2. A statement of the family's strengths and concerns related to enhancing the development of the child.

3. A statement of the major outcomes expected to be achieved for the child and family.

4. A statement of the specific early intervention services necessary to meet the unique needs of the child and the family and to achieve the outcomes identified.

5. Other services deemed appropriate to assist the child and family to achieve identified outcomes.

6. Projected dates for initiation of the services and the anticipated duration of those services.

7. The name of the case manager (service coordinator) who will be responsible for the implementation of the IFSP and coordination with other agencies and persons.

8. Steps to be taken to support the transition of the child, upon reaching age 3, to the next program of services recognized to be appropriate.

The case of Alisa, which is given in Figure 5–2, illustrates one format that encompasses the requirements.

Case Management

Case management is considered to be an integral part of the IFSP process. P.L. 99-457 Part H rules and regulations state that case management consists primarily of activities designed to assist and enable an eligible child and the child's family to receive the rights, procedural safeguards, and services that are authorized to be provided through each state's early intervention program. The case manager who is assigned during the IFSP meeting is responsible for coordinating all services across agency lines and is to serve as the single point of contact in helping parents to obtain appropriate services.

Case management is to be an active, ongoing process that involves helping parents to gain access to services identified in their IFSP, coordinating these services, and facilitating timely delivery of appropriate services throughout the duration of the child's eligibility. In many areas, early childhood special education teachers may be expected to become case managers. Those who have not had training in family systems theory,

INDIVIDUALIZED FAMILY SERVICE PLAN

Date: 12-20-91

Child's Name: Alisa Jones
Birthdate: 12-7-89   *Age:* 24.5 months
         (Three months premature)   (adjusted age: 21.5 months)

Team Members: Services begin 1-5-92
    Mother: M. Jones   Speech Therapy
    Case Manager: K. Harris   (biweekly @ home)
    Educator: C. Kraft   Early Education
    Speech-Language Pathologist: B. Lauren   (biweekly @ home)
    Nurse: J. Herrera

DEVELOPMENTAL LEVELS

Assessment Instruments
    Carolina Infant Assessment
    Child observation in multiple settings
    Parent interview

Gross Motor: 20 months   *Cognitive:* 18 months
Fine Motor: 20 months   *Language:* 6 months
Self-help: 18 months   *Social/Emotional:* 6 months

Vision Status: normal
Hearing Status: normal

FAMILY CONCERNS AND PRIORITIES

Mrs. Jones is very concerned about Alisa's increasing temper tantrums. They occur at least once a day, and the length of each episode is increasing. She is also very concerned about her lack of language development. Mrs. Jones reports that she frequently spends time trying to get Alisa to imitate words, but that Alisa rarely complies.

Mrs. Jones indicated that despite interactions with many professionals, she really does not understand Alisa's problems, nor does she know what to do to help her.

FAMILY RESOURCES

Though Mrs. Jones is a single parent, she has a close and effective network of friends and family that provides important support. She has two close friends who live in her apartment building. Her own parents and sister live within walking distance. Her oldest child, Sharon, is 12 years old, and often cares for her other two children, Missy (4 years) and Alex (6 years). Mrs. Jones is highly motivated to help Alisa.

CHILD STRENGTHS AND NEEDS

Alisa is an energetic and determined 2-year-old. She is curious and loves to explore her physical environment. She tries to do everything independently (which often gets her into trouble).

Her greatest needs appear to be in the areas of social/emotional development and communication skills. She is socially and emotionally immature. She prefers objects to people and engages in relatively few social interactions. Her primary mode of communication appears to be through negative behavior. Occasionally, when her efforts to reach some object are thwarted, she will reach toward and make eye contact with a caregiver or sibling, and whine, as a request for assistance.

Figure 5–2 (pp. 164–166)

MAJOR GOALS (DESIRED OUTCOMES) FOR ONE-YEAR PERIOD
#1. MRS. JONES WILL HAVE A CLEARER UNDERSTANDING OF HER DAUGHTER'S BEHAVIOR AND DEVELOPMENT.
#2. MRS. JONES WILL FEEL CONFIDENT IN HER ABILITY TO FACILITATE HER DAUGHTER'S HEALTHY GROWTH AND DEVELOPMENT, PARTICULARLY IN THE AREA OF COMMUNICATION SKILLS.
#3. ALISA WILL SEEK THE ATTENTION OF OTHERS AND WILL APPROPRIATELY INITIATE POSITIVE SOCIAL INTERACTION.
#4. THE RATE OF ALISA'S TEMPER TANTRUMS WILL BE REDUCED TO NO MORE THAN ONE PER MONTH.
#5. ALISA WILL CONSISTENTLY USE A MINIMUM OF 15 WORDS TO EXPRESS A RANGE OF COMMUNICATIVE FUNCTIONS.

SHORT-TERM (QUARTERLY) OBJECTIVES

Outcome #1
Short-Term Objective A: Mrs. Jones will have the opportunity to review all medical and developmental records related to Alisa.

Strategies: Mrs. Jones will be invited to either examine Alisa's files in the Regional Center Office with her case manager, K. Harris, or she can receive copies of reports and documents which she can examine at home. K. Harris will encourage her to ask for clarification of information that she does not understand and to discuss any aspect of the files or issues raised by her reading of the files.

Timeline: by 1-30-92

Person(s) Responsible: K. Harris, Case Manager

Criterion: Mrs. Jones will indicate that she has examined and understood all materials related to her daughter's case history.

Short-Term Objective B: Mrs. Jones will receive information related to Alisa's needs.

Strategies: C. Kraft, the early childhood special educator, will provide Mrs. Jones with access to appropriate written materials, videotapes, conferences, and lectures, and will introduce her to representatives of parent groups.

Timeline: Ongoing, throughout the year

Person(s) Responsible: C. Kraft, early childhood special educator

Criterion: At the end of one year, Mrs. Jones will express an understanding of her daughter's behavior and development and of the kinds of intervention that may be helpful. By the end of the first quarter, Mrs. Jones will have made contact with one parent group representative and will have been given information from at least two sources.

Outcome #2
Short-Term Objective: Mrs. Jones will be introduced to specific strategies which may be helpful in (a) managing Alisa's tantrums and (b) facilitating social-communicative interaction.

Strategies: C. Kraft (educator) and B. Lauren (speech-language pathologist) will describe and model intervention strategies for Mrs. Jones several times, in a variety of situations.

Timeline: by 3-30-92

Person(s) Responsible: C. Kraft and B. Lauren

Criterion: During a home visit, Mrs. Jones will spontaneously demonstrate use of at least one strategy for each area of concern.

Outcome #3
Short-Term Objective: Alisa will participate for one minute in a turn taking game which involves a favorite toy or activity.

Strategy A: Use Alisa's existing interest to establish turn-taking (e.g., stacking blocks, blowing bubbles, eating a cookie)

Figure 5–2 *(Continued)*

a. Identify object or material that Alisa is interested in.
b. Briefly assist or participate with her in some way (e.g., blow a bubble for her, or break off a piece of cookie and give it to her).
c. Discontinue your participation and wait.
d. If Alisa hesitates or looks up briefly, say "Oh, it's my turn." Briefly take a turn, then say, "Now it's your turn."

Strategy B: Identify non-object-related activities that Alisa enjoys and encourage turn-taking by having her request "more" (e.g., being pushed in the swing, pulled in a wagon, or swung in a blanket).
a. Engage in activity briefly.
b. Interrupt activity (e.g., stop swing).
c. Wait for Alisa to respond in some way to request "more." [In this activity, any response should be accepted (e.g., brief eye contact, moving her body forward, etc.) to avoid a temper tantrum]
d. Repeat activity saying, "Ok, you want to swing some more."
e. If possible, reverse roles (e.g., have Alisa push adult or sibling in the swing).

Strategy C: Try to interest Alisa in social-interaction games appropriate to the social developmental stage she is in, e.g., playing "peek-a-boo." Use of puppets as the interaction partner may facilitate her interest if she avoids face-to-face interaction with adult.

Timeline: by 3-30-92

Person(s) Responsible: M. Jones (mother) and C. Kraft (educator)

Criterion: Alisa will engage willingly in turn-taking interactions with adults or siblings at least three times per day, for at least one minute each time.

Outcome #4 and #5:
(NOTE: Because the team feels that Alisa's tantrums may be related to her lack of communication skills, initially goals #4 and #5 will be addressed using the same short-term objective.)

Short-Term Objective: About one-third of the time (i.e., in at least one out of every three tantrum situations), Alisa will use a consistent non-cry signal (such as a sound, pointing to the object, reaching toward mother, etc.) to indicate frustration or need for assistance.

Strategy:
1. For a period of one week, mother and teacher will carefully observe tantrum episodes to determine the following:
   a. Precipitating events/situations.
   b. Child's movements or expression immediately preceding trantrum.
2. If it is discovered that Alisa uses a consistent behavior to signal the onset of the tantrum, assist her immediately in response to that signal before that tantrum behavior has a chance to occur.
3. If #2 is not possible or is not successful, attempt to anticipate a tantrum episode and quickly model or motor the child through a "help" signal, such as pointing to the object or making the sign for help.

Timeline: by 3-3-92

Person(s) Responsible: M. Jones (mother) and C. Kraft (educator)

Criterion: For a two-week period, one-third of the time Alisa will signal her frustration and her need for assistance without tantrums.

DATE OF NEXT PLANNED TEAM MEETING: 3-30-92

SIGNATURES OF TEAM MEMBERS:

Margaret Jones _____ (Parent or Guardian)
Karla Harris _____   _Catherine Kraft_
Bobbi Lauren _____   _J Herrera_

Person completing this form: Catherine Kraft

Figure 5–2 (Continued)

in understanding the requirements of P.L. 99-457, and in local service delivery systems must seek this training before accepting such a responsibility.

Specific functions of case management listed in the law include (a) coordinating the performance of evaluations and assessments; (b) facilitating and participating in the development, review, and evaluation of IFSPs; (c) assisting families in identifying available service providers; (d) informing families of the availability of advocacy services; (f) coordinating with medical and health providers; and (g) facilitating the development of a transition plan to preschool services, if appropriate.

TRANSITION PRACTICES

Early childhood special education teachers are in a unique position to help families and children make the move from programs for infants and toddlers to programs for preschool-aged children. Families who are coping with their children's special needs in a demanding environment can be especially stressed in times of transition. They have many questions and are faced with the unknown. Teachers and other early in-

tervention personnel can encourage parents to visit and become familiar with possible new settings for their child. They can directly prepare children and families by first understanding the environmental expectations of the placement possibilities. Whenever possible, children can be exposed to new routines and requirements ahead of time. Exiting teachers can work directly with receiving teachers in person, via telephone, and through reports to smooth the way and provide reassurance and support to parents. Putting parents in direct touch with parents who already have children in the new environment can be invaluable. These same concerns and strategies should be used when children move from preschool programs into public elementary school programs and beyond.

The focus of this chapter was on collaborative identification of the early intervention goals and objectives of individual families and their children. Chapter 6 discusses effective intervention strategies for realizing the stated goals and objectives. Considerable attention is given to describing generic instructional strategies while recognizing the importance of play as a primary context for learning.

Summary

Before activity planning can begin for children with special needs, Public Law 94-142 requires that an Individualized Education Program (IEP) be developed. Each child must be seen for a diagnostic study by members of a multidisciplinary team. This team considers the child's current educational needs, determines eligibility, and specifies goals and objectives to guide program implementation. Early education teachers and specialists carefully observe each child and, in collaboration with the child's parents, outline a program that is reviewed and revised periodically. The child's teachers, both

special and regular, carry the primary responsibility for program implementation.

For children from birth to age 3, Public Law 99-457 specifies that an Individualized Family Service Plan (IFSP) be developed to guide early intervention services for each child and his or her family. While similar in intent to the IEP, the IFSP differs in many important respects. First, it is family focused rather than child focused. That is, the concerns and priorities of the family are to be jointly determined and are to serve as the frame of reference for all child-oriented services. Rather than goals and objectives, outcome statements based on changes family members want to see for their child and themselves are stated.

While basic requirements of the IFSP and case management process are the focus of the second part of this chapter, it is important to realize that final regulations of the IFSP have not been written. States will carry out the mandates of P.L. 99-457 differently because definitions and eligibility criteria will vary. An example is pro-

vided to illustrate the basic format. Readers are advised to refer to the annotated bibliography and to follow updates from such groups as the National Early Childhood Technical Assistance System (NEC*TAS) to keep abreast of the rules and regulations as they become finalized. NEC*TAS is coordinated by the Frank Porter Graham Child Development Center at the University of North Carolina at Chapel Hill.

Discussion Topics and Activities

1. Consider the following problems: The IEP conference for David has concluded. The parents are pleased with the suggestions made by the multidisciplinary team. These include continued placement in your preschool class for 3 year olds. An early childhood special education teacher has been assigned to help you plan activities for David. Test results indicated that David is lagging in all developmental areas. What questions will you want to ask the special education teacher when he or she visits you the first time?

2. Interview parents who have participated in an IEP meeting. Try to find out how they felt about the experience. Did they feel comfortable? If not, what bothered them about the process? Ask them what advice they would give to a new early interventionist for making families feel welcomed and a true part of the team. Share your findings with class members.

3. Work with your instructor in setting up an opportunity for you to sit in on an IEP meeting. Try to determine just what the teacher and others do to

make parents feel that their opinions are important and that they are critical to the decision-making process. If possible, interview the early childhood special educator to ask the questions that occurred to you throughout the meeting.

4. Ask your instructor for assistance in determining whom to contact in your local area to become involved in the P.L. 99-457 planning and implementation process.

5. Compare the IFSP process with that of the IEP. Determine what would be necessary to carry over the family-focused approach into the IEP process.

6. Become thoroughly familiar with the local agencies that provide services to young children with special needs in your area. With a class member, visit at least one local agency to become familiar with how services are accessed, exactly what services are available; and what the eligibility criteria are. By collaborating with class members, develop a directory of services useful to parents as well as early intervention professionals.

Annotated Bibliography

Arena, J. (1989). *How to write an I.E.P.* Novato, CA: Academic Therapy Publications.

Included in this clearly written book are samples of the ways that goals and objectives can be written to facilitate effective programming. Also included are activities for parent use outside of the classroom.

Bailey, D. B., & Simeonsson, R. J. (1988). *Family assessment in early intervention.* Columbus, OH: Merrill.

This innovative text is designed to provide the information needed to assess family needs and plan goals jointly with families. Thorough coverage of the entire assessment procedure is offered, together with specific strategies for assessing family concerns and family communication, determining and stating family goals, and evaluating family services.

Lovitt, T. (1980). *Writing and implementing an IEP.* Belmont, CA: David S. Lake.

This paperback book presents a step-by-step analysis of how to prepare the contents of an IEP. Included is a model form that can be adapted for specific uses. Lists of goals and objectives, record-keeping techniques, and sequences of skills also can be found.

McGonigel, M. M., Kaufmann, R. K., & Johnson, B. H. (Eds.). (1991). *Guidelines and recommended practices for the Individualized Family Service plan* (2nd ed.). Bethesda, MD: Association for the Care of Children's Health.

This monograph represents a consensus about the best practices for providing family-centered, comprehensive early intervention services. It is not a blueprint for implementation. Rather, it suggests a philosophy and conceptual framework for the IFSP and provides recommendations for practices and procedures that are consistent with the intent of Public Law 99-457.

McNamara, B. E. (1986). Parents as partners in the IEP process. *Academic Therapy, 21,* 309–319.

To enhance communication between professionals and parents this article presents strategies that can be employed prior to, during, or after the IEP conference. Included are questionnaires to help teachers gain insight into their own attitudes toward parent involvement and to help evaluate the success of parent participation in IEP meetings.

Maher, C. A., & Barbrack, C. R. (1980). A framework for comprehensive evaluation of the individualized education program (IEP). *Learning Disability Quarterly, 3,* 49–55.

This article describes a process for the comprehensive evaluation of the IEP. It provides for collection of a range of evaluation information about the design, implementation, practicality, and effectiveness of the program. Useful suggestions are made to those who are charged with evaluating the appropriateness of services provided to children with disabilities.

School, B., & Cooper, A. (1981). *The IEP primer and the individualized program.* Novato: CA: Academic Therapy.

This is a down-to-earth, practical book that shows how to set up and conduct an IEP conference, how to write agreed-upon goals and objectives, and how to carry out the plan. There are sample IEPs and a useful list of *do's* and *don'ts.* This is a very helpful and inexpensive resource.

Strickland, B. B., & Turnbull, A. P. (1990). *Developing and implementing Individualized Education Programs.* Columbus, OH: Merrill.

This book is designed to help educators answer the question, How can I effectively carry out my responsibilities associated with the IEP? It is organized into three major parts: (1) procedural guidelines for IEP development, (2) mechanics of IEP development, and (3) implementation of the IEP. Also included is a comparative description of the IFSP as outlined by P.L. 99-457.

References

Bailey, D. B. (1987). Collaborative goal setting with families: Resolving differences in values and priorities for services. *Topics in Early Childhood Special Education, 7*(2), 59–71.

Bailey, D. B., & Simeonsson, R. J. (1988). *Family assessment in early intervention.* Columbus, OH: Merrill.

McGonigel, M. J., Kaufmann, R. K., & Johnson, B. H. (Eds.). (1991). *Guidelines and recommended practices for the Individualized Family Service Plan.* Bethesda, MD: Association for the Care of Children's Health.

Public Laws 94-142 and 99-457. Washington, DC: U.S. Government Printing Office.

Strickland, B. B., & Turnbull, A. P. (1990). *Developing and implementing Individualized Education Programs.* Columbus, OH: Merrill Publishing Co.

Vincent, L. (1990, October 6). *Collaborating with families: A challenge of the 90's.* Keynote address delivered at Santa Clara University, Santa Clara, CA.

Chapter 6

Implementing Intervention and Instructional Strategies

Key Points

▶ A clear conceptualization of desired outcomes and appropriate educational strategies is necessary before a curriculum is designed or adapted.

▶ Curriculum content should include goals that are meaningful and relevant to each child.

▶ Curriculum content should also focus on the development of the underlying cognitive and psychoemotional processes that enable children to engage in self-directed learning and establish positive human relationships.

▶ Long-term goals must be broken down into appropriate short-term behavioral objectives that can be observed and evaluated easily.

▶ Programs should utilize an "activity focus" by working on several objectives simultaneously in the context of a pleasurable and motivating activity.

▶ Professional practice in early childhood special education requires good record-keeping systems that can be used to evaluate children's ongoing progress.

▶ Identification of motivations is critical to successful intervention with infants and young children with special needs.

▶ Young children must be motivated to act upon the environment and to initiate interaction.

▶ Adults play a crucial role in facilitating the development of infants and young children through responsivity to children's cues, use of communicative interactions, and social mediation of experiences.

▶ Creating a predictable environment through the use of routine and repetition is essential to children's learning and adjustment.

▶ One of the most important contexts for learning in the early education program is children's play.

▶ In addition to certain generic strategies, the early childhood special education professional must also have a thorough understanding of disabilities and must master intervention strategies specific to each disability.

Key Topics

▶ Definition of curriculum.

▶ Moving from annual goals to daily activities.

▶ Writing goals and objectives.

▶ Providing a wide range of activities and experiences for each en-route behavior.

▶ Keeping records.

▶ Developing schedules.

▶ Generic instructional strategies, including motivation, behavior modification, effectance motivation, social medication, adult-child communication, and routines.

▶ Play as an important teaching context.

▶ Arranging the physical environment.

▶ Considerations for adapting curricula for young children with specific needs.

The previous chapters introduced some of the major issues surrounding the processes of identification, diagnosis, assessment, and evaluation. Attention was given to preparing early childhood special educators for their primary role as astute observers of children's behavior. The options available for assessment within the classroom were discussed. Finally, the process of developing individualized programs and plans was illustrated.

This chapter suggests practical instructional strategies. The focus in the first part of the chapter is on choosing goals to meet individual needs, writing instructional objectives, and using these objectives in the development of instructional plans. The second part of the chapter focuses on the use of certain generic instructional strategies that can provide the methodological foundation for educational programs for all children.

Emphasis is placed on using clearly stated objectives and sound teaching strategies to individualize instruction while working with a group of children. The overall approach presented in this chapter makes it possible to include children with disabilities or developmental delays in a wide range of early education programs.

CURRICULUM

Definition

Curriculum has been defined in various ways. Wolery (1983) defined it as an organized description of what to teach. It should also include basic strategies and activities for teaching, but the primary emphasis of a curriculum definition is generally on what to teach. Mori and Neisworth (1983) suggested that an acceptable early childhood curriculum is not simply a hodgepodge of objectives. It should provide a clear plan for programming; meet the needs of the child, parent, ethnic group, and general culture; and match teacher style and theoretical approach.

Vincent (1988) has aptly described curriculum as a "road map"—a tool that helps us know where we are going and how to get there. The desired outcomes for children and families are the destination. The instructional objectives and teaching strategies are the routes by which we get there.

Choice

Many types of curricula have been developed for infants and young children, both with and without special needs. These curricula are based on the theoretical approaches described in Chapter 2. Many curricula have been designed in a comprehensive way and include criterion-referenced assessments, detailed, step-by-step behavioral objectives, and suggested activities and materials. These are often commercially available as packaged programs, many of which are listed and described in Appendix F. It is important for early intervention professionals to understand, however, that such so-called "self-contained" curricula may or may not meet the needs of children in their particular programs. First educators must clearly identify their own, as well as parents' educational goals for their children. Second, they must examine the strengths and learning styles of children, as well as their own teaching styles. A clear conceptualization of both the desired program outcomes and the best educational strategies must be generated before a curriculum is selected. Educators will find that packaged curricula need modifications and adaptations in order to meet unique needs of a particular group of children. They may also choose to design their own curricula.

Philosophy of This Text

In practice, most programs for young children with special needs combine elements of several curriculum models. The philosophy of this text is based on the following assumptions.

1. The content of the curriculum must include goals that are meaningful and relevant to each child within the context of his or her home and community. That is, they must be **functional** and **ecologically relevant.** (Refer to Chapter 4 for a review of these concepts.) In addition, curriculum content will also include the development of children's underlying cognitive and psychoemotional processes, which enable them to eventually engage in self-directed learning and establish positive human relationships.

2. The designing of specific behavioral objectives and en-route behaviors will consider information related to the stages and processes of **development.** In addition, principles and techniques from the field of behavior analysis (e.g., task analysis) will be used as tools when necessary.

3. Teaching strategies used to reach targeted goals will reflect a strong **social-transactional** approach, with the primary method of instruction being rooted in the social interactions between children and significant adults (i.e., teachers and caregivers) as well as between children and their peers.

FROM ANNUAL GOALS TO DAILY ACTIVITIES

Once educators have defined their program philosophy and designed or adapted curriculum, it is often helpful to generate working checklists against which the progress of individual children in the program can be measured easily.

When choosing or developing a checklist, early childhood teachers need to consider what skills are needed for their children to function adequately in whatever environmental circumstances they may be placed. The IEP meeting, of course, helps teachers gain insight into the needs and desires of parents. Choosing target behaviors

important to parents will ease the child's functioning at home and should bring positive reinforcement. Skills necessary to function in other environments such as the neighborhood or grandparents' home should also receive consideration. In other words, educators must be concerned not only with what is developmentally appropriate, but also with what is necessary for daily living.

Checklists may be arranged sequentially according to the ages at which particular skills and behaviors are expected to emerge. Typically, these sequences of behaviors are grouped according to four or five major categories. The divisions usually include motor, cognitive, language, social-emotional, and self-help skills. Since there is always overlapping between one division and another, the segregation is somewhat arbitrary. For example, self-help skills require motor skills, and language and cognitive skills interrelate and overlap.

Checklists may also include objectives that pertain only to one child. For example, a child's family may identify particular goals such as pronouncing the name of a favorite aunt and recognizing her picture. These goals may be extremely important for their child, but they would not be appropriate for all children in the program.

It is most useful if the checklist is arranged by curriculum area in a **criterion-referenced sequence.** Reference to the ages when the subskills should have developed is irrelevant to the teacher who is planning an individual's program. If the child is 4 years old, knowing that he or she should have developed a particular skill at age 18 months is not germane to the teacher's task. What is important is discovering what the child can do (**entry behavior**) and planning the shortest journey (the **en-route behaviors**) to the destination (the **terminal objective** or the most difficult related items on the checklist).

By matching the checklist to the curriculum objectives, a quick and easy way to keep track of the progress of individual children is provided. By placing the items on the checklist in a column down the left side of the page and the names of the children across the top, it is easy to record progress and to identify each child's current en-route behavior (see Figure 6–1). The teacher (or aide) simply records the date and level of accomplishment for each item. Some prefer to include only the date of achievement. Then, the next item on the list becomes the current en-route behavior to be practiced. The parent's checklist (Figure 6–2) provides a combination curriculum guide, overall plan, and reporting system. Unlike report cards, it informs in a useful way. By helping parents to keep their checklist up to date with the teacher's, they have a consistent picture of what their child's education includes. They are better able to understand the teacher's objectives as well as things they can do to be supportive.

The example of the parent's checklist includes pictures. We have found that parents appreciate these, and they tell us that they can understand what is wanted more easily. Other suggestions for including parents as effective partners in fostering their child's growth were discussed in Chapter 3.

CURRICULUM DOMAIN: Fine motor

Goal: To learn cutting skills

Key: + = Skill already established
☐ = Current target behavior
▧ = Date achieved

	Meg A.	Mary C.	Danny D.	Bobby J.	Vicky M.	Eric R.
Tongs and cotton balls	+	+	+	+	+	+
1-inch snipping	10/91	9/91	10/91	+	☐	+
1-inch snipping on heavy line	☐	10/91	10/91	+		+
3-inch cutting on heavy straight line		☐	☐	10/91		+
3-inch cutting on heavy curved line				☐	10/91	
Cutting out 3-inch-diameter circle, heavy line						☐

Figure 6–1

	Date achieved
1. When I give my child tongs, a bowl and five cotton balls and help by showing and guidance, my child can pick up the balls with the tongs and drop them into the bowl.	
2. When I give my child blunt-tipped scissors and a strip of paper 1 inch wide, my child can snip the paper into little pieces.	
3. When I give my child a strip of paper 1 inch wide with heavy, black lines on it, my child can cut on the line, cutting through the paper.	
4. When I draw a straight line 3 inches long on a strip of paper, my child can cut on the line.	

Figure 6–2

Using the Curriculum Checklist to Plan Daily Activities

After skills on the checklist have been grouped according to the curriculum, philosophy, and goals of the preschool program, the skills must be listed in sequential order and translated into **behavioral objectives.** By reviewing the missed items from the formal tests given during the diagnostic stage and by carefully observing the child, the teacher can check those items that the child has already achieved, those that appear to be emerging, and those that show no evidence of development at that time. Most teachers develop a code like that illustrated in Figure 6–1 to designate these different levels of accomplishment.

Initially teachers identify developmental levels in each area of the curriculum. After identifying these entry behaviors, they are ready to plan daily activities.

A recording system that provides opportunity for continuous assessment is automatically provided by the checklist. In addition, children who are either on the same step or on steps close to each other can work together, and children who are significantly ahead in one or more areas of the curriculum may assist those who have not yet reached their level of development. The age of the child becomes irrelevant when behavioral objectives are linked to developmental levels. The child is not compared to others and thus does not have to experience the feelings of failure that can come from such comparison. Instead, the child's successes are recognized, recorded, and emphasized as he or she progresses from step to step.

Individualizing Daily Activities

Children whose skills have been assessed carefully are likely to be taught more efficiently. Teachers who have a clear picture of individual needs can be more effective in planning as well as teaching. However, teaching one child at a time is neither suggested nor implied by the special education rules and regulations. The intent is to provide an education in the least restrictive environment. To do this, it is inevitable that children will be learning in the same class with others who have a range of skills. If they are to learn from those who are more advanced, they must be able to watch them, interact with them, and participate in mutually satisfying ways.

Each child can be both teacher and learner at some time during the day. A spirit of mutual caring can be established in a class of very young children. Learning to give and receive help develops naturally.

Occasionally a teacher may prefer to work with one or two children at a time. However, if goals have been defined and objectives appropriately sequenced, it is possible to teach a group of five or more children at the same time. This is true even if each child is working toward a different behavioral objective. The goal and terminal objective may be the same for all of the children even though each one is receiving equivalent practice on a different en-route behavior. For example, consider the small-group lesson outlined in Table 6–1.

By writing the goal and objectives for cutting with scissors on one page, the teacher has a helpful one-page reference to guide him or her in planning the lesson to be useful to a group of children with widely varying skills. The terminal objective is an appropriate skill for a 5 year old, whereas lifting cotton balls with the tongs can be accomplished by most 3 year olds.

However, some 5 year olds with developmental delays may find it difficult to learn to use the tongs. They may require help and physical guidance as well as encouragement and verbal guidance for many days or weeks before they can proceed to the second objective. By being included in the activity with children who can do the more difficult tasks, they observe and discover that they also can learn.

It is critical to remember that one of the reasons for the sequence of carefully planned en-route behaviors is to provide each child with a task until criterion is reached. It is possible to develop difficult skills gradually and without the pain of failure. Beginning by expecting each child to "cut on the line" guarantees failure for many of them.

To teach five or more children to cut on the line, it is necessary to provide each one with the materials needed, demonstration at his or her level of performance, and continued encouragement. In this way, no one fails; rather, each child succeeds. Most will recognize the challenge of the next step and be eager to try it.

In addition to the usefulness of the clearly written behavioral objectives to the teacher, as the lesson is planned and conducted, these same objectives help in pinpointing necessary **branching** or smaller steps.

The basic set of goals and objectives should be designed to be useful guides in teaching the majority of the children. But some children will need even smaller steps. By analyzing the existing objectives, the teacher can identify what these more precise steps should be.

The format of the page of objectives is a help in analyzing the task. If the child is not succeeding, where is the breakdown? Should a change be made in what the teacher is providing or restricting? Or is the quantity of work or time allowed inappropriate? Sometimes the en-route

Table 6–1   Example of using goals and objectives to individualize an activity

Given (the teacher will provide or restrict)	The child will	Criterion
Goal: To develop cutting skills.		
Terminal objective: Blunt-tip scissors; paper with a 3-inch straight line, a 3-inch curved line, and a 3-inch-diameter circle; and directions to cut on the line and cut out the circle.	Cut as directed.	Cut within 1/4 inch of lines within 5 minutes.
En-route objectives *(least to most skilled)*:		
1. Tongs, 5 cotton balls, 4-inch bowl, teacher's guidance in placing fingers and thumb and forefinger in cutting position, and help in opening and closing tongs.	Open and close tongs around cotton ball, lift it to bowl, and release it into bowl, accepting teacher's assistance as needed.	Keep fingers in correct position and accept help.
2. Same as above, except restrict teacher's help to verbal directions, encouragement, and reminders.	Same as above.	Keep fingers in correct position and complete action (no time limit and no penalty for "dropped" cotton).
3. Same as above.	Same as above.	Maintain correct position, lift and drop cotton into bowl (no more than one ball outside bowl within 2 minutes).
4. Blunt-tip scissors and strips of construction paper 1 inch wide and 11 inches long.	Cut paper.	Cut at least 10 pieces within 5 minutes.
5. Same as above, with heavy black lines marked on paper at 1-inch intervals.	Cut paper on lines.	Cut within 1/4 inch of lines, one cut per line (no time limit).
6. Blunt-tip scissors and construction paper 3 inches wide and 11 inches long, with heavy black lines at 1-inch intervals the width of the paper.	Make three cuts per line.	Cut within 1/4 inch of lines, severing each piece within 10 minutes.
7. Same as terminal objective (except longer time criterion).	Cut as directed.	Cut within 1/4 inch of lines within 10 minutes.
8. Same as terminal objective.		

Adaptations for children with physical disabilities include squeeze scissors instead of traditional scissors. For some children, scissors with four finger holes may be useful because they allow the teacher to cut with the child. Children with visual impairments should be provided buff-colored paper with a heavy brown line for necessary contrast.

behaviors become more difficult because the task changes. At other times only the time limitations change. By evaluating the task, the criterion, and what the teacher does or does not do, it is possible to establish a much better sense of successful teaching for the teacher as well as the children.

Throughout all of the activities, teachers attempt to help children establish independence, accuracy, patience, and persistence. These qualities can be nurtured more successfully when enroute behaviors are clearly stated.

WRITING GOALS AND OBJECTIVES

The obvious reason for writing goals and objectives is that the law requires them to be included in educational plans for children with special needs. However, there are even more compelling reasons. These reasons are contained in the following characteristics of a well-written behavioral objective:

1. What is to be taught is described precisely and accurately. Anyone reading the objective knows what to do and the conditions in which it is to be done.

2. What the children will be doing when the objective has been achieved is defined and described.

3. The time allowed to complete the task is stated. How well the child must perform (the criterion) is clearly identified.

4. Because the task, the performance expected, and the criterion for success are clearly stated, accountability is facilitated.

In addition to these advantages are the following two less obvious but equally important benefits:

1. After writing objectives and working with them, teachers often discover that they are able to analyze learning problems more

efficiently. They recognize the critical importance of small changes in what they are doing. These seemingly small changes, sometimes referred to as *branching*, can make enormous differences in teaching success. In effect, practice in thinking in the manner required to write behavioral objectives enhances teaching skills.

2. Once a series of performance (behavioral) objectives has been developed, it can be used to teach other children with similar needs. A well-written file of objectives can be a tremendous time saver in lesson planning.

Basics of Writing Behavioral Objectives

Mager (1984) stated that "you cannot concern yourself with the problem of selecting the most efficient route to your destination until you know what your destination is" (p. 1).

Behavioral (or performance or instructional) objectives require that the teacher state the destination precisely. "Fuzzy" terms are appropriate in goals. They are not allowed in behavioral objectives. For example, a correctly written *goal* might read, "To teach the colors red, yellow, and blue." But the *objective* related to the goal must contain the following three components:

1. What the teacher will *provide*, *restrict*, and *do*.

2. What the learner will be *doing* or *saying* when the objective has been achieved (a behavior that can be seen or heard).

3. *How well* or *how often* the learner must perform in this manner to convince the teacher that the task has been learned (within what time frame this performance must occur).

An example of a correctly written objective related to the goal "To recognize the colors red, yellow, and blue" might be "When the teacher points to any one of 15 different items (5 of each color red, yellow, or blue) and asks 'What color is this?' the children will answer within 20 seconds, stating the color correctly on 80% of the trials." Exhibit 6–1 illustrates terms useful in writing goals and objectives.

The standard that must be achieved to accomplish this objective is 80% of the trials. This standard is referred to as the **criterion.** Eight of ten (or 80%) correct performances are usually described as "proficiency" on the task. Ten of ten or (100% accuracy) are defined as "mastery level." (The level required must vary with the needs of individual children. Some cannot be expected to reach 100%.)

The following is an example of an objective and goal related to a motor skill:

Goal: To improve eye-hand coordination.

Objective: Given a pencil and paper the children will watch as the teacher draws a 2-inch circle (counterclockwise) and then imitate the teacher's model, using the same directionality, holding the pencil in the same manner, and completing a circle between 2 and 3 inches in diameter. The circle will be no more than 1/2 inch out of round.

Criterion: Four of five trials correctly.

In some cases a time limit becomes part of the criterion for judging successful performance, for example, within 2 minutes.

Guidelines for Choosing and Writing Behavioral Objectives

Teachers will want to write objectives to meet particular needs. Norm-referenced tests and preschool curriculum guides suggest similar goals for all early childhood classes. However, each class and each program are unique and special.

The following procedure has been useful in writing objectives for preschool children. Each objective must contain the basic components, but the manner in which they are recorded may vary. Several different forms are suggested, but the process of choosing them and sequencing them remains the same.

1. *Identify a particular goal.* Goals should state in general what you want the children to learn. Examples of goals include to improve self-esteem, to express feelings, and to develop expressive language. Goals are not specific. They do not describe what teacher or child will do.

EXHIBIT 6–1 _____

Appropriate Verbs for Writing Behavioral Objectives

1. **Goals**
   The verbs suggested in this category are useful for writing goals but are *not* appropriate for writing behavioral objectives:

| To decrease | To discover | To improve | To practice |
| To develop | To demonstrate | To increase | To understand |

2. **Behavioral objectives**
   The verbs suggested in this category are useful for writing behavioral objectives and can be used to describe observable behaviors:

To answer	To follow	To name	To recall
To color	To hold (as directed)	To pick up	To say
To complete	To imitate	To place together	To sort
To cut	To list	To point to	To use
To draw	To look at		

2. *Decide what you want the children to learn in relation to the goal.* Choose the most difficult task you want them to be able to do. Visualize exactly what they will be doing when you look at them doing it and say "Now they *know* that." Write a description of what you have visualized in your mind's eye. This will be the observable behavior.

3. *Think about what you will give them and tell them when you want them to perform this observable behavior.* This will become the part of the objective that identifies what the teacher will do, provide, or restrict. Often this section begins with "Given" or "When the teacher."

4. *Write what you have visualized in the form you have chosen.* At first, it seems helpful to write the objective in one long sentence that includes all of the components. Later, you may prefer the shorter versions. Each must be complete. It is important to state a criterion or standard within each objective. Each criterion must be reasonable, and it must fit that particular objective.

5. *Begin task analysis.* So far you have chosen a goal, decided on the most difficult of the objectives you want to achieve in relation to the goal, and written all of this in the form you have chosen. What you have written is the terminal objective. Next, think about what you would need to do if the children could not achieve this objective in the way you have written it. Assume that it was too difficult for any of them. But you do want all of them to achieve it at least by the end of their experience in your program. How could you make it a little bit easier? Write this slightly easier en-route behavior (one of the objectives on the route to the terminal objective). Sometimes it is helpful to actually do the task yourself or carefully watch another do it to determine the en-route objectives.

6. *Continue task analysis as suggested in the previous guideline.* Write en-route behaviors that are simple, and include so many prompts (cues)

that you are certain every child you teach will be able to do at least the easiest one.

7. *Do not try to write every possible step.* Choose steps between objectives that you feel the majority of the children will be able to take. (Analyze the samples offered with this consideration in mind.) If you have a child who can perform a specific objective but seems unable to do any part of the next one in your sequence, you may need to plan another *branch*. That is, for an occasional child it may be necessary to insert additional objectives. Usually these need not be added to your sequence but rather recorded separately on the child's record. If you discover that you need this particular branch for a number of the children, add it to your sequence. (As noted earlier, keeping each en-route behavior on a separate card makes it easier to add or delete objectives.)

8. *Assemble your objectives.* At first, putting the en-route behaviors on individual cards makes it easier to arrange them in sequential order. Later, as your skill in task analysis grows, it becomes less necessary. However, if the en-route behaviors are on separate cards, it is easier to insert additional steps for children who need tasks broken into tiny steps. After assembling the en-route behaviors (objectives), it is helpful to actually do the task as outlined to verify the initial sequence and detect any missing steps.

Write the goal at the top of the form you have chosen. Beginning with the simplest one, write the objectives in sequence from the easiest to the most difficult. Remember, the most difficult one is your terminal objective. All of the others are called en-route behaviors. They are similar to en-route destinations on a trip. The terminal objective is your final destination, and the other objectives are specific places you will proceed through on your way to this destination. When you are headed toward a particular place on a trip, it may be your "target" for that day or week. In the same way, you may refer to a particular objective for a certain child as a target behavior.

This process of analyzing terminal objectives and discovering and sequencing en-route behaviors is referred to as the process of **task analysis.**

9. *Identify the entry behaviors of each child.* Each of the children will enter your preschool or center with some awareness of the information or behavior you have chosen to teach. A few will be able to demonstrate the skills described in some of your terminal objectives the very first day. Others will be completely unaware of any facet of that particular target behavior. This is why you must analyze the terminal objective and write the en-route behaviors. Attempts are then made to determine which of the en-route behaviors each child can do (assessment). Dates must be recorded. When this is done, each child's entry behavior has been identified. Now you know where to begin.

10. *Provide a variety of equivalent practice.* Use many different materials and toys until you feel your criterion has been achieved. Don't rush. At first, some children will progress very slowly. When you feel confident that an individual has achieved criterion on the entry behavior (the objective this child was able to do when entering your class), record the date next to the name and begin working on the next objective in the sequence.

11. *Provide as much equivalent practice as necessary.* The sequence of the objectives is intended to be useful to you in planning for all of the children. Some of them may learn quickly. Do not be surprised if some children move through a whole series of en-route behaviors and right through the terminal objective in a very short time. Others may take days or weeks on each en-route behavior. For accelerated children, a variety of activities and materials should be provided. Maintain the same level of difficulty your written objective states as you provide this equivalent practice.

Your written objective describes particular materials to be used in checking for criterion performance (at least in some instances). But

you should *feel completely free to use any materials you choose in lessons, games, or spontaneous play.* The intent is to provide each child with many successful experiences (equivalent practice) on each level. The critical task is to *maintain the appropriate level of challenge.* A well-planned sequence of behavioral objectives serves as a very helpful frame of reference for working effectively and efficiently with individual children.

12. *Sometimes use Montessori's "periods" as a guide in planning.* Although Montessori (1972, p. 126) did not know the terminology of behavioral objectives, she used a guide that is helpful in planning and sequencing objectives. She referred to the following periods:

Period 1. Naming ("This is ____.")
Period 2. Recognition ("Show me the ____" or "Give me the ____.")
Period 3. Recall (Montessori referred to this as "The Pronunciation of the Word." She asked "What is this?")

This outline is helpful in thinking about the sequence of objectives. First activities require that the teacher provide experiences or activities that involve *naming* things in an explicit way. Recognition is easier than recall, but practice in recognition makes recall possible.

13. *Use the objectives you have written as the basis for daily lessons.* As soon as you have written your first goals and objectives, use them. Experiment with them. Use them as the basis for lessons with individual children. Try using them with a small group of children who are working on adjacent en-route behaviors. Next, attempt working with a larger group, all of whom are working on two or three adjacent objectives. Gradually, as you feel comfortable with this new way of planning lessons, attempt to include one or two children who are working toward the same terminal objective but are working on widely separated en-route behaviors.

14. *Evaluate your objectives continuously as you use them.* Writing a series of objectives be-

comes easier with practice. Trial and error can be an efficient teacher. However, failure by the children must be interpreted by the teacher as an indication that the objectives must be changed in some way. Asking the following questions can be helpful if problems occur:

a. Could the children do any part of the task?

b. Did they listen and look, or were the directions too long?

c. What modality or modalities were involved in the teacher's directions, that is, visual, auditory, tactile-kinesthetic, or combinations of these?

d. Which modalities were required in the response?

e. What distractors interfered?

f. What additional cues might have helped?

g. Did both the teacher presentation and the expected response allow for individual adaptations because of disabling conditions? For example, if the child had a visual impairment, were auditory and tactile-kinesthetic clues provided? If the child had a hearing impairment, were visual and tactile-kinesthetic clues available?

h. Was the time allotted adequate?

i. Was the content limited and specific to avoid misunderstanding?

j. Were the related subskills well learned before the presentation?

In practice, children should be able to demonstrate proficiency performance or 80% accuracy on one objective before proceeding to the next. The new objective should be partially achievable on the first try. That is, if the next en-route behavioral objective is a total mystery to the children (or to any one child), more branches or tinier steps are needed. A well-written sequence allows for continued success experiences. A limited amount of failure can be instructive. It can lead the children to use their mistakes as clues in the discovery of what they need to do differently. But for children who have experienced a great deal of it, failure must be kept to a minimum for a long time.

15. *Add new goals and objectives to the curriculum as the need for them appears.* Remember, your goals and objectives are your curriculum. You will want to add to them regularly. You will also want to delete or remove some from time to time. As you become accustomed to thinking in terms of what the children say and do (or do not do) as a result of your teaching, you will feel more effective as a teacher. Planning will be simplified. Individualizing lessons, based on the en-route behaviors you have written, will be much easier. En-route behaviors that do not work can be deleted. More steps can be inserted, if needed, for some children. Many children will be able to achieve each en-route objective rapidly. When the steps are small enough for the slowest to "climb," many children will achieve each level within a brief time.

PROVIDING A WIDE RANGE AND VARIETY OF ACTIVITIES AND EXPERIENCES FOR EACH EN-ROUTE BEHAVIOR

Choosing Appropriate Activities

In choosing appropriate activities or "equivalent behaviors" for each en-route behavior, the following two guidelines should be kept in mind:

1. What the teacher does and what the child is expected to do must be at the same level of difficulty as the written objective.

2. Any difficulties encountered will be corrected by a smooth return to a simpler objective.

When these two guidelines are considered, the appropriate activities and experiences to be provided are limited only by the teacher's imagination and creativity. For example, the following objectives might be chosen to achieve the goal "To learn the names of body parts":

Terminal objective: When the teacher points to any body parts (eyes, ears, nose, mouth, arms, hands, or feet) and says, "Tell me what this is called," Danny will name them correctly with no more than 2 errors in 10 trials. Each body part will be checked on a doll, the child, and another child.
En-route behaviors *(all criteria equal 8 of 10):*

1. When the teacher points to any of the body parts listed and says, "This is a ____," Danny will imitate the teacher's spoken model.
2. When the teacher points to any of the body parts listed and says, "Is this the ____?" Danny will name the part.
3. When the teacher says, "Show me your ____," Danny will point to his own named body part.
4. When the teacher asks, "What is this?" while pointing to his or her own, another child's, or a doll's features, Danny will name the features correctly.

The following list of activities could be used to provide equivalent practice on any of the objectives just described. It should be remembered that each activity will be accompanied with as many verbal labels as possible.

1. Bathing a doll.
2. Dressing a doll.
3. Washing hands and faces.
4. Doing a puzzle (that includes body parts).
5. Drawing at the chalkboard.
6. Drawing on paper.
7. Making a jack-o'-lantern.
8. Pasting features on a teddy bear made of construction paper.
9. Singing a song ("Made up" chants are fun, for example, "I touch my nose and blink my eyes. I clap my hands and say 'Surprise!' ").
10. Making a gingerbread man.
11. Telling stories, and encouraging the children to act them out.
12. Puppet plays.

As illustrated in the following dialogue, these activities will allow children to work on different en-route behaviors while participating in an activity together.

The Activity: Bathing a Doll

Equipment: Aprons, warm water, soap, wash cloths, towels, a doll bathtub, and a dirty doll

Teacher: Sally, will you help me wash our doll? She is so dirty. Look at those hands and feet. (Pointing.)

Sally: I get the water and soap.

Danny: Wa-er (water).

Teacher: Get the towel, Danny.

Vicky: Where? (Grabbing the doll.)

Teacher: Hold her very carefully, Vicky. Be gentle. (Pointing to the arm.) See, her arm is all wet.

Danny: Dere no (nose). (Pointing.)

Teacher: Right Danny, that's her nose.

Danny: Wha da? (What's that?)

Teacher: That's her ear (Pointing.) Can you find her other ear?

Danny: Dere (There.)

Teacher: Right!

Using the objectives, the teacher can individualize any activity by applying the expected level of performance (criterion) requirements to the activity.

Evaluating the Effectiveness of Each Activity

The usefulness of any activity is determined largely by its appeal to children. In addition, the activity should lend itself to repetition with minor variations. (Children enjoy a meaningful amount of repetition.) Each activity should be chosen to develop skills in ways that are a challenge but do not overwhelm the least capable child in the group. Participation is a prerequisite for effective learning with young children. "Just watching" is a useful beginning for some very shy or young children. With gentle encouragement these children can be helped to become full participants.

Using an Activity to Achieve More Than One Objective

Bricker (1989) has suggested using an **"activity focus"** for program planning. This approach suggests that programs must be built around activities that are *appropriate* and *motivating*.

Most activities can be used to achieve several objectives at the same time. For example, learning to follow two- and three-stage directions is an important skill. Counting and learning colors and other concepts are goals included in every preschool curriculum.

In bathing the doll, teachers might say "Get the blue towel. It is under the sink" (emphasizing color and the preposition *under*). She might say, "Take off both socks. See, one sock is on her foot, and the other is on the floor" (emphasizing one-to-one correspondence, foot, and the preposition *on*).

Of course, most preschool teachers do many of these things spontaneously and without much conscious planning. However, when the program includes children with special needs, this important emphasis on specific skills cannot be left to chance. These children require explicit examples, meaningful repetition, and a variety of related experiences. One experience is inadequate. The ability to generalize from one experience to the next must be conscientiously nurtured.

KEEPING RECORDS

Each early intervention program has unique needs for record keeping. Some require a great deal of detailed information to be recorded about each child each day. Others rely on occa-

sional notes to parents and brief comments in the children's files. Individual preferences often determine both the kinds of records kept and the frequency with which they are updated. However, if children with special needs are included in the class, certain information must be recorded, kept up to date, and made available to those responsible for the children's education. Doing this in the simplest manner possible is important. Unwieldy systems are time consuming, difficult to understand and ineffective.

Choosing a System

During the first years of early childhood special education classes, many federal grants were available. Schools, universities, and private facilities developed model programs. Many of these model programs became available for replication in other schools. Most of these subsidized programs provided time for teachers to plan, analyze problems, write objectives, experiment, and revise at each step. Volumes of objectives were recorded in each domain. As a result of this, very bulky curriculum guides filled many shelves.

The intent to be thorough somtimes resulted in record-keeping systems that required a computer or many hours of a teacher's time each day. This luxury is rarely available to most preschool and child care teachers today. If many hours are required for record keeping, these are hours that the teacher would prefer to be doing other things. The best system is the simplest and easiest to maintain, but it must be effective and complete.

Factors to Consider. The first consideration should be the purpose of the records. Will they be used with children with special needs as the basis for lesson planning, or will they be used primarily to report to parents at the end of specified times? As preschool teachers discover the advantages of using the developmental checklist as a basis for curriculum planning, it is probable that

this system will be used for all children. Thus, the record-keeping purposes expand for all those attending the preschool, not just those needing IEPs.

Deciding who will maintain the records is important. If a secretary is available, perhaps records can be more elaborate. But if the teacher is expected to keep all of the records up to date, the process must be streamlined.

For some children quarterly reports to parents are adequate. For others a number of people may need to be continuously informed. Determining who will need to be regularly informed is a deciding factor in style and method of record keeping.

It is important to ask, "How will the information be distributed?" Will a phone call suffice, or must written reports be made? Is it enough to have the information available in the classroom for those who need to review it regularly?

Although teachers will want to be able to check the children's skill levels daily, it is useful to consider how often others will need to be informed of progress. Teachers must ask, "How frequently should this information be reported?"

Other important questions to ask and factors to consider when planning a record-keeping system include the following:

1. Where will the records be kept?
2. What provisions for privacy of records must be made?
3. Can the record-keeping system be used to enhance teaching and planning for all members of the group?

Suggestions for Record Keeping

Usually a readily available checklist that includes a brief statement about each objective and the names of all the children is adequate for daily use. The more available it is, the more useful it is. Some teachers prefer to keep this checklist in a notebook; others find it useful to have it on a bulletin board beside the teacher's desk.

By itself the checklist is inadequate for record keeping for children with special needs. It *is* adequate for daily recording, but unless it is written in behavioral objectives, it is not acceptable for children who need IEPs. If the checklist includes a complete set of objectives, it is too long and bulky!

A workable solution to the problem just described is to have the checklist as described and have the correctly written behavioral objectives associated with each item on the checklist filed in an accessible cabinet. For example, the checklist item might simply read "Recognizes colors." The complete objective, filed under the cognitive domain, might read "Given five items of each of the primary colors mixed together and the teacher's direction 'Give me the/a (color name) (item name),' the children will do as directed 8 out of 10 trials for each color."

In addition to the checklist and the behavioral objectives, some form of report designed especially for the parents is useful. Some schools prefer an abbreviated version of the checklist. The form and the arrangement of the items usually parallel the longer checklist used in the classroom.

Although it is important to keep accurate records of each child's skills as they develop, it is inappropriate to "grade" them in the usual sense of that word. An "A" in "learning colors" is meaningless. The only relevant information is whether or not the child can perform in the manner and under the circumstances described in the objective. As a result, there should be no place for a letter grade on the report.

One type of report to parents (Figure 6–2) that has been particularly useful can serve in three very different ways. Designed to be useful as long as the child is attending preschool, this report form includes all of the items on the curriculum checklist. However, each is written in a simplified objective form and illustrated with a cartoon drawing. First, this report form serves to acquaint the parents with all of the goals and objectives of the curriculum. Second, with a minimum explanation it enables the parents to identify their child's entry behavior. Third, it allows them to keep track of their child's progress as it occurs. By using this form, parents feel they understand the curriculum.

Developing Daily and Weekly Schedules

Traditionally, preschool schedules identified the activities to be included, the songs to be sung, the games to be played, and the snack to be eaten. Although it was expected that the children would develop cognitive, language, motor, and social skills, it was not considered necessary to individualize the lessons in any structured or formal way. The children were expected to grow and develop normally. Children with special problems were rarely included, and if they were it was up to each teacher to figure out how to deal with the unusual ones.

With the advent of P.L. 94-142, many preschools and child care centers, as well as the early childhood special education classes, have found it necessary to plan their daily lessons in a highly structured manner. Individualizing each activity has become the necessity.

Teachers planning for a group of preschoolers rarely have the luxury of hours for planning on school time. Teaching young children is demanding work at best. It is important to develop efficient, effective ways to plan. To do this requires a well-organized curriculum and a set of related goals and objectives. These have been described and defined throughout this chapter.

The suggestions for preparing and writing daily plans that follow are based on experience. At first, each day's plan required several hours to complete! Gradually, greater efficiency developed. Finally, each weekly lesson plan required only a few minutes to complete.

The first step in planning is to ask the following questions:

1. How will the day be divided into the various activities?

2. How much time will be allowed for each activity?

3. Which routines and activities will be repeated daily (for example, greeting the children as they arrive, bathroom routines, playtime, and outdoor time)?

4. Will a theme be used to provide focus for the activities each week?

5. What use will be made of small and large groups for specific teaching?

6. Which activities must be repeated frequently over time to allow for increasingly complex skill development? (Examples include most motor skills, many cognitive skills, and all language and social skills.)

7. Who will have to follow these activity plans?

By answering these seven questions, a system appropriate for the classroom will emerge. First, consider question 7: Who will have to interpret and follow your activity plans? Of course, the teacher will. But so will substitutes when the teacher is away. Teacher aides and volunteers will need to understand what is being done and why. The supervisor or principal will want to know what the teacher is planning. So while writing plans, you should consider the answer to question 7 continuously. Ms. McLynn's unique planning considerations are discussed in Exhibit 6–2.

EXHIBIT 6–2 _____

A Week's Plan and Individualized Activities

Ms. McLynn plans activities a week in advance. She is careful to choose things that the children are able to do and will enjoy.

Each week she chooses a theme. Vocabulary, concepts to be emphasized, and gross and fine motor activities as well as music and stories are chosen in relation to the theme. For example, if the theme is "See signs of spring and learn about them," she will plan a walk to look at buds and spring flowers, plant seeds, do a craft (fine motor) activity such as make crepe paper flowers, and learn a song about spring.

Many of the objectives for each child require practice over time. Each day, Ms. McLynn chooses materials and games that promote these skills. This equivalent practice makes it possible for the children to do many different things at essentially the same skill level. They are not bored, even though they are practicing the same skills daily. The needed repetition never becomes meaningless drill.

Ms. McLynn found it difficult to include each child's individual objectives on the weekly lesson plan. She prefers to list the activity, such as "numerals and counting," on the plan. Then, she uses her checklist and objectives to provide individualized lesson targets for each child. This does not mean that she works with them one at a time. She conforms her directions and questions to each child on the basis of individual skills during the group activity. Experience has taught her that she can match the appropriate en route behavior to each child without writing each objective on her weekly plan.

Ms. McLynn's friend Ms. Watts has less experience in teaching young children with different individual needs. She prefers to have a separate page for each child. She writes the specific objective for each part of the weekly plan on the individual child's plan. Then, she writes a comment each afternoon about the effectiveness of her planning. In this way she is learning to evaluate and adjust her planning. Each of these teachers chooses a theme and plans individualized activities within group lessons. However, they prefer a different system for organizing and record keeping.

EXHIBIT 6–3

Example of a Daily Time-Use Plan: Preschool Classroom

Time-use plan and description of daily routines for both morning and afternoon classes*

8:30 A.M. or 12:15 P.M.	*Greeting.* Children are greeted individually as they arrive. Welcome by name, encourage to respond with eye contact, and use a smile and "Hello" or "Good morning." Help them only as much as necessary to hang up their coats and get ready for their special work. Ask whether they have brought a note from home. Some (as needed) go to the bathroom. Active conversation with them about everything they are doing is a must, since their primary need is to develop social, language, and cognitive skills about their everyday experiences. Encourage them to look into the mirror to see whether they are neat and ready for school. During the first 30 minutes children will appear to be playing, some alone and some in small groups of *their choice.* This open classroom is an important teaching time, because children choose "lessons," games, or toys. Teachers, aides, and parents may play or work with them, but it is each child's option to choose what to do. Encourage children to choose carefully, complete an activity, then return toys and games to the shelves. They are not required to share what they have chosen and may play alone if they prefer. It is important to enjoy conversation with children about what they are doing, although this will be a bit one-sided at first. Interactive conversation (which includes the adult's listening) is the optimum way to teach speech and language skills. Concepts to be emphasized are listed on the weekly theme page and on the *concept board* behind the teacher's desk. The intent of the concept board is to provide a "prompt sheet" for adults in the classroom to use these words continually in appropriate ways throughout the day. Contrive occasions for children to use these concepts correctly. Spontaneity is important. Repeated use is requisite.
8:45 A.M. or 12:30 P.M.	*Clean-up time.* Children take turns ringing the bell to announce the end of play time. Sing the "clean-up" song. All participate in cleaning up and moving chairs to form a semicircle facing the bulletin board. Reward with praise those who arrive first with their work completed. *Circle time.* Sometimes children sit on their own carpet squares on the floor or under a tree to allow for variety. The purpose of this period is to give children practice in participating, listening, and controlling themselves in a large group. This takes time. "Dailies" include a

Next, how the day will be divided and how much time will be spent on each activity (questions 1 and 2) should be considered. To avoid having to fill in a blank space each week with repetitive comments such as "Greet children individually" or "Take care of bathroom needs" or even "Sing the Clean-Up Time Song," it is helpful to write a *time-use plan* that can be used for many weeks. Any activities that are repeated daily should be included. Enough detail should be included so that a substitute will be able to have a clear picture of what is expected during each time segment. Exhibit 6–3 and 6–4 give examples of time-use plans.

In addition to the time-use plan, a form with blanks, including places to write specific activites, themes, or vocabulary, is needed. It is helpful to focus on particular cognitive and motor skill areas each day. These also can be printed on the form. For example, note "Colors" on the sample plan (Exhibit 6–5). This is a helpful reminder to plan an activity that focuses on colors at that time each week. However, whatever the teacher does during that lesson must reflect individualization of the lesson. Here, reference to the checklist and the related behavioral objectives will serve as a guide.

Regardless of the materials used or specific

9:00 A.M. or 12:45 P.M.	review of the weather, days of the week, the calendar, learning names, recognizing who is absent, and "show and tell." These activities not only help children become socially aware but also help develop their language expression, memory, and just plain everyday knowledge. *Small-group time.* Children choose from activities previously set up by the teacher. These usually include a fine motor activity, language activity, problem-solving activity, and combination activity such as cooking, which builds fine motor skills, language, and concepts. Some children may work individually with the teacher, aide, or therapist at this time. For children with special needs, choices may be narrowed to develop target behaviors such as cleaning up, toileting, and washing hands.
9:30 A.M. or 1:15 P.M.	*Snack time.* A wide variety of nutritious foods are eaten to encourage conversation and understanding of differences, for example, in color, texture, taste, and shape. As children finish, they brush their teeth and select a book from the shelf.
9:50 A.M. or 1:35 P.M.	*Story time.* Sometimes all children "read" to themselves. At other times, some read to themselves while others join an adult to listen to a story. When enough adults are available, several stories may be listened to in small groups around the room.
10:10 A.M. or 1:55 P.M.	*Movement time.* Depending on the weather, movement activities may be inside the room, in the gym, or outside. Music may accompany such activities. The physical therapist may work with some children, as noted on the physical therapy list.
10:30 A.M. or 2:15 P.M.	*Music and art time.* Music and fingerplay activities may be done in the group circle. Art activities are usually done in small groups. Sometimes parents will share special interests with children at this time. Choice is given, when possible.
10:50 A.M. or 2:35 P.M.	*Dismissal preparation.* Children clean up and then join others in the circle. One at a time, children get their belongings and put on their coats while others exchange feelings about the day and sing the closing song.
11:00 A.M. or 2:45 P.M.	*Dismissal.* Children are released to parents or bus drivers.

* NOTE: Times suggested are approximate. Young children should not be rushed. Flexibility is necessary to capture "teachable moments" and to accommodate special events such as field trips.

activities, teaching will be guided by the specific objectives for each child. For instance, if the teacher chooses to teach colors this week by baking cookies and icing them with the colors being taught, he or she will conform to the objectives by asking some children to "Show me the blue icing' " or "Use the yellow icing." For children who have demonstrated that they can *recognize* colors (for example, "Show me") the teacher will be ready to ask, "What color did Joe use on his cookie?" This, of course, reflects individualizing because Joe is asked to *recall* the color, a more difficult objective than to merely recognize it when the color is named. When the teacher plans

in this way, it becomes unnecessary to write objectives for each different activity because the teacher is providing **equivalent practice.** That is, the teacher is expecting each child to perform on the level identified on his or her column of the checklist.

However, some activities will involve cooking, whereas others involve dressing the doll, sorting different color toys, or choosing paper for a fine motor project. While teaching, the teacher is continually assessing the individual performances. He or she can be very creative in the activities chosen but will not need to write each one in detail. The checklist, with its related ob-

EXHIBIT 6–4 _____

Example of a Daily Time-Use Plan: Infant Toddler Center

B. Ammons	D. Tison
Teachers	Physical Therapist
A. McKail/C. Rodriquez	M. Briggs
Assistants	Speech Therapist

DATE: Sept 20

Time	Daily Activities	Notes
9:00	1. Arrival	1. Staff will greet bus and assist children and parents in coming to classroom.
	2. Facilitated Play • Puzzles • Blocks • House play • Mirror activity: old hats • Manipulative toys	2. • Optional areas: floor, table, and room areas. • Assistance given to individual children or small groups—Encourage participation. • Objectives: language, socialization, fine and gross motor.
9:25	3. Transition	3. • Give signals/cues to end play. • Allow time to leave play areas. • Bring chairs to circle. • Assist in positioning children who need help.
9:30	4. Large-group circle A. Music (with guitar) "Good Morning"/"Buenos Dias" "Where Oh Where?" (Sing each child's name) "Wheels on the Bus" B. Activity "What's in the Box?" (Balloons hidden in decorated box.) Blow up balloon and pass around.	4. A. • Parents may be encouraged to sit with the children. B. • Objectives: language concepts, social interaction, attention, motor activity, problem solving.
9:45	5. Outside Play yard: facilitated and self-directed play: • Sand box • Water play • Trikes, cars, wagons • Playground equipment (slides, ladders, swings, etc.)	5. • Objectives: gross motor, social interaction (encourage children with disabilities and those without to interact with toys, games, equipment); exploration through movement and space. • Parents are encouraged to participate.

jectives, saves time and repetitive effort. The weekly lesson plan identifies the activities and the themes.

GENERIC INSTRUCTIONAL STRATEGIES

A wide body of research and theoretical work in fields such as developmental and experimental psychology, child development, neuropsychology, and education has generated an extensive knowledge base from which we can develop a catalog of principles and strategies for early intervention. These strategies and principles are generic in that they apply not just to young children with special needs, but to all children. They are based on several key principles that describe how children learn. Students wishing to develop expertise in the field of early childhood special education cannot hope to do so without understanding, first, how all young children learn, and second, how teaching strategies can be adapted and fine tuned to meet the needs of children with special needs.

Time	Daily Activities	Notes
10:15	6. Small-group activity (4-5 children in each group). • Make pudding (choose flavor, open box, mix, taste)	6. Objectives: language concepts, choice, taste, social interactions, fine motor.
10:40	7. Clean-up Toilet	7. This is time for children to help clean up - wash pans and hands. As clean-up proceeds, 2-3 children go to "potty room." This is an important time for teaching self-help skills, language, etc.
11:00	8. Lunch Clean-up	8. Good teaching opportunity: • Encourage self-help, language, socialization. • Attention to positioning and feeding techniques (as needed).
11:45	9. Closing: Large-group (three classes) music/ activities	9. Parents, children, and staff join together in music, rhythms, rhymes, and relaxation. Bilingual songs and games.
12:00	10. Going home	10. Staff assists parents and children in going to bus.

Important Components Underlying Daily Program

1. Physical Therapists and Speech Therapists work in classrooms throughout the morning.

2. Parents participate in classroom or observe through one-way mirror or socialize with other parents in parent room.

3. Bilingual interactions throughout morning activities.
   • Spanish/English
   • Chinese/English

4. Each child has individual goals within daily activities.

5. Signal transition times.

Motivation

One of the most powerful keys to learning is **motivation,** one of the oldest notions in the field of psychology (Maslow, 1968). Motivation is an incentive or inducement to action. Human organisms behave and act on the environment for certain reasons. Young children with no disabilities are typically easily motivated; early childhood educators may not need to spend a great deal of conscious effort identifying and understanding the motivations of such children.

For young children with disabilities, however, the identification of high-preference objects, people, and activities is crucial to intervention success.

It is helpful to view motivation as being of two types: external and internal. The techniques of behavior analysis and behavior modification rely primarily on externally provided motivators. These might include primary **reinforcers** such as food and water or socially conditioned reinforcers such as praise or tokens. Also to be considered is effectance motivation, which, instead,

EXHIBIT 6–5

Example of Weekly Activity Plan

Activities for week of: _Feb. 8–12_   Teacher: _Mc Lynn_

Theme for this week: _Valentines – "Caring"_   Teacher aide: _Coia_

Vocabulary to be emphasized: _valentine, heart, lace, caring, love, sharing, kind_

Concepts to be emphasized: _match, doesn't match, corner, center, middle, edge_

Please note: All work is individualized, even during group activities. See the checklist and the sequenced behavioral objectives

	Daily Activities	Monday	Tuesday	Wednesday	Thursday	Friday
8:30 A.M. / 12:15 P.M.	Shelf choice and greetings—open choices	playdoh	easel painting	large blocks	puzzles	cutting pasting
8:45 A.M. / 12:30 P.M.	Circle time (All together)		The "DAILIES": weather; day of the week; calendar of who's here, who's absent; and show and tell			
	Special emphasis (for example, holiday, field trip, or visitor)	(Colors) pink red white	(Shapes) "heart shape"	(Numbers) addresses	(Listening) post office	(Feelings) happy faces love, sharing
9:00 A.M. / 12:45 P.M.	Small, group-choice time	match colored valentines	crawl-through shapes	addressing valentines	field trip	long exp. story post office
9:30 A.M. / 1:15 P.M.	Snack time	raspberry yogurt	toast shapes milk	fruit	making cran-berries	mothers' treat
	(Note: This is an important teaching time. In addition to teaching children to prepare and eat a wide variety of foods, spontaneous and directed conversations are used to teach concepts [above], math readiness, colors, textures, shapes, and categories of foods.)					
9:50 A.M. / 1:35 P.M.	Story time	Peek #50	"I'm glad I'm me"	"Jenny's Val. Party"	Peek #90	"What color is love?"
10:10 A.M. / 1:55 P.M.	Movement time	tunnel	parachute	balance beams	free play	dancing
10:30 A.M. / 2:15 P.M.	Music and art time	band	coloring valentines	cutting/pasting valentines	records	"Love Somebody"
10:50 A.M. / 2:35 P.M.	Dismissal preparation	self-help		zippers, buttons →→→		
11:00 A.M. / 2:45 P.M.	Dismissal	buses	wait for bus in front hall →→→			

is thought to be dependent on internal motivational factors.

Behavior Modification

The contributions of techniques of **behavior analysis** and **behavior modification** to the field of special education have been substantial. The ability to describe behavior objectively, analyze antecedent events and consequences, and shape children's behavior is a basic skill requirement for all educators. While space does not allow a thorough presentation of the principles and applications of behavior modification in this text, early interventionists must acquire competence in the use of such techniques as successive approximations, the use of cues and prompts, and the provision of contingent reinforcement (see Walker & Shea, 1991.)

Briefly, this approach is based on the principle that immediate consequences of a specific behavior can either strengthen or weaken that behavior. Consequences that are pleasurable are called *reinforcers.* Consequences that are unpleasant or aversive are called *punishers.* The use of punishers or aversive control is not appropriate for infants and very young children. However, the use of **positive reinforcement** can be very helpful in increasing the strength and frequency of certain behaviors. For example, giving a thirsty child a sip of juice each time he or she makes a sound might help increase vocalizations.

Whenever possible, the positive reinforcer should be a logical or "natural" consequence of the particular behavior, rather than an artificial one. An example of a natural reinforcer for making the correct sign for a favorite toy would be providing the opportunity to play with the toy rather than receiving a piece of candy. Another example would be giving the child a glass of juice for saying "juice," rather than telling the child "Good talking."

Another key component of behavior modification is the planning and selection of specific cues and prompts. Again, whenever possible, the child should learn to respond to natural rather than contrived cues and prompts. Earlier behavior modification programs utilized highly structured programs aimed at so-called "errorless learning." Teaching of specific skills was broken down into many small steps, beginning with highly contrived prompts that were to be faded gradually until the child could perform the behavior without prompts. Unfortunately, such procedures often produced children who were "cue bound," that is, they continued to be extremely dependent on specific prompts. Generalization to other settings was difficult. For example, a child could be taught to say the word "cookie" in response to the prompt "Say 'cookie,'" but would not spontaneously request a cookie without a cue in another setting. Thus, more recently emphases have been placed on teaching children to recognize the appropriate situation in which to use the behavior, respond to more natural cues such as an adult's expectant look or saying "Is there something you need?", and teaching in natural contexts (Falvey, 1986).

Another key component of behavior modification is reinforcement of the child's **successive approximations.** This is a solid principle of learning based on recognition of the importance of starting with whatever the child can do and gradually encouraging closer and closer approximation to the correct behavior. For example, initially a child may only be able to swipe at a paper with a colored marker. Gradually the child can be reinforced for behavior that comes closer and closer to making a circle.

Behavioral principles are also very useful in our attempts to understand certain behaviors by carefully observing both the **antecedents** of the behavior (i.e., the events that occur immediately prior to the behavior) and its **consequences** (i.e., what occurs immediately following the behavior). For example, a child who has tactile defensiveness (i.e., is very sensitive to touch) may have frequent episodes of crying. Careful recording may reveal that these episodes are brought on by situations in which the antecedent event is the child's being crowded by other children. Observation may also reveal that the usual consequence of this crying is for the child's favorite adult to start talking to him. A simple intervention that may reduce the crying and increase the child's tolerance for crowding would be the following: When the favored adult notices the antecedent situation (crowding) occurring, she could approach the child *before* he begins to cry, commenting on how she is pleased he's having such a good time with the other children. Such a rearrangement of **contingencies** (i.e., what behavior or event follows or precedes what other behavior or event) both reinforces the child for participating and not crying, *and* conditions the child to associate crowded situations with the pleasant experience of being talked to by a friend.

Behavior modification techniques can be powerful influences on children's behavior. It is extremely important that they not be used in isolation from a thorough understanding of the *whole* child. For example, one would not use behavior modification strategies to control tantrums without also exploring all possible causes of these tantrums (e.g., medication effects, pain, or fear).

Effectance Motivation

The theory of **effectance motivation** holds that all young children innately have an internal drive toward effectance or achievement (White, 1959). Children internalize or feel personally responsible for the mastery they have over their own behavior and the resulting impact on their environment. If free of disabling conditions, children can more easily feel pride in accomplishments they can attribute to their own effort or ability (Cook, 1983). It is this personal feeling of control over one's self and pride in one's efforts that provides inducement to act (motivation).

The existence of an internal drive to have an effect on one's environment suggests the importance of encouraging young children to initiate interactions with both the animate and inanimate world around them. For nondisabled children, the key to this type of motivation lies both in the opportunity for self-initiation and exploration and in the existence of a responsive environment. For children with special needs, teachers and caregivers must be able to read cues that are often ambiguous and may occur infrequently. These cues must be perceived in order to identify situations in which a child with disabilities is attempting to act upon the environment. It may also be necessary to manipulate the child's environment in ways that increase the likelihood that the child will initiate an interaction and experience success.

The teacher may have to, verbally and in other ways, call the child's attention to the fact that his or her actions really do make a difference. Only when the success of an action is attributed to one's own efforts can pride resulting in motivation or the desire to try again be realized (Cook, 1983). The following examples may help illustrate the importance of understanding children's motivations.

Johnny is a healthy, energetic, typical 4 year old. Most of his interest is in large muscle activities. He loves being outside, riding tricycles, and climbing. One rainy day he wandered over to the cupboard where the play dough was kept, managed to climb precariously up on the counter, and opened the cupboard. Mrs. Hunt's first inclination was to reprimand Johnny for climbing, but instead she said, "What are you looking for? Can I help you?" She then realized that he was trying to get the play dough. This was uncharacteristic of Johnny, since he typically had no patience for this kind of fine motor activity. So Mrs. Hunt decided to encourage his interest, and she provided him with the play dough. She also stayed close to him while he rolled it into balls and "snakes," assisting him and praising him occasionally. Thus, she was able to encourage participation in a new activity by taking advantage of Johnny's own drive to act upon his environment.

Another child, Robert, has cerebral palsy. He has very limited movement in all four extremities. He cannot walk and is just beginning to reach and attempt to grasp objects. Even though he has severe physical impairments, he has a great sense of humor and loves attention. During free-play time, he is placed prone on a bolster so he can watch two of his nondisabled peers, Maria and Jeff, playing with blocks. The teacher enters the group and begins to build a block tower just within Robert's reach. She demonstrates to Robert that if he reaches and contacts the block tower, he can knock it down. She pretends to be dismayed by the destruction of the tower. Robert beams. Now the teacher rebuilds the tower and, without prompting, Robert reaches to knock the tower down again, thoroughly enjoying the game. Very shortly, Maria and Jeff want to get into the game, each building towers for Robert to knock down.

These scenarios demonstrate the use of motivation and the importance of having an effect on one's environment. In the first example, the teacher recognizes Johnny's interest in the play dough and responds to that interest, thus allowing him to have an impact on the objects and people around him. She then assists his development in a new skill area. In Robert's case, he becomes motivated by his impact on both the physical and the social environment. He experiences *effectance* by successfully making the tower fall down and also by initiating a turn-taking game (social interaction) with both his teacher and his nondisabled peers. This is a result that is often difficult for young children with disabilities to achieve.

Social Mediation of Experience

The literature in the field of developmental and cognitive psychology is rich with both theoretical explanations and empirical descriptions of ways in which adults mediate (i.e., assist in making meaningful) the environment and the events that young children experience. Feuerstein, Rand, Hoffman, and Miller (1980) referred to these phenomena as "mediated learning events" or MLE, in which adults carefully enhance a child's understanding and mastery by translating events both physically and verbally as the child experiences them.

Another theorist, Vygotsky (1978) stated that cognition develops within a social context. He described that "zone of proximal development," which is the realm of abilities that the child is able to exhibit while interacting with a significant adult but cannot perform independently. As sensitive adults interact with young children they become aware of this "zone" and are able to facilitate development by providing just the right degree and type of support necessary to assist the child's progress toward independent mastery of a task. Bruner (1982) referred to this as "scaffolding," or the providing of graduated cues to assist a child through problem solving. Such **social mediation** of the child's experience is important for all infants and young children, regardless of their particular capabilities. Note the two examples that follow.

Jose is a highly gifted, somewhat rambunctious 3 year old. He is trying to use three blocks to build a sort of archway for his truck to go under, but it is too narrow. He glances around briefly for a solution but quickly gives up and starts to move on to something else. His teacher notices and says, "Gee, the space is too narrow, isn't it? The truck can't fit through there. The truck is too big. Hmm. What can we do?" While making these comments, the teacher finds a long piece of cardboard, which, if substituted for the block across the top, will make it possible to widen the opening. She does not say this, but simply offers the piece of cardboard to Jose. She waits, giving him the opportunity to discover the solution himself, which he promptly does. He pushes the truck through, and his teacher comments, "Oh, good. Now the opening is big enough for the truck to go through."

A second child, Min, has severe developmental delays and multiple disabilities. She is blind and nonambulatory. She is able to reach and grasp, but does so infrequently. Her favorite activity is eating. She appears to be sensitive to food aromas, because she becomes much more alert as lunchtime approaches and food carts are moved through the hallways. Her teacher helps Min organize and understand her experiences around lunchtime, mediating the environment around her. As the teacher notices Min becoming alert to the smell of the approaching food, the teacher says "Lunch! It's lunchtime, Min. Let's get ready." The teacher first introduces Min's bib, encouraging her to touch and feel it, saying "here's your bib." The teacher puts on the bib, encouraging as much independence as possible by getting Min to push her arms through the holes. Next, as the cart enters the room, she taps its side so Min can hear it, then moves her close to it so she can feel it. The teacher says, "Good, our food cart is here. Now we can eat. I'll push you over to the lunch table."

In this way, the teacher is mediating what might otherwise be simply a confusing blur of sounds, smells, touches, and position changes. By doing this consistently, the teacher will eventually assist Min in understanding and anticipating these events.

Adult-Child Communication Strategies

As can be seen in the preceding examples, another critical factor in assisting children's learning is the use of language. How adults and older children talk to infants and young children has a major impact on their development, particularly in the areas of language and cognition. These strategies will be discussed in some detail

in Chapter 9. However, it is appropriate to summarize them here as well.

1. *Use referential language.* That is, use the names of things and actions; be specific and concrete. For example, a child is enjoying rolling a ball down the slide. Teacher A might say something like "Wow! That's neat. Look at it go." While this is an enthusiastic and positive response to the child's involvement, it is not referential. This comment would have a less positive effect on the child's language development than would teacher B's response: "Wow! the ball's rolling down. Down the slide. The ball's rolling down fast!"

2. *Use redundancy and repetition of key words and phrases.* It is not sufficient to refer to something only once. Language needs to be redundant, mentioning key concepts and events several times. In addition, repetition of key words and phrases is important. Redundancy and repetition are important to all children, and even more important for children with disabilities. In the example above, the word "ball" is used two times; "down" is used three times; and "rolling" is used twice. Ideally, these three concepts would be introduced again during the play situation, in a slightly different context. For example, the teacher could roll a different ball down an inclined board, or the children could roll themselves down a hill, and so on.

3. *Utilize routines.* Some degree of routine and predictability is important for all children. For children with special needs, the careful use of routines becomes an important teaching strategy. Repetition of key words and phrases within a familiar sequence of daily events facilitates language development. Both play routines and caretaking routines are effective strategies for encouraging many areas of children's development and will be discussed in more detail later.

4. *Provide comprehensive input.* The impor-

tance of comprehensive input was first described by MacNamara (1972). It is important for children to be tuned in to and understand what you are talking about, even if they don't actually understand all the words. Several strategies facilitate this. For example, adults can follow the child's lead and talk about what the child is paying attention to and experiencing. Sometimes this is called "mapping language onto experience" (McLean & Snyder-McLean, 1978, p. 193). Another strategy is to talk about concrete things that can be seen, felt, or heard. In this way words can be associated easily with their referents.

5. *Match adult language to the child's language level.* For children who are just beginning to learn language, adult language input must be short, consisting of one- and two-word utterances and short, simple sentences. As the child's language develops, adult language can become more complex. MacDonald (1989, p. 173) referred to this as **progressive** matching. For example, John has just begun to use single words.

As he is playing catch with his teacher, she says "Catch. Catch the ball. Catch the ball, John." John's friend Theo, who speaks easily in simple sentences, joins the game. The teacher says, "Here Theo. Catch the ball, then throw it to John." In this way, the teacher models more complex utterances for Theo.

6. *Establish turn taking.* For very young children or children with severe disabilities, it may be necessary to first establish turn-taking skills before the strategies previously listed can be used effectively. Turn taking provides the social basis upon which communication skills develop. In a nondisabled child, turn-taking skills are well established within the caregiver-infant dyad in the first 3 or 4 months of life. For some children, however, this may need to be established as a specific teaching goal. Several strategies can be used to establish turn taking: (a) imitating something the child is already doing; (b) engaging in a pleasurable activity and then interrupting that activity and waiting un-

til the child makes some kind of response; or (c) physically prompting the child to take a turn. Chapter 9 will elaborate on other ways to develop communication skills.

Routines

Daily living routines are important in designing educational programs for young children. For infants, daily living routines may be referred to as *caregiving routines.*

Daily Living Routines. Daily living routines are the kinds of routines that occur as part of carrying out the daily activities of life. Families may vary in the extent to which their lives are characterized by a predictable routine or schedule. While some home environments may be quite predictable (e.g., wake up, eat breakfast, go to school, come home from school, have a snack, take a nap, play with Dad, eat supper, watch television, take a bath, read a story, go to bed), others may be chaotic and unpredictable. Some degree of predictability is thought to be important to young children. It helps them feel secure and gives them a sense of mastery and control over their environment. As will be discussed in Chapter 7, it facilitates both emotional and cognitive development.

Daily living routines are also important in the center or classroom for the same reasons that they are important at home. In addition, they provide useful contexts for teaching language and cognitive concepts. A familiar routine is a necessary background against which children with disabilities can experience novel and special events. For these children, such events can be attended to and processed more easily when they are experienced as different from the norm. On the other hand, when such events occur as simply one of many unexpected and unfamiliar events in a day, they are meaningless at best and probably confusing.

Play Routines. Play routines provide another way to utilize repetition and routine in the classroom. Play routines can be designed specifically to teach language and concepts, and social skills. A play routine often revolves around a pretend play theme, such as going shopping, going on a camping trip, finding something lost, hunting for treasure, and so on. The possibilities are endless. The purpose of a play routine is to provide a familiar activity sequence within which to teach specific concepts, vocabulary, social behaviors or pragmatic communication skills. The play routine requires a great deal of work and planning initially, but as the routine is repeated over and over it becomes easier to implement while it becomes more powerful as a teaching strategy. The complexity and content of the play routine will be dependent upon the needs and characteristics of the children in the class.

Exhibit 6–6 demonstrates how the generic strategies discussed here can be incorporated into the medium of play, the context that is most normal to young children.

PLAY AS AN IMPORTANT TEACHING CONTEXT

Skilled use of the strategies described here presents a significant challenge to the early childhood special education professional. There is no better context in which to use these strategies than the context of play. In fact, in many ways play is probably the single most important concept in early childhood special education. It is important both as a teaching context and as an end in itself. Play is an important skill. Typical young children can often learn play skills with little guidance from adults. Many children with special needs, however, must be assisted in learning these skills. Thus, the teaching of play as a social skill is considered an important part of the early education curriculum. This aspect of play will be discussed further in Chapter 7.

Play is an ideal context in which to discover and mobilize children's motivations. It also creates a rich environment where teachers can

EXHIBIT 6–6 _____

Use of Generic Instructional Strategies During Playtime

Event	*Strategy*
The children in Mr. Curtis's class have finished lunch. Mr. Curtis announces that it is time to clean up the tables and go to recess.	Signal for transition
The children are very familiar with this routine, so with little assistance they throw away their napkins and milk cartons and bring their cups and plates to the sink.	Use of routines
Andrea, a 4 year old who has Down syndrome, heads out to the playground. On her way she notices the bottle of bubble soap on the shelf. She loves blowing bubbles and tries to grab the bottle.	
Miss Chinn, the aide, notices and asks, "Would you like to take the bubble soap outside?" "Okay. Can you get the bottle for us?"	Response to child's interest
Andrea reaches with one hand, but has difficulty getting hold of the bottle. Miss Chinn gently moves Andrea's other hand toward the bottle, encouraging her to grasp with both hands.	Scaffolding
Andrea gets the bottle and carries it outside.	Child experiences success
Andrea's friend Alex notices that she has the bubble soap. He comes over and offers to help her get the top off. He blows some bubbles, then hands the wand to Andrea so she can try.	Peer interaction
The teacher approaches and sits down on the grass with the children. He says, "Andrea, look at these bubbles. Many, many bubbles! Oops! One popped. The bubble popped. Pop! Pop!"	Use of short sentences Repetition of key words
Andrea looks at Alex pointing to a bubble on the ground, saying "Buh!" Alex says, "Bubble. Right!" Then the bubble pops and Andrea says "Pop! pop!"	Child responds and is heard
Later that same day, Miss Chinn finds a balloon. She brings the balloon to Andrea, saying, "Let's blow up the balloon." Andrea does not seem interested at first, but she becomes intrigued as Miss Chinn starts to blow. She blows it up a little bit, then stops. She looks expectantly at Andrea.	Redundancy Generalization practice
Andrea waves her hand toward the balloon. Miss Chinn says, "Shall I blow some more?" Andrea says, "More."	Reading child's nonverbal cues Responsivity
The aide finishes blowing up the balloon. Then she says, "I'm going to *pop* the balloon." "I'm going to *pop* it."	Repetition Foreshadowing events
Andrea looks at her quizzically. Miss Chinn then takes a pin and pops the balloon. She says, "It popped!" Andrea claps her hands excitedly. She runs off to find her friend Alex at the sand table. She looks at Alex and says, "Pop!"	Social interaction Use of language to describe past events

use the interaction and mediation strategies described earlier.

Within the field of early education there is a strong historical precedent for a focus on play. Froebel, a German educator in the 1800s, believed that the principles of early education include the following:

1. Education should primarily protect and nurture.

2. It should not prescribe and control.

3. Play should constitute the heart of the curriculum.

4. Play is the means by which children gain insight.

5. Play is the means of mental development.

This is a strong endorsement of the role of play in education, and it has continued to influence the field of early education throughout its history (Weber, 1971).

It is equally important to apply this concept to the field of early childhood *special* education. This application requires some refinement. First, as mentioned before, some children with special needs do not engage in play easily. Thus, teachers must develop strategies not only for utilizing play as a context, but also for encouraging its occurrence. Second, it is necessary to understand how the elements of play can be achieved for all children.

There are some 40 definitions listed in the dictionary for the word *play.* An operational definition that might be useful for our purposes would be the following: Play is a situation in which an infant or child is actively engaged with his or her environment—either animate or inanimate—but for which there is not an intended or predetermined outcome or goal.

There are several key elements in this definition that parallel the principles and strategies discussed earlier and that demonstrate why play is such a powerful teaching and learning context. First, the child must be engaged. This suggests that, at the very minimum, there must be some information processing occurring; the child is paying attention to something. Furthermore, active engagement requires initiating and acting upon the environment in some way. The term *environment* refers not only to the physical world of objects, space, and sensory stimuli, but also (and perhaps more important) to the social environment. The social, or animate, environment consists of the people (and pets), communication, emotions, facial expressions, touches, and so on, that impinge in some way upon the infant's or child's experiences.

The element of play that perhaps most distinguishes it from other contexts or activities is the final element: there is no predetermined outcome or goal. In play, goals may emerge and unfold or arise spontaneously; outcomes are discovered through exploration and trial and error.

Given this definition of play, it can range from the simple exploratory behavior of the infant to the complex pretend scenarios of the preschooler. Playing peek-a-boo or putting blocks in a can may be play for one child, while pretending to be an alien from outer space is play for another.

Thus, play must be viewed as an important and necessary component of early childhood special education. It is, of course, not the only component. Routine daily living events are equally important contexts for learning. For busy parents, these contexts are possibly more important than play. There is also an important place for more structured, traditional learning contexts, particularly as children reach preschool age or are enrolled in behaviorally designed programs that focus on particular skills or behaviors. But the hallmark of the competent professional in the field of early childhood special education will be the ability to unleash the full potential of play not only to facilitate learning but also to enhance the joy and quality of life for young children with special needs.

ARRANGING THE PHYSICAL ENVIRONMENT TO MAXIMIZE LEARNING

There is substantial evidence that the social environment, as reflected in the preceding discussion, has great impact on children's development. It is also important to consider how the *physical* environment can influence both children and adults in ways that will enhance children's opportunities to learn and to interact socially with one another. Generally, physical arrangements and facilities that are effective for typical young children (NAEYC, 1984) will be suitable for children with special needs. However, some adjustments may have to be made, depending on the nature of the children's special needs. There may also have to be greater space within the classroom area to accommodate a larger number of adults, especially if active participation of family members is expected. A two-way mirror is very helpful in allowing for unobtrusive observation by families and teachers in training. The discussion that follows is meant to further highlight some of the unique considerations that might accompany integration of young children with special needs.

When integrating children who have physical challenges, ramps may have to be provided and enough space made available for children who need to maneuver equipment such as walkers or wheelchairs. Some may even need special positioning devices, which take additional space within the classroom. Materials should be at eye

level. Shelves and tables-must be sturdy enough to support children who have difficulty standing and maintaining balance. Sand and other activity tables should be set away from walls so that children may get to them from all sides. Tables with semicircular "bites" out of them and rims around the edges allow children to get closer to materials while also preventing items from rolling to the floor. In some cases, materials should be put on the floor. Nonslip floor coverings are necessary to prevent tripping or catching crutches. Adaptable equipment will be necessary to ensure full participation of all children.

For centers attended by children with visual impairments, room arrangements should be fairly fixed. Clutter must be eliminated. When changes must be made, it is important to assist children with visual impairments with adaptations to these changes. Routes from one area to another should be direct, minimize cross traffic, and be free of obstacles. Doors should be either fully open or completely shut. Sharp edges of tables should be padded. Auditory or tactile cues should be used to designate areas. For example, a carpet might mark the quiet corner while the bubbling of an aquarium signifies the science center. Groups should be kept small and noise levels controlled to allow for maximal use of hearing. Noisy, chaotic environments reduce opportunities for children with visual impairments to learn.

It is usually not necessary to make adaptations in facilities or equipment for children with cognitive, health, communication, or social-emotional differences. Children who are experiencing difficulties in self-control or overactivity do require more clearly defined limits and greater consistency in caregiving in order to feel safe. Opportunities for as much natural social interaction as possible are essential to the success of an integrated program. Teachers will find that while acting as guides they can use flexibility of setting and materials to help children develop social skills.

Special Considerations for Infants and Toddlers

Some special concerns for infant and toddler environments are worthy of note. Healthy and safety issues are of primary importance. Floors need to be padded, sharp edges and table corners eliminated, and elevated areas no more than 2 feet in height. Sinks and soap for handwashing and diapering must be conveniently located to encourage good hygiene. Diapering areas should not be located near food preparation centers. Carpets of short pile material will facilitate ease of cleaning. Storage areas that are easily accessible help to avoid clutter and hazards in traffic areas.

Environments for infants and toddlers should be designed to encourage movement and interaction with one another. Movement can be facilitated by providing carpeted steps and ramps that lead to interesting play areas. Places to crawl through, such as tunnels, and cozy spaces to crawl into, such as a specially designed box or cubby, will serve to motivate movement. Use of multiple elevations also encourages easier interaction between very young children and their caregivers by facilitating eye contact. Water beds set on the floor are effective movement motivators and can be comforting at the same time. Adult rockers and couches not only provide additional places for toddlers to climb into, but also encourage adults' holding, reading, and talking to infants and toddlers. "Adopted grandparents" might be just the right people to provide needed encouragement to move and verbalize.

Providing choices for infants and toddlers whose disabilities may be confining is essential. They need incentives for body movement and a variety of toys. Toys and other interesting objects should be displayed clearly on shelves that are neutral in color so that the objects stand out. To avoid visual confusion, only a few toys should be visible at any one time. Hart (1985) has also suggested keeping some interesting toys in cupboards or on high shelves to encourage children's communicative behaviors as they request objects that they cannot reach.

Room acoustics can be optimized by use of absorptive materials on floors, walls, and ceilings to reduce resonance and ambient noise. Many children with and without disabilities (as well as many adults) find noisy environments distracting and disorganizing. This may be especially true of those who have visual impairments and those who are easily overstimulated. Constant background noise from radios and record players encourages children and adults to talk louder, thus increasing the overall noise level in the classroom. This, in turn, increases stress and fatigue. Of course, it is important that efforts be made to reduce environmental noise without inhibiting children's exuberance. Readers are referred to Bailey and Wolery (1989) for an excellent presentation of guidelines for assessing environments.

Before integrating young children with special needs, directors would be wise to assemble an advisory panel made up of a physical therapist, an occupational therapist, a child psychologist, a speech and language pathologist, a nurse, and an early childhood special educator. This committee can make recommendations for adaptations to be made in the physical setting and the program. The following section outlines some of the considerations necessary for adapting curricula for children with specific special needs. In addition, illustrations of effective accommodations are found throughout the remaining chapters of this text.

CONSIDERATIONS FOR ADAPTING CURRICULA FOR CHILDREN WITH SPECIFIC SPECIAL NEEDS

It must be remembered that a child with disabilities is first a child. The suggestions given here are designed to help teachers, parents, and other caregivers meet those special needs that can get in the way of a child's opportunity to experience the best possible childhood. These ideas are only suggestions to be accepted, rejected, or modified to meet each child's unique needs. Of course, only some of the many possible considerations are included here. We hope they will serve as a stimulus to the development of many other successful adaptations.

Health Impairments

Common chronic health problems include allergies, anemia, asthma, cancer, cystic fibrosis, juvenile diabetes, epilepsy, heart defects, hemophilia, pituitary problems, juvenile rheumatoid arthritis, muscular dystrophy, and sickle-cell disease. No attempt will be made here to describe each of these problems in detail. A number of them are defined in the glossary. For more details, readers are referred to medical and nursing reference books. The suggestions made here are appropriate for almost any child with chronic health impairment, regardless of its specific nature.

Caregivers must work very closely with health care providers not only to ensure coordination of care of the primary disorder, but also to assist in the maintenance of general health. Remember that children with health impairments are more prone to common illnesses such as colds, ear infections, or diarrhea than are typical children. Children with chronic health needs usually miss more school, spend more time convalescing at home, and are hospitalized more frequently than are children with most other disabling conditions. Repeated separation and trauma create emotional and physical stress.

Much greater responsibility is placed on parents, who must continually monitor the child's health, chauffeur the child to and from appointments, endure the anxieties of medical routines, and sometimes perform daily therapy. In addition, some chronic health problems are life threatening. Caregivers must, then, be more sensitive and supportive than usual.

Specific Intervention Strategies for Working with a Child with Health Impairments

1. Find out as much as possible about any health problems experienced by children in your program. Read widely and personally visit health care agencies. Ask questions and record answers. Pay attention to the role of diet, medication, possible side effects of medication, physical restrictions, and behaviors indicating that a chronic illness is becoming acute.

2. Consult the child's parents and the primary care physician in planning the child's program. Become aware of what may cause a health crisis such as a seizure or insulin reaction. Caregivers must be completely prepared to deal with any such health-related crisis. They must know what warning signs to look for, what accommodations are appropriate, and how to follow through on emergency measures.

3. Prepare classroom aides and other children for the possibility of crisis events so that no one will be frightened and everyone will receive appropriate care. Perhaps a curriculum unit can deal with emergencies including fire protection, earthquake procedures, and so forth. Then the child who has a health impairment is not made to feel different.

4. Prepare a list of typical classroom activities. Ask the parents and the physician to note which activities should be avoided and to suggest adaptations so the child can participate as fully as possible.

5. Encourage the child to be as independent as possible.

6. Some children fatigue rapidly. Arrange the class schedule so that vigorous activites are followed by less strenuous ones. Do not restrict a child unless there is clear physical or emotional danger.

7. Help children to understand the implications of their health problems. Be open and encourage them to discuss or act out (in play) their fears and anxieties. Children who understand what foods they can or cannot eat, what activities they must avoid, and so on can begin to make decisions for themselves and thus feel more in control of their lives.

8. Review the suggestions in Chapter 7 as you help children prepare for hospitalization.

9. Develop a plan for keeping in touch with children who must be absent for long periods of time. Telephone calls, cards, and tape recordings can go a long way toward helping children cope with isolation.

Hearing Impairments

A hearing loss ranges from mild (hard of hearing) to profound (deaf). Specialists (audiologist, otologist, speech and language pathologist) can assist caregivers in understanding the degree to which development of communication skills will be affected by the disabling condition. Parents should be consulted to determine how much hearing capacity the child does have and which teaching methods and communication system (oral vs. total communication) to use with those who have more severe impairments. Early developmental milestones will be similar to those of the hearing child. The impact of a hearing impairment is most obvious in language development. Actual cognitive ability is hindered only to the extent that performance depends on language comprehension and use. Children with hearing impairments may exhibit inappropriate behavior due to lack of understanding or resulting socialization problems.

Specific Intervention Strategies for Working with a Child with Hearing Impairments

1. Seat the child up close for good visibility of teacher, activity, or other children.

2. Experiment to find out or ask parents how close a speaker must be for the child to hear.

3. Provide the child with experiences that make use of residual hearing.

4. Speak at normal speed and volume without exaggerating lip movements.

5. Avoid speaking with your back to the child or with a bright light behind you. Don't inadvertently cover your mouth when speaking. Realize that moustaches and beards do interfere with visibility of lip movements. Lipstick may enhance visibility.

6. Use normal vocabulary and sentence structure. Be prepared to repeat, rephrase, point out, or demonstrate if the child does not understand.

7. When seeking the child's attention, be certain to use his or her name. Teach the child to attend to your face, and do not give any directions until the child is obviously attending.

8. When teaching the child, use visual and tactile aids. Model the desired behavior whenever possible.

9. Learn to change a hearing aid battery and/or cord.

10. Encourage speech in group activities by allowing time for the child to start and finish speaking.

11. Work closely with the audiologist and speech and language specialist in planning programs for any child with a hearing impairment.

12. Adaptations made for children with speech and language delays will also be effective with children with hearing impairments.

Learning Impairments

Children with learning impairments are those who may be at risk for the development of learning disabilities or who for some reason learn "differently." Such children may exhibit excessive motion, find it difficult to attend or concentrate, lack coordination, experience difficulties in visual or auditory processing of information, have poor memories, and have difficulty in abstract reasoning and in making generalizations. Such disabilities are often difficult to detect and accept because they may be invisible.

Specific Intervention Strategies for Working with a Child with Difficulties in Learning

1. Be consistent in the use of behavior management techniques to increase or decrease movement. Structure and consistent classroom organization helps these children to feel secure and to respond appropriately to their environment.

2. Present content in short segments using a multisensory approach (audio, visual, manipulative). Provide for as much overlearning or repeated practice as necessary.

3. Analyze tasks. Break them down into as many small steps as needed for success. Use short sentences and simple vocabulary.

4. Use concrete examples when presenting new concepts. Choose functionally important concepts, not just those next on the developmental scales.

5. Praise the child's progress, no matter how small.

6. Concentrate on each child's strengths, not weaknesses.

7. Be patient when it is necessary to show a child how to do something many times. Don't expect children to generalize easily.

8. Give directions one at a time until a child can

handle more than one. Provide physical help if necessary.

9. Consult with speech and language specialists in planning the child's program. Suggestions for the children with hearing impairments, visual impairments, and speech and language impairments are also useful for those with learning impairments.

10. Help parents to understand that such children are not just "dumb" or stubborn. Encourage the establishment of consistency and opportunities for multisensory learning experiences at home. Help parents to recognize their children's small successes.

Physical Impairments

Orthopedic impairments (of the bones, joints, or muscles) may be the result of such conditions as arthritis, cerebral palsy, muscular dystrophy, spina bifida, and spinal cord damage. Characteristics will vary by the nature and severity of each condition. Children with physical impairments acquire information and manipulate the environment through other sensory modes. Children who are severely involved communicate and signify learning through breathing changes and eye blinks.

Of course, the most obvious developmental disabilities are in the motor area. Such children may attain motor milestones at a different rate or in a qualitatively different way than typical children. Some will never attain certain milestones. Certain aspects of language and cognitive development will be delayed due to motor impairment. For example, inability to grasp and manipulate the environment contributes to delayed problem solving. Alternative responses using adaptive equipment may be necessary to enhance cognitive development.

Delays in postural control and inability to use the muscles necessary to imitation may hinder development of communication skills.

Speech itself may be directly affected. Children with physical impairments who are unable to cuddle with their caregivers may not receive the positive interaction so necessary to all aspects of early development. Frustration may be a major part of life for both children and parents.

Specific Intervention Strategies for Working with a Child with Physical Disabilities

1. Review the suggestions made for working with the child with health impairments.

2. Proper handling and positioning of the child is extremely important. The child needs to feel comfortable and well balanced to be able to concentrate. Consult the parents and physical therapist in order to determine appropriate positions. For example, a prone position over a bolster will allow the child to make visual contact with the environment. A side-lying position may assist arm and leg movements. Each child's position will usually need to be changed every 20 to 30 minutes.

3. Arrange activities and the environment so that minimal movements will produce effects on the environment.

4. Use adaptive equipment that allows the child to interact with the environment as much as possible. Consult specialists in making the most appropriate physical adaptations to the classroom and its equipment.

5. Become proficient in the use of wheelchairs, crutches, braces, artificial limbs, and other mechanical aids.

6. Consult speech and language specialists in order to identify a successful response mode for the child. Special language boards will need to be constructed for some children.

7. Work toward realizing the goal of maximum physical and social-emotional independence for each child. Positive self-regard may be

the key to future motivation and self-fulfillment.

8. Do not underestimate a child's capabilities; do be realistic.

Visual Impairments

Legally, a person who is partially sighted is one with corrected visual acuity between 20/200 and 20/70. The term *partially sighted* is used when there is enough usable vision for learning with the help of magnification. A person who is legally blind has corrected visual acuity no better than 20/200 in his or her better eye. Such a person sees at 20 feet what those with normal vision see at 200 feet. Vision loss may result from common refractive errors (nearsightedness or farsightedness) or from such impairments as amblyopia (lazy eye), cataracts, cornea damage, detached retina, glaucoma, and retinitis pigmentosa.

Many of the children enrolled in mainstreamed programs will have some functional vision. Visual impairments do affect other areas of development. Delays have been noted in motor milestones that require self-initiated mobility, such as elevation of self by arms, raising to a sitting position, or running. Delay in the use of the hands results in delay of concept development. Language differences may become more noticeable after the age of 3, approximately. Many children with severe visual impairments experience difficulty with personal and possessive pronouns. In general, both cognitive and language development are hindered by lack of stimulation.

Specific Intervention Strategies for Working with a Child with Visual Impairments

1. Consult with the child's parents and vision specialists to determine just what the child can see. Many children can at least see shadows, color, and sometimes large pictures.

2. For some children, peripheral vision may be best. Therefore, do not assume that a turned-away head means inattention.

3. Be aware of lighting conditions and their effect on the child.

4. Orient the child to the classroom layout and materials location. Give a new orientation whenever changes are made.

5. Areas of the classroom can be identified by different floor coverings, different mobiles, and so on.

6. Provide the child with a rich variety of tactile, manipulative, and auditory experiences.

7. Facilitate auditory localization, reaching for sound, and auditory discrimination skills.

8. Try to keep the general noise level down, since a child with visual impairments relies heavily on auditory cues.

9. Encourage independence both by your actions and in the way the room is arranged. For example, giving the child the cubbie at the end of the row will make it easier to find. Experiment with bright, shiny, and lighted objects of various sizes and shapes.

10. Encourage children to identify themselves when they approach a child with severe visual impairments.

11. Be alert to the need for physical prompts. When teaching new self-help skills, work from behind the child and gradually reduce the help given.

12. Before beginning a new activity, simply say what is going to happen.

13. Consult with specialists to develop aids for the child who is partially sighted. For example, black pen marks on the edges of paper will help the child to know the boundaries of the drawing pad.

14. Be creative in finding ways to help the children develop a positive concept of self.

The principles and strategies described in this chapter are powerful and effective for *all* children. They represent some of the basic competencies of all early educators. Because this is a text in early childhood *special* education there are additional skills and methods that must be mastered by the early childhood special education professional. These include environmental manipulations, use of special methods and adaptive devices for children with specific disabilities, microanalysis of children's behavior and of teaching effectiveness, and, especially, parent-professional partnership in the design and implementation of programs for children with special needs. These will be addressed throughout the remaining chapters of this book.

Having focused on strategies common to all high-quality early education programs and on specific adaptations for those with unique needs, in the next chapter we will discuss techniques for promoting healthy social and emotional development.

Summary

Curriculum can be considered to be a clear description of what we teach (goals) and how we teach (strategies). Goals and strategies are to be developed in accordance with a clearly defined philosophy based on assumptions about human nature and how young children learn. The philosophy of this text assumes that goals must be functional and ecologically relevant. Strategies will be built on what we know about each child's development and the most appropriate techniques for helping each child reach his or her goals. Instruction is thought to be rooted in the social interactions between children and significant others in their environment.

It is important for professionals in the field of early childhood special education to plan instructional programs carefully. Instructional objectives will reflect a curriculum that has been adapted to meet the needs of individual children and classrooms. Instructional objectives must specify what the teacher will do (or refrain from doing) and what behavior the teacher will observe when the children know or have learned what was taught. Objectives also include criteria for performance and are precise and graduated.

It is often helpful to generate a checklist reflecting the major instructional goals in the curriculum. After the checklist has been developed, goals and objectives written, and a parent report form devised, it becomes a simple matter to link assessment with individualized lesson planning. The important questions are: (1) Can this child perform this behavior? and (2) If he or she cannot, what related simpler objective can be identified as the entry behavior?

By using a set of well-planned objectives, groups of children at different developmental levels can be taught together. In both small and large groups it is possible to individualize lessons. Children with developmental lags in one or more areas can be successfully included in classes with children who are more advanced. By making it possible for the teacher to pinpoint what needs to be taught, teaching is greatly simplified.

A sound philosophy also generates instructional strategies that are guides for action with *all* children regardless of the early education setting. Careful thought must go into understanding how children are motivated, how to guide their behavior, and how to use communication to mediate their experiences. The importance of using routines and play as instructional strategies is worthy of emphasis. Specific suggestions for adapting the environment and curricula smooth the way for effective integration of young children with special needs.

Discussion Topics and Activities

1. Choose something about which you know a great deal. Consider activities such as baking a cake, playing a simple tune on a musical instrument, roller skating, or coloring in a coloring book. Write an appropriate goal and a terminal objective. Then, write five en-route behaviors. Remember to work backward from your terminal objective. Then arrange your en-route behaviors in sequence from the easiest step to the final, terminal objective. Try to teach someone, using your sequence of objectives. Identify any missing steps, look for incomplete objectives, and be aware of the appropriateness of the sequence.

2. Describe the difficulties you encountered in your attempt to write and sequence the objectives for the activity you chose.

3. Now consider this problem. You have a girl with a mild hearing impairment assigned to your class of typical 4 year olds. You can understand some of what she says, but most of her efforts to communicate result in confusion for you. Describe three things you can do if she runs from the doll corner to tell you something in a happy, enthusiastic manner but you are unable to understand her. Write an objective for her that reflects your desire to teach her first how to attempt to tell you something. Then, if you do not understand, assume that you want her to show you what she is trying to say. Last, you want her to attempt to imitate your spoken model of what she was trying to say.

4. You are a teacher in a newly established preschool. You have been asked to help design a system for record keeping. You must consider the following: who will maintain the records, who will read the records and maintain confidentiality, how the information will be distributed, how frequently the information must be gathered, and how often it must be reported. Develop a system for record keeping and discuss it with other class members.

5. Observe a teacher in an early childhood program. Describe how she utilizes each of the generic strategies discussed in the chapter.

6. Prepare a drawing of an ideal physical environment for an integrated early education setting.

Annotated Bibliography

Falvey, M. A. (1986). *Community-based curriculum: Instructional strategies for students with severe handicaps.* Baltimore: Paul H. Brookes.

This concise informative text represents important guidelines for implementing appropriate educational programs for individuals of all ages with severe disabilities. Throughout, the emphasis is on acquisition and performance of age-appropriate and functional skills within a variety of integrated community environments. Also included are strategies for moving students and staff from segregated to integrated school sites and facilitating interactions between students with severe disabilities and their nondisabled peers.

Fredericks, H. D., Baldwin, F. L., Grove, D. N., & Moore, W. G. Record keeping. In J. B. Jordan, A. H. Hayden, M. B. Karnes, & M. M. Wood (Eds.), *Early childhood education for exceptional children.* Reston, VA: The Council for Exceptional Children.

This chapter presents records and record-keeping systems used by the First Chance Network projects. Numerous examples are included to illustrate various approaches to the documentation of children's progress. Review of this chapter is useful to anyone setting up a record-keeping system.

Goplerud, D., & Fleming, J. E. (1980). *Mainstreaming with learning sequences.* Belmont, CA: Fearon Pitman.

This book presents a "how to" approach to the development of learning sequences. Concrete examples are illustrated through sequential scripts. While most of the 13 sequences present concepts appropriate to kindergarten and first grade, the process of lesson development can easily be generalized to prekindergarten tasks.

Howell, K. W., Kaplan, J. S., & O'Connell, C. Y. (1979). *Evaluating exceptional children: A task analysis approach.* Columbus, OH: Merrill.

This text was written for use in a course on evaluation of children with exceptionalities. Of particular value are the chapters on task analysis and the clear, concise instructional program on the basics of writing good behavioral objectives.

Linder, T. W. (1990). *Transdisciplinary play-based assessment: A functional approach to working with young children.* Baltimore: Paul H. Brookes.

This book presents a practical and innovative guide to assessment and intervention within the context of play. It is appropriate for infants and young children developmentally between the ages of 6 months and 6 years. The book contains descriptive observation guidelines for assessment and program planning in the areas of socioemotional, cognitive, communication, and sensorimotor development through child-directed play. It is intended for use by a transdisciplinary team.

Lillie, D. L. (1975). *Early childhood education.* Chicago: Science Research Associates.

The focus of this book is on a specific individualized approach to developmental instruction. The Carolina Developmental Profile is included as a base from which to organize educational activities. This book is an excellent resource for anyone wishing to individualize curriculum for young children.

MacDonald, J. D. (1989). *Becoming partners for children: From play to conversation.* San Antonio, TX: Special Press.

This book describes play- and conversationally based strategies for facilitating the development of social and communicative competence in young children with disabilities. The book is intended as a guide for professionals for planning intervention programs, as well as working with parents. Techniques are based on turn taking and communicative interaction within a play context.

Mager, R. F. (1984). *Preparing instructional objectives.* Belmont, CA: David S. Lake.

This small paperback is a "must." The author has provided much-needed specific instruction in how to select goals and clearly state objectives. It answers questions about what as well as how to write. Included is a self-test to assist readers in determining whether they have met acceptable criteria in the preparation of instructional objectives.

Mori, A. A. (Senior Ed.). (1983). Curricula in early childhood special education. *Topics in Early Childhood Special Education,* 2(4).

This entire issue of *Topics* is devoted to curricular concerns not usually addressed. Especially important are the issues of selection, use, and evaluation of curriculum. The advanced student will appreciate the consideration given to curriculum design, objectives, selection, models, and adaptations suggestions for the special needs of young children with visual, hearing, and physical impairments.

Mori, A. A., & Olive, J. E. (1980). *Handbook of pre-school special education.* Rockville, MD: Aspen Systems.

The authors focus on the need for early intervention with infants and toddlers. Presented are the essential steps involved in effective use of the developmental checklist and curriculum lesson plans they have devised for use with children from birth to 26 months of age.

Neisworth, J. T., Willoughby-Herb, S. J., Bagnato, S. J., Cartwright, C. A., & Laub, K. W. (1980). *Individualized education for preschool exceptional children.* Rockville, MD: Aspen Systems.

These authors stress the importance of linking developmental diagnosis with curriculum planning. Half the book is comprised of a curriculum of developmentally sequenced objective for children from birth to 5 years of age. This curriculum is organized into four domains: communication, personal and interpersonal skills, motor development, and problem solving.

Odom, S. L. (1988). *The integrated preschool curriculum: Procedures for socially integrating preschoolers with or without handicaps.* Seattle: University of Washington Press.

This is a practical guide for teachers describing procedures for arranging play activities in ways that facilitate social interaction among peers. It also provides intervention strategies for use with children who interact at very low rates. The guide includes two assessment approaches useful in monitoring social integration within the classroom.

Odom, S. L., & Karnes, M. B. (1988). *Early intervention for infants and children with handicaps: An empirical base.* Baltimore: Paul H. Brookes.

This book reviews the research bases for effective practices in early childhood special education. Several topics are reviewed, including research design issues, intervention practices across skill domains, issues related to families, program efficacy, and teacher training.

TenBrink, T. D. (1986). Writing instructional objectives. In J. M. Cooper (Ed.). *Classroom teaching skills.* Lexington, MA: D.C. Heath.

This chapter serves as an excellent resource for those wishing to perfect their skills at writing behavioral objectives. Written in a self-teaching format, it allows the reader to use exercises that help in the selection of appropriate instructional objectives from available sources, and it teaches how to write these objectives in a useful and well-defined manner.

References

Bailey, D. B., & Wolery, M. (1989). *Assessing infants and preschoolers with handicaps.* Columbus, OH: Merrill.

Bailey, D. B., & Wolery, M. (1984). Designing preschool environments: Physical space and materials. In D. Bailey & M. Wolery (Eds.), *Teaching infants and preschoolers with handicaps.* Columbus, OH: Merrill.

Bricker, D. (1989). *Early intervention for at-risk and handicapped infants, toddlers and preschool children.* Palo Alto, CA: Vort.

Bruner J. (1982). The organization of action and the nature of the adult-infant transaction. In E. Tronick (Ed.), *Social interchange in infancy: Affect, cognition and communication* (pp. 23–35). Baltimore, MD: University Park Press.

Cook, R. E. (1983). Why Jimmy doesn't try. *Academic Therapy. 19*, 155–163.

Falvey, M. (1986). Community-based curriculum: *Instructional strategies for teaching students with severe handicaps.* Baltimore, MD: Paul H. Brookes.

Feuerstein, R., Rand, Y., Hoffman, M., & Miller, R. (1980). *Instrumental enrichment.* Baltimore, MD: University Park Press.

Hart, B. (1985). Naturalistic language training techniques. In S. F. Warren & A. K. Rogers-Warren (Eds.), *Teaching functional language: Generalization and maintenance of language skills.* Austin, TX: Pro-Ed.

Klein, M. D., & Briggs, M. (1987). Facilitating mother-infant communicative interaction in mothers of high-risk infants. *Journal of Childhood Communication Disorders, 10*(2), 95–106.

MacDonald, J. (1989). *Becoming partners with children: From play to conversation.* San Antonio, TX: Special Press.

MacDonald, J., & Gillette, Y. (1984). Conversation engineering: A pragmatic approach to early social competence. *Seminars in Speech and Language, 5,* 171–183.

MacNamara, J. (1972). Cognitive basis of language learning in infants. *Psychological Review, 79,* 1–13.

McLean, J., & Synder-McLean, L. (1978). *Transactional approach to early language training.* Columbus, OH: Merrill.

Mager, R. F. (1984). *Preparing instructional objectives.* Belmont, CA: David S. Lake.

Maslow, A. H. (1968). *Toward a psychology of being.* New York: Van Nostrand Reinhold.

Montessori, M. (1972). *Dr. Montessori's own handbook.* New York: Schocken.

Mori, A., & Neisworth, J. (1983). Curricula in early childhood education: Some generic and special considerations. *Topics in Early Childhood Special Education, 2*(4).

NAEYC. (1984). *Accreditation criteria and procedures of the National Academy of Early Childhood Programs.* Washington, DC: The National Association for the Education of Young Children.

Vincent, L. (1988, March). *Curriculum development.* Inservice training for early childhood special education teachers, Los Angeles Unified School District.

Vgotsky, L. (1978). *Mind in society: The development of higher psychological processes.* Cambridge, MA: Harvard University Press.

Wachs, T. G., & Chan, A. (1985). *Physical and social environment correlates of three aspects of twelve month language functioning.* Paper presented to the annual meeting of the Society for Research in Child Development, Toronto.

Walker, J. E., & Shea, T. M. (1991). *Behavior management: A practical approach for educators.* Riverside, NJ: Macmillan/Merrill.

Weber, L. (1971). *The English infant school and informal education.* Englewood Cliffs, NJ: Prentice Hall.

White, R. (1959). Motivation reconsidered: The concept of competence. *Psychology Review, 66,* 297–333.

Wolery, M. (1983). Evaluating curricula: Purposes and strategies. *Topics in Early Childhood Special Education, 2*(4), 15–24.

Chapter 7

Promoting Social and
Emotional Development

with contributions by Carol Cole

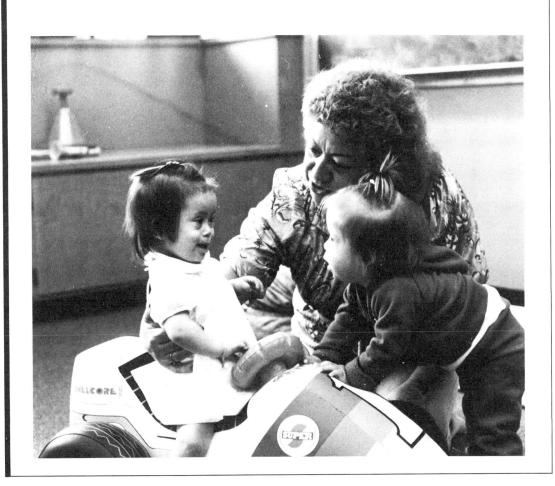

Key Points

▶ The most crucial social-emotional event in a young child's life is the development of an attachment bond.

▶ The earlier writing of Erik Erikson and current work of Stanley Greenspan have made significant contributions to the understanding of children's emotional development.

▶ Effective strategies for creating a healthy emotional environment include consistency and routines, limit setting, responsive adults and constructive consequences, and encouragement of the expression of feeling.

▶ Early childhood special educators must master a variety of strategies that develop positive social skills and effectively assist children who have emotional and behavioral problems.

▶ Play is not only an important context for development, it is also a social skill and therefore an important educational goal.

▶ Children who are maltreated often suffer disorders of attachment and may display a variety of maladaptive behaviors ranging from extreme withdrawal to assaultive behavior.

▶ Maltreated children need consistency and predictability in their educational environments and should be provided with a primary provider who can serve as an attachment figure in the classroom or center.

▶ Labels such as "drug exposed" or "crack babies" and the use of segregated classrooms for infants and young children who have been exposed to drugs prenatally are inappropriate practices.

▶ The effects of prenatal exposure to drugs and alcohol are unpredictable and highly variable; while many children suffer a variety of ill effects (e.g., irritability and attention disorders), others show no effects.

▶ Many characteristics of children who have been exposed to drugs prenatally may be related more to postnatal environmental factors than to prenatal influences.

▶ The characteristics of children who have been exposed to drugs prenatally are not necessarily unique to that population and may be similar to characteristics typical of other risk factors such as prematurity and low birthweight, perinatal medical complications, and child maltreatment.

▶ Many intervention techniques that may be effective with infants and children who suffer effects of prenatal drug exposure are the same techniques that have been effective with other high-risk populations.

▶ Group homes and multiple placements can have extremely damaging effects on social and emotional development.

▶ One of the great challenges to early childhood special educators working with children who have been maltreated and those who have been prenatally drug influenced is developing an understanding of the child's family and avoiding blame.

▶ The problems of children who have been maltreated and those who have been prenatally drug influenced and their families are complex and must be dealt with by a collaborating interdisciplinary team.

Key Topics

▶ Developing a healthy personality.

▶ Erikson's stages of psychosocial development.

▶ Greenspan's model of affective development.

▶ Building a healthy environment.

▶ Facilitating social skills.

▶ Encouraging developmental play behavior.

▶ Helping children with emotional and behavior problems.

▶ Special needs of children who are maltreated.

▶ Special needs of children influenced by prenatal substance abuse.

The promotion of social and emotional development means helping children to develop a healthy personality and a "sense of self" (Stern, 1985). Numerous attempts have been made to describe the attributes of a healthy personality. The work of such early theorists as Erik Erikson, as well as the more recent work of Stanley Greenspan and Daniel Stern, provide useful foundations for the understanding of infant and child emotional development. From the initial attachment to a primary caregiver in infancy through the establishment of mutually responsive interaction patterns and communicative strategies, the emotionally supported preschooler achieves a strong and healthy sense of self and the ability to express and understand a wide range of emotional experiences and ideas.

With this emotional strength and healthy autonomy, the young child begins to develop effective social skills. For many children, preschool is their first experience in a group setting. They may need assistance in handling this new experience. All children are in the process of learning to recognize and to cope with their feelings in environments that require that they also learn to manage their own behavior.

This chapter aims to help professionals and parents understand how adults can help children to be emotionally and socially well adjusted. We present techniques for dealing effectively with emotional and behavioral needs. We recognize the influence of the environment and emphasize the importance of play in the creation of a secure, growth-producing early education experience.

DEVELOPING A HEALTHY PERSONALITY

Understanding emotional development and the growth of personality in infants and young children must begin with a careful look at the process of **attachment.** The infant's strong, positive feeling for a primary caregiver provides the seed from which all aspects of development can grow. For children with special needs—children with disabilities as well as those at risk due to factors such as maltreatment and prenatal drug exposure—the establishment of a strong caregiver-infant attachment relationship may be threatened. It is important for early childhood special educators to understand the nature of the attachment process and to be able to facilitate its development.

Attachment

Over the years, the development of an attachment bond between the child and the caregiver has been thought by developmentalists to be perhaps the most pervasive early social and emotional event in the child's life (Connor, Williamson, & Siepp, 1978; Ulrey & Rogers, 1982). Attachment is most commonly assessed using the Ainsworth Strange Situation paradigm (Ainsworth & Wittig, 1969). In the "strange situation," the infant's response to a series of separations and reunions with a stranger and parent are carefully observed. The paradigm consists of the following seven 3-minute episodes:

1. The mother brings the infant to the playroom and puts the infant down.

2. A stranger enters the room and attempts to play with the infant.

3. The mother leaves the room.

4. The mother returns and the stranger leaves.

5. The mother leaves the infant alone.

6. The stranger returns.

7. The mother returns and greets and picks up the infant.

As a result of early studies conducted by Ainsworth (1973) and her associates, three categories of attachment were defined. Group B infants greeted parents in an unambiguous manner upon reunion. For example, the child might smile, greet, approach, or establish physical contact. These infants were considered to be *attached*. Group A infants demonstrated pointed avoidance of the caregiver upon reunion characterized by aborted approach, averted eye gaze, or ignoring. These infants were labeled *insecurely attached-avoidant*. Group C infants could not be comforted by caregivers, and upon reunion they directed angry, resistant behavior at the parents through such behaviors as pushing away, kicking to be put down, or refusing a toy. These infants were described as *insecurely attached-resistant*. Some recent researchers have suggested the existence of a fourth group of infants who are disorganized and demonstrate both avoidant and resistant behaviors (Lyons-Ruth, Connell, Zoll, & Stahl, 1987).

Ainsworth (1973) described the insecurely attached infant as a child who becomes greatly distressed when separated from the caregiver; at the same time, this child is not easily comforted by the caregiver. It is as if the child's sense of trust has been disturbed or never fully developed. More securely attached children, on the other hand, fuss less when left and cease crying more quickly. There is an interesting parallel between Chess and Thomas's descriptions of easy and difficult children (discussed later in this chapter) and Ainsworth's description of securely and insecurely attached children. Some children, then, may be predisposed by temperament to influence the attachment process negatively or positively.

Connor, Williamson, and Siepp (1978) offered a glimpse of the importance of the reciprocal relationship between the young child and the primary caregiver:

The baby signals his need for some kind of caretaking by crying or fussing; the mother responds by picking up the child; the child responds in turn with some kind of bodily reaction such as cuddling. The baby's bodily adjustments signal to the mother that he is ready for the next step, be it diapering, feeding, bathing or just cuddling and stroking. The baby responds to the caregiving by quieting, which reinforces the mother's caregiving. (p. 253)

The importance of such a chain of cues and responses is readily apparent. Any breakdown in the signaling and response system may affect the whole bonding and attachment process. Fraiberg (1974), in her classic research on blind infants, notes that their mothers frequently have difficulty feeling attached because of the lack of eye contact and delay in the development of the infant's social smile. Other disabilities and difficult temperament can delay the attachment process. Children with cerebral palsy may not be able to give warm reinforcement to the caregiver, since cuddling may be more difficult. Children with hearing impairments cannot respond with eye contact and other attachment signals when the mother uses her voice. Resultant attachment patterns, then, are an end product of a complicated interactional process. Not only do the child's innate mannerisms influence the response of the parents, but, of course, the adult's natural tendencies help determine the child's view of self and environment. The self-esteem of one affects and is influenced by the other.

One of the goals of many early intervention programs is to encourage and support the development of a strong affectional bond between caregivers and children, especially in those instances when disabling conditions adversely affect attachment. Educators can help parents become tuned in to the child's cues so that their responses can produce an enjoyable response in the child. When parents can learn to understand unclear or confusing cues from their child who has special needs, they have a chance to respond in appropriate ways, allowing them to develop higher parental self-esteem. Bromwich (1981) has developed a process of identifying the level of mutually positive and pleasurable interactions between parent and child. Teachers can use such an observation technique as they plan intervention strategies that may include modeling of recognition, sensitivity, and responsiveness to young children's signals and cues.

Erikson's Stages of Psychosocial Development

In his developmental outline, Erikson discussed three stages of psychosocial development thought to be characteristic of the young child. Each stage includes the solution of a problem involving conflicting feelings and desires. The resolution of the central problem of each state creates a favorable disposition for adjustment at the next developmental stage. Table 7–1 presents Erikson's stages of personality development along with adult behaviors that can help children come to a healthy solution of each stage's problems of conflicting desires and feelings.

Sense of Trust Versus Mistrust. The first year of life was considered by Erikson (1963) to be the crucial time for the development of a **sense of trust.** During this time, an environment characterized by consistency and dependability fosters the development of trust in those responsible for the child's care. The quality of caregiving is more important than the quantity of food or love given. Caregiving that is basically consistent and sensitive to an infant's needs promotes a view of the world as dependable and safe. Negative, inconsistent, or insensitive caregiving, by contrast, stimulates a fearful, suspicious view of the world.

The child's development of a sense of trust (or mistrust) in the world is only one of the personality attributes developed during infancy. Erikson also discussed the importance of children's perceptions of their ability to control their own body movements. Through such actions as continuous repetition of grasping and holding objects, children learn that they can depend on their bodies to do their bidding. It is not difficult

Table 7–1   Adult behaviors to promote child's personality growth

Erikson's Stage	Appropriate Adult Behaviors
1. To promote sense of *trust*	Be consistent and sensitive in caretaking.
	Play trust-building games (playful repetition such as peek-a-boo).
	Provide prompt relief of discomfort.
	Provide genuine affection.
	Establish climate of stability and predictability.
	Avoid showing favoritism.
	Provide for choice making.
2. To promote sense of *autonomy*	Allow opportunities to explore.
	Forbid only what really matters.
	Couple firmness with tolerance.
	Avoid shaming.
	Let child set pace, try developing skills.
	Be accepting of individuality.
3. To promote sense of *initiative*	Provide leeway for imagination.
	Encourage role playing.
	Serve as an appropriate model.
	Hold punishment to a minimum.
	Talk about feelings and dreams.
	Answer questions.

to imagine the frustration experienced by children with physical disabilities during their quest to develop a sense of trust in their own bodies. A curriculum that incorporates specialized body movement activities encourages even children with disabilities to become more trusting in their body control.

Interventionists who provide an atmosphere of consistent, sensitive caring help to further a young child's development of trust in the environment. Conversely, helter-skelter experiences in the program can make a fearful child even more fearful or a basically secure child question his or her relationship to others. A trustful atmosphere is easily developed through establishing reasonable, enforceable rules of conduct, the regularity of a basic schedule of activities, and sensitive, immediate responses to children's needs.

Sense of Autonomy Versus Shame and Doubt. From the end of the first year of life through the second and third year of life most children are busy exploring their environment and trying to establish some independence. Children who are primarily trustful usually do not hesitate to join "the terrible twos" if encouraged to develop skills at their own pace. Children of this age who are given opportunities to make simple choices, to exercise their expanding sensorimotor abilities, and to experiment with their new-found verbal skills will become confident enough to assert themselves appropriately.

Children who are shamed (e.g., being called a "bad boy") or told "no" continuously will begin to doubt themselves and their abilities. They may react by defiance or act ignorant of authority. Children who are not allowed to make choices when they are young may become overdependent and fearful when they need to make major life choices. Some children may withdraw into their feelings of worthlessness, whereas others may strike out aggressively.

Interventionists can assist children in developing **autonomy** with a reasonable degree of self-control by creating opportunities for young children to explore, to make decisions, to ask questions, and to exercise appropriate self-restraint. Curricula and room arrangements that provide centers with materials to manipulate and activities from which a child can choose ideally promote autonomous, confident behavior. Establishing firm, reasonable guidelines for classroom exploration and conduct encourages autonomy while not letting children become overwhelmed by their need for independence and by their lack of mature judgment. Children of this age who are readily propelled by their more mature large muscles may be easily frustrated when their smaller muscles do not react so efficiently. Interventionists must lend assistance that does not create conditions for loss of self-esteem. Children with disabilities may need special incentives to venture into the activities so easily enjoyed by unencumbered children.

Although controls and gentle firmness are essential protections for young children, these controls must have meaning. In this regard, Erikson (1971) suggested that the most constructive rule an adult can follow is "to forbid only what really matters and, in such forbidding, to be clear and consistent" (p. 126).

Sense of Initiative Versus Guilt. Children who have developed a basic trust in their environment and in themselves and who have experienced a growing self-confidence in their ability to explore and experiment are ready to develop a **sense of initiative.** Around 4 or 5 years of age, children experience a heightened period of imagination and fantasy. It is a time for reaching out and intruding both physically and verbally. Children with healthy personalities and healthy bodies vigorously try out their developing ideas of themselves. They are great imitators, as evidenced by their "superhero" play and their use of any and all four-letter words.

Children of this age are also beginning to develop what is termed a *conscience*. Since they often have difficulty separating fantasy from reality, they may feel guilty about merely thinking unkind thoughts. Teachers who are aware of this tendency try to avoid overreacting to a child's characteristic statement of "I hate you." When difficulties occur in the home such as death or a divorce, children need to be helped to realize that their actions or thoughts did not cause the unpleasant event to happen. This is also an age of nightmares and dreams. These children need extra comfort and reassurance in separating fantasy from reality.

Teachers who allow leeway within secure guidelines for children's developing sense of initiative can contribute significantly to their motivation to achieve (Cook, 1983). This motivation is important to the next stage of industry versus inferiority, and it is necessary to the development of self-esteem and the desire to try out the freedom to explore, to imagine, to question, to help plan, to make choices, to participate in meaningful activities, to create, and to engage in role-playing behavior. Teachers of young children with special needs must be aware of the need to teach some children to explore, to play, and to attempt what may be difficult. Children whose abilities or environments are limited may have to be helped directly if they are to develop feelings of trust, autonomy, and initiative. Usually these qualities develop spontaneously in nondisabled children through nurturing environments.

Greenspan's Model of Affective Development

Stanley Greenspan has been an important contributor to the understanding of infant/child emotional development. His work has been particularly important because he has addressed the specific needs of infants and young children with disabilities and developmental differences (Greenspan, 1988, 1990). Like Erikson, Greenspan has proposed a developmental model of the stages of emotional growth (Greenspan & Greenspan, 1985), which are summarized here. Greenspan's model parallels in many ways Piaget's stage theory of cognitive development (Greenspan, 1979).

Self-Regulation and Interest in the World. During the period from birth to approximately three months, healthy infants develop the ability to regulate their internal states in ways that allow them to take in and attend to the world around them. Through sight, vision, sense of touch, and smell, infants experience their environment. This experience is best achieved when they are in a calm, alert state.

Babies who are neurologically overresponsive and are easily overstimulated may experience great difficulty maintaining a calm, alert state. As a result, such babies will have less opportunity to take in the world around them. They may not develop a natural interest in their world if that world is painful or irritating.

Babies who are hyperirritable will need special handling techniques that assist them in self-regulation and maintenance of a calm, alert state. For example, swaddling them, placing them in a tucked and flexed position, applying firm pressure to the chest, using deep pressure massage (rather than light stroking), and rocking can be helpful in calming hyperresponsive infants. Some premature babies, babies who have been exposed to certain drugs prenatally, and babies who have experienced certain neurological insults may benefit from the use of such techniques.

Some infants may be hyporesponsive, that is, they are difficult to arouse. They have trouble becoming fully awake and maintaining an alert state. They are sleepy and passive. Such babies may respond more to certain types of sensory stimulation than to others. For example, a baby might remain sleepy through parents' exhaustive efforts to interest him or her in their sounds and funny faces. Such a baby might be more aroused by touch and kinesthetic stimulation (movement and position). Thus, it may be possible to assist the baby in reaching an alert state by massaging or tickling and frequently changing his or her position. Once in an alert state, the baby may find voices and faces more interesting.

In summary, during this early stage of development, infants must be supported in their efforts to achieve a calm, alert state and to experience the sensations provided by the world around them without being overwhelmed.

Falling in Love (Attachment). During the period from approximately 2 to 7 months, infants who have been successful during the first stage in regulating internal states (homeostasis) will begin to be very familiar with their primary caregiver. In addition, they begin to associate sensations of the primary caregiver—face, voice, odor, touch—with pleasurable sensations of being cuddled and fed. As a result, as Greenspan said, the babies "fall in love" (Greenspan & Greenspan, 1988, p. 16). This is the essence of infant attachment. The reciprocal of this experience for a caregiver, as an infant responds to the caregiver's presence and behaviors, is what is called **bonding** (Klaus & Kennell, 1979). As a caregiver bonds with the infant, he or she becomes more responsive to the infant, both behaviorially and affectively, and, in turn, strengthens the infant's attachment. As discussed earlier, the development of attachment and bonding progresses over time and is dynamic and interactive. Each partner influences the other in powerful ways.

Infants who have disabilities such as blindness or deafness or who have difficulty responding in positive ways to caregivers' behaviors (e.g., infants who are born very prematurely or who have been affected by prenatal exposure to drugs) may be in some jeopardy during this stage. For example, an infant who is hyperirrita-

ble may cry or turn away when his mother brings her face close or talks to him. He may look at her only fleetingly and may avert his gaze when she smiles. Such an infant may have difficulty developing a preference for the human world, which is an important outcome of this stage of attachment. According to Greenspan and Greenspan (1988, p. 16), parents of such infants may need special assistance in learning how to "woo" their infant in order to ensure this attachment process.

Purposeful Communication. From approximately 3 to 10 months of age, as their behavior consistently elicits feedback from significant caregivers, one can observe the gradual development of intentionality in infants. They learn that they can do things that have an impact on the environment, and particularly that they can use actions to communicate with the social world. Caregiver responsiveness to this intentional communication is crucial to infant development.

Specifically related to children's healthy emotional development is a type of caregiver response referred to as **affect attunement.** According to Stern (1985), by the time infants reach 9 or 10 months of age, the nature of their caregivers' interactions begins to include mirroring of the infant's affect (emotional state). Parents no longer simply imitate or respond to the baby's behavior, but also accurately reflect the baby's feelings. When the baby is happy, Mother smiles and reflects this feeling. When the infant is crying and upset, Mother may furrow her brow and frown, saying "Oh, poor baby." When the infant is startled or surprised, Mother may pull back quickly, with her eyes opened wide, saying "Oh, my goodness!" In this way, the infant can begin to learn that it is okay to express a wide range of emotions. As caregivers match and reflect their emotions, infants also learn to recognize emotions in others. Most important, they learn that not only their behavior, but also their feelings can influence others.

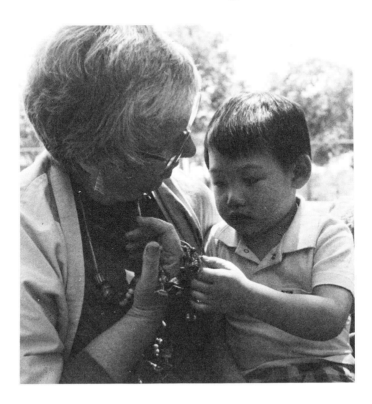

It is extremely important that adults learn to read the affective cues of infants with disabilities. For example, an infant with severe motor impairment may have difficulty giving clear cues of joy or sadness. Parents may be extremely frustrated by not being sure whether the child finds an experience pleasurable or not. Sometimes only the greatest extremes of emotions, such as anger, can be understood easily. Early interventionists from several fields may need to work together as a team with parents to help make this kind of emotional communication clear so that parents can respond appropriately. Failure to do this enhances the risk that the infant will give up and become passive and withdrawn. Such a reaction will significantly interfere with the child's ability to fully realize the next stage of emotional development—an **organized sense of self.**

The Emergence of an Organized Sense of Self. The period from 9 to 18 months (the transition from infancy to toddlerhood) is an important period of development in which infants achieve a clearer sense of themselves as individuals who are separate from others. They begin to be able to move away from caregivers by using **distal communication.** That is, they can crawl across the room and look back at Father who, in turn, smiles and vocalizes to them. In this way, toddlers learn that they can be separated from caregivers but still experience their love and support. Thus, they eventually learn that it is safe to be separated by physical space and that they, themselves, are separate beings.

Children with certain disabilities may need special assistance during this stage. For example, a child who is blind may need to be assisted in learning to communicate distally and in learning that he or she has a separate identity. A toddler who has been in neglectful environments or who has had multiple placements may have been thwarted at every stage of emotional development. If the toddler's social environment has been unresponsive and he or she has not been successful in expressing and understanding a wide range of emotions, development of a sense of self will be significantly threatened.

As toddlers develop a sense of self, they become increasingly able to associate and utilize more complex chains of behavior around emotional events. For example, when their mothers return home, toddlers do not simply smile, but they smile, vocalize, toddle over, and reach their arms up to be held. They initiate and carry out these behaviors in competent ways. Their sense of ways of interacting in various circumstances begins to be internalized and organized. Their self-image is forming.

Creating Ideas and Emotional Thinking. Greenspan's final stage (which in some of his writings appears as two stages) emerges during the period from 18 months to 4 years. During this period, toddlers become increasingly able to think, that is, to represent experience and knowledge internally (mentally). They become much more independent and autonomous. They develop a more sophisticated understanding of themselves as emotional beings and of the emotional characteristics of significant others. That is, not only can they see themselves as "sometimes naughty and sometimes nice," but they also know that although mommies are sometimes happy and sometimes sad, they are still the same person. They also have learned that certain ways of behaving will make mommy mad and others will make her happy. Children who have not experienced consistent reactions to their behavior, or who have not been allowed express a wide range of emotions, will be hampered in this stage of development.

During this stage, children's participation in pretend play plays an important role in their development of emotional thinking. Pretend play is also a critical educational and therapeutic activity. Through pretending, a child can act out his or her own range of emotions as well as practice elaborated relationships between mothers and fathers, parents and children, brothers and sisters, and so on. Pretend play can provide the child with the opportunity to learn to say "I'm really mad at you!" rather than hitting someone to express anger.

Children can also act out their own emotional crises and frustrations. Children from abusive and neglecting environments may learn important coping strategies by playing out themes of abandonment or violence. For these children, as well as children with severe emotional disorders, it will be important for the early educator to work in collaboration with mental health professionals in determining appropriate intervention strategies.

BUILDING A HEALTHY ENVIRONMENT

A review of the literature suggests that early education specialists are shifting their focus away from a skill-based approach to a more interactional view recognizing the importance of the child-environment fit (Sainato, 1985). This **ecological perspective** recognizes the need to create a healthy environmental climate conducive to preventing emotional and behavioral problems. Such a climate can not only prevent the occurrence of problems, but also be the major factor in resolving conflicts that develop between children and their environment. The following sections discuss characteristics that most researchers consider essential to optimum growth during the early childhood years. These are highlighted in Figure 7–1.

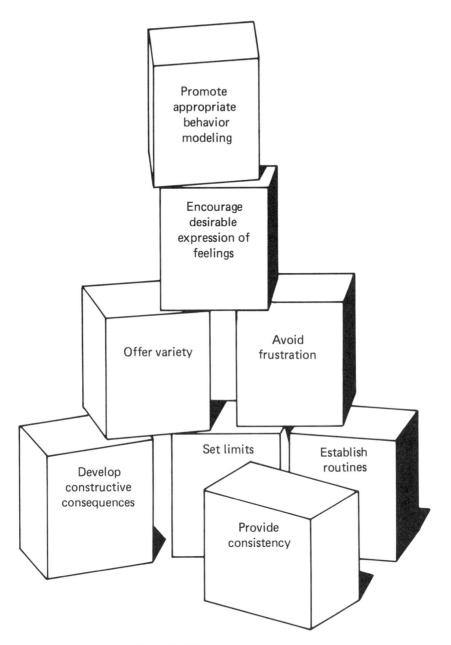

Figure 7–1   Building a healthy environment.

Consistency

Blackham (1968) pointed out why **reasonable consistency** is an absolute prerequisite to effective teaching: "Nothing upsets a child more than not knowing what is expected of him and what he can expect from his teacher" (p. 109). Consistency means predictability. In instructing parents and teachers in techniques for effective child management, Smith and Smith (1976) equated predictability with the feeling of being safe. Like Maslow, they saw the expectation for safety as a basic bodily need. When we cannot predict what will happen next, we are usually constantly ready to defend ourselves. "If our predictions come true, we feel safe. If they don't come true, it is upsetting—we become angry. If we can't make any successful predictions at all, we are in a constant state of turmoil" (Maslow, 1968, p. 7).

From a practical point of view, caregivers must be consistent for children to learn the rules of conduct for social acceptance. Children are as baffled by inconsistent rules as we would be if we were trying to learn the rules of baseball and the batter sometimes ran to third base instead of first base after a hit. If it is sometimes all right for a child to jump up and down on the sofa and if other times a spanking results, the rule the child learns is to "try and see."

Instead of the "terrible twos," we should call toddlers the "testing twos." Given consistent responses to their testing, they learn the rules and usually try to function within them. At the same time, consistency fosters their understanding of the basic relationships between cause and effect.

Routines

To develop Erikson's sense of trust or the feelings of being safe, professionals must plan carefully. Routines or schedules that allow children to predict within reason what will happen next help them to relax and to handle transitions from one activity to another with relative ease. Although schedules should not be so rigid that teachers cannot take advantage of "teachable moments," children can be prepared for changes in routine and for the times between activities when movement, a change of pace, or grouping is required.

Misbehavior often results when children do not know when or how to change to the next activity. Children should be given a signal such as a flick of the lights or a soft word that they will soon need to stop the activity in which they are engaged. Young children need time to become uninvolved just as they need time to become involved. Teachers should discuss obvious changes in the daily schedule with children so that they can develop the understanding that change can be predictable.

Limits

Reasonable limits or rules help provide consistency. Rules or limits not only contribute to children's emotional needs for security, but also create conditions for bodily safety. While children have a strong need to be autonomous, they lack the cognitive judgment to control their own behavior enough to avoid harming themselves or others at times. Behavioral limits offer children guidelines they can imitate and internalize in their development of appropriate self-control. As pointed out earlier, teachers must establish a delicate balance between necessary limits and the freedom to explore.

Only rules that are absolutely necessary to a positive learning environment for both children and teachers should be established. Too often teachers and parents establish so many rules that none can be learned or enforced consistently. Teachers should remember that if children are to follow a rule or a direction and have no choice, they should not be given a choice. Inadvertently, adults sometimes make the mistake of saying something such as, "It is time to go home. Wouldn't you like to put your coat on?" What if the child replies "No"?

Smith and Smith (1976) suggested that a good rule should fulfill the following three requirements:

1. *It must be definable.* Rules have to be at the developmental level of the children both in vocabulary and expectations. They must state specific behaviors that are expected or not allowed. For example, we often hear parents or teachers tell children to "be good." What does "be good" mean to the child or to the adult? To the child it may mean not running in the building because that is what he or she got into trouble for yesterday. To the parent it may mean eating all his or her lunch because the parent has noticed many leftovers in the lunch pail. Rules or expectations must be clearly stated in behavioral terms. If teachers want children to stay within a certain area while sitting on the carpet, then they should mark the area with a piece of tape so the child knows exactly what the limits are. Concrete, visual aids help young children learn rules of conduct just as they help them develop cognitive skills.

2. *It must be reasonable.* Teachers must judge the developmental level of children before rules can be established. It is not reasonable to expect many 2 1/2 year olds to share to the extent that many parents and teachers would like them to. A constant reference to developmental norms is necessary. It must be remembered that children with developmental delays require extra patience as they learn to adapt to limits that others may adapt to more easily. For example, some children may only be able to listen to a story for 5 minutes, whereas other children may still be engrossed 20 minutes later.

3. *It must be enforceable.* Teachers and parents must assume that not all children can or will adhere to all limits. Some rules will be broken. For limits or rules to help children feel safe and trustful, any established rule must be enforceable. When children observe that teachers cannot or will not do anything about a broken rule, they cannot predict what will happen and become anxious. Children seek and enjoy limits. Some will break a rule just to see whether they can indeed predict what will happen. This is generally called "testing the limits," and it happens in every classroom. As suggested earlier, teachers should see a certain amount of this as normal in children's establishing predictability. Teachers should react firmly, consistently, and calmly. This reaction will define for children the consequences of their behavior. It will tell them what will happen if rules are broken. Seeking to avoid the consequences will motivate them to control their behavior. They feel secure when others are helping them to develop self-restraint. Of course, only developmentally appropriate rules can be enforced. If a special circumstance causes a teacher to change the rules or limits, a discussion with the children will help them to understand the need for flexibility within consistency.

Constructive Consequences

Dreikurs (1964) advocated using natural and logical consequences as an effective means of helping children to develop social responsibility. **Natural consequences** occur when an adult does not interfere at all and a child learns from what naturally happens in a situation. For example, children who do not cooperate when games are played soon learn that other children avoid playing with them. If a child does not eat the prepared snack, becoming hungry may help him or her to learn to eat when food is available.

Logical consequences, conversely, are those developed by adults who find that natural consequences either are not readily available or are harmful. These usually help to keep or to restore order and avoid chaos. For example, children who insist on throwing sand must be removed from the sandbox. Consequences that help children to learn to control their own behaviors must be both logical and immediate. If a consequence does not bear any logical relationship to the misbehavior, then it will be difficult for the child to learn the logical relationship between cause and effect. A consequence that occurs long after the misbehavior will not be associated with it by the child. If the child cannot remember what it was that caused the consequence, then he or she will not make the link between cause and effect. This is one of the reasons why the threat "Father will punish you after he gets home" does not work.

Logical Connections. A **logical connection** between an act and its consequences provides a number of advantages to establishing and maintaining a healthy relationship between children and their environment. Children who are denied the use of materials after being careless with them are less likely to see the teacher as arbitrary than when they are told to sit in the corner for being careless. Children will only feel "picked on" if ordered to sit in the corner. Removing the materials, however, can be seen as necessary to the protection of the other children. A logical connection also helps children to focus on the behavior to be changed, making it easier to interpret the misbehavior as the cause of the consequence.

A child who is also given some control over the extent of the consequence will be more likely to feel the ability to do something about terminating or preventing such consequences in the future. For example, children who are asked to remove themselves from the group for being disruptive, and told they may return when they feel they can control themselves, have an opportunity to take part in their own rehabilitation. They can learn not only that disruptive behavior will cause removal, but also that self-control can create return. Conversely, children who are told to sit in the "time-out" area for 20 minuts or until the teacher comes for them feel that immediate self-control will not help and that only passage of time changes events.

Variety

Careful planning to include a change of pace during the day is essential to motivating children to learn. A variety of both individual and group activities consistent with the children's developmental level should be included. Young children need to have active involvement interspersed with quiet activities. Children whose senses or physical mobility are limited will fatigue more quickly and need an opportunity for rest. Others may need additional opportunities to move freely to release inner tension.

By nature, young children generally have short attention spans. (Of course, there are exceptions). This needs to be considered carefully when planning the daily schedule. If children's attention wanders and they are bored or frustrated, they become restless. This restlessness can become contagious, influencing the behavior of a number of children. This is one of the reasons why learning theorists recommend that practice of any kind be distributed over time.

Carlson (1980) reminded us that novelty, newness, and change enhance motivation. It has been found that young children are more likely to explore novel objects than familiar objects (Henderson & Moore, 1980). Some mothers are surprised to find that the usually unwanted vegetables disappear when served in a special dish or arranged to resemble a happy face.

Finally, a change of pace also means including activities that are just plain fun and full of laughter. Most adults are guilty of being in too much of a hurry or so intense that they miss the occasional opportunities to laugh with children or to turn a mistake into a learning experience. Even shoes on the wrong feet often appear funny enough for a chuckle and for encouragement to try again rather than the usual response of "Your shoes are on the wrong feet."

Avoiding Frustration

Teachers who are astute observers of children are able to plan and implement a therapeutic environment. They are alert to individual signs of frustration and stress. Understanding the developmental level of each child makes it possible to plan appropriate activities. Even the best matched activities, however, can produce frustration in a tired, hungry, or sick child. Teachers should quickly recognize such warning signs as fussing, crying, nail biting, sighing, fidgeting, thumb sucking, and tantrums. Usually a prompt change of activity will reduce the frustration and thus *prevent* disruptive behavior.

Frustration can be avoided by teachers' reducing clutter and noise, keeping directions simple, providing meaningful activities that are relatively short, and being available if the child needs help. They should analyze tasks and break them into manageable subskills that are appropriately sequenced. Efforts, regardless of outcomes, should receive recognition. Competition should be avoided. Activities that guarantee success can not only make a child's day but also make the day of the teacher.

Transition times can be periods of frustration for children if not smoothly organized. Distractible children can become unruly if left to wander or wonder. Withdrawn children may become fearful. Routines for transition times must be explicitly taught. As discussed earlier, signals such as flickering the lights help children to wind down from one activity to get ready for the next. Hurrying young children only frustrates the teacher who forgets that preschoolers have not developed the inner time clocks that often become the bosses of adults. Scheduling major activities to end at natural breaks during the day makes transitions smoother. For example, it is easier to gain children's cooperation in cleaning up art materials if they know lunch will follow.

Encouraging Desirable Expression of Feelings

In spite of an appropriately planned schedule of activities, consistency, and well-defined limits, unpredictable things do happen. Children need to learn to cope constructively with feelings that arise from interpersonal situations. Anger, jealously, depression, fear, and other unpleasant feelings are common interpersonal emotions. Teachers choose either to provide an opportunity

for helpful expression or to insist on at least temporary suppression. The success and choice of teachers' approaches often depend on how well they can handle their own unpleasant feelings. Teachers who have confidence in their abilities to handle negative feelings and have carefully created a trustful relationship with their children can handle stressful situations in ways that promote emotional growth (Biehler & Snowman, 1982).

Sensitive teachers find many opportunities to help children accept and express their feelings appropriately. Practically any unpleasant experience in the classroom can be a source of discussion. Young children cannot assimilate long lectures explaining feelings or behavior. Short statements or a warm physical touch will help a child to know that having feelings is all right. A simple acknowledgment of feelings and inquiry about coping behaviors will help a child understand and express emotions appropriately while feeling accepted. For example, the teacher might say, "It is okay to be mad when Johnny rips your paper, but I can't let you hit him. Can you think of another way to let Johnny know how angry you are?"

Numerous well-written books are available that help children learn to cope effectively with their developing feelings. Even difficult topics such as death and divorce are subjects of sensitive presentation. Puppets, role-playing activities, art activities, punching bags, and imaginative, unstructured play also give children opportunities to work through their feelings acceptably. Figure 7–2 and Exhibit 7–1 illustrate some lessons that can be planned to help children learn to understand, label, and constructively express their feelings.

Promoting Appropriate Behavior Modeling

Young children with disabilities often learn new and more adaptive behavior through imitating their nondisabled peers. The modeling effect is a strong argument for integrating children with

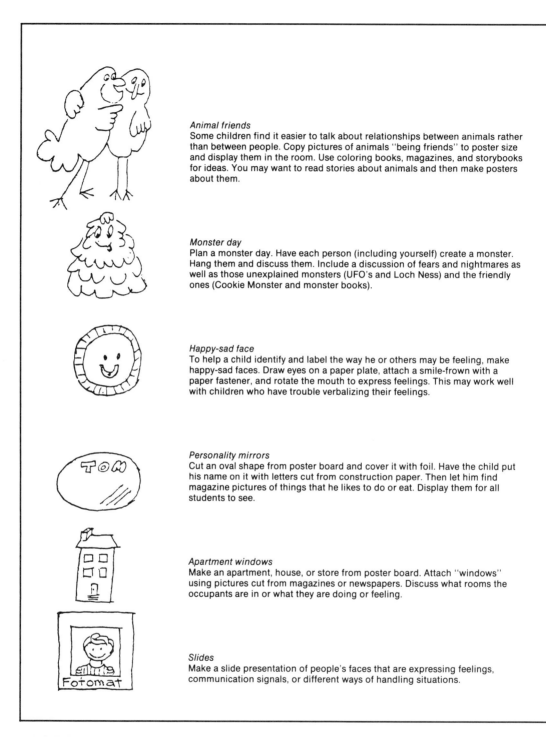

Animal friends
Some children find it easier to talk about relationships between animals rather than between people. Copy pictures of animals "being friends" to poster size and display them in the room. Use coloring books, magazines, and storybooks for ideas. You may want to read stories about animals and then make posters about them.

Monster day
Plan a monster day. Have each person (including yourself) create a monster. Hang them and discuss them. Include a discussion of fears and nightmares as well as those unexplained monsters (UFO's and Loch Ness) and the friendly ones (Cookie Monster and monster books).

Happy-sad face
To help a child identify and label the way he or others may be feeling, make happy-sad faces. Draw eyes on a paper plate, attach a smile-frown with a paper fastener, and rotate the mouth to express feelings. This may work well with children who have trouble verbalizing their feelings.

Personality mirrors
Cut an oval shape from poster board and cover it with foil. Have the child put his name on it with letters cut from construction paper. Then let him find magazine pictures of things that he likes to do or eat. Display them for all students to see.

Apartment windows
Make an apartment, house, or store from poster board. Attach "windows" using pictures cut from magazines or newspapers. Discuss what rooms the occupants are in or what they are doing or feeling.

Slides
Make a slide presentation of people's faces that are expressing feelings, communication signals, or different ways of handling situations.

Figure 7–2   Affective domain activities. (Reprinted with permission of Cathi Effinger Steinmann, St. Louis.)

EXHIBIT 7–1

Teaching Thoughtfulness

Goal: To create daily opportunities to nuture thoughtfulness in children.

How to begin:

1. *Be* what you wish to see children express. If you want them to be thoughtful, be thoughtful yourself.
2. Notice nearly every expression of *that* quality. Call attention to the child who expresses it in a spontaneous way. Do not make a major production of it. Rather, touch the child gently or hug lightly. Say "That was thoughtful. You helped Susie with her coat," or "That was thoughtful." You may think that the other children are not paying attention, but they are. In no time they will try to figure out ways to get you to tell them how they are being thoughtful. And of course they will be learning the subtle meaning of "thoughtful."
3. Avoid calling attention to thoughtlessness. Ignore it.

After a few days:

1. Reduce the frequency with which you call attention to the target quality. Continue to do all of the things suggested above, just less often.
2. Make up short stories about children who are thoughtful. Use puppets, flannel boards, or Polaroid pictures. Catch a child expressing thoughtfulness. Paste the picture on one page and write a brief story below it telling what happened:

   "Susie couldn't get by. Tommy moved his chair. Then she could get through. That was thoughtful."

3. Read stories and comment about the examples of thoughtfulness as you read. ("Little Red Riding Hood was thoughtful. She shared her cookies with her Grandma.")
4. Occasionally with puppets and stories, mention lack of thoughtfulness (or whatever quality you are focusing on at the time). Then ask the children to suggest a thoughtful thing to do. Be careful. At this point, do not lecture. Do not try to relate it to something they should have done.

NOTE: Remember, you are not only nurturing thoughtfulness, but you are also helping the children to learn the names of their feelings and actions. All too often adults tell children to "be thoughtful," or "That was a thoughtless thing to do." Children may not have the slightest idea what they are talking about. Labeling the good behaviors makes it easier for children to express them spontaneously and purposefully.

From then on:

1. Continue to call attention to examples of the qualities you wish to see expressed. Of course, as these qualities increase in number, it becomes impossible to call attention to each of them constantly. It also becomes unnecessary. There seems to be a special magic to the expression of positive qualities. If a once-established quality seems to be diminishing, however, merely begin to call attention to it again, and do so on a regular basis.
2. Introduce new targets regularly. Watch them expand. You may discover quickly that even some of the naughtiest children express some of the target qualities from the first day. You may not have noticed before.

and without disabilities in early education programs. Bricker (1978) emphasized that "children can acquire new responses from observing and modeling others' behavior; however, the opportunity for watching and imitating more complex behavior must be available" (p. 19).

The teacher's responsibility is to understand the dynamics of learning through imitation and to ensure that appropriate models of desired behavior are available. A number of variables help determine whether or not a child will reproduce the observed behavior. Researchers have found that simply placing children with and without disabilities together does not necessarily result in the desired peer imitation (Jenkins, Speltz, & Odom, 1985; McLean & Hanline, 1990). In fact, studies are demonstrating that teachers who directly reinforce children for imitating appropriate behavior and who manipulate the environment to ensure desired peer interaction increase the chances for positive social behavior (Peck, Apolloni, Cooke, & Raver, 1978; Vaughn, 1985).

FACILITATING SOCIAL SKILLS

Several principles should be kept in mind as beginning teachers set out to provide classroom experiences that promote the development of positive behavior.

1. *Keep the groups relatively small* (from two to four children) when structured learning activities are involved. Small groups make it possible for teachers to facilitate ongoing positive social interactions without interrupting them.

2. *Provide materials appropriate to the skills or interaction desired.* Children must learn to use play materials before they can be expected to play with them in cooperative situations. Children who become frustrated because they do not have the skill to use a material may become disruptive or withdrawn. Research has also revealed that some materials are more conducive to positive social interaction than others. For example, simple table games such as Lotto or Candyland, with specific rules, may be more

conducive to cooperative play than more unstructured play materials such as sand. Children with disabilities who have not developed imaginative play may need to move gradually from structured to unstructured play when positive interpersonal relationships are a high-priority goal. Teachers will need to observe carefully to determine which materials are most conducive to fostering the desired behavior.

3. *Make sufficient materials available to promote cooperation and imitation.* When children outnumber the materials available, cooperative play obviously is dependent on children's willingness to share. If sharing is not one of the priorities for the play activity, then abundant materials should be available. Imitation is also not immediately possible and cannot be reinforced if children must wait to use the materials.

4. *Plan definite activities that require cooperation.* Hewett and Taylor (1980) described a number of tasks that require at least two children to communicate and cooperate to reach a mutual goal. Each one's actions are indispensable to the other. For example, the pan-sorting task requires one child to sit on each side of a screen. Each has three different colored pans and a number of objects. One child is the dispatcher who describes what he or she is doing as objects are placed in the pans (e.g., "I am putting the yellow car in the red pan"). The other child attempts to follow these directions to imitate the actions of the dispatcher. Such an activity is particularly helpful to children who have difficulty cooperating and paying attention long enough to follow directions. Of course, the more verbal the children, the easier the task. Remember, some children must be taught how to imitate or to model the behavior of others.

5. *Quickly reinforce specific desired behavior.* The role of positive reinforcement or reward in guiding and directing children's behavior is well documented. Behavior is thought to be a function of its consequences (Ross, 1977). Behavior that brings positive reinforcement to children directly or vicariously is likely to be strengthened, whereas behavior that goes unnoticed or is punished is likely to be weakened or possibly not repeated again or as often. Teachers must therefore be prepared to reinforce the behavior of those children modeling a desired behavior, whether this behavior occurs spontaneously or is programmed by the teacher. Merely being in the presence of a good model does not ensure imitation.

When a child exhibits a desired behavior, the teacher must act quickly to give attention to this behavior by saying or doing something that will help the child to feel better about himself or herself and to see that he or she is capable of worthwhile behavior. This reward or reinforcement must be done as soon as possible and should include specific verbal statements. Words should clearly tell children exactly what behavior the teacher wishes to see repeated. A statement such as "Vicky, you may be the first to choose your free-play toy because you cleaned up and then sat still and waited so nicely" is useful because it tells the children exactly what Vicky did that was helpful. Consider this statement: "Vicky, you may be first to choose your free-play toy because you were so helpful." The other children, and even Vicky, may not know exactly what behavior the teacher considered helpful.

6. *Identify potential reinforcers.* To do this, teachers need to observe children carefully to determine their interests, desires, and dislikes. Most young children thoroughly enjoy physical reinforcement such as a hug or a pat on the shoulder, but some find this to be aversive. Children usually respond to smiles and words of praise. Tangible reinforcement such as raisins or peanuts usually are not necessary and should not be used without accompanying social rewards, (smiles and words of praise). Tangible rewards, however, especially food, may be the only thing that some children will work for at first. Each child and each situation are different. Exhibit 7–2 lists some of the many effective reinforcers

EXHIBIT 7–2

A Sample of Reinforcers

Social Activity	*Concrete Activity*	*Rewarding Statements*
Giving verbal praise	Giving food or special treat	"You are really trying hard. I like that."
Giving physical praise: hug, pat, smile	Giving toys	"Thank you very much."
Showing and telling	Stamping smiling face on hand	"Wow!"
Helping the teacher with special task or errand	Giving gold stars	"That's right. Good for you."
Clapping by others	Playing with special puppet or game	"You should be proud of your good work today."
Going to head of the line	Giving a special hat or cloak to wear	"I appreciate your help."
Displaying child's art work or photo	Going on a special field trip	"Give yourself a smiling face for being so helpful."
Choosing songs to sing or play	Giving parties	"Thank you for using an inside voice."
Phoning parents	Sending happy note to parents	"I like the way Johnny is sitting."
Inviting parents to class	Playing records	

for young children along with useful, specific rewarding statements.

ENCOURAGING DEVELOPMENTAL PLAY BEHAVIOR

"As research and theory become more refined, children's play is increasingly seen not only as a normal part of development but also as an instrument *for* development" (Garwood, 1985, p. ix). Recognizing the critical role of play in the enhancement of every aspect of a child's development, researchers are investigating play behavior from a variety of viewpoints.

The Importance of Play

The importance of play has been noted in the early literature as far back as Plato and Aristotle (Cherry, 1976). Freudians view the repetition of experiences in play as a means of gaining mastery over painful events. Eriksonians consider play to be a method by which children organize and integrate life experiences. Piagetians see play

as an essential means of mastering one's environment. Sutton-Smith has emphasized the role of play in developing creativity and in increasing the child's repertoire of responses (Bergstrom & Margosian, 1977; Smith, 1975). The importance of play as a context for teaching and learning was discussed in Chapter 6.

In addition, the crucial role of play in the development of skills leading to social competence is receiving considerable attention (Neisworth, 1985; Rogers & Ross, 1986). Teachers are directed to become social engineers who can help young children play appropriately with others as a means toward ensuring the development of acceptable social skills (Burstein, 1986).

The importance of creating an environment that promotes spontaneous and appropriately directed play cannot be underestimated. Early childhood educators have long realized the need for play activities as a part of all preschool curricula. The issue of accountability, however, has jeopardized the role of spontaneous play in some classrooms. Teachers feel pushed to judge the value of a play activity by what is learned. Perhaps the challenge now is to create a three-way balance among less structured creative activities, freedom of choice, and directed tasks designed to remedy developmental deficits.

The Nature of Play

Piaget (1963) placed play into three broad categories. First, *practice play* accompanies the sensorimotor stage of cognitive development. Practice play is characterized by the exploration and repetition involved in mastering an activity. The game of taking things out and putting things in is typical practice play.

Symbolic play describes the second type of play, which occurs during the preoperational stage of cognitive development. Preschool children involved in symbolic play can be seen using one object to represent or symbolize another. A child might attribute the qualities of a camera to a small wooden block and go around "taking pictures." The child's increased verbal ability allows imitating and reenacting experiences, thus facilitating pretending and dramatic play. Greenspan and Greenspan (1985) have emphasized the importance of pretend play.

The third kind of play is referred to as *games with rules*, which requires more complex communication and cooperation. Whereas some children may engage in rule-oriented play during preschool, interest in this behavior is thought to heighten during the concrete operational stage of cognitive development near 7 years of age.

Development of Social Interaction Skills Through Play

A current review of the literature readily suggests that investigators have shifted their focus from emphasis on the cognitive competence of children with disabilities as a predictor of future functioning to concern for social development. Despite the good intentions of mainstreaming, we find again and again that "mere exposure to a peer displaying the desired (social) behaviors

is no guarantee the handicapped child will select, observe, and imitate the behaviors desired" (Vaughn, 1985, p. 170). Special programming strategies are necessary to increase interaction and promote social skill development of children with special needs. They are just less adept at developing the interpersonal skills typical children may acquire through usual play behavior. To understand the developmental levels of social play behavior, we will discuss a variation of the classic work of Parten (1932). Parten's seven levels of social participation provide a sequence for reference, but they need more empirical support to be followed without caution. At least they do provide guidelines for observation and selection of intervention strategies. The following discussions of each level elaborates on the work of Bailey (1978):

1. *Unoccupied behavior.* At this level there is no interpersonal interaction. The child may watch anything that attracts his or her attention. Some children will engage in self-stimulating behavior. Even at this level, children should be placed near other children and reinforced for manipulating a toy and staying within the social environment.

2. *Solitary independent play.* Again the child plays alone and with toys that are probably different from those being used by other children. He or she may be within speaking distance of other children but is unlikely to interact with them. Teachers should encourage involvement with toys even if the child is not interacting with others. Toys must be carefully chosen and reinforcement given for appropriate use. Not only will encouragement of appropriate use of toys and objects help children enhance their cognitive skills, but it will make them better prepared to become socially integrated.

3. *Adult-directed behavior.* Burstein (1986) found that children with disabilities interact more with adults than do nondisabled children in all settings investigated. This may be related to

the fact that, in general, children with disabilities spend more time with adults than peers. Teachers are also very good at initiating adult-child interaction, but may spend less time involving children with their peers. Interaction with adults should be encouraged for children who would otherwise engage only in solitary activities. However, the environment should be manipulated as soon as possible to encourage involvement with peers.

4. *Onlooker behavior.* On this level, children are definitely observing the play of others and may even engage in conversation with them. As a step toward actual involvement with others, adults should place children where they can clearly observe and should encourage any attempts at interaction. One promising approach to increasing the social interaction of young children with disabilities has been to teach non-disabled peers to be the initiators of social exchanges (Odom, Strain, Karger, & Smith, 1986). McHale and Olley (1982) reported that "peers even briefly trained to use behavioral procedures can elicit social responses during play from young children with a variety of handicaps" (p. 84). However, generalization to new settings is still questionable. Thus, these authors suggested that a more effective procedure might involve play with an untrained nondisabled peer who possesses the "natural" initiations to which the children with disabilities might respond.

5. *Parallel activity.* Behavior on this level includes independent play among other children that utilizes toys like those used by the other children. To move children toward complete involvement, the teacher should encourage the nondisabled children to share toys with the children who have disabilities and to ask for toys from the children with disabilities. In this way the nondisabled children act as initiators of involvement. Children with disabilities should be placed clearly within the group and not on its fringes.

6. *Associative play.* On this level, children are playing with other children. There is borrowing, loaning, sharing, engagement in similar activities, and interest primarily in association rather than activities. To facilitate such involvement, teachers must deliberately structure the environment. They must provide toys and objects such as blocks, dress-up clothes, and games that encourage interaction. Space must be adequate, as crowding tends to lead to disruptive play. Nondisabled peers should be reinforced for conversation and sharing with playmates who have disabilities. Children with disabilities may need extra reinforcement and redirection if they begin to wander from the group.

7. *Cooperative or organized play.* On the final level of Parten's continuum, children play in a group that is organized in some way. There are common goals and a division of labor. All members usually feel part of the group even though it is led by one or two players. Typical activities include building structures during block play and dramatization. The teacher's role in facilitating cooperative play centers around preparation of the environment and providing appropriate space and "social" toys requiring cooperative interaction between two or more children.

Some Ways to Get Children to Play. Education usually emphasizes structured, teacher-directed play because some children do not appear to learn readily through spontaneous play. Langley (1985) suggested that inappropriate toys and play materials may contribute to the limited play behavior of children with disabilities. Toys that are not durable fail to withstand rough treatment, and toys such as dolls designed for symbolic play are not developmentally appropriate for some children. Children who still need to engage in practice play must be provided with toys strong enough to accommodate repeated use. Children who lack attending skills, imitation skills, or communication skills cannot be expected to share or take turns. Developing these abilities takes time and is taught deliberately through modeling and reinforcement. Teachers need to assess a child's developmental strengths and weaknesses to encourage the most appropriate play activities.

Once the teacher notes that a child has begun to explore the environment and effectively uses a variety of different toy objects, Wehman (1978) has encouraged the development of "(a) more sophisticated and sustained toy play and (b) greater frequency of social interaction patterns" (p. 284). Exhibit 7–3 suggests some guidelines to enhance productive free-choice play.

Imagining and pretending may be difficult for many children. Granting this freedom to be somebody else or something else is often a good way to lead a withdrawn child out of his or her shell. Dress-up clothes, an assortment of hats (fireman, cowboy, train conductor, or nurse), and old costumes left from Halloween are appealing. Pretending to be animals during story times and participating in musical activities allow many children to romp and move freely. With freedom of movement comes greater ease in being around other children.

A large box with holes for windows provides a sense of protection. As the children crawl in and out they discover new ways of looking at things. Looking through the window in the box restricts the view in unexpected ways. Moving becomes purposeful. Seeing what is inside intrigues some children. If the box is large enough, a small carpet and a place for a snack will encourage some children to enter.

Teachers may want to tell short stories using a flannel board or pictures. Then, as the teacher provides simple props and withdraws from the center of the activity, children usually accept the suggestion to "play the story."

Role playing is a form of pretending and imagining. An apron and play kitchen equipment make it possible for children to be Mom or Dad. A plastic hammer or a wrench enables a

child to be a carpenter or a garage mechanic. Some children pretend to be their big brothers and sisters.

Much insight into fears and frustrations can be gained by encouraging role playing without evaluating it. Of course, the insights gained may not be pleasant. Judgment about how to use such knowledge requires compassion, understanding, and wisdom.

Puppets are therapeutic and fun for most children. A box with a "stage" cut out, an old television with the insides removed, or a table with a curtain becomes the puppet theater. Of course a real puppet stage can be constructed by a willing parent. The puppets can be made from socks or sewn from a simple pattern. Commercial puppets are enchanting, although most are expensive. Children enjoy merely playing with

EXHIBIT 7-3

Setting the Stage for Productive Free Playtimes

A. *Arrange the play area thoughtfully.*
   1. Provide adequate space indoors and out. Avoid crowding.
   2. Arrange small play spaces separated by shelves or other dividers. Puzzles, books, and other things to do alone should be available.
   3. Prepare larger spaces for cooperative play with blocks and other building materials.
   4. A play kitchen in a corner encourages group play. Provide some full-sized pans and spoons and child-sized equipment.
   5. Maintain the same basic room arrangement over time, but vary the play materials available. Have a storage area where toys may "rest." Sometimes allow the children to choose what will be stored and what will be available.
   6. Include clay and easels, but monitor their use.
   7. Puppets, dolls and doll houses, and barns and animals should be regularly available. These imagination stimulators require set-up space, whether used alone or with a group.
   8. Remove toys that appear to encourage an activity or noise level incompatible with the best interests of all the children. In small areas, large cars and trucks usually generate too high an activity level for safety.
   9. Plan to alternate indoor and outdoor play whenever possible. Outdoor areas should provide safe climbing and running spaces, as well as tricycles and structures for crawling in, over, and under.
   10. Be alert for special needs. Provide special equipment for children with physical disabilities.

B. *Establish rules or guidelines from the beginning.*
   1. Keep the rules simple and limited in number.
   2. Telling children rules is important, but not very effective. They will need to learn the guidelines by observation and experience. But the teacher should have the rules firmly in mind.
   3. Rules should be designed to establish thoughtful, kind, and courteous behavior. The following are some we have found useful:
      a. The child who chooses a toy first may decide whether he or she wants to play alone or with others. The child's decision will be respected.

the puppets, but if a teacher puts on the first show, they will have a better idea of how to be puppeteers.

It is not unusual for withdrawn children to say their first words with a puppet on their hands. Often they will find it necessary to use the puppet for days whenever they want to talk. A change of puppets should be offered with care. If a particular puppet is effective, the teacher should not rush into expecting the child to assume many roles with other puppets. Some children require prolonged encouragement before they can venture out.

Peers and play often draw children out of their shells. Suggesting that one child help another by picking up a spilled puzzle leads to later spontaneous kindnesses. Some children notice the needs of other youngsters more completely than most adults believe. Consider this experience of Lance and Carla:

Lance was enrolled in kindergarten, but over a period of several months he stood quietly and firmly in one corner of the room. The kindergarten teacher was patient and experienced, but with 32 other children, the situation was overwhelming to Lance. Because of Lance's continued withdrawn behavior, his parents placed him in a preschool. When he entered school his eyes were unsmiling and his lips were taut. For several days the other children played around him.

b. Sharing is not required, especially if the item to be shared belongs to a particular child. Sharing is, however, encouraged.

c. Children wanting to join an established group must be invited to join. The newcomer may ask to play, but cannot move in without a welcome.

d. Good manners are modeled and expected. "May I," "please," and "thank you" are routinely used by teachers. Children absorb these courtesies quickly.

e. When a child or a group is finished with an item, the item must be returned to its place on the shelf before a different toy or game is chosen.

f. Sometimes children like to just watch for awhile. This wish is respected. A rocker and a beanbag chair are often used by watchers.

g. Just as child newcomers may not barge into an established group, so adult (teacher or parent) newcomers must ask permission and be accepted.

C. *Some attitudes for teachers and parents during free play.*

1. Respect the children's ability to choose an activity suited to their present learning needs. By providing a range of materials and possible activities, the teacher allows the self-knowledge of each child to function.

2. Trust each child to use good judgment. Interfere only if real danger or unkindness is imminent. Anticipate and prevent trouble rather than punishing it after the fact.

3. Be aware of what is happening throughout the room. Even when attending to a particular child, the teacher must be alert to everyone and everything. Evidence of this awareness from the beginning leads children to follow the rules consistently.

4. Avoid overprotecting the child who lacks assertiveness. By "making" more aggressive children share, the teacher rewards the child who fails to assert himself or herself for this lack of assertiveness. Rather, suggest to the quiet ones that they ask for a turn. If they begin fussing, remove the object of the argument for a time. Explain that they will have to find a way to resolve the problem.

5. If an unacceptable behavior persists, reevaluate the whole situation. If things are being thrown in the wrong place, find a place where it is appropriate to throw and move the throwers there. If loud noises inside are a problem, be outside more often.

6. Avoid making children self-conscious. Calling everyone's attention to a mistake or a mess is unkind.

7. Avoid comparisons. Respect uniqueness consistently.

He refused snacks, special treats, and all efforts to involve him in play. Then Carla took over. She was 4 years old. She walked right up to Lance and said, "I like blocks. Play with me." Without further ado she pulled Lance abruptly to the floor, pushed the blocks to him, and began to build. Smiling and chatting away (definitely a monologue) she told him all about the wonderful house she was building. Lance stared emotionless, but Carla was not disturbed. After a while Carla said, "Help put the blocks back. We'll do a puzzle." Lance did not move. A few minutes later Carla announced, "Lance likes grapes." The teacher did not discover how Carla knew of Lance's liking for grapes, but promised to bring the fruit the next day.

The following day, Carla asked for some grapes "for Lance." Carrying the grapes with one hand and dragging Lance with the other, she moved to the puzzle corner. She said, "We'll do a puzzle first." With the grapes plainly in sight, but out of Lance's reach, they began a puzzle. "When we finish we eat grapes," said Carla. Lance smiled and slowly pushed a puzzle piece to Carla. He also ate grapes with Carla.

Carla's mothering continued for weeks as she ignored Lance's rebuffs. She regularly told everyone, "Lance is my friend," and busily planned things to do with him. She alternately insisted and cajoled. Frequently, when Lance ignored her she walked away, only to return as if nothing had happened a few minutes later. Carla literally planned and executed therapy for Lance. No doubt, Carla's natural inclinations accomplished more than many well-planned teacher-directed lessons.

Facilitating Play and Social Skill Development in Children with More Severe Disabilities

Children with obvious or more severe disabilities may have had little opportunity to play with other children. Some may have spent a lot of their short lives in hospitals, while others may have been overprotected by parents who fear their child might experience ridicule or rejection. Of course, many disabling conditions by their very nature make it difficult for children to play in ways that lead to social skill acquisition. For instance, children with severe hearing, speech, or cognitive impairments may not have the lan-

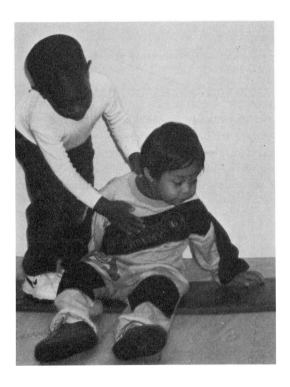

guage necessary to make their needs known or to engage in appropriate verbal interchange. Children with physical disabilities or lack of behavior control may have problems making friends because their behavior or necessary adaptive equipment has become a barrier to social interaction. Therefore, caregivers must make special efforts to facilitate effective involvement of children with more special needs.

Instructors from Texas Tech University listed the following target skills to be given special consideration when working with children with more severe disabilities:

1. Start and sustain play with other children.
2. Follow another child's lead or model.
3. Pretend in creative dramatic play.
4. Share materials and take turns.
5. Let other children know what they think and feel. (1984, p. 104)

Several strategies for developing these skills have already been discussed. Of course it is necessary to begin by carefully observing to find out what social skills each child already has and which ones need to be developed. In addition, Fewell (1984) developed an assessment scale especially designed to evaluate play behavior of children from birth through age 3. More recently, Linder (1990) compiled guidelines for an approach to assessment of observation of play. A number of the commercial instruments annotated in Appendix E do assist in the observation of social skills.

Physical Prompting and Fading. Sometimes children with more severe disabilities do not become involved because they do not know how to play with the available toys or respond to others. When they do not react, there is no play behavior for the caregiver to reinforce and encourage. The caregiver, then, may have to physically guide the child through the desired response. For example, if the game is to roll a ball from one child to another, the caregiver or a trained peer may manually guide the child's hand until the child can approximate the behavior on his or her own. The guiding hand should be gradually removed as the approximation becomes closer and closer to the desired behavior. If during this fading or gradual removal of the physical prompting, the child becomes upset or apparently is not ready to continue alone, the fading should be discontinued temporarily. Such an approach can be very effective with children who experience severe physical, visual, hearing, or mental impairments. It is much easier for these children to follow directions illustrated through physical prompting.

Initiating and Sustaining Play. Sometimes physical prompting is not enough. Children may need to be given the words they need to initiate and sustain play behavior. When a child doesn't seem to have the words to invite another to play, the caregiver must supply them for the child. For example, when Danny wanted Brad to help him build a road in the sand, he kept looking and motioning to him. Brad, who often does not follow nonverbal cues, did not respond. Then Ms. McLynn said, "Danny, go and say to Brad, 'Come help me build the road.'" Danny modeled Ms. McLynn who, in turn, reinforced both Danny and Brad as both began to build a road. When another child began to step on the road, Ms. McLynn said to Danny, "Say, 'Stop!'" Danny again modeled Ms. McLynn, and the children played on.

HELPING CHILDREN WITH EMOTIONAL AND BEHAVIORAL PROBLEMS

No matter how consistent and positive a teacher and the environment are, there will be children who continue to need additional help as they strive to develop a healthy, well-adjusted personality.

Individual Temperament

Like Thomas, Chess, and Birch, we believe that "the personality is shaped by the constant interplay of temperament and environment" (1970, p. 2). Through intensive parent interviews and observation of children, these researchers identified nine characteristics of temperament, which they clustered into three basic types describing approximately 65% of the children studied. The other 35% just did not show a basic constancy of temperament or style of behavior.

Thomas, Chess, and Birch (1968) described the *easy* child as one whose behavior is low in intensity and who is adaptable, approachable, predictable in bodily functions, and positive in mood. This kind of child easily makes parents believe they are good at parenting. Obviously, such a child (who accounted for approximately 40% of the sample studied) would be a pleasure in the classroom.

The second type of temperament is that of the *difficult* child, who made up approximately 10% of the sample studied. This type of child is often negative in mood, adapts slowly to change, has unpredictable biological functions, and often exhibits intense reactions to environmental demands. Such a child not only requires that teachers and parents exercise extra effort and patience to keep the child's self-esteem intact, but behaves in such difficult ways that the self-esteem of involved adults is often threatened. When adults are unable to provide firm guidance by building the environment discussed throughout this chapter, they may experience a sense of helplessness when such children appear unhappy or out of control. The threat of becoming burned-out caregivers is very real (White & Phair, 1986). This possibility is even more acute in the case of at-risk children who have exhibited early developmental delays. When children are unable, due to disabling conditions or prematurity, to give forth the early social signals necessary to establish early attachment, their difficult behavior later on is even more of a threat to parents who may already be feeling uneasy about their parenting skills.

The third type of child discussed by Thomas, Chess, and Birch is the *slow-to-warm-up* child, who accounts for approximately 15% of the sample. Such a child typically exhibits negative responses to new situations but, given time and patience, eventually adapts. Patience and understanding of the child's tendency to withdraw seems to be the key to helping this child become well adjusted.

The stability of these temperamental traits is thought to be dependent on particular experiences of the individual. Thomas, Chess, and Korn (1982) stated that

the concept of difficult temperament as a within-the-infant characteristic in no way implies a fixed immutable trait . . . but can be modified or altered by post-natal genetic or maturational influences, situational context, or the effect of the child-environmental interactional process. (p. 15)

It is the responsibility of caregivers to influence the child-environment interactional process so that difficult temperamental traits can be modified toward healthy adjustment to environmental demands now and in the future. Therefore, the following sections suggest some practical methods of giving additional assistance to children whose behavior interferes with learning or can be described as disruptive or harmful.

Children Who Lack Sufficient Self-Control

Children who lack sufficient self-control are usually thought of as aggressive, hostile, overactive, impulsive, or hyperactive. Such children find it difficult to follow the classroom rules of conduct. Some, such as hostile and aggressive children, may deliberately strike out at others or damage equipment. Others, such as hyperactive or impulsive children, may merely be unable to control extraneous movements. The basic problem for the classroom teacher or parent is the same—

helping the child to control his or her own behavior. Many of the same techniques for behavior control can be used effectively with all children who have these problems. Some children, however, will need individualized help. We will begin with those techniques that will be useful with a number of children and then follow with special considerations.

Do Not Permit Aggressive Behavior. Not permitting aggressive behavior should be the first rule toward helping children control the expression of unacceptable, possibly harmful behavior. From the very beginning, adults must make it perfectly clear that hitting, kicking, pushing, and shoving will not be allowed. Then teachers and parents must act swiftly in the face of the expression of such behavior to demonstrate consistently and firmly what the consequences of such actions will be. Children thus learn that such acts will not be tolerated, as they lead to nonpunitive but effective consequences. Firm consistency helps children develop trust in themselves and in others.

Despite the teacher's best efforts toward preventative discipline, aggressive acts do occur and must be dealt with immediately. The key to dealing with aggressive children is to be nonaggressive oneself. Nonhurtful discipline such as a time out is considered to be effective (Marion, 1981). Children learn that aggressive behavior will not be tolerated of anyone, not even of the teacher. They also learn that the teacher can be trusted to be nonhurtful. If teachers are to give attention, they should give it to nonaggressors. That is, the teacher should give attention to the victim rather than to the aggressor. Throughout this chapter, other examples of nonaggressive methods of behavior control are discussed. These merit consideration.

Prepare the Child's Environment. Teachers need to prepare the child's environment. Children who are hyperactive, anxious, or angry often find it almost impossible to sit still, to take turns, or to wait for explanations. They may constantly squirm, turn, or wiggle. Such children may be easily overstimulated if they have difficulty filtering out extraneous sounds or sights (Cruickshank, Bentzen, Ratzeburg, & Tannhousser, 1961). Teachers must take care to limit the noise level in their classrooms and the visual stimuli surrounding these children. Inabilities to filter out extraneous stimuli and to control impulses may be the reason some of these children can be so difficult for parents to handle when shopping in department or grocery stores. Conversely, Zentall (1977) found that some hyperactive children may actually need *more* stimulation. He hypothesized that some children produce their own stimulation through activity because they are understimulated. Such different views again require that teachers be astute observers to consider each child's needs when preparing the environment.

Concentration can be improved by providing a quiet place to work free from distraction. Ample equipment and materials should be available so that these children do not have to do too much waiting or sharing. Teachers should limit the use of toys or games with many small pieces to manipulate that can create frustration. They must space tables or desks far enough apart so that extraneous movements will not bother others. They should eliminate toys such as guns and soldiers that elicit aggressive behavior. They should place impatient children in a position to receive snacks or working materials relatively early in the waiting time. As these children show signs of increasing their capacities for self-control, waiting time can be increased.

Carefully Consider Curriculum Implementation. Teachers must carefully consider curriculum implementation. Children who find it difficult to concentrate may fall behind in developing pre-academic skills and may be labeled as learning disabled later on. Sometimes their speech is so fast that words and thoughts become a jumble,

resulting in excessive use of gestures. Children's frustrations may develop into aggressive behavior and a loss of self-esteem from being ashamed of their lack of self-control. To avoid these frustrations, directions must be extremely clear and given one by one. Teachers should analyze tasks and present them in sequential steps so they can reinforce success intermittently and frequently. Using the child's name often while working with a group helps the child to focus his or her attention. A calm voice is a must. A raised voice will only create anxiety and heighten the child's level of activity.

Unstructured free playtimes or transition times can be especially difficult for impulsive children. Choices for these children may have to be limited. It helps to establish definite procedures for transition times, such as those suggested in Exhibit 7–4. A teacher or paraprofessional will need to stay with the most impulsive children until they have become involved in their new activities. Hewett and Taylor (1980) described "order tasks" that can be especially useful in "helping children learn to adapt to routines, follow directions, complete assignments, and control their behavior" (p. 189). These are tasks that usually involve eye-hand coordination and are simple enough to complete so that children can readily realize success. Examples include picture puzzles, pegboard designs, bead stringing, and most of the activities included in *Workjobs* (Lorton, 1974). When children are losing control during either free play or work time, they can be directed to these order tasks to help them gain composure acceptably and nonpunitively.

Using loud, lively records during music time can be upsetting for children who have difficulty with control. Some activity records require children to be able to process auditory information quickly to participate. For children who lack self-control, these records may be inappropriate or can be used for only a very short time. Teachers must remember that many behavior problems are simply children's responses to overstim-

EXHIBIT 7—4

Daily Activity Transition Techniques

A. When children are playing (free play or free choice activities):

1. Five minutes before clean-up time, quietly say, "It's almost clean-up time." Speak to small groups and individuals—do *not* make a group announcement.

2. Have a child ring a bell to signal "Clean-up time, *now.*"

3. Sing a "clean-up song."

4. Move among the children, helping them find containers and properly sorting and replacing toys. As children learn where things belong, teacher assistance should be reduced.

   SUGGESTIONS: Early in the year, have a limited number of toys and games available. As the children learn to replace those correctly, add new ones and remove some things. Avoid clutter. Provide variety, that is, puzzles, games, blocks, beads, or coloring materials. Have a specific container for each kind of toy. Provide a particular place to which each container is returned as the children clean up.

B. Transition from circle time or a group activity to another directed activity such as a small-group lesson, snack time, or individual lessons:

1. As the activity in progress draws to a close, tell the children, "It's almost time for ____."

2. Establish brief eye contact with each—a look and a smile at the same time. Then say, "Listen for the directions. It is ____'s turn."

3. Give each child in turn specific directions for moving to the next lesson or activity location. For example:
   Teacher: "Matt, clap your hands two times, touch your ear, and walk backward to the table for a snack."
   (Others watch as Matt follows the directions. The directions are given in one long sentence. Matt must wait until the teacher finishes speaking before he begins.)
   Teacher (To Danny, who has a learning problem): "Danny, jump two times."
   (Danny's directions are shorter and spoken more slowly.)
   When the teacher gives specific directions for going to the table or the next activity location, children learn to listen to and follow directions while being able to "let off a little steam." The transition occurs in an orderly way and enhances a sense of appropriate behavior.

---

ulation or frustration. Why create or accentuate such problems?

Teachers can use visual aids to help children control themselves. Carpet squares or pieces of tape on the floor give them a definite, visual, and tactile space in which they are to keep themselves. Having a definite location for their belongings is also important to all children. It helps them to control their things and themselves. While on field trips, overactive children should be in small groups and close to adults. If they are verbally engaged, they usually have better body control. Similar-style name tags for groups of two or three help these children to feel a manageable sense of belonging to a small group.

Deescalate Play Behavior. Caldwell (1977) offered several useful suggestions for working with children who lack sufficient self-control, especially those who are aggressive or hostile. She outlined a number of reasons why ignoring or physically punishing aggressive behavior is ineffective. Generally, ignoring may imply approval and physical punishment certainly models aggressive behavior while producing unwanted side effects. Caldwell suggested that, instead, teachers work closely with parents to develop cooperative, consistent efforts toward behavior control, because otherwise parents may be encouraging the very behavior teachers are trying to stop. Activities that involve altruism (helping and cooperating) also should be planned and reinforced systematically.

Children need to be helped through active adult participation to deescalate their play when it gets out of hand. To illustrate the need to help children refocus their play when they become too involved, Caldwell described the all too familiar sandbox scene. Children begin innocently making sand pies and then one child steps on or otherwise destroys a child's product. Then hostility erupts and aggression occurs. Caldwell suggested that involved adults should not only catch the behavior before it escalates but also return children to positive playfulness by not making judgments and reading intent into every aggressive act.

Use Time-Out Effectively. Marion (1981) discussed a number of steps that should be considered when developing effective **time-out procedures.** These include the following:

1. Simply explaining to the child that he or she will be placed in time-out every time the unacceptable behavior occurs.

2. Designating a nonfrightening time-out area away from activity but within view of the teacher.

3. Calmly insisting that the child take a time-out if resistance is shown.

4. Praising the child who participates in a time-out as planned.

5. Keeping the time-out short.

6. Rewarding positive behavior when the child returns to an activity after a time-out.

Several conditions increase the likelihood of success of this approach: Teachers are cautioned to warn the child only once; to describe the child's probable feelings with kindness; to restate clearly the broken rule; to make the child responsible for knowing when he or she is once again in control; and to actively assist the child's return by helping him or her become involved in the ongoing activities. Hewett and Taylor (1980) added the importance of allowing the child to return without lecturing or attempting to obtain promises to be good in the future. They also suggested that when the child returns the teacher should make an effort to engage him or her in a task in which the child is interested and can be successful.

Maintain Physical Proximity and Touch Control. An adult's physical proximity or a gentle touch will help some children maintain control over their behavior. This is especially useful when young children are placed in situations that require extra efforts at control. Many public-supported early childhood programs are placed within elementary schools. As a result, children may be expected to stand and walk in lines and to control their behavior in ways that usually are not expected until they reach kindergarten age. Teachers may even need to take the hands of some children to help them maintain the needed control. This should not be done as a punishment for misbehavior, but should be done before problems arise, as a help to the child. If the teacher uses handholding as a punishment, the teacher might become an aversive stimulus and the child might feel less worthy.

Use Signal Interference to Prevent Loss of Self-Control. **Signal interference** can be very effective with impulsive children if teachers have observed carefully to see what usually "sets off" such children. Sometimes patterns in behavior are obvious, such as excessive frustration or activity just before a snack, during circle time, or near the time to go home. Environmental factors such as overstimulation, lack of sufficient movement space, or lack of time to complete a task might be a part of the patterns. Nonverbal (and sometimes verbal) signals such as a nod or a wink can be especially effective if used in the beginning stages of misbehavior and with children who are capable of understanding them and can remember why the signal is being given.

Signals must be used before a child becomes so emotional that he or she is unable to stop the behavior. A warm relationship between the teacher and the child contributes to the effectiveness of this approach. As children mature, they can be taught to understand their own signs of impending loss of control. They can then be encouraged to signal the teacher that they need a time-out or a change in activities.

Deal Consistently with Temper Tantrums. Temper tantrums that are only bids for attention may go away when they are consistently ignored. If the tantrums persist, then the child becomes a candidate for the six-step time-out process just outlined. Nonthreatening statements are preferred, such as, "It seems that you are unable to play with us right now. I hope you will be able to work with us after some time in the 'thinking corner.'" Once the child is back and participating appropriately, reinforcement should be given for the constructive behavior in progress.

Mutual cooperation with parents is essential to establishing firm, consistent guidelines. Above all, adults must be certain that a tantrum does not result in the child's getting his or her own way if that way is inappropriate. The child's day should be programmed so that numerous opportunities exist for the child to get attention in constructive ways. Exhibit 7–5 reveals how one teacher and parent worked together to improve behavior at home and at school.

Help Overactive Children to Feel Good About Themselves. Many children who overact are angry underneath and expend energy covering up feelings of inferiority or fears of being vulnerable. Possibly the primary objective for such children is to help them see themselves as worthwhile people capable of developing self-control. Experience has shown that when these children begin to feel like responsible individuals their needs for negative behavior is diminished (Glasser, 1969).

Healthy young children enjoy pleasing adults whom they can trust. When these children misbehave, teachers should ask themselves whether something they are doing or not doing is causing the problem. Have the children been allowed to change activities frequently enough? Is too much being demanded? Are the children being allowed to constructively express their feelings verbally and physically by pounding clay or knocking down tenpins? Is the reward-to-punishment ratio at an optimum level? The teacher's responsibility is to prevent children from losing control of their behavior. Loss of control creates shame, guilt, and lowered self-esteem.

The curriculum needs to be reviewed periodically to ensure realistic expectations. During a meeting of the National Association for the Education of Young Children, leading experts cautioned educators to beware of stressing academics to the detriment of social and emotional development. Elkind suggested that teachers "avoid emphasizing academics during the preschool years. Instead they should concentrate on certain prerequisites like listening, being able to relate past experiences to present activities and using and respecting the tools of learning." Nimnicht encouraged education to "promote positive self-concepts for children and help them solve their problems." He further urged that children's self-confidence be the object of "loving, tender care" (Harris, 1980, p. 10).

Finally, helpful teachers will (a) express their acceptance of children's feelings, negative and positive, (b) reassure overactive children that one of the teacher's jobs is to protect children from harming others or themselves; (c) exhibit confidence in children's abilities to improve self-control; and (d) demonstrate that children will be allowed greater opportunities to control their own behavior as they exhibit increased self-restraint and appropriate expressions of feelings.

A Word About Medication and Nutrition

Medication. Perhaps the most controversial method of handling children who lack sufficient self-control involves using psychotropic drugs. Stimulants such as methylphenidate hydrochloride (Ritalin) and dextraamphetamine sulfate (Dexedrine) seem to have a paradoxical effect on children who are overactive. Such drugs do not actually act as a sedative because they do not slow down or suppress a child's initiative. Instead they "may inhibit production of substances that interfere with the normal work of neurotransmitters" (Swanson & Reinert, 1984, p. 142). The child is then able to focus on meaningful stimuli and organize bodily movement. Possible side effects include insomnia, stomach upset, dizziness, and nervousness.

Tranquilizers such as chlorpromazine hydrochloride (Thorazine) and thioridazine hydrochloride (Mellaril) are used with some children. These drugs seem to decrease aggressive and destructive behavior, but they can create drowsiness (Swanson & Reinert, 1984). Response to medication is specific to the individual child. Because one of the primary purposes of medication is to help children to respond appropriately in the classroom, teachers become the primary observers of the effects of the medication. The systematic physician depends on the teacher to observe and record changes in the child's behavior. The dosage level must be monitored regularly because effects are different at different dosage levels. Teachers must be alert to possible side effects and report their occurrence.

When school opens, teachers should request that parents keep them informed of any child's medication and its possible effects. If teachers are expected to administer any medication, the

EXHIBIT 7–5 _____

Dialogue: Parents and Teachers Working Together

Most often it is the mother who comes to the preschool to talk about behavior problems. Sometimes she has carefully avoided letting the teacher know that "her Tommy" is prone to temper tantrums, and it is necessary to ask her to come. Let us assume that Tommy's mother has been asked to come because Tommy has some temper tantrums each day. He is disrupting the class. The tantrums must be stopped.

SCENE: It is 11A.M. Mrs. Jones has agreed to come for a conference about Tommy. Over the phone she noted that Tommy is "all boy." She described him as "just like Uncle Joe. When he doesn't get his way he blows his top." She said that he has tantrums at home, too, and it really upsets everyone. She said that the worst times are at the supermarket. If she doesn't buy everything he wants, he kicks her and yells right in the store. She has "done everything" and "nothing works." Tommy is 4 years old and strong for his age.

Mrs. Jones: "Tommy really is a darling boy, you know. He just can't help it. He has a short fuse. Things make him so mad."

Ms. McLynn: "What kinds of things make him angry at home?"

Mrs. Jones: "Oh, just everything. If his little sister touches his toys he screams and hits her. If his big brother won't let him play with his train, he knocks it on the floor. They just fight all the time."

Ms. McLynn: "This really makes you angry, doesn't it?"

Mrs. Jones: "It sure does. But he doesn't act that way when his daddy is home. My husband really can settle him."

Ms. McLynn: "Oh? What does Mr. Jones do that stops the tantrums?"

Mrs. Jones: "It really makes me nervous. He uses his slipper, and really spanks him hard. Then I get all upset and cry, and he stomps out of the house."

Ms. McLynn: "This whole thing really makes you miserable, doesn't it?"

Mrs. Jones: "Yes, and it's getting worse. I just don't know what to do."

Ms. McLynn: "Well, Tommy has been having tantrums here, too. We can't let him disrupt classes several times a day. We have some ideas about teaching Tommy to control himself, but we need your help."

Mrs. Jones: "You have my permission to spank him. It's the only thing that works. Just don't hit him too hard."

proper procedures must be followed. Nurses, principals, and directors can help teachers be certain that parent consent forms are on file and that policies are followed. A recording system should be developed. The teacher must be certain that objective communication of observed behavior is maintained among the teacher, the parents, and the doctor.

Remember: Drugs do not teach. Teachers ought to be certain to prepare the environment carefully, to look for positive behavior to reward, and to treat the child as one who is learning to develop self-control. Beware of the self-fulfilling prophecy, "Oh, you forgot to take your pill this morning. I guess this will be a bad day." Too many children and parents come to believe that the child's improved concentration is totally the result of medication. Teachers should remember that without the child's effort, improvement would not be possible. More than ever, credit must be given where credit is due. It is essential to help children believe in themselves so that the medication can be withdrawn as soon as possible. The more times the child feels he or she is

Ms. McLynn: "Oh, no. We never hit children."

Mrs. Jones: "Well, you must really have a mess. If you never spank you must have tantrums all the time."

Ms. McLynn (laughing): "Oh, no. In fact, tantrums here at preschool are actually rare and do not last very long. We just make it very unprofitable to act that way."

Mrs. Jones: "Well, what do you do?"

Ms. McLynn: "First, we never let a tantrum 'work' for a child. The minute one begins, we move the child to our time-out room. One of us stays with the child, but we give him no attention. Usually we read a book or write a note until things quiet down. Then, we may say, 'Are you ready to go back to the room now?' Sometimes, the child begins to scream again, and if that happens, we just go back to our reading. After a while, when the child is in control, we explain quietly and in a very few words, "You may not act that way around here. We just don't do that.' "

Mrs. Jones: "How can I stop Tommy's tantrums?"

Ms. McLynn: "Let's plan a series of trips to the supermarket designed to limit the tantrums there. First, plan to purchase only two or three items of interest to Tommy. Before you go, make a shopping list. Use pictures to show Tommy what you will buy, and talk about those things. Using can labels provides an opportunity for a matching lesson. He can look for the same label on a can at the store. When you arrive at the store, park as near to the door as you can. Sit quietly in the car for a few minutes, and tell Tommy what you will do in the store. Say something like this:

'Tommy, we need to find three red apples, a can of green beans, and a can of peaches. You will walk beside me. We will look for things together.'

Avoid saying something about being good or bad. Rather, tell him exactly what to do. Walk into the store, and show him (as you tell him) to 'walk beside me.' Talk about everything you see. Try *not* to hold his hand, but do hold it if you must. *Converse* with him as you look for the three things on your list together. Then, go immediately to the checkout line. Again, talk about what you are doing. Leave as soon as you have checked out. Tell Tommy what a good helper he was, but don't call attention to any misbehaviors. The intent is to have a happy shopping trip together. Be certain to tell Tommy's father how helpful Tommy was. You may wish to let Tommy choose what you will have for dinner or in some other way reward him.

Of course, if he misbehaves at the store, pick him up. Move quickly. Say nothing, but go directly to the car. Behave very quietly—even if he screams. Go directly home and put him in the 'time-out' spot. Do not get into a discussion or scold. Just act.

Several days later, try again."

responsible for the improved behavior, the more likely he or she is to work toward self-control.

Nutrition. A number of efforts have been made to determine the significance of the relationship between foods consumed and behaviors produced. Possibly the best-known attempt to regulate behavior through diet control is the Feingold diet (Feingold, 1974). The basic premise of those who monitor the reactions of children to various foods is that difficult behavior such as hyperactivity, fatigue, irritability, and nervousness may be the result of adverse reactions to various food substances. Eliminating food colors, additives, sugar, and milk products is found to help relieve and control the symptomatic behavior in some children (Crook, 1975).

Although the relationship between nutrition and behavior or learning problems currently is a matter of controversy, results of diet control do seem to be dramatic. Teachers are encouraged to pay close attention to the research as it is reported and to encourage parents to talk to their doctors about the possibility of allergic reactions to food. In the meantime, teachers will want to choose carefully the snacks offered in the classroom. Most teachers are convinced that sugar promotes tooth decay, if not hyperactivity. This alone is a good enough reason to eliminate sugar from snacks. A local director of a nursery school eliminated milk, sugar, and red dye from the snack list altogether. The children quickly adjusted to the variety of fruits, vegetables, juices, and other nutritious snacks (Lansky, 1978). Most parents were delighted to find their children being introduced to new foods and building better eating habits. Some even found themselves trying something new at the request of their child. Anyone who doubts the wisdom of reducing the intake of sugar should visit an elementary school the day after Halloween.

Involve Parents. Many parents would gladly improve their children's nutrition of they knew how to. One effective way to gain parents' interest and cooperation is to sponsor a tasting party. Begin by obtaining a book from the local library that lists the basic food nutrients such as protein,

---

EXHIBIT 7–6 _____

Preparing Young Children for Hospitalization

Hospitalization and illness can produce great emotional stress in children, especially during the early years. Caregivers are encouraged to consciously prepare young children for the possible, if not certain, event of hospitalization or a visit to an emergency room. The following suggestions should lead to discussion and generate even more fruitful ideas.

1. Be aware that even young children need information, opportunities to express their feelings, and consistent emotional support from adults.

2. Deliberate preparation should be given once or twice each year and then periodically throughout the year. Although for all children a visit to an emergency room is just an accident away, hospitalization is a common experience to children with physical and health impairments.

3. Effective means of preparation include visits to hospitals, films, specially designed books, dramatic play, circle time discussions, and drawing. Commercial materials are available to help preschools set up a "hospital corner." Many local medical centers will loan or give many materials to early education programs. Hospital masks should definitely be included since these are often scary. Thinking of doctors, nurses, and hospitals as sources of "fixing" hurts and aches can be very comforting to young children.

4. Parents should definitely be involved in the ongoing preparation program. A parent meeting might be devoted to discussion of how to comfort children in an emergency room or how to prepare a child for impending surgery. Parents will appreciate a lending library of appropriate books and play materials.

5. Caregivers can help parents and children through the experience of offering emotional support. Parents should be encouraged to be with their child as much as is realistically possible. However, they should not be made to feel guilty as they attempt to fulfill other essential obligations. Prior visits to become acquainted with hospital procedures help to ease the stress on both child and parents. Many hospitals have well-designed previsit experiences that should be advertised.

6. While in the hospital, children find comfort in a favorite toy or something that belongs to their parents. Telephones and television sets are welcomed by children old enough and well enough to enjoy them. One 2 year old especially appreciated and was soothed by tape recordings of music and parent-read stories, which were normally a part of "sleepy time" at home.

7. Finally, caregivers should provide opportunities for young patients to talk about, act out, or draw about their experiences after they have returned to the program. Fears can remain and often need to be mastered through play.

minerals, vitamins, and carbohydrates and the important food sources of each. Then make charts with pictures of the food sources included under each nutrient (e.g., iron: liver, dried beans and peas, and green, leafy vegetables). Ask each parent to bring a food source to be set on a table under the appropriate chart and to be sampled by children and parents together. The larger the number of samples the more the parents will realize how much they need to increase their understanding of nutrition. This experience is even more effective when teachers are able to conduct a diet analysis of each child through cooperation with area doctors or universities. Such an analysis is obtained by asking parents to record what a child eats over a specific period of time. A computer responds by printing out the child's abundance or lack of certain nutrients. With an analysis in hand, parents are encouraged to pay closer attention to the foods they are sampling. They may then encourage their child to try foods containing nutrients found to be deficient in the child's diet.

Children Who Are Reluctant to Participate

Children who are reluctant to participate are rarely a bother to teachers and classmates. Shy or timid children are easily overlooked. Special attention is important for children whose behavior ranges from timid and inhibited to completely withdrawn; otherwise their needs may go unnoticed. Such children usually separate themselves physically, avoid group activities and verbal interaction, seem afraid to try new tasks, sometimes appear disinterested, and may seek comfort through self-stimulation (e.g., rocking, twisting their hair, or thumb sucking). Kauffman (1985) described these children as those who lack the very behaviors that bring them into social contact such as looking, talking, playing with, and touching. He saw them as "lacking in responsiveness to others' initiations of

social contact" (p. 207). Teachers often find themselves responsible for helping these children to develop approach and responsiveness behaviors.

In addition to lacking social contact behavior, some of these children may be preoccupied with self-stimulation or with daydreaming and fantasy. By being so absorbed in their imaginations or their repetitive acts of sensory stimulation, they miss social cues. This lack of attention prevents them from the social learning available to children who are not isolated either physically or emotionally. Children who also experience language delays are at an even greater disadvantage. Even if they are paying attention, they may not be able to understand directions or to ask necessary questions. They have or take few opportunities to demonstrate what they know and understand. Skill and patience are absolutely necessary to help these children develop the trust they so desperately need.

Prepare the Child's Environment. Swap (1974) sought to explain the tasks of teachers working with these overly controlled children to prepare their environment by combining the theoretical approaches of Hewett (1968) and Erikson (1963). This combination encourages teachers to help children develop trust in themselves and their environment at the same time they are being taught how to listen and respond. "On the one hand, the teacher needs to establish a climate of safety, predictability, and consistency. . . . On the other hand, the teacher needs to extend . . . an acceptance of his [the child's] responses, however limited, and provide nurturance, nourishment, and individual attention regardless of the quality or quantity of the child's initial output" (p. 165).

Children who are reluctant to participate will appreciate a small, safe place into which they can retreat. The place must not be like the time-out area. The child should be able to view the classroom activities from the safe place. Many inhibited children learn a great deal from watching others. Through watching they may develop the confidence necessary to attempt a new or different task.

As the child becomes more trustful, the "watching chair" can be moved closer to the ongoing activity. At an intermediate point, identical play materials can be placed within the child's reach. The teacher should not coax the child. No attention should be given to the child unless he or she attempts the activity either alone or with the others. If this occurs, then positive reinforcement should be given quietly and inconspicuously. The teacher must know what the child enjoys. A smile rather than a public announcement of the child's participation would probably be more appropriate.

These children will feel more secure if materials are kept in the same place day to day. They want a definite place for their own objects, including crayons and coats. The teacher should not force them to share until they are ready to do so. Consistency in routines and procedures helps them to predict and therefore feel more comfortable. The child must be prepared in advance for any new or strange situations such as visitors, field trips, or tornado drills.

Promote Peer Assistance. Seating nonparticipating children near relatively quiet but competent children can do wonders in promoting peer assistance. Experience has shown that extremely shy children often respond to another child much more quickly than to an adult. Caring, concerned children who do not move too loudly or quickly are excellent models and they do not threaten the insecure child. Such children can be prompted to invite the reluctant child to participate without begging for involvement. Sometimes the best approach is for the child or maybe the teacher to ask for help, for example, "Johnny, will you please help me clean up this paint," or "Please hold the picture." Help can begin with an independent activity such as passing snacks and can graduate to a cooperative activity such as two children going to get the

juice. Helping others gives the child an easy basis to establish relationships; at the same time self-esteem can be enhanced.

Consider Curriculum Adaptations. Like most children, inhibited children need a predictable schedule that includes both group time and individual time. Group size can be increased as the child builds confidence. Some children who are unwilling to express themselves in conversation will join in a song because they feel less conspicuous. They may sit on the edge initially. The teacher should not rush them. In the beginning, peripheral involvement such as holding pictures rather than naming them can be encouraged. Many of these children will participate physically before they will participate verbally. If a story is being read and followed by questions, call on the reluctant child last and then do not coax. Teachers must remember that the child must set the pace.

Many young children will interact with pets before they will interact with people. Letting such children take care of pets helps them to feel they are contributing to the welfare of the pets and to the classrooms. Their involvement also gives them a chance to receive the approval they seek.

Research suggests that socially isolated children respond to the social learning principles of modeling and imitation (Kauffman, 1985). Teachers should therefore seriously plan opportunities for these children to observe positive, pleasant social interaction as discussed earlier.

Individual attention is sometimes the key to getting reluctant children to participate in instructional activities. Teachers should approach them calmly, speaking slowly and clearly, and state exactly what they expect. They should present activities that they are reasonably certain are interesting to the child. Teachers must try to couple their attention to the child with something pleasant. They should help children to be reminded of good things when they see or think of their teacher. If the child refuses to become

involved, then the teacher should merely place the materials nearby and let the child watch. This procedure should be followed at snack time as well. The teacher should not become anxious if the child does not eat. The more uncomfortable attention the child receives, the less he or she is likely to eat.

Walsh (1980) offered the following suggestion for helping isolated children become a part of the group: Begin by standing close to the isolated child. Then suggest that

he or she join a group: "Tim and Laura could use someone to help build a bridge. . . . Why not give them a hand, Bob?" At this point, the teacher should move away, returning to give more attention only if the child acts on the suggestions. (p. 11)

Teachers then may wish to give additional suggestions if they seem to facilitate involvement.

Provide Opportunities for Expressing Feelings. As mentioned earlier, the expression of a full range of emotions is essential to healthy emotional de-

velopment (Greenspan & Greenspan, 1985). Inhibited, withdrawn children typically experience many unexpressed emotions. Special encouragement thus must be given to self-expression. Drawing, painting, puppetry, clay, water play, fingerpainting, and music can provide opportunities for this expression. Of course, these children must not be forced, and their efforts must be rewarded without regard to their products. As trust develops, teachers can gradually encourage verbal expression by asking such questions as "Is the girl in your picture very upset or unhappy today?" Like "active listening" (Gordon, 1975), this approach helps children to feel understood and accepted. They can attribute their unpleasant feelings to the object in the drawing and thus find these feelings to be less threatening.

Pictures, especially photographs of the children themselves, are especially useful when talking about feelings. Pictures that show clear facial expressions, definite gestures, or obvious effects of the child's actions on others should be chosen.

Such pictures help the child to perceive how another may feel and to discover cause-and-effect relationships. Guided discussion should focus on describing what is happening, what will happen, and how those in the picture might feel.

Help Reluctant Children Feel Good About Themselves. Above all, teachers must be conscious of the need to help reluctant children feel good about themselves so that they may find the courage to develop the social contact and attention skills critical to healthy social involvement. The teacher should begin with step-by-step presentations of noncompetitive tasks that can be achieved by the child. Nonthreatening rewards for effort coupled with a trusting relationship developed through dependability are essential. When children participate little, it is extremely difficult to manipulate the environment to ensure an optimal reward-to-punishment ratio. Avoiding punishment may be the most efficient means toward helping the child build confidence and trust in the beginning. Reinert (1980) listed the following five methods that do *not* work with reluctant children:

1. Forcing the child to become involved.
2. Embarrassing the child.
3. Ignoring the behavior.
4. Asking the child why he or she does not want to take part.
5. Comparing the child to other children. (p. 137)

Because a child's inhibited, withdrawn pattern can be a developmental pattern later associated with serious disturbance, it is imperative that teachers work closely with parents, counselors, and psychologists. When a child's severe reluctance persists after a couple of months of consciously structuring the environment and creating nonthreatening opportunities for involvement, the teacher should not hesitate to seek help. After giving the child a reasonable time to become adjusted, considering the child's age and previous experiences (or lack of them),

the teacher takes careful observational notes. The teacher should study these carefully to see whether any progress is being made, and he or she should discuss minimal progress with the school psychologist or with some other mental health worker to determine whether additional evaluation or a change in programming is necessary.

USE OF REINFORCEMENT

Research suggests that lack of achievement may be related to children's failing to link acceptable performance with their own efforts or abilities. They may instead attribute their successes to chance, task ease, or powerful others (Cook, 1983). Given this tendency of some children to attribute performance to external causes, teachers must be extremely careful in phrasing their praise.

Give Credit Where Credit Is Due

The praise must describe in specific terms the behavior that the teacher wishes to have repeated either by the child being praised or by those who are watching at the time. Furthermore, the praise must give the child credit for his or her efforts or abilities. Consider these statements: "Danny, you should feel happy. You listened carefully to my directions and then tried to do exactly what you were asked to do." Such statements point out to others what behavior is expected at the same time Danny is helped to realize that his efforts are important. Note that effort rather than outcome was emphasized.

Young children, and especially young children with special needs, must be encouraged to focus on effort rather than on outcome. After all, they may be able to control their efforts even though successful outcomes are sometimes out of reach. Consider this statement: "Danny, I'm so glad you have a new hearing aid. You were able to follow my directions." Danny now feels that he could succeed because of the hearing aid, not necessarily because of his effort. He may or may not put forth effort in the future, especially once his hearing aid is no longer a novelty.

Minimize the Use of Negative Consequences

To minimize negative side effects of any form of punishment, teachers and parents must make careful efforts to control each child's **reward-to-punishment (R-P) ratio.** According to Kirkhart and Kirkhart (1972), rewards are considered to be any action or statement that builds a child's self-esteem or anything that makes the child feel good about himself or herself. Punishment may refer to any action or statement that decreases a child's self-esteem or makes him or her feel less worthy.

Kirkhart and Kirkhart (1972) clearly pointed out the importance of the reward-to-punishment ratio in the development of a healthy personality:

5 – 1

> A reward to punishment ratio of five rewards for every one punishment is about optimal in guiding and directing a child's behavior. However, when the R-P ratio falls down to only two rewards for every one punishment, neurotic symptoms begin to develop, especially those of inferiority and inadequacy and a generalized fear of failure. (p. 152)

They further stated that predelinquent behavior is often observed in children whose reward-to-punishment ratio falls to one-to-one or below.

Observations of classrooms readily suggest that many teachers are unaware of the reward-to-punishment ratio they are using. This is especially a problem when a child does very little that merits reward and functions as if negative attention is better than none at all. To control the reward-to-punishment ratio, teachers must plan carefully to ensure that such children are attempting tasks for which their efforts can be rewarded.

Preventative observation is essential. When a teacher sees children begin to lose control or interest because of frustration, fatigue, or hunger, the teacher must quickly change the child's activity. The reward-to-punishment ratios can approach optimal levels by preventing punishment and by increasing reward. Teachers can develop special nonverbal signals such as a nod or a wink to be given as reminders to children who seem about to misbehave. Then immediate reward or reinforcement can be given when a child increases the effort to control his or her behavior.

Ignore Truly Nondisruptive Behaviors

Some irritating behaviors will disappear if they receive no attention or reward from anyone. Teachers must be astute observers. Even though a teacher may ignore a behavior, it does not mean that other children are not giving attention to it. Simply ignoring the behavior will not work in such a situation. The child is getting attention of some kind and is possibly modeling inappropriate behavior for other children.

Some children will use troublesome four-letter words, stick out their tongues, or tap their tables merely to get a reaction from the teacher. Observant teachers usually guess when this is the case. Ignoring behavior can be effective as long as the teacher realizes that the child may go on until some kind of attention is given. The answer is to find a way to give the child positive attention. This can be done by directing the child into an activity while simultaneously ignoring the undesired behavior. Depending on the child, ignoring alone may just bring on more disruptive behavior.

Keep Negative Consequences to a Minimum

As discussed earlier, punishment needs to be kept to a minimum to assure a satisfactory reward-to-punishment ratio. Punishment is thought only to decrease the rate at which inappropriate behaviors occur and can also produce negative side effects such as fear, tension, and withdrawal. Any aggressive acts by an adult also provide undesirable models for children to imitate (Miller, 1984).

Punishment in the form of logical and natural consequences can have an informative effect if used wisely. Punishment that is part of rule setting in the classroom can be a natural consequence predicted by those who do not follow classroom rules. When linked directly to their behavior, they can see the relationship between their causative act and the resulting effect.

If children know that hitting others or otherwise fooling around during circle time will cause them to be asked to go to the time-out seat, then they will see the punishment as justified and directly caused by their behavior. They will not see the teacher as arbitrary or themselves as unresponsible for the outcome. They will know how to prevent the punishment in the future if the teacher has said specifically exactly why they were punished. The teacher might say, "Vicky, you must take time-out. You have hit Susie and we cannot hurt others."

Walker and Shea (1984) offered the following guidelines to those who find it absolutely necessary to use punishment:

1. Specify and communicate the punishable behavior to the children by means of classroom rules for behavior.
2. Post the rules where the children can see them, and review them with the group frequently.
3. Provide models of acceptable behavior.
4. Apply the punishment immediately.
5. Apply the punishment consistently, not whimsically.
6. Be fair in using the punishment (what is good for Peter is good for Paul). (pp. 112–113)

Of course, these rules have to be adapted for use with very young children. Picture symbols might be used instead of words when listing the rules. Walker and Shea also listed 14 reasons why teachers should avoid using either physical (spankings) or psychological (derogatory statements) punishment. Basically, other forms of behavior management are more effective and avoid damaging effects. More important, punishment bruises the already fragile developing self-images of children.

Punishment that is in any way derogatory or demeaning should be avoided at all costs. Only punishments that are logical, natural, and unattached to the child's person or personality should be used. Table 7–2 illustrates the importance of this suggestion. Acceptable punishments, when kept to a minimum and used as a last resort, include deprivation of privileges (including time-out) and compensation for intentional wrongdoing such as picking up deliberately spilled puzzle pieces. It should be remembered, however, that any form of punishment should be administered with firm kindness to avoid becoming derogatory or demeaning.

SPECIAL NEEDS OF CHILDREN WHO ARE MALTREATED

In the 1990s early childhood special educators unfortunately will be faced with many children who are having special difficulty with the development of emotional and social skills: children who have been abused and/or neglected and children who have been influenced by prenatal exposure to drugs and alcohol. The social environments provided by abusive and/or drug-addicted parents, as well as the multiple caregivers often experienced by children in residential placements or foster care homes, are particularly threatening to children's social and emotional development. In addition, for some (though not all) drug-exposed children, there may be neurological differences that interfere with the development of healthy emotional thinking, behavior organization, and self-

Table 7–2   Logical consequences versus punishment

The Behavior (What Happened)	Logical and Natural Consequence	Punishing the Personality
Child spills milk	Child cleans up spill	"You are so clumsy." "Don't you ever watch what you're doing?" "You messed up again."
Child grabs another child's toy	Returns the toy	"You're a brat again." "Must you be so bad?" "You're always the selfish bully."
Child "forgot" to hang up coat	Hangs up coat	"Can't you remember anything?" "You're such a slob." "How many times have I told you. . . ?"
Child yells loudly at supermarket	Softly say, "Let's practice soft noises." Return to market and practice being quiet	"Shut up; you're a bad girl." "Good girls are quiet in public." "I'll never take you to the store again."

control. The following sections will describe these children and suggest educational strategies that can support their development.

According to a report by the Clearinghouse on Child Abuse and Neglect (1985), 1 in 10 children in the United States has been abused or neglected. According to Steele (1987),

The most serious and long lasting effects of maltreatment follow significant neglect and abuse [that occur] during the first three years of an infant's life. The unempathic, neglectful, abusive caregiving experience of early infancy leaves the child with a poor sense of self, a shaky identity, a lack of basic trust in people, difficulty in finding pleasure, a propensity for depression, fears of intimacy, and long lasting feelings of emptiness and dependency. (p. 14)

Both attachment theory (Bowlby, 1969) and social learning theory (Patterson, 1986) would predict that infants of maltreating caregivers are significantly at risk for disturbances of the parent-infant relationship as well as peer relationships.

Characteristics of Maltreating Families and Their Children

Youngblade and Belsky (1989) pointed out that child maltreatment patterns include abuse (acts of commission), neglect (acts of omission), and, in most cases, both abuse and neglect. Approximately 15% of maltreating families engage in abuse only, without neglect. Such families have been described by Crittendon (1989) as highly motivated to be recognized as good parents. They place extreme pressure on their children to be obedient and to perform well. They view human relationships in terms of power and coercion, and they are often intrusive and demanding. Their infants initially respond with resistance, which is punished as disrespectful behavior. Parents then attempt to reestablish their control through increased demands for compliance. By 1 year of age, some infants learn to inhibit their negative affect and comply with parental demands. In effect they learn to manage their abusive caregivers. Such children often become relatively compliant in the classroom but are often aggressive and bullying with peers. Other children of abusive parents become more and more defiant, and by school age they have a "chip on the shoulder." They may be disruptive and antisocial.

Another 20% of maltreating caregivers neglect, but do not abuse, their children. These parents often have mild retardation (Crittendon, 1989). They have few expectations for themselves or their children. They behave as though they are helpless to influence the course of their own lives. Because there is little contingent responsiveness, children of these neglecting caregivers are often developmentally delayed by age 2. In school they typically are inattentive and socially unskilled. According to Crittendon, unlike abused children, who learn to manage powerful adults, neglected children learn to ignore them.

Still another 50 to 60% of maltreating parents engage in both abusive *and* neglecting behavior (Crittendon, 1989). Children of these parents experience both parent aggressiveness and unpredictability. They are often withdrawn and aggressive. They are unable to manage adult behavior effectively, and they often defy authority.

Children who are maltreated have significant difficulty with peer relationships. Youngblade and Belsky (1989), summarizing the literature, reported that they are more aggressive, less prosocial, and display more inappropriate responses to other children's distress. Children who are abused are more likely to avoid both peers and caregivers in response to prosocial initiations. For example, a peer's friendly approach might cause the abused child to turn and walk away. Children who have been abused are also more likely to engage in assaultive behavior and to be aggressive in response to other children's distress, rather than sympathetic.

Special Considerations for Working with Children Who Have Been Maltreated

Probably the single most important intervention strategy for children who have been abused and neglected is the establishment of a predictable and safe environment. Over a period of time, a responsive, predictable environment may provide the child with the support necessary to enable him or her to explore the physical environment as well as relationships with others.

Earlier discussions of classroom routines, both in this chapter and in Chapter 6, provide important suggestions for designing and implementing predictable environments. Programs that depend primarily on children's own self-direction or that require children to accept major responsibility for their use of time may provide too much freedom and ambiguity for children who have been maltreated. For children with attachment disorders, it will be important to assign a **primary provider**—one person who is consistently available to the child to greet the child, assist with self-help skills, and especially to be available in moments of frustration and loss of control.

It is also important for children to learn how to influence people and events in appropriate and effective ways. Other important program goals for these children will be to assist them in learning how to self-control and to express and understand a wide range of emotions. Children who have been maltreated will often engage in disruptive behavior that interferes with the learning of others. Both punishment and sympathy should be minimized. The need for discipline should be prevented when possible. Coercion and power struggles should be avoided. When negative consequences are necessary, they should be predictable, consistent, mild, and brief.

Discipline should be carried out in an affectively neutral environment so that positive expressions are not paired with negative consequences. Children who have been abused and neglected often receive mixed messages from caregivers. For example, a parent may be physically abusive one moment and overly solicitous the next, or the parent may assume a false sweetness to induce the child to comply or perform some task. Thus, a teacher should not apply a discipline strategy such as removal from an activity while at the same time saying something positive such as "You know I love you very much."

In addition, staff members should be clear and consistent in their expression of such emotions as happiness, sadness, or fatigue. This will assist the child who has been maltreated in understanding human emotions and will provide models for the child's expression of his or her own emotions.

Cicchetti and Toth (1987) have emphasized the importance of a **transactional model of intervention** for maltreating families. In a transactional model, all elements of the system (i.e., child, family, and environment) are viewed as exerting reciprocal influences on one another. A transactional model does not isolate one element of the system, such as the child, for intervention. Rather, such a model attends to all components of the dysfunctional family system, including child, family, and environmental characteristics. Thus, it will be necessary for the classroom teacher to work in close collaboration with other team members and social service agencies to meet the many needs of the child who has been maltreated and his or her family. Exhibits 7–7 and 7–8 provide information on recognizing signs of physical abuse and following up after a case of abuse has been reported.

SPECIAL NEEDS OF CHILDREN INFLUENCED BY PRENATAL SUBSTANCE ABUSE

Unfortunately, terms such as *drug babies, crack babies,* and *crack kids* have almost become household words in our society. It is important for early educators to avoid using these highly pejorative labels, which reveal virtually nothing about an individual child's characteristics or developmental patterns. It is also important for professionals in this field to be careful to avoid stereotyping these children and to understand and express the complexity of the problems associated with this population. The following is a summary of issues and concerns presented by Poulsen (1989):

EXHIBIT 7–7 _____

Recognizing Signs of Physical Abuse

1. Be alert for signs of sadness or anger, as well as bruises, burns, and cuts. Listen to what the children say. Be especially alert for changes in behavior that cannot be explained by impending illness or a happening at school. Begin *at once* to record specific details of your observations. Be certain to make a written note of the date, time, and manner of observation. These may be necessary if a report must be made to authorities. Keep these confidential and under lock and key.

2. Cigarette burns are usually round. Small round burns should always be investigated.

3. Bruises on legs and buttocks can be the result of falls. The frequency and the severity of the bruises are useful criteria. Even clumsy children stay unbruised most of the time. If the child is nearly always bruised, be suspicious.

4. Black eyes do result from bumping into things. So do bumps on heads. Again, the severity and the relative frequency of the bruises dictate the degree of teacher concern.

5. Little children usually "tell all," but even 3 year olds can be frightened into lying about how they were hurt. It is not unusual for parents to tell little ones that if they say that mommy or daddy hurt them a big bad person will come and take them away. When this happens, the children's explanations are usually and obviously "dictated." If the story changes, be suspicious.

EXHIBIT 7–8

Follow-Up

1. After a report to the proper authorities has been made, the teacher should seek help and guidance from the principal or the director of the school. Next steps with the parents should not be decided by the teacher alone. Home visits should be discontinued at least for some time. This is a needed safety precaution for both the teacher and the parents.

2. On subsequent visits, after conferences with persons who are competent to advise the teacher on what to do and how to do it; the teacher should not go alone to the home. An aide should accompany the teacher and should be alert to what is said. Confidential notes made by the teacher after the meeting should not become part of the child's file but should be kept in the teacher's personal possession. These can be destroyed when the need for them is ended.

3. Regardless of the nature or severity of the case, if the child continues to attend school, it is the teacher's responsibility to continue to try to encourage the parents to participate in parent meetings and volunteer at school. The teacher should have the help of persons trained and skilled in helping these parents. If the school or center does not offer this service, the teacher should insist on receiving it from some public or private source. Skill in teaching does not imply that the teacher must be all things to all people. Trying to be so can result in disaster.

---

1. While the maternal use of drugs during pregnancy places the fetus at risk, there is no one-to-one relationship between either type of drug or frequency of use and the child's developmental outcome.

2. The developmental outcome of infants who have been exposed to drugs prenatally may range from no or little effect to significant developmental, learning, behavioral, or psychosocial problems. Other factors that influence outcome include inherent vulnerability of the fetus, prenatal care and nutrition, gestational age at time of drug exposure, and additional pre- and perinatal risk factors such as maternal infection.

3. The developmental outcome is affected as much by the postnatal social environment as it is by the original perinatal insult. Group homes and multiple placements can also provide compounding psychosocial risks.

4. Children prenatally exposed to drugs, as a group, are neither homogeneous nor unique. Many of the characteristics of these children are similar to those of other children labeled as high risk, including those who were born prematurely or small for gestational age (SGA).

5. Since these children are more like other at-risk children than they are a separate category, programs should *not* be designed that segregate and label them.

6. All children at biological risk will be more vulnerable to adverse environments than nonrisk children will be. Many natural and foster mothers cannot meet the needs of these children for predictable, consistent, and responsive caregiving without special intervention support.

7. If the child is placed in foster care, there should be only one placement until reunification with the natural parents or relinquishment takes place.

8. Substance-abusing parents will often have many additional life stresses that interfere with parenting, such as drug recovery, poverty, housing issues, and domestic violence.

9. The problems of the infant who has been exposed to drugs prenatally and his or her family are complex and must be addressed via a collaborative interagency team.

Characteristics of Infants and Young Children Prenatally Influenced by Drugs*

Babies who have been exposed to substances prenatally can be difficult. They may have poor eating and sleeping patterns. Some may be hypersensitive to touch, sound, and light. They are easily overstimulated and difficult to soothe. Some may lack organized responses to environmental stimuli and have poor arousal, depressed interactive abilities, and few vocalizations. Still others display tremors, decreased quality of movement, and hypertonia. As discussed earlier, Greenspan's model suggests that these characteristics impact parent-infant attachment and how an infant learns about people, objects, and events in the world.

The variety of drugs used, amount and time of use during pregnancy, and individual constitution all influence fetal outcome. Many children who have been exposed to drugs prenatally have also been abused and/or neglected. The characteristics presented in the previous section on maltreatment may also be present in these children (Weston, Ivins, Zuckerman, Jones, & Lopez, 1989). Fetal development may also be affected by other toxic substances such as alcohol, and some infants may experience developmental and learning problems due to lead poisoning. These conditions will be discussed in Chapter 10.

While there is no typical profile of children prenatally exposed to drugs, there seems to be a developmental continuum of vulnerabilities that persist into the preschool years. Some children

* The authors wish to thank Carol Cole, Early Intervention Specialist, Los Angeles United Public Schools, for contributing the essence of this section.

are identified as having moderate to severe disabilities before 3 years of age. They often receive early intervention services through programs developed for children with disabilities. However, other children who were prenatally exposed appear to be typical in their acquisition of major developmental milestones during the first 3 years of life.

Some children display fine motor difficulties and gross clumsiness. Tremors, which are common in infancy, may continue into the preschool years. Word retrieval difficulties and articulation problems are displayed by others. Many children appear disorganized. They seem unable to focus on classroom tasks and are impulsive and easily distracted. Such children may eventually be labeled as having learning disabilities or attention deficits.

Children who have been prenatally drug exposed may be chronically irritable. Often how they try to soothe themselves may not be seen as acceptable classroom behavior. For example, a child may simply remove himself or herself from an ongoing classroom activity, even when there is a teacher directing the activity. Some of these children insist on carrying an object with them wherever they go, often manipulating and twisting it. Others may tap their fingers, jiggle their feet, or suck their thumbs when they are overly stressed. These behaviors do not have to be stopped before an activity can proceed.

During the preschool years, the children continue to be easily overstimulated and often have difficulty modulating their behavior. For example, giggles can turn into uncontrolled laughter, pleasant moods into sullen ones, independence into extreme dependence. Achievement of developmental milestones may become more uneven during the preschool years. Particularly in the area of social-emotional development, these children show delays and exaggerated reactions to events. For example, they often display more difficulty with transitions within the school day (e.g., changes in routine and changes in staff) than is expected for children their age.

Assessment of children who have been prenatally exposed to drugs is complicated. Many display sporadic mastery of skills—displaying a skill one day and not the next, even when the cues and context are the same. The behavioral and emotional unpredictability of these children make assessment by unfamiliar examiners very difficult. At times, they will "pass" the assessment because they can do the isolated types of skills often measured on developmental scales. When more complex skills and problem solving are involved, the children may refuse to participate or may behave erratically at best.

Special Considerations for Working with Children Influenced by Prenatal Exposure to Drugs

It is important for professionals to avoid stereotyping and labeling children who have been exposed to drugs. Each child is unique. Without stigmatizing labels, many prenatally drug-exposed children might not be thought of as different from other normally developing children. When providing services for this population of children, care must be taken to suspend moral judgments as to why they are at risk. However, it is important to understand each child's past experiences. In utero, the fetus reacts to the mother's ingestion of drugs by rapid increase in heartbeat and extreme startle reaction. After birth, the infant may be moved abruptly to a foster home. Frequent changes of caregivers are the rule rather than the exception for this population. Often, just as attachment and trust begin to develop, the infant is moved again, increasing mistrust and behavioral unpredictability. Young children being raised in group care with multiple caregivers can show a decrease in appropriate use of adults for support and indiscriminate expressions of affection. Languishing in the court system until permanent placement is determined can delay them from receiving the kind of stable environment they need for optimal growth. Children who have been maltreated often have similar early experiences with multiple caregivers and dependency court processes.

By the time these children reach preschool age, the short 1,095 days since birth often have been complicated by environmental instability. They have feelings about these experiences that must be acknowledged as real, important, and legitimate by the early intervention staff. It is important to remember that children behave and misbehave for a reason, even if it cannot be figured out. In responding to misbehavior, the first priority should be to acknowledge what the child seems to want and feel before dealing with the misbehavior. Doing so allows the child to recognize that feelings are real and valid. Being understood facilitates self-esteem and promotes a willingness to function within prescribed limits.

Intervention services, to be effective, must attempt to counteract prenatal risk factors and stressful life events. It is important to build protective factors into the classroom environment and provide facilitative ways for these young children to cope with stress appropriately. Some of these include (a) respecting children's work and play space by keeping interruptions and adult distractions to a minimum; (b) keeping demands, both cognitive and social-emotional, within developmentally appropriate limits; and (c) providing opportunities for children to learn by doing through interaction, exploration, and play.

The number of rules that children need to adhere to in order to be successful should be limited. The children's social-emotional needs necessitate ample time for facilitated exploration and play in which adults actively participate with them. Adults must be consistent and nurturing while explaining what will happen in the classroom or center. They must be specific about when events will occur and who will be involved. Rituals and routines must be used to provide continuity and reliability. These strategies, over time, strengthen children's self-control and sense of mastery over the environment.

Developing a working home-school partnership in which professionals share their expertise but also listen to what caregivers want and need is essential. Through this partnership, the teacher learns an individual child's story. As with children who have been maltreated, a team-based, transactional approach is crucial to working with these families. Family, child, and environmental characteristics are all interrelated, and they *must* be viewed as a system. Caregivers who continue to use drugs may have little energy for meeting the needs of their children. Drug addiction is all-consuming. Caregivers may be enslaved by both the physical addiction and their debilitating lifestyle.

Viewing children within the larger ecological system helps teachers frame reality when engaging in mutual discussions with them. They should let the child's history and actions guide the kind and intensity of reassurance, support, and intervention to be provided. Children who have experienced disrupted attachment or sudden changes in caregivers will test limits repeatedly. Their background must be remembered when teachers respond. Isolating a child for misbehavior may convey the wrong message. Teachers may be more successful dealing with these episodes if they recognize when children may be seeking reassurance that they will not be removed. If a child's home placement is to be changed, teachers can help by preparing the child emotionally for the move and by providing support to the receiving caregivers. Maintaining a child's early education placement during such moves may be of great assistance. Acknowledging reality validates the child's experience and feelings while enhancing his or her ability to deal with whatever stress reality brings. Ignoring a child's reality will not make it go away.

In working with this population, as with children who have been maltreated, it is important to accept the child and family as having unique strengths and needs. Most are doing the best they can. The solution is not to be punitive or to demand that the child catch up quickly, but to work with the child and the family. Early childhood special educators can make a difference, even though the problem is great. It is important to remember that while we may not be able to remediate organic deficits caused by prenatal exposure to drugs or inoculate children against adverse childrearing conditions, we can create intervention services for children and families that can significantly improve children's self-esteem, self-control, and ability to solve problems in the real world.

As thoroughly discussed in this chapter, children who have developed healthy self-concepts through nurturing environments will develop more readily in all areas. The next chapter will, however, outline the concerns most essential to the promotion of motor skills.

Summary

This chapter provided an overview of the essential elements of a home and school climate conducive to developing healthy personalities. Some of Erikson's (1963) growth stages were reviewed to emphasize the interaction between forces within the child and conditions from without. These necessitate early warmth and consistency in caregiving, encouraging autonomy within reasonable guidelines, and developing initiative tempered with gentle direction.

More recent theory proposed by Greenspan has described five major stages of emotional development: self-regulation, attachment, intentional communication, an organized sense of self, and emotional thinking. Greenspan stressed the importance of a responsive environment and the infant's need to learn to express and recognize a wide range of human emotions. Using a Piagetian framework, such cognitive milestones as intentionality and pretend play assume important roles in affective growth.

The essential blocks that build a growth-producing environment were illustrated and described. Teachers were urged to prevent inappropriate behaviors by building security through the use of a number of behavioristically oriented principles including establishing limits, routines, variety, constructive consequences, avoidance of frustration, behavior modeling, and opportunities for appropriately expressing feelings.

Some children arrive at preschools and child care centers with behaviors and emotional characteristics that interfere with learning. They may be too active or too withdrawn. They may be impulsive. Some are overly dependent on adults for direction, whereas others refuse all directions from their teachers. Techniques for working with unique ways of behaving were suggested. These range from effectively using time-out to using puppets and play. Throughout, the role of positive reinforcement and appropriate modeling of behavior was emphasized. Enhancing self-esteem is an ever-present goal.

Guidelines were offered to assist teachers in creating an environment that fosters the development of spontaneous play behavior considered to be essential in the development of emotional well-being.

The final section addressed the characteristics and needs of children who have been abused and neglected and/or influenced prenatally by exposure to drugs or alcohol. Issues and concerns related to the dangers of stereotyping and labeling these children were presented, and the complexity of problems and circumstances related to these children and their families were described. Specific behavioral and learning characteristics observed in some of these children were considered, as were specific teaching and intervention strategies.

Discussion Topics and Activities

1. Make a list of necessary classroom limits or rules. Be certain that each is definable, reasonable, and enforceable. Role play the explanation of these limits to determine whether they are indeed definable.
2. List and discuss any special adaptations that will have to be made in classroom structure and management for children with disabilities.
3. Develop a workable classroom schedule that provides a balance between active and passive involvement, experiences that require visual attention, those that necessitate auditory attention, and group and individual activities. Exchange constructive criticism with classmates.
4. Make a chart of as many natural and logical consequences for behavioral difficulties as you can think of. Use Table 7–2 to help you begin. Keep the chart handy. Observations in classrooms should help you expand your list. A review of one of Dreikurs's excellent books will convince you of the importance of these alternatives to punishment.
5. Role play how you would deal with a parent who insists his or her child should settle arguments by fighting.

6. Try to identify toys that might be frustrating to some children. Make a list of these toys and the types of children who might have difficulty with them.
7. Develop a repertoire of techniques to effect smooth transitions. Role play some of these with classmates.
8. Study one of the many excellent texts on behavior management techniques. Conduct a behavior management project to increase or decrease a designated behavior. Report the results of your project in graphic form to your classmates.
9. Visit a school supply center or obtain catalogs from toy companies. Develop a list of "social" toys and a list of "isolate" toys. Share with your classmates in the development of a master list for all to keep.
10. Observe children engaged in pretend play. Describe the range of emotions expressed.
11. Observe the caregiver-infant interaction of three dyads. Identify the stage of emotional development of each infant. Cite the behavioral evidence for your conclusions.

Annotated Bibliography

Developing a Healthy Personality

Dinkmeyer, D., & Losoncy, L. E. (1980). *The encouragement book: Becoming a positive person.* Englewood Cliffs, NJ: Prentice-Hall.

This book is designed to "show you how to be there when someone needs your emotional support." It provides exercise and examples designed to "bring out the encouraging person in you." Parents and teachers will find the ideas useful as they work with young children, although the book was not written specifically for this purpose.

Erikson, E. H. (1963). *Childhood and society.* New York: W. W. Norton.

Erikson, E. H. (1971). A healthy personality for every child. In R. H. Anderson & H. G. Shane (Eds.), *As the twig is bent: Readings in early childhood education.* Boston: Houghton Mifflin.

These readings contain original source material offering the reader a glimpse of Erikson's eight stages of man that are considered to be the impetus for much of today's lifespan research. The 1971 reference is extremely well written and a fascinating digest of major contribution to the understanding of children's emotional development.

Greenspan, S., & Greenspan, N. T. (1985). *First feelings: Milestones in the emotional development of your child from birth to age four.* New York: Viking Penguin.

This book is written primarily for parents of children from birth to 4 years of age. It presents the stages of emotional development as conceptualized by child psychiatrist Stanley Greenspan. The book describes how to recognize key stages of a child's emotional growth and how to enhance and support that growth. It also includes examples of strategies for optimally supporting the development of infants who vary in neurophysiological make-up (such as the hyperresponsive infant) and temperament.

Hendrick, J. (1988). *The whole child: Developmental education for the early years.* Riverside, NJ: Macmillan.

This comprehensive textbook offers sound philosophy and practical suggestions in a number of critical areas for teachers of young children. Of particular interest are the sections on nourishing emotional health and fostering social development. Topics such as self-esteem, helping children master emotional crises, what to do about aggression, and the establishment of self-discipline are addressed. An overview chapter on working with exceptional children is also included.

Honig, A. S. (1986). Stress and coping in children. *Young Children, 41*(4), 50–63; (6), 47–59.

This most welcome two-part review of research examines the components and stages of stress in young children. Research findings are used to illustrate varieties of intrapersonal, ecological, catastrophic, and interpersonal stress factors in the lives of children. Some measures of stress are also given. Of greatest value are the suggestions offered to help caregivers recognize, prevent, and alleviate child stress while enhancing children's coping skills.

Samuels, S. C. (1977). *Enhancing self-concept in early childhood.* New York: Human Sciences Press.

The author has effected a well-organized integration of the relationship between empirical knowledge and practical classroom situations related to the development of self-concept. Various means of understanding a child's self-concept and suggestions for creating a healthful classroom climate are presented. The easy reading style makes the book useful for paraprofessionals, parents, and teachers.

Stern, D. N. (1985). *The interpersonal world of the infant.* New York: Basic Books.

This text presents a view of infant emotional development that combines the theories of psychoanalysis and developmental psychology. Psychiatrist Daniel Stern describes the emergence of a sense of self in infants and young children and relates this to the development of personality. He not only integrates the thinking from the two fields of psychiatry and child development, but incorporates the major findings of infant research as well.

Promoting Positive Social and Emotional Development

Brenner, A. (1984). *Helping children cope with stress.* Lexington, MA: Lexington Books.

Given the assumption that the range of everyday stressors children experience has broadened, this book seeks to provide caregivers both understanding and techniques to enable children to cope more effectively. A variety of viewpoints and strategies is presented for the reader to adapt to children's specific needs. Situations discussed range from low-level stress to more acute stresses such as abuse, parental alcoholism, divorce, and death. It is a well-organized, useful reference book.

Brown, C. C., & Gottfried, A. W. (Eds.). (1985). *Play interactions: The role of toys and parental involvement in children's development.* Skillman, NJ: Johnson and Johnson Baby Products Co.

This Pediatric Rountable #11 publication is organized around five concepts: (1) origins of play; (2) play and developmental processes; (3) social significance of play; (4) parent-child interactions; and (5) stimulation through play. Advanced students will be interested in the current theorizing, speculation, and empirical findings supporting the conclusion that play materials and parental involvement are two of the most potent home environmental factors related to child developmental status.

Chess, S., & Thomas A. (1986). *Temperament in clinical practice.* New York: Guilford.

This comprehensive volume contains the wisdom of over 25 years of research and clinical practice. It stresses the importance of dynamic, interactive understanding of temperamental and environmental factors, with particular emphasis on the "goodness of fit" between parents and children. Of particular interest are the sections on understanding temperament in infancy and toddlerhood and in the child with disabilities. Methods of assessment, intervention, and handling difficult children are most valuable.

Essa, E. (1990). *A practical guide to solving preschool behavioral problems.* Albany, NY: Delmar.

This "how-to" manual uses a situational approach for solving specific behavior problems that commonly occur in the preschool setting. Each behavior is discussed in a separate chapter, with step-by-step recommendations provided to correct the problem. The reader is encouraged to consider the influences of developmental, environmental, and health factors on children's behavior.

Field, T., Roopnarine, J., & Segal, M. (Eds.). (1985). *Friendships in normal and handicapped children.* Norwood, NJ: Ablex.

The value of this edited text is the knowledge it provides on the peer interactions of preschoolers with disabilities. The focus is on issues relating to social competence and social skill development rather than on friendship selection or popularity. The attention given to the importance of friendships in the lives of children with disabilities is refreshing.

Garwood, S. G. (Ed.). (1985). Developmental toys. *Topics in Early Childhood Special Education.*

The entire issue of this most pertinent journal provides a cross section of theory and practice related to the developmental use of toys. Topics include a review of how toys can influence types of play activity, an examination of the social and cognitive benefits of play materials, and the important functions of books as toys. The final article, which provides detailed information on selecting, adapting, and using specific toys in relation to specific special needs, is especially helpful.

Halperin, M. (1979). *Helping maltreated children: School and community involvement.* St. Louis: C. V. Mosby.

In a brief, useful format the author defines maltreatment, describes ways of recognizing it, and offers practical suggestions for dealing with it. The author also includes strategies for preventing maltreatment.

Hendrick, J. (1986). *Total learning: Curriculum for the young child.* Columbus, OH: Merrill.

The in-depth text helps the reader to more fully understand regular early childhood education. It introduces a developmentally based curriculum emphasizing multicultural/multiethnic education. The chapters on play, designing a supportive environment, achieving emotional and interpersonal competence, and the sense of self are of particular interest.

Hewett, F. M., & Taylor, F. D. (1980). *The emotionally disturbed child in the classroom.* Boston: Allyn and Bacon.

The authors provide a behavioral-educational approach to the management of any child whose behavior stands in the way of receiving an effective education. Teachers in early childhood programs may find it beneficial to consider designing centers that correspond to the attention, response, order, explorations, and social hierarchy discussed and illustrated in this book.

Hildebrand, V. (1985). *Guiding young children.* Riverside, NJ: Macmillan.

This book is designed for students who are learning to communicate and interact with young children. Readers learn how to handle ordinary daily routines to cope with behavior problems, and to guide children toward self-direction. One section is devoted to the mainstreaming of young children with disabilities.

Honig, A. S. (1985). Compliance, control, and discipline. *Young Children, 40*(1), 50–58; (3), 47–52.

Advanced students will appreciate this extensive research review of the effects of child care on the development of compliance, control, and self-discipline. The first half of the article appears in the January issue and focuses primarily on mother-child interaction and its influence on compliance. The second part, in the

March issue, focuses on group programs for children and discipline methods conducive to the development of cooperation and compliance. Readers will find the practical techniques for effective discipline most useful to their efforts to help young children become ego-resilient, self-disciplined people.

Johnson, D. W., & Johnson, R. T. (1975). *Learning together and alone: Cooperation, competition, and individualization.* Englewood Cliffs, NJ: Prentice-Hall.

Although this is an older book, it still fosters the current interest in engaging children in cooperative learning. The basic principles are adaptable to all age levels and to almost any school situation. The advantages of cooperative over competitive or individualized learning activities are clearly supported by research. Cooperative learning experiences appear to promote far more positive interaction between children with disabilities and those without than do more traditional approaches to classroom structure. The essential components and implementation steps of cooperative learning are presented by Johnson and Johnson in the April 1986 edition of *Exceptional Children.*

Kauffman, J. M. (1985). *Characteristics of children's behavior disorders.* Columbus, OH: Merrill.

This text is designed to provide insight into the problems and characteristics of children who are emotionally disturbed. It is intended for the student interested in theory and research related to behavioral disorders. Although it is not a "how-to" methods book, there are examples of how to control disruptive behavior throughout the book.

Lecroy, C. W. (1983). *Social skills training for children and youth.* New York: Haworth.

This volume synthesizes practical knowledge and research in the development of social skills within the context of the family, the classroom, and in special settings. Of particular interest are the chapters "Social Skills Development in Young Children: Prevention and Therapeutic Approaches" and "Remediation of Social Withdrawal in Young Children: Considerations for the Practitioner."

Marion, M. (1981). *Guidance of young children.* Columbus, OH: Merrill.

This well-written, brief paperback is based on the assumptions that adults want to help children learn to control themselves; to like and value themselves; and to be humane, caring, competent, independent, assertive, cooperative, and helpful. The child, the adults

in his or her life, and the environment are considered the essential components in the guidance system. The book is enormously helpful to anyone involved in early childhood education. It is soundly based on theory and research while offering a great variety of well-received practical suggestions for guiding young children.

Mori, A. A. (Ed.). (1982). Play and development. [Special issue]. *Topics in Early Childhood Special Education, 2*(3).

Anyone who desires to gain a more in-depth understanding of the importance of play in the lives of children with special needs will find this volume intriguing. It begins with a review of Piaget's speculations on the development of play, continues with descriptions of the unique aspects of the play of children with special needs, and ends with specific suggestions for designing play environments for young children. Throughout, the author develops the role of play as a facilitator of social development.

Morris, L. R., & Shulz, L. (1989). *Creative play activities for children with disabilities.* Champaign, IL: Human Kinetics Books.

This book includes 250 games and activities designed to help children from infancy through age 7 grow through play. Many activities incorporate special adaptations for children with visual, hearing, emotional, and mental challenges.

Musselwhite, C. R. (1985). *Adaptive play for special needs children.* San Diego, CA: College-Hill.

All categories of disability are addressed in this practical and comprehensive resource book. The primary focus is on the therapeutic and educational value of play for children and adolescents with disabilities. The author surveys empirical research and theoretical articles and discusses the practical applications of the theory, giving specific play strategies to meet specific goals. Methods of organizing toy lending libraries, adaptive toy workshops, annotated bibliographies, and a resource list make this a highly valuable reference book.

Rogers, D. L., & Ross, D. D. (1986). Encouraging positive social interaction among young children. *Young Children, 41*(3), 12–17.

This article explores two questions: Why is it important to help children who are socially isolated develop more effective social skills? How can we encourage children's positive social interactions? It identifies the elements of effective social interaction and discusses strategies to help children develop social skills in a natural context and receive immediate feedback.

Segal, M., with W. Masi, R. C. Leiderman, & C. K. Sokolowski. (1985). *Your child at play, birth to one year.* Segal, M., & Adcock, D. (1985). *Your child at play, one to two years.* Segal M., & Adcock, D. (1985). *Your child at play, two to three years.* New York: Newmarket.

Here is a well-illustrated, readable series of books for parents about ways to play with their young children. Easy-to-understand developmental sequences, simple activities, and strategies for managing problem situations make this series a worthwhile resource.

Smith, C. A. (1982). *Promoting the social development of young children: Strategies and activities.* Palo Alto, CA: Mayfield.

This practical text is a much-needed resource of over 100 strategies and activities designed to encourage the development of body and sensory awareness, emotional awareness, empathy for others, friendship, conflict resolution, cooperation, and the expression of kindness.

Soderman, A. K. (1985). Dealing with difficult young children. *Young Children, 40,* 15–20.

This practical article does a nice job of summarizing classic research in temperament and applying it to the management of difficult young children. Caregivers are provided with several commonsense techniques that stress understanding and building on children's strengths.

Swanson, H. L., & Reinert, H. R. (1984). *Teaching strategies for children in conflict: Curriculum, methods, and materials.* Columbus, OH: Merrill.

The authors discuss various alternatives to meet the individual needs of children with emotional and social problems. They draw methods from a variety of conceptual approaches and intend a match between the child and the most appropriate intervention. This is an excellent text for those who wish to obtain an excellent overview of the theory and practice relevant to children with social and emotional problems.

USA Toy Library Association, 5940 W. Touhy Avenue, Chicago, IL.

This is a rather new organization designed to provide play experiences and materials that stimulate growth and development. Individual and institutional memberships are available. Members receive monthly newsletters detailing new toys and toys adapted for children with special needs. Included are a toy library operator's manual, discounts on toy purchases, an annual membership meeting, and workshops on toy library operations, therapeutic play, and intervention programs.

Walker, J. E., & Shea, T. M. (1984). *Behavior management: A practical approach for educators.* Columbus, OH: Merrill.

The specific purpose of this text "was to provide experienced teachers, teachers-in-training, and paraprofessionals with a guide for the application of behavior modification techniques in special and general educational settings" (p. ix). The authors have managed to translate the often misunderstood principles of behavior modification into classroom practices readily usable by practitioners. This is a handy tool for those wishing to become more effective managers of behavior.

Walsh, H. M. (1980). *Introducing the young child to the social world.* New York: Macmillan.

This well-written book offers theoretical ideas and practical suggestions for facilitating young children's social competence. Walsh believes that "a major goal of early childhood is to help young children grow beyond considerations of themselves only toward a concern for the welfare of others and a knowledge of the social world around them" (p. vi). It is a refreshing change from the emphasis on the development of cognitive and preacademic skills.

Wolfgang, C. H. (1977). *Helping active and passive preschoolers through play.* Columbus, OH: Merrill.

This inexpensive book suggests a number of schemes for general environmental design, classroom strategies, and organization of time. These ideas can be helpful to the teacher who has time to implement one-to-one interactions. The strategies outlined give teachers options to try even though the theoretical basis is somewhat unclear and possibly too simplified.

Yawkey, T. D., & Pellegrini, A. D. (Eds.). (1984). *Child's play: Developmental and applied.* Hillsdale, NJ: Erlbaum.

This book is intended for those who seek in-depth study of play in early childhood. Each of the 19 articles includes thorough literature reviews and extensive references. Part 1 addresses theoretical issues of pretend play, assessment procedures, and the development of the social self. Part 2 investigates play-related actions, while Part 3 contains articles that critically review the applied nature of play.

References

Ainsworth, M. D. (1973). The development of infant-mother attachment. In B. M. Caldwell & H. Riciutti (Eds.)., *Review of child development research* (Vol. 3, pp. 1–94). Chicago: University of Chicago Press.

Ainsworth, M. D., & Wittig, B. A. (1969). Attachment and exploratory behavior in one-year-olds in a strange situation. In B. M. Foss (Ed.), *Determinants of infant behavior* (Vol. 4, pp. 129–173). London: Metheum.

Bailey, E. W. (Ed.). (1978). *Ongoing data collection in the classroom.* Seattle, WA: Western States Technical Assistance Resource.

Bergstrom, J. M., & Margosian, R. K. (1977). *Teaching young children.* Columbus, OH: Merrill.

Biehler, R. F., & Snowman, J. (1982). *Psychology applied to teaching.* Boston: Houghton Mifflin.

Blackham, G. J. (1968). *The deviant child in the classroom.* Belmont, CA: Wadsworth.

Bowlby, J. (1969). *Attachment and loss, Vol I: Attachment.* New York: Basic Books.

Bricker, D. D. (1978). A rationale for the integration of handicapped and nonhandicapped preschool children. In M. J. Guralnick (Ed.), *Early intervention and the integration of handicapped and nonhandicapped children.* Baltimore: University Park Press.

Bromwich, R. (1981). *Working with parents and infants: An interactional approach.* Baltimore: University Park Press.

Burstein, N. D. (1986). The effects of classroom organization on mainstreamed preschool children. *Exceptional Children, 52,* 425–434.

Caldwell, B. M. (1977). Aggression and hostility in young children. *Young Children, 32,* 4–13.

Carlson, N. A. (1980). General principles of learning and motivation. *Teaching Exceptional Children, 12,* 60–62.

Cherry, C. (1976). *Creative play for the developing child.* Belmont, CA: Fearon.

Cicchetti, D., & Toth, S. L. (1987). The application of a transactional risk model to intervention with multi-risk maltreating families. *Zero-to-Three, 7*(5), 1–8.

Clearinghouse on Child Abuse and Neglect (1985). *Child abuse: An informed approach to a shared concern.* Washington, DC: National Center on Child Abuse and Neglect.

Connor, F. P., Williamson, G. G., & Siepp, J. M. (1978). *Program guide for infants and toddlers with neuromotor and other developmental disabilities.* New York: Teachers College Press.

Cook, R. E. (1983). Why Jimmy doesn't try. *Academic Therapy, 19,* 155–163.

Cook, R. E. (1986). Motivating children to succeed. *Santa Clara, 28,* 7–10.

Crittendon, P. M. (1989). Teaching maltreated children in the preschool. *Topics in Early Childhood Special Education, 9*(2), 16–32.

Crook, W. G. (1975). *Can your child read? Is he hyperactive?* Jackson, TN: Pedicenter.

Cruickshank, W. M., Bentzen, F., Ratzeburg, F., & Tannhousser, M. A. (1961). *A teaching method for brain-injured and hyperactive children.* Syracuse, NY: Syracuse University Press.

Dreikurs, R., (1964). *Children: The challenge.* New York: Hawthorn.

Erikson, E. H. (1963). *Childhood and society.* New York: Norton.

Erikson, E. H. (1971). A healthy personality for every child. In R. H. Anderson & H. G. Shane (Eds.), *As the twig is bent.* Boston: Houghton Mifflin.

Feingold, B. (1974). *Why is your child hyperactive?* New York: Random House.

Fewell, R. R. (1984). *Play assessment scale.* Seattle, WA: University of Washington Press.

Fraiberg, S. (1974). Blind infants and their mothers: An examination of the sign system. In M. Lewis & L. Rosenblum (Eds.), *The effect of the infant on its caregivers.* New York: Wiley.

Garwood, S. G. (Ed.). (1985). Developmental toys. *Topics in Early Childhood Special Education, 5*(3), ix.

Glasser, W. (1969). *Schools without failure.* New York: Harper & Row.

Gordon, T. (1975). *Parent effectiveness training.* New York: New American Library.

Greenspan, S. I. (1979). Intelligence and adaptation: An integration of psychoanalytic and Piagetian developmental psychology. *Psychological Issues.* Monograph 47/48. New York: International Universities Press.

Greenspan, S. I. (1988, September). Fostering emotional and social development in infants with disabilities. *Zero-to-Three, 9*(1), 8–18.

Greenspan, S. I. (1990, September). An intensive approach to a toddler with emotional, motor and language delays: A case report. *Zero-to-Three, 1*(1), 20–26.

Greenspan, S. I., & Greenspan, N. T. (1985). *First feelings: Milestones in the emotional development of your baby and child from birth to age four*. New York: Viking Penguin.

Harris, E. C. (Ed.). (1980). *Report on education research*. Washington, DC: Capitol.

Henderson, B., & Moore, S. G. (1980). Children's responses to objects differing in novelty in relation to level of curiosity and adult behavior. *Child Development, 51*, 457–465.

Hewett, F. M. (1968). *The emotionally disturbed child in the classroom*. Boston: Allyn and Bacon.

Hewett, F. M., & Taylor, F. D. (1980). *The emotionally disturbed child in the classroom*. (2nd ed.) Boston: Allyn and Bacon.

Jenkens, J. R., Speltz, M. L., & Odom, S. L. (1985). Integrating normal and handicapped preschoolers: Effects on child development and social interaction. *Exceptional Children, 52*, 7–17.

Kauffman, J. M. (1985). *Characteristics of children's behavior disorders*. Columbus, OH: Merrill.

Kirkhart, R., & Kirkhart, E. (1972). The bruised self: Mending in early years. In K. Yamamoto (Ed.), *The child and his image* (pp. 121–177). Boston: Houghton Mifflin.

Klaus, M., & Kennell, J. (1979). *Maternal-infant bonding*. St. Louis: Mosby.

Langley, M. B. (1985). Selecting, adapting, and applying toys as learning tools for handicapped children. *Topics in Early Childhood Special Education, 5*(3), 101–118.

Lansky, V. (1978). *The taming of the C.A.N.D.Y. monster*. Wayzata, NY: Meadowbrook.

Linder, T. (1990). *Transdisciplinary play-based assessment: A functional approach to working with young children*. Baltimore: Paul H. Brookes.

Lorton, M. (1974). *Workjobs*. Atlanta: Addison-Wesley.

Lyons-Ruth, K., Connell, D. B., Zoll, D., & Stahl, J. (1987). Infants and social risk: Relations among infant maltreatment, maternal behavior and infant attachment behavior. *Developmental Psychology, 123*(2), 223–232.

Marion, M. (1981). *Guidance of young children*. Columbus, OH: Charles E. Merrill.

Maslow, A. H. (1968). *Toward a psychology of being*. New York: Van Nostrand Reinhold.

McHale, S. M., & Olley, J. G. (1982). Using play to facilitate the social development of handicapped children. *Topics in Early Childhood Special Education, 2*(3), 76–86.

McLean, M., & Hanline, M. F. (1990). Providing early intervention services in integrated environments: Challenges and opportunities in the future. *Topics in Early Childhood Special Education, 10*(2), 62–77.

Miller, C. (1984). Building self-control. *Young Children, 40*, 15–19.

Neisworth, J. T. (Ed.). (1985). Social competence: Development and intervention. [Special issue]. *Topics in Early Childhood Special Education, 4*(4).

Odom, S. L., Strain, P. S., Karger, M. A., & Smith, J. (1986). Using single and multiple peers to promote social interaction of preschool children with handicaps. *Journal of the Division for Early Childhood, 10*, 53–64.

Parten, M. B. (1932). Social participation among preschool children. *Journal of Abnormal and Social Psychology, 27*, 243–269.

Patterson, G. R. (1986). Performance models for antisocial boys. *American Psychologist, 41*, 432–444.

Peck, C., Apolloni, T., Cooke, T., & Raver, S. (1978). Teaching retarded preschoolers to imitate the free play behavior of nonretarded classmates: Trained and generalized effects. *The Journal of Special Education, 12*, 195–207.

Piaget, J. (1963). *Play, dreams, and imitations in childhood*. New York: Norton.

Poulsen, M. K. (1989, December). *Perinatal substance abuse: Social policy and service delivery issues*. Paper presented to the California Early Intervention Technical Assistance Network Work Group, Sacramento, CA.

Reinert, H. R. (1980). *Children in conflict*. Columbus, OH: Charles F. Merrill.

Rogers, D. L., & Ross, D. D. (1986). Encouraging positive social interaction among young children. *Young Children, 4*, 12–17.

Ross, A. O. (1977). The application of behavior principles in therapeutic education. *The Journal of Special Education, 1*, 275–286.

Sainato, D. M. (1985). The behavioral ecology of preschool classrooms. *DEC Communicator, 12*, 2.

Smith, J. M., & Smith, D. E. (1976). *Child management*. Champaign, IL: Research Press.

Smith, L. (1975). *Human development: 2 1/2 to 6 years*. Costa Mesa, CA: Concept Media.

Steele, B. F. (1987). Abuse and neglect in the earliest years: Groundwork for vulnerability. *Zero-to-Three, 7*(4), 14–15.

Stern, D. N. (1985). *The interpersonal world of the infant*. New York: Basic Books.

Swanson, H. L., & Reinert, H. R. (1984). *Teaching strategies for children in conflict*. Columbus, OH: Merrill.

Swap, S. M. (1974). Disturbing classroom behaviors: A developmental and ecological view. *Exceptional Children, 41,* 163–172.

Texas Tech University. (1984). *The special child: Student laboratory manual.* Lubbock, TX: Home Economics Curriculum Center.

Thomas, A., Chess, S., & Birch, H. G. (1968). *Temperamental and behavior disorders in children.* New York: New York University Press.

Thomas, A., Chess, S., & Birch, H. G. (1970). The origin of personality. *Scientific American, 223,* 102–109.

Thomas, A., Chess, S., & Korn, S. J. (1982). The reality of difficult temperament. *Merrill-Palmer Quarterly, 28,* 1–20.

Ulrey, G., & Rogers, S. J. (1982). *Psychological assessment of handicapped infants and young children.* New York: Thieme-Stratton.

Vaughn, S. R. (1985). Facilitating the interpersonal development of young handicapped children. *Journal of the Division for Early Childhood, 9,* 170–174.

Walker, J. E., & Shea, T. M. (1984). *Behavior management: A practical approach for educators.* Columbus, OH: Merrill.

Walsh, H. M. (1980). *Introducing the young child to the social world.* New York: Macmillan.

Wehman, P. (1978). Play skill development. In N. H. Fallen & J. E. McGovern (Eds.), *Young children with special needs.* (pp. 277–303). Columbus, OH: Merrill.

Weston, R., Ivins, B., Zuckerman, B., Jones, C., & Lopez, R. (1989). Drug exposed babies: Research and clinical issues. *Zero-to-Three, 9*(5), 1–7.

White, B. P., & Phair, M. A. (1986). "It'll be a challenge!" Managing emotional stress in teaching disabled children. *Young Children, 41,* 44–48.

Youngblade, L. M., & Belsky, J. (1989). Child maltreatment, infant-parent attachment security, and dysfunctional peer relationships in toddlerhood. *Topics in Early Childhood Special Education, 9*(2), 1–15.

Zentall, S. (1977). Environmental stimulation model. *Exceptional Children, 43,* 502–511.

Chapter 8

Helping Young Children Develop Motor Skills

Key Points

▶ Infants learn from the sensations of movement, which come primarily from active rather than passive movements.

▶ Motor development follows a highly predictable sequential and overlapping pattern.

▶ Physiological maturation and environmental factors influence the rate and quality of physical and motor development.

▶ Assessment of motor skills is a team effort using a variety of approaches.

▶ Therapeutic intervention should encourage functional behaviors, including gross and fine motor skills, and their use in daily living.

▶ Positioning and handling are important considerations in normalization of muscle tone, prevention of deformity, and stabilization of the body.

▶ Adaptations of materials and environmental considerations should be a vital concern in program planning for children with motor impairments.

Key Topics

▶ Development of motor skills including reflexes and gross motor, fine motor, perceptual-motor, and self-help skills.

▶ Atypical motor development.

▶ Assessment of motor abilities.

▶ Therapeutic intervention.

▶ Movement education with adaptations.

Working with young children to develop motor skills requires a special kind of planning. Competition and "winners," often associated with physical education in schools, are inappropriate. Infants and young children need to learn about their bodies. They need to develop balance and coordination. It is important for them to discover themselves in relationship to space. Care must be taken to help children develop an inner awareness of the difference between the two sides of the body, since moving through space requires both sides of the body to act as a team.

Coordination of movement skills contributes to children's development of confidence and trust in themselves and their bodies. This sense of bodily trust is considered to be important to the emergence of healthy personalities (Erikson,

1963). These are just some of the reasons that sensorimotor activities have held a dominant place in early education. For many children with motor problems or delays (cerebral palsy, mental retardation, orthopedic disabilities, etc.), movement experiences are often limited. Additional instruction, therapeutic intervention, and encouragement are essential to minimize the disability and maximize children's potential in all aspects of development.

Motor skills are usually divided into at least two general categories. **Gross motor skills** refer to activities that involve the use of the large muscles of the neck, trunk, arms, and legs. Included are basic body movements such as lifting the head, rolling, crawling, creeping, walking, running, leaping, jumping, hopping, galloping, and skipping. Large muscle strength and endurance are also important in climbing, pushing, pulling, hanging, and lifting.

Fine motor skills involve more precise movements of the small muscles, especially those of the eyes, speech musculature, hands, fingers, feet, and toes. Movements such as blinking, focusing, sucking, grasping, releasing, pinching, and writing are considered to be fine motor activites. Many fine motor skills, including cutting, copying, stringing beads, and pasting, require the eyes to direct the hands. These activities are referred to variously as those that require perceptual-motor, visual-motor, sensorimotor, ocular-motor, or eye-hand coordination.

This chapter reviews normal motor development, including gross and fine motor skills and perceptual-motor integration, and suggests activities to enhance development. Identification and problems of atypical motor development are emphasized, with suggestions for intervention. Special efforts are taken to encourage the integration of movement skills with other areas of the curriculum as well as in day-to-day functional activities.

THE DEVELOPMENT OF MOTOR SKILLS

Babies learn from the sensations of movement, which come primarily from active rather than passive movements. In this developmental process, the ability of the higher centers to mature is in part dependent upon sensory information brought to them (Connor, Williamson, & Siepp, 1978). Sensory input (such as tactile, proprioceptive, visual, or auditory) is sent through the nervous system and integrated at appropriate levels of the brain and spinal cord. As messages are received and processed, responses are sent back in the form of motor acts. Voluntary motor activity is controlled by upper brain centers located in the cerebral cortex, while involuntary or

unconscious muscle movements (e.g., digestion of food, eye blinking, reflex movements) are controlled by lower brain centers, that is, the cerebellum and parts of the brain stem (Thurman & Widerstrom, 1990).

According to Espenschade and Eckert (1980), in general, the development of motor skills proceeds according to the laws which govern the physiological maturation of the child, with the development of movement patterns progressing from simple arm or leg actions to highly integrated total body coordinations (p. 135).

The rate of development is thought to depend not only on the quality of environmental stimulus but also on the stage of brain development (Wolff, 1979). No distinction is usually made in the motor abilities of boys and girls in infancy and early childhood because the differences are not very great. During the late preschool years, girls appear to perform better on tasks requiring manual dexterity, whereas boys are more adept when using large (gross) muscles. The extent to which this difference may be culturally determined is still being questioned. Fallen and Umansky (1985) have pointed out that parents' expectations and interactions with infants generally differ according to the sex of the child. These expectations are reflected in play activities.

Environmental factors such as amount of sleep and exercise, quality of medical care, and adequacy of nutrition may influence the rate and ultimate degree of physical, and thus, motor development. In addition, childrearing practices that vary among cultures also should be taken into account when viewing differences in motor skill development. In general, a child's potential for motor skill development is considered to be the result of genetic origin and specific environmental influences.

By the time a child is 5 or 6 years of age, many motor behaviors have been established and require only refinement and mastery at a higher, more complex level. During these early

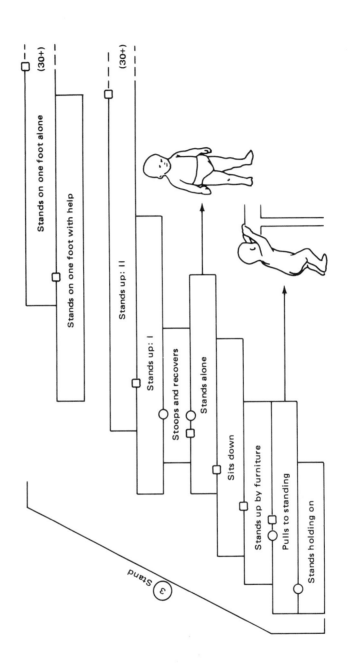

3 Stand

Stands on one foot alone (30+)

Stands on one foot with help

Stands up: II (30+)

Stands up: I

Stoops and recovers

Stands alone

Sits down

Stands up by furniture

Pulls to standing

Stands holding on

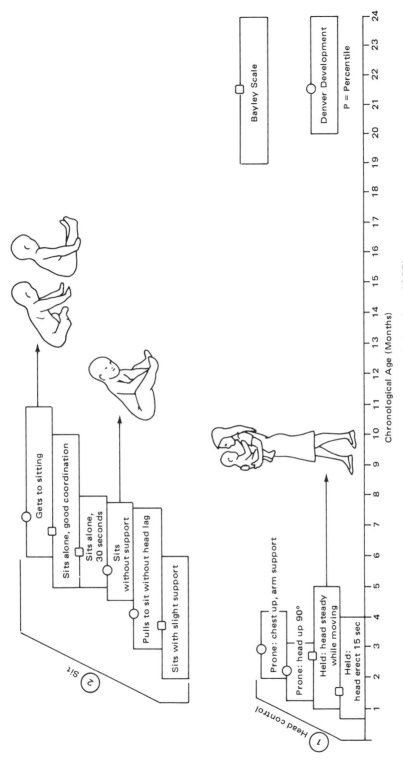

Figure 8–1 Progressions of change: Postural control. (*Source:* Keogh & Sugden, 1985)

277

years, motor development follows a highly pre-dictable sequential and overlapping pattern (Connor, Williamson, & Siepp, 1978). Although the rate at which typical children progress varies, the sequence remains fairly constant. The litera-ture on motor development contains many de-scriptions and timetables for the stage/age at which motor abilities are attained. Variation in developmental rate is well documented. It is not unusual to hear mothers compare walking age variations from 8 to 18 months. For example, Figure 8–1 clearly shows the sequence and varia-tion in postural control.

Sequential Trends of Motor Development

O'Donnell (1969) discussed seven basic prin-ciples that govern the sequence of motor devel-opment:

1. *Cephalocaudal pattern.* Muscular develop-ment proceeds from the head to the foot. For example, infants have voluntary control over their heads before lower parts of their body. Similarly, children can usually throw before they can catch.

2. *Proximo-distal pattern.* Growth and devel-opment tend to proceed from the spine (proximo) to the outer extremities (distal). That is, voluntary movement begins in the shoulder, then moves on to the elbow area, wrist, and finally, the fingers.

3. *Mass-to-specific pattern.* Body movement of young infants is undifferentiated, involving the total body. Later, specific patterns of movement develop out of these generalized mass movements. When learning new skills, it takes time for children to inhibit the un-wanted extraneous movements.

4. *Gross-motor-to-fine-motor pattern.* Children usually gain control over large muscle activ-ity before fine or small muscle activity. In

addition, a child must gain differential con-trol. That is, movement of muscles on one side of the body should occur without simi-lar movement on the other side of the body, unless desired.

5. *Maximum-to-minimum-muscle-involvement pattern.* Like the mass-to-specific pattern, body movement becomes increasingly more efficient. With practice, children learn to eliminate unnecessary expenditures of energy. Where it once took a whole bodily effort to catch a ball, children learn to catch with the use of just one arm and hand.

6. *Bilateral-to-unilateral pattern.* Children pro-gress from undifferentiated use of both sides of the body to unilateral preference, referred to as the *establishment of laterality.*

7. *Orderly development pattern.* Children differ in the rate of their development but do tend to follow a similar pattern if environmental conditions are adequate and no organic def-icits are present.

Helping Parents to Understand

In teaching or talking to parents about various aspects of child development, early intervention-ists often find themselves caught up in lengthy, detailed descriptions of developmental domains. As a result of parents' requests for jargon-free explanations of sequential development, Lacy (1981) put together a manual describing devel-opment from the view of the growing infant. *Dear Mom and Dad* includes extensive recom-mendations for parent-child activities and is in-cluded here (Figure 8–2) as a summary of the area of early motor development.

Reflexive Development

Early motor activity of infants is structured by a variety of primitive and automatic reflexes.

Dear Mom & Dad

a baby's Letters to her Parents

(Gross Motor Development)

Dear Mom and Dad,

I'm sure that one of the first things you noticed when I was born was that I came out moving and haven't stopped yet! Those early movements weren't really planned out by me, though. A lot of that thrashing about was because of my immature nervous system and getting into certain positions was because of reflexes. Remember how you used to put me on my back to change me and I would jump? Well, that was my startle (Moro) reflex. And also that position on my back where I looked like a fencer (head turned toward bent arm and leg-- opposite ones straight)? Well, that was my ATNR reflex. I really began to notice things around me with my senses before I could act on them with my body, and that was frustrating--let me tell you!

As I did get going, though, I developed from my head down to my toes and from the center of my body to the outside muscles--"head down" and "inside out" is how I remember it. You see, my control was first with eye muscles, then with facial, on to neck, and finally down to trunk, legs, and feet. So I could focus my eyes and make faces, then balance my head before my body, and after that drag my body on the ground before creeping on hands and knees, and finally pull up to stand before walking. The side-ways growth showed up in arm-waving, then batting, then using wrist, hands, and finally individual fingers to manipulate objects. (I'll tell you more about arms and hands later.)

In those early months, my physical performance depended a lot on whether I was crying, sleepy, active, or alert. I really wasn't tuned in too much back then. But you kept on trying just the right activities for my abilities, giving me opportunities for new growth by the way you placed my body, praising and encouraging me, but always you found out very early that the way I felt about myself (my self-concept) depended so much on how well I could move

— Infant Development Program —

Figure 8–2 (pp. 279–281)   Summary of early motor development. (With gratitude to Virginia McDonald, Ann Lacy, and Project Hope, Department of Education, San Diego County, California)

my body by myself. So, you used a "hands-off" policy when you could, helping me to crawl or walk with a towel around my waist, etc. Then I really began to feel that I could make things happen in my new world.

Well, that whole first year seemed to be a time of learning more and more about how to use my body. My social growing and use of objects and language weren't quite as important to me yet. But I was really doing some learning as I thought out and planned all of those movements. A couple of things were going on all at once. First of all, I began to take in (integrate) those reflexes that I mentioned earlier, and also some others and started doing motions that I had control over. At the same time, I was gradually changing from being sideways to being upright as I got control over my head and trunk and then arms and legs. This ability to move and choose my actions and to move toward being vertical in my second year affected all parts of my life. It helped me to explore more with objects and try out new experiences through my senses (fine motor and cognitive), I could see people better and get to know them (visual and social), and my inside breathing organs were in a better position to help me talk (language). The best part of all was being able to move about by myself and have many more chances to explore things that had been out of reach or range--and just be more independent on my own.

As I learned each new step, you must have wondered why I sometimes did things so slowly--and also the same thing over and over. Well, I went slowly because I really needed to concentrate on my new accomplishments. (Sometimes I even wanted to give up eating and sleeping, too, to concentrate on my new physical miracles.) And the reason I practiced so much is that I wanted to make sure that each movement really became a part of me so that I wouldn't forget it. Sometimes I tried a new movement, like standing, only once and then dropped it for awhile (maybe even two months) because my new independence frightened me.

No, it wasn't all easy. I went along first wanting to take on the world, then needing to slow down or stop, and sometimes even drop something I had learned. I know you

Figure 8–2   (Continued)

could tell, Mom, as I often cried, clung to you and acted difficult, that sometimes this new independence brought by a new movement was a little scary; I needed to slow down and come back to you for some reassurance. You probably came to realize that my shakiness and unsureness was sure to pop up right before a new "motor milestone." Thanks, Mom and Dad, for understanding and going along with my difficult times of wanting to move away from you and then being scared and returning for the comfort and love only you could give.

Thanks, too, for finding that nice balance between freedom and limits. It must have been hard for you to give me the chance to explore and learn, while also teaching me about rules and dangers. But you did a great job of protecting me and also giving me a nice environment to want to learn about. And best of all, you watched my own individual signals and trusted me. From the top of my head to the bottom of my toes and from the inside out, I thank you.

Love,

Your Growing Child

Infant Development Program

Figure 8–2 (Continued)

Primitive reflexes are evident in early infancy at or soon after birth. It is not known whether these reflexes are the framework for further motor maturation or must be inhibited for the development of coordinated voluntary control (Taft, 1982). There is a wide range of variation in reflex responsiveness among infants as well as within the same infant, depending on the behavioral states of the child being observed (Malina, 1980). These reflexes are expressions of the immaturity of the infant's nervous system and provide a basis for assessing the integrity of the developing neuromuscular system early in life.

Although the teacher may have difficulty understanding the complexities of neurological development, it is important to have some idea of how coordinated movement evolves and what factors may interfere with normal functioning. Appendix C summarizes major reflexes and potential problems. Concerned early interventionists may consult a physical or occupational therapist who is specifically trained to assess reflexive behavior.

Developing Gross Motor Skills

Gross motor skills refer to the involvement of the large muscles of the neck, trunk of the body, arms, and legs. Early childhood affords the time and practice for emerging skills to become accomplished before rapid bodily changes begin to occur. Children develop postural control and learn to walk, run, catch, and jump with relative skill (See Figure 8–1 for progressions of change in postural control.) The extent to which children become proficient in these skills is dependent on muscle development as well as opportunity for muscle use. However, it must be remembered that even in the most optimal situations, large and uneven growth spurts do occur. To provide the stimulation needed, safe environments free from obstacles and full of encouragement are needed. References at the end of the chapter suggest how to facilitate the development of growth-producing play areas.

Proficiency in gross motor skills is influenced by changes in body proportions. The 2-year-old's

head accounts for about one fourth of the child's height. By the time the child is 5 years old, it accounts for only about one sixth of the total height (Cratty, 1970). As children become less top heavy, their ability to balance themselves develops. Children entering kindergarten have usually experienced an increase in muscle tissue, creating a larger potential of muscle energy available for movement (Keogh & Sugden, 1985).

Developing Fine Motor Skills

Fine motor skills involve small muscles. Most fine motor skills, as far as preparation for manual control is concerned, involve hands and fingers. (See Figure 8–3 for progression of change in manual control.) Coordination of hands and fingers is often described as requiring strength, flexibility, and dexterity. The coordination of eye-hand movement is referred to as a visual-perceptual skill.

Handedness. When observing children engaged in fine motor activities, the question of "handedness" or hand preference usually arises. Preschool teachers can relax, for research indicates that it is usual to find children frequently interchanging the use of hands throughout early childhood. Hand dominance is often not achieved until the age of 6. Even then, some children develop functional ambidexterity (Espenschade & Eckert, 1980; Westphal, 1975). The fact that children tend to use their right hands more often in taught activities such as cutting and throwing suggests the influence of our cultural bias.

Practice Payoff. Long before a baby can walk, her mother may report, "Sally picked up a raisin today." Surprised that the child could pick up something so tiny, mothers become more alert about leaving beads and other nonedibles around. Later, this ability to see small things and pick them up will become the foundation for grasping and holding crayons, pencils, and other small objects.

Although merely having things available to pick up is all that is necessary for most young children to learn important fine motor skills, they must have opportunities to practice. Building with small blocks, manipulating small toys, and using crayons, chalk, and scissors all lead to the improvement of essential skills.

Snap-together beads, geoboards, puzzles, beads for stringing, button and lacing boards, and large nuts and screws offer interesting and challenging fine motor practice for young children. Even cooking activities help children to develop skills such as stirring, cutting, pounding, and rolling, while learning a variety of concepts. A sample list of typical motor skill activities is found in Table 8–1. A chart of normative expectations can be found in Appencix A.

Developing Perceptual-Motor Skills

Much has been written about the integral relationship between developing motor and perceptual skills (perceptual-motor skills) as well as visual and auditory perception. To comprehend the dynamic role of sensorimotor and perceptual skills in a child's development and in typical preschool curricula, it is necessary to have a basic understanding of perception.

Perception. Lerner, Mardell-Czudnowski, and Goldenberg (1987) explained perception as follows:

Perception is an interpretive function of the brain. It is the translation of sensory impressions into some representational level that is easily stored and recalled. In reality, the functions of sensation, motor activity and perception are so closely related that it is difficult to separate one from the other. (p. 160)

Perception is a learned cognitive process. Encountering sensory stimulation of a particular

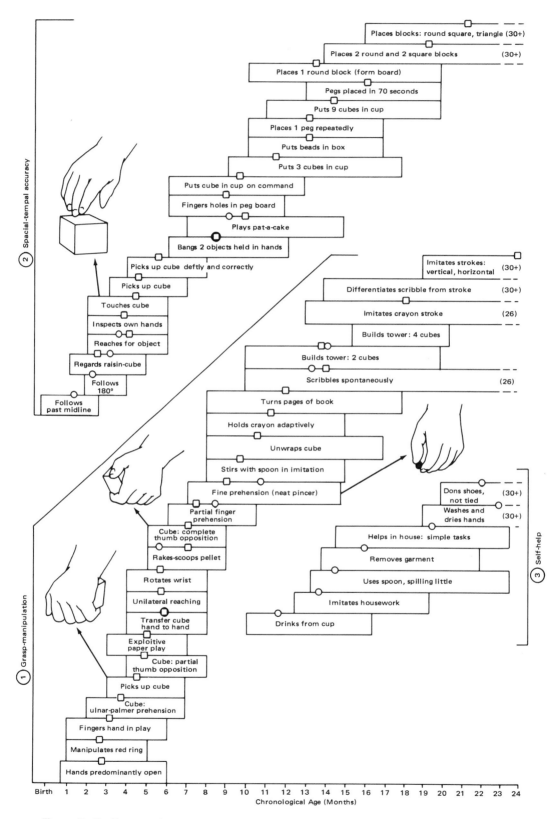

Figure 8–3 Progressions of change: Manual control. (*Source:* Keogh & Sugden, 1985)

Table 8–1   Typical motor skills activities

Gross Motor Development

Eye-Foot Coordination	*Eye-Hand Coordination*	*Body Awareness*	*Balance*
Kicking	Climbing	Crawling in and out of	Standing on tiptoe
Climbing	Hanging	things	Walking the balance beam
Jumping	Striking balloons	Crawling through and	Riding wheeled toys
Hopping	Throwing	around things	Walking around tire edges
Dancing	Catching	Moving like an animal	or sandbox rails
Walking the balance beam	Using tools	Mirroring activities	Moving and carrying
Jumping over ropes	Block building	Playing "Simon Says"	something without
	Rolling balls	Steering wheeled toys	spilling it
	Pounding		Walking with bean bag on
	Stirring		head or shoulder

Fine Motor Development (Eye-Hand Coordination)

Cutting	Lacing	Outlining with stencils or templates
Coloring	Geoboards	Copying
Drawing	Tracing	Pasting
Sewing	Painting	Building block towers
Puzzle building	Paper folding	Stacking
Bead stringing	Copying designs	

Self-Help Skills

Dressing (buttoning, zipping, snapping, buckling)
Eating
Personal hygiene (brushing teeth, washing hands)
Toileting

kind for the first time, children *receive* (sense) the stimulation. Subsequent encounters usually result in their *perceiving* (interpreting) the stimulus. If any of the senses are impaired, even slightly, children may not be able to sense the initial stimulus accurately. If they do not receive an accurate first impression, later interpretations of that stimulus will be wrong or confusing to them.

Failure to develop accurate perceptions has been observed in children described as learning disabled. The early works of Strauss and Werner (1942) and Strauss and Lehtinen (1947) emphasized that perceptual deficits interfere seriously with all learning. Cruickshank (1967) also has supported this belief.

Perceptual-Motor Skills. In an effort to enhance perceptual-motor skills (coordination of what is perceived with movement of body parts) or remediate deficits, there have been numerous teaching systems and techniques proposed (see Ayres, 1972; Cratty, 1970; Frostig, 1974; Kephart, 1964).

In the past, perceptual-motor skill instruction was the primary focus of curricula in many special education programs. In summarizing his review of research on perceptual-motor instructional programs, Mercer (1983) warned:

Many of the perceptual-motor training programs commonly used, then, do not directly improve academic achievement or perceptual-motor development. Until further research, the inclusion of academic content in motor activities is desirable. (p. 278)

After considering more than 60 studies, Larsen and Hammill (1975) concluded that the relationship among visual, perceptual, and academic performance is not significant. Therefore Hammill and Bartel (1975) urged teachers "to implement perceptual-motor training on a remedial basis in only those few cases where improvement in perception is the goal" (p. 230). They further suggested that such training is more acceptable for preschoolers than for kindergarten or school-aged children.

Or, as Piazza (1979) suggested,

If perceptual, motor, or psycholinguistic skills are to be trained they should be done for their own sake and not for some projected transfer to an academic area. Chidren do need to be taught the difference between the left and right sides of their bodies, and . . . such tasks as cutting. (p. 47)

It is for these reasons that we encourage the development of perceptual-motor skills as tasks in and of themselves, but in association with language and concept development.

Developing Self-Help Skills

Self-help skills include both fine and gross motor skills. Many children entering early education programs can take care of most of their personal needs. They can put coats and sweaters on and take them off. Some children continue to need help with getting zippers started and small buttons buttoned. Many need help tying shoes. Of course, those with motor disabilities may need special instruction in order to develop essential self-help skills.

Parents should be encouraged to provide clothes that are easy for their children to manage. Some parents will need encouragement to allow their children to do things for themselves. This may be especially true if the child has a physical problem of any kind. It is helpful to show parents where to begin with a child who has special needs. For example, long before children can put socks on, they can take them off. Show parents how to pull the sock part way off and then put the child's hand on the toe and pull.

Smiles and praise for success, combined with "You pulled your sock off," encourage self-help and build language. The Portage Preschool Project (Shearer & Shearer, 1976) was provided a series of steps to teach a number of self-help skills.

Reverse Chaining. The most complete curricula developed for teaching self-help skills have been contributed by those who work with individuals with moderate and severe disabilities. A sample is found in the annotated bibliography at the end of the chapter. These guides are especially helpful to professionals working with young children because they present complete sets of task analyses directly useful in preschool classrooms and early childhood centers.

Task analyses in the areas of dressing, eating, and personal hygiene are usually offered. Sometimes toileting is included. Self-help skills are usually taught through the process known as **reverse chaining.** As pointed out in the example of taking socks off, the last part of the task is done first. Consider the following steps outlined by Fredericks and colleagues (1976, p. 36):

1. Child puts on sock when just above heel.
2. Child puts on sock when just below heel.
3. Child puts on sock when toes started in.
4. Child puts on sock when handed to him with heel in correct position.
5. Child puts on sock (heel in correct position).

In addition, the authors of this resource suggested that oversized clothing be used when children are having considerable difficulty. They further questioned the use of dressing form boards because such practice is difficult to transfer to clothing on one's body. Some preschool teachers have had success with the placement of form board fronts on pillows that can be held by the child in front of himself or herself. A piece of elastic around the child and attached to either side of the pillow is also helpful.

Think back to the steps outlined for putting on socks. Reverse chaining means that the child

would initially be helped at step one and reinforced for success. When this step has been accomplished, then teaching would begin at step two the next time socks needed to be put on. Of course, astute observation allows the teacher or parent to know which step to begin with in the process of reverse chaining.

ATYPICAL MOTOR DEVELOPMENT

Atypical motor development or motor differences can occur for a variety of reasons. Brain damage, orthopedic problems, genetic defects, mental retardation, and sensory impairments can potentially interfere with motor skill acquisition.

Deviations in movement patterns affecting the young child usually originate in the prenatal or perinatal period. Neuromuscular dysfunction originating in the central nervous system, specifically cerebral palsy (CP), is the most common motor disability among children of all ages. Cerebral palsy is a general term given to nonprogressive brain lesions. It generally causes complex problems in all aspects of development (Molnar, 1982). Adnormal movement patterns seen in children with CP are related to primitive reflex retention and problems of motor incoordination and muscle tone. A continuum of motor dysfunction due to insult to the brain may include on one end a child with clumsy and awkward movements and on the other a child with CP who has such severe impairments that any coordinated movement is next to impossible. In between are varying degrees of movement problems.

Although the severe form of CP affects many other developmental areas, it is important to be cautious not to equate the degree of motor disability with cognitive deficits. According to Martin (1982), many studies show that central nervous system insult is not an accurate predictor of cognitive growth and later academic performance.

Problems in Muscle Development

Muscle characteristics of tone, control, and strength are significant concerns in development and eventual intervention. Causes of problems vary from central nervous system damage and genetic disorders to nonspecific delays in development. Hanson and Harris (1986) discussed the deviations in muscle development that require consideration when programs are planned.

1. *Deficits in muscle tone.* The degree of tension in the muscle at rest defines muscle tone. Three types of muscle tone deviation are noted. The first, **hypotonicity,** describes low tension or flaccidity in muscles. The "floppy" child usually demonstrates generalized weak, flabby muscles, and often hypermobile joints, especially in shoulders, hips, and ankles (Rogers, 1982). The child with Down syndrome, Prader-Willi syndrome, or those classified as having ataxic cerebral palsy are good examples of "floppy" children. The hypotonic child is usually less active than his or her peers and may become fatigued easily by motor activities.

Motor milestones such as sitting, creeping, and walking are usually delayed because of the affected child's generalized low muscle tone. Other areas affected may be the chest and face muscles. Because of low muscle tone, breathing tends to be shallow. The child may also have difficulty sustaining sounds when attempting to cry, babble, or talk.

Conversely, the child with **hypertonia** has too much muscle tone. Another name for hypertonia is **spasticity.** A high percentage of children with CP have spasticity. The affected muscles are characterized as feeling stiff and rigid. For instance, when the child tries to passively extend

the flexed arm, it feels "locked," and a slow, steady pressure at the elbow is necessary to perform this motion. In children with spastic hemiplegia, one side of the body is affected. In spastic diplegia, the legs are primarily affected, but trunk and arms may also be involved. In spastic quadriplegia, all four extremities and trunk are involved.

Children with hypertonia are frequently delayed in achieving motor milestones. They often have difficulty assuming and maintaining postures that go against gravity, such as sitting, creeping, and standing. Breathing may also be impaired due to decreased movement of the ribs and chest. If facial and oral muscles are involved, as is often the case in spastic quadriplegia, articulation, chewing, and swallowing also may be affected (Hanson & Harris, 1986).

Rogers (1982) described **fluctuating muscle tone,** which can be seen in children who are generally hypertonic or hypotonic. Usually in these cases, an attempt at voluntary movement sets off increased muscle tone. However, when the child is resting, muscles may be hypotonic. The incoordination of contraction and relaxation may be seen in *athetoid* movement patterns, which are repetitive, poorly coordinated voluntary movements. The most common type of motor disability in which fluctuating tone occurs is athetoid cerebral palsy.

2. *Deficits in muscle control.* Writhing movements, tremors, and fluctuating muscle tone are abnormal motor characteristics that interfere with voluntary movements. As the child with CP tries to do something, for example, not only is fluctuating tone present, but also uncoordinated movements and abnormal posture caused by increased or decreased tone. Involuntary facial movements (mouth opening and closing, the tongue moving in and out) are often related to general muscle tone fluctuation throughout the body. Attempts at fine motor activities tend to increase problems in overall coordination in some children with CP.

3. *Deficits in muscle strength.* There may be differences in muscle strength among and within children. Certain degenerative diseases such as muscular dystrophy have a progressive effect on muscle strength. Paralysis of muscles related to spinal cord damage such as spina bifida or contagious diseases such as polio often cause permanent loss of strength in certain muscle groups. The inactivity of a child wearing a cast for a broken bone will cause losses of strength and muscle tone that quickly return to normal with exercise and movement.

Hyperactivity

"He is just never still a minute! He's always running, getting into things, pushing and kicking other kids. He's even been expelled from nursery school." This is a frustrated mother talking about her 3-year-old son. Children exhibiting these behaviors over time may suffer from a disorder so complex and confusing that few professionals can diagnose, treat, or even name it.

The misunderstanding may also be aggravated because the condition has many names: hyperkinetic syndrome, minimal brain dysfunction, minimal cerebral dysfunction, and, more recently, attention deficit disorder (American Psychiatric Association, 1980).

Hyperactivity has no single known cause and is therefore classified as a *syndrome* because it has a cluster of symptoms. It is generally characterized by excessive motor activity, short attention span, and impulsive behavior. All the symptoms must be weighed in relation to the child's age and proven absence of mental retardation or mental illness (Hadley, 1984). Because of this complexity, it is important that parents, teachers, therapists, and physicians work as a team to diagnose, treat, and cope with the child who is hyperactive.

According to Campbell (1985), there is a high probability that untreated early signs of overactivity, distractibility, and impulsivity will continue to be problematic throughout the early years of elementary school. Rosenberg, Wilson, and Legenhausen (1989) have suggested that rather than waiting and hoping for hyperactive behaviors to disappear developmentally, parents, early interventionists, and pediatricians should make active use of the preschool years. These years can be used to assist the child with hyperactivity in developing appropriate patterns of behavior.

There are several types of recommended treatment ranging from medication and diet changes to behavior management. Renshaw (1974) made several practical recommendations for those who work with hyperactive children. She advised parents and early educators to be consistent in rules and discipline, to speak quietly and slowly, and to have a clear routine for the child (playtime, naptime, mealtime, worktime, and bedtime, interwoven with physical activity to release excess energy). Long periods of sitting in a preschool class will certainly tax the tolerance level of a child who has the need to move. A sensitive teacher will provide for extra physical activity rather than punish lack of "good sitting behavior." More recent literature highlights possible neurological differences between young boys and girls, again supporting the importance of opportunities for and tolerance of movement, especially for boys (McGuinness, 1985).

ASSESSMENT OF MOTOR ABILITIES

In educational planning or therapeutic intervention, it is important to assess the young child in all developmental areas and to determine how the absence or delay of motor abilities will affect overall learning and social interactions. No matter what type of assessment approach is used (observation checklist or standardized tests), the information should be translated into optimal learning experiences.

As emphasized throughout this text, the responsibility for assessing the child should be a team effort. The parent, teacher, physician, and allied health professionals all contribute information essential in identification, diagnosis, and remediation of motor problems. As with all assessment, care must be taken not to pin on diagnostic labels until all pertinent information is obtained. The high-risk premature infant, for example, is too often given an early diagnosis of cerebral palsy based on symptoms characteristic of an immature but developing nervous system. Imagine the impact of that incorrect diagnosis on the parents!

Early education program staff often become coordinators and synthesizers of assessment information. Information from parents on early developmental milestones, family history, and current behavior, plus hospital records and diagnostic assessment from medical specialists, add up to a more comprehensive view of a child's physical development.

Infants and Toddlers

Probably the earliest assessment of motor development is performed routinely at 1 minute and at 5 minutes after birth. The newborn baby is assessed for appearance (color), heart rate, reflex irritability, activity, muscle tone, and respiratory effort to determine whether or not further medical assistance is needed. A practical scoring system usually used to assess these attributes is the Apgar score (Apgar & James, 1962). Table 8–2 shows the five criteria and point values used to measure the effect of loss of oxygen and damage to the circulation in newborns. Each characteristic is rated 0, 1, or 2 (2 being best). These are added together to obtain an overall score that varies from 0 to 10. The 5-minute score has been shown to predict future developmental progress quite accurately (Batshaw & Perret, 1981). More extensive observation of the newborn may be accomplished with an instrument such as the Brazelton Neonatal Behavioral Assessment Scale (Brazelton, 1973). The Brazelton Scale helps identify problems in the central nervous system and the sensory abilities of the newborn.

When infants or young children lack obvious or visible impairments, it is much more difficult to detect possible problems related to motor development (Taft, 1982). Usually a parent or early educator detects the more subtle behaviors that can be observed over time and are not seen in a short office visit with a medical specialist. Some of the behaviors that should be noted and considered as indicators of the need for referral include the following:

1. Delayed motor milestones. (Although delay is an important indicator, normal developmental variations must be kept in mind.)

2. Abnormal posturing of arms and legs during rest or activity.

3. Tremor of hands or arms when performing a task.

4. Significant difference in skill between right and left arms or legs.

5. Early hand preference (before 13 months of age).

6. Poor balance and equilibrium.

Table 8–2   Apgar scoring system

Points	0	1	2
Heart rate	Absent	Below 100	Above 100
Respiratory effort	Absent	Slow, irregular	Normal respiration
Muscle tone	Limp	Some flexion	Active motion
Gag reflex	No response	Grimace	Sneeze, cough
Color	Blue all over; pale	Blue extremities, rest of body pink	Pink all over

7. Difficulties in eye tracking.

8. Poor coordination in gross or fine motor activities.

9. Poor motor control of tongue, lips, or mouth muscles (e.g., drooling).

10. Inability to inhibit movements, as shown by jerking, mirroring, or fidgeting.

11. Poor visual-motor integrative skills, often seen in drawing.

12. Weakness or extreme fatigue during movement activities.

The more of these signs a child displays, the more likely he or she is to have some type of neurological dysfunction. Any of these behaviors should be noted and communicated to the child's primary care physician. In addition, various medications can cause side effects that may appear to be symptoms of neuromotor or attentional problems. Early childhood program staff and parents should know about the possible side effects of any medication a child may be taking.

Severe Motor Impairments

Young children with severe motor impairments present some difficult assessment problems—especially if cognitive or communication skills are also being evaluated. Because many assessment tasks require both fine and gross motor skills, the child with severe motor problems is penalized for inability to perform on standardized items. An understanding of primitive reflexes and abnormal movement patterns helps the educator to place the child in the *best position* for achieving optimum voluntary motor responses. A physical or occupational therapist can provide ways to help the child improve motor performance and demonstrate skills in other developmental areas.

Videotaped records of a child's behavior and performance in informal play settings can also be very helpful in understanding the qualitative aspects of his or her ability. The evaluator may require several sessions to properly assess the child's strengths. Because the child's psychological and physiological state can drastically influence muscle tone and coordination, movement abilities may differ considerably from day to day (Rogers, 1982).

General Considerations for Assessment of All Young Children

Effective observation of motor skills requires observers to keep in mind that the *process* or *approach* to motor tasks is significant. How a child goes about trying to catch a ball is much more revealing than whether or not the ball is caught. There is a great difference in ability between (a) the child whose eyes are following the path of the ball and whose hands are working together to attempt a catch and (b) the child who seems not to be looking at the ball and whose hands hang loose or do not seem to work together. Although neither one may actually catch the ball, their differences in attempts must be carefully noted and considered. They are clearly at different levels developmentally. A child's lack of experiences in such activities as climbing stairs or using scissors also influences performance. The child's level of excitement or fear of strangers and/or new tasks could be further inhibitors to motor processes.

Since the quality of performance is dependent on physiological maturation and experience, assessment for the purpose of developing instructional objectives must depend on individually referenced criteria. Although comparison with group norms can provide the early childhood educator with a general frame of reference, it cannot determine whether individual progress is adequate in light of changes that take place within that individual. For example, a 3 year old who has the body height and weight of a 2 year old cannot be expected to perform balance tasks with the ease of most 3 year olds. Considering lack of balance to be a weakness and including objectives to teach balance would be inappropriate until a shift in bodily proportion takes place. In short, educators are expected to "combine data from normative tests with [their] knowledge of individual differences in [their] class and develop a set of *criterion-referenced* objectives" (O'Donnell, 1969, p. 53).

Developmental Task Analysis. Once a teacher has used a developmental checklist derived from normative expectations and has observed very carefully while considering individual levels of maturation, interests, and experiences, program activities can be determined. The checklist may include only broad curriculum objectives that may be stated more as goals, or it may contain a more specific task analysis that breaks each broader goal into teaching steps. The checklist

then becomes a teaching as well as testing or assessment tool.

In utilizing task analysis as an observational tool to establish appropriate motor goals and objectives, a sample formula may be helpful for both interventionists and parents. Hanson and Harris (1986) suggest five basic steps as illustrated in Exhibit 8–1.

Play-Based Assessment

This approach provides many opportunities to observe a wide range of infants and young children in both structured and unstructured play activities. It is especially useful in observing movement behaviors. Linder (1990) and her colleagues have developed observation guidelines for sensorimotor development that encompass categories of (a) general appearance of move-

---

EXHIBIT 8–1 _____

Example of Five Basic Steps in Task Analysis

BEHAVIOR: Child Rolls from Back to Stomach

1. **Decide which behavior you want to teach.**
   Debbie will roll from back to stomach without assistance.
2. **Decide on the cue you will use to prompt the child.**
   Say, "Roll over, Debbie," while physically assisting her. Favorite toys are lying out of reach in the direction Debbie will roll to encourage rolling.
3. **Decide on consequences to follow the behavior.**
   Debbie will play with the toy obtained by rolling.
4. **Break the behavior into small steps and order the steps.**
   a. When Debbie is lying on her back, physically bring her arm across her chest and, by bending her at her knee, gently roll her all the way over from back to stomach.
   b. Debbie is physically rolled one half way over. She rolls the last half of the way on her own.
   c. Debbie rolls on her own from back to stomach.
   d. Debbie rolls on her own from back to front.
   Note: The verbal cue "Roll over, Debbie" is used during each step.
5. **Decide how well Debbie must do the behavior.**
   a. The number of seconds you will wait following the cue. Debbie will roll within 30 seconds of the cue.
   b. The number of times Debbie should perform correctly. Debbie will perform correctly 8 out of 10 times. When Debbie does this 8 out of 10 times for 3 days in a row, she can go on to the next step.

ment; (b) muscle tone/stength/endurance; (c) reactivity to sensory input; (d) stationary positions used for play; (e) mobility in play; (f) other developmental achievements; (g) prehension and manipulation; and (h) motor planning. The **sensorimotor observations** are integrated into the overall transdisciplinary play-based assessment, which includes cognitive, language, and social development.

THERAPEUTIC INTERVENTION

What is the purpose of therapeutic intervention? Who should provide the therapy? How is it used in home- or center-based intervention programs? Early childhood educators ask these critical questions when planning for children with physical limitations.

Therapists and teachers have shifted the focus from *developmental* goals to **functional independence.** Work on functional motor goals should begin as early as possible, especially for young children with severe disabilities. Examples of functional goals might include picking up Cheerios, turning a doorknob, and holding a crayon. Such skills enable the child to be more independent or to better interact with his or her environment. Perry (1986) has pointed out that too often professionals persist in trying to "normalize" the muscle tone and movement patterns of young children with severe brain damage. We must relinquish responsibility for trying to "fix" this brain damage and instead work toward setting realistic functional goals for the child, the parents, and ourselves.

In planning intervention for an individual child, one should look carefully at the child's functional level, considering activities for daily living, interactions within home and community environments, skills needed to support other developmental areas (i.e., positioning for problem-solving activities or social interaction), and types of assistive devices needed to enhance performance. After reviewing this information, teachers have a better picture of the functional level and the type of motor goals to be initiated for the child.

Role of Therapists

As part of the team approach in early childhood special education, the therapist must help teachers and parents to understand the objectives and techniques for development of functional motor skills. In consultation with physicians, the occupational or physical therapist will provide the expertise for implementing gross and fine motor activities and offer advice on positioning and use of therapeutic devices (braces, wheelchairs, etc.) as well as facilitating the development of feeding and other self-help skills. He or she will also work with families in both home and school settings to help integrate the therapy prescriptions into the daily routine of the child's care.

In working with infants and young children, there is considerable overlap in the roles of physical and occupational therapists. In institutional programs or in working with older children and adults, the **physical therapist** is usually concerned with large muscle movement and gross motor activities, while the **occupational therapist** is more often involved in evaluation and treatment of perceptual-motor (fine motor) functioning and activities of daily living.

The current trend in many early intervention programs is to have the therapist actually work in the center beside the teacher or in the home with the parents. In this way the therapist also demonstrates how the therapeutic activities can be integrated into the daily routine of the classroom or the home. In addition, the therapist can observe and participate in classroom or home activities that may lead to better understanding of other developmental concerns.

Therapy must be an integral part of the early childhood special education program, with the teacher understanding the rationale and serving as a promoter and translator of therapeutic objectives in the child's daily program. Ongoing staff training in the classroom or in special meetings should be a significant part of the therapist's responsibility.

Approaches to Therapy

There are a number of widely differing therapeutic techniques to improve motor performance of young children with physical disabilities, including exercise, skill instruction, use of adaptive devices, drug therapy, and often surgery.

Proper positioning, inhibition of abnormal reflexes, and facilitation of active movement are major concerns in working with a child who has cerebral palsy or other neurological disorders. Among several techniques for dealing with these, the most popular is the Neurodevelopmental Treatment Approach (NDT) developed by Bobath and Bobath (1975). Although skillful use of the NDT approach requires extensive training, the basic principles and practical application can be utilized by both teachers and parents.

Sensory integration is another approach used often in the therapeutic repertoire and training of the occupational therapist (Ayres, 1972). Ayres expressed the belief that learning disabilities are related to deficits in sensory integration. Many of the special activities are designed to provide tactile (touch) and vestibular (balance) stimulation. The therapist uses multisensory approaches that enhance the nervous system's abilities to organize and interpret sensory input in order to improve motor output effectiveness. Swings, rotary equipment, scooters, and other play equipment are used in the child's therapy.

Jones (1983) outlined several other approaches to therapy, usually classified by the name of their promoter (i.e., Phelps, Rood, and Doman-Delacato). The Doman-Delacato latter approach has been popular with some parents of neurologically impaired children, but has been highly controversial among professionals. Techniques consist of several periods of daily "patterning" involving four or five adults to assist in carrying out specific movement patterns such as creeping or crawling.

One of the most important considerations in optimizing performance of a child with motor delays is proper positioning and handling. The following section provides some guidelines that are appropriate for all early intervention specialists.

Positioning and Handling

Although it is often important to encourage movement, there are times when the young child should remain in a static position. For infants and young children with motor impairments, one area of significant concern is positioning and handling. In order to modify excessive or insufficient muscle tone and to control the predominance of abnormal reflexes, certain positions and specific handling techniques should be integrated into the child's home and school or center activities.

Positioning is the placement of the child in carefully selected positions (e.g., side-lying, sitting, standing) in order to normalize muscle tone, prevent deformity, and stabilize the body (Copeland & Kimmel, 1989). Careful positioning will also allow a child to function more efficiently during toileting, feeding, play, and other functional activities. For example, if a child's trunk is not stablized for sitting, control of arms and hands for self-feeding and playing with toys may be compromised.

Handling, according to Copeland and Kimmel (1989), is a dynamic process with goals of normalizing muscle tone, preparing the child for movement, and facilitating movement.

Use of hands on an appropriate key point of the body can control or inhibit undesirable postures and movements. In addition to specific activities for the positioning and handling of individual children, Hanson and Harris (1986)

have suggested the following general guidelines to consider in planning intervention:

1. *Key points of control* refers to parts of the body nearest the center of the body, including the *head and neck*, the *shoulder girdle*, and the *legs*. These are the key points to think about whenever you move, carry, or position a child. Paying close attention to these points will aid in normalizing muscle tone as well.

2. *Symmetry* of the child's body means that both sides of the body are positioned similarly so that one side looks like a mirror image of the other. Symmetry is also a consideration in developing muscle tone, as well as in inhibiting primitive movement patterns.

3. *Midline positioning* is important. Many young children with motor impairments are unable to bring their hands together at the midline (the middle of the body). Activities using hands in midline will help develop motor and self-help skills. Side-lying positioning is one way to facilitate midline activities. Hanson and Harris (1986) and Finnie (1975) have offered specific tech-

niques and equipment to encourage activities at the midline.

4. Use only *minimal support* when positioning and handling the child. Providing too much support will not allow children to use the muscle control they have already developed. For example, if a child has adequate trunk control to sit independently, a corner chair with a high back is not necessary. Using such a device will only inhibit trunk muscles and not provide the practice needed to develop strength and endurance.

Based on these guidelines, Copeland and Kimmel (1989) have suggested asking the following questions during assessment:

1. Is the head at midline and can the child visually focus on the desired target, e.g., toy, object, playmates.

2. Is the trunk symmetrical and well-aligned with the rest of the body?

3. Are the lower extremities properly aligned? If seated, kneeling, or standing, are the lower extremities bearing weight equally?

4. Are the upper extremities properly aligned and in functional positions for weight bearing or manipulation of objects?

5. Does this position promote the development of tightness, contractures, deformity, or pressure sores? (p. 48)

Whenever possible, parents and professionals should consult with the therapist to determine the child's individual needs for positioning and handling. There are also several excellent resources that give detailed guidelines and activities. Some of these include Bigge (1991); Finnie (1975); Hanson and Harris (1986); and Scherzer and Tscharnuter (1982).

Proper Lifting

In using correct lifting and carrying techniques, especially with young children who have severe motor impairments, the early interventionist or parent has an opportunity to provide support as well as therapy. According to Landecker (1980), "When a child is picked up correctly, abnormal reflexes are not stimulated, and the child looks more normal and actually is under less stress (and so are you)" (p. 9). Some important steps recommended by Landecker (1980) in lifting and carrying are as follows:

1. Speak to the child, telling him or her what you are going to do and where you are going.

2. Wait for some response and encourage the child to assist in the process (e.g., "You need to help. Give me your hand.").

3. Praise the child for any attempts to help.

4. Lift the child gently.

To protect yourself from injury, practice the following:

1. Bend your knees and keep your back straight.

2. Avoid twisting; approach the child straight on.

3. Keep the child's body as close to yours as possible.

4. Do not try to carry the child by yourself if he or she is too large or too heavy.

5. Give the *least* amount of help needed.

Proper and improper lifting techniques are shown in Figure 8–4.

Positioning for Feeding

Positioning is critical in feeding the child with motor problems. If proper positioning tech-

NOT RECOMMENDED

Improper Lifting   Proper Lifting

Figure 8–4   Proper and improper lifting techniques. (*Source of drawings: From Positioning for Infants and Young Children with Motor Problems (Videotape manual), pp. 8–11.* Courtesy of the University of Colorado School of Nursing, Marilyn Krajicek, Director, First Start)

niques are not used during feeding, many children with abnormal muscle tone will have problems with gagging, choking, or swallowing (Copeland & Kimmel, 1989). Everyone who feeds the child must have an understanding of the child's movement patterns in order to respond appropriately to changes that may occur from day to day and hour to hour. The positions in which a child can be fed will depend on the child's age, physical size, postural tone, and movement patterns (Bigge, 1991). Figure 8–5 shows the most usual positions for feeding—lap, arm, or chair.

Other issues to be considered in an effective feeding intervention program (Bigge, 1991) are

- Feeding techniques.
- Selection of feeding utensils.
- Choosing food textures and consistencies.
- Normalizing oral tactile sensitivity.
- Cup drinking.
- Spoon feeding.
- Receiving solid food.
- Coordinating respiration and early sound production.
- Social interactions.
- Diet.

In addition to consultation with therapists and nutrition and feeding specialists, more extensive intervention approaches are described in Bigge (1991), Copeland and Kimmel (1989), Finnie (1975), and Morris (1977).

Adaptive Equipment

Appropriate early intervention program planning for children with motor problems may involve a diverse array of equipment. Children may require *prostheses* (aids designed to function as limbs), *orthoses* (aids for assistance), *mobility devices* such as walkers and wheelchairs, positioning aids, or *academic aids* to help function in

a classroom. Dykes and Venn (1983), Copeland (1982), and Bigge (1991) have illustrations of adaptive equipment.

It is especially important for teachers of children with severe disabilities to learn about and use **adaptive equipment.** Basically, the value and purpose of this type of assistance are to: (a) help maintain normalized muscle tone; (b) inhibit primitive reflexes; (c) allow the child to use voluntary movements; (d) provide optimal positioning to interact more effectively with the environment; and (e) encourage independence.

Equipment to aid in positioning is now commonly found in almost every program serving children with special needs. The wedge, the bolster, the prone board, and modified chairs are used in a variety of ways as required. These types of equipment can be purchased commercially or made by a skillful teacher or parent. The choice of adaptive equipment should be made in consultation with a therapist, who can also help the teacher to identify its purpose, explain its use for a particular disability, and describe any special precautions to be observed while the child is using the equipment. (Inappropriate use of adaptive equipment can often do more harm than good.)

Adaptations for Fine Motor and Self-Help Activities

Adapted materials for fine motor and self-help skills are also an important consideration in program planning. A Velcro strap to hold a crayon or paintbrush in the hand, a large knob on a wooden puzzle piece, or a simple switch attached to a mechanical toy are examples of adaptations that may help a child participate more fully in learning experiences. Incorporating specific fine motor skills into daily activities, rather than giving isolated therapeutic exercises, provides more practice and consistency at home and school (Bailey & Wolery, 1984).

For children with significant neuromuscular problems, self-help skills become one of the primary concerns of caregivers and early interven-

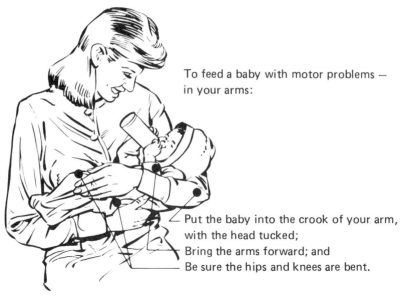

To feed a baby with motor problems —
in your arms:

Put the baby into the crook of your arm,
with the head tucked;
Bring the arms forward; and
Be sure the hips and knees are bent.

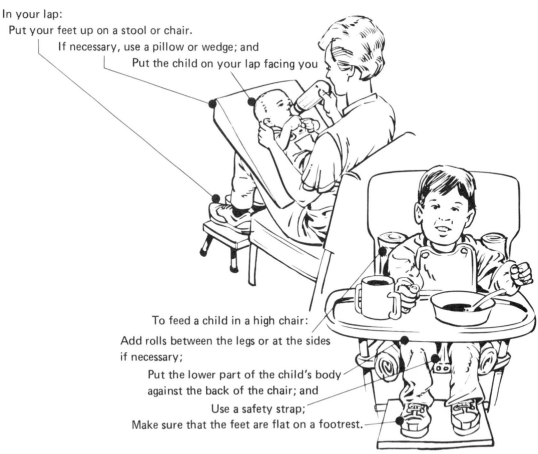

In your lap:
Put your feet up on a stool or chair.
If necessary, use a pillow or wedge; and
Put the child on your lap facing you

To feed a child in a high chair:
Add rolls between the legs or at the sides
if necessary;
Put the lower part of the child's body
against the back of the chair; and
Use a safety strap;
Make sure that the feet are flat on a footrest.

Figure 8–5 Most common positions for feeding. (*Source of drawings:* From *Positioning for Infants and Young Children with Motor Problems* (Videotape Manual), pp. 8–11. Courtesy of the University of Colorado School of Nursing, Marilyn Krajicek, Director, First Start)

tionists. Persistent premature reflexes, limited hand use, poor head control, and poor sitting balance all interfere with the development of self-help skills. Many parents (and children) find eating and self-feeding skills an area of great frustration. Positioning, adapted eating utensils, and special chairs are part of the overall instructional plan. Because of the complexity of these critical developmental skills, parents, teachers, and therapists should work together to maintain consistency between home and school or center programs.

Many publications discuss assessment, intervention, and adaptive equipment for motor skill development. Finnie (1975), Fallen and Umansky (1985), Hansen and Harris (1986), and Bigge (1991) are worthy resources.

Adapting the Environment

Because most disabling conditions require children to work extra hard to utilize the learning resources in their environment, most programs for children with special needs attempt to identify obstacles to learning and facilitate children's involvement in the learning process.

The Classroom. The integrated early education classroom is a dynamic system that includes both physical and social components. According to Rogers-Warren (1982), physical components include the actual classroom space, the arrangement of activity areas within the space, the furniture and fixtures, the play and work materials, the activities of the program and their sequence, the number of adult participants, the number and types of children (with and without disabilities), and the grouping of staff and children. Social components are the behaviors of adults and children in the classroom setting.

The classroom environment can facilitate movement and independence by providing opportunities for children to determine their own behavior and manage some of their own materi-

als. Even a child with the most severe disabilities needs a chance to have some effect on the environment. Accessible bathrooms, drinking fountains, and play materials will encourage independence and learning. Rogers-Warren (1982) suggested a checklist to help teachers accommodate young children with physical disabilities in the classroom:

• How does the setting appear at a child's level? Are there interesting things to see and touch, such as windows, mirrors, mobiles, aquariums and toys?

• Is there room for a wheelchair-bound or awkwardly mobile child to negotiate in and out of spaces and turn around?

• Are shelves and tables at a comfortable level for a child's height? Is there a place (preferably more than one) that can accommodate a child in each activity area?

• Are shelves, tables, sinks, and other fixtures sturdy enough to hold the weight of a minimally mobile child who may need support?

• Are prosthetic devices (such as a standing cuff) easily accessible in the areas where children might gain practice standing or sitting without an adult's assistance while engaged in an activity?

• Are some of the materials and toys accessible to a child without assistance even if he or she is minimally mobile?

• Is the sound level and acoustic arrangement of the room satisfactory for a child with a hearing impairment or a hearing aid? Are there some special quiet areas for children to work with minimal noise distraction?

• Does the environment contain sufficient contrasts to attract the notice of a visually impaired child? Do color and light contrasts corroborate texture and height contrasts?

• Are the cues (use of color, change of levels, dividers) that designate different areas clear and consistent?

• How much of the environment is designed for self-management or self-engagement? How frequently do children use these opportunities? Does a child need training to use these opportunities?

• Does the arrangement of the room allow for quiet places and social places to meet the changing moods and needs of children? (pp. 29–30)

In an effort to make integrated classrooms appropriate for the young child with motor impairments, Safford (1989) suggested that activities involving movement should allow the child to be involved as much as possible without accentuating the inability to move well. For example, the leader can combine sitting activities with floor locomotion activities such as rolling or combat crawling. (These movement activities are enhanced by music or rhymes.) If a child is unable to perform movements voluntarily, an adult should assist in motoring the child through the activities.

The Home. In home-based programs, the primary learning environment is the home and its surroundings. Lynch, Brekken, Drouin, and Wolfe (1984) have suggested that although program staff may have little control over the child's home, the home interventionist may recommend ways to make the home safe and facilitate learning. Burns, cuts, falls, electrical shock, and poisoning are some of the major home hazards. An interventionist who reviews such hazards

with the family and explains what to expect from children at different ages promotes safety concerns. Other things that the home interventionist may wish to explore with parents are:

1. The kinds of toys and objects in the home that stimulate exploration and learning.

2. Toys that are age and developmentally appropriate and can be adapted to accommodate special needs.

3. The level of visual and auditory stimulation in the home.

4. Modification to the environment that may allow the child greater independence and freedom of action.

5. Adaptive equipment such as chairs, prone boards, and self-help aids should be included in home-based programs to encourage opportunities for social interaction and participation in family life.

Exhibit 8–2 describes a model therapeutic home-based program.

MOVEMENT EDUCATION

Whenever infants and young children move any part of their bodies, there is potential for two kinds of learning to occur: learning to move and learning by moving. Bailey and Burton (1989) expanded on this:

Learning to move involves the emergence and refinement of movement skills and the development of general movement abilities. Learning by moving consists of infants forming associations and making cognitive relationships. This is the process whereby they gradually construct their reality. (p. 1)

Thus, **movement education** as a critical component of early intervention and preschool programs should also be viewed as a means of providing growth in self-image, concept development, language development, perceptual dis-

EXHIBIT 8–2 _____

Model Therapeutic Home Program

Since therapeutic intervention for young children with significant physical disabilities must include more than a once-a-month clinic visit or prescribed routines in a center-based program, emphasis on the integration of occupational and/or physical therapy into a functional home-based program seems critical to the provision of consistent, ongoing therapy. As suggested by Vincent, Salisbury, Laten, and Baumgart (1979), a desirable approach is for the therapist and family to work together to identify the times and contexts within which to apply therapeutic methods and work on therapeutic goals that are relevant for the child and realistic for the family. By assessing the family's typical routine, the therapist and family can identify naturally occurring teaching opportunities (Rainforth & Salisbury, 1988).

One approach to assessment and implementation is the Family Daily Routine model (Vincent et al., 1979). Rainforth and Salisbury (1988) have described the process in detail. An example of embedding home programming recommendations into existing family routines can be seen in the case of Frankie R.

Frankie is a 2-year-old boy with severe cerebral palsy (spastic quadriplegia) and a mental retardation. He is enrolled in a home- and center-based early intervention program where he receives physical therapy on a weekly basis. The therapist and Frankie's parents identified several goals for home and center. Two of the goals included in the family plan are:

1. To increase range of motion in shoulders and hips.
2. To establish symmetry and head control while sitting.

5:30 P.M.: Television, Relaxing with Dad

Method: Position Frankie straddling Dad's leg, side-lying on the couch, or prone-lying over Dad's lap.

Rationale: Mr. R. agreed that these procedures would not conflict with his need to relax and also would provide an opportunity for him to interact with Frankie. The physical therapist indicated that both goals were being addressed.

7:00 P.M.: Bath with Mom or Dad

Method: Stretch Frankie's shoulders and hips while bathing and drying him; also stretch his trunk by hip and shoulder rotation. Facilitate head control and reaching by playing in the water and touching body parts.

Rationale: The warm water and terrycloth towels tend to help Frankie relax, and, while he is undressed, this is a good opportunity to work on range of motion. Bathtime provides a natural motivation to maintain head control and to move arms in the water. It is also an excellent time for communication.

Adapting this type of model for all home activities allows the maximum benefit from parent-identified activities that, with minimal intrusion, can be used to provide practice of important developmental skills (Rainforth & Salisbury, 1988).

crimination, socialization, and recreation. This section will highlight adaptations in movement education and include the significant role music and imagination play in young children's development.

Adaptations in Movement Education

Popovich (1977) suggested the use of prompts (cues) when assisting children who are having difficulty developing motor skills that should be within their behavioral repertoire. If a child does not respond to a normal verbal direction and modeling of desired responses, the verbal direction is repeated and accompanied by gestures. If there is still no response or an inadequate one, the verbal request can be accompanied by physically helping the child to perform the act. Positive reinforcement is given at whatever level the act is attempted. Of course, physical or gestural prompts are removed (faded) as soon as possible. Other adaptations are included in the following list. Some of these guidelines are patterned after those offered by Frostig (1974).

1. Carefully plan lessons consistent with classroom guidelines for behavior.

2. Incorporate some degree of movement education into each day's plan.

3. Alternate vigorous activities with more relaxing ones.

4. Give attention to all attributes of movement. None should be left out in the total week's plan.

5. Vary body positions in on-the-floor activities as well as during activities that involve locomotion.

6. Intersperse activities in a group with activities alone or with a partner. This variation creates opportunities for cooperation without too much repetition.

7. Use equipment and music to allow for creative variations, but not as a part of every lesson. Children need time to concentrate on their own bodily actions.

8. Conscious teaching of concepts does not need to be included in every activity. Instead, integrate concepts logically into the day's schedule.

9. Take care to allow for repetition and modeling when giving directions to children who may have perceptual or linguistic delays. Move from the known to the unknown and from the simple to the complex. Do not expect transfer from one activity to another.

10. Use physical, tactile, and verbal prompting as needed. Break tasks into simple, sequential steps. Give positive reinforcement with each step of progress. Be patient with those who are slow or reluctant. Keep vocabulary within the children's level. Do not expect understanding of the verbal labels "left" and "right."

11. All young children, especially those who are medically fragile, need adequate rest periods. Do not try to cover too much at once or continue an activity for too long.

12. Provide varied but structured activities for children who have difficulty paying attention and/or controlling bodily movements. Activities should be simple and free from distractions. Maintain eye contact. Be gentle but firm. Do not give the child a choice if a choice is not intended. For example, saying, "Do you want to _____?" allows the child to say "No."

13. If a child has a visual impairment, be certain to use his or her name when verbally directing activities. Minimize eyestrain by not standing where the child must look into a glare. Give the child an extra dose of body awareness activities.

14. Use visual cues such as "stop" and "go" signs in red and green not only as attention getters but also to assist those with hearing impairments. Also be certain children with hearing impairments can read your lips when giving directions. Be certain that shadows are not in your face, and stand relatively still. Be certain to get the child's attention before beginning an activity. Withdrawal or hyperactivity can be the result of not being able to distinguish words.

15. Include children with physical impairments whenever possible. For example, when others are running under a parachute, these

children can be pushed under. When possible, substitute a sitting or lying position for a standing position.

16. Most important of all is the need for lessons to be enjoyed by everyone. Do not attempt activities that involve movement and noise if you are not in a mood to tolerate what they create.

Exhibit 8–3 provides an example of an adapted gross motor activity.

Movement Skills and Music

Dancing, marching, imitating, and imagining are often more enjoyable with music. Most commercially prepared records and tapes move a bit too fast for preschoolers, at least at first. If so, sing the songs without the records and say the directions first. Gradually, as the children's ability to listen and move quickly grows, the recording can be used. Some children feel lost with the recorded voice. Young children with mild hearing losses or perceptual problems, particularly, find recorded voices difficult to understand.

Rhythm bands, whether they include real instruments or pans with spoons, are exciting to children. Banging on something is an excellent way to develop awareness of body movement. The music may not be concert hall quality, but it certainly pleases the performers. Learning to make different kinds of noises by stamping feet loudly and then tiptoeing quietly leads to other kinds of body awareness.

A number of books are available to assist teachers in movement skills activities with the accompaniment of music. Nelson (1977, 1978) has cautioned that because it is difficult to define dances or other rhythmic activities in terms of age, teachers must carefully think through their children's developmental characteristics. Even the most appealing jingle can frustrate children if the accompanying movements are too difficult. For children with special needs, Nelson has sug-

gested beginning with the most simple and gradually working up to the more difficult songs or games. Reluctant children may need a personal invitation to join by offering them your hand. If they do not accept, they should not be forced to join. Rather, she has suggested the use of song games that invite children to join by name.

Movement Skills and Imagination

Children often need help in imagining things, since some have had little opportunity to pretend. They enjoy pretending to be engineers on trains, bus drivers, animals, and robots. Dress-up clothes add to the fun but are not necessary. Films and filmstrips can start an idea. Stories and flannelboard materials can lead to stimulating ideas. Pretending to put out a fire with an imaginary hose is almost as exciting as the real thing, and much safer.

Children discover the motions people make through seeing a combination of real people,

EXHIBIT 8–3 _____

A Gross Motor Activity with Adaptations

Goal: *To develop body image; to increase awareness of moving in different directions (directionality).*

Objectives: Given directions to move forward, backward, and sideways, each child will do the following:

1. Do as directed when the teacher prompts (physically, with gestures, or with additional words, as needed).
2. As a member of a group, follow the teacher's spoken and gestured signal.
3. As a member of a group, follow spoken directions (no gestures).
4. Throughout this lesson, stop and remain still in the exact position he or she was in at that moment when asked to "freeze." (This condition helps children learn to inhibit unnecessary movements.)

Procedure: Begin with children sitting in a line facing the teacher. Then the activity may proceed according to the following steps (of course, variations will be determined by the individual needs of the children):

1. "Susie, come stand here" (point to a masking tape X on the floor).
2. "Good, now walk forward" (physically prompting and gesturing to Susie).
3. "Right, you walked forward. Thank you. You may sit down. Tommy, it's your turn. Come stand on the X."
4. "Tommy, can you walk backward?" (Gesturing—but because Tommy begins to move backward, no physical prompting is needed.)
5. "Tommy, you did that just the right way. You walked backward."

Procedural notes: The teacher's enthusiasm and encouragement are of critical importance. The lessons will be individualized as each child's movements are observed. Physical prompts, gestures, and demonstrations will be faded as quickly as possible. Children will be encouraged to verbalize their understanding of their body movements through natural conversation as the activity progresses. Other considerations include the following:

1. Initially each child should be given a brief individual turn. Children will learn from watching. Begin with the child who is most likely to succeed with little or no help. This child serves as a model for the others to follow.

films, and pictures. Then they take turns pretending. Gradually, they become more creative. The fireman has to put out a fire on the roof, so he stretches up high. Next, the fire is in the basement, so he aims the hose down low. A robot, walking with stiff legs, may move very slowly. Then as someone turns the controls, he moves faster or even more slowly. Although the teacher may need to suggest ways to move at first, the children's use of imagination improves quickly.

Because so many teachers think they cannot encourage imagination and creativity through movement without being musicians, they sometimes do not try. Cherry (1971) offered step-by-step assistance to teachers who are "nonmusicians." She gave specific guidelines to assist children to originate their own ways of moving and exploring body capabilities. Motor and movement activities combine with imagination to enrich learning of personal, spatial, language, and social interactions.

2. Next, pair two children at a time to follow the directions. The children may be given the same or two different directions, depending on their stage of development. (Keep the activity moving.)

3. As soon as possible (but for some children this may take several days), have groups of three to five children moving at the same time.

4. To add variety, a 4/4 march or dance rhythm can be introduced with records, a drum, or by singing. A square dance calling format can be included with the help of another adult. Guide children as needed, using modeling or prompting as well as calling the directions.

5. New directions should be introduced following this same sequence, before incorporating them into the dance.

Lesson adaptations:

1. For the child with a hearing impairment:
   a. Be sure the child can see your face and gestures.
   b. Place a child with normal hearing on either side.
   c. Let this child feel the drum or other musical instrument as the rhythm is played. It sometimes helps to set record players on the floor and let the child perform with bare or stocking feet.

2. For the child with a visual impairment:
   a. Use physical prompts until the verbal prompts can be followed. (Fade physical assists as soon as possible.)
   b. Assign a sighted partner. Holding hands will be helpful.
   c. Be certain the space used is free from tripping and falling hazards.

3. For the child with a motor impairment:
   a. Encourage as much participation as possible.
   b. Use supports (for example, walkers and crutches) as needed.
   c. Have an adult push a wheelchair, if necessary.
   d. Assign the child to be caller or drum beater.

4. For the child with learning delays:
   a. Continue the prompting as needed.
   b. Place excellent models beside the child.
   c. Give directions slowly and one at a time.
   d. Repeat directions as often as necessary (with kind enthusiasm).
   e. Demonstrate patience if the child cannot do what he or she could do the day before.
   f. Socially reward each small step of progress.

The purpose of the next chapter is to convey the complex nature of the development of communication skills. Focus will be on the importance of helping young children develop functional communication skills that will enable them to initiate and influence social interaction.

Summary

Professionals who work with children with a wide range of abilities and disabilities in various early intervention settings should understand physical and psychological factors that may interfere with the normal developmental process. Because infants are now in many programs, knowledge of the beginning behaviors is critical in planning intervention and assisting parents effectively. All early educators should study the development and interrelationship of the nervous system and motor skills.

The young child with a motor delay requires a team approach involving the physician, therapists, nutritionists, parents, and teachers to meet special needs at home and school. Observations and team planning assure consistency and selection of appropriate intervention strategies. Mutual understanding of therapeutic and educational goals serves to strengthen motor skill development.

Adaptations of materials and environmental considerations should be a concern for all early education programs, but more specifically when children who are medically fragile or have motor delays are included. Finding ways for these children to interact, respond, and develop will require more than the few activities usually listed in curriculum guides. Gross and fine motor skills, self-help skills, and movement experiences must be an integral part of each child's day-to-day home and school activities. Its relationship to other aspects of development makes movement an essential component of an effective early education program.

Discussion Topics and Activities

1. Thoroughly review at least three developmental checklists. Pay special attention to the sequential order of the motor skills. Adopt a checklist that seems to be complete or compile your own. Observe a typical child and a child with a disability or children of two different ages. Were you able to detect differences in skill development? If not, your checklist needs to be broken into smaller steps.

2. Now take a major skill such as throwing and break it into subskills as directed in Chapter 6. Sequence these skills. After your task analysis is complete, try to teach the skill to a friend or a child. What subskills did you leave out? Did the order of your skills need to be changed? With adults, skipping is a good skill to analyze.

3. Interview or ask a physical and occupational therapist to visit class. Ask for information, for example, about positioning techniques, adaptive equipment, and special teaching procedures. Be certain to ask the therapist to explain his or her view of motor development.

4. Investigate the relationship between motor skills and body awareness. Begin a file of activities specially designed to teach body awareness and contribute to self-esteem.

5. There are several suggestions in the literature that instruction in perceptual skills may not be defensible. Research this matter. Discuss and debate the issue with classmates.

6. Try to explain the sequential trends of motor development to another person, deriving and using specific examples. If you can explain them clearly to another, then you probably understand them well.

7. Research and discuss the various disabling conditions, such as cerebral palsy, muscular dystrophy, and visual impairment, that have an impact on motor skill development. If possible, invite a member of the community who has experienced difficulties from such an impairment to discuss ways teachers can be of assistance.

8. Plan a motor activity. Be creative. Consider parachutes, isometric exercises, and dances. Teach this lesson to your classmates. Discover the fun some movement activities really are. Do your lesson with children.

9. Design a playground that would be suitable for children with a variety of disabling conditions. The work by Jones listed in the Annotated Bibliography can help you to begin.

Annotated Bibliography

Bailey, R. A., & Burton, E. C. (1989). *The dynamic infant.* St. Paul, MN: Toys' n Things.

An easy-to-read, practical approach to understanding and providing appropriate movement activities for the infant and toddler. A good book for parents.

Baker, M. J., Banfied, C. S., Killburn, D., & Shufflebarger, K. J. (1991). *Controlling movement: A therapeutic approach to early intervention.* Gaithersburg, MD: Aspen.

This looseleaf manual provides precise therapeutic activities for parents and early interventionists to use in systematic programs for infants and toddlers. It is easy to read and has excellent illustrations.

Bigge, J. L. (1991). *Teaching individuals with physical and multiple disabilities.* New York: Macmillan.

Although this book focuses more on school-aged children with disabilities, it is highly recommended to early interventionists for the comprehensive, readable discussions on therapeutic management, adaptive and assistive devices, prespeech and feeding techniques, and augmentative communication. Useful lists of resources are included throughout the text.

Blackman, J. A. (Ed.). (1989). *Medical aspects of developmental disabilities in children birth to three.* Rockville, MD: Aspen Systems.

This manual summarizes health information that is important in the day-to-day care of children with developmental disabilities. The authors give the description, cause, incidence, detection, course, accompanying health problems, usual medical management, and implications for education of approximately 40 developmental disabilities. Illustrations accompany its clear explanations.

Copeland, M. E., & Kimmel, J. R. (1989). *Evaluation and management of infants and young children with developmental disabilities.* Baltimore: Paul H. Brookes.

Since both authors are occupational therapists, the focus is on abnormal motor development and instructional methods designed for infants and young children with developmental disabilities. Detailed discussions on movement, feeding, toileting, and dressing are particularly useful.

Cryer, D., Harms, T., and Bourland, B. (1987). *Active learning for ones.* Menlo Park, CA: Addison-Wesley.

The *Active Learning* series is made up of activity books for infants and 1-, 2-, and 3-year-olds. For each age group there is a planning guide and four activity sections. *Active Learning for Ones* includes the following sections, which contain ideas suitable for use with toddlers from 12 to 24 months: "Planning for Ones," "Activities for Listening and Talking," "Activities for Physical Development," "Creative Activities," and "Activities for Learning from the World Around Them." Included are over 300 activities that are easy to read and do with one toddler or a small group. Ideas on setting up environments for toddlers in this age group and an easy system for writing plans help caregivers set the stage for a good activity program. Developed at the Frank Porter Graham Child Development Center in Chapel Hill, NC, the complete planning guides contained in each volume are essential reading for all teachers of toddlers.

Curtis, S. (1982). *The joy of movement in early childhood.* New York: Teachers College Press.

This book includes a series of photographs exploring stages involved in each of the fundamental motor patterns—walking, running, jumping, kicking, throwing, and catching. It offers suggestions for incorporating these patterns into a total motor activity program and discusses other facets such as setting up creative play spaces and making one's own equipment.

Endres, J. B., & Rockwell, R. E. (1985). *Food, nutrition, and the young child.* Columbus, OH: Merrill.

This book focuses on nutrition as an integral part of early childhood programs. It stresses a team approach in which nutritionists, teachers, and parents work together to ensure an effective program. The section on nutrition discusses needs of the child from birth to 5 years of age. It includes excellent ideas for incorporating food and nutrition into the overall learning environment.

Frostig, M., & Maslow, P. (1970). *Movement education: Theory and practice.* Chicago: Follett.

This book remains an excellent resource for teachers who wish to develop programs of movement education that truly consider individualized development. Research current to the time is well summarized. Teachers will be pleased with the ideas for specific activities designed to promote coordination, rhythm, flexibility, speed, agility, balance, strength, and endurance without fear of failure or competition. A handy file of cards that contains some of these and other activities can also be obtained through the same publishing company. They are called *Move, Grow, Learn.*

Hansen, M. J., & Harris, S. R. (1986). *Teaching the young child with motor delays.* Austin, TX: Pro-Ed.

This easy-to-read guide is written primarily for parents of children from birth to age 3 who have motor impairments. The book provides information to parents on how motor development influences other areas of child development, teaching strategies, and therapeutic activities. Resource lists and diagnostic materials are useful to both parents and professionals.

Jaeger, L. (1987). *Home program instruction sheets for infants and young children.* Tucson, AZ: Communication and Therapy Skill Builders.

The home instruction sheets represent some of the more common exercises and activities for young children with motor dysfunction. The instruction sheets are generally used with parents as a reminder of recommended home activities generally prescribed by the physical therapist. Teachers may also use the positions and activities in the classroom.

Jones, M. (1977). Physical facilities and environments. In J. Jordan, A. Hayden, M. Karnes, & M. Wood (Eds.), *Early childhood education for exceptional children.* Reston, VA: The Council for Exceptional Children.

This chapter presents a clear analysis and description of several well-planned First Chance and other programs' playgrounds and equipment. The requirements for suitable environments for children with disabilities are discussed along with detailed illustrations. Resources for more in-depth information are included.

Keogh, J., & Sugden, D. (1985). *Movement skill development.* New York: Macmillan.

This scholarly text provides a comprehensive view of the dynamics of motor skill development from birth onward. The chapters on early movement development are especially important to educators of young children.

Lacy, A. (1981). *Dear Mom and Dad.* San Diego, CA: Project Hope, Superintendent of Schools, Department of Education, San Diego County.

Individual introductory letters "written by the baby" from birth to 2 years about various aspects of development including touching, movement and balance, big muscle movement, learning, hearing, and making sounds are presented. Each section contains suggestions for intervention. This is an excellent resource for parents of infants both with and without disabilities.

Linder, T. W. (1990). *Transdisciplinary play-based assessment: A functional approach to working with young children.* Baltimore: Paul H. Brookes.

This book contains descriptive observational guidelines for assessing a young child's development through child-directed play. The chapter on sensorimotor development by Susan Hall provides an excellent framework for assessing both the qualitative and quantitative components of this area of development.

Marotz, L., Rush, J., & Cross, M. (1985). *Health, safety, and nutrition for the young child.* Albany, NY: Delmar.

This comprehensive guide for child care providers and parents emphasizes prevention. It is useful as both text and practical reference. The topics of health, safety, and nutrition are interrelated with the concept of preventive health. Involvement with parents is stressed through the coordination of planned classroom experiences with home-based incidental learning.

Petrie, P. (1987). *Baby play: Activities for discovery and development during the first year of life.* New York: Pantheon.

This is a book to be enjoyed and used by all who are interested in infant development. Excellent illustrations and photographs are included, as well as valuable suggestions for developmentally appropriate activities and toys.

Physical and occupational services. (1988). In *Topics in Early Childhood Special Education, 7*(4).

This entire journal is devoted to issues related to therapeutic intervention in programming for young children with developmental disabilities. Such topics as training for therapists, evaluation of effective therapeutic approaches, and assessment are addressed.

Seaman, J. A., & Depauw, K. P. (1989). *The new adapted physical education: A developmental approach.* Mountain View, CA: Mayfield.

The authors present an extensive discussion of neuromotor development as a basis for understanding the needs of individuals with motor disabilities. Approaches to intervention provide a useful resource for early intervention specialists. The role of well-trained adaptive physical education specialists is clarified.

Tansley, A. E. (1986). *Motor education.* Tucson, AZ: Communication and Therapy Skill Builders.

This handbook emphasizes the importance of motor skills in growth and development, especially in the formative early years. It also provides suggestions for remedial programs involving both motor and language development.

Zimmerman, J. (1988). *Goals and objectives for developing normal movement patterns: A manual of gross motor behavior objectives with emphasis on the quality of movement.* Gaithersburg, MD: Aspen Systems.

This manual is a useful resource for pediatric occupational and physical therapists as well as other interventionists working in educational settings. It helps to set behavioral objectives to develop normal movement patterns and components necessary for functional skills.

References

American Psychiatric Association. (1980). *Diagnostic and statistical manual of mental disorders* (3rd ed.). Washington, DC: American Psychiatric Association.

Apgar, V., & James, L. S. (1962). Further observations on the Newborn Scoring System. *American Journal of Diseases of Children, 104,* 419–428.

Ayers, J. (1972). *Sensory integration and learning disorders.* Los Angeles: Western Psychological Services.

Bailey, D. B., & Wolery, M. (1984). *Teaching infants and preschoolers with handicaps.* Columbus, OH: Merrill.

Bailey, R. A., & Burton, E. C. (1989). *The dynamic infant.* St. Paul, MN: Toys 'n Things.

Batshaw, M. L., & Perret, Y. M. (1981). *Children with handicaps: A medical primer.* Baltimore: Paul H. Brookes.

Bigge, J. L. (1991). *Teaching individuals with physical and multiple disabilities.* New York: Macmillan.

Bobath, B., & Bobath, K. (1975). *Motor development in the types of cerebral palsy.* London: Heinemann.

Brazelton, T. B. (1973). *Neonatal behavioral assessment scale.* Philadelphia: Lippincott.

Campbell, S. B. (1985). Hyperactivity in preschoolers: Correlates and prognostic implications. *Clinical Psychology Review, 5,* 405–428.

Cherry, C. (1971). *Creative movement for the developing child.* Belmont, CA: Lear Siegler/Fearon Pitman.

Connor, F., Williamson, G., & Siepp, J. (1978). *Program guide for infants and toddlers with neuromotor and other developmental disabilities.* New York: Teachers College Press.

Copeland, M. (1982). Development of motor skills and the management of common problems. In K. E. Allen & E. M. Goetz (Eds.), *Early childhood education: Special problems, special solutions.* Rockville, MD: Aspen Systems.

Copeland, M. E., & Kimmel, J. R. (1989). *Evaluation and management of infants and young children with developmental disabilities.* Baltimore: Paul H. Brooks.

Cratty, B. (1970). *Perceptual and motor development in infants and children.* New York: Macmillan.

Cruickshank, W. (1967). *The brain-injured child in home, school, and community.* Syracuse, NY: Syracuse University Press.

Dykes, M. K., & Venn, J. (1983). Using health, physical, and medical data in the classroom. In J. Umbreit (Ed.), *Physical disabilities and health impairments: An introduction.* Columbus, OH: Merrill.

Erikson, E. (1963). *Childhood and society.* New York: Norton.

Espenschade, A., & Eckert, H. (1980). *Motor development.* Columbus, OH: Merrill.

Fallen, N. H., & Umansky, W. (1985). *Young children with special needs.* Columbus, OH: Merrill.

Ferry, P. C. (1986). Infant stimulation programs: A neurological shell game? *Archives of Neurology, 43,* 281–282.

Finnie, N. (1975). *Handling the young cerebral palsied child at home.* New York: E. P. Dutton.

Fredericks, H., Riggs, C., Furey, T., Grove, D., Moore, W., McDonnell, J., Jordan, E., Hanson, W., Baldwin, V., & Wadlow, M. (1976). *The teaching research curriculum for moderately and severely handicapped.* Springfield, IL: Charles C. Thomas.

Frostig, M. (1974). *Movement education, Its theory and practice.* Workshop presented at The Marianne Frostig Center of Educational Therapy, Los Angeles.

Hadley, J. (1984). Hyperactivity. *Children Today,* 9–13.

Hammill, D., & Bartel, N. (1975). *Teaching children with learning and behavior problems.* Boston: Allyn and Bacon.

Hanson, M. J., & Harris, S. R. (1986). *Teaching the young child with motor delays.* Austin, TX: Pro-Ed.

Jones, M. H. (1983). Cerebral palsy. In J. Umbreit (Ed.), *Physical disabilities and health impairment: An introduction.* Columbus, OH: Merrill.

Keogh, J., & Sugden, D. (1985). *Movement skill development.* New York: Macmillan.

Kephart, N. (1964). Perceptual-motor aspects of learning disabilities. *Exceptional Children, 31,* 201–206.

Lacy, A. (1981). *Dear Mom and Dad*. San Diego, CA: Project Hope, Superintendent of Schools, Department of Education, San Diego County.

Landecker, A. W. (1980). Lifting and carrying. In J. Umbreit & P. J. Cardullias (Eds.), *Educating the severely physically handicapped: Basic principles and techniques*. Columbus, OH: Special Press.

Larsen, S., & Hammill, D. (1975). The relationship of selected visual perceptual skills to academic abilities. *Journal of Special Education*, 9, 281–291.

Lerner, J., Mardell-Czudnowski, C., & Goldenberg, D. (1987). *Special education for the early childhood years*. Englewood Cliffs, NJ: Prentice-Hall.

Linder, T. (1990). *Transdisciplinary play-based assessment: A functional approach to working with young children*. Baltimore: Paul H. Brookes.

Lynch, E., Brekken, L., Drouin, C., & Wolfe, S. (1984). *A resource guide for early childhood special educators*. Sacramento, CA: Infant/Preschool Special Education Resource Network.

Malina, R. M. (1980). Biological correlates of motor development during infancy and early childhood. In L. S. Greene & F. E. Johnstone (Eds.), *Social and biological predictors of nutritional status, physical growth and neurological development*. New York: Academic Press.

Martin, H. P. (1982). Neurological and medical factors affecting assessment. In G. Ulrey & S. Rogers (Eds.), *Psychological assessment of handicapped infants and young children*. New York: Thieme-Stratton.

McGuinness, D. (1985). *When children don't learn*. New York: Basic Books.

Mercer, C. (1983). *Students with learning disabilities* (2nd ed.). Columbus, OH: Merrill.

Molnar, G. (1982). Intervention for physically handicapped children. In M. Lewis & L. T. Taft (Eds.), *Developmental disabilities: Theory, assessment and intervention*. New York: SP Medical and Scientific.

Morris, S. E. (1977). *Program guidelines for children with feeding problems*. Edison, NJ: Childcraft Education.

Nelson, E. (1977). *Movement games for children of all ages*. New York. Sterling.

Nelson, E. (1978). *Dancing games for children of all ages*. New York. Sterling.

O'Donnell, P. (1969). *Motor and haptic learning*. Sioux Falls, SD: Adapt Press.

Piazza, R. (1979). *Three models of learning disabilities*. Guilford, CT: Special Learning.

Popovich, D. (1977). *A prescriptive behavioral checklist*

for the severely and profoundly retarded. Baltimore: University Park Press.

Rainforth, B., & Salisbury, C. L. (1988). Functional home programs: A model for therapists. *Topics in Early Childhood Special Education*, 7(4), 33–45.

Renshaw, D. (1974). *The hyperactive child*. Chicago: Nelson-Hall.

Rogers, S. (1982). Assessment considerations with the motor-handicapped child. In G. Ulrey & S. Rogers (Eds.), *Psychological assessment of handicapped infants and young children*. New York: Thieme-Stratton.

Rogers-Warren, A. K. (1982). Behavioral ecology in classrooms for young handicapped children. *Topics in Early Childhood Special Education*, 2(1), 21–32.

Rosenberg, M., Wilson, R., & Legenhausen, E. (1989). The assessment of hyperactivity in preschool populations: A multidisciplinary perspective. *Topics in Early Childhood Special Education*, 9, 90–105.

Safford, P. (1989). *Integrated teaching in early childhood*. New York: Longman.

Scherzer, A., & Tscharnuter, I. (1982). *Early diagnosis and therapy in cerebral palsy: A primer on infant developmental problems*. New York: Marcel Dekker.

Shearer, D. E., & Shearer, M. S. (1976). The Portage Project: A model of early childhood intervention. In T. D. Tjossem (Ed.), *Intervention strategies for high risk infants and young children*. Baltimore: University Park Press.

Strauss, A., & Lehtinen, L. (1947). *Psychopathology and education of the brain-injured child*. New York: Grune & Stratton.

Strauss, A., & Werner, H. (1942). Disorders of conceptual thinking in the brain-injured child. *Journal of Nervous and Mental Disease*, 96, 153–172.

Taft, L. T. (1982). Neuromotor assessment of infants. In M. Lewis & L. T. Taft (Eds.), *Developmental disabilities: Theory, assessment and intervention*. Jamaica, NY: Spectrum.

Thurman, S. K., & Widerstrom, A. H. (1990). *Infants and young children with special needs*. Baltimore: Paul H. Brookes.

University of Colorado Health Sciences Center School of Nursing. (1988). Manual to accompany videotape *Positioning for Infants and Young Children with Motor Problems*. Lawrence, KS: Learner Managed Designs, Inc.

Vincent, L., Salisbury, C., Laten, S., & Baumgart D. (1979). *Designing home programs for families with handicapped children*. Unpublished manuscript. Madison, WI: University of Wisconsin, Department of Rehabilitation, Psychology, and Special Education.

Westphal, R. (Ed.). (1975). *Human development: 2 1/2 to 6 years.* Costa Mesa, CA: Concept Media.

Wolff, P. (1979). Theoretical issues in the development of motor skills. In L. Taft & M. Lewis (Eds.), *Developmental disabilities in the preschool child.* Symposium presented by Rutgers Medical School, Educational Testing Service, and Johnson and Johnson Baby Products, Chicago.

Chapter 9

Nurturing Communication Skills

with contributions from Virginia B. Armbruster

Key Points

▶ Communication and language are very complex skills that are best understood as occurring within a context of social interaction.

▶ Communication skills develop in predictable stages beginning at birth; the foundation of language is laid during the first year of life.

▶ The development of language during the preschool years consists not simply of more words and longer sentences, but of pragmatic skills that enable the child to communicate effectively and appropriately in a variety of social contexts.

▶ The focus of communication intervention must be on the development of functional communication skills that enable the child to initiate social interaction and influence his or her environment.

▶ Key adult behaviors that facilitate communication skills are listening and responding to children's communication attempts and carefully mapping language onto children's experiences.

▶ The learning of a second language proceeds in much the same fashion as the acquisition of the first language, and, like the first, the second language is best learned in interactive social environments.

▶ All children can communicate. For young children with severe and multiple disabilities, alternative modes of communication may have to be established.

Key Topics

▶ The subskills of language, including pragmatics, semantics, syntax, morphology, phonology, content, use, and form.

▶ Stages of the development of communication skills.

▶ Characteristics that interfere with speech and language development.

▶ Techniques for nurturing speech, language, and conceptual skills.

▶ The role of caregiver-child interaction.

▶ Classroom strategies that facilitate communication.

▶ Facilitating communication in children with severe and multiple disabilities.

▶ Facilitating social communication between children with special needs and their non-disabled peers.

▶ Working with children with hearing and visual impairments.

▶ Assisting children who have language differences.

▶ Collaborative consultation with speech/language specialists.

In the past decade, probably no aspect of child development has received more attention than the area of communication. Similarly, a great deal of interest has been generated regarding intervention strategies to facilitate the development and acquisition of speech and language skills. Despite the wealth of information and insights gleaned from these efforts, much remains to be learned about the processes underlying the fascinating development of communication skills in children. And there is much to learn about which techniques and strategies best support the efforts of the young child with disabilities to communicate with those around him or her.

This chapter will consider several interesting areas of research and apply them to the design of early childhood curricula for children with special needs. However, we must first review some basic terminology used to describe the various subskills of language.

THE SUBSKILLS OF LANGUAGE

It is important to keep in mind that the separation of language into subskills is arbitrary and

the complexity of the skills is impressive. Presented in Exhibit 9–1 are definitions of the speech and language subskills that should be developing during the preschool years.

Pragmatics

Learning how to use language in appropriate ways within various contexts is crucial to the successful development of communication skills. **Linguistic pragmatics** refers to rules and conventions that govern how language is used for communication in different situations. Pragmatic communication skills also include many nonverbal behaviors.

Speakers and listeners follow a set of unconscious guidelines as they talk to each other. These include such behaviors as looking at each other

EXHIBIT 9–1

Subskills of Language: Key Concepts

pragmatics: The gamut or whole range of functions language serves in social contexts. Anthropologists, as well as psycholinguists and sociologists, study the ways in which people use language in their efforts to communicate. Factors such as the situation, the relations of speaker to hearer, and the speaker's intent influence the manner of communication. Learning to take turns in conversation, as well as recognizing what is appropriate or inappropriate in specific situations, involves the development of pragmatic language (communication) skills.

semantics: The meanings of words. Meaning is influenced by use and the place in the utterance where the word is used.

syntax: The rules that organize morphemes. Without the rules, utterances would be unintelligible. *Grammar* and *syntax* are terms usually used interchangeably in traditional language (grammar) teaching in English classes. Current theories define three major divisions of syntax: morphological rules, phrase structural rules, and transformational operations. The study of syntax is the study of sentence structure.

morphology: Morphology is one aspect of syntax. It is the facet that enables speakers to create words from morphemes. For example, *s* is a morpheme when it is used with another word to indicate "more than one." Psycholinguists disagree on a definition of morpheme. One frequently used description of a morpheme is "a minimal unit of meaning." Thus *boy* is one morpheme, and *boys* is composed of two "minimal units of meaning." Morphemes provide inflectional information as well as content information.

phonology: The sound patterns of a language. In all languages song patterns can be found that convey meaning. For example, in English a rising tone at the end of an utterance indicates that a question has been asked. Pitch changes that convey meaning are referred to as prosodic features *(prosody)* or *suprasegmentals.* Speech sounds or *phonemes* are the smallest discernible segments of speech. English has approximately 44 phonemes (varied by regional differences). Prosody (song patterns) and phonemes (individual speech sound) are two facets of phonology.

and looking away, and waiting for the speaker to pause before the listener begins to speak. These behaviors require attention to subtle cues. Facial expressions and body language appropriate to particular circumstances must be learned. Sensing this nonverbal communication, children are often quick to perceive insincerity.

The situation, the specific topic, the relation of listener to speaker, and many other variables determine *what* is said as well as *how* it is said. Children who have not acquired these pragmatic skills stand out as "different" in preschool groups almost as much as those whose speech is unintelligible. But it is more difficult for parents and teachers to pinpoint how and why they are different.

Hopper and Naremore (1978, p. 63) presented a useful introduction to pragmatics. They listed the following ways in which the situational context influences how a person communicates: (a) the people present; (b) what was just previously said; (c) the topic of conversation; (d) the task that communication is being used to accomplish; and (e) the times and places in which the communication occurs. Observation suggests that young children readily use these contextual clues to enable themselves to understand much more than words alone.

As Bates (1976) described it, the acquisition of pragmatic skills begins to develop well before childrens' first words. Bates described various prelinguistic communication acts such as pointing and reaching, combined with vocalizations and directed eye gaze. These behaviors, which typically emerge in young children around the 10th month of age, lay an important foundation for later language development.

Semantics

Learning the meanings of words (semantics) is very dependent on interactions with adults who make their meaning clear. For example, talking about the ocean to a child who has never seen one will result in little understanding of *ocean.* Young children do not learn word meanings through vicarious experiences. Things they see must be named while they are looking at them and touching them. Activities must be described while they are happening. And then children must have the opportunity to experiment with the words, to discover whether they have learned what each really means.

Bloom and Lahey (1978) described several **semantic relations** typically expressed in children's early two-word combinations. These include such meanings as *recurrence* (e.g., "more juice" or " 'nother birdie"), *disappearance* (e.g., "cereal gone" or "no dollie"); *appearance* (e.g., "that Mommy" or "there ball"); *rejection* (e.g., "no want!" or "don't wash!"); *actions,* (e.g., "baby fall" or "push Daddy"), *locations* (e.g., "cookie 'frigerator" or "doggie bed"), *possession* (e.g., "Teddy mine!" or "Mommy shoe"), and occasional *descriptors* (e.g., "cereal hot" or "pants dirty").

Syntax

Learning the rules for correct word order in sentences is one aspect of **syntax.** Syntax includes knowing that it is correct to say "We are going to the ball game" rather than "Game ball to going we the are." Of course, children learning to utter syntactically correct sentences are really just trying to communicate. They are not consciously practicing the rules they are learning.

But as they learn, children everywhere develop in essentially the same manner. Between ages 9 and 14 months, most of them use single words to communicate. By age 2, they string two or three words together, and by age 4 they are creating grammatically correct sentences that follow the rules of the language they have been hearing and practicing. Their word order matches that of the adults with whom they have been living. They rearrange word orders to ask questions. The word order is obviously rule governed.

Morphology

Learning the rules for changing the form of individual words (rules of **morphology**) makes it possible for children to understand and communicate singular and plural meanings. They discover when to add *s*, when to add *es*, and when to change the word *man* to *men*. They discover how to form possessives and how to use number and tense in verbs (e.g., he walks, they walk, he walked, he is walking, or we walked). Children learn comparatives (long, longer, longest) and how to add prefixes and suffixes to alter meaning. They use pronouns as possessives (his or hers), as subjects (I, he, or they), and as objects (him or her).

As they learn these rules of morphology, children make many interesting mistakes. They overgeneralize, saying, "We wented" and "The mans." However, their errors are logical and confirm that they are not just imitating what they are hearing. They are learning rules. Exceptions to the rules such as irregular verbs and irregular plurals will be learned in time. Often very young children can be heard using irregular nouns and verbs correctly (men, ran, or fell). As they begin to internalize language rules, they may change to rule-governed forms (mans, runned, or falled). Then the adult models around them must help them to discover these exceptions to the rules all over again.

Phonology

Learning the rules of the sound systems of speech and language (**phonology**) involves discovering that pitch and rhythm changes make a difference, along with the individual speech sounds, or *phonemes.* The song patterns (*prosodic features* or *suprasegmentals*) are learned very early. Babies just a few months old babble in ways that sound almost like the patterns adults use. A conscientious listener can hear questions and statements in the intonation patterns of babies long before words can be heard. Careful listening will also detect exclamations! They sound much like a radio that is too soft to understand but transmits the rhythm and pitch changes.

As they near 6 months of age, many babies begin to babble in syllables that include some of the phonemes of the adult system. Their production is usually somewhat wide of the mark. By age 1, they have learned to use some sounds accurately some of the time, and the first words begin to appear. Skill in producing speech sounds accelerates rapidly during the preschool years.

However, the accuracy of children's production is highly dependent on being able to hear the sounds they are trying to produce clearly, accurately, and often. They do not need to hear the sounds in isolation or even in syllables. Hearing them in words and connected speech (phrases and sentences) appears to be enough. But they do need to hear the phonemes, and they do need lots of opportunity to practice them. Most children learn to produce nearly all of the 44 phonemes of English by the time they are 4 years old.

Content, Use, and Form

Lahey (1988) described three dimensions of language: content, use, and form. The *content* of language is its meaning—what it refers to or what it is about. *Use* refers to the purpose or function of language—what it is used for. The *form* of language refers both to its syntactic and morphological structure (i.e., the order and forms of words) and to the phonological form (i.e., the particular sounds, or phonemes, and the sound sequences that occur in spoken language).

Every utterance can be analyzed according to these three dimensions. Take for example the child who, hoping for a second helping of ice cream, looks at her mother and says, "Is there more ice cream?" The *content* of this utterance refers to the existence of a frozen, sweet dairy product called "ice cream"; its *use*, or purpose, is to obtain a second helping; and its *structure* is a five-word interrogative sentence. This theoretical framework is helpful in making clear the multidimensional and complex nature of language.

CONTRIBUTION OF SOCIAL INTERACTION THEORY TO UNDERSTANDING EARLY COMMUNICATION DEVELOPMENT

The past 2 decades of research have reflected an important shift from emphasis on speech and language to emphasis on communication. A second important shift of interest has been away from the child in isolation and toward the **dyad** (significant pair of individuals)—in this case the parent-child or teacher-child dyad. Research in these areas has revealed exciting new information—in addition to confirming many age-old intuitions—regarding the contributions of conversation and interaction to children's development of communication skills and the role of early caregiver-infant and caregiver-child interactions in children's development.

A third shift of focus in the study of children's development of communication has been away from the study of the form and structure of language toward the study of the purposes of children's communicative behaviors and the functional uses of communicative behavior within social contexts. This area of focus is referred to as **developmental pragmatics** (Bates, 1976; Ochs, 1979).

These areas of emphasis have generated information and theories with important implications for the field of early childhood special education. First, they have provided a much greater understanding of the precursors of language development occurring during the child's first year of life. Second, studies of the effect of caregiver input on children's development have important implications for intervention strategies and the design of early intervention curricula.

STAGES OF DEVELOPMENT OF COMMUNICATION SKILLS IN YOUNG CHILDREN

Early childhood special educators must thoroughly understand the development of communication skills in normally developing children. Several available texts provide detailed descriptions of typical communication development within each of the five subskills previously defined (see, for example, Owens, 1988). Table 9–1 also provides development information for the major language subskills.

The following section will briefly describe the major accomplishments in communication skills development from birth to 3 years of age. Because space does not allow for a detailed description of this process, the section is intended only as a review. Students are encouraged to supplement their background with the readings listed in the annotated bibliography at the end of this chapter.

Prelinguistic Communication

It is important for early childhood special educators to recognize that the infant begins the process of learning to communicate long before the onset of true or conventional speech and language. Literally from the moment of birth, communication takes place between infant and caregiver. Research in the areas of mother-infant interaction and developmental pragmatics has suggested that the communication patterns established during the first year or two of life are crucial to children's later development in several areas, including language, cognition, and social skills.

During the first few months of life, the infant's communications are not really intentional. Nevertheless, they can be easily understood by those around the infant. For example, crying, smiling, cooing, looking, and eventually reaching are behaviors that often have great meaning for

Table 9–1 (pp. 319–321) Normal language development: expected sequence and approximate age norms*

Age in Months (Approx.)	Pragmatics	Phonology	Grammar Morphology-Syntax	Semantics
1	Gazing, crying, "comfort sounds"	Begins to play with pitch change		
3	Laughs, smiles when played with; looks at speaker; sometimes responds to a speaker by vocalizing	Vocalizes two or more syllables		
6	Babbles and smiles at a speaker; stops (begins turn taking) when someone speaks	Babbles four or more syllables at one time; plays at making noises; labial (/p/, /b/, /m/) consonants emerge; vowels		
8	Plays "peek-a-boo" and "pat-a-cake"; listens to adult conversations; turns toward speaker; understands gesture	Intonation patterns for questions and commands; jargon includes vowels and consonants (five or more of each)	(No real words, but vocalizing sounds as if forming a sentence or question)	Recognizes names of some common objects
10	Follows simple commands; enjoys clapping to music; begins to "send message" by pointing	Uses a varied jargon, with pitch and rhythm		
12	Responds to manner and attitude of speaker (e.g., joy, anger, or hurry)	Consonant-vowel and consonant-vowel-consonant jargon	Holophrastic speech (one word stands for a whole sentence)	Says first words; tries to imitate words
12 to 18	Follows one- and two-step directions	Imitates noises and speech sounds	Some begin to use two-word sentences	Uses two or more words; learns new words every few days
				Recognizes and points to many familiar objects; learns new words almost daily

Table 9–1 (Continued)

Age in Months (Approx.)	Pragmatics	Phonology	Grammar Morphology-Syntax	Semantics
18 to 24	Jargon and some echolalia; "dialogue" uses speech to get attention; "asks" for help	Uses /p/, /b/, /m/, /h/, /t/ and vowels	Two-to three- word sentences, but omits articles and most modifiers; begins to use personal pronouns; telegraphic speech	Says 10 to 20 words at 18 months, but some say as many as 200 words by 24 months; understands many more
24 to 36	At 2, speech is not used for social control, but at 2 1/2, demands and attempts control By 3, language is linguistically and contextually contingent, and 70% of speech is intelligible, although articulation errors are still common. Short sentences (three to four words) are common. All vowels are correct, but /r/, /s/, /ch/, /j/, /v/, /l/, /x/ are often incorrectly spoken. Vocabulary ranges to as many as 1,000 words. Sentence types include agent-action, action-object, and agent-object	Many begin to use additional consonants; add /f/, /k/, /d/, /w/, /g/; vowels 90% intelligible	By 2 1/2, grammatical morphemes begin to appear: -ing (present progressive) -s and -es (plurals) -ed (past tense) a, an, the (articles) my and 's (possessives) auxiliary verbs prepositions	Recognizes names and pictures of most common objects; understands 500 words

Table 9–1 (Continued)

Age in Months (Approx.)	Pragmatics	Phonology	Grammar Morphology-Syntax	Semantics
36 to 48	Social control; whispers; tells name; "explains" what happened; asks questions, sustains topic; systematic changes in speech depend on the listener; some role playing; metalinguistic awareness (ability to think about language and comment on it); "hints" at things through smiles and gestures as well as words	All vowels correct; although many children articulate most consonants accurately, articulation errors on the following are still within normal range: /l/, /r/, /s/, /z/, /sh/, /ch/, /j/, /th/; pitch and rhythm variations similar to adults, but this age enjoys extremes—yells and whispers	Expands noun phrases with tense, gender, and number; conjugates "to be" correctly; uses pronouns, adjectives, and plurals; near age 4, begins using longer and more compound and complex sentences; begins to interrelate clauses (uses *and*, *because*, *when*, and *then*)	Vocabulary grows rapidly; actively seeks to learn new words; likes to experiment and makes many charming errors; continues process of differentiating lexical types; knows between 900 and 1,000 words
48 to 60	Seeks information constantly; "why" is a favorite; becomes aware of behavior listeners attent to; begins to grasp relevance	Begins to use stress contours, pitch changes purposefully; articulation errors still common, but diminishing; nonfluency not unusual; blends difficult	Uses comparatives (big, biggest); uses all sentence types, including relative clauses; grammar approximates that of adults	Size of vocabulary varies widely with experiences; many know 2,000 or more words

* From Brown (1973), Bzoch and League (1970), Dale (1976), Hopper and Naremore (1978), Prutting (1979), and Wilkinson (1979).

the infant's caregivers, even though the infant may not be doing them "on purpose." A term often used to describe these kinds of communicative behaviors is *perlocutionary* (Bates, 1976).

These perlocutionary behaviors are responded to and interpreted by caregivers as though they *were* intentions. As the infant gains greater control, voluntary behaviors eventually become intentional communicative acts. By 9 or 10 months of age, most children are engaging in a variety of intentional (but still unconventional) behaviors such as pointing, use of directed eye gaze, and use of vocalizations to get attention, to exclaim, or to accompany their own actions or expression of wants and needs.

Precommunicative Functions. These types of intentional communicative behaviors are often referred to as *illocutionary*. Halliday (1975) described several categories of communicative functions that infants may use even prior to the acquisition of first words:

1. The *interactional function* is also referred to as the "you and me" function. By using this function the infant is attempting to elicit interaction and attention from others in his or her immediate environment. For example, an infant may look at mother, clap his hands, and vocalize in an attempt to play "pattycake." Or he may wake from his nap and call from his crib in order to get some company.

2. The *instrumental function* is also referred to as the "I want" function. Here the infant uses communicative behaviors to obtain something he or she wants from the environment, such as food or a favorite object. For example, an infant's looking toward his bottle, pointing, and saying, "Uh" is an instrumental communicative behavior.

3. The *regulatory function* is the "Do as I tell you" function; it is used by the infant to control others' behaviors. For example, an infant may be requesting someone to push her in her stroller, or pick her up.

4. The *personal function* is called the "Here I come" function. The infant uses this function to simply express some emotion or to accompany his or her own actions. For example, an infant tastes a bite of ice cream and says, "Mmmm," or drops something and says, "Uh oh!"

5. The *heuristic function* is an important function because it sets the stage for the infant's use of communication to obtain information from adults in his or her environment. This is referred to as the "Tell me why" function. By use of such strategies as a vocalization with question-like rising intonation, or raised eyebrows, the infant learns to solicit additional information such as a label or explanation, from people nearby.

6. The *imaginative function* may be used by some infants during this prelinguistic stage of communication development. The imaginative function is referred to as the "Let's pretend" function; it accompanies the older infant's pretend play activities (e.g., car sounds).

The Onset of Language

Somewhere around 1 to 1 1/2 years of age, the infant learns his or her first "real" words. After this point, communication becomes symbolic and conventional. The toddler continues to use all the communicative functions just described, but now many of these functions are expressed using recognizable words such as *peek, bottle, up, oh oh, whaddat?* and *night night.* In addition, a new function is now added to the toddler's repertoire: the *informative function.* Halliday has called this the "Let me tell you" function, because the child can now truly share information via symbolic language behavior.

Around this same time, the child also begins to move toward a new stage of cognitive development: the **preoperational stage.** Now the infant becomes increasingly able to represent things mentally. As a result, he can also use his newly found symbolic behavior to refer to things that are not immediately present in the environment, and very shortly, to events that happened in the past.

Thus the onset of conventional speech and language skills also typically coincides with several other exciting milestones in the infant's development. The infant's communication is no longer tied to the here and now. In addition to using social interaction and manipulating her environment to meet her basic wants and needs, she can now share her experiences with others.

It should be noted that the speech of a toddler at the early one-word stage is often unintelligible to anyone not involved with the toddler on a regular basis. Some words may even be idiosyncratic, bearing little phonemic relationship to the conventional word (e.g., "da" for bottle). Real words may also be combined with jargon, or strings of unintelligible speech sounds (often consonant-vowel syllables such as "da" or "tee"). The toddler may sound as though she is uttering whole sentences, although she really is not.

Combining Words

Sometime around 20 to 24 months, when the infant has learned approximately 50 to 100 words, he will begin to put them together. Often his first combinations will be words he already uses. For example, instead of saying "juice" or "more" to get another glass of juice, he will say "more juice." Just why the infant begins to combine words in this way is not clear. For many years, child language acquisition research focused on this process of learning to produce longer and longer utterances that conform more and more closely to adult language.

The *structure* of language refers to the way in which words are combined into sentences (syntax) and the various forms of words (morphology). The young child must learn to say, "I want juice," rather than "Want juice I," and "The boys are running," rather than "The boys is run." There is much literature from the 1960s and early 1970s that described in some detail the evolution of children's grammar. While teachers of young children need not be familiar with all the specific details of children's grammatical development, it is important that they know the major stages of language structure development as described in the following paragraphs.

1. *Telegraphic language.* When children begin to combine words, they are most likely to use words that have the most meaning. In earlier writings on child language acquisition, these utterances were called "telegraphic" because they appeared to omit unessential words. Utterances such as "Baby like bottle" are typical of children in this stage.

2. *Grammatical morphemes.* Around 2 years of age, children begin to include grammatical morphemes in their utterances. Words such as *the* and *an*, word endings such as plural *s*, present progressive *ing*, past tense *ed*, and others are gradually included. As a child first begins to use grammatical morphemes, she may often use them incorrectly. For example, she may say, "The boy runned" or "an apples." The teacher should be aware that incorrect use of grammatical morphemes nevertheless represents a more sophisticated stage of grammatical development than the earlier telegraphic stage in which grammatical morphemes were omitted altogether.

3. *Simple sentences.* Gradually, by the age of 3 years, children learn to produce sentences that resemble simple ones used by adults. These sentences will contain a subject and a predicate and will include the necessary grammatical morphemes, although still not always in the correct form. The 3 year old says, "I want some milk, please," or "Let's go outside," or "My dollies is mad!"

The 3 year old has also learned to make *sentence transformations*, that is, to ask questions ("Do you have my doll?") and give commands ("Give me my doll!"), as well as to make simple declarative statements ("This is my doll.")

4. *Complex language.* By the age of 4 years, young children can easily combine words into sentences and produce them intelligibly. In addition, they can produce complex sentences such as, "I don't want to go to the store if I can't buy a new toy." Perhaps even more important is their increasing linguistic flexibility. They can now adjust the structure and content of their language according to the nature of the situation and the age and status of the listener. For example, to his 2-year-old sister, the 4 year old might say, "Give me the ice cream!" But when talking to an older adult he would change the structure of his language (e.g., "Could I have some more ice cream, please?").

The 4- or 5-year-old child is also capable of carrying on a conversation: the child can take turns, extend the topic, and return the conversational floor to his or her partner. The following dialogue demonstrates these conversational strategies, which are so crucial to the young child's development of social skills:

Danny: "Did you see 'Kit' on TV last night, Erin?"

Erin: "No, 'cause I watch 'Highway to Heaven.' "

Danny: "It was great! Kit got all smashed up."

Erin: "How come?"

Danny: "Some guys was chasin' him. He flew right off this cliff!"

Erin: "Gee, maybe I'll watch it sometime."

Finally, the 4- or 5-year-old child can engage in *narrative*—stories that have a beginning, a middle, and an end. The child is now not only able to use language to manipulate the environment and obtain social interaction, but also to express emotions and to share his or her experiences and ideas with others. Language and cog-

nition now become inextricably woven together as a means of problem solving and learning about the world.

Hopefully, the 4 year old has acquired the kinds of linguistic skills that will also support academic achievement. These autonomous or literate-style language skills are discussed in Chapter 10. The child's words and sentences can now stand alone. He or she can tell a story or describe a situation clearly and successfully to a listener who has no previous knowledge or shared reference regarding the event being described.

Many of the milestones described in this section will be communication goals for young children with special needs. Strategies for helping children develop these communication skills will be described later in the chapter.

NECESSARY CONDITIONS FOR THE DEVELOPMENT OF COMMUNICATION SKILLS

Because of the tremendous complexity of speech and language skills, several necessary conditions must exist in order for these skills to develop normally.

First, the peripheral sensory system must be intact. Hearing is of greatest importance, of course, for the development of language. In addition, the vision and oral musculature sensitivity must function well.

The central nervous system must also be intact. Speech and language development depend on the ability not only to receive incoming auditory information but also to process, organize, and store it. Of particular importance in the development of speech production (i.e., articulation skills) is the motor system. The production of speech involves incredibly precise coordination of many muscles and muscle groups making up the speech production mechanism, including those involved in movement of the tongue, lips, jaw, velum, larynx, and muscles of respiration.

The production of speech sounds in the rapid sequence necessary to the production of intelligible speech requires synergistic split-second timing and smooth control of these muscles. For children with motor impairments such as those associated with many forms of cerebral palsy, the production of speech is extremely difficult.

Cognitive abilities are crucial to the development of language skills. The content of a child's language is dependent on what the child is able to represent, organize, understand, and recall of the world around him or her.

Social/affective growth must also be normal in order for communication skills to develop. Communication development during the first year of life, and many of the precursors of language, depend on the infant's or young child's seeking out the attention of and interaction with others in his or her environment. The child who lacks this drive toward social intercourse, as, for example, in many cases of autism, will most likely be significantly impaired in the development of communication skills.

Finally, the environment itself must be responsive to the infant's and young child's needs, and the linguistic input provided by caregivers must be appropriate to the infant's ability to process information. Recent research has suggested that several interaction strategies, particularly caregiver responsiveness, can enhance children's later development. These interaction strategies are also important to teachers in the field of early childhood special education, and they should be incorporated into the daily activities of the classroom. We will discuss these interaction strategies in more detail later in this chapter.

Characteristics That Can Interfere with Language Development

Characteristics of common communication disorders are summarized in Figure 9–1. The following sections discuss these disorders in more detail.

Hearing Impairments. Hearing loss can interfere with both speech and language development. Even mild or intermittent hearing impairments such as those associated with otitis media can interfere with the learning of speech and language. Children who are hearing impaired can be taught to speak and to understand language, but the task is not an easy one and requires the help of parents and highly trained specialists. Although children who are deaf are eventually identified, lack of language development in children with mild hearing losses frequently goes undetected (Davis, 1977).

Children with mild hearing losses cannot hear all phonemes with equal clarity. The distorted speech pattern they hear is inconsistent and incorrect. Downs (1977) and Bess and McConnell (1981) discussed the effects of mild, intermittent hearing loss and its long-term interference with language development. If a child fails to develop normal communication skills at expected ages, regardless of what other factors seem to be involved, the child's hearing should be checked and regularly rechecked by a competent audiologist. If any hearing deficit is detected, the causes should be discovered and removed. If this is not possible, parents should receive guidance, and the child's language development should be monitored and directed by a speech-language pathologist or a trained teacher of children who are deaf. Children who are unable to hear normally during the first years of life are disabled in all aspects of language and speech development. According to Davis (1977), "The effects of hearing loss are such that the longer the hearing impairment is undetected and untreated the more serious is the problem and the less likely it is to be remediated optimally" (p. 27).

Chapter 4 pinpoints some high risk signals that professionals should review often.

Auditory-Perceptual Impairments. Auditory-perceptual impairments are presumed to be the cause of specific language disorders in some children. A review of the literature on this topic by

Figure 9–1   Characteristics of common communication disorders. (From public information materials of the American Speech-Language-Hearing Association. Reproduced with permission.)

Lubert (1981) noted that a diversity of labels and assessment instruments has led to some confusion. This article reported that these disorders have been studied by researchers from several disciplines, including neurology, psychiatry, psychology, speech pathology, audiology, and linguistics. Terms used include *developmental aphasia, congenital aphasia, aphasoid children, developmental dysphasia, language deficit, language delay, learning disability, verbal auditory agnosia,* and *central auditory dysfunction.*

The perceptions and observations of the various specialists have led to different conclusions, theories, and remediation approaches. Lubert (1981) reported,

The above research suggests that language-disordered children may be characterized by an impaired rate of processing for rapidly changing acoustic information. . . . An obvious treatment implication is that the signal should be slowed down to facilitate its perception by the language-disordered child. (p. 1)

Thus, parents and teachers should avoid presenting stimuli too rapidly. Fast talking and chaotic environments may be difficult for some children to process, and they may be overwhelming. As a result, these children may eventually develop the habit of "tuning out" their environments, which can cause additional learning problems.

Visual Impairments. While visual impairment does not produce the same degree of interference as hearing impairment, it does affect concept and vocabulary development. If the child cannot see clearly, it is difficult to recognize the things and events being discussed. Because blind children, by virtue of their disability, have a deprived experiential base, they need special help to acquire speech and language. Like children with a partial hearing loss, children who are partially sighted have special needs that often go unnoticed. Fraiberg (1977) has offered specific and useful information to aid early identification of children with visual impairment. Chapter 4 lists warning signs of possible visual impairment.

Cognitive Impairments. Mental retardation is presumed to be the cause of delayed speech and language in some children. Since many tests of intelligence rely heavily on verbal interactions between examiner and child, it is difficult to tell cause from effect. Qualified examiners should be able to make this distinction, but many find it difficult. Thus a young child without speech and language may be judged to have developmental delays due to lack of communication skills. Davis

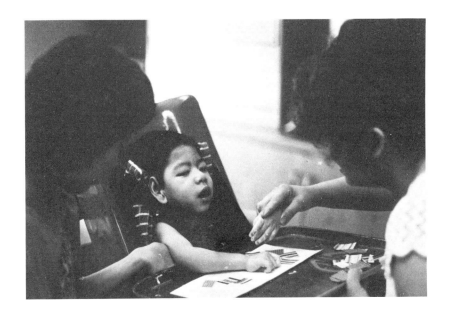

(1977) cautioned that tests containing verbal items reflect the child's linguistic age, not necessarily his or her intellectual status.

Children with slower than average cognitive development need thoughtfully planned and carefully provided individualized opportunities and challenges. Children who have moderate and mild retardation will often be able to learn to talk and understand speech and language in the expected sequences, although at a slower pace. It is especially important to provide these children with a **language-nurturing environment** matching their linguistic age, rather than their chronological age. Thus, if they are just beginning to use two words, they should be talked to, listened to, and played with in a manner appropriate to that level of language development. Children who have been described as having retardation may need special help in the pragmatic skills of language, as well as with vocabulary, grammar, and articulation. Helping them to understand when to talk, as well as what to say, should be an important part of curriculum planning.

The child with more severe retardation poses very different problems and challenges for the early childhood special education teacher. When there is severe impairment of cognitive and perceptual processes, the impact on the development of communication skills is great. In many children who have severe or profound retardation, rule-governed symbolic language skills may never develop. However, it is important to recognize that these children, too, must have some means of communication. We will discuss young children with severe and multiple disabilities in a later section.

Emotional Problems. Deviant language development or the refusal to communicate at all may result from emotional problems. Although these problems require the skillful and caring therapy of persons especially trained to help children and their parents, much can be done to support mental health in a preschool environment. Chapter 7 offers a number of classroom support strategies for children with emotional or social problems. Cooperation among therapists, parents, and teachers is especially critical in this area.

Autism. One of the identifying characteristics of children who have autism is the atypical development of social skills and language. Current theories regarding etiological factors in autism suggest that its basis is neurophysiological, that is, that there are differences in how the child's central nervous system responds to incoming stimuli. These differences result in serious information-processing deficits (Rutter, 1986).

Many children with autism are particularly sensitive to tactile and auditory stimuli, which can result in major interference with the processes of attachment and social interaction as well as development of communication skills. In addition, the problems with social responsiveness typical of these children also contribute to particular difficulties with the development of functional uses of communication.

Lack of Stimulation. Lack of appropriate stimulation limits communication development. Recent studies in many areas support the importance of loving, emotionally satisfying stimulation from birth. However, some parents simply do not know how to talk to their young children. It is not uncommon to have them say, "What can you say to a baby?" or, "My friends will think I'm crazy if I talk to a 2 year old."

It is usually assumed that people who speak a language, children as well as adults, instinctively know how to talk to children. This is not always true. Later, suggestions for teaching parents and others how to talk to their children will be given. In any case, when a child is not talking, be alert to help parents create a language-nurturing environment.

Regardless of other causes for poor oral communication skills, the lack of stimulation should be considered as an ongoing contributor to the delay. This may be especially true if the child has physical problems, including hearing and visual deficits that have delayed normal language acquisition. Once language development is "off schedule," parents may feel helpless and fail to provide the stimulation that would have come naturally and intuitively to them otherwise. Kleffner (1973) reported that a child's lack of communication ability, when added to parental fears and anxieties, can result in parents' changing their family lifestyle. They may become oversolicitous, do fewer things together, and talk less or differently.

Parents can learn to use everyday experiences to teach communication skills. Cooking, cleaning, and gardening are excellent experiences for children. Conversation during these activities becomes an excellent language-teaching time. Washing the car or working with tools provides additional excellent opportunities to foster speech and language learning. But parents need encouragement, effective examples, and thoughtful reminders if they are to make their child's language-learning environment stimulating.

Characteristics That Interfere with Speech

Structural Abnormalities. Craniofacial deformities of any kind interfere with speech skill development. A child who cannot imitate and reproduce speech sounds will be less skilled in using language as well. For example, if deviant mouth structure precludes placing tongue and teeth in the correct position to pronounce /s/, as in boys and shoes, the child cannot use the language rule "Add /s/ to form plurals."

Hypernasality, often associated with cleft palate, also interferes with learning speech. Only three English speech sounds are intended to have this characteristic nasal quality: /m/, /n/, and /ng/ (as in ring). When most of the sounds of speech are nasalized, listeners usually characterize the speech as unintelligible. Conditions other than cleft palate can cause this. If a child seems to be "talking through the nose," the causes should be discovered and corrected.

Motor Problems. Normal control of the muscles necessary for speech is needed for correct articulation. This develops so spontaneously in most children that its significance is not recognized. Playing the violin skillfully is far less complex than pronouncing a word correctly. To apreciate this muscular achievement, shut your lips lightly and pay attention to your tongue as you say, "Look at Larry's new green coat." (Shutting your lips helps to focus on the tongue activity.)

Cerebral palsy interferes with muscle coordination. Injury, other physical problems, and certain drugs also interfere. Teachers will want to work closely with therapists when children have problems of this kind.

Voice Problems. The effect of a cleft palate and/ or lip may result in a nasal voice even if a surgical repair was accomplished early in the child's life. Children who have frequent respiratory infections may lack nasal resonance. Children who scream a lot may be hoarse. All of these problems deserve skillful attention and remediation from professionals.

Stuttering. Stuttering is speech with disturbed rhythm. When a speaker repeats a sound or syllable, prolongs it more than is typical of other speakers, or blocks (a complete halting of the speech flow), many people describe this as stuttering. Some stutterers develop patterns of grimaces and gestures in an effort to avoid disturbing their flow of speech. Sometimes described as *secondary characteristics*, these behaviors are often thought of as habits that reflect the speaker's anxiety and an effort to break tension.

Stuttering usually begins between the ages of 2 and 4, although it may happen much later. All speakers normally repeat, hesitate, and sometimes prolong sounds. This is especially true of young children. They are in a hurry. Finding the right word is difficult for little children, and this is reason enough for them to hesitate and repeat.

Some speech-language pathologists believe that calling attention to the perfectly normal disfluencies of young children may result in more repetitions. Telling children to slow down or to think before they speak may cause them to stumble even more. Then parents become even more anxious and so do their children. The following suggestions are useful to both parents and teachers of young children who are beginning to stutter:

1. Reduce the pressure to communicate.

2. Slow down your own rate of speech.

3. Avoid watching the child's effort to speak in obvious ways.

4. Avoid reacting with anger, shock, or distaste to speech blocks or repetitions.

5. Avoid suggesting by word or touch that you "know she has a problem, but you love her anyway."

6. Do not make comments such as "stop and start over" to a stuttering child.

7. If the stutterer is so disturbed by the disfluency that a reaction from you is expected, say something like, "That was a hard word," or "Sometimes my words get stuck too."

8. Refuse to feel anxious yourself. It won't help.

NURTURING SPEECH, LANGUAGE, AND CONCEPTUAL SKILLS

There is a large body of information available to the early childhood special education professional regarding ways of facilitating the development of communication skills in young children. Some of this information will be presented in the following sections.

The Important Role of Caregiver-Child Interaction

The importance of the early caregiving environment, and particularly caregivers' use of responsive communicative interactions, has been well established. Earlier research in the field of de-

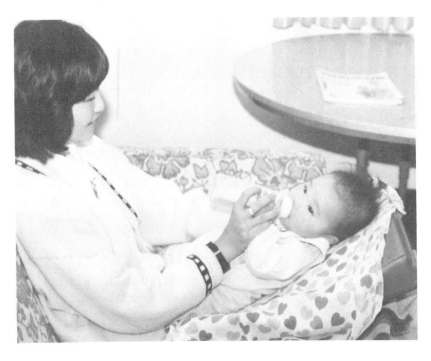

velopmental psychology (e.g., Clarke-Stewart, 1973; Yarrow, Rubenstein, & Pedersen, 1975) and more recent research with populations with special needs (e.g., Mahoney, Finger, & Powell, 1985) have clearly demonstrated relationships between certain kinds of caregiver-infant/child interactions and the development of young children. A longitudinal study reported by Coates and Lewis (1984) demonstrated relationships between mothers' interaction behaviors with their infants at 3 months and the children's school achievement and cognitive skills at 6 years of age. As many studies of this type have found, maternal responsivity appeared to be the strongest factor.

Particularly important to the development of children's language skills are caregivers' uses of certain **communicative interactions,** which will be described in the following section. For more detailed understanding of this important area, students are referred to descriptions of several intervention programs designed to assist parents of children with special needs in developing and refining these skills (e.g., Klein & Briggs, 1987; Klein, Briggs, & Huffman, 1988; MacDonald, 1989; Manolson, 1985) Figure 9–2 gives examples of the kinds of interactions often targeted for infants and very young children.

The caregiver-child interactions described in the following sections are equally important for teachers and other early interventionists. Early interventionists must not only develop the ability to recognize and encourage the use of interactive behaviors between parents and children, but just as important, they must be able to demonstrate and consistently use these strategies themselves.

Encouraging Conversation. The literature on so-called "motherese" and mother-infant interaction has described several specific strategies mothers use to encourage and maintain a dialogue with their infants (Cross, 1984). These include such behaviors as (a) use of rising intonation "yes/no" questions (e.g., "Wanna eat now? or "Is baby tired?"); (b) pausing expectantly after each utterance to give the infant a turn;

and (c) imitating the infant's vocalizations or responding to the infant's vocalizations as though they were intelligible (e.g., "Oh yeah?", "Is that right?", "No kidding!", etc.).

Responding Contingently to Child's Behavior. Maternal responsivity has frequently been found to be a robust correlate of later development in young children. Particularly important for the early childhood special educator is a sensitivity to all communicative attempts on the part of the child. For example, a child with severe disabilities who is nonverbal and rarely initiates interaction or attempts to get attention should receive *immediate* attention for any communicative effort, including gestures, changes in body position, vocalizations, and so forth. The child who communicates only by crying or pulling the teacher's sleeve should receive an enthusiastic response for making a grunting sound or pointing to get a drink of juice, because this is a new behavior for the child. MacDonald (1989) described an interaction strategy called "upping the ante," in which the teacher or parent encourages a slightly more sophisticated response than the one the child typically uses.

Modifying Interaction in Response to Negative Cues. Another important aspect of maternal responsivity, albeit a more subtle one, is the ability to change or terminate interaction with an infant in response to such cues as gaze aversion, changes in body tension and facial expression, or lack of response from the infant. Interventionists, too, must be able to read children's cues of disinterest, overload, or distraction. Continuing a particular cue or prompt such as "Show me the doll" when the child is clearly not attending to the stimulus is wasted effort and may eventually teach the child to "tune out" as a generalized strategy to overwhelming or meaningless stimulation.

Using Communication to Teach Language and Concepts. Much has been written about the maternal language patterns that are typical of mid-

OBSERVATION OF COMMUNICATIVE INTERACTION (OCI)
Mother-Infant Communication Project

Infant's Name _____ Birthdate _____ Age _____

Setting _____ Date _____ Adjusted Age _____

Observer _____

	Rarely/Never	Sometimes	Often	Optimally	Not Applicable
1. **Provides appropriate tactile and kinesthetic stimulation (e.g., gently strokes, pats, caresses, cuddles, rocks baby).**	1	2	3	4	N/A
2. **Displays pleasure while interacting with infant.**	1	2	3	4	N/A
3. **Responds to child's distress.**	1	2	3	4	N/A

a. changes verbalization
   b. changes infant's position, attempts to distract.
   c. provides positive physical stimuli (e.g., patting, rocking).
   d. avoids negative physical or verbal response.					

4. **Positions self and infant so eye-to-eye contact is possible (e.g., facing and 7 to 12 inches away).**	1	2	3	4	N/A
a. attempts to make eye contact. b. reciprocates eye gaze.					
5. **Smiles contingently at infant.**	1	2	3	4	N/A
a. consistently returns infant's smile. b. smiles in response to infant vocalization.					
6. **Varies prosodic features.**	1	2	3	4	N/A

a. uses higher pitch.
   b. talks more slowly.
   c. exaggerates 'intonation'.					

7. **Encourages "conversation".**	1	2	3	4	N/A

a. uses rising intonation questions.
   b. waits after saying something to infant, and looks expectantly, providing infant turn.
   c. imitates child's vocalizations, or words
   d. repeats own sounds, words or phrases (e.g., "Here's the bottle. Bottle."
   e. answers when infant vocalizes (e.g., "Oh, year?", "Okay.", "Is that right?").					

8. **Responds contingently to infant's behavior.**	1	2	3	4	N/A

a. touches or responds with facial expression within 2 seconds after infant vocalization.
   b. vocalizes within 2 seconds after infant moves arms, head, etc.
   c. vocalizes within 2 seconds after infant vocalization.
   d. stops own activity or verbalization in response to interruption by infant's vocalization or movement.
   e. responds vocally to infant from a distance of more than 2 feet.					

9. **Modifies interaction in response to negative cues from infant.**	1	2	3	4	N/A

a. changes activity.
   b. reduces intensity of interaction.
   c. terminates attempts at interaction.					

Figure 9–2 Communicative Interaction checklist. (*Source:* Klein & Briggs, 1987)

10. Uses communication to teach language and concepts.   1   2   3   4   N/A

a. interprets infant's behavior appropriately (e.g., "Oh, you're hungry, aren't you.")
b. re-casts own sentences (e.g., adult says, "Shall we turn on the light? Turn on the light. There's the light.").
c. comments on infant's attention to immediate environment and *labels* objects (e.g., "You see the doggie? That's the doggie.")
d. matches infant's vocalization, or word with slightly more elaborate language (e.g., baby says, "Ball", and adult says, "That's a ball." or "Big ball.")

Figure 9–2   (Continued)

dle class mothers as they interact with their young children. Some of these communicative interaction strategies appear to be correlated with later language development (Nelson, Bonvillian, Denninger, Kaplan, & Baker (1984).

Caregivers and professionals should use these language behaviors in response to the infant's or toddler's interest and attention, as demonstrated by the child's eye gaze, gestures, and vocalization or words. These interaction strategies include:

1. *Commenting* on what the infant or child appears to be attending to (e.g., "Oh, you hear that doggie barking, don't you?").

2. *Re-casting* one's own words or phrases in different ways in order to emphasize important words (e.g., "Yup, that's the *doggie*. Hear the *doggie? Doggie!*").

3. *Matching* the child's vocalization or word with a slightly more elaborated response, thereby interpreting the utterance (e.g., the child says "buh" and the teacher says "Bottle, yes bottle").

4. *Expanding* the utterance syntactically (e.g., the child says "cookie" and the teacher says "That is a cookie"); or *semantically extending*, that is, adding meaning to the utterance (e.g., the child says "doggie" and the teacher says "Yeah, that's a *big* doggie!").

Several instructional programs have been designed around the interaction strategies described here. For more information, refer to MacDonald (1989), Manolson (1985), and Weiss (1981).

CLASSROOM STRATEGIES THAT FACILITATE COMMUNICATION

The social interactionist theory of language development and knowledge about the stages and major achievements of language acquisition generate a useful approach to early language intervention. Before describing some of the strategies suggested by this approach, let us consider three important principles related to the development of communication skills.

1. *Interaction* is the first key to the development of communication skills (Reike & Lewis, 1984). Infants and young children must learn to experience the pleasures of turn taking and reciprocal interaction.

2. True communication skills must be *functional* for the child. The ability to provide rote answers to stereotyped questions is not really communication. Infants and children must have opportunities to *initiate* communication. Observation of early childhood special education classrooms reveals that children are too often

---

EXHIBIT 9–2

Some Ways to Promote Syntactic Development

Tony uses many two- and some three-word sentences, and he loves to talk. Both his parents and his teachers have many conversations with him throughout the day. They *listen* to him with obvious interest. Some of the time they *expand* what he has said. When he says "Falled down," they may say "Your big tower fell down. That was noisy." They do this in a way that suggests "You're right, it fell down," never in a manner that indicates "Now, say it the right way."

As the adults do things while Tony is present, they may use *self-talk*. They talk about what they are feeling and doing, as they do it. "Time for supper. I'll take the plates to the table, now. The meat and the green beans are almost ready, and it's time to make the salad. I'll cut the carrots, first." Of course, the speaker pauses after each sentence and *listens* if Tony starts to say something.

Sometimes his teachers and parents use *parallel talk*. They talk about what Tony is doing. "Tony, you put the toys on the shelf just the right way. I like the way you are picking up those blocks. You put the biggest ones on the bottom."

When Tony says something incorrectly, they rarely correct him directly, but they do use *corrective echoing*. If he says "Her frew dat ball," they might say "You saw Susie. *She threw* the ball." And although they may exaggerate the "she" and the "th" slightly by saying them slowly, they are really just confirming that they understood.

placed in a respondent role. That is, they are taught to respond to specific prompts and cues provided by the teacher. Communication used only in this way cannot be a learning tool for children. They must be encouraged to initiate interaction, to use language and other communicative behaviors to appropriately manipulate the environment, to ask questions and obtain information, and to solve problems. Children must learn to use language for purposes other than simply answering questions.

3. Language develops best in a *responsive environment.* The teacher who is most sensitive to the infant or child's communicative intentions will be most successful in facilitating language development. Many specific ways of responding are suggested by the literature describing "*motherese*" (the speech and language characteristics typical of mothers' communication with infants and young children described earlier).

Beginning Where the Child Is

Our understanding of appropriate practices in nurturing receptive and expressive language suggests that teachers should attend to children's levels of development. Thus, if 4-year-old Sean does not yet try to tell adults anything, one thing to nurture is the "telling" of things as very young children do. If Susie cannot produce any speech sounds distinctly, she may need to be encouraged in simple vocal play and babbling. If Tommy does not try to ask for things, perhaps he should be expected to make some kind of sound before he is given what he wants.

Developmental scales of speech and language can be checked to determine whether a child has a developmental lag. Speech and language pathologists can assist as questions arise. Table 9–1 can be used as a basis for constructing a checklist for evaluating language development. However, instructional objectives for language development should also be based on the functional needs of the child; they should not be limited to items on a developmental checklist.

The Importance of Conversations

Conversations about familiar things that interest young children are a critical tool in helping them to learn communication skills. Nelson (1974) reported that children's first verbal labels or names are of objects, people, events, and actions they know and can associate with. Unless they are truly interested and can make associations, they will not attend. And attention is a prerequisite for learning anything.

Choosing What to Talk About

Communication skills develop around objects and events that interest children. For the really reluctant talker, food can be a good place to begin. Sitting around a table with other children while the teacher cuts an apple into pieces can be a powerful stimulator. Conversation can focus on such things as the name of the fruit, the smooth, red skin and small, black seeds, the sharp knife, and how the apple will taste. Pragmatic skills also can be nurtured in this "social situation" (e.g., turn taking and use of polite requests).

Any game, dollhouse, play kitchen, or toy barn can be used as the conversational focal point. At first, the teacher should join the children in an ongoing activity with toys they have chosen, following the children's lead. Later, when rapport has been well established, the teacher may choose the activity. Introducing variety is important. But at first, joining into the children's choice of things to do is best.

For adults who find it difficult to converse with young children, the following suggestions may prove useful:

1. Listen attentively. Even if the things children are saying are unintelligible, look at them with interest and listen.

2. Speak slowly and distinctly, using natural or

slightly exaggerated intonation patterns (the prosodic features).

3. Keep sentences short, no more than three or four words. Sometimes use single words. Repeat frequently.

4. *Do not ask questions*, unless you really want to learn something you do not know. Avoid asking, "What color is your shoe?" or "Where is the ball?" when both of you can see the answer. Questions asked one after another do not constitute conversation. In fact, just as with adults, too many questions result in no conversation. But good questions do lead to problem solving and planning.

5. Talk about the here and now. Vicarious experiences are not useful as conversation starters with young children.

6. Use a calm and pleasant tone of voice. Bring fun to every conversation.

7. Use words the children are interested in, because they can see or understand what they refer to as you talk. Tell them the names of actions as well as things.

8. Pause between sentences. Don't be in a hurry.

9. As the children understand and speak more, gradually make your sentences longer and use a larger vocabulary.

Listening

Adults should listen to children *with great interest*. This is especially true if the children have not developed speech and language skills at the expected rate. If they are unable to talk, every effort on their part requires more than the usual amount of trying. The reward most likely to accelerate the growth of speech and language is *not* an M & M; it is an interested listener. Presenting an alert facial expression, remaining quiet, staying in one position, and even just looking at the children are also important considerations.

Developing Pragmatic Skills

Pragmatic skills are the social skills of language. Taking turns during a conversation, refraining from interrupting, and saying the appropriate thing cannot be learned in isolation. Children require social experiences and are dependent on social interaction. By modeling correct pragmatic skills, adults can direct attention to courteous and effective ways of conversing.

Expanding Skills

Ideally, children's language skills are expanded through increasingly complex conversations using longer sentences and a larger vocabulary. MacDonald (1989) has referred to this strategy as "progressive matching" (p. 174). If children have the opportunity, the process expands their skills. If their development has been delayed, the rate may continue to be slower than is expected, but the developmental sequence probably will not differ. Exhibit 9–3 suggests ways to promote children's syntactic development.

FACILITATING COMMUNICATION IN CHILDREN WITH SEVERE AND MULTIPLE DISABILITIES

Many special education preschool programs include children with severe and multiple disabilities who demonstrate very few communicative behaviors. Many of these children will never develop the use of intelligible speech. Some may never be able to use any formal symbolic system of communication such as signing or graphic symbols. Nevertheless, these children *can* learn to communicate using nonverbal, nonspeech systems of communication.

In planning communication instruction programs for children with multiple disabilities, it is perhaps easiest to consider two types of children. The first group includes those who have the cog-

EXHIBIT 9–3

Arrival Time to Build Language Skills

The Scene: Children are arriving, and the teacher and aide are greeting them individually.

The Teaching Strategy: A warm greeting and a brief conversation with each child are designed to make each child feel welcome and expected. Modeling, expanding what the children say, and listening to them are some of the strategies to be used to promote communication skills. Direct correction of articulation errors or grammatical mistakes will be avoided.

Ms. McLynn: Good morning, Sally. I am so glad you brought your doll. Do you want to take her coat off?

Sally: Me do. Coat dirty.

Ms. McLynn: I know you can take her coat off. Her coat *is* dirty, isn't it? We can brush the dirt off.

Sally: Wed shoes. (Pointing to her new shoes)

Ms. McLynn: I like those new red shoes. They are shiny.

Timmy: Hey, looka dat! Dat nose wiggles.

Ms. McLynn: I see our rabbit. She *is* wiggling her nose!

Nancy: Ms. McLynn, my mommie said that she couldn't come today but she will call you afterwhile. She has to go to the supermarket 'cause we're having company tonight.

Ms. McLynn: I'm glad you told me she couldn't come. Would you like to pretend that you are at the supermarket, too? We have lots of things in our store, too.

nitive skills necessary for the development of language (i.e., some formal system of symbolic communication) but do not have the fine oral-motor skills required for the production of intelligible speech. The largest number of children in this group would be those with severe forms of cerebral palsy but no mental retardation.

For these children, some form of **augmentative communication system** must be designed and developed (Schiefelbusch, 1980). In recent years there has been a tremendous growth in technology available for such children, including electronic communication boards and computerized systems. A number of nonelectronic systems can also be tailored to meet the physical and communicative needs of each child.

It is important that the necessary prerequisite skills for using augmentative systems be learned early. Teachers should not wait to see whether or not efforts to teach speech are going to be successful before beginning augmentative communication instruction. There is currently no evidence that teaching nonspeech communication strategies interferes with speech development. There is some suggestion that such instruction may actually facilitate vocalization and speech development (Klein, 1985). Space does not permit detailed descriptions of augmentative systems or intervention procedures shown to be effective in establishing children's use of these systems. Teachers are encouraged to seek out recent information on this topic (Baumgart, Johnson, & Helmstetter, 1990; Reichle, York, & Sigafous, 1991).

The second group of children are those whose disabling conditions produce a poor prognosis for the development of any formal symbolic system. The group includes children with severe and profound mental retardation and some who demonstrate a number of different disabling conditions (e.g., a child with deafness, severe visual and motor impairments, and moderate mental retardation). For such children, the goal of either intelligible speech production or any formal symbolic system of communication such as sign language or graphic symbols may be unrealistic. However, they *can* learn to utilize specific behaviors in functional ways to communicate basic wants, needs, and feelings.

A classroom teacher who is unfamiliar with children who have severe multiple disabilities is often initially overwhelmed with the apparent difficulty of working with such children, especially in the area of communication skills. Again, while space does not permit a thorough descrip-

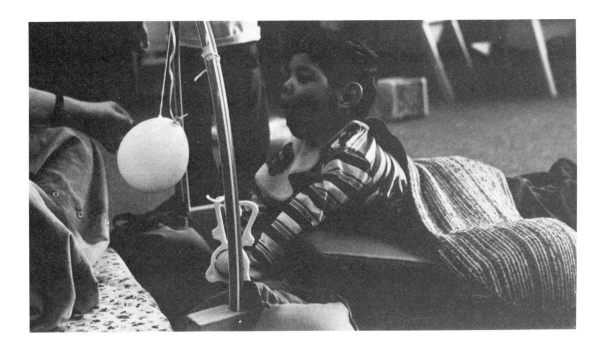

tion of intervention strategies for this group of children, several keys to facilitating communicative behaviors are presented in the following sections. In addition, the strategies included in Exhibit 9–3 can encourage communication in *all* children, regardless of the nature of their disabling conditions.

Verbal Input Strategies

Many of the input strategies discussed earlier are also appropriate for children with severe impairments. When an infant or young child demonstrates a low response rate (i.e., just doesn't seem to "do much"), the teacher's *response* to the child's cues of interest and attention, and to any attempts to communicate, becomes crucial. Teachers must be more vigilant with such children and be ready to respond with appropriate communicative input.

For example, let us consider a child who has severe motor and visual impairments. The child's voluntary behavioral repertoire consists of moving his head from side to side and a few vocalizations. He does not appear to understand any verbal input, but he does respond to sudden loud sounds, to the sound of his mother's voice, and occasionally to food odors as lunch is prepared. The teacher must be very alert to cues from this child that he is recognizing and processing some incoming stimulus. For example, if another child in the classroom drops her tray on the floor, the child with severe disabilities is startled and begins moving his head from side to side. The teacher should provide some verbal input appropriate to the situation and its meaning to the child. In this case, the teacher might say something like, "Oh oh! That was loud, wasn't it? That was a loud crash! Maria dropped her tray." In this way, the teacher comments on the most salient aspect of the situation (in this case the sound, since the child cannot see well), repeats his or her comment in a slightly different way, and semantically extends his or her own comment by adding information about the source of the sound.

Repetition, redundancy, and responsiveness are important input strategies in working with infants or young children with severe disabilities. Certain key words and phrases should be used repeatedly to make significant the events of the day. Certain verbal cues should always be associated with certain events. In this way the teacher establishes **verbal routines** (Snow, Midkiff-Borunda, Small, & Proctor, 1984), which are important as children begin to learn to decode language.

For example, the greeting activities that begin the classroom day should include parts that are always repeated. The transition from music time to lunch should always be accompanied by many predictable cues such as, "OK, who knows what time it is now? It's lunch time. It's time to eat," followed by a sequence of predictable events (e.g., chairs moved, bibs put on, table set, etc.). After lunch, the input might be, "OK, we're all done. All done eating. Let's go outside. We'll play outside." Tables are cleaned, chairs pushed in, coats put on, and so forth, while appropriate verbal input strategies accompany these key events.

Careful verbal input (in response to cues provided by the child that indicate interest and attention or attempts to communicate) is an important key to facilitating communication development. However, for children with severe disabilities, facilitative input strategies are not enough. For these children, it is also necessary to manipulate objects and events in the environment to create the opportunity and the need to communicate. Some of the strategies for doing so are described as follows.

Identifying High-Preference Objects and Activities: Making Communication Functional

Normally developing young children first develop communicative behaviors around the objects, activities, and persons they are most interested in and most desire. The young child's call for "Mama" and requests for "bottle" and "cookie" reflect the importance of high-preference events as motivators for the development of communication skills. The desires and preferences of the typical child are numerous and easily identified. However, identification of **high-preference items and events** for a child with severe disabilities can often present a major challenge. Nevertheless, designing an environment that creates a need to communicate is not possible without first determining those things about which the child is most likely to communicate.

Thus it is necessary to devote time to the systematic identification of high-preference items and activities for each child. To do this, parents should be interviewed carefully with regard to their child's schedule and activities at home. This effort may uncover clues related to possible preferences. In addition, the teacher should devote time to systematically identifying high-preference items and activities. Food is often assumed to be a high-preference item, and indeed it often is for many children. But the teacher should be aware that there are many other objects, persons, and activities that may motivate the child who has severe disabilities to communicate. Table 9–2 lists some examples of these. The teacher must also be aware that, as with all individuals, children's preferences change over time and vary with circumstances. The search for high-preference, motivating objects, activities, and persons to use in teaching functional communication skills must be a continuous process in any program that includes children with severe and multiple disabilities.

High-preference objects and activities can be identified and verified using a number of strategies. These same strategies can simultaneously be used to determine what voluntary behaviors a child with severe disabilities may be capable of using in a communicative way. The teacher must realize that the mere presentation of a potential high-preference object or activity will not necessarily evoke a positive response

Table 9–2 Examples of High-Preference Activities for Preschoolers with Severe Disabilities

Motor/Kinesthetic	Manipulables
Bouncing	Playing with cause/
Riding in a wagon	effect toys
Swinging in a blanket	Operating knobs
Auditory/Visual	*Setting Changes*
Singing	Going outside
Listening to records	Reduction of discomfort
Listening to radio	*Tactile/Physical*
Watching television	*Interaction*
Operating a music box	Stroking
Playing with percussion	Hugging
toys	Tickling
Listening to tapes of	Brushing hair
familiar voices	Blowing air
Watching flashing	Playing with water
lights	Playing with sand
Watching mobiles	
Playing with a Jack-	
in-the-box	

from the child. In many cases, interrupting or withholding an item or activity will be much more effective in determining the child's desire for it.

Identifying Behaviors That Can Be Used Communicatively

Whether to activate some augmentative communicative system or simply to find a communicative signal, the teacher must identify which behaviors the child can voluntarily control. Even in a child with the most severe disabilities, there is probably some behavior that can be voluntarily controlled, such as directed eye gaze, head turning, reaching, or vocalization. *Any* behavior can be used as a communicative signal.

Three simple procedures can be utilized to determine which behaviors the child may be able to use by creating "communicative context" (Constable, 1983).

1. *Presentation.* An obvious technique is simply to present an object to the child and observe the child's behavior. However, the presentation of an object or event, even if desired by the child, may not evoke any voluntary response.

2. *Interruption.* Another way is to present an object or activity believed to be high preference, and then to stop the activity or remove the object. For example, a child who enjoys being pushed in a wagon is pushed for a moment or two; then the wagon is stopped. The child's behavior is carefully observed, in the event that she attempts to reinstate the activity. She may vocalize, move her head, change her body position or tension, attempt to reach out, and so on. The teacher can systematically observe which behaviors are under some degree of voluntary control.

3. *Withholding an anticipated event.* If there are regularities and predictable events in the child's daily life that he or she enjoys, and if the child is able to anticipate those events given certain cues, then withholding such an event may also be a way of evoking the same kinds of behaviors as those described in item 2. For example, assuming that snack time is a high-preference activity for that child, seating everyone else at the snack table and "forgetting" the child would provide another opportunity to observe potential communicative behaviors.

Such procedures are sometimes referred to as "violations of routine events" (Raver, 1987, p. 229).

Another strategy that can be used to create motivation for spontaneous communication is called "violation of object functions" (Raver, 1987, p. 230). An example would be using a shoe to brush your hair or putting a cup on a doll's foot. Such ridiculous situations can often serve as powerful elicitors of communicative behavior. Raver has also suggested that such a strategy may promote the development of humor.

Teaching Communicative Behaviors: Creating Opportunity and Need for Communication

The simple strategies just described are powerful basic tools for both assessment and beginning intervention. Presentation, interruption, and withholding of an anticipated event provide simple, systematic procedures to be used not only to identify and verify high-preference items and activities, but also to begin teaching rudimentary communicative behaviors. When a child's preferences have been inventoried and at least one voluntarily controlled behavior identified, the environment can be systematically manipulated and designed to provide opportunities for the child to use the important communicative function of *requesting*. Teachers should keep in mind that, in most children, the use of language or gestures to request some desired object, event, or person emerges long before the use of language or gesture for the purpose of labeling or sharing information.

Because space prohibits giving detailed descriptions of many specific intervention techniques and procedures, the reader is encouraged to refer to other resources related to this area (e.g., Rogers-Warren & Warren, 1984; Klein et al., 1981). Here is a brief description of several techniques:

1. Even a child with the most severe impairments can be taught to request more of a desired object or activity, as described previously. It is not necessary that the child make this request again and again in each setting. For example, the child need not request every single bite of a favorite food. Rather, four or five opportunities could be provided several times per day. There is some evidence that this *distributed practice* is more effective than intensive training blocks of what are called *massed trials.*

2. Another important technique is to provide *choices.* In as many situations as possible

throughout the child's day, give opportunities to make choices. Choices of activities, food items, toys, and people can easily be incorporated into classroom programming.

3. Pausing and waiting for the child is another important technique. All too often teachers bombard children with questions, commands, prompts, and cues without giving them ample time to respond. Many children with severe disabilities require a longer time than others to process incoming information and organize a response. An expectant look on the teacher's face accompanied by silence can often be an amazingly powerful provocateur for communicative behavior.

4. Finally, it is extremely important to make sure that the child with severe disabilities, particularly the nonambulatory child, is provided with some means of getting adults' attention. The child who is at the mercy of others in the environment to initiate communication cannot really engage in functional dialogue. Many children will be unable to produce an audible vocal signal as an attention-getting device, and they will need to be provided with some other type of auditory signal such as a bell or buzzer. The ability to *initiate* communication is critical to the success of any communication instruction program.

Use of Structured Instructional Steps in Shaping Specific Communicative Behaviors

Some authors have described sequential instructional steps to teach specific communicative behaviors and shape them toward more conventional or symbolic behaviors. Wulz, Hall, and Klein (1983) have described a sequence of cues and prompts that may be used with any of the situations and strategies just described. These steps, similar to those described by Rogers-Warren and Warren (1984), are as follows:

1. *Create the need or opportunity to communicate.* Using the kinds of strategies just described, manipulate environmental variables to encourage attempts to communicate. Keep in mind that indentifying the objects, persons, and events that interest and motivate the infant or young child is a critical prerequisite to this step.

2. *Pause and wait.* Give the child an opportunity to initiate communication. For children with severe disabilities, this may take 10 to 20 seconds (as opposed to individuals without disabilities, who can organize and produce a behavior in 1 or 2 seconds). There are two ways in which the pause and wait strategy can be used. Early in teaching it is often helpful to look expectantly at the child. Many teachers will find it very difficult to look at a child without saying anything for 10 to 20 seconds. However, in some children the use of this procedure will produce previously unseen communicative behaviors. (See Halle, Alpert, & Anderson, 1984.)

When the child has acquired the behavior, (e.g., directed eye gaze, pointing at an object, pointing at a picture, etc.), move or turn away from him or her as though busy doing something else. This procedure can be used to encourage the use of an attention-getting behavior such as vocalizing, ringing a bell, or activating a buzzer. Initially, this procedure may require two teachers, since one teacher will be unable to observe the child's unsuccessful attempts or to provide prompts and cues.

3. *Provide a natural cue.* Initially in teaching a communicative behavior, cues and prompts can be provided when the child is unable to respond or responds inappropriately during the pause period. It is important, however, that cues and prompts *not* be provided every time, lest the child learn to simply wait through a series of prompts to eventually obtain the desired communicative consequence. Occasionally, the opportunity to communicate should simply be terminated until a later time during the day. This is particularly appropriate for optional situations such as choosing a toy or a dessert.

When a child does not respond during the pause period, employ a *natural* cue. A natural verbal cue is one that is likely to occur in the natural environment, for example, someone asking, "What do you want?" or "Can I help you?" or "Tell me what you want to do now." If the child still does not respond, prompts may be used.

4. *Use prompts and assistance.* A wide variety of prompts may be used to assist the child in communicative behavior. Many of these are borrowed from behavioral teaching strategies. Perhaps the most commonly used prompting strategy is the use of **modeling.** Modeling can be an effective prompt for children who have a generalized imitation strategy, and who will attempt to imitate the teacher's model. Unfortunately, many children with severe disabilities do not have a generalized ability to imitate a model. For these children, physical prompting and shaping may be necessary.

Physical prompting involves physically guiding the child through the behavior. For example, if you are teaching a child to reach or point toward a desired object, a physical prompt moves the child's hand and arm through the motion of pointing. Using traditional behavioral methods, gradually fade this physical prompt until the child can produce the behavior on his or her own.

To use physical prompting effectively, the "topography" of the behavior must be accessible. Unfortunately, vocalization—one very important communicative modality—does not lend itself to physical prompting. Control of vocalization is completely internal. A teacher cannot force or assist a child in vocalizing other than by use of an imitative prompt. Thus, it is important to realize that when physical prompts must be used, communicative behaviors other than vocal behaviors must be selected.

5. *Comply with the communicative request.* Within this sequence of steps, provide the desired object or activity at any point at which the child produces an acceptable approximation to the

targeted communicative behavior. That is, the child should get the toy, be moved to a favorite location, have the record player turned on, or whatever is desired.

In addition, the teacher should always accompany his or her compliance with the appropriate verbal input. The input strategies described earlier are very important here, particularly the use of repetition and re-cast sentences. As the teacher provides the desired item, he or she should say, "Oh, you want the *doll*, huh! Here's your *doll*. What a cute doll." If the child then appears to be paying attention to the doll, the teacher can semantically expand these utterances by adding a bit more information. For example, "Oh, the *doll* has a new *dress*. Look."

The use of these steps increases the likelihood that several necessary conditions will be met for effective communication instruction. First, the child is *actively processing* incoming information and recognizes the *need* to communicate. Next, the child *initiates*, or is helped to initiate the communicative interaction and is not forced to wait for a specific stimulus to which to respond. Third, the child's communicative behavior has an *impact* upon the environment, because the teacher complies with the request. The child thus experiences *effectance*, perhaps the most powerful reinforcer of all. Finally, the opportunity is created for the teacher to use verbal input to map language onto the child's experience.

Use of the strategies described earlier with regard to natural environments and daily routines is referred to as a milieu approach. According to Warren and Kaiser (1988) the term *milieu approach* represents an array of approaches characterized by (a) distributed practice rather than massed trials, (b) following the child's lead, (c) teaching within conversational contexts, and (d) teaching within natural communicative situations.

While the strategies and approaches described in this section have been most frequently reported in association with children with more severe disabilities, they can be equally effective with children who have mild to moderate disabilities.

Some specific strategies for encouraging young children to talk are given in Exhibit 9–4.

Facilitating Social Communication Between Children with Special Needs and Nondisabled Peers

In order for successful social interaction to take place between a child and his or her peers, two components must be in place. First, the child must be able to *respond* to a peer's initiation in an appropriate way. Second, the child must be able to *initiate* interaction in a way that is likely to obtain a positive response (Odom & Strain, 1986).

Some children with disabilities may lack these skills, and they may need direct instruction related to these important social communication behaviors. Odom and colleagues (1988) have developed a curriculum that is specifically designed to socially integrate preschoolers with special needs and their typical peers. An important section of the curriculum describes procedures for direct instruction of social skills.

Familiar procedures of modeling, prompting, and reinforcement are used. The teacher first talks to a small group of children about appropriate play behaviors, demonstrating "good" and "bad" social behaviors and familiarizing the children with classroom behaviors related to playing together cooperatively. Both children with disabilities and those without can then be taught to initiate (e.g., "Jose, can you ask Mary to help you with the tower?") and respond (e.g., "Jose, Mark is sharing his cookie with you. Tell him 'Thank you.' ") appropriately in actual play situations. Initially, children's appropriate social behavior may need to be reinforced externally by the teacher (e.g., saying, "Jose, that was very nice of you to say 'Thank you' to Mark," giving the child a sticker for being polite, etc.). However, these contrived reinforcers should be discontinued as quickly as possible. The goal ul-

EXHIBIT 9—4

Promoting Specific Reasons for Talking

Using Language for Finding Out About Things
Curiosity is expected of young children. Hide something in a box or bag, and then encourage them to guess what is inside. Ask, "Is it round?" "Can it swim?" Offer the opportunity to teach how asking questions leads to answers. If "why?" and "how?" questions are not being used by some children, games and experiments with different toys can initiate them.

Using Language for Getting Involved
As young children often play beside each other rather than with each other, sand, water, and block play encourage "getting involved." As they learn to express intentions, tell others what to do (directing), and report what has happened, they learn new language quickly. Combining verbal children and those who speak less well provides a natural language learning opportunity.

Using Language for Getting Help
Wanting something that is put away or too high to reach provides the need to ask for it. Zippers that stick and shoes that come untied create the need to ask for help. This becomes the opportunity for you to act as if gestures, helpless looks, and even tears do not communicate. However, any attempt to say something should be rewarded. (Of course, for the child who usually does not even use nonverbal attempts at communication, *any* effort should be rewarded.)

Modeling "Tie my shoe" and accepting the child's "Tie oo" at first encourages greater effort. Gradually, if you are absolutely certain that the child is able to say it better, you may appear to be puzzled until the child makes a better attempt.

Using Language to Get Attention or Approval
Some children poke and pull at adults as well as other children. Children need something to take the place of a habit that needs to be changed. The words "Look" or "Watch me" can be used in many situations. Each time they attempt to get attention in other ways, avoid responding immediately. Turning away, ask "Do you want me to look?" (pause) "Tell me (pause) *look*." Then, refuse to watch unless they say *something*.

Using Language to Tell Something
If there are interested listeners, most children want to tell them something. Asking parents to write a note about interesting events at home is helpful. Then, you can initiate the discussion. Sometimes a picture or a favorite toy from home serves this purpose. Formal show and tell is not usually effective with young children, but informally telling the teacher or a friend is popular.

Using Language to Defend Themselves
"Stop that" needs to be learned early. "Move, please" is better than shoving. Teaching children how to defend themselves verbally instead of with a push or shove results in more pleasant homes and classrooms. They will need examples, models, and teachers' insistence that saying something is better than just shoving.

Using Language to Learn New Things
Children who know how to express themselves in one way are quicker to learn other ways to talk about things. When a wide range of new experiences are provided throughout the year, new ideas and new words are learned. The vocabulary of taking care of the science corner is not the same as the vocabulary for music time. For children with very limited speech and language, initially focus on things they need to know and say in the classroom and at home, and then expand the horizon.

Using Any Utterance to Begin Communication
For some children with severe disabilities, any attempt to make a sound will need to be rewarded with instant encouragement. If it appears that a child wants something and is attempting to ask for it, give it to the child immediately. If you know what word was attempted, model (say) it to confirm that you understood. First efforts should never be the occasion for an attempt to improve the child's production. That comes *much* later. But letting the child know that he or she has in fact communicated is rewarding in itself.

timately is for the natural consequence of the child's appropriate interaction and communication to be its own reward.

WORKING WITH CHILDREN WITH HEARING IMPAIRMENTS

A preschool teacher whose class includes a child with hearing impairment will find that a teacher trained in this specialty is vital to assist in planning the child's overall education. Although special training and experience are necessary in teaching children with severe hearing impairments, the following list identifies several techniques that teachers can use to help communicate with children who have hearing losses:

1. Be sure that windows or other light sources are not behind you or shining into the eyes of the children. If children are to read lips or to interpret signs, the light must be on the speaker or signer, not in the children's eyes.

2. Speak at your normal rate and loudness, unless you typically speak too quickly to be appropriate for any language teaching/ learning situation. Your rate of speaking and/or signing should consider the age and skills of the children. But don't speak so slowly that the normal rhythm and stress of speech are lost.

3. Stand or sit still! It is very difficult to focus eyes on a moving target.

4. Don't ask, "Do you understand?" (Children will say "yes" regardless.) Rather, discover how much has been understood by asking questions or giving directions that show how well you have been understood by what the children do.

5. Do not exaggerate lip movements or pause after each word. This makes lipreading more difficult. It also establishes poor expectations. Rather, speak carefully. Articulate

clearly. Your lips must move to allow for speechreading.

6. If the children appear to be puzzled, add clues in the following order:

   a. Repeat what you said.
   b. If more clues are needed, say the same thing in a slightly different way.
   c. If confusion continues, combine telling and showing if at all possible.
   d. If you are attempting to teach something, make a mental note to use this particular communication frequently until it is usually understood. Be explicit.

7. Remember to follow the suggestions made for nurturing the learning of speech and language among children who do not have hearing impairments.

Children Who Are Deaf

There is much controversy about the way in which children with profound hearing losses should be taught to communicate. It is not appropriate here to consider the debate about oral versus manual communication versus total communication. Within each of these communication styles there are complex divisions, subdivisions, methods, and variations on methods. The annotated bibliography at the end of this chapter includes a number of suggested additional readings for those who wish to pursue this study.

Although manual communication has many advantages, the person limited to its use may not experience the same opportunities he or she would have if spoken communication were the modus operandi. The suggestion that signing or fingerspelling expedites language learning in the young child has been debated for more than 200 years. For purposes of working with a young child with a hearing impairment in a preschool setting, the decision about signing or speaking must be made by the parents. The teacher should accept their decision and work with them and the trained teacher of the child with hearing impairments.

Children with Intermittent Hearing Losses

Often young children have hearing losses that come and go. Fluid in the middle ear, wax in the ear canal, and frequent colds, no matter how mild, may result in a hearing loss that comes and remains awhile. Usually physicians are unaware of this condition unless parents report it to them. And parents are unaware because the child is not complaining. However, they often report that "Johnny has been so stubborn this week. He doesn't come and do what I tell him unless I yell at him." Or they may say, "Sandy has been so grumpy all week. She won't listen. She just pretends not to hear me."

All Hearing Losses Are Serious

In addition, there is growing evidence that children with losses of 10 to 15 decibels, which are not even considered a loss by many examiners, show academic retardation, limited vocabulary, less well-developed language skills than their peers, and attention deficits. Typical hearing screening tests check the child's ability to hear the frequencies at 20 to 25 decibels. An alert child may have a mild loss and yet respond at this level. Downs (1977) expressed the belief that that mild fluctuating hearing loss in the region of 15 to 26 decibels can cause delays in both language and educational achievement. Bess and McConnell (1981) and Naremore (1979) stressed that much more should be known about mild hearing losses before their negative effects are considered "mild." Naremore (1979) stated, "The consequences of hearing loss in these early years can be striking. Roughly 60% of the children who come through our clinic with language problems, many labeled 'learning disabled,' have

some degree of hearing loss, and most of these have histories of chronic otitis media." These observations indicate that screening tests are missing many children who do indeed have problems hearing.

WORKING WITH CHILDREN WITH VISUAL DISABILITIES

Much has been learned in the past decade regarding the development of communication skills in children with severe visual impairments (see, for example, Andersen, Dunlea, & Kekelis, 1984). Considerable attention is being given to facilitating communicative interactions between young children who are blind and their caregivers (Dote-Kwan, 1991).

It is important that early intervention professionals work collaboratively with specialists in visual disabilities to ensure that optimal adaptations are made. It is wise to involve orientation and mobility specialists as well as those who specialize in teaching children with visual disabilities. The following suggestions may be helpful in facilitating communication skills in children with visual impairments:

1. Utilize the strategies already described in this text.

2. During vocalizations, touch the child to let him or her know you are there listening. Converse or interact with the child verbally, just as you would with any other youngster of the same language development level.

3. Play interaction games, for example, rhythm games and hand-clapping activities, that allow the child to feel the motion of an adult's hands as well as his or her own.

4. Talk about what you are doing and what the child is doing as it happens. Label actions as well as things.

5. Be certain the child uses vision to the maxi-

mum extent possible, and then combine looking with touching and talking.

6. Be certain that children with visual impairments see and feel all parts of an object and understand the relationship of parts to the whole.

7. Spatial relations are difficult to demonstrate. Place the child in various positions and encourage touching and manipulating. Sometimes use toys to demonstrate concepts such as on-off, up-down, and in-out.

8. Use language and the auditory modality to facilitate children's beginning understanding of directionality and distance, e.g., "I'm across the room, far away." "Now I'm coming closer!"

9. Avoid "bombarding" the child with too much talk. Pause frequently and avoid talking too rapidly.

10. Teach the child to localize sounds and recognize their source, direction, and distance.

Chapter 4 also includes a list of high-risk signals of possible visual impairments. Such a checklist should be readily available and studied frequently.

WORKING WITH THE CHILD WHO HAS AUTISM

In establishing communication intervention goals and strategies for children with autism, professionals first must consider the possible need to manage problems of tactile defensiveness and auditory sensitivity. Assistance should be sought from occupational or physical therapists in designing strategies to reduce and manage tactile sensitivity. In addition, staff members should work with parents to identify and understand the child's aversions and sensitivities to certain sounds.

The primary intervention goal related to communication interaction will be helping children develop the important early social interaction skills that are crucial to the later development of language skills. Especially important are turn taking, social initiation, and the development of instrumental and regulatory functions of communication, that is, using gestures and vocalizations to express wants and needs and to influence the behaviors of others. (See Prizant & Wetherby, 1988.)

The use of traditional modeling approaches to language instruction that rely on elicited imitation may be problematic, since children with autism often develop so-called "echolalic" speech (i.e., the immediate or delayed exact repetition or "parroting" of another person's speech). While they may respond easily when the teacher models a cue such as "say 'cookie,'" generalizing the response to functional and meaningful spontaneous use of the word *cookie* is often extremely difficult. Techniques that may be more helpful include a combination of modeling and environmental manipulation techniques such as those presented earlier in the discussion of strategies for children with severe disabilities. (For a discussion of the uses of echolalia by children with autism see Prizant, 1983.)

WORKING WITH THE CHILD WHO HAS LANGUAGE DIFFERENCES

The English spoken by the majority of people in the United States is usually called Standard American English. Realistically, there is little question that people who speak standard English have advantages in school and in the job market. Awareness of this has led many who speak a dialect to want their children to learn both the dialect and standard English. The same concern applies to families for whom English is a second language. As will be described in Chapter 10, in the discussion of literacy, there are also important differences in how families *use* language.

Because demographics in the United States are changing so dramatically, it is imperative that professionals working with young children be prepared to respect and celebrate diversity, while at the same time preparing children to succeed in the mainstream.

Dialectal Variations

Through the years, delineating which dialect speakers have speech and language disabilities and which are merely "different" has become a recognized necessity (Mattes & Omark, 1984). Teachers are being encouraged to consult with speech-language pathologists to separate language deficiencies from language differences before initiating a program of language development. In turn, the speech-language pathologist is expected to be aware of the limitations of culturally biased tests currently used in determining whether or not a child has a language deficiency.

In 1979, a federal judge in Michigan's Eastern District Court ruled that the Ann Arbor School District must develop a plan for teaching standard English to dialect speakers while respecting differences in dialect (Bountress, 1980). This decision was in response to African-American parents' contention that their children were experiencing academic difficulties as a result of teacher insensitivity to the students' dialects. "The best recommendation appears to be that the teacher should respect the black child's dialect just as she respects the Mexican or Puerto Rican child's Spanish, yet while doing this, also make it possible for him (or her) to learn standard English" (Hendrick, 1980, p. 239).

There is growing acceptance of various social dialects, and attempts are being made to assist children in the development of both their native dialect and standard English (Taylor, 1986). Adler (1979) has been an avid proponent of **bidialectalism,** which is an approach to the teaching of standard English while maintaining the native dialect. According to him, "the espoused goal of such programs is to increase language skills *in general*—to teach children to use standard English in appropriate contexts while respecting and maintaining the native dialect" (p. 125). The intent is to teach children to be competent in any social situation by being able to use whatever form of language is appropriate to the participants and the setting.

English as a Second Language

The same degree of respect is necessary for children who are learning English as a second language. In addition to learning the vocabulary, grammar, and syntax of the new language, these children must discover acceptable social behaviors in the new culture. Learning two sets of social-language interactions as well as two sets of grammar can result in confusion and discomfort, unless the transitions are developed tenderly.

More and more programs expect either the teacher or an assistant to be bilingual. When this is not possible, teachers should study the basic social differences and hold conferences with parents and others who can explain the cultural expectations. For example, one difference often noticed is the degree to which speakers of different languages expect or avoid eye contact. Teachers who do not understand social differences may accuse the Indian or Puerto Rican child of not paying attention when he or she is avoiding eye contact in an effort to show respect to adults. This is only one of many pragmatic functions of language that influence a child's desire and ability to learn.

Learning a New Language

Richard-Amato (1988) has emphasized the notion that second language learning must be an *interactive* process. It should be clear that the strategies already described in this chapter can make important contributions to children's learning a second language.

The most efficient way to help children learn a second language uses conversations about the things they are interested in throughout the day. Tough (1977) and Krashen and Terrell (1983) have contended that the same principles that undergird the fostering of language in all children should be the basis of teaching. They emphasized that the dialogue between teacher and child should be in situations that maintain the child's interest and attention. However, they pointed out some important differences in the way the teacher might use the same situation with a first and a second language learner. The teacher may help the child who is already using the language (first language learner) to think and speak beyond the immediate situation. Such a child can be reminded of similar past events or helped to anticipate future similar situations. On the other hand, a child who is learning a new language may need to focus only on present situational clues to understand what is being said. The teacher should use language that makes the meaning clear for each specific time and place.

As we have emphasized throughout this chapter, consideration of each child's unique needs is necessary, whether the child is a first or second language learner. Similarly, "other conditions that help the child learn his first language seem likely also to help a child learning a second language" (Tough, 1977, p. 84). The conditions referred to by Tough include giving the child ample opportunity to hear the same phrases again and again; encouraging practice of well-formed phrases at appropriate times; modeling and expanding; and concentrating on a small number of phrases at first, and then extending the variety and precision of what the child is able to say and understand. (For an excellent summary of current approaches to facilitating communication skills and literacy in the bilingual, bicultural child, see Bunce, 1990.)

COLLABORATIVE CONSULTATION WITH SPEECH AND LANGUAGE SPECIALISTS

Nurturing the development of communication skills in young children requires a team approach. Major contributions can be made by a qualified speech and language specialist who has received training in early intervention. The speech/language specialist can make a particularly important contribution in the area of assessment, using both formal and informal measures.

In the field of communication disorders, growing emphasis has been placed on the use of **collaborative consultation models** (Marvin, 1987). A collaborative consultation model differs from a more traditional "expert" model of consultation, in which the consultant assumes the role of a professional who provides information or services that the teacher does not possess. The collaborative model emphasizes the parity between the teacher and the speech/language specialist, who work as a team and contribute different skills and information to the processes of assessment, planning, and intervention, as well as solving specific problems. The following are examples of the types of collaboration that might occur in such a model.

As part of the assessment, the speech/language specialist would carefully interview the classroom teacher regarding the child's communicative behavior and observe the child in the classroom. Communication goals and objectives would be generated as a team, involving the parents, who meet with the teacher and the speech/language specialist together. Innovative teaching strategies and activities might be demonstrated in the classroom by the speech/language specialist, who would receive feedback and suggestions for adaptation from the classroom teacher.

Collaborative consultation models are also becoming increasingly important to the success of efforts to mainstream children in all types of educational environments. In such programs, collaboration must also take place between special educators and regular classroom teachers. For further information related to the growing area of collaborative consultation, the reader is referred to Heron and Harris (1987).

Although some professionals might argue that cognitive skill development precedes develop-ment of language skills, we chose to discuss the development of communication skills first. It is fitting, then, that the next chapter will concentrate on techniques for encouraging the development of cognitive skills and literacy. Understanding of the dynamics of language development will assist in obtaining insight into children's developing mental capacity as they journey toward becoming literate beings.

Summary

Communication, language, and speech are highly complex skills that develop as a function of many underlying processes including cognitive, fine motor-perceptual, and especially, social interaction. There is perhaps no area of development as crucial to the young child with special needs as communication skills.

The early education teacher, in close partnership with parents, can have a major impact on this area of development. For the child who has less severe disabilities, providing language input finely tuned to the child's perceptual and cognitive level, in a style that follows the child's lead and within a context of social interaction, can greatly facilitate communication skills development.

For the child who has more severe and multiple disabilities, in addition to these input strategies it will also be necessary to structure the environment in ways that encourage the child to communicate his or her basic wants and needs. Once this important motivational factor has been provided, specific communicative behaviors can be shaped. Often these are not conventional speech or language behaviors. Nevertheless, they can be used in functional ways, and can form the basis of augmentative communication systems.

With careful planning, the strategies that facilitate communication can be incorporated into all classroom activities. Furthermore, monitoring of children's communicative behaviors within a variety of *naturally occurring contexts* can provide the most meaningful assessment of progress.

Discussion Topics and Activities

1. Using a good quality tape recorder, record conversations of mothers and young children. Look for mothers who have more than one preschool-age child. Record the verbal interactions with each child, alone. How are they similar? How do the conversations differ?

2. Analyze the children's responses to mother's speaking pattern. Consider length, grammar, and syntax, using tapes made for Activity 1.

3. Record your own conversations with children 1 year, 2, 2 1/2, 3, and 4 years of age. Attempt to interact intuitively with these children. Then analyze what you have done in response to the feedback from the children.

4. Bring the tapes to class. Listen to them and critique the appropriateness of the adult's utterances with the children. Consider vocabulary, length of sentences, speed, pauses, interest to the children, and the effect on the children's vocalizations.

5. Record a 15-minute conversation with one 4 year

old and an adult as they make cookies or do something similar. Play the tape for the class. What *new* concepts were introduced?

6. Record the conversations of several 4 year olds as they play together. Analyze the speech and language used from the frame of reference of each of the subskills of language.

7. Write dialogues to demonstrate appropriate conversations with children from ages 2 through 5.

8. Select a child who has severe and multiple disabilities. Conduct interviews with the child's teacher and parents to try to identify three high-preference activities or objects. Systematically present each to the child and observe his or her behavior. Also, observe the child's behavior as you take the object away or as you interrupt an enjoyable activity. What behavior can you identify that could be used by the child as a communicative system?

Annotated Bibliography

Adler, S. (1979). *Poverty children and their language: Implications for teaching and treating.* New York: Grune & Stratton.

This textbook is designed to provide a strategy for working with children whose language processes are different from those who speak standard English. A bidialectal or bicultural approach to be used along with conventional "enrichment" programs is described in detail. Of particular interest is the linguistic description of social dialects found in the appendix.

Baumgart, D., Johnsom, J., & Helmstetter, E. (1990) *Augmentative and alternative communication systems for persons with moderate and severe disabilities.* Baltimore: Paul H. Brookes.

This is a straightforward, easy-to-understand text dealing with designing augmentative communication systems. The text includes separate sections for preschool-aged, elementary-school-aged, and adolescent students. Particularly helpful are case studies included in several chapters that demonstrate successful planning and implementing of augmentative communication systems.

Bernstein, D. K., & Tiegerman, E. (1985). *Language and communication disorders in children.* Columbus, OH: Charles E. Merrill.

This text provides an excellent review of the social and cognitive bases of language development, as well as the stages of language acquisition in children. It focuses on types of communication disorders in children, including those associated with mental retardation, autism, hearing impairment, and learning disabilities. Two chapters on intervention are also included.

Bess, F. H., & McConnell, F. E. (1981). *Audiology, education, and the hearing impaired child.* St. Louis: C. V. Mosby.

This book fulfills a need to combine critical information about individuals with hearing impairments with descriptions and discussions that will be useful to parents and teachers as well as physicians and audiologists. The authors identify effective procedures to implement services for children with hearing impairments. Throughout the book, vignettes provide clear and concise examples of the topics discussed. The organization of this textbook includes a description of normal hearing, the major causes of hearing impairment, and factors that relate to classifying hearing loss. The first part of the book includes a useful description of the interrelationship between the development of audition and the establishment of language skills. Later chapters emphasize ways of meeting the challenges of identification, management of varied services, and appropriate educational planning.

Butler, K. G. (Ed.). (1984). Communication management with mentally retarded children. *Topics in Language Disorders, 5*(1), 1–95.

This entire journal issue is devoted to communication intervention with children who have mental retardation. Three articles are particularly important for early interventionists. Kahn describes strategies for encouraging communication skills through teaching of early cognitive skills and provides specific suggestions for teaching object permanence and means-end behaviors. An article by Spinelli and Terrell emphasizes the importance of language instruction in natural contexts rather than in highly structured formats. Reike and Lewis describe how early communicative functions provide the basis for language intervention.

Cazden, C. B. (Ed.). (1981). *Language in early childhood education.* Washington, DC: National Association for the Education of Young Children.

This is an excellent reference for anyone who works and plays with young children. The various authors cover nearly every facet of language development and suggest numerous ways to promote oral communication. A section about day-care programs includes useful ideas for working with children whose language style or dialect is different.

Chen, D., Friedman, C. T., & Calvello, G. (1989). *Parents and visually impaired infants.* Louisville, KY: American Printing House for the Blind.

These are excellent materials for parents of infants who are blind. They offer strategies for helping parents observe their own infants and set parent-infant interaction priorities. Included are an excellent section on strategies for assessment of infants' communication, sections on hearing and vision screening, and assessment of the infant's interaction with objects. The program is unique in that it allows parents to take primary responsibility for goal setting and observation.

Cheng, L-R. L. (1987). *Assessing Asian language performance: Guidelines for evaluating limited-English-proficient students.* Rockville, MD: Aspen Systems.

This text, while not aimed specifically at very young children, not only contains valuable information related to the characteristics of Asian languages and dialects, but also includes discussion of the culture and history of the various Asian groups. Strategies and materials for nonbiased informal assessment of communication skills and language background are provided. Appendixes include a variety of helpful resources such as questionnaires, language elicitation pictures, checklists, and so on. This book should be useful for both speech/language pathologists and teachers.

Conant, S., Budoff, M., & Hecht, B. (1983). *Teaching language disabled children: A communication games intervention.* Cambridge, MA: Brookline.

While this book is aimed primarily at school-aged children with disabilities, the excellent strategies describing use of games as language learning contexts are easily adaptable for use with preschool children, both with and without disabilities. The book provides an excellent rationale for the games approach, and it is theoretically sound. The specific games are described in detail and are categorized as hiding games, communicative lotto and bingo games, matching games, identical arrangement games, action-directive games, and guessing games. The book describes not only how to play the games, but also how to set up the game situation and the materials needed for each game.

Fraiberg, S. (1977). *Insights from the blind: Comparative studies of blind and sighted infants.* New York: Basic Books.

Careful research, thoroughly described, forms the basis for a very useful book. The effects of visual deficits on the child's organization of early experience and on ego development are reported. Specific suggestions for promoting the mental and physical development of infants and young children are explicit. The section on language acquisition is a must for anyone working with children who have visual impairments.

Hendrick, J. (1986). *Total learning: Curriculum for the young child.* Columbus, OH: Charles E. Merrill.

Chapter 14 concentrates on developing verbal competence. In addition to offering many useful ideas, the book provides specific lesson plans. Particularly helpful is the section on African-American English and bilingualism. Resources, including books, music, and poetry, are abundantly presented.

Klein, M. D., Briggs, M. H., & Huffman, P. (1988). *Facilitating caregiver-infant communication: A model program to facilitate positive communicative interactions between caregivers and their high-risk infants.* Los Angeles: Division of Special Education, California State University, Los Angeles.

This publication provides specific guidelines, techniques, and materials for carrying out a program designed to facilitate positive communicative interaction between caregivers and their high-risk infants. The program is particularly helpful in working with high-risk families. It includes specific strategies for observing the infant in the neonatal intensive care unit, establishing center-based groups, developing a home visit program, and using videotape feedback as an intervention technique. The program also includes simplified handouts for parents related to caring for and playing with their infants, the Observation of Communicative Interaction (OCI), a parent booklet entitled *Help Your Baby Learn to Talk,* and two videotapes: "Talking to your Baby" and "Talking to Toddlers."

Lansky, B. (1986). *Baby Talk.* Deephaven, MN: Meadowbrook.

This is an excellent description of communication skill development in infants from birth to age 3. Intended for parents, it also provides suggestions for simple activities parents can use to encourage communication at each age.

MacDonald, J. D. (1989). *Becoming partners with children: From play to conversation.* San Antonio, TX: Special Press.

The work of this author during the past 20 years has

provided the basis for numerous language intervention programs developed in the past decade. In this text, he presents a detailed description of a communication assessment and instructional program that applies many of the strategies found in typical parent-child interaction. The program includes the following levels of instruction for parents and their children: play, turn taking, communicating, using language, and becoming conversational partners. This text provides an excellent rationale and literature review as well as detailed descriptions of each level of instruction. It is soundly based on social interaction theory and developmental pragmatics.

Manolson, A. (1985). *It takes two to talk.* Toronto: Hanen Early Language Resource Center.

Built on the work of Dr. James MacDonald, this is a program for parents of young children with disabilities. It is designed as a step-by-step instructional program to teach parents to encourage their own children's language development through the careful use of certain caregiver-child interactions such as turn taking, following the child's lead, and prompting for better turns.

Mattes, L. J., & Omark, D. R. (1984). *Speech and language assessment for the bilingual handicapped.* San Diego, CA: College-Hill.

This text addresses many issues related to assessment of limited-English-speaking students, including language difference versus disorder, the importance of assessment teams, use of interpreters, assessment of cultural and environmental influences, and limitations of and alternatives to standardized texts. A chapter is also included on educational planning. Appendixes are included that critique available assessment instruments, provide guidelines for interviewing parents, and describe characteristics of minority languages spoken in the United States.

McCormick, L., & Schiefelbusch, R. L. (1990). *Early language intervention* (2nd ed.). Columbus, OH: Charles E. Merrill.

This is an excellent text on early language intervention aimed at teachers and beginning communication specialists. It provides an easily understood review of language acquisition as well as descriptions of different types of communication disorders. Included are excellent chapters on bilingualism, literacy, augmentative communication, and strategies for working with children who have severe disabilities.

Odom, S. L., Bender, M. K., Stein, M. L., Doran, L. P., Houden, P. M., McInnes, M., Gilbert, M., Deklyen, M., Speltz, M. L., & Jenkins, J. R. (1988). *The*

integrated preschool curriculum. Seattle: University of Washington Press.

This is a curriculum specifically designed to facilitate the social interaction of preschool children with and without disabilities. It contains detailed strategies and activities that can be used to encourage social interaction and play. It is appropriate for use with children with all types of disabilities.

Owens, R. E., Jr. (1988). *Language development* (2nd ed.). Columbus, OH: Charles E. Merrill.

A comprehensive text describing communication and language development, this book contains a good chapter reviewing research in the area of "motherese" and mother-child communicative interaction. Children's functional language use and pragmatic skills are considered in all stages of language development. Also included is a chapter on dialects and bilingualism.

Prizant, B. M., & Wetherby, A. M. (1988). Providing services to children with autism (ages 0 to 2 years) and their families. *Topics in Language Disorders, 9*(1), 1–23.

This is an excellent article describing the characteristics of and communication intervention strategies for young children with autism. The article discusses the potential of early intervention as prevention. Practical and meaningful suggestions related to assessment are provided. Intervention approaches described in the article focus on facilitating functional communication skills and on the important social relationship between caregiver and child.

Reichle, J., York, J., & Sigafoos, J. (1991). *Implementing augmentative and alternative communication: Strategies for learners with severe disabilities.* Baltimore: Paul H. Brookes.

This text describes strategies for planning and implementing augmentative communication systems for individuals with severe disabilities. It includes a section on decision making related to planning an augmentative system and conducting ecological inventories of functional communication behaviors and needs. Five chapters are dedicated to strategies for facilitating initiating behavior, particularly requesting and rejecting. Also included are sections related to communicative exchanges and generalization. The last section of the book deals in some detail with specific instructional strategies for students with particular kinds of needs, such as those who have very severe physical disabilities.

Richard-Amato, P. A. (1988). *Making it happen: Inter-*

action in the second language classroom. New York: Longman.

This is an important text in the area of teaching English as a second language. It takes a strong position supporting an interactional, context-based approach to language learning. The text is unique in that it provides an excellent review and critique of existing theories regarding second language learning as well as detailed suggestions for practical classroom applications. While it does not focus exclusively on the preschool-aged child, it is an excellent resource for anyone wishing a current review of this field.

Schiefelbusch, R. L. (Ed.). (1980). *Nonspeech language and communication: Analysis and intervention.* Baltimore: University Park Press.

This edited text provides an overview of issues and techniques related to augmentative communication. Sections are included describing strategies useful for children with severe physical disabilities as well as those with severe mental retardation. Both manual communication systems and communication board systems are described. The text also includes sections on assessment.

Schulman, B. (Ed.). (1987). Making the collaborative consultation model work: The speech-language pathologist as consultant and teacher in mainstream education. *Journal of Childhood Communication Disorders. 11*(1).

This entire journal issue is devoted to articles describing various ways in which the speech/language pathologist can work as a consultant in the classroom. Several articles address the role of the speech/language pathologist in working with the teacher to facilitate literacy.

Schuyler, V., & Rushmer, N. (1987). *Parent-infant habilitation: A comprehensive approach to working with hearing-impaired infants and toddlers and their families.* Portland, OR: IHR Publications.

This is a state-of-the art and comprehensive text dealing with the development of infants and toddlers with hearing impairments. It describes an approach to early intervention that emphasizes the role of parent-infant interaction and relationship as the key to development and learning. Use of both speech and manual sign language are included, and the stress is on a highly individualized approach to each infant and family. The text includes chapters dealing with parental reactions to the infant with a hearing impairment and the importance of the parent-professional partnership. It provides strategies for helping parents develop observation skills and for using naturalistic interactions as opportunities for language teaching. The relationship between language and cognition is also discussed.

Snow, C., & Butler, K. (Eds.). (1984, Sept.). Language development and disorders in the social context. *Topics in Language Disorders, 4.*

This entire issue is devoted to the consideration of various applications of research on mother-infant interaction and language development within the social context. It considers remediation of communication disorders in young children who have visual impairments, hearing impairments, and language delays.

Tough, J. (1977). *Talking and learning: A guide to fostering communication skills in nursery and infant schools.* London: School Council Publications.

Through dialogues, discussions, and examples, this book emphasizes fostering communication skills for all young children. In addition, it includes chapters on children with special needs and an excellent section on children learning English as a second language. Curriculum planning and classroom practice are explained. Based on practices in British nursery and infant schools, the information is directly useful to anyone working with young children. Useful chapters on the nurturing of reading, writing, and mathematics readiness skills are included.

Warren, S. F., & Rogers-Warren, A. K. (1985). *Teaching functional language.* Baltimore: University Park Press.

This edited text first presents a functional communication perspective and then provides several chapters describing various intervention strategies used with children with severe disabilities who have autism, language delays, and are difficult to teach. Two chapters also discuss naturalistic and conversational teaching strategies. The final section of the book considers methods for facilitating and measuring generalization of language behaviors.

References

Adler, S. (1979). *Poverty children and their language: Implications for teaching and treating.* New York: Grune & Stratton.

American Speech-Language-Hearing Association Ad Hoc Committee on Language/Learning Disabilities. (1980). Language and learning disabilities ad hoc develops position statement. *American Speech-Language-Hearing Association, 22*, 628–636.

Andersen, E. G., Dunlea, A., & Kekelis, L. S. (1984). Blind children's language: Resolving some differences. *Journal of Child Language, 11*, 645–664.

Bates, E. (1976). Pragmatics and sociolinguists in child language. In D. Morehead and A. Morehead (Eds.), *Language deficiency in children: Selected readings.* Baltimore: University Park Press.

Baumgart, D., Johnson, J., & Helmstetter, E. (1990). *Augmentative and alternative communication systems for persons with moderate and severe disabilities.* Baltimore: Paul H. Brookes.

Bess, F. H., & McConnell, F. E. (1981). *Audiology, education and the hearing impaired child.* St. Louis: C. V. Mosby.

Bloom, L., and Lahey, M. (1978). *Language development and language disorders.* New York: Wiley.

Bountress, N. G. (1980). The Ann Arbor decision: Implications for the speech-language pathologist. *American Speech-Language-Hearing Association, 22*, 543–545.

Brown, R. (1973). *A first language: The early stages.* Cambridge, MA: Harvard University Press.

Bunce, B. (1990). Bilingual/bicultural children and education. In L. McCormick & R. L. Schiefelbusch (Eds.), *Early language intervention* (2nd ed.) (pp. 473–500). Columbus; OH: Charles E. Merrill.

Bzoch, L. R., & League, R. (1970). *The Bzoch-League Receptive-Expressive Emergent Language Scale.* Gainesville, FL: Tree of Life.

Clarke-Stewart, K. A. (1973). Interactions between mothers and their young children: Characteristics and consequences. *Monographs of the Society for Research in Child Development, 38*(6 & 7, Serial No. 153).

Coates, D. L., & Lewis, M. (1984). Early mother-infant interaction and infant cognitive status as predictors of school performance and cognitive behavior in six-year-olds. *Child Development, 55*, 1219–1230.

Constable, C. (1983). Creating communicative context. In H. Winitz (Ed.), *Treating language disorders: For Clinicians by clinicians.* Baltimore: University Park Press.

Cross, T. (1984). Habilitating the language-impaired child: Ideas from studies of parent-child interaction. *Topics in Language Disorders, 4*, 1–14.

Dale, P. (1976). *Language development: Structure and function.* New York: Holt, Rinehart & Winston.

Davis, J. (1977). *Our forgotten children: Hard of hearing pupils in the schools.* Minneapolis: University of Minnesota Press.

Dote-Kwan, J. (1991). *The relationship between early experiences and the development of young children with visual impairments.* Unpublished doctoral dissertation, University of California, Los Angeles.

Downs, M. P. (1977). The expanding imperatives of early identification. In F. H. Bess (Ed.), *Childhood deafness: Causation, assessment and management.* New York: Grune & Stratton.

Fraiberg, S. (1977). *Insights from the blind.* New York: Basic Books.

Halle, J. W., Alpert, C. & Anderson, S. (1984). Natural environment language assessment and intervention with severely impaired preschoolers. *Topics in Early Childhood Special Education, 4*, 36–56.

Halliday, M. A. K. (1975). Learning how to mean. In E. Lenneberg & E. Lenneberg (Eds.), *Foundations of language development* (Vol. I). New York: Academic Press.

Hendrick, J. (1980). *The whole child: New trends in early education.* St. Louis: C. V. Mosby.

Heron, T. E., & Harris, K. C. (1987). *The educational consultant: Helping professionals, parents, and mainstreamed students.* Austin, TX: Pro-Ed.

Hopper, R., & Naremore, R. J. (1978). *Children's speech: A practical introduction to communication development.* New York: Harper & Row.

Kleffner, F. R. (1973). *Language disorders in children.* Indianapolis: Bobbs-Merrill.

Klein, M. D. (1985, April). *Teaching severely handicapped preschoolers to communicate nonverbal requests.* Paper presented to the annual conference of The Council for Exceptional Children, Anaheim, CA.

Klein, M. D., & Briggs, M. H. (1987). Facilitating mother-infant communicative interaction in mothers of high-risk infants. *Journal of Childhood Communication Disorders, 10*(2), 95–106.

Klein, M. D., Briggs, M. H., & Huffman, P. (1988). *Facilitating caregiver-infant communication.* Los Angeles: California State University, Los Angeles, Division of Special Education.

Klein, M. D., Wulz, S., Hall, M., Fox, T., Waldo, L., Carpenter, S., Lathan, D., & Marshall, A. (1981). *Comprehensive communication curriculum guide.* Lawrence, KS: Early Childhood Institute Document Reprint Service.

Krashen, S. E., & Terrell, T. (1983). *The natural approach: Language acquisition in the classroom.* Oxford: Pergamon.

Lahey, M. (1988). *Language disorders and language development.* Columbus, OH: Macmillan.

Lubert, N. (1981). Auditory perceptual impairments in children with specific language disorders: A review of the literature. *Journal of Speech and Hearing Disorders, 46*, 3–9.

MacDonald, J. D. (1989). *Becoming partners with children: From play to conversation*. San Antonio, TX: Special Press.

Mahoney, G., Finger, I., & Powell, A. (1985). Relationship of maternal behavioral style to the development of organically impaired mentally retarded infants. *American Journal of Mental Deficiency, 90,* 296–302.

Manolson, A. (1985). *It takes two to talk.* Toronto: Hanen Early Language Resource Center.

Mattes, L. J., & Omark, D. R. (1984). *Speech and language assessment for the bilingual handicapped.* San Diego, CA: College-Hill.

Marvin, C. A. (1987). Consultation services: Changing roles for SLPs. *Journal of Childhood Communication Disorders, 11*(1), 1–16.

Naremore, R. J. (1979). Influences of hearing impairment on early language development. In D. G. Hanson & R. F. Ulvestad (Eds.), Otitis media and child development: Speech, language and education. *The Annals of Otology, Rhinology and Laryngology, 88,* 54–63.

Nelson, K. (1974). Concept, word and sentence: Interrelations in acquisition and development. *Psychological Review, 81,* 267–285.

Nelson, K. E., Bonvillian, J. D., Denninger, M. S., Kaplan, B. J., & Baker, N. D. (1984). Maternal input adjustments and non-adjustments as related to children's linguistic advances and to language acquisition theories. In A. Pellegrini & T. Yawkey (Eds.), *The development of oral and written language in social contexts.* (Vol. XIII). *Advances in Discourse Processes.* New Jersey: Ablex.

Ochs, E. (Ed.). (1979). *Developmental pragmatics.* New York: Academic Press.

Odom, S. L., Bender, M. K., Stein, M. L., Doran L. P., Houden, P. M., McInnes, M., Gilbert, M. M., Deklyen, M., Speltz, M. L., & Jenkins, J. R. (1988). *The integrated preschool curriculum.* Seattle: University of Washington Press.

Odom, S. L., & Strain, P. S. (1986). Using teacher antecedents and peer initiations to increase reciprocal social interaction of autistic children. A comparative treatment study. *Journal of Applied Behavior Analysis, 19,* 59–71.

Owens, R. E., Jr. (1988). *Language development* (2nd ed.). Columbus, OH: Charles E. Merrill.

Prizant, B. (1983). Language acquisition and communicative behavior in autism: Toward an understanding of the "whole" of it. *Journal of Speech and Hearing Disorders, 48,* 286–296.

Prizant, B. M., & Wetherby, A. M. (1988). Providing services to children with autism (ages 0–2 yrs.) and their families. *Topics in Language Disorders, 9,* 1–23.

Prutting, C. (1979). Process: The action of moving forward progressively from one point to another on the way to completion. *Journal of Speech and Hearing Disorders, 44,* 3–23.

Raver, S. A. (1987). Practical procedures for increasing spontaneous language in language delayed preschoolers. *Journal of the Division for Early Childhood, 11,* 226–232.

Reichle, J., York, J. & Sigafoos, J. (1991). *Implementing augmentative and alternative communication: Strategies for learners with severe disabilities.* Baltimore: Paul H. Brookes.

Reike, J. A., & Lewis, J. (1984). Preschool intervention strategies: The communication game. *Topics in Language Disorders, 5*(1), 41–57.

Richard-Amato, P. A. (1988). *Making it happen: Interaction in the second language classroom.* White Plains, NY: Longman.

Rogers-Warren, A. K., & Warren, S. (1984). The social basis of language and communication in severely handicapped preschoolers. *Topics in Early Childhood Special Education, 4,* 57–72.

Rutter, M. (1986). Infantile autism: Assessment, differential diagnosis and treatment. In D. Shaffer, A. Erhardt, & L. Greenhill (Eds.), *A clinical guide to child psychiatry* (pp. 314–332). New York: Free Press.

Schiefelbusch, R. L. (Ed.). (1980). *Non-speech language and communication: Analysis and intervention.* Baltimore: University Park Press.

Snow, C., Midkiff-Borunda, S., Small, A., & Proctor, A. (1984). Therapy as social interaction: Analyzing the contexts for language remediation. *Topics in Language Disorders. 4,* 72–85.

Taylor, O. L. (Ed.). (1986). *Treatment of communication disorders in culturally and linguistically diverse populations.* Boston: College-Hill.

Tough, J. (1977). *Talking and learning: A guide to fostering communication skills in nursery and infant schools.* London: School Council Publications.

Warren, S. F., & Kaiser, A. P. (1988). *Research in early language intervention.* In S. L. Odom & M. B. Karnes (Eds.), *Early intervention for infants and children with handicaps.* Baltimore: Paul H. Brookes.

Weiss, R. S. (1981). INREAL intervention for language handicapped and bilingual children. *Journal of the Division for Early Childhood, 4,* 40–51.

Wilkinson, L. C. (1979). Theoretical bases of language and communication development in preschool children. In L. Taft & M. Lewis (Eds.), *Developmental disabilities in the preschool child*. Symposium presented by Rutgers Medical School, Educational Testing Service, and Johnson and Johnson Baby Products, Chicago.

Wulz, S. V., Hall, M. K., & Klein, M. D. (1983). An instructional communication strategy for severely handicapped children. *Journal of Speech and Hearing Disorders*, 48, 2–10.

Yarrow, L. J., Rubenstein, J. L., & Pedersen G. (1975). *Infant and environment: Early cognitive and motivational development*. New York: Wiley.

Chapter 10

Encouraging the Development of Cognitive Skills and Literacy

Key Points

▶ Understanding the development of thinking and reasoning, from the infant's first reflexes to the 5-year-old's problem-solving strategies, is critical to the effectiveness of the early childhood special educator.

▶ The three cognitive processes of attention, perception, and memory work together to enable the child's development of cognitive skills.

▶ The most significant single contribution to the understanding of children's cognitive development has been the theory of Jean Piaget.

▶ The early childhood special education professional must master techniques that facilitate such critical cognitive skills as intentionality, means-end discovery, trial-and-error exploration, object permanence, and imitation in infants and toddlers with special needs.

▶ Critical cognitive skills for the preschool child include symbolic representation (particularly pretend play), problem solving, cognitive subskills related to academic readiness, and expansion of referential language skills.

▶ Early childhood special education professionals must be able to utilize specific strategies for adapting learning environments for infants and young children who are cognitively different.

▶ Preschool programs should *not* emphasize the direct instruction of reading; rather, the preacademic focus should be on facilitating emergent literacy (i.e., an appreciation of and interest in the nature and purposes of writing and reading) within naturalistic daily activities.

▶ Children's early experiences with literacy and literate oral language styles such as narrative will greatly influence their later academic success.

▶ Facilitating children's successful transition to kindergarten requires a thorough understanding of expectations of the receiving classroom (particularly with regard to school language skills and social skills, careful planning for the transition, and collaboration with parents and the receiving teacher.

Key Topics

▶ The basic cognitive processes of attention, perception, and memory.

▶ The developmental theory of Piaget.

▶ Facilitating cognitive skills in infants and toddlers.

▶ Facilitating cognitive skills in preschool children.

▶ Facilitating cognitive and information-processing subskills related to academic achievement.

▶ The development of literacy.

▶ The relationship between oral language and literacy.

▶ Cultural differences in early language and literacy experiences.

▶ Strategies for facilitating emergent literacy.

▶ Transition to kindergarten.

Kim: "When we talk on the phone how does our words get to the telephone pole wires and to our house?"

Mom: "Well, that is hard to explain. Our voice travels by what we call sound waves."

Kim: "Oh, it must be like on the ocean. Our talk rides like a surfer."

As this interaction between mother and child demonstrates, cognitive development of young children is evidenced in their attempts to use what they know to solve new problems. New information is taken in and related to what was learned earlier. New knowledge and old knowledge are adapted to solve problems more efficiently. Or, as Kodera and Garwood (1979) explained, "Acts of cognition are thought to represent an individual's attempts to make sense of experience" (p. 153).

WHAT IS COGNITION?

Cognition is defined in the dictionary as "the act of knowing." Piaget (1954) referred to the development of cognition as the child's construction of reality. These simple definitions belie the great complexity of human cognitive processes. How the young child develops the ability to mentally represent and understand the world around him or her is by no means simple. Understanding the evolution of thinking and reasoning from the infant's first reflexes to the development of complex problem-solving strategies is critically important to our effectiveness as educators of young children. Many children with special needs have cognitive impairments that interfere with the development of the conceptual and reasoning skills necessary for mastery of academic skills. The early childhood special education professional can recognize these challenges and provide the support necessary for the achievement of important cognitive skills.

BASIC COGNITIVE PROCESSES

Three basic processes related to information processing are important to the development of cognition: attention, perception, and memory.

Infants must be able to pay attention to the world around them; they must also be able to receive, recognize, and discriminate stimuli. Eventually, they must be able to organize and interpret those stimuli and store them for later retrieval.

Attention

Attention is the focusing of the individual's perceptual processes upon a specific aspect of the environment. Learning cannot take place unless the individual is able to focus attention on the important elements of a task or situation. Attention is basic to many cognitive tasks and is a prerequisite for effective intervention. Attention in the form of concentration requires that the developing child learn to master two somewhat contradictory skills: (1) the ability to focus on those aspects of his or her environment that are relevant and have the greatest functional value to the task at hand and (2) the ability to ignore the multitude of irrelevant stimuli around him or her. *Selective attention* begins almost at birth, and the kinds of stimuli and the way babies look at them change in predictable ways. When a child attempts to attend and respond to too many irrelevant stimuli, the child is considered to be distractible.

Much recognition is given to what are sometimes called *attention deficit disorders* (American Psychiatric Association, 1980). Such disorders are very common and may be present when extreme inattention, impulsivity, and hyperactivity characterize a child's behavior. However, an attention deficit disorder may also be present when a child is withdrawn and unable to respond (Swanson & Reinert, 1984). This hypoactivity may be related to the child's tendency to become fixated on stimuli that are no longer relevant, or to be preoccupied with some inner need that in extreme cases may be suggestive of autism.

Teachers of young children must consider these behavioral descriptions cautiously. The concept of normal development must be ever present as the model of reference. Young children are, by nature, very active, inattentive, and impulsive. Yet the inability to focus selectively on relevant stimuli is among the developmental learning disabilities discussed by Kirk and Chalfant (1984). These learning disability specialists offer a number of useful suggestions for children who are clearly more inattentive than what is considered typical. Some of these are described later in the chapter.

Perception

Perception is the "process of becoming aware of and interpreting objects and events that stimu-

late the sense organs" (Silverman, 1975, p. 366). Perceptual abilities are dependent on the sensory systems of touch, taste, proprioception, smell, hearing, and vision. These systems actually develop in utero, thus enabling the newborn infant to begin the processes of perceptual development at birth. Each sensory system (tactile, visual, auditory, olfactory, and gustatory) is associated with a different mode of perception. For perception to occur, some information must be stored in the nervous system. Sensations are then interpreted in the context of stored information.

The interpretations or perceptions of individuals may differ depending on what is stored and on the strength of the perception modality, such as visual and auditory, which develop unevenly. Thus, one child may perceive more accurately through the visual channel while another may gather information more efficiently through the auditory channel. As stated earlier, young children may find it easiest to interpret physical cues, followed by visual and finally verbal cues. Unfortunately, most teachers tend to teach predominantly through talking and expecting responses to verbal directions. Teachers who attempt to match teaching input to the developmental needs of their children will contribute greatly to the progress of children with perceptual disabilities, who usually have difficulty interpreting and obtaining accurate meaning from their environment.

Discrimination Abilities. "Discrimination is the process by which one perceives the likenesses and differences among related stimuli" (Kirk & Chalfant, 1984, p. 112). Children who learn to visually discriminate characteristics such as shape, size, distance, and color while in preschool will be prepared for the subtle discriminations between printed letters, numbers, and words necessary to success in kindergarten and first grade. Likewise, children who learn to perceive the differences and similarities in pitch, loudness, rhythm, melody, rate, and duration of sound will likely be successful in learning to read by phonetic methods. Most prereading activities, by design, assist children in developing discrimination skills. For example, when a child is asked to find a picture illustrating a spoken word, he or she is discriminating among details in the picture while also practicing sound discernment, association, and memory skills. A majority of the activities discussed in this book, found in early childhood methods books and highlighted in Appendix F, give children practice in developing perceptual efficiency and accuracy.

Memory

The third basic cognitive process is **memory.** Memory is the process by which information that is received through attention and perception is stored in the central nervous system. Atkinson and Shiffrin (1968) suggested the following model of memory:

1. Incoming sensation is perceived briefly (about 1 second).

2. If attended to, it will be placed in short-term memory, which can store information for 10 to 15 seconds.

3. Depending on a number of factors, some information will be placed in long-term memory where it can be stored indefinitely.

Very young children have few memory strategies and may need repeated experiences of the same event or information before it can be stored in long-term memory. As children get older they develop so-called "rehearsal" strategies (Atkinson & Shiffrin, 1968). Information in short-term memory is purposely repeated or practiced, which then assists in long-term storage.

The ability to learn is highly associated with memory. The most common kinds of memory include long-term, short-term, sequential, auditory, visual, rote, recognition, and recall. When assessing a child's difficulties in memory, several

important questions must be considered. Are environmental conditions such as noise, excitement, emotional upset, or interpersonal problems interfering with retention? Is the content to be remembered meaningful, concrete, and short enough to be developmentally appropriate? What kind of response is required? Is it immediate or delayed? Does it require recognition or recall, a motor or vocal response?

For very young children, little in the way of rote memory should be expected. The developmental sequence prepared by Montessori (see Chapter 6) and this chapter's guidelines for facilitating concept development help in the preparation of memory-strengthening lessons.

As Thurman and Widerstrom (1990) pointed out, the three processes of attention, perception, and memory are interdependent. Individuals cannot pay attention if they are not able to perceive incoming stimuli; they cannot store information that they do not perceive; they cannot further develop perceptual skills of recognition and interpretation if they do not have information stored in memory, and so on.

DEVELOPMENT OF COGNITIVE SKILLS

The Developmental Theory of Piaget

The most prominent cognitive theorist to influence the fields of child development and early education was Jean Piaget, a Swiss scientist interested in epistemology, or the study of human knowing. He was neither a learning theorist nor a maturationist. Rather, he combined these two views and believed that human cognitive development is a product of the interaction between the environment and the infant's biological capacities.

Two important concepts developed by Piaget's theory are the **schema** and the process of **adaptation.** The schema can be defined as a psychological structure that provides the individual with a template for action in similar circumstances (Piaget & Inhelder, 1969). Schemata, which are initially infant reflexes, gradually become differentiated, combined, organized, and under the child's control. They also eventually become internalized, that is, they become mental processes. This occurs through adaptation, a twofold process comprised of **assimilation** and **accommodation.**

During the assimilation part of adaptation, experiences are taken in by infants or young children through the application of existing schemata. For example, the infant applies his "sucking schema" to his thumb. However, not all experiences can be assimilated to existing schemata. For example, if the infant tries to apply his existing sucking schema to the corner of his blanket, he will not be successful. Thus, the infant must change, or "accommodate" his existing schema in order to adapt to this new situation. Thus, through the complementary processes of first using existing schemata and then modifying them to adjust to new experiences, the infant adapts to the world around him. In Piaget's view, this is the process of learning.

In addition to his important theory of cognitive development, Piaget also contributed an important research methodology that included naturalistic observations of infants and young children combined with presentation of situations in which to test his hypotheses. Information related to the sensorimotor and preoperational periods was based on his observations of his own children. His descriptions of the development of mental operations was based on his observations of school children.

Piaget described several stages in the development of cognition. Each stage of development builds upon the previous one. This is referred to as the "spiral of knowing" (Gallagher & Reid, 1981, p. 35). As children mature and interact with their environment, they construct and reconstruct reality through the processes of assimilation and adaptation, in accordance with their cognitive capabilities at each stage.

The Sensorimotor Stage. Piaget reportedly believed that the most creative period of an individual's life is between birth and 18 months of age (Anisfeld, 1984). The **sensorimotor stage** is divided into six substages. The first five of these stages lay the foundation for the beginning of representational thought—the mental representation of objects and events. The sixth stage, with its full achievement of object permanence, marks the transition from sensorimotor "knowing" through patterns of action to mental knowledge and symbolic ability.

Sensorimotor substage 1: use of reflexes (0–1 month). During the first month of life, the infant interacts with his world primarily through reflexes. As the nipple touches his lips, he sucks; he "roots" or turns automatically to the side of the cheek that is touched; sudden loud sounds or loss of support elicit a startle, or "Moro" reaction, and so on.

Sensorimotor substage 2: primary circular reactions (1–4 months). During the second substage, the infant's reflexive behavior leads accidentally to new experiences. For example, the infant discovers his thumb and assimilates this experience to his existing nipple-sucking schema. He accommodates to the new object (his thumb) and thus *learns* to suck his thumb. Such primary circular reactions are always centered on the infant's own body.

Sensorimotor substage 3: secondary circular reactions (5–8 months). During this substage the infant becomes increasingly interactive with events and objects in the external environment, outside his own body. Secondary circular reactions are those behaviors in which the infant engages in order to repeat an interesting event. For example, the infant accidentally hits a mobile hanging above his crib, which provides the visual experience of seeing the mobile move. The infant then tries to hit the mobile again to recreate this experience.

Sensorimotor substage 4: intentional adaptations (8–12 months). During this substage, the infant begins to utilize and coordinate his secondary circular reactions in order to achieve a specific goal. This represents a major milestone in the development of cognition: the development of **intentionality.** Now the infant can look at the mobile and utilize the "looking-and-swiping" schema acquired through his secondary reactions of substage 3 and *intentionally* activate the mobile. He now has the goal in mind *before* he engages in the behavior. He has discovered the means-end relationship.

Also during this stage, the baby demonstrates the earliest ability to search for hidden objects. However, he will search in the place in which he last discovered the object. For example, an interesting object is covered with a blanket, and the infant is assisted in rediscovering the object. In full view of the infant, the object is then hidden under a box. Despite observing this, the infant will again search for the object under the blanket. He does not engage in a systematic search based on where he sees the object disappear.

Sensorimotor substage 5: discovery of new means (12–18 months). In substage 5, rather than simply repeating a behavior in order to recreate an interesting event, the infant searches for novelty through tertiary circular reactions. He systematically changes his behavior and observes the effect. This is sometimes called **trial-and-error exploration.** The following is a familiar example of this type of behavior. An 8-month-old infant, sitting in a highchair, drops, then tosses his food onto the floor, first from one side of the tray, then from the other. While parents may interpret this as willful naughtiness, it is actually evidence of the growing cognitive abilities of the infant. It enables him to learn about cause and effect. Through such trial-and-error behavior, the infant discovers new means, or strategies, for achieving goals. For example, the child learns that he can crawl *around* a barrier to reach

something on the other side if he is unable to crawl *over* it.

Continued development of the concept of object permanence can also be seen during this substage. Now the infant will more systematically search for the object at the place where he sees it disappear. However, if the infant does not see the object being moved, he will not search for it.

Sensorimotor substage 6: rudiments of representational thought (18–24 months). Substage 6 marks the end of the sensorimotor period. By the end of this substage, the toddler has mastered the full concept of **object permanence.** He clearly understands that objects exist whether or not he can see them. He will search systematically for an object even when he has not seen it disappear. This important cognitive capability now frees the infant from his dependence on sensorimotor actions for discovery and understanding. It frees him from the "here and now" world and enables him to develop memory skills.

The 18- to 24-month-old toddler now has the capacity for **mental representation**—the ability to think. This mental representation ability is particularly evidenced in two types of behavior observed toward the end of substage 6: deferred imitation and pretend play. The ability to imitate something observed at an earlier time reflects the toddler's mental representation and memory for that event; deferred imitation also provides a mechanism for learning.

The ability to act out previously experienced events through pretend play (e.g., putting the doll to bed or pretending to serve breadfast) also is clear evidence of the ability to think about and remember such events. Like deferred imitation, pretend play provides important contexts in which to learn.

The Preoperational Stage. The second major stage of cognitive development in Piaget's theory is called the **preoperational stage.** This term simply reflects the fact that while preschool children are clearly more capable than sensorimotor infants, they are not yet able to perform the mental operations required of logical thinking and reasoning. Piaget was more intrigued with what the preoperational child could *not* do than with the important achievements of this period. In Piaget's later writing, this stage was divided into two periods: the preconceptual and the intuitive.

The preconceptual period (2–4 years). A major accomplishment during this period is the development of **symbolic ability.** The child learns that one thing can represent another thing. This symbolic ability is evidenced both in her pretend play and in increasing language development. The child can now use a block as a truck, or she can *imagine* that a cloud is a bear floating in the sky. Language becomes freed from the immediate context. Words as symbols can now be used to describe and share experiences that occurred in the past.

The intuitive period (4–7 years). During this period, the child makes an important transition into the period of concrete operations. She learns to categorize objects on the basis of certain features. Toward the end of this period, she begins to be able to **decenter.** That is, she no longer is only able to focus on one feature of an object at a time, but will begin to demonstrate the ability to consider more than one characteristic simultaneously, as well as some reversibility in her thinking.

The classic conservation experiment demonstrates this. Throughout most of the period from 2 to 7 years of age, the child is unable to respond successfully to the following experiment: Two identical beakers are filled with equal amounts of water. The water from one of the beakers is poured into a narrower, taller beaker. When asked whether the tall beaker now contains more or the same amount of water as the short, wide beaker, the child invariably responds "More," despite repeated demonstrations of pouring wa-

ter back and forth. According to Piaget, the preoperational child lacks the ability to attend to both height and width and centers only on height (tallness). She also lacks reversibility of thought and cannot realize that the width of the shorter beaker would compensate for its lack of height and vice versa.

The lack of ability to decenter is also observed in the preschooler's egocentrism. She has difficulty taking another person's perspective and views the world in relationship to herself. She does not understand that someone else may not be able to see what she can see, and her language is often insufficiently referential.

During the **intuitive period,** the preschool child experiences a gradual shift in the ability to perform mental operations. Also during this period the child's thinking becomes more elaborated, as is particularly demonstrated in dramatic play episodes. The preschooler can orchestrate long and complex interpersonal sequences that provide opportunities for practicing social routines and solving problems. Another characteristic of children during this period is their inability to think logically. Children's thought is sometimes referred to as *transductive.* While truly logical thought is either inductive (proceeding from the specific to the general) or deductive (from the general to the specific), young children's thought often proceeds from the particular to the particular, with no logical connection. For example, a 4 year old trips as she comes in the door and announces, "I just ate a whole candy bar so I can't walk too good!" Although the child cannot think logically at this stage, she clearly recognizes that events have causes and perceives the need for explanations.

The Stages of Concrete Operations and Formal Operations. Once the child moves into the stage of **concrete operations** (which extends from the ages of 7 to 11 years), he has achieved the mental flexibility necessary to perform the operations required in reading and mathematics and the ability to think logically. This significantly enhances his problem-solving capability. The child in this stage of cognitive development is able to decenter and to consider many dimensions of an object or a problem simultaneously.

The final stage of **formal operations** is achieved somewhere between 11 and 15 years of age. The young adolescent is now capable of performing the mental operations mastered during the concrete operations stage on more abstract material. He can now think about complex moral dilemmas that often have more than one "right" answer, depending on the situation. He can also think scientifically, using processes of the scientific method such as hypothesis testing.

The developmental theories of Piaget and his associates are complex, and their development spanned a time period from the early 1930s to the 1970s. These works have been addressed here in the briefest manner. The student of early childhood special education is encouraged to examine such texts as Gallagher and Reid (1981), Piaget and Inhelder (1969), Ginsburg and Opper (1969), Piaget (1977), and Bell-Gredler (1986).

Alternate Views of Cognitive Development

While the theory of Piaget continues to provide the cornerstone of our understanding of the intellectual development of young children, several theorists have offered alternative or supplementary views of development, particularly with regard to the preoperational period of development (Cole & Cole, 1989). For example, **Neo-Piagetian theorists** (Case, 1985) have suggested that Piaget's stages of development are domain specific—that subareas of development such as drawing, language, and mathematics may have their own developmental schedules. An **information-processing approach** developed by Klahr and Wallace (1976) used a model of development that is analogous to the processes of a computer: input, sensation, short-term memory, strategies for long-term memory stor-

age, and retrieval and association. A current **biological approach** suggests that the human brain consists of a vast collection of "mental modules" (Fodor, 1983), which are specifically tuned to respond and make sense of certain kinds of environmental input. Such modules might include number concepts, language, causality, and so on. Finally, the **cultural context view** has much in common with Piaget's views, but it places greater emphasis on the role of social context, and particularly on children's participation in "social scripts" that are created by adults (Nelson, 1986).

DEMONSTRATION OF COGNITIVE SKILLS THROUGH THE DEVELOPMENTAL STAGES OF CHILDREN'S PLAY

One of the easiest ways to observe the development of children's cognitive skills is through the observation of their play. There are many ways of categorizing play, some of which were mentioned in Chapters 6 and 7 in this text. Westby (1980) described strategies for assessing cognitive and language abilities through observation of children's play. She described 10 stages of play ranging from the intentional manipulations of the 9 to 12 month old to the complex symbolic play orchestrations of the 5 year old. Fewell (1984) developed a scale for the assessment of the stages of play. Linder (1990) described strategies for assessment of all domains of development through observation of play.

The stages of cognitive development can be readily observed using the following taxonomy: simple manipulation, exploratory play, functional play, and symbolic play.

Simple Manipulation. Simple manipulative behaviors such as mouthing, poking, waving, banging, or throwing are examples of secondary circular reactions that are typical of sensorimotor substage 3. As the infant reaches substage 4,

around 8 to 10 months, these sensorimotor schemata become combined and under her intentional control. She now clearly *intends* to bang or throw. For example, the infant notices a ball and purposely moves toward it, picks it up, and throws it.

Exploratory Play. As the infant moves into the fifth substage of sensorimotor development, she engages in trial-and-error exploration. She notices some blocks and a can. She picks up the can and bangs it on the floor, then puts it on her head. She picks up the block and puts it in the can. She dumps the block out of the can. She is also capable of inventing new means to achieve her goals. For example, she can't reach a ball that has rolled under the sofa, so she takes her mother by the hand to solicit her help.

Functional Play. By the end of the fifth substage, the child can demonstrate appropriate object use. She pushes the truck, pounds with the hammer, dials the telephone, combs her hair, and so on. She may also demonstrate autosymbolic play, pretending to engage in some familiar activity such as sleeping or eating.

Symbolic Play. By the end of the sixth substage, the child has achieved the ability to represent objects and events internally and to engage in symbolic behavior. Symbolic play develops through several stages from the end of the sensorimotor period through the preoperational period.

Initially, the child engages in pretend play activities in which she is the actor, engaged in some highly familiar activity such as going to sleep. During the next stage, she focuses the pretend play activity on some inanimate recipient of her actions such as a doll or teddy bear. Now she pretends to put the doll to bed or pour coffee for the bear. Next, the doll will be the agent, not just the recipient, of the child's actions (i.e., the doll washes herself, or puts the teddy to bed).

After 24 months, there is a gradual increase in the preoperational child's ability to use non-realistic objects to represent real objects, as symbolic skills improve. Eventually, after 36 months, the child uses imaginary objects or people. There is also an increase in the length and complexity of pretend play sequences in the preoperational period. After 24 months, the child can play the roles of different individuals and reenact events from the past. After 36 months, the child begins to plan pretend scenarios in advance and organize who will do what. Play sequences begin to look more like a story, with a beginning, a plot that evolves (e.g., a problem to be solved or a special occasion), and an ending. By this stage, language becomes an essential element of play.

By age 4 or 5 the child begins to act out possible *future* scenarios (i.e., "what would happen if . . . ?" situations) and can act out multiple roles (e.g., play the mother who is also a doctor).

CAUSES OF COGNITIVE IMPAIRMENT

Many children with special needs demonstrate impairments in cognition. Generalized impairment of intellectual functioning is called **mental retardation.** There are many causes of mental retardation, including (a) genetic disorders such as Down syndrome; (b) prenatal in utero influences such as maternal illness (e.g., rubella) or exposure to toxic substances (e.g., drugs and alcohol); (c) perinatal complications (e.g., anoxia); and (d) postnatal causes (e.g., poisoning or head injury).

Space does not permit discussion of the many causes of cognitive impairment in this text. However, two sources of cognitive impairment in infants and young children are of increasing concern in the 1990s: fetal alcohol syndrome (FAS) and lead poisoning.

Jones and Smith (1975) discovered that a high proportion of infants born to women who are chronically alcoholic manifest many of the following symptoms:

- Low birthweight (less than 2,500 grams).
- Continuing growth deficiencies in weight and height.
- Mild to moderate mental retardation; frequent microcephaly.
- Characteristic facial features, including narrow eye slits, drooping eyelids, sunken nasal bridge (causing the face to appear flat), and thin lips.
- Organ and limb malformations, including frequent heart defects.
- Hyperactivity and poor attention span.

According to Vaughan, McKay, Behrman, and Nelson (1979), 10% of all children between the ages of 1 and 6 years have absorbed excessive amounts of lead. Sources of lead include older paints and plaster, glazes on some cookware, and leaded gasoline. Repeated exposure to lead may eventually cause blindness, convulsions, spasticity, and brain damage. Children living in impoverished urban environments are most at risk for lead poisoning.

FACILITATING THE DEVELOPMENT OF COGNITIVE SKILLS IN INFANTS AND TODDLERS

Several cognitive milestones are particularly important targets for early intervention. Certain disabling conditions may begin to interfere with children's achievement of these important cognitive skills early in infancy. For example, a child who is blind may have particular difficulty with the achievement of object concepts and object permanence. A child with motor impairments may have difficulty discovering means-end strategies, and his or her opportunities to practice trial-and-error exploration will be limited.

The following section describes several key cognitive milestones during the period from birth to 3 years of age and provides suggestions for facilitating these cognitive skills. In addition, the reader is encouraged to review earlier chapters that have described generic strategies such as scaffolding (Chapter 6), communicative interactions (Chapters 6 and 9), and naturalistic milieu approaches to intervention (Chapter 9). These strategies are particularly effective in the development of cognitive skills. Many of the specific suggestions in this chapter reflect those approaches.

The reader is also again reminded that teaching must be activity-based. That is, intervention goals and objectives are integrated and incorporated into pleasurable, developmentally appropriate *play* activities. They are *not* isolated as bits of behavior to be learned.

Intentionality

As discussed earlier, somewhere around 8 to 10 months of age typically developing infants achieve the ability to do things intentionally. They no longer must discover things by chance in order to repeat them. They can now perform an action on purpose. Achievement of **intentionality** is a prerequisite to almost every other skill. The ability to deliberately act upon the environment is an important key to continued development.

Some children with severe disabilities may need assistance in the development of intentionality. For such a child, the importance of intentionality cannot be overemphasized. Learning that the individual can produce a behavior volitionally and that such behavior has an effect on the world around him or her is a major accomplishment. The following strategies are examples of ways to facilitate this important cognitive milestone.

1. *Increase motivation by use of high-interest objects and activities.* Begin by taking a careful inventory of high- and low-preference objects, people, and activities. It will be necessary to interview caregivers to obtain a good understanding of the child's likes and dislikes. Once these are identified they may be used to create the need or desire to act upon the environment in some way.

2. *Create the desire or need to perform intentional acts.* The following are examples of strategies:

    a. Place a high-preference object within the child's view but out of reach.

    b. Begin a pleasurable activity, then abruptly stop it. Wait for the child to do something in an attempt to continue the activity. For example, push the child in the swing, then stop the swing. Wait for some kind of signal from the child that he or she wants to continue, then resume the activity.

    c. Engage in an unpleasant activity such as washing the child's face, then discontinue the activity if the child indicates rejection (e.g., pushes your hand away).

    d. Interpret even unintentional cues such as head turning or arm waving as intentional; respond as though the child did it purposely. For example, if the child inadvertently moves his or her arm toward a toy, respond by handing the child the toy.

    e. Adapt favorite toys, tape players, television sets, and so on so that they can be activated by a switch requiring only minimal movement from the child.

3. *Allow ample time for the child to initiate a purposeful behavior.* Some children appear not to demonstrate intentional behavior simply because they have learned that there will not be enough time to organize a response. Adults frequently anticipate chil-

dren's needs or perform actions for them, interfering with their initiation of intentional acts.

Means-End Behavior

As infants learn to act intentionally on their environment, they discover that these actions have certain effects upon objects and people. As they become familiar with these causes and effects, they are able to engage in an action intentionally in order to bring about a desired end and, when necessary, to modify that action to create new means to achieve the desired end. For example, a child may use a stool to help her climb onto a counter so she can reach the cookies, or she may pull at mother's hand and take her to the counter to get the cookies.

These kinds of behaviors are important manifestations of the child's ability to cognitively associate certain events with their consequences. Children with disabilities often need assistance with both understanding these relationships and engaging in **means-end behaviors.** It may be necessary to structure the environment carefully in ways that clearly demonstrate cause and effect and consistently reinforce the child for attempts to achieve certain goals.

Simply constructed toys and devices that produce an interesting response to a specific type of manipulation can be effective. These include infant toys such as a "Busy Box," a "Jack-in-the-Box," and an easily activated musical toy.

Equally important is the contribution of a responsive social environment. Caregivers who respond quickly to an infant's signals of discomfort or to an older child's bids for attention will support the development of means-end behaviors.

Trial-and-Error Exploration

The ability to systematically explore objects and space is crucial to the development of the child's

ability to learn from experience and develop problem-solving skills. Systematic manipulation of objects and modification of the individual's own actions lead to self-directed learning and the discovery of new behaviors and solutions.

In attempting to assist children in learning these exploratory strategies, teachers must understand that they are teaching a *process* rather than a specific behavior. For example, a jar containing pieces of candy is offered to a child. The jar has a tightly fitted lid. To teach the child to take off the lid would simply require task analyzing this skill and teaching it step by step until the child had mastered unscrewing the lid. On the other hand, encouraging **trial-and-error exploration** requires a different approach. It is necessary for the teacher to use several of the generic strategies described in Chapter 6. The teacher must assist the child in initiating different attempts to open the jar and reinforce *persistence*, not just success. The teacher must be able to read the child's cues of boredom or frustration and know when to finally scaffold successful unscrewing of the lid. Other opportunities must be created later on in which to generalize this trial-and-error process.

The following example demonstrates a way of encouraging trial-and-error behavior as a problem-solving strategy.

Nathan is sitting at the snack table with several nondisabled peers. Each child is handed a fruit roll in a wrapper as a special treat. The children eagerly tear open their wrappers. Nathan has motor coordination difficulties and typically cannot manage such a task. He has become accustomed to seeking help in such situations, so he hands the package to his teacher. This time, the teacher does not immediately open the package. She hands it back to him and says, "I'm sorry Nathan, I can't help right now. I'll help in a few minutes." She signals to the aide to sit next to Nathan. Nathan fiddles briefly with the wrapper, then looks at the aide, who says, "Well, try it this way." She turns it around and hands it back to him. He tugs at one end of the wrapper unsuccessfully. The aide says, "Boy, that's hard to do, isn't it?" He pulls at the other end of the wrapper, again to no avail, then bangs it on the table. At this point the aide takes the package and makes a small tear in one corner. She hands it back and points to the torn corner. Nathan pulls at that corner and opens the wrapper. The teacher then approaches Nathan, saying, "Well, you got that unwrapped all by yourself, didn't you!" Hopefully this child has learned something about the value of trying different solutions and the importance of persistence.

Object Permanence

The achievement of the concept of **object permanence** is critical to the child's continued development of important mental processes including memory and mental representation. Throughout the first year of development, chil-

dren learn about the existence and properties of objects. As they continue through the sensorimotor period, they eventually discover, by the end of the second year, that objects and people continue to exist even when they are out of sight and their removal was not observed.

At this point, which marks the end of the sensorimotor period, children have the ability to represent objects and events internally. They can conjure mental pictures in their minds. They no longer must see an object to know it exists. This is obviously important for the development of memory skills.

There are many simple ways in which object permanence can be demonstrated for young children. Perhaps one of the first such activities introduced to infants is the game of peek-a-boo, a simple way to demonstrate that a person continues to exist even when the infant cannot see the person's face. Other ways to demonstrate object permanence include searching for something missing from its expected storage container, playing hide and seek, or hiding cookies in your pocket and asking children to guess what you have.

Deferred Imitation

The ability to recreate an action observed at a previous time reflects the development of important cognitive skills. It requires an understanding of object pemanence, the beginning development of memory skills, and the ability to mentally represent a sequence of events. **Deferred imitation** eventually plays an important role in the development of pretend play and language development.

The development of imitation skills, both immediate and deferred, may be encouraged by using the following sequence:

1. Begin by imitating the child's behavior, encouraging turn taking and then encouraging the child to continue the game. Children

who have no disabilities will happily see this as a sort of "Simon Says" game.

2. Next, introduce a variation of the behavior to see whether the child will attempt to follow suit.

3. Once the child can do this easily, you can be the initiator of the imitation game, rather than imitating the child's behavior first. (Over the years, many programs have been developed that teach imitation at this level, using modeling, physical prompts, and reinforcement techniques.)

4. When the child has acquired a generalized imitative response (i.e., the child will attempt to imitate novel behaviors in addition to those that have been trained) and has developed the concept of object permanence, it may be possible to teach *deferred* imitation. The length of time between presentation of a model and imitation of the model can be increased gradually. For example, at recess, children can pretend to "walk like a duck." Later, you can say, "Can you remember what we did at recess?" This requires the child to use both memory and imitation skills.

FACILITATING THE DEVELOPMENT OF COGNITIVE SKILLS IN PRESCHOOLERS

Symbolic Representation

As children enter the preoperational stage of cognitive development, two major achievements reflect emerging symbolic skills: (1) increasing use of language to represent objects and events that are not present in the immediate environment or that occurred in the past and (2) the ability to engage in symbolic, pretend play. The topic of language, which was discussed in some detail in Chapter 9, will be addressed later in this chapter.

Much has already been said about play in this text. Play is important as a context for teaching (Chapter 6), as an end in itself in the development of social skills, and as means for facilitating healthy emotional development (Chapter 7). Through symbolic play, children express their understanding of the world around them and the interrelationships of people and events. In addition, symbolic play provides an important context within which to experience and express emotions, both one's own and those of others.

In this chapter we have discussed symbolic play as an important cognitive milestone. The ability to allow one thing to stand for something else, such as a block representing a car, or a tissue representing a blanket, is evidence of the child's developing symbolic representation skills. Other evidence of symbolic skills can be observed in drawing, language, mental images, and eventually in reading, writing, and mathematics.

It is important for the early childhood special educator to be aware of the importance of facilitating play skills in general, and particularly pretend play. As we discussed earlier in this chapter, symbolic play moves through various stages. The first is **autosymbolic play,** in which children themselves are the actors. These play episodes reenact highly familiar activities such as pretending to eat or go to sleep, and they incorporate materials that are real (e.g., a pillow) or that closely resemble real objects (e.g., a small plastic spoon or tiny cup from a tea set). For children who are functioning developmentally at the end of the sensorimotor period, these are the kinds of activities that can be modeled both by the teacher and by other children. The use of play routines discussed in Chapter 6 can be helpful in establishing this early type of pretending.

The simple level of pretending can also be encouraged in group activities. For example, the teacher can say, "Let's pretend to be a snake" or "Let's pretend to swim." For children with special needs, it will be important to select pretend activities that represent very familiar activities or concepts. Children cannot pretend to do or be something they have never experienced.

Gradually, the teacher should introduce pretend play scenarios that involve other actors, such as dolls and stuffed animals, as well as other children acting out familiar roles in relationship to one another. The classroom should include dramatic play centers that include materials that encourage pretending, such as dress-up clothing, a toy stove, a sink and cupboards, dishes, brooms, telephones, dolls and doll beds, and so on.

Also, the teacher should gradually encourage the use of objects that are more and more abstract. For example, instead of toy cars that crash and have to go to the Fisher-Price garage for repairs, wooden blocks can be used for cars and an upside-down box can become a garage. The ability to use the same blocks for a fence and the box for a doll bed represents the emergence of the kind of mental flexibility (i.e., reversibility and understanding of transformations) that is a hallmark of the next stage of cognitive development, the stage of concrete operations.

The following example demonstrates the facilitation of symbolic play skills in a child with severe disabilities.

Jason and Monique love to play house in the dramatic play center. Andrea, who has many autistic-like behaviors, loves to sit in the rocking chair in the classroom and rock. The teacher decides to move the rocking chair into the dramatic play area and suggests to Jason and Monique that maybe Andrea could be the mother today: she could help put the baby to bed by rocking her. After rocking for awhile, while Jason and Monique are "cooking," Andrea is encouraged to put the doll in her own bed. Now it is time for everyone to go to sleep. Jason and Monique lie down with their pillow, and they encourage Andrea to do the same. The baby then wakes up crying in the night, and, since Andrea is the mother, she must rock her back to sleep.

Such a scenario as the one just described could also be worked into a play script, which is repeated several times. In this way, Andrea could be assisted not only with pretending but with language development and cooperative play as well.

Problem Solving

As preschoolers face increasing demands to develop greater and greater independence, the cognitive skills that enable them to engage in **problem solving** become increasingly important. Typical preschoolers often have little difficulty *recognizing* problems to be solved; they may need help only with generating more effective solutions. Children who have disabilities or are at high risk, however, may need assistance not only in the development of problem-solving strategies, but also in recognizing that a problem exists and that they have the capability to solve that problem through their own focused efforts.

Problem solving is distinctly different from academic learning. Academic skills represent external knowledge that must be taught; problem-solving opportunities during early childhood encourage the child to create new mental relationships by interacting with the environment. Meaningful problems stimulate children's mental activity as they relate new understandings to previous ones (Goffin & Tull, 1985, p. 28).

Conditions Necessary for Problem Solving to Occur. It is all too easy to structure activities with young children so carefully that they never have the opportunity to solve problems or to realize the relationship between cause and effect. Alert parents and teachers often prevent problems so consistently that young children seldom have the chance to recognize a problem, let alone solve it. Yet everyday activities at home and at school can offer many opportunities to teach children these important skills. Even if problem-solving opportunities are readily available, children will only respond when the following conditions are met.

Freedom from fear of failure. Freedom from fear of failure is the most essential condition basic to learning new things. Failure should be interpreted as a clue to try another way, according to Bruner (1960) who wrote, "Yet it seems likely that effective intuitive thinking is fostered by the development of self-confidence and courage in the student. . . . One who is insecure, who lacks confidence in himself, may be unwilling to run such risks" (p. 65).

Taking risks is natural to young children. That is why they must be watched so carefully. But taking risks in trying new things requires courage for some children. This is especially true if their early explorations resulted in pain and punishment. Sometimes the punishment has been a part of their disability.

A young child with a hearing impairment who cannot understand what is said fails when trying to talk. Unless adults understand the reasons for this and offer adaptations, that child may be severely frustrated. The child with visual impairments who bumps into things but whose disability was not detected and understood may also resist exploring. Children with physical disabilities may be overprotected, or abused children may be afraid. Children who have had limited opportunities to play, to use a variety of different toys and materials, and to discover need help in freeing their natural talents and curiosity.

Opportunities to experience cause and effect. Young children readily learn the relationship between cause and effect through inquiry and experimentation. Teachers and caregivers must take time to listen to and act on children's questions. Safe conditions, inside and out, should allow for experimentation. Noise and mess often are a sign of cognition in action. Children learn when they can dig and pile up things. Pouring and stirring with sand and water teach new concepts. The opportunity to discover is controlled in part by what there is to discover. Clearly marked areas may encourage experimentation.

But the freedom to "do it myself" must be taught to some. Merely standing back and letting children "try" is an important teaching skill central to encouraging them to understand cause and effect.

Encouragement and reinforcement. Encouragement and reinforcement are also necessary for cognitive learning. Cognitive learning is disrupted if children fear punishment. The natural consequence of making a mess should be cleaning it up, never a teacher's scolding or saying, "I warned you not to do that." Encouraging experimentation may merely require making the materials available, but some children need to be told repeatedly that it is all right to play with particular things that were (and perhaps are) forbidden at home. Both these children and their parents need to understand that some things are appropriate at school and not at home.

Teachers should be alert to provide social and tangible rewards for progress in expressions of curiosity and resilience and for the learning achievement. Just as structured, sequential lessons are needed for children to learn to recognize shapes and colors, so prompting and supporting are needed for children to learn qualities such as curiosity, experimentation, and problem solving (Zimmerman & Pike, 1972).

Problem-Solving Skills to Be Nurtured. In speaking of the problem-solving skills to be nurtured, Cook and Slife (1985) concluded that

Most research about problem solving suggests that the five steps are practically a universally endorsed process: (1) recognition of the problem, (2) analysis of contributing factors, (3) consideration of possible solutions, (4) choice of optimal solutions, and (5) evaluation of feedback to determine results. Not only is problem solving a natural logic, but the motivation to overcome obstacles appears to be natural as well. (p. 5)

Recognizing problems. Recognizing problems in everyday situations as they occur is the first step in nurturing problem-solving skills. The

child who stands helplessly waiting for someone to hang up a coat needs help in thinking about alternatives. The child who cries when the milk is spilled has a basic problem-solving opportunity misinterpreted as a threatening-punitive situation. If the teacher uses the words "We have a problem. What shall we do?" and then encourages the children to define the problem and to clean up the mess, progress can be rapid. Children basically enjoy solving problems.

Deciding where to have a snack or the best place for playing with clay presents opportunities to talk about why one place is better than another. This is the beginning of problem solving. "Staging" or contriving problems to solve is a useful addition to those problems that occur spontaneously. Having too few cartons of milk at snack time creates the need to count the children before going to get the milk. Losing pieces of puzzles can become the occasion to talk about how this problem could be avoided in the future.

Children can then be helped to see that puzzles should not be put away unless they are finished and complete. Discovering that the taller children can reach things whereas others cannot leads to problem solving, an arithmetic lesson, and a lesson on concept comparatives (e.g., Who is tallest? John is tall, but Timmy is taller. Bill is the tallest child in the class).

Although problem solving itself is considered to be a cognitive (thinking) skill, it involves language learning, social awareness, and motor activities. The alert teacher sees the distinct opportunities to develop many skills from the simplest situations.

Defining problems. Defining the problem is a skill that precedes effective problem solving. One afternoon in a classroom, the children complained of being hot. They were sitting around a table near a large west window playing with clay. It would have been easy for the teacher simply to say, "Oh, you are sitting in the sun. That's why you are hot. Here, I'll move the table into a shady spot." Instead she asked "Why are we uncomfortable? I'm hot, too." (Note that she used the long word "uncomfortable" but coupled it with the word they knew, "hot.")

One of the boys responded, "That old window is stuck," but he did not add that it was bitter cold outside and energy conservation forbade opening windows. A little girl made the good suggestion that the heater should be turned off. But after the thermostat was turned down they were still uncomfortable. Finally, one announced, "We got too much solar energy in here." Earlier the teacher had told them about how the sun could be used to provide energy. She had explained that the sun heats water and other things. It was not long before the children were agreeing that solar energy was the reason (cause) they were hot (effect). They had defined the problem. They were ready to think of ways to solve it.

Attending to critical features and conditions. Facilitating attending to critical features and conditions of the problem is the teacher's role. In the case just mentioned, she suggested that one boy feel the table where the sun was hitting it. Before she could suggest it, another boy decided to feel the floor where the sun was not hitting it. He reported it was cold. Then three children at once saw the solution. "Move the table into a spot where the sun wouldn't hit the table," they offered. But the little boy who had made the first comment about solar energy had another idea. "Let's sit under the table. It's cool down there." And they did.

Sitting under the table would not have occurred to the teacher. It was a temporary solution but a good one. The children were very pleased they had thought it up themselves.

Considering alternative solutions. Children can consider alternative solutions as soon as they have learned how to recognize and state a prob-

lem. Creative thinking is a result of thinking about alternatives.

According to Raudsepp (1980),

The importance of creativity to professional and personal success cannot be overestimated. Professionally, creativity plays a fundamental role in the problem-solving and decision-making that are intrinsic to technical and managerial activities. Personally, creativity supplies the insight and variety that help make life interesting and meaningful. (p. 73)

Raudsepp was not talking about preschool! He was describing the importance of nurturing creativity in business managers and engineers. He pointed out the need to overcome personal and environmental factors that inhibit the development of creativity.

1. *Creativity.* If creativity is so essential, it should be systematically cultivated from earliest experiences. Raudsepp suggested playing games that develop the ability to discover principles linking different situations and things. He emphasized that recognizing simple solutions (such as sitting under the table to avoid the sun) is a skill that can be taught.

One of the games Raudsepp suggested is Tangram, which originated in China around 1800. The game consists of a seven-piece set of "tans." With these seven pieces over 1,600 designs can be arranged! Very young children enjoy doing this, and with encouragement they create fascinating figures. After a few experiences with Tangrams, they begin to play more creatively with blocks, clay, and all other manipulables. The mere awareness that the same pieces can be put together in different ways creates a mental set that establishes the habit of thinking creatively.

2. *Divergent thinking.* Seeking divergent solutions is important in developing problem-solving skills. Divergent thinking (Guilford, 1967) is a form of creative thinking involving an opportunity to go off in different directions exploring various strategies to solve problems.

After one group of 4 year olds had grasped the knack of divergent thinking, a whole carton of milk spilled on the floor. One creative thinker quickly suggested that the best solution was to find a hungry cat. Another used the concept of osmosis and suggested placing a terrycloth towel in a pan with one corner placed into the puddle. She had previously noticed that when her towel had just one corner in the bathtub the water "climbed up the towel" and made a mess on the floor. She translated this observation into a way to clean up the spilled milk.

3. *Brainstorming.* Brainstorming in preschool is exciting. As soon as children understand that the teacher really respects their ideas and will adopt them, they express unbelievable creativity. We find it useful to let them watch us write their suggestions on the chalkboard in a column. After they have made a number of suggestions, we read them together to see whether one is better than the others. If all of the suggested solutions to a problem are similar, the teacher may offer a very different idea, even an obviously silly one.

Choosing the best alternative. Discussing the suggested alternative solutions to a particular problem provides opportunities for developing language, vocabulary, and cognitive skills. As children talk about the different ways of meeting a particular need, they become engrossed in what they are thinking about and add new ideas. But one alternative must be chosen and given a fair trial. Reasons for the choice should be discussed. Verbal children usually take the lead in telling their ideas. Even nonverbal children, however, can be encouraged to suggest different ways to solve a problem.

One teacher who contrived a problem placed the tumbling mats beside a shelf so that, to get around them, everyone had to walk several feet out of the way. The teacher even pretended to stumble over them several times. Then she announced, "Boys and girls, we have a problem."

Fifteen pairs of feet marched over to see what was happening. The teacher explained, "These mats are in the way, and we don't have any place to put them away. What shall we do?"

Silence. Then, one very small boy announced, "We could open 'em up and walk on them."

"No," said another child. "They'd get dirty."

Another boy said, "Let's just frow [throw] them away." (He did not enjoy tumbling.)

A little girl who could speak very little pointed up and said, "Up dere." She had noticed that the top shelf had some space. Everyone quickly agreed that "up dere" was indeed an effective answer.

Evaluating results. Evaluating the "up dere" solution did not take long. When they tried to get the unwieldy mats to the top shelf, they discovered it would not work. Just as adult engineers go back to the drawing board, so did the children. They reviewed all of their ideas. None seemed useful. So they decided to think about it some more. The next day one little girl came bouncing into the room. "I'se got sootion [solution]," she said. "Puts dem over dere by da books. Den we can sit soft while we read." And they did.

Developing flexibility and independence. Teaching effective problem solving requires teachers to accept some solutions that do not seem appropriate to adults. Surprisingly, children quickly develop a sense of things that will work and things that will not. But at first they must be encouraged to try the things that occur to them. The boy who suggested that the cat should clean up the milk forgot one thing: the school did not have a cat! When this was remembered, he suggested more conventional means of mopping up spilled milk. But if she had had any way of anticipating his suggestion, the teacher vowed that she would have brought a cat to school that day. Rewarding creative thinking causes it to blossom. The reward is as simple as seriously accepting the suggestions and trying them.

Avoiding critical attitudes and fault finding. If a teacher does not laugh at or ridicule a suggestion, neither will the children. If one child observes, "That's a dumb idea," the teacher may quickly respond, "There are no dumb ideas around here. Remember, we're brainstorming." If the teacher uses this term for a few days, the children will add it to their vocabularies, but more important, they will add it to their way of thinking. They will learn to withhold critical judgment until several ideas are expressed.

Nurturing affective development through conflict resolution. If children are accustomed to thinking in terms of alternative solutions, they will transfer this learned skill to the task of solving personal problems. If two children are determined to play with the same toy, problem-solving skills should be brought to bear on the resolution of this "problem." If they are used to thinking in terms of alternatives, it will not be long before you will hear them calmly suggesting that they can "take turns," play together, or find something else to do for awhile.

Nurturing language and reasoning through problem solving. Nurturing language and reasoning through problem solving is as simple as encouraging a great deal of discussion about "what to do." At first the discussions are likely to be brief, simple, and monopolized by a few children. The teacher can prevent this, however, by insisting that everyone have the chance to say something or to "help solve our problem." New vocabulary, new concepts, and new ways of looking at old problems grow out of the process. The product (the solution) may be less than the best for a while, but with patience and continued encouragement, young children can become excellent evaluators. They can also become a genuine help in keeping things running smoothly.

The ability to judge and reason wisely is a skill that can be developed very early. Consistent management by persons important to the children is basic. Teachers must recognize that problem solving in the best sense facilitates both cognitive learning and language development. Expecting young children to use good judgment, setting the stage for it in thoughtful planning, and then allowing them to experiment and evaluate what they do helps develop intelligent behavior.

WORKING WITH CHILDREN WHO ARE COGNITIVELY DIFFERENT

Two groups of children may be identified during the early childhood period who have special needs related to differences in cognitive abilities and characteristics. These are children with significant cognitive impairment and children who are highly gifted.

Children Who Have Cognitive Impairments

Identifying and labeling infants and preschoolers as having mild to moderate cognitive impairments or learning disabilities is difficult to do with accuracy prior to formal schooling, and it should be avoided. However, some young children will clearly demonstrate significantly delayed or impaired cognitive functioning early in life. The primary identifying characteristic of these children is significantly slowed development of cognitive skills, hence the term **mental retardation.**

A precise definition of mental retardation is difficult due to several factors, including lack of agreement as to the definition of intelligence as well as cultural variations in expectations regarding so-called "normal" intellectual functioning. In this section we are referring to children who, very early in life, demonstrate significant difficulty with the kinds of skills discussed in this chapter. These cognitive deficits can be caused by many factors, including genetic disorders (e.g., Down syndrome); prenatal insult to the fetus from toxic substances (e.g., alcohol) or viral infections (e.g., rubella); perinatal complications (e.g., anoxia); and postnatal influences such as head injury, asphyxia (e.g., near-drowning), and poisoning (e.g., lead poisoning). While these factors do not always cause significant cognitive impairment, it is a possible outcome.

Characteristics of Children with Significant Mental Retardation. The following are characteristics commonly associated with children who have significant mental retardation.

1. According to Peterson (1987), the most obvious characteristic of children with retardation is their slower rate of development. They learn slowly and require repeated, systematic instruction (Ford & Mirenda, 1984).

2. They experience significant difficulties with the kinds of basic cognitive processes described earlier in the chapter. They experience short-term memory deficits and difficulty attending to relevant stimuli.

3. Children with significant mental retardation experience particular difficulty with language development. While for most developmental domains the child will be functioning at a level similar to his or her mental age (i.e., cognitive level), language development is often below the child's mental age.

4. Many children with retardation process information more slowly than their normally developing peers and require more time to produce a response.

5. They often do not demonstrate learned skills spontaneously, and they do not *initiate* easily. They have difficulty generalizing skills to new situations (Horner, Sprague, & Wilcox, 1982).

Adapting Instruction

In light of these learning characteristics, several strategies can be effective in assisting young children who have significant cognitive impairments. These are summarized in Exhibit 10–1. These adaptations are easily incorporated into any preschool program. Nondisabled peers can often benefit from them as well. For example, during activities designed to facilitate classification skills, familiar, functional materials can be used, such as forks, knives and spoons, or different-colored socks. Another simple adaptation is to remind all staff to speak more slowly and increase the length of pauses. This adaptation will make it easier for all children to understand, and it will provide ample time for children to organize their ideas and communications. Particularly important are the use of repetition, creating a predictable environment, and facilitating active learning by teaching the child to initiate.

EXHIBIT 10–1

Special Considerations for Children Who Need Extra Time and Spaced Practice

1. *Provide concrete, multisensory tasks.* Preschool-aged children naturally learn more easily when tasks are three-dimensional and concrete rather than abstract.

2. *Find the child's most efficient mode of learning.* Observe carefully to determine each child's strongest mode of learning. If it is visual, then use visual cues to assist auditory directions. If auditory, then accompany visual tasks with auditory assists. If motoric, then use movement as much as possible to teach language and cognitive skills.

3. *Monitor pacing.* Children who must work extra hard to concentrate or to process information usually tire easily. The amount of effort exerted should be varied to allow for occasional rest times, quiet activities, or soft music. Children who process information more slowly should receive less information or should receive it over a longer time.

4. *Provide repetition.* Some children need to try things again and again or need to have something repeated several times before it can be grasped. Intermittent practice helps children to remember skills they have learned.

5. *Plan for modeling and imitation.* Some children do not acquire information incidentally. If a specific response is desired, plan experiences in which the behavior is demonstrated and positively reinforced. Once the child imitates the desired behavior, be certain to give the expected reinforcement.

6. *Task analyze.* Tasks must be broken into simple, short steps that can be sequenced from the easiest to the most difficult.

7. *Give explicit directions.* For some children it is necessary to give nearly all directions slowly and in small steps. One step can be completed before the next direction is given.

Children Who Are Gifted

Nearly every early education center has children who are gifted enrolled. However, giftedness is difficult to identify during the early years. Not only are official definitions somewhat unclear, but they vary from state to state. In addition, some children who are gifted have not yet participated in experiences that reveal their talents. Others may have such a discrepancy between their cognitive development and their social-emotional development that their giftedness is masked behind withdrawal, aggression, or other forms of inappropriate behavior. Some states do support formalized identification procedures through screening and in-depth testing. (Recall the cautions surrounding the use of standardized tests discussed in Chapter 4).

Given the inadequacies involved in testing young children and the lack of financial support, most teachers must turn to informal checklists to identify children who are potentially gifted. However, professional literature does contain criteria to help teachers identify these young children. Merle Karnes and her associates (1978), from the University of Illinois, have developed a Preschool Talent Checklist designed to identify preschoolers with talents in specific academic areas.

Even though a series of so-called typical "gifted" behaviors may be described, remember that not every child who is potentially gifted will display all or even most of the behaviors. Children from different cultural backgrounds will also display their giftedness in different ways from that of the majority culture (Torrance, 1977). In general, children who are potentially gifted tend to have large vocabularies, a great ability to concentrate, a high level of curiosity, and a good memory. They learn rapidly, show a mature sense of humor, are alert, and enjoy the challenge of problem solving and abstract thinking.

Children who are gifted need the special encouragement described in Exhibit 10–2. Enrichment of the regular early education environment will meet the needs of most young children who are gifted. This chapter contains numerous suggestions for the development of cognitive skills through active learning and problem solving. Teachers can increase the depth, complexity, or abstractness of these activities when children who are gifted are involved. "Questions and activities designed to elicit fluent, flexible, original, and elaborated thinking can be readily incorporated into many regularly scheduled activities, such as sharing, art, weather, and story reading" (Kitano, 1982, p. 19). Indeed, all of the steps described in the development of problem-solving skills are perfectly suited to the needs of children who are gifted.

In summary, the following recommendations made by Kitano reaffirm the appropriateness of most of the curriculum suggestions in this chapter as an appropriate foundation for any program serving young children who are gifted. Kitano recommends providing activities that enhance creativity; higher cognitive processes; and forecasting, planning, and decision making, as well as activities that promote inquiry, problem solving, and affective development.

ACADEMIC READINESS

For the preschool child, one of the greatest concerns regarding the development of cognition has to do with the cognitive skills that will ultimately support the learning of academic skills of reading, writing and mathematics, and classroom language skills. Many of the mental operations and thinking skills that evolve throughout the preschool years will be critical to school performance and the development of academic skills. This section addresses the teaching of these cognitive subskills.

However, it is important to realize that the development of academic skills—and literacy skills in particular—does not depend on levels of

EXHIBIT 10–2

Children Who Are Gifted Need Special Encouragement

Children who are gifted are usually curious about everything. They want to experiment all of the time. They are persistent in problem solving. They have a large fund of information, often more than the teacher does, about things that particularly interest them. They are not easily distracted, and they want to remain at a particular task until they have mastered it. Their ability to attend and concentrate is usually greater than that of others.

If their insatiable curiosity is not rewarded, their unique abilities may be limited. If the messes they create as they experiment are the occasion for punishment, they may stop experimenting.

Young children who are gifted need expanded opportunities. The materials they can enjoy, the books they like to have read to them, and the conversations they will seek should be appropriate to their level of development. Often these children are particularly sensitive to the feelings of adults. They can be skillful manipulators. Be alert to help them to use their special gifts, but not abuse them.

Almost any material can be adapted to meet the needs of children who are capable of creative or divergent thinking. Attribute blocks are an obvious example. Most children who are gifted will quickly learn to sort by color, shape, and size. Advanced children can learn to sort the differences among more than one attribute. Making an alternating chain of one and two differences does challenge the minds of most preschoolers.

cognitive development alone, but also on the social and linguistic experiences of the child. Thus, to truly understand academic readiness and to develop strategies for facilitating academic skills in young children, it is also necessary to understand the early development of literacy (currently referred to as "emergent literacy" [van Kleeck, 1990]) within the social context of the young child's family and culture.

The reader is reminded also that the early caregiver interactions described in Chapters 6 and 9 play a critical role in children's later development of cognitive and academic skills.

FACILITATING COGNITIVE AND INFORMATION-PROCESSING SUBSKILLS RELATED TO ACADEMIC ACHIEVEMENT

The preschool years can be viewed as a period of preparation for the formal academic achievement that must take place in the early elementary school years: reading, writing, and mathematics. In addition, there is a fourth area that we now realize to be crucial to children's academic success. It is referred to as *school language.*

Significant debate exists regarding to what extent academics should be stressed during the preschool years. Preschool programming approaches often reflect one of two polar views. One view suggests that academic skills should be directly taught in preschool programs emphasizing learning the alphabet, sound-letter relationships, counting, and reading and writing numbers and letters. At the other end of the continuum are programs that stress that neither academics nor academic readiness skills are appropriate for the preschool classroom. These programs emphasize self-directed play and exploration and exclusively child-centered activities.

In light of the growing concern regarding the lack of school preparedness of millions of young children from impoverished environments who are at risk for a variety of biological and social reasons, there is probably an important middle ground somewhere between the two views. There is much that can be done within a child-centered program to enhance the child's cognitive, social, and linguistic foundations for the later development of academic skills. It is our position that the early childhood special educator must understand the nature of these foundations and be able to design educational programs that facilitate them, yet stop short of emphasizing the formal teaching of academic skills.

Basic information-processing skills such as attention and memory, as well as certain mental operations such as seriation, categorization, one-to-one correspondence, and transformations, form the cognitive bases for academics. The following sections provide specific classroom strategies for facilitating these processes and concepts.

Facilitating Attention Skills

Assessing Problems of Attention. To help young children develop appropriate capacities for concentration, the teacher must identify the factors that may be contributing to lack of attention. First, the teacher must be certain that the child has no health problems and no interference with normal vision or hearing. Obviously, many young children with special needs do have physical problems that affect their concentration. The guidelines in Chapter 6 offer some assistance in developing an environment most responsive to particular special needs.

Assuming that their attention expectations take into consideration each child's special needs, teachers will want to assess whether tasks match the child's abilities and are broken into manageable steps, directions are clear, vocabulary is at an appropriate level, and amount of stimulation is reasonable.

Stimulus Selection. Teachers should analyze the amount and complexity of stimuli to which the child is being asked to respond. Some distractible children may not be able to attend to a very colorful puppet with a very high voice while seated on the floor in a large group far away from the teacher. The same puppet might get a totally different response in a small group with two or three children seated at a table with a volunteer aide who uses a soft voice. Decreasing the amount and complexity of impinging stimuli will make it easier for the child to separate relevant from irrelevant stimuli.

When children have difficulty figuring out what stimuli are relevant, using novelty in the form of concrete objects, touch, and movement can help focus and sustain attention. It is believed that children first learn to interpret stimuli received through the sense of touch (tactually). Then around the age of 3 or 4 months, they integrate information presented visually and auditorally as well (Rowbury, 1982). Even so, for many children, touch continues to help isolate the relevant features of a stimulus and increase the child's ability to focus on them. When trying to teach children how to walk across a street safely, giving each child a teddy bear to "instruct" in role plays might be an effective means of focusing attention and recall.

Duration of Attention. Initially the amount of time required for a task should be in keeping with the child's natural ability to sustain attention. Then, using positive reinforcement and in some cases a timer, the *time on task* requirement can be increased. Remember that often children do not sustain attention because the task itself is inappropriate. For the very young child, learning tasks need to have visually concrete (obvious) beginnings and endings. Because some children just do not know how to start an activity and have poor visual organizing skills, they are easily distracted. Through careful structuring of environmental demands, teachers can help children to have productive contact with early learning materials.

When environmental demands do not exceed children's response capabilities, frustration can be avoided and involvement sustained. Puzzles exemplify a type of material that often places inappropriate demands on children. Teachers are surprised at the difficulty level of many puzzles supposedly designed for young children. Even though puzzles do have concrete beginnings and endings, their difficulty level may be conducive to only limited involvement. Perhaps an appropriate puzzle is just not available when the child decides to visit the puzzle corner. He or she may then wander around or try to take another child's puzzle. This child's so-called "attention deficit" may be more related to the characteristics of the activity than to those of the child.

Active Looking and Listening. One of the ways we have found to encourage active looking, listening, and thinking is through cooking activities. For example, children love to crack eggs. This is a learned skill; it is messy but worth the effort.

Properly attired with an apron, and after protecting the table and floor with paper, each child is allowed to go to the refrigerator (one at a time) to get an egg. First, the teacher shows how, and then each child is encouraged to describe what he or she will do, and later, what was done. "Tap the egg on the edge of the bowl. Put your thumbs in the broken place. Pull it apart." Demonstrated and talked about, egg breaking is a fine motor lesson, a language lesson, and a sequence lesson all rolled into one.

Other cooking lessons teach many things. One class has a yellow bowl, a purple spoon, a green measuring cup, a red-handled scraper, and a shiny beater. Before the cooking lesson, these implements are lined up about 10 feet away from the cooking table. Ten children at a time sit around the rectangular table. The teacher asks, "What do we need first?" and at least one child says "The bowl." That child is directed, "Get the yellow bowl." This process is continued until the needed items are on the table. Each child has a particular part to play in making the simplest food. Making muffins is a good place to begin.

All of the concept words on the bulletin board are included in some way in the cooking lesson (see Exhibit 10–3 later in this chapter). Each child does at least one thing, although all should have a turn at stirring and beating. Putting the mix into the oven is part of the project, and of course eating the finished product is the reward. Using the experience as the basis for an experience story chart also makes it possible to combine reading and mathematics readiness into the lesson.

Hearing. Hearing what happens is far more difficult for most children, even if they have perfectly normal hearing. The activity just described is also an excellent way to teach children to listen. If they fail to attend to the directions, they may lose their turn to do something they really wanted to do. Of course, it is important to be careful to avoid punishing children who truly cannot understand.

For a child with a hearing impairment or a child with limited language comprehension, this lesson offers the teacher the opportunity to give the directions first and then lead the child through the activity. As the child completes what he or she was told to do, the teacher should say, "Good work. You brought the green measuring cup," or "You broke the egg just the right way." The teacher should be alert to model and expand what the child says. But the teacher should not stop the activity to insist on "good speech." Rather, the activity should be used simultaneously to develop thinking skills and listening skills.

Critical Observation. This is an advanced observation skill that can be taught. Even very young children know when they have been fooled. Learning to listen, see, touch, taste, smell, and observe carefully is a prelude to thinking critically. Understanding that some things are safe and others dangerous involves observation and critical thinking. Conversation that nurtures this awareness is needed. Asking "Do you think we should _____?" and "Is everything ready?" helps children to begin to solve problems. The teacher should avoid doing things for them whenever the opportunity to think and make choices is a possibility.

Imaginative Observation. Imaginative observation is basic to nurturing creativity. Just lying on one's back seeing animals in the clouds is a good place to begin. Seeing funny things in the shape of puddles after the rain and noticing the way a crumpled piece of paper looks are not expensive activities. But doing this consistently teaches children to observe imaginatively.

Often, teachers are careful to show children pictures as they read to them. But sometimes it is fun to offer them crayons and paper and see whether they can draw something about what has just been read. Perhaps they can look at a squashed tennis ball and, with a little help, see a mountain or a spaceship. Then, as they show and talk about their creations with friends, they will develop additional observations. Observation through the senses of smell, touch, and taste also enlivens the products of children's imaginations.

Structuring Learning Experiences

Young children who have not yet developed adequate attention, concentration, perceptual, or memory skills may not be making effective contact with their learning environment. By structuring the curriculum, teachers can help these children to become active problem solvers and effective learners. O'Connell (1986) has advocated the scheduling of a structured, isolated, small-group instructional session by restructuring the periods of the day traditionally called "free play time" or "center time." In a typical mainstreamed early education class, there might be 4 or 5 children with disabilities in a group of 20. While there may be only two teachers, volunteers are usually available so that one adult can be involved in each of three small groups. Ideally, each group would contain a mix of children with and without disabilities. The nondisabled children would function as models and could assist the children with special needs.

The children with disabilities would then be assigned to whichever small-group activity promotes skill development in their personal areas of weakness. As discussed in Chapter 6, many activities such as puzzles, cutting, and color recognition already provide for individual differences through the process of task analysis. Children can work side by side with puzzles of differing difficulty level or can cut with scissors designed to accommodate different levels of skill. O'Connell (1986) has further suggested that children with special needs be seated closest to the adult at the table, so that sufficient opportunities for reinforcement and prompts are available.

Rowbury and Baer (1980) suggested as an alternative that half the class group come to the work area, while the other half continues in free play. The second group comes to the work area after the first group has completed a designated number of individually prescribed tasks. The resulting advantage of having peer models for both preacademic tasks and social free play deserves consideration.

Planning Instruction. Many young children with special needs have to be helped to begin a task, stay with it, and recognize when it is completed. They may see a task as endless and fail to recognize when they should take pleasure in a product or in the process of learning to learn. To promote successful contact with the task and recognition of accomplishment, it may be best to begin with learning tasks that have visually concrete starts and completions. Functional activities such as picking up all the blocks after play time, putting them in their proper container, putting the top on, and returning them to the shelf can be broken down into small units that are gradually combined as children develop increasing attention and concentration skills. Research suggests that helping a child to recognize and feel responsible for his or her own successes stimulates motivation or the desire to learn (Cook, 1983; Weiner, Graham, Taylor, & Meyer, 1983).

Structuring the Environment. To structure the learning environment, the teacher must match its features with the learning characteristics of the children. Rowbury (1982) discussed the following factors as important elements in the organization of an optimal learning environment:

1. *Location for learning.* A constant assigned location will reduce distraction and help to cue attentiveness and task orientation.

2. *Selection of materials.* Materials most appropriate for learners with delays include those that

   a. are concrete representations of the concept being taught.

   b. provide a maximum of tactile and visual information with little verbal interpretation.

   c. incorporate frequent but easily performed manipulative responses from the child.

   d. easily isolate the concept being taught.

   e. can be arranged in steps and presented to the child as specific, visible products to be completed.

3. *Visual arrangement of materials.* The following suggestions will be helpful to the child who has difficulty organizing his or her own work area. Such a problem is common to children who have delays in perceptual development.

   a. Limit materials to only those needed to complete the task.

   b. Arrange initially needed materials before the child arrives or ask the child to bring the red tub (which contains necessary materials) to the center. This prevents distractible children from having to wait and possibly beginning to lose interest.

   c. Be certain that all materials are within the child's reach and at eye level.

   d. Put loose materials in a container to avoid spills and their resulting distraction.

   e. Use visual supports and guidelines such as the placement card holders that come with some visual matching cards to help the child develop necessary organization skills such as left-right progression.

Teaching Classification, Seriation, and Concept Development

Whatever the theoretical orientation of and the skills expected by kindergarten teachers, nearly every preschool curriculum has similar pre-academic (or cognitive) goals. In one way or another activities are included related to classification (grouping) including sorting and matching, categorization, and seriation (ordering), and the development of concepts related to color, shape, space, time, number, opposites, and letters. In general, expectations move from the concrete to the abstract, from the simple to the complex, and from the here and now to the remote in time and space (Hohmann, Banet, & Weikart, 1979).

Matching (a form of discrimination) and then putting things together that are the same or alike is among the first of the expected skills. Identical things are matched, whereas things that are alike in some way are *grouped*. *Sorting* is also a form of discrimination followed by separating according to differences. Both matching and sorting activities are described within the broader context of *classification* (distinguishing characteristics of things, then sorting, matching, or otherwise grouping them). Note that the ability to understand the concepts of "same" and "different" is essential to performing on tests and following directions. Teachers should carefully teach the verbal labels of "same" and "alike" and "different," "not the same," and "not alike." Children cannot understand these concepts without using the verbal labels unless prompted to do so.

As children learn to classify, they are encouraged to begin with concrete, multisensory objects. Attention must be called to the various *attributes* (features or characteristics) of the objects. It is a pleasure to watch children as they move from the concrete to the abstract or from the simple to the complex in their thinking. For example, very young children are dominated by what they see, hear, smell, or touch. This is known as being "perceptually dominated." They will describe an orange as something that is orange in color, round, or rough (depending on the words within their vocabulary). Later they will be interested in its function and will classify it as "something to eat." Finally, it will become part of a whole class labeled "fruit." This cognitive hierarchy is reflected on intelligence tests that award a greater number of points to the answer "It's a fruit" than are awarded to "It's orange."

Seriation (ordering according to relative differences) is thought to be preliminary to understanding number concepts. Practice in serialization helps children to coordinate relationships as they begin to understand size, position, and time comparisons. Teachers begin with highly dissimilar objects and move gradually toward the discrimination of finer and finer differences.

Making comparisons to see what goes together and what does not enhances thinking skills. *Grouping* and *regrouping* in many different ways require flexibility of thought. This flexibility is basic to successful reasoning, judging, and problem solving.

Once critical preacademic skills are identified as preschool objectives, the next step is to translate them into a workable curriculum. The following sections present pragmatic suggestions for teaching and developing necessary preacademic skills in young children. Exhibit 10–1, presented earlier in the chapter, can help teachers implement their curriculum with children who need extra time and spaced practice.

Facilitating Classification

Classification is basic to making analogies. Classification instruction should stress teaching children to organize (group or sort) the same information in different ways. Most preschool curricula emphasize teaching colors, shapes, and sizes. Initial classification of things by these attributes should include a wide range of items. As children become adept at sorting things by color, they should be introduced to colored shapes. As they learn to sort by shapes, they should be provided with shapes of different sizes and thicknesses.

Sorting activities should never be limited to one set or one kind of materials. Matching socks of different colors and sizes is as useful as using more elaborate teaching materials. Sorting colored balls into two boxes can be both a learning experience and a useful clean-up activity. The teacher should encourage children to think of *their own* criteria for grouping. In this way the teacher can reward their tendencies toward divergent or creative thinking.

Attribute Blocks. A good set of attribute blocks includes red, yellow, and blue circles, squares, rectangles, and triangles. Each shape is provided in two sizes and two thicknesses. Children can sort them into several identical plastic boxes with low sides to make it easy to see them. At first the children are taught to put all the red shapes together, mixing all the shapes in the same container but keeping the color constant. The blocks are mixed together on the floor in a pile, in equal amounts of red, yellow, and blue. The teacher begins by saying, "Let's put all the red ones here," and then picks up three or four red blocks one at a time, saying, "This one is red," each time. Next a child is directed to "Find another red one" and place it into the correct box. The process is continued until all of the blocks have been sorted according to color.

After a few days of doing this, circles and squares are contrasted. Again, blocks of all three colors and both shapes are mixed in a pile on the floor. The teacher sets the stage in the manner just described, except that now *shape* is the criterion.

As soon as the children are secure in this classification, multiple criteria can be introduced. Using the identical materials and boxes, they sort the blocks according to color *and* shape.

Blue squares can be placed in one box and yellow circles in another. Later, big blue squares and little blue squares may be segregated. Yellow circles and yellow triangles should be sorted before thin yellow circles are segregated from thick yellow circles. We stress beginning with the attribute of color because research suggests that children focus on this attribute earlier than they focus on shape and other attributes (Pick, Frankel, & Hess, 1975).

Adapting Instruction. Individualizing behavioral objectives is important, because as in all teaching activities, the teacher's skill in making the activity interesting and enjoyable is important. There should never be a sense of solemnity or serious importance with games. It is critical for the teacher to be alert to support each child at his or her success level. If the lesson includes children of more than one skill level (and it should), all of the suggestions made for individualizing within the group should be followed.

A well-organized set of performance objectives enables the teacher to move forward or backward in providing the appropriate challenge while avoiding the overwhelming obstacle of failure. For example, the teacher may hand a red circle to Willie and say, "Let's put this big red circle with the other big red circles here" as she points and guides Willie's hand to the right box.

But she may say to Susie, sitting next to Willie, "Susie, what should go into this box?" as she points to the box with big red circles. Susie likely will respond, "Big red circles." In this way, each child is challenged but no child fails. They also learn from each other. Groups of 4 or 5 are optimum, but as many as 10 can enjoy this kind of classification lesson. Table 10–1 suggests the sequencing of the development of shape concepts that makes individualization possible.

Attending to Relevant Features

"Knowledge of the rule enables attention to be directed to the appropriate information" (Pick, Frankel, & Hess, 1975, p. 356). Using the attribute blocks to develop the understanding of rules has been useful. During the beginning sorting activities, the teacher can say, "My rule (criterion) in this box is everything yellow," or, "My rule in this box is only circles." After several sessions using the term *rule* the teacher may ask, "What is my rule in this box?" as she points to a box with blocks of one characteristic. If the children seem puzzled, the teacher can simply answer the question, "My rule in this box is _____," and then call one child to "follow the rule" and choose a block to add to the box.

The teacher should continue to use the term *rule* and to assist any child who does not grasp the idea. Usually several children will begin to understand and use the word correctly. They provide continued practice for the others. For those who grasp the idea quickly, a new dimension can be added. By providing them with an assortment of blocks and boxes, the teacher can encourage the children to make up a rule and make the teacher figure out their rule. But this is difficult for many children long after they can quickly identify the teacher's rules. The teacher should be patient. Continuing to play with the blocks in this manner leads to a firm grasp of an important principle: The same things can be sorted (categorized or classified) in different ways.

Table 10–1   Example of en-route objectives leading to a terminal objective

Sequential Steps	Descriptions
Area: Cognitive	
Goal: To teach children to identify shapes in the environment	
Terminal objective: The child will name shapes (circle, square, triangle, and rectangle) in his or her environment with 100% accuracy, no matter what size or color the shapes take.	
1. Matches shapes	Given an assortment of 10 objects of 2 different shapes and the teacher's statements "This (object) is (shape name)" and "Put all of the (shape's name) in this box," the child will place all of the items of the designated shape together.
2. Sorts shapes with verbal directions	Given 10 items of each of 2 shapes and the same relative size, and the teacher's request "Give me a (shape name)," the child will choose an item of the shape named and give it to the teacher. The teacher will randomize his or her requests to reduce the chances of successful guessing.
3. Imitates shape name	Given the teacher's spoken word model, "This shape is (shape name)" and the request for the child to "Tell me about this shape," the child will imitate what has been said.
4. Recalls shape name	When asked "What shape is this?" as the teacher shows one of the shapes, the child will respond correctly, naming the shape.
5. Recognizes shapes of toys	When told to "Show me something that is (shape name)," the child will respond by pointing to a toy, furniture, or any other item he or she can see of the shapes named.
6. Recalls shape names	When asked, "What shape is the (any environmental item)?" the child will respond correctly by saying the appropriate shape name.

Grouping the Same Things Using Different Rules. Awareness of grouping the same things using different rules is necessary for reading. After all, the same letters can be grouped in many different ways. Children must recognize that they can group things according to one category such as animals, food, things that go (transportation), and toys, and then that these things can be grouped in other ways. As soon as children grasp the idea of primary categories, they should be introduced to sorting each category into sub-classifications. Foods divide into fruit, meat, and vegetables. Animals can be classified as farm and zoo, tame and wild, or pets and nonpets. Clothing can be sorted into things for the head, things for the feet, things to wear outdoors, and things to wear inside. Each of these cognitive skills requires knowing the names of things, the uses of things, and the ways in which they can be sorted. Remember, these are readiness activities for true hierarchical grouping that occurs later.

Encouraging Flexibility in Thinking. Teachers should encourage flexibility in thinking. Sorting toys into different storage containers at different times is one useful way of doing this. For example, a class had been keeping toy animals in a box with pictures of animals on it and Lincoln Logs in their special box. One day, two boys insisted that Lincoln Logs belonged with the animals. Their reasoning: "We plan to use the logs to make a fence in our zoo tomorrow." Because teaching children to think in flexible, creative ways is a major goal, the logs stayed with the animals. That is, until someone else decided they were just right for the farm. Then they sorted the zoo animals and the farm animals separately with no direction from the teacher. The logs moved to the farm.

Children enjoy the challenge of sorting anything if the teacher is enthusiastic and excited when they grasp new ideas. For example, a teacher laminated a large piece of cardboard and divided it into four sections. Pictures were chosen from categories the children had been studying. At first, the cardboard merely took the place of the boxes used in the first lessons. (For some children, it is useful to actually place the boxes on the cardboard at first.) Then, when they recognized that the task was the same (sorting according to categories), the boxes were removed. The teacher continued to refer to the divisions on the cardboard as boxes.

Problem Solving in a Montessori Classroom

A visit to a Montessori classroom would reveal an array of attractive materials. Each would emphasize teaching one dimension. Each would be "self-correcting" in that the material would reveal the error, allowing the child to correct himself or herself by further experimentation. For example, the knobbed cylinders shown in the picture fit snugly in only one corresponding hole. Focus between the ages of 3 and 6 would be on self-directed concentration.

Later, the children will need to know that rectangles and squares in their kindergarten workbooks arecalled boxes. These earlier experiences help them to bridge the gap between real boxes and boxes on paper. Children who learn less quickly than some of their peers will benefit from a larger variety of materials. Not only does this help them to see more relationships, but it also lessens the likelihood of boredom in doing the same thing in the same way over a longer period.

Facilitating Seriation

Introducing children to serial ideas such as first and last should be done in the context of everyday activities, especially those that involve whole body movement. *First* and *last* may refer to place in line or when one does something. These concepts are critical for young children entering kindergarten. Most of the problems involved in lining up or being allowed to do something are caused by children's lack of understanding and experience with these terms. Understanding the concept (cognition) and using the correct label (language) cannot be separated. Without the concept words, one cannot talk about the concept. Without the idea, the word is useless.

Montessori cylinders and "nesting" toys are typical seriation materials. Hardware stores often provide sample paint cards that can be used to seriate from dark to light. The teacher should not overlook using household measuring cups or variously sized nails.

Facilitating Concept Development

Providing children sufficient experiences with the many concepts they must learn and the association with the words is a challenge. Merely keeping track of the concepts requires a system. A system for teaching concepts includes the following features:

1. Identify the concepts to be taught.

2. Plan a large number of activities and experiences that make explicit the idea of each concept.

3. Use the associated concept word throughout many class sessions as the need for the word occurs. That is, grasp the moment most likely to demonstrate the concept meaning to the child and use the word at that moment.

4. Provide many experiences involving a particular concept close together, but in natural, spontaneous ways.

5. When half the children seem to grasp the idea, plan a structured drill-like activity. The intent is to emphasize the common features associated with the different activities, but to concentrate on one target concept. For example, if grasping the idea of "first" is the target, play many different games requiring lining up in serial order. Focus on "first" in moving from one activity to another in the room. Lining toy animals in a row, identifying the animal that is "first," and then turning all the animals around to discover that the one that was first is last helps to make the concept clear.

6. Provide for contrived uses of the concept word by the children. That is, create the occasions when spontaneously using the target word throughout the day is appropriate.

7. When most of the children use the word some of the time and most of them appear to understand it, establish a system for regular review. Of course, if the concept words are used frequently because they are needed and useful, the review is spontaneous and effortless.

Each playgroup or classroom will want to focus on many of the same concept words. Needs are quite universal. An examination of teachers' manuals for kindergarten and first grade reading and arithmetic yields a large number of necessary concept words. These should be introduced through real-life and play activities at least 2 years before the children encounter them in school. "Put your finger at the top of the page" is a much harder direction to understand if children have not learned about "the top shelf" or "the top of the page" in a book as someone read a story. A review of the Boehm Test of Basic Concepts (Boehm, 1986) or the work of Bangs (1968) will be helpful in selecting target concepts.

Record the Concepts Being Taught. The system for recording the concepts being taught that we have found useful is described as follows:

1. Identify the concepts to be taught, and print each one large enough to be seen across the room. Write the words on individual pieces of cardboard. (We use pieces about 1 × 5 inches.)

2. Choose a bulletin board that is high and not of particular interest to the children. Divide it vertically into four sections. (See Figure 10–1.)

3. The first section (on the left) might be labeled "Provide experiences." The second section might be called "Fun drills." The third column might say "Contrived experiences," and the last row "Monitor children's use."

4. Place the target concept words in the first column, "Provide experiences." Alert parents, teachers, and aides to use these words at appropriate times throughout the day both at home and at school. Begin with only two or three simple concepts.

5. When half the children demonstrate that they understand a concept, move the card with that concept word to the next column. Add a new concept to the first column.

6. Continue moving each concept from left to right, allowing it to remain in the columns as long as necessary. If a concept is not used by the children when it is in the "Monitor

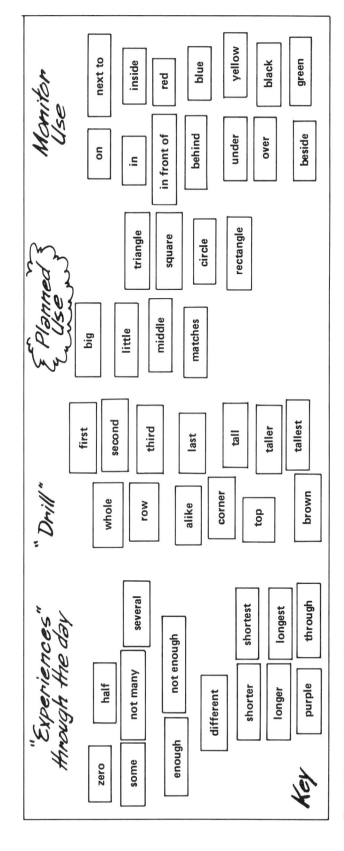

Figure 10–1 Concept recording board.

393

use" column, simply move it back to the left to the "Contrived experiences" column.

Avoid Stereotyped, Labored Teaching of Concepts. Teachers should provide opportunities for children to learn the concepts through experiences appropriate to a particular setting. (See Exhibit 10–3 for an example.) They should not leave the learning of important concepts to chance. The basic procedure that should be followed is to

- Identify the concepts.
- Use them.
- Make meanings clear.
- Monitor use over time.

DEVELOPMENT OF LITERACY

The previous section considered certain cognitive subskills related to academic readiness. In this section, we consider social and linguistic factors related to literacy.

Morrison (1991) has suggested that literacy has become the current "hot topic" among early educators (p. 91). According to him, this is at least partly in response to the fact that 50 million Americans are functionally illiterate. It is also related to the growing numbers of children who enter school without the necessary prerequisite communication skills and early experiences that prepare children to participate in formal literacy education.

A term that reflects the increasing emphasis on the relationship of early experience to literacy is **"emergent literacy"** (van Kleeck, 1990). Literacy is not simply an accumulation of the specific skills related to reading and writing, but rather evolves through both social and cognitive processes that begin at birth. Literacy evolves gradually as a function of exposure to and interaction with print materials and exposure to other children and adults who are *using* print, that is, "literacy events."

Anderson and Stokes (1984) have described the types of early literacy materials and experiences to which young children may be exposed, including the following categories:

EXHIBIT 10–3 _____

Snack Time: A Perfect Time to Develop Concepts

Most early education centers focus on teaching children how to enjoy a wide variety of foods. They stress good nutrition and encourage social manners. In addition, snack time provides a unique opportunity for developing concepts. Although different foods are eaten, the routine remains essentially the same each day: arranging the table, deciding how much food is needed, and discussing the qualities of the food. Eating is a multisensory experience that should not be taken for granted.

Unlike nouns, concept words cannot be taught directly, as they are not objects with names. Instead, concepts must be experienced and appropriate concept words applied to the experiences. Snack time provides an ideal opportunity for many children to become directly involved in concept-related experiences. For example, a child's glass may be *full* or *empty*, the grapefruit is *larger* than the apple, there are *not enough* straws, but there are *more* on the table. Through lively conversations, observations can be guided, comparisons made, and concept words practiced. Meaningful questions readily bring light to number, size, and placement concepts.

Of course, snack time is not the only time to focus on concept development. It is just one of the best and often overlooked times. The ability to attend is greatly enhanced when touchable favorite foods can be smelled, seen, and tasted. Even children who are very easily distracted become intently involved when they have good things to eat.

1. Daily living activities, such as making lists for grocery shopping; reading labels and recipes; going to various public services offices such as the departments of welfare, employment, and motor vehicles; and paying bills.

2. Entertainment, such as reading newspaper movie listings, television guides and books; doing crossword puzzles; and reading subtitles or credits on films or videos.

3. Religious activities, such as attending Bible study groups, singing hymns, and reading daily devotions books.

4. Work-related activities, such as writing checks, reading instructions, following delivery instructions, and stocking shelves.

5. School-related activities, such as doing homework or playing "school."

6. Interpersonal communications, such as writing and reading notes, letters, and birthday cards.

7. Storybook time, in which children are read to, primarily for their entertainment.

8. Literacy techniques and skills, which include activities in which reading or writing is the specific focus of the interaction. Such activities are often initiated by the child (e.g., the child asks "What is this word?" or "How do you make a "T"?).

Van Kleeck (1990) has pointed out that mere exposure to literacy materials and experiences is not sufficient for the development of literacy. Rather, it is the adult-child interaction around such events that is important.

Chall (1983) has described six stages of learning to read. The first stage, "Stage 0," extends from birth to 6 years of age. According to Chall, early in this stage children learn to read signals; for example, a certain facial expression means mother is angry, or the car in the driveway means father is home. Later this visual recognition becomes more abstract. For exam-

ple, the child recognizes the McDonald's arches or the Pepsi logo. Also in this stage children begin to become aware of sound segments through rhyming and songs, and they become aware of sources of print. It is not until grades one and two that most children actually learn sound-letter relationships. Of course, some children may develop a substantial sight vocabulary much earlier.

Relationship Between Oral Language and Literacy

Much has been written about the relationship between oral language skills and literacy, (e.g., Cook-Gumperz, Gumperz, & Simons, 1981; Tannen, 1982) as well as the nature of the school discourse style, or "school language," that is required for successful performance in schools. Young children need to be familiar with certain types of language, sometimes referred to as **literate style language** or *autonomous language*, in order to learn to read and write. This type of language is more decontextualized than language that is used in the home. Language used in the home often has a great deal of shared understanding among speakers. Such language does not depend solely on the *words* used in the communication, but also on gestures, facial expression, and intonation, as well as the shared knowledge and experience of the speakers. The examples in Exhibit 10–4 demonstrate two types of communication style: *interpersonal language style* typical of that used in the home or with close friends and *literate style*, which is the type required in the classroom and serves as the basis for the development of reading and writing. In addition, school classrooms require certain kinds of communication skills. These include answering questions, using language to "show and tell," raising hands before speaking, using language to talk about language and thinking, and so on.

EXHIBIT 10–4

Demonstration of Literate and Interpersonal Language Styles in a 4 Year Old

Interpersonal Style

Kisha: (Spilling chocolate milk on her dress) "Oh darn!"

Mother: "Oh oh. Take it off."

Kisha: "Should I put some of that stuff on it?"

Mother: "Good idea."

Kisha: "Hope it's not ruined."

Literate Style

Kisha: (Returning from a visit to her grandmother's) "Hi mom!"

Mother: "Did you have a good time? Tell me all about it."

Kisha: "Well, Grandma took me shopping at the mall. We went to the new Disney store there. They have the same stuff as in Disneyland. I saw a really cute Minnie Mouse doll, but it was awful expensive, so Grandma couldn't buy it for me. I did get a silver necklace though. It has lots of things on it, like Mickey and Minnie and Pluto and even Goofy. After the mall we had supper at McDonald's."

In the first example, language is characterized by short utterances and frequent use of pronouns. There is little specificity or explicitness, because it is not necessary. Mother and child both share the same reference—the spilled milk and the stain on the dress.

In the second example, Kisha is engaging in a narrative; she is describing past events, much as she would tell a story. Her narrative has a beginning, a middle, and an end, and it represents the sequence in which events actually occurred. She is using explicit and specific language, which is necessary because her mother has not shared her experience. This type of language use is said to be more *decontextualized* since there are fewer contextual cues. It is also referred to as *autonomous* language because the words and sentences must stand alone without the assistance of shared context or visual props.

It is also important to note that in the second example there is clearly an expectation on mother's part that Kisha will "perform" the narrative account of her experiences. This helps prepare Kisha for the kinds of academic performances that will be required of her in school.

The Nature of School Language

To be successful in school, children must be able to demonstrate certain kinds of communication skills. Some of these skills are linguistic and some are social or pragmatic.

Certain kinds of interactions required in classrooms may be unfamiliar to some children. The following are examples:

- Children are required to raise their hands before speaking.

- Children are expected to answer questions individually, addressing the group at large. (Many children may be more accustomed to demonstrating their understanding through action rather than words.)

- Children are expected to respond very quickly.

- Teachers ask questions that are "test questions"; that is, the teacher already knows the answer and is using the question to evaluate the child's knowledge. Such a format is unfamiliar to many children.

The linguistic skills required are those that have been alluded to earlier in the chapter, including the following:

- The child must use and understand language in the classroom that is often decontextualized (i.e., not embedded in the immediate context). For example, the teacher often gives instructions using only words, or the child is asked to describe a past event.

- Vocabulary is expected to be specific and precise.

- Syntax and grammar are used to carefully mark the relationships among sentences (e.g., "if," "but," "because," etc.).

- Narratives are expected to reflect sequence accurately and be coherent.

These literate language skills are built on the symbolic, referential language concepts that emerged during the preschool years. In turn, reading and writing skills, which must be learned in the primary grades, will be based on literate-style language. Many children do not have the kinds of early language experiences that prepare them for success in the early grades. In part this may be due to cultural differences. The following section addresses some of the ways in which children's early experiences with language and literacy may be different from what is expected in the classroom.

CULTURAL DIFFERENCES IN EARLY LANGUAGE AND LITERACY EXPERIENCES

Infants and young children are exposed to a wide variety of early experiences related to language use and reading and writing. Some of the most important research related to cultural differences in these early experiences was reported by Heath in her book *Ways with Words* (1983). Using the classic ethnographic research method of participant observation, Heath carefully observed families in two communities in the Piedmont area of Appalachia. Heath provided detailed descriptions of the interactions between adults and young children in a working class white community and in a rural African-American community. She compared these interactions with the types of interactions that are typical of what she referred to as white middle class "mainstream" families.

Differences in Children's Early Use of Narrative

Of particular importance, according to Heath, are differences found in the types of narratives that young children are encouraged to use. Narratives are important both because they are believed to form the foundation for learning to read and write and because children are expected to be able to perform certain types of narratives when they enter school.

Heath (1986) summarized the kinds of narratives most common among different cultures as follows.

1. *Recounts.* A **recount** is a report of an experience from the past. It is commonly parent initiated (e.g., "Jenny, tell Daddy about your field trip"). Recounts are the most common form of narrative required in the public school. Unfortunately, they are the least common form of narrative in nonmainstream cultures. In middle class mainstream families, however, children are not only encouraged to produce recounts frequently, but also encouraged to use literate-style language, that is, language that is precise, highly referential, and in proper sequence.

2. *Eventcasts.* An **eventcast** is a description of a current activity. It describes situations or activities that are immediate or obvious, for example, "I'm building a tower," or "Mommy's making pudding now." This type of communication is also common in mainstream families

and in public schools (e.g., "John, tell us what the boy in the picture is doing"). It is very *un*common in many nonmainstream cultures, in which it is often considered ridiculous to talk about the obvious. Consider the effect of the following classroom scenario on a child who is not accustomed to the use of eventcasts. Paul is making a ball out of a piece of clay. The teacher notices and says to Paul, "Oh Paul, tell us what you're making!" While a middle class child might easily launch into a detailed description of what he was doing, Paul is somewhat bewildered and probably not sure he understood the teacher's question. He might even be concerned that describing such an obvious thing would be insulting to her.

As children get older, they learn to use eventcasts in **metalinguistic** and **metacognitive** ways. That is, they use language to reflect upon language or thinking (e.g., "Let me think about how to do that," or "Oops! I said that wrong"). This is an important school language behavior, and it is useful in learning how to learn.

Somewhat related to eventcasts is the kind of response required by the typical classroom test question format—the familiar teacher-student interaction consisting of a question-reply-evaluate sequence that predominates in school classrooms. The following is an example:

Teacher: "Sean, what is the first word?"
Sean: "Trucks."
Teacher: "No, that's wrong."

In this format, the child is being asked to answer a question that the adult already knows the answer to. For many children this is bizarre.

3. *Accounts.* **Accounts** are similar to recounts in that they tell about a past event. However, accounts are initiated by the child, rather than by an adult. Accounts are often accompanied by communication strategies designed to get and hold the listener's attention (e.g., "Hey, ya know what?!"). While these types of narratives are much more common in nonmainstream families than are recounts and

eventcasts, they are discouraged in many public school classrooms and are often punished as interruptions or off-task behavior.

4. *Stories.* According to Heath (1986), the most common type of narrative among nonmainstream families is the story. **Stories** are often handed down from generation to generation, or they may evolve over a period of time within the child's early experience. Stories may begin with an adult teasing a child about a particular event. Stories evolve and change over time, and eventually some parts may be fictionalized. Stories contain strong elements of performance; the narrator's style is important, and listener participation in the story is often expected. Needless to say, such language activities do not follow the rules of school language, and they may be viewed as lying or attention-getting behavior.

Cultural Differences in Early Caregiver-Infant Interaction

Long before children learn to use narratives, important cultural differences can be observed in how parents interact with their infants and young children. These differences can determine whether or not young children have opportunities to learn literate-style language prior to school entry.

Middle class caregivers are typically verbally responsive to their infants and young children. This may not be the case in certain other cultures. While caregivers from other cultures may be responsive physically through touch or through facial expression, they may not respond verbally. Westby (1985) pointed out many such differences among non-middle-class cultures.

Middle class caregivers are also more likely to use highly referential language than are caregivers who are members of some nonmainstream cultures. **Referential language** is characterized by use of frequent labels and precise vocabulary with clear referents. Thus, typical middle class communication practices expose children to both a large quantity of language and the quality of language that facilitates eventual development of literate school language skills. Examples of these different kinds of caregiver-child interaction are presented in the following dialogues:

Sample 1

Jason, 12 months old, sitting in his high chair, starts to whine.

Mother: "Jason, what's wrong?"

Jason: Looks down at the floor.

Mother: "Oops! Your cookie, huh? You dropped your cookie." (Mother picks up the cookie.) "Yuk. This cookie's all dirty. See, it's dirty 'cause it was on the floor."

Sample 2

Alice, 12 months old, sitting in her high chair, starts to whine.

Mother: Looks up at Alice.

Alice: Looks and reaches toward the floor.

Mother: Picks up the cookie and hands it to Alice, saying, "Here it is."

In both these examples, the caregiver is responsive to her infant's cues. However, in the first example the mother is both *verbally* responsive and *referential*. She uses the word *cookie* several times and uses other key words that specifically refer to the key features of the experience—*dropped*, *dirty*, and *floor*. In the second example, although the mother is responsive, her language is limited. When she does verbalize, it is non-referential in that she does not explicitly name the object (cookie) or the location (floor). Instead, she uses the words *here* and *it*.

Cultural Differences in Uses of Print

Cultural differences can also be observed in children's early experience with reading and writing. While reading books for pleasure or information

and using writing for communication are common in middle class homes, they may not be common in some nonmainstream homes. Anderson and Stokes (1984) described the kinds of reading and writing experiences that occurred among three different cultural groups. In this study, Anglo families engaged in twice as many literacy activities as did the other two cultural groups. More specifically, Anglo adults initiated significantly more interactions directly related to teaching literacy skills such as helping the child read food labels or words in books. They were also more likely to use print for purposes of personal communication (i.e., writing notes and letters). Other cultural groups were more likely to engage in literacy events in religious contexts such as Bible reading.

In the 1990s, teachers commonly encounter children whose native language is not English. It is important to realize that the native language of the child is often not the only difference. The kinds of cultural differences just described can create a serious mismatch between teacher and child, and they may be even more problematic in the child's attempts to achieve school success (Iglesias, 1985). Saville-Troike (1979) suggested that American schools are designed primarily to prepare middle class children to participate in their own culture.

The ways in which nonmainstream families provide early language and literacy experiences for their children are not wrong; they are simply *different* from those expected in our school systems. It is particularly important that teachers of young children with special needs understand these differences and be aware of educational strategies that can help children make a successful transition to public school settings.

STRATEGIES FOR FACILITATING EMERGENT LITERACY

In early childhood programs, the major goals related to the development of literacy are *not* learning to recognize letters and learning sight vocabulary. Rather, the more important goals, particularly for children with special needs, are to develop an awareness and understanding of the functions of reading and writing and to develop literate-style oral language skills. These skills will provide the foundation for reading and writing, as well as the skills necessary for successful teacher-student interaction in the classroom.

In order to help children achieve these goals, teachers must begin by determining which kinds of language and literacy activities are already familiar to the children in their classes and then building on these experiences. As Heath (1986) stated, educators must find ways "to use what children do with language in their homes and communities to extend and enrich the school's repertoire of narrative genres" (p. 93). In addition, teachers must help young children understand the *value* of reading and writing. The following are examples of such strategies.

• *Demonstrate the functional uses of print.* This is one of the most powerful strategies teachers can use in the classroom. It includes such activities as reading the daily menu to see what will be served for lunch, listing on the board the names of children who are present or absent, writing notes to themselves as reminders to do something later, writing notes to other teachers, and so on. In these activities, children are *not* expected to read; more important, they are developing an understanding of the *functions* of reading and writing. As they observe the power of the printed word, children develop a fascination with decoding the mysterious symbols.

• *Work with parents to identify the ways in which print is used in each child's home.* This might include such activities as reading the television guide, reading recipes, reading food labels at the grocery store, reading comic books, and so on. Similar activities and materials can easily be incorporated into the classroom.

• *Incorporate literacy events into children's play.* Treasure hunts are exciting ways to demonstrate the use of print. Again, children are not expected to actually read the clues, but to experience their effectiveness in leading to the treasure. Other examples of play activities include playing postal service (letters are "written," placed in the mailbox, and delivered), going to the grocery store with a shopping list, and pretending to read a bedtime story to a doll. Reading recipes during cooking activities and writing notes that have been dictated by children to take home to parents are other good activities.

• *Play games that require referential language to facilitate literate-style oral language.* For example, two children can be separated by a screen. The child who is "It" draws a picture and instructs the other child to draw the same thing (e.g., "Make a big circle and color it blue. Now put two black eyes on it," etc.). The object of the game is to see how closely the pictures match. The same format can be used in playing with different shapes and colors of blocks or setting up a doll house. For children with severe disabilities, the game can be made simpler by using familiar objects and performing very simple tasks, for example, selecting objects such as a cup and a shoe to be placed in a box, then comparing to see whether both children end up with the same objects in the box.

• *Structure other activities that facilitate literate language style.* These might include helping children explain the rules of a game to someone else, go to the school office and deliver a verbal message, describe an exciting event to a student who was absent, and play the "telephone" game. Simpler versions might include having children feel objects in a sack and guess what they are or playing "Simon Says." These activities facilitate the use of specific autonomous language. For children who are less verbal, they demonstrate the functional uses of language for the purpose of sharing information and regulating others' behavior.

• *Read stories to both large and small groups and to individual children.* The importance of doing this cannot be overestimated. The stories selected must be meaningful to the children. They should be short, and they should be repeated often. Stories should also include props, such as a flannelgraph board, or actual objects to highlight important story points. Involving children's actions at key story points is also important. Including props and actions will make storytime more interesting for all children. As stories are repeated, pause at key points to allow the children to fill in the familiar phrases. Familiar storybooks should also be available to children during free-play time so they can "read" the stories to themselves or to a friend or doll. (This will necessitate having several copies of favorite books available.)

Exhibit 10–5 provides examples of activities that can be used during "Calendar Time" to facilitate learning.

Whole-Language Approaches to the Development of Literacy

Early childhood special educators must be aware of current trends in teaching reading and writing in the primary grades. An understanding of emergent literacy leads naturally to a view of reading and writing as a complex natural process related to social and communication processes and experiences. Goodman and Goodman (1986) described a **whole-language approach** in which reading, writing, speaking, and listening are viewed as interactive and interdependent. Reading and writing are not taught separately, nor are they broken mechanistically into subskills. (See Moran, 1990, for a discussion of recoding versus interactive approaches.) Bunce (1990) has suggested the following examples of whole-language activities that are becoming common in early primary grades:

• Language experience stories that children dictate to the teacher based on shared experiences. Stories are written by the teacher on flipcharts so they can be read again and again by the class. Students may copy the stories for their own reading later on.

EXHIBIT 10–5 _____

Making Calendar Time Meaningful for All Children

Calendar time is an almost universal activity in preschool programs. Because of the abstractness of concepts of time, children with special needs often have difficulty relating to this activity. The following is an example of how calendar time might be made more meaningful for children with cognitive disabilities.

1. Rather than presenting the entire calendar month, highlight only the current week.

SUNDAY	MONDAY	TUESDAY	WEDNESDAY	THURSDAY	FRIDAY	SATURDAY

   Each day should be a different color, with Saturday and Sunday easily distinguishable from the days of the school week(e.g., they might be pastel, while the week days are primary colors).

2. Identify one activity for each school day that is only done on that day. For example, Monday is "Pudding'" day; Tuesday is "Walk-to-the-Park" day; Wednesday is "Popcorn" day; Thursday is "Hat" day; and Friday is "Clean-Up" day.

3. Each of these days has a special symbol or picture representing that activity. The symbol is placed on a cardboard square of the same color as the corresponding day on the calendar and with the name of the day printed on the bottom.

4. Introduce the calendar activity by saying, "Who knows what day it is today? Right! It's Monday. What do we do on Monday? We make pudding. It's Monday and we're going to make pudding. Who can find the Monday card?"

5. Teach the children to learn to recognize the appropriate day-of-the-week card by relating the activity symbol to its matching color and word.

- Choral reading of familiar stories or poems. Choral reading can play the same positive role that singing favorite songs plays for younger children. Choral reading combines this pleasurable repetition and predictability with written words.

- Use of predictable storybooks that include repetitions of sentences and key words.

- Journal writing and writing picture captions on students' own pictures.

TRANSITION TO KINDERGARTEN

Much has been written regarding the importance of collaborative planning and parent support for transition from preschool to kindergarten (e.g., Spiegel-McGill, Reed, Konig, & McGowan, 1990). Salisbury and Vincent (1990) have stressed the importance of teaching for the next environment, and many studies have described the survival skills necessary for kindergarten adjustment (e.g., Rule, Fiechtl, & Innocenti, 1990). While such skills are not the only goals important

(For children with severe disabilities, show a duplicate of the activity card during the actual activity. This will help with symbolic representation and memory.)

6. At the end of the day, again say, "What day is it today? It's Monday and we made pudding." Then foreshadow a *future* event by saying, "Who knows what day it will be tomorrow? It's Tuesday. And what do we do on Tuesday?" Encourage the children to find the Tuesday card, but do not hang it on the calendar until the next day.

7. At the beginning of the next day, begin by asking, "Who knows what day it was *yesterday?* What did we do?" Point to the Monday activity card already placed on the calendar the previous day, and review the Monday activity. This facilitates children's learning of past tense.

8. Repeat steps 4, 5, and 6 for Tuesday, and so on.

9. As the week progresses, have the children mark the sequence of days and the passage of time as the activity cards fill up the calendar. As the week comes to a close, briefly review the week's events and talk about weekend plans.

   With this activity, a child who has severe cognitive disabilities can work on matching and eventually associate the activity symbol card with the activity and a particular day of the week. Nondisabled children can learn the days of the week; use language to describe past, current, and future events; and learn to read the names of the days of the week.

for preschool programming for children with special needs, they should be included to increase the likelihood of successful adjustment in kindergarten classrooms.

Establishing and maintaining contact with the staffs of the new environments can help children adjust to their new classrooms. When special considerations are necessary, it is helpful to have a preliminary meeting that includes the child's present and future teachers and the parents. Receiving teachers can be informed of each child's current social and academic skills, while present teachers learn what remains to be done to prepare the child for transition.

Early education teachers can plan activities designed to prepare children for more structured environments. This preparation is not intended to be academic or like an early kindergarten; it is designed to acquaint children with new expectations, routines, schedules, and patterns of reinforcement. They will require increased independence and self-sufficiency as the ratio of children to teacher increases.

Such preparation could include gradually

decreasing teacher attention, praise, instruction, and prompts. Children can learn to raise their hands when they wish to respond, if that is the expectation in the new environment. Practice in following such behavioral directions as standing in line or asking to be excused to the restroom can save children from some embarrassing moments later on. Attention spans will need to be lengthened gradually by increasing expectations for on-task behavior or requiring more self-sufficiency at free-play time.

It is the preschool teacher's responsibility to determine what skills children will need to develop before they move on. Exhibit 10–6 lists some representative skills. After these are determined, the teacher should try to incorporate practice in "kindergarten skill" development in ways that are as natural as possible. Ideally, continued contacts between kindergarten and preschool teachers will ensure a smooth transition. While we have addressed the importance of collaboration among professionals and between professionals and family members, it is necessary to consider the collaborative relationship that must be built between early intervention professionals and the paraprofessionals so crucial to effective service delivery. The final chapter offers practical techniques designed to ensure effective utilization of aides, students, and volunteers in early intervention programs.

EXHIBIT 10–6

Behaviors Needed for School Achievement*

1. Follows directions.
2. Concentrates long enough to complete a task.
3. Observes and remembers.
4. Answers questions about a simple story.
5. Contributes to conversations.
6. Directs and pays attention.
7. Solves simple problems.
8. Tolerates failure sufficiently to persist with a task.
9. Makes transitions easily.
10. Works on a task over a reasonable period.
11. Accepts adult direction without objection or resentment.
12. Works without constant supervision.
13. Accepts classroom routine.
14. Suppresses tendencies to interrupt others.

*Adapted from Adelman and Taylor (1986), p. 173.

Summary

All preschool and child care teachers share the responsibility of developing cognitive, active learning, and problem-solving skills together with academic readiness in young children. This task is especially important for teachers of children with developmental delays or disabilities. This chapter focused on practical ways to identify and teach these skills.

Piaget's stages of cognitive development were reviewed, as well as ways of observing cognitive development through children's play. Strategies for facilitating early cognitive skills were described, as were later skills related to problem solving and academic readiness.

Cognitive skills in preschoolers can be enhanced readily within a seemingly natural environment of play and curiosity. Elements from the major theories of child development help in devising strategies to stimulate problem-solving skills and academic readiness.

By giving children the freedom to explore and opportunities to learn from failure while remaining free from anxiety, early educators can easily incorporate problem-solving skill development into the curriculum. Examples and rationales are provided to illustrate how children can develop the skill to identify and define problems, consider alternative solutions, choose among alternatives, and evaluate results with flexible judgment. The relationship between problem solving and academic readiness becomes apparent as concepts and abstract images are translated into words that facilitate movement through the stages of problem solving.

The section on emergent literacy describes the importance of encouraging children's appreciation of the purposes of reading and writing. Also important is the development of literate-style language skills, which are necessary for school success. Teachers must be aware of the many cultural differences in children's early language and literacy experiences. These differences will significantly influence children's social adjustment and academic success in school.

If a preschool is to be successful in preparing children for the transition to kindergarten and beyond, it must identify the preacademic skills relevant to any local school district. In addition to "pays attention" and "follows directions," the curricula of most early childhood classrooms provide readiness activities involving classification (including sorting, matching, categorization, and serialization), colors, shapes, space, time, numbers, opposites, and letters. Suggestions for promoting a child's awareness of various attributes or relevant features necessary for generating and following rules used to manipulate concepts are included. Finally, special consideration is given to the needs of those who have cognitive skill deficits or potential for giftedness, or who will be making a transition to a new environment.

Discussion Topics and Activities

1. Think of several ways to create the need to solve a problem. Design situations appropriate for a 2 year old and a 4 year old.

2. Observe a preschool classroom and identify ways in which functional uses of print can be incorporated into the existing schedule and activities.

3. Think of ways to involve a child with severe cognitive impairments with nondisabled peers in a pretend block play activity in which children are building streets and houses.

4. Design some preschool lessons that will encourage children to experience cause-and-effect relationships. If possible, carry these out with children. What improvement could be made in your lesson design? Did you get the results you desired? Discuss the children's involvement with classmates. Perhaps a recording of the children's responses will help you to analyze the children's reactions in greater detail.

5. Why is it important to maintain a balance between social-emotional and intellectual activities in the preschool? This is a critical issue that is receiving attention nationally and should be thought through periodically. Recognize your own philosophy and investigate its implications for young children.

6. Role play your answer to a parent who insists that reading per se should be taught in preschool. Ask colleagues for constructive criticism.

7. Go on a "trust walk" to help develop your observation skills. Children also enjoy this exercise.

8. Visit and observe a local kindergarten class. Be alert to the behavioral and academic expectations. Compare these expectations with the "exit" goals of preschool classrooms you have observed. Discuss what you learned with classmates.

Annotated Bibliography

Views of Human Learning

Allen, K. E., & Goetz, E. M. (1982). *Early childhood education: Special problems, special solutions.* Rockville, MD: Aspen Systems.

This book outlines the basic principles of behavior analysis including prompting, stimulus control, and reinforcement. It is based on an integrated behavioral program at the University of Kansas. Practical suggestions for a variety of problems are given. Of special interest are the chapters on preacademic skills for the reluctant learner and transition from preschool to kindergarten for children with special needs.

Ashton-Warner, S. (1965). *Teacher.* New York: Bantam.

Readers who can find a copy will delight in this old classic. Sylvia Ashton-Warner captures the imagination with her exciting description of the way she helped young Maori children bring meaning into the process of learning. Her approach illuminates the motivation readiness so important to the relationship between learning and life.

Bell-Gredler, M. E. (1986). *Learning and instruction: Theory into practice.* New York: Macmillan.

This welcome volume seems to take a fresh look at the application of learning theory to the classroom. Its goal is to present each contemporary theory's contribution to our understanding of human learning. Theories discussed include those of Thorndike, Skinner, Gagné, Piaget, Bandura, Weiner, and others. This is an informative and useful text because it clearly discusses educational applications, giving examples of related classroom strategies.

Hohmann, M., Banet, B., & Weikart, D. P. (1979). *Young children in action.* Ypsilanti, MI: High/Scope.

This comprehensive volume is designed as a manual to present the Cognitively Oriented Preschool Curriculum, which is organized around a set of key experiences. These key experiences are derived from Piaget's theory and are thought to be the primary cognitive characteristics of children in the preoperational stage of development. They are the guidelines for the development and evaluation of the Cognitively Oriented Preschool Curriculum. All related classroom activities are built on concrete, active experience.

Saunders, R., & Bingham-Newman, A. M. (1984). *Piagetian perspective for preschools: A thinking book for teachers.* Englewood Cliffs, NJ: Prentice-Hall.

This comprehensive book is designed to get early childhood practitioners cognitively involved in the teaching experience. Advanced students will enjoy the opportunities to participate in experiences that encourage construction of their own theories. The authors suggest that the critical features of Piagetian classroom environments are activity, diversity, change, and intellectual honesty rather than classification, seriation, and number. Familiar activities are

described and subtle shifts in focus are suggested to enhance the potential for thinking.

Wadsworth, B. J. (1984). *Piaget's theory of cognitive and affective development.* New York: Longman.

Here is one of the more popular introductions to Piaget's theories, including affective as well as cognitive development. The four central concepts—schema, assimilation, accommodation, and equilibrium—are described. Piaget's four stages are explained in detail and with much appeal. The relationship between cognitive development and such factors as heredity, action, motivation, and developmental stages are considered. Finally, some of the implications of Piaget's work for child care and education are presented.

Facilitating Cognitive Skill Development, Problem Solving, and Literacy

Berk, L. E. (1985). Why children talk to themselves. *Young Children, 40,* 46–52.

This article presents an excellent overview of the research into what psychologists call *private speech.* It gives clear illustrations and helpful implications for practice. Besides being fascinating to the observer, private speech is an important way in which children organize, understand, and gain control over their environment. This article helps caregivers set the stage for constructive use of private speech as an effective learning tool.

Bradbard, M. R., & Endsley, R. C. (1980). How can teachers develop young children's curiosity? *Young Children, 35,* 21–32.

This excellent article reviews the implications of research for the development of curiosity in young children. Specific suggestions are made about how teachers can foster the growth of this important attribute. The tone of this article makes it perfectly clear that teachers can actively influence the expression of exploratory types of behavior. Such behaviors are not necessarily a result of intellectual capacities.

Chalfant, J. C., & Kirk, S. A. (1984). *Academic and developmental learning disabilities.* Denver: Love.

Although most of the suggestions for classroom implementation are intended for use with children of school age, this book presents a much-needed view of developmental learning disabilities. Teachers in early education will gain much useful background information from the chapters on attentional, memory, perceptual, thinking, and oral language disabilities. There is welcome emphasis on observation and informal assessment without reliance on formal testing. Specific suggestions for good, solid observation are given throughout. A brief but helpful section on how to identify developmental learning disabilities in preschool children is included.

Copple, C., Sigel, I. E., & Saunders, R. (1979). *Educating the young thinker: Classroom strategies for cognitive growth.* New York: Van Nostrand.

This supplementary text combines a theoretical perspective with a practical approach. It demonstrates strategies to foster thinking and problem-solving skills. With a Piagetian orientation, it integrates problem-solving skills into daily activities including art, music, imaginative play, and science.

Gibson, L. (1989). *Literacy learning in the early years.* New York: Teachers College Press.

Connections and continuity within the total process of learning to read and write, from birth to age 8, are stressed. The book is organized into age-level performance components with each phase examined in relation to its unique contributions to and constraints on the potential growth of literacy in young children. Teaching strategies and programs appropriate for literacy acquisition are emphasized.

Goffin, S. G., & Tull, C. Q. (1985). Problem solving: Encouraging active learning. *Young Children, 40,* 28–32.

This timely article regards problem solving as distinctly different from academic learning. It clearly discusses such helpful topics as the importance of problem-solving possibilities, characteristics of good problems, the creation of problem-solving situations, and teacher strategies to challenge children to think.

Heath, S. B. (1983). *Ways with words: Language, life and work in communities and classrooms.* Cambridge, England: Cambridge University Press.

This book provides rich detail in describing the author's qualitative observations of culturally different communities in the Piedmont mountain area of Appalachia. Heath carefully describes the early communicative interactions between families and young children in the two communities of Roadville and Tracton. She also discusses the mismatch between these family and community experiences and early school experiences.

Kail, R. (1984). *The development of memory in children.* New York: W. H. Freeman.

This unique book details the relationship between changes in memory development and cognition. Advanced students will appreciate the chapters on the development of mnemonic strategies, metamemory, early memory, mechanisms of memory development, and memory in children with mental retardation.

Pick, A. D., Frankel, D. G., & Hess, V. L. (1975). Children's attention: The development of selectivity. In E. M. Hetherington (Ed.), *Review of child development research.* Chicago: University of Chicago Press.

This excellent chapter allows the more advanced student to obtain a view of what is known about the process of attention and its importance to problem solving and learning in general. The developmental changes revealed through research are directly applicable to curriculum design. Of note is the importance of deliberate attempts to accentuate relevant features when specific concepts are being taught.

Sparling, J., & Lewis, I. (1979). *Learning games for the first three years.* New York: Berkeley.

This is a handy paperback with illustrated ideas and activities for parents and teachers to enhance infant-toddler development. The games include 100 experiences a child can enjoy from birth to 36 months of age. Child-caregiver interaction is encouraged. Most activities are adaptable for young children with special needs.

van Kleeck, A. (1990). Emergent literacy: Learning about print before learning to read. *Topics in Early Childhood Special Education, 10*(2), 25–45.

This article clearly describes ways in which young children are exposed to early literacy experiences and the role of caregiver-child interaction in learning to read and write. The author discusses the role of the preschool in the development of literacy and describes strategies for encouraging children's understanding of literacy.

Encouraging Active Involvement of the Young Child Who Is Gifted

Clark, B. (1983). *Growing up gifted: Developing the potential of children at home and at school.* Columbus, OH: Merrill.

This extremely thorough text is a classic. Especially appreciated is the in-depth discussion of the importance of early learning to the development of giftedness. Early environmental influences, understanding of early sensitive periods, specific suggestions for nurturing very young children who are gifted, and the problems their unique characteristics create receive much-needed attention. Guidelines to help parents select an appropriate early education program are included. Most impressive is the author's ability to consider giftedness within an overall understanding of child development.

Kitano, M. (1982). Young gifted children: Strategies for preschool teachers. *Young Children, 37,* 14–24.

This article briefly reviews the literature on education for young children who are gifted and offers specific methods for working with these children in regular early education settings. Since children who are gifted are found in nearly every early education program, all teachers should read an article such as this. Its specific suggestions will help both beginners working with young children who are gifted and more experienced

teachers who realize how much of any good program is already appropriate for the special needs of children who are gifted. (Inquiry, problem solving, affective development, and the incorporation of process objectives into the curriculum are worthwhile goals for any new or existing program.)

Kitano, M. K., & Kirby, D. R. (1986). *Gifted education: A comprehensive view.* Boston: Little, Brown.

This thorough text contains a brief section on the young child who is gifted, outlining basic characteristics of this population and existing programs for children of preschool age. Other sections are devoted to children who have disabilities as well as being gifted and those who are underachievers, rural residents, low-income, or culturally diverse.

References

Adelman, H. W., & Taylor, L. (1986). *An introduction to learning disabilities.* Glenview, IL: Scott, Foresman.

American Psychiatric Association. (1980). *Diagnostic and statistical manual of mental disorders* (3rd ed., rev.). Washington, DC: APA.

Anderson, A., & Stokes, S. (1984). Social and institutional influences on the development and practice of literacy. In H. Goelman, A. Oberg, & F. Smith (Eds.), *Awakening to literacy.* Exeter, NH: Heinemann.

Anisfeld, M. (1984). *Language development from birth to three.* Hillsdale, NJ: Erlbaum.

Atkinson, P. C., & Shiffrin, P. M. (1968). Human memory: A proposed system and its control processes. In K. W. Spence & J. T. Spence (Eds.), *The psychology of learning and motivation: Advances in research and theory (Vol. 2).* New York: Academic Press.

Bangs, T. (1968). *Language and learning disorders of the pre-academic child.* Englewood Cliffs, NJ: Prentice-Hall.

Bell-Gredler, M. E. (1986). *Learning and instruction: Theory into practice.* New York: Macmillan.

Boehm, A. E. (1986). *Boehm test of basic concepts.* New York: Psychological Corporation.

Bruner, J. (1960). *The process of education.* New York: Alfred A. Knopf.

Bunce, B. H. (1990). Bilingual/bicultural children and education. In L. McCormick and R. L. Schiefelbusch, (Eds.), *Early language intervention* (2nd ed.). Columbus, OH: Merrill.

Case, R. (1985). *Intellectual development: A systematic reinterpretation.* New York: Academic Press.

Chall, J. (1983). *Stages of reading development.* New York: McGraw-Hill.

Cole, M., & Cole, S. (1989). *The development of children.* New York: American Scientific Books.

Cook, R. E. (1983). Why Jimmy doesn't try. *Academic Therapy, 19,* 155–163.

Cook, R. E., & Slife, B. D. (1985). Developing problem solving skills. *Academic Therapy, 21,* 5–13.

Cook-Gumperz, J., Gumperz, J., & Simons, H. (1981). *School-home ethnography project.* (Final Report to the National Institute of Education). Washington, DC: U.S. Department of Education.

Fewell, R. R. (1984). *Play assessment scale* (4th ed.). Unpublished document. Seattle: University of Washington.

Fodor, J. (1983). *The modularity of mind.* Cambridge, MA: MIT Press.

Ford, A., & Mirenda, P. (1984). Community instruction: A natural cues and correction decision model. *Journal of the Association for Persons with Severe Handicaps, 9,* 79–88.

Gallagher, J. M., & Reid, D. K. (1981). *The learning theory of Piaget and Inhelder.* Monterey, CA: Brooks/Cole.

Ginsburg, H., & Opper, S. (1969). *Piaget's theory of intellectual development.* Englewood Cliffs, NJ: Prentice-Hall.

Goffin, S. G., & Tull, C. Q. (1985). Problem solving: Encouraging active learning. *Young Children, 40,* 28–32.

Goodman, K., & Goodman, Y. (1986). *What is whole about whole language*. Portsmouth, NH: Heinemann.

Guilford, J. P. (1967). *The nature of intelligence*. New York: McGraw-Hill.

Heath, S. B. (1983). *Ways with words: Language, life and work in communities and classrooms*. Cambridge, England: Cambridge University Press.

Heath, S. B. (1986). Taking a cross-cultural look at narratives. *Topics in Language Disorders, 7*(1), 84–96.

Hohmann, M., Banet, B., & Weikart, D. P. (1979). *Young children in action*. Ypsilanti, MI: High/Scope.

Horner, R. H., Sprague, J., & Wilcox, B. (1982). General case programming for community activity. In B. Wilcox & G. T. Bellamy (Eds.), *Design of high school programs for severely handicapped students* (pp. 61–98). Baltimore: Paul H. Brooks.

Iglesias, A. (1985). Cultural conflict in the classroom: The communicatively different child. In D. Ripich & F. Spinelli (Eds.), *School discourse problems* (pp. 79–87). San Diego: College-Hill.

Jones, K. L., & Smith, D. W. (1975). The fetal alcohol syndrome. *Teratology, 12,* 1–10.

Karnes, M. B., & associates. (1978). *Preschool talent checklists manual*. Urbana, IL: Publications Office, Institute for Child Behavior and Development, University of Illinois.

Kirk, S. A., & Chalfant, J. C. (1984). *Academic and developmental learning disabilities*. Denver: Love.

Kitano, M. (1982). Young gifted children: Strategies for preschool teachers. *Young Children, 37,* 14–24.

Klahr, D., & Wallace, J. G. (1976). *Cognitive development: An information processing view*. Hillsdale, NJ: Erlbaum.

Kodera, T. L., & Garwood, S. G. (1979). The acquisition of cognitive competence. In S. G. Garwood & colleagues (Eds.), *Educating young handicapped children*. Rockville, MD: Aspen Systems.

Linder, T. (1990). *Transdisciplinary play-based assessment*. Baltimore: Paul H. Brookes.

Moran, M. R. (1990). Facilitating literacy in the primary grades. In L. McCormick & R. L. Schiefelbusch (Eds.), *Early language intervention* (2nd ed.). Columbus, OH: Merrill.

Morrison, G. S. (1991). *Early childhood education today*. (5th ed.). Columbus, OH: Merrill.

Nelson, K. (1986). *Event knowledge: Structure and function in development*. Hillsdale, NJ: Erlbaum.

O'Connell, J. C. (1986). Managing small group instruction in an integrated preschool setting. *Teaching Exceptional Children, 18,* 166–171.

Peterson, N. L. (1987). *Early intervention for handicapped and at-risk children*. Denver: Love.

Piaget, J. (1954). *The construction of reality in the child*. New York: Basic.

Piaget, J. (1977). *The development of thought: Equilibration of cognitive structure*. New York: Viking.

Piaget, J., & Inhelder, B. (1969). *The psychology of the child*. New York: Basic.

Pick, A. D., Frankel, D. G., & Hess, V. L. (1975). Children's attention: The development of selectivity. In E. M. Hetherington (Ed.), *Review of child development research*. Chicago: University of Chicago Press.

Raudsepp, E. (1980, July). Creativity games: A little imagination goes a long way. *Machine Design,* 73–77.

Rowbury, T. G. (1982). Preacademic skills for the reluctant learner. In K. E. Allen & E. M. Goetz (Eds.), *Early childhood education: Special problems, special solutions* (pp. 201–228). Rockville, MD: Aspen Systems.

Rowbury, T. G., & Baer, D. M. (1980). The applied analysis of young children's behavior. In D. S. Glenwick & L. A. Jason (Eds.), *Behavioral community psychology: Progress and prospects*. New York: Praeger.

Rule, S., Fiechtl, B. J., & Inocenti, M. S. (1990). Preparation for transition to mainstreamed post-preschool environments: Development of a survival skills curriculum. *Topics in Early Childhood Special Education, 9*(4), 78–90.

Salisbury, C. L., & Vincent, L. J. (1990). Criterion of the next environment and best practices: Mainstreaming and integration 10 years later. *Topics in Early Childhood Special Education, 10*(2), 78–89.

Saville-Troike, M. (1979). Culture language and education. In H. T. Trueba & C. Barnett-Mizrahi (Eds.)., *Bilingual multicultural education and the professional: From theory to practice* (pp. 139–148). Rowley, MA: Newberry House.

Sigman, M., & Mundy, P. (1987). Symbolic processes in young autistic children. In D. Cicchetti & M. Beeghly (Eds.), *Symbolic development in atypical children: New directions for child development* (No. 36). San Francisco: Jossey-Bass.

Silverman, R. E. (1975). *Psychology* (3rd ed.). Englewood Cliffs, NJ: Prentice-Hall.

Speigel-McGill, P., Reed, D. J., Konig, C. S., & McGowan, P. A. (1990). Parent education: Easing the transition to preschool. *Topics in Early Childhood Special Education, 9*(4), 66–77.

Swanson, H. L., & Reinert, H. R. (1984). *Teaching strategies for children in conflict*. Columbus, OH:

Merrill.

Tannen, D. (1982). The oral/literate continuum in discourse. In D. Tannen (Ed.), *Spoken and written language: Exploring orality and literacy*. Norwood, NJ: Ablex.

Thurman, K., & Widerstrom, A. (1990). *Infants and young children with special needs: A developmental and ecological approach* (2nd ed.). Baltimore: Paul H. Brookes.

Torrance, E. P. (1977). *Discovery and nurturance of giftedness in the culturally different*. Reston, VA: The Council for Exceptional Children.

van Kleeck, A. (1990). Emergent literacy: Learning about print before learning to read. *Topics in Language Disorders, 10*(2), 25–45.

Vaughan, V. C., McKay, R. J., Behrman, R. E., & Nelson, W. E. (1979). *The Nelson textbook of pediatrics* (11th Ed.). Philadelphia: Saunders.

Weiner, B., Graham, S., Taylor, S., & Meyer, W. (1983). Social cognition in the classroom. *Educational Psychologist, 18*, 109–124.

Westby, C. (1980). Assessment of cognitive and language abilities through play. *Language, Speech and Hearing Services in Schools 11*, 154–168.

Westby, C. (1985, August). *Cultural differences in caregiver-child interaction*. Paper presented at the annual meeting of the American Speech-Language-Hearing Association, Albuquerque, NM.

Zimmerman, B. J., & Pike, E. C. (1972). Effects of modeling and reinforcement on the acquisition and generalization of question-asking behavior. *Child Development, 45*, 892–907.

Chapter 11

Effective Use of Paraprofessionals and Volunteers in Early Intervention Programs

Key Points

▶ Both paid and unpaid paraprofessionals can make significant contributions to the effectiveness of early intervention programs.

▶ The effectiveness of the paraprofessional's contribution depends primarily on how well the teacher or director prepares for and develops a working relationship with the paraprofessional.

▶ Clear, well-thought-out job descriptions that consider the strengths and desires of the paraprofessionals can serve to motivate and guide volunteers and aides.

▶ Early interventionists serve as role models for paraprofessionals.

▶ The creation of an optimal working relationship is highly dependent on effective communication of expectations, desires, and needs between the early interventionist and the paraprofessional.

▶ Feedback and evaluation can strengthen team relationships.

▶ Aides and volunteers deserve to be recognized for their contributions to early intervention services.

Key Topics

▶ Preparing to work with paraprofessionals.

▶ Recruiting paraprofessional services.

▶ Providing an orientation to job expectations.

▶ Defining the interventionist's responsibilities to the aide or volunteer.

▶ Evaluating paraprofessional services.

▶ Preventing burnout among paraprofessionals.

It would be difficult to find a teacher of young children with special needs who is not grateful for and even dependent on the help of paraprofessionals and volunteers in the classroom or center. Teachers or other interventionists who hesitate to sing the praises of those who assist them either have not learned how to incorporate their assistance into the classroom routine effectively or have a unique situation. Teachers must do more than be grateful for the assistance they receive; they must also realize that they have an important responsibility for guiding paraprofessionals and helping them develop their skills. Resourceful work is required to launch a successful volunteer program, but teachers typically do not know where to begin. This chapter provides guidelines for effectively developing and using paraprofessionals and volunteers in the center or classroom.

Paraprofessionals are individuals who by assistance or aid extend the capacity and effectiveness of teachers and other interventionists. By definition, paraprofessionals do not have the training and expertise of professional teachers, and they receive less in monetary compensation. Another category of auxiliary personnel is the volunteers who also assist or aid in classrooms and centers. Volunteers may be parents, students in training, or interested community members. They usually serve on a part-time or sporadic basis, while paid assistants or aides work according to a consistent schedule. Most of these people delight in caring for children, are patient with their fumbles, and understand their special needs. These basic qualities of respect, caring, and desire to serve are essential to effective involvement in early childhood education.

The motivation to serve in and of itself is not enough. Paraprofessionals and volunteers need guidance in effectively using their talents and may need to be willing to learn new skills. Some will need a willingness to change attitudes and philosophies about how to manage child behavior. Simply responding to special problems according to one's parental experience or values about "good" and "bad" behaviors may run contrary to the professional aims of the program and the teacher. For example, paraprofessionals and volunteers frequently have strong ideas about such matters as discipline and issues related to sex that may need tempering to be consistent with the goals and philosophy of the teacher.

The teacher or director has the responsibility to explain special needs, to provide specific guidelines, and to demonstrate desired techniques of behavior management. In effect, when working with paraprofessionals and volunteers, the teacher is a leader and a manager. For this adult-to-adult role relationship to work effectively, mutual respect among the participants is needed. Each will bring specific skills, interests, and talents to the tasks to be performed. Each will have a unique role to play in making children's experiences pleasant and educationally appropriate. But it remains the teacher's responsibility to guide, develop, and use the interests, talents, and motivation of any and all paraprofessionals and volunteers who seek to contribute.

WHO ARE
THE PARAPROFESSIONALS?

Paraprofessionals, those who lack the full training and certification necessary to teach young children with special needs, provide three levels of assistance (Greer, 1978). A *teacher assistant*

has limited decision-making authority but is responsible for directly assuming whatever instructional and support tasks are granted by the supervising teacher. Teacher assistants often are involved in directly instructing children as part of their training before becoming professionals.

Teacher aides have less authority and responsibility than teacher assistants. Typically aides are not directly involved in supervised instruction because they may have no teacher training. They commonly handle less sophisticated instructional activities such as supervising play, feeding, toileting, and preparing materials. However, in many programs there is no distinction between the roles of the teacher assistant and the teacher aide. In fact, all auxiliary personnel may be called aides and may be functioning in a variety of instructional support capacities.

Volunteers provide a broad range of assistance for which they receive no salaries. As established by the National School Volunteers Program, the following four principal objectives are reached by the tasks performed by volunteers (Carter & Dapper, 1974):

1. Relieving professional staff members of nonteaching duties.

2. Providing to individual children needed services that supplement the work of the classroom teacher.

3. Enriching the experiences of children beyond what would normally be available (such as sharing special talents).

4. Building improved understanding of school problems in the community and stimulating citizen support for educational improvement.

Throughout this chapter the term *paraprofessional* will generally refer to any of the three levels of assistance by those of nonteacher rank. However, where the handling of paraprofessionals and volunteers differs, the distinctions will be clearly stated. For example, schools typi-

cally do not have to recruit *paid* teacher aides and teacher assistants. Volunteer recruitment may be a critical element, however, in having sufficient adult resources to carry out needed instructional and support activities within budget limitations. Usually, the performance effectiveness of volunteers is not evaluated formally. Volunteers are most often thanked and praised for their help. With paraprofessionals who may aspire to become teachers, however, specifying tasks and formalizing the evaluation of their performance are fundamental parts of the learning-development process.

PREPARING TO WORK WITH PARAPROFESSIONALS

Recruiting, developing, and effectively involving paraprofessionals often places the teacher of young children in a role for which he or she may be ill-prepared (Lindeman & Beegle, 1988). The prevailing emphasis in the education of teachers is toward theories of learning and child development, instructional methods, curricula, and behavior management. When paraprofessionals are used in any capacity to supplement and extend pupil-teacher contact, however, the teacher is thrust into the role of leader and manager of adults. In this leadership role, the responsibilities of the teacher differ only in degree from many of the functions required of a manager in a business, a hospital, or a government agency.

The remainder of this chapter explores the avenues for successfully working with paraprofessionals through the planning, organization, and leadership skills of the supervising professional. Before the teacher aide or volunteer can begin to offer a major contribution to the classroom or center, several essential steps should be taken by the supervisor. These include the following:

1. Developing clear and appropriate job descriptions.

2. Recruiting selectively to find people with needed job qualities.

3. Becoming involved in a thorough orientation program and clearly defining the teacher's responsibilities to teacher aides and volunteers.

4. Attempting continually to discover and match classroom responsibilities with the special skills, talents, and interests of paraprofessionals and to provide evaluative feedback (Karnes & Lee, 1978; Krupicka & Fimian, 1987).

Designing and Defining Jobs

Designing and defining jobs is the starting point for effectively using paraprofessionals (Blalock, 1991). There are two primary reasons why **job design** is the appropriate point of departure. First, careful consideration of job design elements provides the criteria for recruiting and selecting paraprofessionals, especially paid teacher aides. Second, people work more effectively when they know what they are supposed to do and how and when they are supposed to do it. Job design thus frames the expectations that are so important to job functioning and role relationships. Because this responsibility falls on teachers, it clarifies in their minds the purposes, tasks, and conditions in which paraprofessionals are to be part of the classroom team. Similarly, a clearly defined set of tasks, responsibilities, and relationships establishes for paraprofessionals the framework within which they are expected to work.

Job design refers to specifying the content and relationships of any job, be it the job of teacher aide, volunteer, teacher, principal, or director. Properly conceived, job design considers both the job holder as a person and the performance contributions expected on behalf of the organization (or classroom). A simple way of thinking about job design characteristics is to borrow concepts from a classical study of group dynamics in which Homans (1950) conceived of any work group (e.g., teacher, paraprofessionals, or pupils) as a social system. Homans identified three features common to any small work group: activities, interactions, and sentiments. With slight modification, the following are the basics for defining essential job design elements in centers and schools:

1. *Activities or tasks.* This feature defines the content of what a job holder is to do. What is the scope or breadth of tasks? To what degree are they to be standardized and routinized instead of creative? How often are they to be performed? What results are expected? How are they to be recognized (by both the paraprofessional and the teacher)?

2. *Interactions or role relationships.* This defines with whom the job holder is expected to interact, how often (or under what conditions) this is to happen, and the quality of that relationship. What relationship is the paraprofessional to have with the children? With other adults—staff members and parents? What are the paraprofessional's responsibilities and limits of authority relative to the teacher? How much autonomy or freedom (self-initiative) is given the paraprofessional for certain types of tasks? To what extent is teamwork instead of individual action expected?

3. *Sentiments or values and attitudes.* This defines the conditions under which work is to be performed and sources of satisfaction available to the job holder. By calling attention to sentiments, the teacher is forced to anticipate and build on essential questions that affect the quality of the paraprofessional's involvement in the classroom such as the following: What personal rewards are meaningful to the paraprofessional? How is the paraprofessional expected to view sensitive issues such as discipline methods and toilet habits? What values and attitudes held by

the paraprofessional will contribute best to the program's objectives and be compatible with those of the teacher?

Developing Job Task Descriptions. According to McKenzie and Houk (1986),

Since each paraprofessional brings different skills and expectations to the job and each teacher's needs are different, the paraprofessional's job description must be tailored to reflect their unique interaction. An important part of the paraprofessional's job description is a statement permitting the cooperating teacher and/or coordinator to specify which skills the paraprofessional must acquire, the methods or opportunities available, and the timeline for acquiring this additional training. (pp. 249–250)

The job task descriptions should be expressed in writing, with each participant keeping a copy for reference. These should be rewritten at least once each year following performance evaluation and at any time there is a significant change in assignment. This job description typically conveys more than a trite list of "responsible for" statements. As previously suggested, a written job description provides both the criteria for screening candidates (in the case of teacher aides) and a picture of the job for the candidate. For a starting point in creating a useful statement of job task design, the supervisor should think about the ways in which a teacher aide or a volunteer can be useful. One of the easiest ways to develop such a list of task possibilities is to jot down ideas as they occur during the day. Some of the ways paraprofessionals could be useful might include the following:

1. Preparing the room, including setting up centers, organizing materials needed for special projects, and locating daily supplies.
2. Greeting the children and assisting with all routines.
3. Supervising activities in the classroom and on the playground.
4. Nurturing appropriate behavior, including

dealing with misbehaviors acceptably and effectively.
5. Directing specific activities planned by the teacher.
6. Assisting children with eating and toileting programs.
7. Helping children with orthotic devices.
8. Charting behaviors during the implementation of behavior management programs.
9. Helping to order or build adaptive equipment.
10. Following specialists' instructions in helping to position or transport children.
11. Providing appropriate prompts to help ensure positive social integration.
12. Preparing, cataloging, and filing intervention games and materials.
13. Setting up projectors and other media equipment.
14. Showing videotapes, slides, and special materials.
15. Contacting parents to set up conferences.
16. Helping with end-of-the-day routines, including clean-up.

Once the teacher has identified desirable tasks, he or she should record them to clarify (a) who is to conduct the activity, (b) how often it is to be performed, (c) the manner in which it is to be performed (if standardization or consistency is desired), and (d) how all concerned can recognize successful performance.

Visualizing Role Relationships. After the teacher has defined activity areas, he or she should think carefully about the role visualized for the paraprofessional. Will the paraprofessional be a creative, warm contributor to the children's learning, or merely the person behind the scenes who prepares materials? Will he or she be encouraged to suggest activities, or be relegated to doing only what the teacher has planned?

The answers to such role relationship questions reflect the philosophy and style of the teacher. Figure 11–1 depicts the extreme views of interaction that teachers have of themselves in relation to support personnel. A teacher who wants to be the boss and run a tight classroom or center ought to be aware of this philosophy. Such a situation will definitely restrict the range of freedom and autonomy given to paraprofessionals.

It is helpful if the teacher thinks carefully about his or her role relationship philosophy before completing job descriptions and procedures for paraprofessionals. Whether or not it is recognized and clearly defined, the basic feeling (or sentiment) for what is appropriate and right will

determine what the teacher will do in working with support people.

If the teacher discovers that the role assigned to and accepted by the teacher aide reflects a subtle feeling that the teacher aide cannot actually implement carefully planned and supervised activities, the teacher should experiment. He or she can provide explicit directions, demonstrate what is to be done, and then discuss ways to improve the activity the next time. This may convince the teacher that given helpful supervision, the teacher aide can be an effective assistant teacher. Of course, it is always the teacher's responsibility to determine what the activity should include and what the objectives must be. Techniques of behavior management cannot be

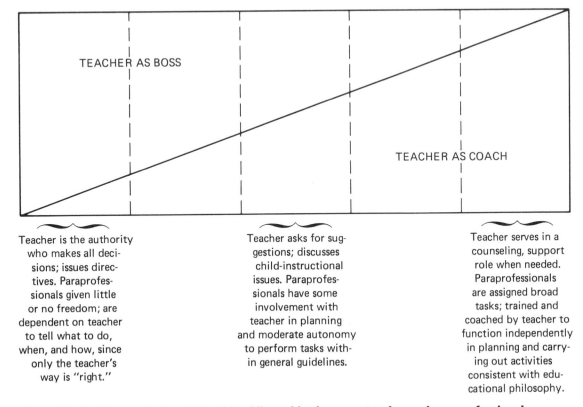

TEACHER AS BOSS

TEACHER AS COACH

Teacher is the authority who makes all decisions; issues directives. Paraprofessionals given little or no freedom; are dependent on teacher to tell what to do, when, and how, since only the teacher's way is "right."

Teacher asks for suggestions; discusses child-instructional issues. Paraprofessionals have some involvement with teacher in planning and moderate autonomy to perform tasks within general guidelines.

Teacher serves in a counseling, support role when needed. Paraprofessionals are assigned broad tasks; trained and coached by teacher to function independently in planning and carrying out activities consistent with educational philosophy.

Figure 11–1   Range of role relationship philosophies between teacher and paraprofessionals.

left to chance or allowed to be inconsistent. These must be the teacher's responsibility. But with planning, guidance, and supervision, teacher aides can provide excellent instruction (McKenzie & Houk, 1986).

Translating Sentiments (Values and Attitudes) into Policy Guidelines. Few dedicated teachers would work without some form of lesson plan or curriculum guide. Similarly, the teacher plans in advance the essential performance tasks expected of paraprofessionals and clarifies intended relationships. This enables planned

rather than reactive use of these potentially valuable people. For optimum effectiveness, however, the teacher should also plan for and codify the *affective* behavior expected of paraprofessionals. This means in part explaining (in writing when possible) the ways in which teacher aides and volunteers are to behave to be consistent with the philosophy and educational aims of the teacher and the school.

The most useful way of expressing such sentiments is to provide guidelines for behavior. Exhibit 11–1 illustrates several specific guidelines that were developed by one preschool director to

EXHIBIT 11–1 _____

Child Interaction Guidelines for Paraprofessionals

1. *Create a pleasant atmosphere.* Tense children cannot become effectively involved. Help them feel comfortable by being warm and enthusiastic. If you relax and enjoy yourself, the children will feel this and follow your example.

2. *Your voice is your assistant.* A soft, confident voice elicits a child's attention more quickly than a high or loud one. First gaining eye contact with a child and then speaking directly and softly to him or her will be more effective than shouting across the room.

3. *Be positive.* Instead of saying, "Don't spill your milk," it is better to say, "Hold your glass with two hands." "Good builders put their tools away carefully" is a better statement than "Don't throw your tools."

4. *Labels are for jelly jars, not for children.* Labels and phrases such as "naughty boy" or bad girl" make children feel ashamed and unworthy. Children with these feelings cannot learn.

5. *Keep competition out of the classroom.* Nothing is to be gained from fostering competition among young children. Discourage children when they say, "I can draw better than Susie," by saying, "Each can draw in his or her own special way."

6. *Choices are for choosing.* When it is time to clean up, do not ask the children whether they want to clean up. Instead say, "It is time to clean up now." If you do not intend to accept no for an answer, do not give them a choice. Give them a choice only when you really want them to choose.

7. *Sharing is not simple.* Preschool-aged children are just learning to share. If they are playing with something, in their minds the toy belongs to them at that moment. Children should be encouraged to ask whether they can have a turn and to tell others when they are through playing with something.

8. *Keep your eyes on the children.* Children must be within the visual range of supervising adults at all times. They need and deserve alert supervision, which is not possible when the responsible adult is engaged in adult conversation. If too many children are entering any one play area, redirect some to other areas.

9. *Do not dominate children's activities.* Children should be allowed to use their active imaginations as they experiment with ideas and materials. Unless you are teaching a specific lesson, stay in the background with supportive but not suppressive comments.

10. *Prevention is perfect.* Be alert so you can redirect behavior that can become a problem. Remember that children should not be allowed to hurt themselves or others.

emphasize the desired behaviors for volunteers to use when interacting with the children. A handout of these and other guidelines was given to each volunteer and explained as part of the orientation process. They subsequently served as criteria the teachers could use to discuss successes and problems with the volunteers. By periodically calling attention to specific guidelines, the teachers were able to guide most volunteers to adopt behaviors that were fairly consistent with the expected patterns.

As suggested by the guidelines in Exhibit 11–1, properly codified policies of role behavior state the way or tone of doing the job and *what* is to be done. They can also indicate *when* a particular behavior is considered appropriate. The volunteer who is supervising outdoor play in the vicinity of the sandbox thus is not caught in the dilemma of wondering, "What do I do now?" when he or she sees Tony throwing sand.

Because they serve as a frame of reference for feedback, policy guidelines not only help in redirecting a paraprofessional's behavior when necessary, but also stimulate job satisfaction. The paraprofessional knows when he or she has done a good job or has handled a difficult situation successfully and consistently with the program's standards. Guidelines also permit teachers to reinforce appropriate behavior. To the extent they allow the paraprofessional to make discretionary choices, the guidelines can help him or her feel more "professional" about being involved in the learning process.

RECRUITING PARAPROFESSIONAL SERVICES

When recruiting paraprofessional services, the teacher or director should keep in mind the necessary qualities of a successful paraprofessional. Agencies that use volunteers regularly are finding that an increasing number of them are generally mature and highly trained. Most volunteers today are middle aged, although retirees increasingly are being recognized as valuable assets to

the classroom or center. They are usually devoted to their work and enjoy sharing their vast knowledge and skills gained from years of experience. Volunteer expenses are even tax deductible for some senior citizens. At the other end of the age-experience spectrum are students from elementary school through college who continue to offer their enthusiasm and desire to learn while working with young children. Many programs are hiring parents of children who have special needs to serve as parent paraprofessionals. Such parents provide invaluable support to parents who are new to the experience of having a child with disabilities (Hanson & Lynch, 1989).

Coordinating Recruitment Efforts

The first step in recruiting and organizing paraprofessional services might be to select a volunteer coordinator. Often a mother will eagerly take such a responsibility. It is helpful to have a coordinator who has previously been an enthusiastic volunteer. The enthusiasm will be most useful in the coordinator's recruiting efforts. The coordinator will also need to have organizational skills and a positive way of working with others.

This person, if not the teacher, works with the teacher in making a list of classroom jobs to be done and in determining the time of day service is needed. The coordinator is then in a position to search for individuals who can fill the needs outlined in the job task description. Exhibit 11–2 lists classroom jobs typically found in preschool or early intervention programs.

Recruitment Techniques

The volunteer coordinator might begin by telephoning parents of children in the program, members of local Parent-Teacher Organizations, and college instructors in the area. Inviting interested individuals to a coffee hour when program needs are presented and sign-up contracts are available may speed up the recruitment process. Holding the meeting in the center will make job

EXHIBIT 11—2 —————————————

Some Services Commonly Provided by Volunteer Workers

Services Requiring Minimal Skills or Training

1. Assisting in decorating rooms.
2. Distributing supplies and snacks.
3. Helping with clothing and toileting.
4. Preparing materials for activity units.
5. Supervising outdoor play.
6. Arranging and helping with field trips.

Services Requiring Some Skills or Training

1. Typing newsletters, forms, and parent notices.
2. Instructing in special arts or crafts units.
3. Organizing and supervising a toy and therapeutic equipment loan program.
4. Assisting in health, vision, and hearing screening programs.
5. Interpreting and conducting classes for non-English-speaking families.
6. Teaching parents to make educational materials for home use.
7. Assisting parents in fundraising activities.
8. Making bibs, aprons, capes, or other sewn items.

and to answer questions. A coordinator who has been volunteering for some time is often more able to answer questions and to generate enthusiasm. It also helps to have on hand brochures or flyers with illustrated samples of job responsibilities, places and times of volunteering, and the name and telephone number of the contact person. The same flyers can be distributed in the local library, medical offices, and churches. At all times, volunteer coordinators should be prepared to sign up individuals who indicate interest. Figure 11–2 offers a sample of one type of recruitment contract.

One effective means of reaching a number of individuals who might be interested in volunteering is to include an eye-catching recruitment letter in the report cards of elementary school children and possibly in report cards of older children. The letter should contain a checklist of skills, interests, and talents. The child can then return the completed form to the teacher. The same letter and checklist can be sent to college students, high school students, and community clubs. In some communities a newspaper advertisement is useful. Figure 11–3 is an example of a letter and checklist that have been used effectively.

Interviewing for a Good Match

McKenzie and Houk (1986) have outlined a four-step placement process that stresses the importance of achieving the best possible match between the supervising teacher and the paraprofessional. Effective involvement of a paraprofessional is based on the degree of correspondence between the paraprofessional's skills and the support needs of the teacher. The first two steps, which involve taking inventories of teachers' needs and paraprofessionals' skills, and the fourth step, developing individualized job descriptions, are discussed thoroughly in other sections of this chapter. The third step, "resolving differences," is often overlooked. The inter-

explanations simple and will help generate necessary enthusiasm. If the teacher is not the coordinator, he or she is spared the uncomfortable feelings of asking for help.

Personal appearances at gatherings of interested service clubs, senior citizen groups, Parent-Teacher Organizations, new members of the community, college and high school classes, and youth organizations can be an effective recruitment technique. The volunteer coordinator should be able to explain clearly what is needed

VOLUNTEER CONTRACT

WHEREAS I believe in the value of nurturing and educating young children and care about their

well-being, and

WHEREAS I seek to contribute my personal talents and energies on behalf of helping the teachers and

children of the Early Childhood Center, in exchange for the joys of sharing a child's happiness,

THEREFORE, I willingly enter into this agreement to volunteer my personal services to the Early

Childhood Center on the following days _____

_____ and times _____ ,

commencing on the _____ day of _____ 199___ , and

continuing until the _____ day of _____ , 199___ .

THIS AGREEMENT entered into at _____ in the state

of _____ between

_____   _____
Volunteer   Date

Who resides at:

_____   _____
                                                                          Phone

_____

and

_____   _____
Volunteer Coordinator   Date

Figure 11–2 A volunteer recruitment contract.

Dear Friends:

This letter is sent to you because I believe that you join me in realizing that children are a most important resource. As a teacher of young children, I feel a special responsibility to recognize and provide for individual needs. The more I learn about child growth and development, the more convinced I become of the need to individualize intervention as much as possible as soon as possible.

Many of the young children in your child's program do need individualized attention. You have many and varied experiences that you could use to help our children here at school. We need volunteer teacher aides to help the children directly and/or to assist the teacher in providing more individual attention.

A list of possible volunteer responsibilities is attached. Please check those duties that you would be interested in doing or add any that have not been included. We invite you to a brief meeting on _____ or _____ to explain the volunteer program in detail. Please check the date that is most convenient for you and return the checklist to school by your child.

Yours truly,

Name _____   Address _____   Phone _____

I would like to:

[ ] Assist in the classroom   [ ] Other: _____
[ ] Help on the playground
[ ] Work with an individual child
[ ] Work with small groups of children
[ ] Help with clerical chores
[ ] Prepare instructional materials
[ ] Share my special talent: _____
[ ] Assist with field trips
[ ] Substitute for a regular volunteer
[ ] Babysit for another volunteer

I prefer to help: [ ] At the center   [ ] At home

Day(s) I can help: [ ] M.   [ ] Tu.   [ ] W.   [ ] Th.   [ ] F.

Hours I can help: _____ _____ _____ _____ _____

Volunteer meeting I prefer to attend:

[ ] _____   [ ] _____
   (Day and time)   (Day and time)

Figure 11–3   Volunteer solicitation letter and checklist.

view process allows the teacher or volunteer co-ordinator to review the job with the applicant and to discuss the appropriateness of the "match." This appropriateness may need to be reviewed occasionally to determine whether or not job descriptions still fit or whether special training should be provided for the paraprofessional.

The interview should be held in the classroom or center, if possible, and should be somewhat informal to ease tension. Interviewers should have a planned procedure and definite questions to ask. Typical situations ("What would you do if . . . ?") should be presented. The response gives the interviewer a feeling for the applicant's natural reactions and provides glimpses of future day-to-day job situations. The teacher should invite the applicant to spend a morning with the children. This is an excellent way to observe not only the adult's behavior, but also children's reactions to the adult. Those who automatically seek to communicate with young children at their eye level show by example that they know how to begin successful involvement with children. Those who resist spending a morning becoming acquainted with the children and the job demands suggest a lack of motivation.

"What am I going to get out of my work in this classroom? How can I make use of my talents and interests so that I am doing something worthwhile and will be resonably satisfied? How can my involvement support the attainment of my personal goals and needs, including learning or growth aspirations?"

MUTUAL LEARNING THROUGH ORIENTATION

Any new teacher aide or volunteer must be socialized into the norms and practices of the teacher and the school or center. Similarly, the expectations and talents of paraprofessionals can never be comprehensively defined during the recruiting or screening stages. These emerge out of discussion and behavior in the classroom. What inevitably happens in the early days of the working relationship is the creation of a **psychological contract** (Hunsaker & Cook, 1986). In framing the psychological contract the paraprofessional typically considers the following:

The classroom teacher's considerations are more along the following lines: "How can I effectively use this person to complement my own skills, talents, and interests? How can I get him or her to accept my philosophies, policies, and goals? What can I do to motivate and develop in this person the abilities and commitments that will help me and the school realize our educational goals?" The terms and conditions of the contract must be favorable to both.

The socialization process of building an effective working relationship is genuinely a mutual responsibility. Both people have to learn about each other. In the process of communicating (verbally, in writing, and through behaviors), they begin to expand their clarification of mutual role relationships. At its very essence, *a role is a set of expectations about what is appropriately to be done and what is to be avoided.* For paraprofessionals, the role can either be reasonably well defined and stimulating or ambiguous, conflicting, and stifling with unpleasant jobs and oppressive supervision.

Communication of Expectations

Both the teacher and the paraprofessional must communicate their expectations. It is an unusual paraprofessional who does not approach the first day of his or her assignment with some feelings of apprehension. For the teacher aide or volunteer, the relationship with the teacher can make the experience rich and fulfilling or miserable and tedious. To help launch the relationship, a planned orientation meeting reaps greater rewards than the cost of the time invested.

If only one teacher and one teacher aide are involved, the orientation may take place in a pleasant corner of the classroom, or it can take place at a restaurant during a planned lunch hour. The number of people involved will influence where the meeting takes place and how it is conducted, but it should not influence what is discussed.

Working as a Paraprofessional in an Early Childhood Special Education Classroom

At least one of the paraprofessionals in this classroom would be paid and expected to conform to professional standards. Most paraprofessionals would be extensions of the teacher helping to provide additional individualized intervention. Many would be invited to participate in conferences, would learn to chart children's progress, and would be expected to model unique techniques of intervention. Some may be assigned to handle extra care needs of children with severe disabilities.

It is a good idea for the teacher to begin with an overview explanation of his or her philosophy and that of the program. The teacher can then lead into a description of the purposes of the program and the plans to be followed in achieving those purposes. Finally, the teacher must describe procedures and role expectations. Here films, slides, or videotapes can be useful (Kelly, 1984). Later the teacher should provide time for discussion and answering questions.

Stressing the importance of communicating common goals, Boomer (1981) discussed specific key items to be considered in the orientation of paraprofessionals. These include design of classroom space, operation of instructional and office equipment, emergency procedures, and the schedule of activities, including the paraprofessionals' hourly responsibilities. One could add to this list the importance of professional conduct. The paraprofessionals who are expected to behave as professionals will usually do so. This includes being prompt, appropriately dressed, and respectful of all aspects of confidentiality regarding children's characteristics and behaviors.

Discovery and Use of Special Skills and Talents

To make the orientation truly an opportunity for two-way communication, the resourceful teacher should encourage new paraprofessionals to reveal their special interests, skills, and talents. Asking about previous work experience is important. Parenting and homemaking skills, however, are equally important in preschools and child care centers. Very few skills cannot be adapted to useful and interesting classroom activities. Everything from sports to needlework fits in somewhere. Hobbies can be the source of exciting lessons. Baking and gardening, as well as sewing and cleaning, can be the basis for preschool science and mathematics lessons.

One effective method of discovering the special skills and talents of paraprofessionals is to develop a simple questionnaire that can be filled out by potential helpers. Many teachers ask parents to complete the questionnaire to encourage parent involvement. Others use the questionnaire with hired teacher aides and with volunteers. The questionnaire in Figure 11–4 was designed to incorporate the needs of an early childhood center while allowing the respondents some latitude of choice.

Once the special interests, skills, and talents of the paraprofessional are known, the teacher may plan to adapt activities to them. A teacher aide in one class loved to garden. An outdoor garden provided lessons in many concepts. Children learned about *straight*, *front*, and *back* rows. They learned about plants that grew *taller* and things that were *shorter*. They discovered the *shortest* stem and the *longest* vine. That garden was the basis of science lessons and nutrition themes, as well as a source of beauty and joy.

Another teacher aide was particularly interested in puppets. She made sock puppets for each child and taught them basic skills. Puppet shows enlivened nutrition lessons and language lessons. Puppets sang the opening song and learned to say "please" and "thank you." Puppets helped with everything, and the teacher aide felt proud of her accomplishment.

When the teacher gives special thought and care to matching classroom responsibilities with the paraprofessional's skills and talents, everyone benefits (McKenzie & Houk, 1986). Ideally a teacher aide will be ready for anything, and many of them are. But even when paraprofessionals are willing to do "anything and everything," relationships and performances are better when interests are allowed to blossom and no one is pushed beyond his or her capacity to perform.

Most teacher aides are expected to take care of many routine matters. Taking attendance,

Name _____

	Mom	**Dad**	WOULD YOU LIKE TO:
1.	[　]	[　]	Read a story to some of the children?
2.	[　]	[　]	Lead a song or some other musical activity?
3.	[　]	[　]	Help children create something in art?
4.	[　]	[　]	Bring the family pet to visit the center?
5.	[　]	[　]	Help set up or supervise a field trip?
6.	[　]	[　]	Make a book of a child's story?
7.	[　]	[　]	Work puzzles or play games?
8.	[　]	[　]	Share your hobby with the class? Hobby:
9.	[　]	[　]	Show children how to use simple carpenter tools?
10.	[　]	[　]	Bring a guitar (or other instrument) and demonstrate?
11.	[　]	[　]	Help cut out and paste pictures?
12.	[　]	[　]	Teach the children something about your occupation?
13.	[　]	[　]	Conduct a simple science experiment?
14.	[　]	[　]	Wear clothing from another country and tell about it?
15.	[　]	[　]	Bring necessary materials and plant some seeds?
16.	[　]	[　]	Demonstrate rug weaving, leather tooling, or other crafts?
17.	[　]	[　]	Make jam or churn butter?
18.	[　]	[　]	Decorate a bulletin board?
19.	[　]	[　]	Sew dress-up and/or doll clothing?
20.	[　]	[　]	Construct special toys or equipment?

And if none of these appeals to you, what would you like to do?

Figure 11—4   Samples from a parent volunteer checklist.

preparing snacks, and supervising the bathroom are often taken for granted. Getting materials ready and cleaning up are duties for many teacher aides. But they can do much more, given encouragement and opportunity. A teacher aide who plays the piano may also find pleasure in choosing songs and musical stories. One who sews will enjoy introducing simple sewing activities. Outdoor games may be the sports-minded paraprofessional's special delight. If the teacher tells the paraprofessional that his or her talents and interests are respected and used, the teacher can generate creative and resourceful suggestions.

DEFINING THE TEACHER'S RESPONSIBILITIES TO TEACHER AIDES OR VOLUNTEERS

So far, we have implied, if not stressed, thoughtful and kindly attitudes on the part of the teacher toward the teacher aide or volunteer. A few of the commonly accepted responsibilities for leadership and guidance are summarized in Exhibit 11–3. However, this genuine caring must not interfere with the teacher's awareness of his or her role as the person on whom ultimate responsibility rests. What is done in and outside of the classroom or center and the way in which it is done are undeniably the teacher's responsibilities. Termination and replacement may be the best solution for the teacher aide who does not share an understanding of this fact. A tug of war for the affections of the children or their parents is destructive and dysfunctional. Differing philosophies of what is best for children lead to subtle and disruptive experiences.

Just as the teacher avoids embarrassing or criticizing the teacher aide or volunteer in front of parents and other adults, so must the paraprofessional avoid undermining the teacher. It is the teacher's responsibility to make this clear from the beginning. The teacher must be alert to recognize any overt or covert attempts to interfere with behavior management or teaching meth-

> ### Working as a Paraprofessional in a Behavioristically Oriented Program
>
> In a highly structured behavioristic program, paraprofessionals might be expected to become proficient in dispensing both concrete and verbal reinforcement. Some would be expected to participate in intensive preservice training designed to teach specific intervention strategies that are to be followed in detail. These would include behavioral management techniques and how to use highly structured procedures.

ods. Such interference should be dealt with immediately. If free and open discussion of the importance of consistent attitudes and management of children is established in the beginning, future problems will be minimized.

We have aimed most of the suggestions thus far at preparing for the entry of volunteers and teacher aides into the early intervention program. These activities are of a managerial planning nature: defining essential tasks, developing policy guidelines for paraprofessional conduct, recruiting volunteers, and orienting teacher aides and volunteers into the philosophy and ways of the program, while also learning of their special talents and interests. What follows is heavily focused on actions the teacher can take to motivate and stretch the abilities of teacher aides and volunteers. These suggestions place the teacher of young children wi h disabilities in a leadership role, guiding, coaching, encouraging, and rewarding the efforts and developing skills of resourceful support personnel. As a starting point, it is useful to think of the teacher as a role model for paraprofessionals.

Being an Appropriate Role Model

Teachers must be appropriate role models. Saying one thing and behaving in a different way is inexcusable. What teachers *do* speaks louder than what they *say*. Advising someone to avoid

EXHIBIT 11–3

Some Responsibilities of Teachers to Paraprofessionals

1. To exert active leadership and guidance to build a team of coordinated helpers.

2. To create an atmosphere in which paraprofessionals feel accepted and motivated to perform effectively.

3. To provide ample structure and direction so paraprofessionals know what is expected of them.

4. To hold an orientation session with new paraprofessionals to discuss program goals, procedures, policies, and what to expect of children with special needs.

5. To plan work in advance of the workday, and to build variety into the tasks paraprofessionals are assigned to perform.

6. To provide adequate information so that paraprofessionals can carry out their tasks, and to provide feedback so they know that you know how they are performing.

7. To have on hand the resources paraprofessionals will need to carry out assigned tasks; to show them where to find materials, how to set up an activity, and how to operate any special equipment. To make known any restrictions or special requirements to accommodate particular children.

8. To assign tasks within the range of competency of a paraprofessional while providing increased responsibility and autonomy as performance indicates increased competence.

9. To provide opportunities for regularly scheduled meetings between the teacher and the paraprofessional. Such meetings will allow for adequate planning and avoid waiting for a crisis to force communication. Impromptu meetings should not become substitutes for regularly scheduled meetings.

spanking, yelling, and fault finding will not achieve the desired results unless the teacher also is consistent in avoiding these negative behaviors when interacting with children. What the teacher does will influence the teacher aide's behavior. If a quiet manner is recommended by the teacher, then a quiet voice must be used by the teacher—at least most of the time.

Often it is useful for the teacher to tell the paraprofessional what will be demonstrated and to pinpoint what is to be observed. The teacher should explain what will be done and why it will be done. Sometimes a particular procedure should be written and available for reference. This is important for new activities.

After the teacher completes a specific demonstration, the teacher aide will want to practice. Usually (at least at first), the teacher should not observe this practice session. But it is helpful for the teacher to suggest that an observation will be made when the teacher aide feels ready. Allow the aide to take the initiative by extending

an invitation such as, "Tomorrow when you feel ready for me to watch you, let me know."

Part of a teacher's responsibility as a role model is to build up, not undermine, the desire and productive energies of paraprofessionals. Just as the teacher's responsibility toward children is to help them to become more fully functioning independently rather than dependently, the same applies to paraprofessionals. But development of the independent skills and motivation of paraprofessionals does not occur through abandonment. A disorganized teacher whose actions reveal that he or she has given little thought to how paraprofessionals are to serve confuses and discourages those who seek to help. Perhaps the best way of looking at effective ways in which a teacher can help to develop and encourage a teacher aide or a volunteer is through the eyes of those who work in paraprofessional roles. Exhibit 11–4 presents just such a perspective in a sensitive but strongly worded message from a practicing teacher aide to teachers generally.

Making Sufficient Planning Time Available

The teacher aide who provided the message for Exhibit 11–4 wrote about the implications of the teacher's planning (or failure to plan) on the motivation of aides. Another facet of paraprofes-

sional motivation and effectiveness comes from the teacher's and the teacher aide's (or the volunteer's) spending some time together to plan. Many federally funded programs in the 1960s and 1970s allowed for whole days for teachers and teacher aides to plan together each week. Money was available for regular evaluation and

---

EXHIBIT 11–4

Advice from a Paraprofessional to Teachers

Note: The comments that follow were written by an experienced teacher aide. She has worked with a number of different teachers and has strong feelings about teacher actions that made her work effective and rewarding and those that interfered with her own effectiveness.

Treating your aides as if they have no common sense will get you little help. Most aides are more intelligent than they are given credit for. Don't give them only menial chores, but also things that are more gratifying. Give them air to breathe and expand themselves and they will be more help to you as the teacher than you can imagine. One time I worked for a teacher just 1 day a week. Often when I came she said, "Oh! Are you here today? I didn't know you came this week." Really made me feel welcome and useful. Sometimes she just said, "I don't have anything for you to do today. Go see if any of the other teachers have something for you to do." So, planning ahead is important. Teachers complain of "having too much to do," and then they don't make good use of the aide's time because they didn't plan.

Treat your aide as an intelligent person. Aides can do much more than set up snacks and wash dirty faces. If you tell them what to do and why and then show them how, they can be really good teachers. Don't expect them to plan the lessons, but with a little help, they can teach little children very effectively. Answer all questions as soon as possible, and answer them as you would any other adult. Don't "talk down" to them. Your college degree doesn't give you the right to belittle their ability to understand. Tell why you do something, and if they don't understand the first time, tell them again in another way. Show them how to do something the right way yourself. Don't just tell them and leave.

Compliment your aide sometimes, but not too much. Too much flattery is insulting. But a genuine "I like the way you showed Susie how to button her coat" helps to make it all worthwhile.

Let your aides learn from their mistakes. Don't "catch them" every time. Just look the other way for a while. Give them a chance to change by themselves. But if they are really doing something wrong, or they are stuck in the same way, suggest, "Sometimes it helps to do it this way." And then show them or tell them again.

Never embarrass them in front of the children or parents, or anybody for that matter. If you must correct them, wait until you can do it when you are alone. Smart teachers know how to make suggestions look and sound like compliments. "You really are teaching Tommy how to wash his hands. Do you think he is ready to learn to use the brush?" is a lot better than "Don't you remember, I told you that you should teach the children to brush their fingernails when they wash their hands."

Listen to the aides' comments. Let them have the satisfaction of suggesting things to you sometimes. An occasional "Oh, I'm so glad you suggested that" is better than a hundred insincere things. Ask your aides' opinions sometimes, and then listen.

Do remember, you are the teacher. You are responsible. You are in charge. Aides need to know "their teacher" knows what to do. They need to respect all that education you've had. Give them a chance.

by Robbie Crane
Alton, Illinois

planning sessions. Few programs today include this necessity. Conversely, time for planning often seems a luxury.

As with everything else, teachers must do what they can. Day-to-day planning usually fits into very small time segments. The time after school, lunch periods, and so-called "breaks" become the scarce moments for planning. These daily time constraints make it necessary for the teacher to do overall planning before the school year begins. Necessary planning before the school year starts includes designing record-keeping systems, choosing basic activity plans, organizing the classroom, scheduling activities, preparing materials, and assigning responsibilities. The paraprofessional must learn how to use the instructional equipment and what to do in case of various emergencies. The paraprofessional's responsibilities within the daily schedule should be written out. There is rarely enough time before and after school for such comprehensive planning, no matter how dedicated the teacher and the teacher aide may be.

Over time, however, teacher aides and even volunteers should be encouraged to plan some of the specific activities. The teacher identifies the goals and objectives, but the "equivalent practice" (Chapter 6) can be suggested by paraprofessionals. For example, one teacher aide raised tropical fish. With her help, the children planned an aquarium. They learned colors as they chose the stones for the bottom. They discovered water temperature as they planned for the fish. Feeding the fish developed measuring skills and a sense of responsibility.

During the months that the aquarium served as an excellent teaching tool, the teacher and the teacher aide discussed many different ways in which it could be used. More than half of the excellent teaching ideas that evolved originated with the teacher aide. The teacher continued to pinpoint specific objectives that could be achieved, but it was uniquely successful because of the teacher aide's knowledge and enthusiasm to take charge of this project.

Planning sessions need not be overly drawn out. At times they focus on preparing for the next day's events for only one or two children. An example of an effective brief planning session is revealed in Exhibit 11–5. This scene also shows how a teacher can provide effective feedback in a helpful but nonthreatening manner.

Providing Constructive Feedback

Just as routine planning time boosts effectiveness, so also does regular and constructive feedback from teacher to paraprofessional. The teacher must build in feedback about how the teacher aide or volunteer is doing. Informal feedback should not be the occasion for a great deal of discussion. It should be specific, clearly stated, and timely. The teacher should identify strengths, behaviors, and attitudes to be changed or developed. The more straightforward the evaluation, the more effective it will be.

Avoid focusing on personalities. Focus on the task behaviors and the procedures that are changeable. For example, telling the teacher aide that he or she is disorganized is not helpful. Explaining why the crayons and scissors should be placed within the reach of each child instead of at the end of the table, however, will help him or her to understand precisely how to become more organized and efficient. The teacher should discuss why specific things are important. If necessary, he or she should reteach and demonstrate again. It is especially important for the teacher to evaluate and provide suggestions to the teacher aide with no other adults or children present or

---

Working as a Paraprofessional in a Piagetian Center

Paraprofessionals in a Piagetian center would most likely function as part of a team. They would participate in small groups and with individual children. A continuous inservice training program would help them understand Piagetian theory and its translation into activity planning. Team members would be expected to become astute observers and promoters of children's natural curiosity.

EXHIBIT 11–5 _____

A Teacher-Paraprofessional Planning Session

The Scene: It is after school. The children have gone home. Ms. McLynn and her teacher aide, Ms. Robbie, are talking about an activity Ms. Robbie just completed.

Ms. Robbie: We were doing the activity from the kit that you had in the plan. The directions said that we should sit in a circle. Then, each child was supposed to roll the ball to a child of his or her choice and say "I'm rolling the ball to _____" and name the child. But Danny and Terry couldn't do it at all.

Ms. McLynn: Did the others understand?

Ms. Robbie: Most of them did. Some just said, "to Susie," but Danny just threw the ball and Terry wouldn't even do that.

Ms. McLynn: What do you think would have made the activity better?

Ms. Robbie: I'm not sure what the point of that activity is. It didn't give a reason for doing it, so I wasn't sure what to emphasize.

Ms. McLynn: Just enjoying an activity is important. Did they seem to like it?

Ms. Robbie: Terry and Danny just seemed confused by the whole thing. When I tried to make them say the whole sentence Danny just got mad and wouldn't do anything. Terry started to cry.

Ms. McLynn: That really wasn't much fun for you either. And activities are usually enjoyed by all when you teach the children. For now, let's just expect that Danny and Terry are learning by being there and watching the others and hearing them. Probably both of them will learn more than we think in that way. Tomorrow, try the activity again with that in mind. When it is Danny's turn, ask him "To whom will you roll the ball?" Do this just before you give him the ball. Gesture with a questioning look and a shrug of your shoulders. Talk to him, too, of course. Expect him to point to a child, and say something. Then you say, "to Jimmy" as a model for him, or name whomever he points to. Again, just before you give him the ball, look expectant, and model "to Jimmy" for him again if necessary. Accept any attempt to say anything now. Later, you can require a better approximation of the speech. Do the same thing for Terry.

Ms. Robbie: What if another child rolls the ball to one of them? Should I take it away from them, and make them listen to me first?

Ms. McLynn: No, but if you have one on each side of you, you could put your hand on the ball while you talk to them. Keep it just as spontaneous and natural as you can. But do contrive it so that they have to say some part of it. As soon as they can do that much, you can make what they say longer—perhaps "rolling to Susie." Part of what they must develop is auditory memory span. Right now, a few sounds are all they can remember. As you play in this way, that skill will grow rapidly.

Ms. Robbie: Okay. I'll try it that way tomorrow.

---

within hearing distance. The teacher's intent is to support and develop the teacher aide's skills, not to undermine needed authority.

It is important not to exaggerate the negative effects of whatever the teacher aide is doing wrong. Rather, state what is wanted, why it is desirable, and how it is to be achieved.

The teacher should not forget to reward effort and abilities as part of success. Things that are easy for the teacher may be difficult for an inexperienced teacher aide. The teacher should not expect everything to be learned at once! Time is needed for practice. Recognition by way of

"thank yous" for regular role-appropriate behaviors is as important as special rewards for exceptional success. But such spontaneous or informal feedback opportunities do not eliminate the need for periodic formal evaluation of paraprofessional behaviors, especially for teacher aides.

EVALUATING PARAPROFESSIONAL SERVICES

Evaluating paraprofessional services is a critical step in developing improved and successful programs for young children. Informal daily feedback helps create an atmosphere in which the paraprofessional feels secure, worthy, appreciated, and professional. But more formal periodic evaluations are helpful for persons whose service is expected to be ongoing. Formal evaluations not only help personnel development, but also can strengthen program development.

Typically, the first evaluation is not too long after initial employment to focus on and correct misunderstandings and confused expectations. (It may be helpful to begin with a 1-month probationary period. This, of course, can be extended or dropped depending on the results of this initial evaluation.) Such a clarification serves the interests of both parties because an effective evaluation acknowledges that the teacher, as well as the paraprofessional, can learn from the experience. The time between subsequent evaluations is lengthened to 3 or 4 months. For an experienced teacher aide, once a year may be adequate.

Using Self-Evaluations

One formal technique is to allow paraprofessionals the opportunity to evaluate their own contributions and feelings. If the paraprofessional feels comfortable in sharing this self-evaluation with the supervising teacher, chances for growth and development can be enhanced. Perceptions of self-performance are tested against the teacher's observations and expectations. The teacher has the opportunity to provide constructive feedback, to offer encouragement, and to coach. The self-evaluation process may be open-ended, or it may be guided by a checklist such as the one illustrated in Figure 11–5.

As noted in the directions in Figure 11–5, using recent critical incidents is typically a practical technique for clarifying role behaviors and learning. By contrasting a successful event with a not-so-successful one, a problem-solving approach can emphasize conditions necessary for future success rather than belabor criticism of a past problem. When a teacher aide or volunteer

has not been doing something felt necessary (e.g., has failed to listen to children), the teacher can probe the consequences of such behavior. The teacher should be prepared to provide an example of when such a failure or neglect led to an inappropriate consequence. Then both the teacher and the teacher aide should work toward a plan of action for reducing the frequency of the undesirable behavior.

Teacher-Initiated Evaluations of Aides

Teacher-initiated evaluations of aides are necessary because some people see their own behaviors in a more positive light than do others. Thus, the self-evaluation conference potentially must deal with distortions in perception between the teacher aide and the teacher. As long as the primary reason for evaluation is personal and team improvement, however, the dangers of conflict due to differing perceptions are reduced. An evaluation initiated by the teacher overcomes the potential clash between views, especially when the teacher uses a form or checklist. However, teacher-initiated evaluation can generate anxiety and defensiveness on the part of the person being evaluated. Success in either case hinges on the manner in which the teacher handles the conference.

It is better for the teacher to focus on specific generalities such as dependability or interpersonal relations. To do this effectively, the teacher needs to take the time to describe specific behaviors of the teacher aide that are helping and hindering performance effectiveness. An easy technique for organizing a face-to-face evaluation conference is for the teacher to list a select few behavioral descriptions under the following three focal areas (adapted from Harrison, 1978):

1. If you would increase or do more often the following things, they would help your performance.

2. If you would decrease or stop doing these things, your performance would be better.

Check the appropriate box for each question as it applies to you. On the back of this page, note briefly two examples (contrasting if possible) of recent experiences for each question.

HOW OFTEN DO I . . .	Usually	Some-times	Seldom
1. Follow directions of the classroom teacher?	[ ]	[ ]	[ ]
2. Observe closely techniques used by the teacher and put them into practice when working with children and groups?	[ ]	[ ]	[ ]
3. Offer my services to the teacher when there is an apparent need for help?	[ ]	[ ]	[ ]
4. Plan for assigned tasks with children rather than wing it on a hit-or-miss basis?	[ ]	[ ]	[ ]
5. Observe closely to realize individual children's likes, dislikes, interests, and limitations?	[ ]	[ ]	[ ]
6. Allow children time to think and act on their own before giving directive help?	[ ]	[ ]	[ ]
7. Find opportunities for giving children choices in daily activities?	[ ]	[ ]	[ ]
8. Really listen to what children have to say?	[ ]	[ ]	[ ]
9. Acknowledge children's successes and appropriate behaviors and minimize failures or inappropriate behaviors?	[ ]	[ ]	[ ]
10. Accept suggestions and criticisms without becoming emotionally upset?	[ ]	[ ]	[ ]

Figure 11-5 Self-evaluation worksheet for paraprofessionals.

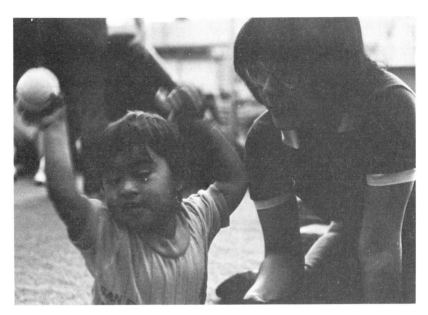

3. To help maintain good performance, keep doing these things much the same as you have been doing.

The teacher and the teacher aide then discuss each of the behaviors to be increased, decreased, or maintained. Specific incidents are used to interpret and demonstrate why the change (or maintenance) would be helpful. The lists for each category should not be too long. The objective is to identify a few important behaviors that conceivably could be changed with concentrated effort. The teacher encourages commitment to some plan of action for changing, but improvement of the aide's performance may mean that the teacher has to change also if he or she is part of the cause of the problem.

The key to a meaningful evaluation is not what is written, but the discussion of the recorded comments between the teacher and the teacher aide. The conference is the basis for developing objectives or intended targets of change (and behavior maintenance) in the future. In a "management by objectives" fashion, any objectives and action plans agreed on by the teacher and the teacher aide can be briefly written, dated, and signed by both (Kelly, 1983; Dyer,

Daines, & Giaugue, 1990). Each subsequent review considers progress toward attaining the previously formulated objectives. Collectively, these periodic evaluations are the basis for the year-end evaluation required for teacher aides in most school districts. As a psychological benefit, however, the periodic conferences reduce the chances that the teacher will take the teacher aide for granted, and they encourage professional-like involvement.

Evaluation of the Teacher by the Aide

Teachers who are dedicated to developing an effective use of paraprofessional services find it valuable to evaluate themselves as responsible models of instructional excellence and supervisors of paraprofessionals. If teachers and the paraprofessionals have developed a relationship of trust and professionalism, teachers can gain much from the paraprofessionals' evaluative feedback. Teachers need to know when their directions are not clear, when they are expecting too much, and when they have been unappreciative or unresponsive. Most teachers do not wish to be negative or ineffective. They are human, however, and do err from time to time. Everyone will benefit if a two-way communication of constructive feedback and positive reinforcement is in effect.

Since the objective of an aide's evaluation of the teacher is to improve their role relationship and team performance, the process needs to be kept simple. Teacher aides need to be given an opportunity to capture their thoughts on paper, however, before any face-to-face meeting. This provides the teacher aide the security of having reflected on and organized thoughts about the quality of the role relationship. A time should be scheduled and the teacher aide should be requested to bring in some written comments or feedback. A most effective way of promoting such preparation is to use a simple three-part variation of the technique mentioned in the previous section. Such an evaluation form is presented in Figure 11–6.

If the teacher and the teacher aide both use a variation of the same three "increase, decrease, or continue" role behavior issues, the process is enhanced. The simplicity of this single-page sheet enables both the teacher and the teacher aide to think in parallel terms, considering what each of them can do to help the other so they both benefit. The concept of increasing, decreasing, or maintaining certain behaviors is easily understood. Not using scales, scores, or rating points reduces the defensiveness or anxiety of either party. The conference focuses on the three levels, inviting objectives and strategies for dealing with the specific identified behaviors. With mutual evaluations, everyone can learn and grow.

RECOGNIZING AND REWARDING TIME AND SERVICE

The importance of daily recognition and praise for time and service cannot be overstressed. Teachers must be careful, however, to be sincere and specific in the comments they make. Each time a teacher aide or a volunteer is told specifically what was helpful, he or she is able to clarify future behavior expectations. Consider the difference between the following two statements:

1. "Ms. Jones, I really appreciated your willingness to help today."

2. "Ms. Jones, I really appreciated your quick response and willingness to help the children clean up the spilled paint. If it had been left on the floor 1 minute longer, two or three children would have walked through it and we would really have had a mess."

Whereas the first comment was obviously positive, it did not tell the teacher aide exactly what was particularly appreciated. The second comment was not only positive but it conveyed to the teacher aide the importance of quick, preventative action. It also helped the teacher aide to know that the teacher is actually observing and really does feel responsible.

Besides daily recognition, paraprofessionals need and deserve some form of more public, tangible recognition and reward. This is especially true of nonpaid volunteers. Many schools choose to publicly honor volunteers at school assemblies, at Parent-Teacher Organization meetings, and at specially planned dinners or coffees. A certificate of recognition is often awarded (Figure 11–7). It is not necessary for the teacher to purchase commercially made certificates. The certificates can be typed, made by teachers, art teachers, or the children themselves.

Names of volunteers and the nature of their service can be listed in the local newspaper or center newsletter. Personal letters from the teacher, director, or school superintendent are always welcome. One early childhood center hosts a special potluck dinner for the staff members and the volunteers once or twice a year. These are festive occasions that everyone anticipates with pleasure. One elementary school features a "Volunteer of the Week" bulletin board to recognize the contribution of a particular volunteer. Of course, permission of the volunteer is obtained first. Another school provides tickets to special performances at the local theater in an effort to say "thank you." The possibilities for volunteer recognition are limited only by imagination and resources.

A TECHNIQUE FOR AN AIDE'S EVALUATION OF TEACHER

To (Teacher): _____

From (Aide): _____

Date: _____

1. You could help my performance and our team effort if you would increase or do more often the following things:

2. I could do a better job of helping you if you would decrease or stop doing these things:

3. To help maintain good performance, keep doing these things much the same as you have been doing:

Figure 11–6   Technique for an aide's evaluation of the teacher.

PREVENTING BURNOUT AMONG PARAPROFESSIONALS

The tendency toward extreme disillusionment with one's job—professional burnout—is common among paraprofessionals. Frith and Mims (1985) outline several reasons for disillusionment, including the following:

1. Stagnation due to lack of opportunity for professional advancement.

2. Inadequate training, which keeps some paraprofessionals from actively becoming involved in the professional team.

3. Poor organizational structure due to undefined role descriptions and unclear understanding of lines of authority.

4. Poor salaries for those who do not have the opportunity to climb a career ladder.

5. Lack of recognition when highly competent paraprofessionals are a threat to those in a position of supervisory responsibility. (pp. 225–227)

Even though teachers may not be in a position to implement a career ladder, they can provide opportunities for paraprofessionals to feel valued and needed. We have discussed the importance of clear job descriptions, the need to discover and incorporate special skills and talents to help the paraprofessional feel like a contributing member of the team, and some helpful ways to show appreciation. Even these basic strategies will go a long way toward preventing burnout for those paraprofessionals who have become creditable members of early education teams.

Summary

Paraprofessionals are potentially valuable resources for extending the teacher's care and development of young children. The extent to which these potentials are realized depends primarily on how the teacher prepares for and develops a working relationship with paraprofessionals.

To initiate a planned program of using paraprofessionals, it is necessary to design the jobs that assistants and volunteers can do. But job design should not be aimed merely at enabling the teacher to eliminate routine or unpleasant tasks. The teacher should remember that effectiveness also involves motivation. Since paraprofessionals work more because of a desire to help young children than for tangible rewards, the jobs they are expected to do should allow for the growth of their abilities. Feelings of competency and learning reinforce paraprofessionals' motivational desires to work thoughtfully with children and to perform other tasks.

The jobs performed by paraprofessionals typically require relationships with either the children or the adult members of the educational team. The teacher should plan the nature of these role relationships so that all participants are behaving appropriately given a common philosophy and a common set of expectations. Guidelines for the ways volunteers and teacher aides are to interact with children should even be formalized in writing.

The following are several advantages to having such job descriptions and policy guidelines in writing and available as handouts:

1. They help in recruiting and selecting paraprofessionals by giving a focused idea of the nature of the work and the working environment.

2. The orientation is focused on those attributes that are important to the teacher and the program.

3. Expectations are clarified and made public to minimize future misunderstandings.

4. They can be a basis for feedback and evalu-

Thank you for being a
LeClaire School Parent Volunteer
and serving the children........

......'N TRUE LOVE.*

Parent Volunteers are a very special breed,
They come forward when there's an urgent need.

No matter what the task or chore,
They're always there to do a little more.

Volunteers add that important extra touch,
That to us all means so very much.

No matter what or which endeavor,
LeClaire School Volunteers should
live on forever!

*(The title of this poem was made
from the letters of the word
"Volunteer")

Figure 11−7 Example of a parent volunteer "certificate." (Poem by Bettie Duncan, LeClaire School, Edwardsville, IL)

ation about how appropriately the teacher aide or volunteer is acting in relation to the needs and standards of the teacher.

As a leader, the teacher is a role model for paraprofessionals, especially in helping them to understand how to work with the children. The degree and quality of preparation for using the time and talents of paraprofessionals set the stage for appropriate behaviors. If the teacher fails to plan how to use a teacher aide's or volunteer's time, paraprofessionals can assume that planning is not a quality necessary for early intervention; that their job is basically babysitting; and that if learning should happen to occur, well, then that is also all right.

If the teacher has planned and organized the tasks of paraprofessionals and clarified the ways of working within the program, then feedback and evaluation can be a natural part of the experience. Rather than functioning as a punishment or as a "here is what you have been doing wrong"

response, frequent feedback and periodic evaluations should be a time for personal development and for strengthening team relationships. Performance evaluation does not have to be a one-way street or something the teacher inflicts on the teacher aide or the volunteer. Quite the contrary, effective teachers will invite teacher aides to evaluate them. After all, the common goal is to discover ways of improving what happens in the classroom and on the playground. If this means the teacher makes some changes in his or her ways of working with paraprofessionals (e.g., being less critical or giving more autonomy), both the teacher and the paraprofessional are probably better off for the change.

Similarly, teacher aides and volunteers need to be recognized for what they contribute. This extends to formal recognition at year's end and at well-spaced times throughout the year. Teacher recognition of paraprofessionals is a way of saying, "Thanks for making my job easier and more successful."

Discussion Topics and Activities

1. Role play an interview with a prospective aide. Be alert to questions that help you get to know something about the individual's talents, skills, interests, motives, and biases. Think ahead and be prepared to be explicit about what you will want the teacher aide to do or not do. Observers may give constructive feedback to the participants by sharing their reactions and what they learned from watching the interaction.

2. Gather or prepare useful techniques for evaluating the success of a paraprofessional program. Refer to Figure 11–5 for suggestions. Check to see that your evaluation elements match the jobs you have designed.

3. Prepare a recruitment letter and an accompanying interest inventory. Discuss with classmates how

these can be used effectively. Try your ideas out on public school personnel who are familiar with or merely interested in paraprofessional services.

4. Prepare an agenda for a volunteer orientation meeting. Take turns role playing various stages of the meeting. Discuss how you would make individuals feel welcome, the "musts" you will cover, and techniques for developing commitments on the part of the participants. Be alert to a tendency to be too technical in your language.

5. Write a paraprofessional's job description. Give specific examples of tasks that are consistent with your philosophy and that of your program. Ask another classmate to check the job description for clarity and adherence to program guidelines.

Annotated Bibliography

Blalock, G. (1991). Paraprofessionals: Critical team members in our special education programs. *Intervention in School and Clinic, 26*, 200–214.

This comprehensive article addresses the question, What should we be doing to ensure that the utilization of paraprofessionals is as fully effective as individuals with disabilities deserve? It outlines numerous steps that can be readily implemented to guarantee that learning takes place and paraprofessionals are effectively involved.

Courson, F. H., & Heward, W. L. (1989). Using senior citizen volunteers in special education classrooms. *Academic Therapy, 24,* 525–532.

This article provides suggestions for recruiting, training, using, scheduling, and retaining senior citizen volunteers in special education settings.

Frank, A. R., Keith, T. Z., & Steil, D. A. (1988). Training needs of special education paraprofessionals. *Exceptional Children, 55,* 253–258.

In surveying 245 special education teacher/paraprofessional pairs, these researchers found that teachers viewed clerical and supervision skills as more important than other paraprofessional skills. While teachers and paraprofessionals tended to agree in their ratings of the importance of various skills, it was evident that the skills needed depended on the type of educational setting.

Frith, G. H., & Mims, A. (1985). Burnout among special education paraprofessionals. *Teaching Exceptional Children, 17,* 225–227.

This brief article is a welcome addition to the sparse literature devoted to the needs of paraprofessionals. The problem of burnout occurs throughout the field of education and especially among those who work with children who have severe disabilities. Frith and Mims offer keen insight into the variables influencing burnout and offer useful ideas on its prevention.

Garber, M., & Perry, M. (1985). Parents help parents help kids. *Exceptional Parent, 15,* 49–55.

This article discusses the Paraprofessional Outreach Program, which shows parents more effective ways of managing behaviors of their children with disabilities. The program uses parents of children with developmental delays as paraprofessionals. They receive a 10-day training program focusing on such topics as goals of community services, behavior modification, and record keeping.

Gartner, A., & Pickett, A. L. (1988). *A comprehensive program of technical assistance to prepare administrators and staff developers to improve the performance and training of paraprofessionals.* New York: City University of New York. Contact the National Resource Center for Professionals in Special Education, Center for Advanced Study in Education, New Careers Training Laboratory, 33 West 42nd Street, New York, NY 10032.

This project offers guidelines and materials to more fully integrate paraprofessional personnel into special education programs. Suggestions for structuring personnel practices and training programs to improve the performance and management of paraprofessionals are included along with five competence-based instructional training modules involving specific activities and handouts.

Jimenez, B. C., & Iseyama, D. A. (1987). A model for training and using communication assistants. *Language, Speech, and Hearing Services in Schools, 18,* 168–171.

A four-phase model for training communication assistants to provide speech and language services in a Head Start center is presented.

Jones, C. B. (1986). Grandparents read to special preschoolers. *Teaching Exceptional Children, 19,* 36–37.

This article describes a program from which both senior volunteers and preschool children with learning disabilities benefited. Seniors rarely missed a session, while the children soon began to select books over toys during free time.

Kellog Model Curriculum Project. (1984). Omaha: University of Nebraska Medical Center. Contact The Meyer Children's Rehabilitation Center, 444 South 44th Street, Omaha, NE 68131.

This project is comprised of five teaching modules covering such topics as child development, legal and ethical issues, behavior management, seizures, and procedures for working with students with developmental disabilities. Each module includes manuals for instructors and trainees.

Kelly, P. M. (1984). *Paraprofessional Facilitator Program.* Topeka: Kansas State Department of Education. Contact the Department of Education at 120 East 10th Street, Topeka, KS 66605.

Included are 26 videotapes covering such paraprofessional inservice topics as roles and responsibilities, instructional and management processes, and working with children with specific disabling conditions. These materials are available for loan.

Krupicka, W. M., & Fimian, M. J. (1987). Using the microcomputer to match special education teacher needs with volunteer interests. *Journal of Special Education Technology, 9*(1), 30–37.

This article describes a user-friendly "index card" software resource that was developed to help local and district school personnel match identified special education classroom needs with volunteer resources.

Lombardo, V. S. (1980). *Paraprofessionals in special education.* Springfield, IL: Charles C. Thomas.

Lombardo discussed the history and status of paraprofessionals in special education. Chapters are training modules to assist individuals who train paraprofessionals. The book is basically a guide that would enable a group to receive training through using several learning stations. Upon completion, trainees would be expected to understand the various characteristics of the diagnostic-prescriptive process and the learning characteristics of the primary disabling conditions. Although the book is intended for those who will work with children older than preschoolers, it can also be useful to trainers of paraprofessionals working with younger children.

McKenzie, R., & Houk, C. S. (1986). The paraprofessional in special education. *Teaching Exceptional Children, 18*, 246–252.

This article outlines a four-step placement process that allows the following three goals to be accomplished: (1) determination of suitable and unsuitable teacher-paraprofessional teams; (2) development of clearly stated job descriptions; and (3) identification of areas in which the paraprofessional may require further training.

Pickett, A. L. (1986). *A training program to prepare teachers to supervise and work more effectively with paraprofessional personnel.* New York: City University of New York. Contact the Center for

Advanced Study in Education, 33 West 42nd Street, New York, NY 10036.

The eight training modules include management and supervision; the instructional team of teacher and paraprofessional; setting goals and objectives for integrating the paraprofessional into the classroom; directing and delegating; interpersonal problem solving; communication and team building; evaluating paraprofessional performance; and helping teacher participants develop a personalized plan for changing and improving their management skills.

Pickett, A. L. (1988). *Paraprofessional bibliography: Training materials and resources for paraprofessionals working in programs for people with disabilities.* New York: City University of New York. Contact The Center for Advanced Study in Education, 33 West 42nd Street, New York, NY 10036.

This annotated bibliography serves as a resource for strengthening and developing systematic training programs for paraprofessional staff. Included are entries on instructional materials, films, and videotapes, as well as items from professional journals, books, and doctoral dissertations on topics ranging from the impact of paraprofessionals on the quality of service delivery, to burnout, to career development and advancement, to personnel practices.

References

Blalock, G. (1991). Paraprofessionals: Critical team members in our special education programs. *Intervention in School and Clinic, 26*, 200–214.

Boomer, L. W. (1981). Meeting common goals through effective teacher-paraprofessional communication. *Teaching Exceptional Children, 13*, 51–53.

Carter, B., & Dapper, G. (1974). *Organizing school volunteer programs.* New York: Citation.

Dyer, W., Daines, R., & Giauque, W. (1990). *The challenge of management.* San Diego, CA: Harcourt Brace Jovanovich.

Frith, G. H., & Mims, A. (1985). Burnout among special education paraprofessionals. *Teaching Exceptional Children, 17*, 225–227.

Greer, J. V. (1978). Utilizing paraprofessionals and volunteers in special education. *Focus on Exceptional Children, 10*, 1–15.

Hanson, M. J., & Lynch, E. W. (1989). *Early intervention.* Austin, TX: Pro-Ed.

Harrison, R. (1978). When power conflicts trigger team spirit. In W. L. French, C. H. Bell, Jr., & R. A.

Zawacki (Eds.), *Organization development.* Dallas: Business Publications.

Homans, G. C. (1950). *The human group.* New York: Harcourt Brace Jovanovich.

Hunsaker, P. L., & Cook, C. W. (1986). *Managing organizational behavior.* Reading, MA: Addison-Wesley.

Karnes, M. B., & Lee, R. C. (1978). *Early childhood.* Reston, VA: The Council for Exceptional Children.

Kelly, C. M. (1983). Remedial MBO. *Business Horizons, 26*, 64–65.

Krupicka, W. M., & Fimian, M. J. (1987). Using the microcomputer to match special education teacher needs with volunteer interests. *Journal of Special Education Technology, 9*(1), 30–37.

Lindeman, D. P., & Beegle, G. P. (1988). Preservice teacher training and use of the classroom paraprofessional: A national survey. *Teacher Education and Special Education, 11*(4), 183–186.

McKenzie, R., & Houk, C. S. (1986). The paraprofessional in special education. *Teaching Exceptional Children, 18*, 246–252.

Appendix A

Chart of Typical Development*

	Gross Motor Skills	Fine Motor Skills	Language Comprehension	Expressive Communication
0–3 Months	Holds head up in prone position. Lifts head when held at shoulder. Kicks reciprocally. Rolls from side to supine position.	Moves arms symmetrically. Follows with eyes to midline. Brings hands to midline in supine position. Activates arms on sight of toy.	Responds to voice. Watches speaker's eyes and mouth. Searches with eyes for sound.	Cries when hungry or uncomfortable. Makes comfort sounds.
3–6 Months	Holds head in line with body when pulled to sitting. Bears weight on hands in prone position. Sits with light support. Holds head steady in supported sitting position. Rolls from supine position to side.	Follows with eyes without moving head. Keeps hands open most of time. Uses palmar grasp. Reaches and grasps objects.	Quiets to mother's voice. Distinguishes between friendly and angry voices. Responds to own name.	Coos variety of vowel sounds. Laughs. Takes turns. Responds to speech by vocalizing. Expresses displeasure and excitement.
6–9 Months	Exhibits body-righting reaction. Extends arms protectively.	Transfers object. Manipulates toy actively with wrist movement.	Looks at pictures briefly. Looks for family members or pets when named.	Babbles to people. Produces variety of consonants in babbling.

* Adapted from the following sources:

CRC Education and Human Development, Inc. for the Administration for Children, Youth and Families. (1978). Mainstreaming preschoolers. U.S. Government Printing Office, 1979620–182/5708

Furuno, S., O'Reilly, K. A., Hosaka, C. M., Inatsuka, T. T., Allman, T. L., & Zeisloft, B. (1985). *HELP Hawaii Early Learning Profile activity guide.* Palo Alto, CA: VORT.

Help for special preschoolers assessment checklist. (1987). Palo Alto, CA: VORT.

Cognitive Skills	Self-Help Skills	Social Skills
Inspects surroundings. Shows anticipation. Inspects own hands.	Opens mouth in response to food stimulus. Coordinates sucking, swallowing, and breathing.	Regards face. Enjoys physical contact; molds, relaxes body when held. Makes eye contact. Expresses distress.
Begins rattle play. Repeats/continues familiar activity. Uses hands and mouth for sensory exploration of objects. Plays with own hands, fingers, toes.	Brings hand to mouth holding toy or object. Swallows strained or pureed foods. Inhibits rooting reflex.	Smiles socially. Discriminates strangers. Demands attention. Vocalizes pleasure or displeasure. Enjoys social play, e.g., "This Little Piggy." Lifts arms to mother.
Works to obtain desired out-of-reach object. Finds object observed being hidden.	Uses tongue to move food in mouth (4–8 months).	Recognizes mother (4–8 months). Displays stranger anxiety.

Johnson-Martin, N., Attermeier, S. M., & Hacker, B. (1990). *The Carolina curriculum for preschoolers with special needs.* Baltimore, MD: Paul H. Brookes.

Johnson-Martin, N., Jens, K. G., & Attermeier, S. M. (1986). *The Carolina curriculum for handicapped infants and infants at risk.* Baltimore, MD: Paul H. Brookes.

Linder, T. W. (1990). *Transdisciplinary play-based assessment: A functional approach to working with young children.* Baltimore, MD: Paul H. Brookes.

	Gross Motor Skills	Fine Motor Skills	Language Comprehension	Expressive Communication
6–9 Months (*Continued*)	Sits independently, but may use hands. Stands holding on. Pulls to stand. Crawls backward. Gets into sitting position without assistance.	Reaches and grasps with extended elbow.	Responds to simple requests with gesture.	Babbles with adult inflection. Babbles reduplicated syllables, "mama," "baba," etc. Vocalizes loudly to get attention.
9–12 Months	Creeps on hands and knees. Moves from sitting to prone position. Stands momentarily. Walks holding on to furniture (cruises).	Takes objects out of container. Uses both hands freely. Tries to imitate scribble. Puts object into container. Releases object voluntarily. Pokes with index finger. Uses neat pincer grasp.	Understands "no no." Listens selectively to familiar words. Enjoys looking at books.	Babbles single consonant-vowel syllables, e.g., "ba." Responds to certain words (e.g., "wave bye bye") with appropriate gesture. Uses behaviors and vocalization to express needs.
12–18 Months	Stands from supine position. Walks without support. Throws ball. Creeps up stairs. Pulls toy while walking. Carries large toy while walking. Moves to music.	Uses two hands in midline, one holding, one manipulating. Scribbles spontaneously. Places pegs in pegboard. Builds two- to three-cube tower.	Responds to simple verbal requests; identifies one body part. Understands many nouns. Brings objects from another room on request.	Combines gestures and vocalizations to express a variety of communicative functions. Says "Dada" or "Mama" purposefully. Uses single words. Uses exclamations, e.g., "Oh oh!" Says "no" meaningfully. Uses 10–15 words (by 18 months).

Cognitive Skills	Self-Help Skills	Social Skills
Touches adult's hand or toy to restart an activity. Plays 2 to 3 minutes with single toy. Follows trajectory of fast-moving object. Shows interest in sounds of object.	Holds own bottle. Mouths and gums solid foods. Bites voluntarily; inhibits bite reflex. Feeds self a cracker.	Smiles at mirror image. Shows anxiety to separation from mother.
Overcomes obstacle to obtain object. Retrieves object using other material. Imitates gestures. Unwraps a toy. Enjoys looking at books.	Finger feeds variety of foods. Holds spoon. Cooperates with dressing by extending arm or leg. Chews by munching.	Enjoys turn-taking game. Resists supine position. Shows like and dislike for certain people, objects, or situations. Shows toys to others; does not release. Tests parents' reactions at feeding and bedtime by new and mischievous behavior.
Understands adult's pointing. Hands toy back to adult. Matches objects. Places round and square pieces in form board. Nests two or three cans. Identifies self in mirror.	May refuse food; appetite decreases. Brings spoon to mouth. Drinks from cup with some spilling. Indicates discomfort over soiled pants. Removes socks.	Displays independent behavior; may be difficult to discipline. May display tantrum behavior. Demonstrates sense of humor. Is easily distractible; has difficulty sitting still.

	Gross Motor Skills	Fine Motor Skills	Language Comprehension	Expressive Communication
18–24 Months	Moves on "ride-on" toys without pedals. Walks upstairs holding railing, both feet on step. Picks up toy from floor without falling. Runs.	Imitates circular scribble. Imitates horizontal stroke. Holds crayon with fist.	Identifies three to six body parts. Matches sounds to animals. Understands personal pronouns, some action verbs, and some adjectives. Enjoys nursery rhymes.	Uses intelligible words about 65% of the time. May use jargon (syllable strings that sound like speech). Tells experience using jargon and words. Uses two-word sentences. Names two or three pictures. Attempts to sing songs with words. Imitates three- to four-word phrase.
24–36 Months	Runs forward well. Jumps in place, two feet together. Stands on one foot, with aid. Walks on tiptoe. Kicks ball forward.	Strings four large beads. Turns pages singly. Snips with scissors. Holds crayon with thumb and fingers, not fist. Uses one hand consistently in most activities. Paints with some wrist action; makes dots, lines, circular strokes. Rolls, pounds, squeezes, and pulls clay.	Points to pictures of common objects when they are named. Can identify objects when told their use. Understands question forms *what* and *where*. Understands negatives *no, not, can't,* and *don't.* Enjoys listening to simple storybooks and requests them again.	Joins vocabulary words together in two-word phrases. Gives first and last name. Asks *what* and *where* questions. Makes negative statements (e.g., "Can't open it"). Shows frustration at not being understood. Sustains conversation for two or three turns.

Cognitive Skills		Self-Help Skills	Social Skills
Finds object not observed being hidden. Activates mechanical toy. Matches objects to pictures. Sorts objects. Explores cabinets and drawers. Remembers where objects belong. Recognizes self in photo.		Scoops food, feeds self with spoon. Chews with rotary jaw movements. Plays with food. Removes shoe when laces undone. Zips/unzips large zipper. Shows awareness of need to eliminate.	Expresses affection. Expresses wide range of emotions including jealousy, fear, anger, sympathy, embarrassment, anxiety, and joy. Attempts to control others; resists control; peer interaction is somewhat aggressive. Engages in parallel play. Enjoys solitary play occasionally.
Selects and looks at picture books, names pictured objects, and identifies several objects within one picture. Matches and uses associated objects meaningfully (e.g., given cup, saucer, and bead, puts cup and saucer together). Stacks rings on peg in order of size. Uses self and objects in pretend play.	Can talk briefly about what he or she is doing. Imitates adult actions (e.g., housekeeping play). Has limited attention span; learning is through exploration and adult direction (as in reading of picture stories). Is beginning to understand functional concepts of familiar objects (e.g., that a spoon is used for eating) and part/whole concepts (e.g., parts of the body).	Gets drink from fountain or faucet unassisted. Opens door by turning handle. Takes off coat. Puts on coat with assistance. Washes and dries hands with assistance.	Watches other children; joins briefly in their play. Defends own possessions. Begins to play house. Participates in simple group activity (e.g., sings, claps, dances). Knows gender identity.

	Gross Motor Skills	Fine Motor Skills	Language Comprehension	Expressive Communication
36–48 Months	Runs around obstacles. Walks on a line. Balances on one foot for 5 to 10 seconds. Hops on one foot. Pushes, pulls, steers wheeled toys. Rides (i.e., steers and pedals) tricycle. Uses slide without assistance. Jumps over 15 cm. (6″) high object, landing on both feet together. Throws ball over head. Catches ball bounced to him or her.	Builds tower of nine small blocks. Drives nails and pegs. Copies circle. Imitates cross. Manipulates clay materials (e.g., rolls balls, snakes, cookies).	Begins to understand sentences involving time concepts (e.g., "We are going to the zoo tomorrow"). Understands size comparatives such as *big* and *bigger*. Understands relationships expressed by *if . . . then* or *because* sentences. Carries out a series of two to four related directions. Understands when told, "Let's pretend."	Talks in sentences of three or more words, which take the form agent-action-object ("I see the ball") or agent-action-location ("Daddy sit on chair"). Tells about past experiences. Uses *s* on nouns to indicate plurals. Uses *ed* on verbs to include past tense. Refers to self using pronouns *I* or *me*. Repeats at least one nursery rhyme and can sing a song. Speech is understandable to strangers, but there are still some sound errors.
48–60 Months	Walks backward toe-heel. Jumps forward 10 times, without falling. Walks up and down stairs alone, alternating feet. Turns somersault.	Cuts on line continuously. Copies cross. Copies square. Prints a few capital letters.	Follows three unrelated commands in proper order. Understands comparatives such as *pretty, prettier,* and *prettiest.* Listens to long stories, but often misinterprets the facts. Incorporates verbal directions into play activities.	Asks *when, how,* and *why* questions. Uses modals such as *can, will, shall, should,* and *might.* Joins sentences together (e.g., "I went to the store and I bought some ice cream"). Talks about causality by using *because* and *so.* Tells the content of a story but may confuse facts.

(Continued)

Cognitive Skills		Self-Help Skills	Social Skills
Recognizes and matches six colors. Intentionally stacks blocks or rings in order of size. Draws somewhat recognizable picture that is meaningful to child, if not to adult; names and briefly explains picture. Asks questions for information: *why* and *how* questions requiring simple answers. Knows own age. Knows own last name.	Has short attention span; learns through observing and imitating adults, and by adult instruction and explanation; is easily distracted. Has increased understanding of concepts of the functions and grouping of objects (e.g., can put doll house furniture in correct rooms); part/whole (e.g., can identify pictures of hand and foot as parts of body). Begins to be aware of past and present (e.g., "Yesterday we went to the park. Today we go to the library").	Pours well from small pitcher. Spreads soft butter with knife. Buttons and unbuttons large buttons. Washes hands unassisted. Blows nose when reminded. Uses toilet independently.	Joins in play with other children; begins to interact. Shares toys; takes turns with assistance. Begins dramatic play, acting out whole scenes (for example, traveling, playing house, pretending to be animals). Comforts peers in distress
Points to and names four to six colors. Matches pictures of familiar objects (e.g., shoe, sock, foot, apple, orange, banana). Draws a person with two to six recognizable parts, such as head, arms, legs; can name or match drawn parts to own body.	Knows own street and town. Has more extended attention span; learns through observing and listening to adults as well as through exploration; is easily distracted. Has increased understanding of concepts of function, time, part/whole relationships.	Cuts easy foods with a knife (e.g., hamburger patty, tomato slice). Laces shoes.	Plays and interacts with other children. Plays dress-up. Shows interest in exploring sex differences.
(Continued)	*(Continued)*		

	Gross Motor Skills	Fine Motor Skills	Language Comprehension	Expressive Communication
48–60 Months *(Continued)*			Understands sequencing of events when told them (e.g., "First we have to go to the store, then we can make the cake, and tomorrow we will eat it").	
60–72 Months	Runs lightly on toes. Walks on balance beam. Can cover 2 meters (6'6") hopping. Skips on alternate feet. Jumps rope. Skates.	Cuts out simple shapes. Copies triangle. Traces diamond. Copies first name. Prints numerals 1 to 5. Colors within lines. Has adult grasp of pencil. Has handedness well established (i.e., child is left- or right-handed). Pastes and glues appropriately. Uses classroom tools appropriately.	Demonstrates preacademic skills.	There are few obvious differences between child's grammar and adult's grammar. Still needs to learn such things as subject-verb agreement and some irregular past tense verbs. Can take appropriate turns in a conversation. Gives and receives information. Communicates well with family, friends, or strangers. Retells story from picture book with accuracy.

Cognitive Skills		*Self-Help Skills*	*Social Skills*
Draws, names, and describes recognizable picture. Rote counts to 5, imitating adults. Describes what will happen next. Dramatic play is closer to reality, with attention paid to detail, time, and space.	Function or use of objects may be stated in addition to names of objects. Time concepts are expanding. The child can talk about yesterday or last week (a long time ago), about today, and about what will happen tomorrow.		
Names some letters and numerals. Rote counts to 10. Sorts objects by single characteristics (e.g., by color, shape, or size—if the difference is obvious). Is beginning to use accurately time concepts of *tomorrow* and *yesterday*.	Begins to relate clock time to daily schedule. Attention span increases noticeably; learns through adult instruction; when interested, can ignore distractions. Concepts of function increase as well as understanding of why things happen; time concepts are expanding into an understanding of the future in terms of major events (e.g., "Christmas will come after two weekends").	Dresses self completely. Ties bow. Brushes teeth unassisted. Crosses street safely.	Chooses own friend(s). Plays simple table games. Plays competitive games. Engages in cooperative play with other children involving group decisions, role assignments, fair play.

Appendix B

Find Your Child's Speech and Hearing Age*

Instructions: Read each question through your child's age group and check yes or no. Add the total and score:

All yes = *Good!* Your child is developing hearing, speech, and language normally.
1–3 no = *Caution!* Your child may have delayed hearing, speech, and language development.
More than 3 no = *Action!* Take your child for professional help.

Check One		Hearing and Understanding	Child's Age	Talking	Check One	
Yes	**No**				**Yes**	**No**
☐	☐	Does your child hear and understand most speech in the home?	*5 years*	Does your child say all sounds correctly except perhaps *s* and *th?*	☐	☐
☐	☐	Does your child hear and answer when first called?		Does your child use the same sentence structure as the family?	☐	☐
☐	☐	Does your child hear quiet speech?		Does your child's voice sound clear, like other children's?	☐	☐
☐	☐	Does everyone who knows your child think he or she hears well (teacher, babysitter, grandparent, etc.)?				
☐	☐	Does your child understand conversation easily?	*2 1/2–4 years*	Does your child say most sounds, except perhaps *r, s, th,* and *l?*	☐	☐
☐	☐	Does your child hear you when you call from another room?		Does your child sometimes repeat words in a sentence?	☐	☐
☐	☐	Does your child hear television or radio at the same loudness level as other members of the family?		Does your child use 200–300 words?	☐	☐
☐	☐	Does your child understand differences in meaning ("go—stop;" "the car pushed the truck—the truck pushed the car")?		Does your child use two- to three-word sentences?	☐	☐
				Does your child ask lots of "why" and "what" questions?	☐	☐
☐	☐	Can your child point to pictures in a book upon hearing them named?		Have your child's jargon and repeating disappeared?	☐	☐

* Adapted from public information materials of the American Speech-Language-Hearing Association. Used with permission.

Check One		Hearing and Understanding	Child's Age	Talking	Check One	
Yes	No				Yes	No
☐	☐	Does your child notice sounds (dog barking, telephone ringing, television sound, knocking at door and so on)?	*2 1/2–4 years*	Does your child like to name things?	☐	☐
☐	☐	Can your child follow two requests ("Get the ball and put it on the table")?	*1 1/2–2 years*	Does your child have 10–15 words (by age 2)?	☐	☐
				Does your child sometimes repeat requests?	☐	☐
				Does your child ask one- to two-word questions ("Where kitty? Go bye-bye? More?")?	☐	☐
				Does your child put two words together ("more cookie")?	☐	☐
☐	☐	Has your child begun to respond to requests ("Come here"; "Do you want more")?	*9 months–1 year*	Does your child say words (8–10 words at age 1 1/2; 2–3 words at age 1. Words may not be clear).	☐	☐
☐	☐	Does your child turn or look up when you call?		Does your child enjoy imitating sounds?	☐	☐
☐	☐	Does your child search or look around when hearing new sounds?		Does your child use jargon (babbling that sounds like real speech)?	☐	☐
☐	☐	Does your child listen to people talking?		Does your child use voice to get attention?	☐	☐
☐	☐	Does your child respond to "no" and her or his name?	*6 months*	Does your child's babbling sound like the parent's speech, only not clear?	☐	☐
☐	☐	Does your child notice and look around for the source of new sounds?		Does your child make lots of different sounds?	☐	☐
☐	☐	Does your child turn her or his head toward the side where the sound is coming from?				
☐	☐	Does your child try to turn toward the speaker?	*3 months*	Does your child babble?	☐	☐
☐	☐	Does your child smile when spoken to?		Does your child cry differently for different needs?	☐	☐
☐	☐	Does your child stop playing and appear to listen to sounds or speech?		Does your child repeat the same sounds a lot?	☐	☐
☐	☐	Does your child seem to recognize mother's voice?				
☐	☐	Does your child listen to speech?	*Birth*	Does your child coo or gurgle?	☐	☐
☐	☐	Does your child startle or cry at noises?				
☐	☐	Does your child awaken at loud sounds?				

* Adapted from public information materials of the American Speech-Language-Hearing Association. Used with permission.

Appendix C

Reflexes, Reactions, and Implications*

Normal Age Range	Reflex	How to Elicit	Motor Response	Implications
Birth to 3–5 months	Biting	Rub index finger on child's upper lateral gum area. Both sides. (Do not attempt on child with teeth.)	Child will rhythmically open and close mouth.	If retained, it will inhibit lateral jaw movement necessary for chewing.
Birth to 3–4 months	Rooting	Stroke with finger from corner of child's mouth to across cheek to earlobe.	Turns head to stimulated side.	If retained, the reflex will interfere with development of natural feeding patterns.
	Grasping	Place object (pencil, rattle, index finger) on palm just below child's fourth and fifth fingers.	Grasps examiner's finger, rattle, pencil, etc.	If not present at birth, indicates abnormality in motor area. If retained, prevents normal grasp and release.
	Stepping	Hold child upright in standing position with weight on feet and lean baby's body slightly forward.	Child will take a few high steps (as if walking).	If not present at birth, indicates neurological problem. If retained, will interfere with gross motor skills.
Birth to 4–6 months	Asymmetrical tonic neck reflex (ATNR)	Child on back with head in midline, arms and legs relaxed.	Child will partially or totally straighten the arm and leg on side of body toward which the head is turned. The opposite arm and leg are partially or totally bent (fencer's position).	Hand use activities in midline, sitting, balance, and control of extremities will be impaired when the head is turned.

Age	Reflex/Reaction	Procedure	Response	Significance
Birth to 6 months	Moro	With child on back with head in midline, arms by side, Examiner places hand on the back of child's neck and raises head off surface. Release support, letting the head drop back. *Catch child's head before it reaches the surface.*	Child's arms straighten out sideways and then move to midline.	If not present at birth, there are indications of neurological immaturity or abnormality. If retained, reflex interferes with general motor control.
Birth to 6 months	Neck righting (log rolling)	Child on back with head in midline, arms straight down by sides. Put your hands on each side of head and turn it to the side.	The body rotates as a unit in the same direction as head is turned.	If retained, reflex will interfere with sequential rolling.
6 months to 18 months	Segmental rolling (body righting on body)	Stimulate as for neck righting.	First head turns, then shoulders, then pelvis.	Becomes voluntary and provides trunk rotation for normal rolling patterns (i.e., leading from hip).
6 months to 24 months	Landau reaction	Hold the child horizontally in space with support under the trunk between the shoulders and pelvis. (Use two hands to support.)	Child fully straightens head, trunk, and hips ("swan dive" position).	If not present, development of extensor pattern necessary for standing and walking will be delayed or possibly prevented.
6 months and beyond	Protective extensor reaction (parachute)	1. Child is held in air, stomach toward ground with support under stomach. Rapidly lower child, head first toward testing table or floor.	Child moves arms forward and catches weight on open hands. Note if child does not use both arms for protection.	If not present, child cannot maintain sitting balance.
		2. Child is sitting independently. Gently push forward or backward or sideways.	Child extends arms and catches weight for support.	

Sources: Ulrey & Rogers (1982); Fiorentino, M. R., (1972); Adaptive Performance Scale (1980). (See Chapter 8 references.)

Appendix D

Competencies for Trainees in Early Childhood Special Education

	Nonexistent	Poor	Satisfactory	Good	Excellent
I. *Appropriately and competently assesses strengths and needs.*					
A. Selects appropriate formal instruments.	1	2	3	4	5
B. Selects appropriate informal strategies.	1	2	3	4	5
C. Monitors child's progress frequently and systematically.	1	2	3	4	5
D. Evaluates family involvement and satisfaction.	1	2	3	4	5
II. *Plans effective intervention programs.*					
A. Works collaboratively with parents in selecting goals and objectives and strategies.	1	2	3	4	5
B. Goals are related to assessment results.	1	2	3	4	5
C. Goals and objectives are clear and relevant to high-priority child and family needs.	1	2	3	4	5
D. Plan is communicated to parents clearly both verbally and in writing.	1	2	3	4	5
III. *Demonstrates understanding of how children learn and ability to utilize generic teaching strategies, including the following:*					
A. Role of social interaction.	1	2	3	4	5
B. Motivation (e.g., identifies high-preference objects, people, and events).	1	2	3	4	5
C. Arrangement of physical environment.	1	2	3	4	5
D. Use of play as both context and method.	1	2	3	4	5
E. Behavioral analysis (including task analysis and identification of antecedents and consequences).	1	2	3	4	5
F. Behavioral analysis (including use of positive reinforcement, use of cues and prompts, shaping, fading, chaining, and stimulus generalization).	1	2	3	4	5
G. Repetition and routines.	1	2	3	4	5
H. Appropriate caregiver-child interaction.	1	2	3	4	5
I. Critical role of family in child's development.	1	2	3	4	5

IV. *Manages classroom environment to optimize learning.*

		1	2	3	4	5
A.	Effectively arranges physical environment.	1	2	3	4	5
B.	Creates appropriate classroom schedule.	1	2	3	4	5
C.	Utilizes daily routines for training.	1	2	3	4	5
D.	Creates effective play routines.	1	2	3	4	5
E.	Provides opportunity for rest and quiet time.	1	2	3	4	5
F.	Creates comfortable atmosphere for parent involvement.	1	2	3	4	5
G.	Takes responsibility for children's safety.	1	2	3	4	5
H.	Effectively manages, coordinates, and involves paraprofessionals, volunteers, and consultants.	1	2	3	4	5
I.	Selects highly motivating activities.	1	2	3	4	5
J.	Utilizes individual as well as small and total group formats appropriately.	1	2	3	4	5
K.	Integrates all developmental domains (i.e., language, cognition, motor, social-emotional, and self-help) into each activity.	1	2	3	4	5

V. *Facilitates the development of communication skills.*

		1	2	3	4	5
A.	Recognizes and correctly interprets communicative cues.	1	2	3	4	5
B.	Understands the stages and characteristics of language and speech development.	1	2	3	4	5
C.	Establishes turn taking.	1	2	3	4	5
D.	Is responsive to child's communicative intents; follows child's lead.	1	2	3	4	5
E.	Uses repetition and recasts.	1	2	3	4	5
F.	Uses appropriate pacing and speech rate; waits for child's response.	1	2	3	4	5
G.	Appropriately labels objects and key events.	1	2	3	4	5
H.	Expands child's utterance.	1	2	3	4	5
I.	Knows how to "up the ante" (i.e., prompt for better turn).	1	2	3	4	5
J.	Utilizes play routines.	1	2	3	4	5
K.	Selects relevant and functional communication goals.	1	2	3	4	5
L.	Develops augmentative communication systems and skills as needed.	1	2	3	4	5
M.	Provides opportunity for choices.	1	2	3	4	5
N.	Facilitates literate, autonomous uses of language (e.g., narrative, explanation, story telling).	1	2	3	4	5

VI. *Facilitates the development of cognitive skills.*

		1	2	3	4	5
A.	Understands the stages and characteristics of typical cognitive development.	1	2	3	4	5

	Nonexistent	Poor	Satisfactory	Good	Excellent
B. Creates opportunities for all children to experience "effectance" (i.e., to develop intentional behavior), and assists child to understand cause and effect.	1	2	3	4	5
C. Effectively encourages exploration and trial and error behavior through modeling, scaffolding, and use of cues and prompts.	1	2	3	4	5
D. Teaches object permanence.	1	2	3	4	5
E. Utilizes activities and materials that encourage mental representation and memory.	1	2	3	4	5
F. Develops symbolic behavior such as pretend play and recognition of graphic symbols.	1	2	3	4	5
G. Creates opportunities for problem solving and assists children in discovering solutions.	1	2	3	4	5
VII. *Facilitates emotional and social growth.*					
A. Understands stages of social and emotional development.	1	2	3	4	5
B. Engages in positive reciprocal interactions with child.	1	2	3	4	5
C. Models and labels a wide range of emotions.	1	2	3	4	5
D. Interprets and validates child's emotional reactions and states.	1	2	3	4	5
E. Uses symbolic play to enhance social and emotional development (at appropriate developmental stage).	1	2	3	4	5
F. Builds self-esteem through emotional nurturing, encouraging trust, and mastery and independence.	1	2	3	4	5
G. Sets appropriate limits and consistent, yet flexible, behavioral guidelines (i.e., "rules").	1	2	3	4	5
H. To the extent possible, assists in providing a stable caregiving environment for child.	1	2	3	4	5
I. Effectively fosters peer-peer interaction, with both peers with disabilities and nondisabled peers.	1	2	3	4	5
J. Encourages altruistic behavior and "manners" in developmentally and culturally appropriate ways.	1	2	3	4	5
VIII. *Facilitates development of motor skills.*					
A. Understands stages and characteristics of typical motor development.	1	2	3	4	5
B. (In consultation with appropriate therapists if necessary), *positions* child appropriately for each activity in order to encourage optimal fine and gross movement and to maximize participation and independence.	1	2	3	4	5

Item	1	2	3	4	5
C. Changes child's position frequently.	1	2	3	4	5
D. Effectively builds child's motor competence and self-confidence by gradually moving toward independent ambulations.	1	2	3	4	5
E. Utilizes appropriate assistive devices.	1	2	3	4	5
F. Utilizes effective teaching strategies to encourage functional fine motor skills and eye-hand coordination.	1	2	3	4	5
G. Utilizes outdoor activities for development of large muscle skills such as running, climbing, and throwing.	1	2	3	4	5

IX. *Facilitates learning of self-help skills.*

Item	1	2	3	4	5
A. Creates positive mealtime environment.	1	2	3	4	5
B. Assists child in development of chewing and swallowing a variety of foods and textures; finger feeding; use of utensils (adapted as necessary).	1	2	3	4	5
C. Establishes appropriate toileting schedule.	1	2	3	4	5
D. In cooperation with parent, develops consistent and appropriate toilet training procedures.	1	2	3	4	5
E. Provides frequent opportunities in natural contexts to learn dressing skills.	1	2	3	4	5
F. Adapts clothing as necessary to support dressing independence.	1	2	3	4	5
(G.) When necessary, applies task analysis and behavioral techniques in teaching self-help skills.	1	2	3	4	5

X. *Facilitates academic readiness.*

Item	1	2	3	4	5
A. Uses developmentally appropriate techniques and materials and everyday contexts to teach cognitive operations such as classification, conservation, and seriation.	1	2	3	4	5
B. Demonstrates functional uses of print (i.e, teacher models use of writing and reading in ways that are meaningful to children and displays print throughout classroom).	1	2	3	4	5
C. Creates opportunity for children to experience function and relevance of literacy behavior (e.g., treasure hunt clues, playing mailman, etc.).	1	2	3	4	5
D. Teaches important preacademic concepts such as opposites ("same" and "different," "big" and "little"); comparative terms ("taller," "tallest"); spatial terms ("in front of," "beside," "behind"); and quantity ("many," "few," "more") in *natural* contexts.	1	2	3	4	5

459

	Nonexistent	Poor	Satisfactory	Good	Excellent
E. Teaches number and quantity concepts in meaningful ways (i.e., teaches "twoness" and "threeness," not simply rote counting).	1	2	3	4	5
F. Teaches auditory recognition, discrimination, and rhyming of sounds and sound combinations.	1	2	3	4	5
XI. Encourages "normalization."					
A. Creates opportunity for involvement with nondisabled peers.	1	2	3	4	5
B. Creates opportunity for child and family to participate in and utilize community resources.	1	2	3	4	5
C. Develops child's ability to engage in age-appropriate and culturally appropriate activities through instruction and environmental adaptation.	1	2	3	4	5
XII. Demonstrates collaborative and interpersonal skills.					
A. Facilitates team approaches and works collaboratively with other disciplines.	1	2	3	4	5
B. Facilitates the development of children with low-incidence disabilities and medical risk conditions in consultation and close collaboration with disability specialists.	1	2	3	4	5
C. Understands roles of each discipline in providing early intervention services.	1	2	3	4	5
D. Effectively manages staff and develops competence and self-esteem of each staff member.	1	2	3	4	5
E. Develops positive work relations with both professional and nonprofessional staff.	1	2	3	4	5
F. Establishes appropriate partnerships with parents.	1	2	3	4	5
G. Communicates with parents in clear and culturally sensitive ways.	1	2	3	4	5
H. Demonstrates flexibility and approaches difficult situations with problem-solving strategies.	1	2	3	4	5

Appendix E

Assessment Techniques for Use with Young Children: A Sampling

Authors' Note: We chose the techniques annotated in this section primarily because they could be used by practicing teachers. We gave preference to criterion-referenced techniques because we believe these are most conducive to program planning. We made no attempt to include tests that take specialized training to administer or to interpret properly.

Because our presentation of these techniques is not an endorsement of their effectiveness, potential users are urged to study their characteristics in detail. To determine which techniques are most appropriate to the purpose and population being tested, potential users should examine test manuals and the *Mental Measurements Yearbook* (produced by the Buros Institute and found in most university or college libraries). Users should take careful note of the test's validity, reliability, characteristics of the normative sample, performance demands, and utility of the techniques.

Arizona Basic Assessment and Curriculum Utilization System for Young Handicapped Children (ABACUS)

Authors: J. McCarthy, C. Bos, K. Lund, J. Glattke, and S. Vaughn
Publisher: Love Publishing Company, 1777 South Bellaire Street, Denver, CO 80222
Ages: 2 to 5 1/2 years
Required Responses: Verbal and nonverbal
Administration: Observations may be made by an individual or a team
Scoring: Easy
Description: This criterion-referenced screening and assessment program covers body management, self-care, preacademics, communication, and socialization skills.
Other Considerations: ABACUS screening Level 1 is designed to determine which children actually need to be observed for in-depth screening and assessment. This is a complete program including prescreening, screening, assessment, and monitoring with a focus on parent involvement.

Battelle Developmental Inventory

Author: Battelle Memorial Institute
Publisher: DLM Teaching Resources, One DLM Park, P.O. Box 4000, Allen, TX 75002
Ages: Birth to 8 years
Required Responses: Verbal and nonverbal
Administration: Individually by teacher
Scoring: Easy
Description: This developmental inventory is a multi-factored assessment based on observations, parent interviews and structured testing in the personal-social, adaptive, motor, communication, and cognitive domains. Separate test booklets for each domain allow independent assessment by various professionals.
Scores: Age equivalents, percentile ranks, and standard scores
Other Considerations: The technical information presented is extensive and the manuals are well organized. The inventory is now available in Spanish.

Bayley Scales of Infant Development

Author: N. Bayley
Publisher: Psychological Corporation, 555 Academic Court, San Antonio, TX 78204-2498
Ages: 2 months to 2 1/2 years
Required Responses: Primarily nonverbal
Administration: Individually by trained examiner in approximately 1 hour with a parent present
Scoring: Moderately difficult
Description: This scale consists of three subparts: mental scale, motor scale, and infant behavior record. It is made up of 163 items including sensory-perceptual activities, manipulation and play with objects, learning and problem solving, the beginning of verbal communication, and motor control.
Scores: Mental Development Index and Psychomotor Development Index
Other Considerations: This is a norm-referenced observation scale with age placements set at the age at which 50% of the normative population passed each

item. High internal consistency. Adequate correlation with the Stanford-Binet Intelligence Scale.

Birth to Three Assessment and Intervention System

Authors: T. Bangs and S. Dodson
Publisher: DLM Teaching Resources, One DLM Park, P.O. Box 4000, Allen, TX 75002
Ages: Birth to 3 years
Required Responses: Verbal and nonverbal
Administration: Individually
Scoring: Easy
Description: This three-part program contains a norm-referenced screening test, a criterion-referenced checklist, and an intervention manual. Test domains include language comprehension, language expression, problem solving, social/personal, and motor skills.
Scores: Standard scores, percentile ranks, and stanines
Other Considerations: This system does focus on parent-teacher interaction in assessment and intervention.

Boehm Test of Basic Concepts-Preschool Version

Author: A. E. Boehm
Publisher: The Psychological Corporation, 555 Academic Court, San Antonio, TX 78204-2498
Ages: 3 years to 5 years
Required Responses: Nonverbal
Administration: Individually by teacher or diagnostician in approximately 15 minutes
Scoring: Easy
Description: This test is intended to measure mastery of basic concepts of time, quantity, and space (direction, location, orientation, and dimension).
Scores: Percentiles for age bands
Other Considerations: Children can point to choices rather than marking with a pencil. It is not suitable for a child with visual impairment. Teachers will find it useful to develop a class profile of concepts to be mastered. It can be used with the resource guide also developed by Boehm.

Brigance Diagnostic Inventory of Early Development-Revised

Author: A. H. Brigance
Publisher: Curriculum Associates, Inc., 5 Esquire Road, North Billerica, MA 01862-9987
Ages: Up to 7 years
Required Responses: Nonverbal and verbal
Administration: Individually by teacher or trained paraprofessional either in its entirety or by individual skills, as needed

Scoring: Easy
Description: This criterion-referenced inventory allows the teacher to determine developmental levels in the areas of psychomotor, self-help, communication, general knowledge and comprehension, social and emotional development, and academic readiness.
Scores: Developmental ages
Other Considerations: It includes developmental record books providing systematic, graphic performance records. Results are readily translated into sequential, individualized lessons.

Carolina Developmental Profile

Authors: D. L. Lillie and G. L. Harbin
Publisher: Kaplan School Supply Corporation, P.O. Box 609, Lewisville, NC 27023
Ages: 2 years to 5 years
Required Responses: Verbal and nonverbal
Administration: Individually by teacher at several different times
Scoring: Easy
Description: This is a criterion-referenced checklist that includes gross motor, fine motor, reasoning, receptive, expressive language, and social-emotional development. It is designed to provide a profile of what a child can and cannot do.
Scores: Developmental ages
Other Considerations: A Spanish edition is available.

Chicago Early Assessment and Remediation Laboratory

Author: Chicago Public Schools
Publisher: Educational Teaching Aids, 199 Carpenter Avenue, Wheeling, IL 60090
Ages: 3 years to 5 years
Required Responses: Verbal and nonverbal
Administration: Individually by teacher or aide in 15 to 20 minutes
Scoring: Easy
Description: EARLY is a 23-item screening instrument that covers gross and fine motor skills, language, visual discrimination, and memory. It has directions in both English and Spanish.
Scores: Percentile ranges that can be recorded on a class summary sheet
Other Considerations: This screening instrument has been normed on 2,000 children in Chicago. The items are coded to items in the 194-activity kit, which is part of the EARLY laboratory. A Spanish version is available.

Cognitive Skills Assessment Battery

Authors: A. E. Boehm and B. R. Slater

Publisher: Teachers College Press, P.O. Box 2032, Colchester, VT 05449

Ages: 3 years to 6 years

Required Responses: Verbal and nonverbal

Administration: Individually by trained aide or teacher in 20 to 25 minutes

Scoring: Easy

Description: This is a criterion-referenced battery intended to provide a profile of skill competencies from which to develop curriculum. Areas covered include orientation of the child to the environment, identification of body parts, visual-motor coordination, auditory memory, story and picture comprehension, knowledge of shapes, numbers, color, letters, and vocabulary.

Other Considerations: A classroom profile is available that enables the teacher to match goals to methods and materials.

Comprehensive Identification Process (CIP)

Author: R. R. Zehrbach

Publisher: Scholastic Testing Service, Inc., 480 Meyer Road, Bensenville, IL 60106

Ages: 2 years to 5 1/2 years

Required Responses: Verbal and nonverbal

Administration: Individually by teacher or trained paraprofessional in 30 to 45 minutes. Specialists are recommended for the vision, hearing, and speech and language subtests.

Scoring: Easy to moderately difficult

Description: This screening test samples cognitive-verbal, fine motor, gross motor, speech, language, social-affective, hearing, and visual development.

Scores: The following three-part system is used to rate the items: pass, evaluate, and refer or rescreen.

Other Considerations: Children are screened individually at different stations. Parents' opinions are considered.

Cooperative Preschool Inventory

Authors: B. Caldwell and J. Freund

Publisher: Macmillan/McGraw-Hill, 2500 Garden Road, Monterey, CA 93940

Ages: 3 years to 6 1/2 years

Required Responses: Verbal

Administration: Individually by teacher in 15 minutes

Scoring: Easy

Description: This test was developed to assess readiness in a variety of basic skills important to school success. The 64 items cover four areas: personal-social relationships, associative vocabulary, concepts-numerical, and concepts-sensory.

Scores: Age percentile norms for the total score

Other Considerations: Directions are verbal and can be given in English or Spanish. Subtests are not individually normed, but teachers can refer to them in informally assessing strengths and weaknesses.

Denver Developmental Screening Test-Revised

Authors: W. K. Frankenburg and J. B. Dodds

Publisher: Denver Developmental Materials, P.O. Box 6190, Denver, CO 80006-0919

Ages: 1 month to 6 years

Required Responses: Verbal and nonverbal

Administration: Individually by teacher or trained paraprofessional in 15 to 20 minutes

Scoring: Easy

Description: This screening test includes items in personal-social, fine motor-adaptive, language, and gross motor development.

Scores: Items are scored as passed or not passed. Developmental levels are obtained.

Other Considerations: The forms and manual have been translated into Spanish.

Detroit Tests of Learning Aptitude—Primary

Authors: D. D. Hammill and B. R. Bryant

Publisher: Pro-Ed, 8700 Shoal Creek Boulevard, Austin, TX 78758-9965

Ages: 3 years to 9 years

Required Responses: Verbal and nonverbal

Administration: Individually by a trained examiner in 15 to 45 minutes

Scoring: Moderately difficult

Description: Contains 130 items arranged in developmental order and divided into linguistic, cognitive, attentional, and motor domains. Contrasts can be made between verbal and nonverbal peformance in each domain.

Scores: Standard scores and percentiles

Other Considerations: Its major purpose is to acquire an estimate of general aptitude. The manual is complete and offers the caution that tests do not diagnose.

Developmental Activities Screening Inventory-II (DASI-II)

Authors: R. R. Fewell and M. B. Langley

Publisher: Pro-Ed, 8700 Shoal Creek Boulevard, Austin TX 78758-9965

Ages: Birth to 5 years

Required Responses: Nonverbal

Administration: Individually by teacher in one or two settings. Instructions may be given either visually or verbally.

Scoring: Easy

Description: The 67 test items assess fine motor control, cause-effect relationships, associations, number concepts, size discriminations, and sequencing.

Scores: Developmental level and quotient

Other Considerations: Tasks can be adapted for use with children who have visual impairments. Simple remedial programs are suggested in the test manual. Has been used successfully with children who have multiple disabilities.

Developmental Indicators for the Assessment of Learning (DIAL-R)

Authors: C. Mardell-Czudnowski and D. Goldenberg

Publisher: American Guidance Service, Inc., P.O. Box 99, Circle Pines, MN 55014-9989

Ages: 2 years to 6 years

Required Responses: Verbal and nonverbal

Administration: Individually by teacher or trained paraprofessional in 25 to 30 minutes

Scoring: Easy

Description: Areas within this revised prekindergarten screening test include gross motor, fine motor, concepts, communication, and social and emotional development.

Scores: Percentile ranks and standard scores

Other Considerations: Strengths and weaknesses can be recorded on a profile sheet. It is necessary to be cautious when scoring the articulation items.

Developmental Profile II

Authors: G. Alpern, T. J. Boll, and M. S. Shearer

Publisher: Western Psychological Services, 12031 Wilshire Boulevard, Los Angeles, CA 90025

Ages: Birth to 9 1/2 years

Required Responses: Rater responses

Administration: Individually rated from direct observation or interview of parents in 20 to 40 minutes

Scoring: Easy

Description: This test is designed to screen quickly for competencies in physical, self-help, social, academic, and communication development.

Scores: Age norms

Other Considerations: Allows for administration, scoring, and interpretation by people without specific training in psychological testing.

Developmental Programming for Infants and Young Children

Authors: S. J. Rogers and D. B. D'Eugenio

Publisher: The University of Michigan Press, 615 E. University, Ann Arbor, MI 48109

Ages: Birth to 35 months

Required Responses: Verbal and nonverbal

Administration: Individually by multidisciplinary team

Scoring: Easy

Description: The purpose of this test is to provide descriptive data in the areas of perception/fine motor, cognitive, language, social/emotional, self-care, and gross motor development.

Scores: Yields a visual portrayal of strengths and weaknesses in the general developmental pattern

Other Considerations: Included is a program providing short-term behavioral objectives that form the basis of daily activities designed to facilitate emerging skills. Caregivers are encouraged to be present during assessment.

Developmental Test of Motor Integration

Authors: K. Beery and N. Buktenica

Publisher: Western Psychological Services, 12031 Wilshire Boulevard, Los Angeles, CA 90025

Ages: 3 years to 8 years

Required Responses: Nonverbal (copying)

Administration: Individually or in small groups in approximately 10 minutes by a teacher, diagnostician, or trained paraprofessional

Scoring: Relatively easy

Description: This test consists of a series of geometric shapes to be copied by the child.

Scores: Age-equivalent scores, standard scores, and percentiles

Other Considerations: Whereas the scoring is relatively easy, trained observers are needed to interpret the results. The child must be able to understand and follow oral or pantomimed directions.

Early-LAP: The Early Learning Accomplishment Profile

Authors: E. M. Glover, J. Preminger, and A. Sanford

Publisher: Kaplan School Supply Corporation, P. O. Box 609, Lewisville, NC 27023

Ages: Birth to 36 months

Required Responses: Nonverbal and verbal

Administration: Individually by teacher or trained paraprofessional

Scoring: Easy

Description: This is a revised version of the Learning Accomplishment Profile for infants. It is a developmental checklist for assessing behaviors in gross motor, cognitive, fine motor, language, self-help, and social-emotional growth.

Other Considerations: The checklist format generates appropriate instructional objectives and task analysis programming.

Early Screening Profiles

Authors: P. Harrison, A. Kaufman, N. Kaufman,

R. Bruininks, J. Rynders, S. Ilmer, S. Sparrow, D. Cicchetti, and G. McCloskey

Publisher: American Guidance Service, Publishers' Building, Circle Pines, MN 55014-1796

Ages: 2 years to 6 years

Required Responses: Verbal and nonverbal

Administration: Individually by teachers or trained paraprofessionals in 30 to 40 minutes

Scoring: Easy

Description: Cognitive/language, motor, and self-help/social profiles are developed and supplemented by articulation, behavior, health history, and home surveys. Separate cognitive and language subscales allow assessment of children who are nonverbal or non-English-speaking.

Scores: Standard scores, percentile ranks, and age equivalents

Other Considerations: Items are similar to those on the Kaufman Assessment Battery for Children, the Bruininks-Oseretsky Test of Motor Proficiency, and the Vineland Adaptive Behavior Scales.

Gesell Developmental Schedules

Authors: H. Knobloch and B. Pasamanick (Eds.)

Publisher: Harper and Row, 2350 Virginia Avenue, Hagerstown, MD 21740

Ages: 4 weeks to 5 years

Required Responses: Verbal and nonverbal

Administration: Individually by trained diagnosticians in 30 minutes

Scoring: Moderately difficult

Description: Administers a broad array of items including copying figures; naming body parts; following commands; matching forms; naming animals; and writing name, address, and numbers.

Scores: Developmental age and developmental quotient

Other Considerations: Reliability appears to depend on the clinical training and experience of examiners.

Hawaii Early Learning Profile—HELP

Authors: S. Furuho, K. O'Reilly, T. Inatsuka, C. Hosaka, T. Allman, and B. Zeisloft-Falbey

Publisher: VORT Corporation, P.O. Box 60880, Palo Alto, CA 94306

Ages: Birth to 3 years

Required Responses: Verbal and nonverbal

Administration: Observations made and recorded by an individual or a team with the assistance of parents

Scoring: Easy

Description: The comprehensive checklist covers over 650 skills in cognition (with receptive language), language, fine motor, gross motor, social, and self-help areas.

Scores: Skills are noted as + if observed, R if reported by parent, − if not observed, or E if emerging.

Other Considerations: Scores are converted to charts to provide a visual picture of each child's abilities.

Help for Special Preschoolers

Authors: Santa Cruz County Office of Education

Publisher: VORT Corporation, P.O. Box 60880, Palo Alto, CA 94306

Ages: 3 to 6 years

Required Responses: Verbal and nonverbal

Administration: Observations made and recorded by individuals or teams of professionals and parents

Scoring: Easy

Description: This comprehensive checklist covers over 600 skills in self-help, motor development, communication/language, social, and learning/cognitive areas.

Scores: Skills are noted as + if mastered, − if not observed, E if emerging, and L if not observed or not fully mastered due to physical limitations

Other Considerations: Skills are developmentally sequenced with age ranges provided. This tool is useful for identifying IEP objectives and resources.

Learning Accomplishment Profile

Author: A. Sanford

Publisher: Kaplan School Supply Corporation, P.O. Box 609, Lewisville, NC 27023

Ages: Up to 6 years

Required Responses: Nonverbal and verbal

Administration: Individually by teacher or trained paraprofessional

Scoring: Easy

Description: This checklist is designed to assist in the development of individualized instructional plans. Areas assessed include language, cognition, self-help, gross motor, and fine motor skills.

Scores: Rate of development equal to developmental age divided by chronological age

Other Considerations: Since this is a checklist, data on reliability and validity were not reported.

McCarthy Scales of Children's Abilities

Author: D. McCarthy

Publisher: The Psychological Corporation, 555 Academic Court, San Antonio, TX 78204-2498

Ages: 2 years to 8 years

Required Responses: Verbal and nonverbal

Administration: Individually administered by a trained examiner in approximately 1 hour

Scoring: Moderately difficult

Description: This norm-referenced test contains six scales: verbal, quantitative, perceptual-performance, general cognitive, memory, and motor development. Determines strengths, weaknesses, and a general level of cognitive functioning.

Scores: Scaled scores yielding a General Cognitive Index (GCI)

Other Considerations: The term *IQ* is carefully avoided. Contents are said to be useful with children of both sexes from various ethnic, regional, and socioeconomic groups.

Motor Free Visual Perception Test

Authors: R. P. Colarusso and D. D. Hammill

Publisher: Academic Therapy Publications, 20 Commercial Boulevard, Novato, CA 94949-6191

Ages: 4 years to 8 years

Required Responses: Nonverbal (pointing)

Administration: Individually by teacher or trained paraprofessional in 10 minutes

Scoring: Easy

Description: This test consists of 36 items in the following areas: spatial relationships, visual discrimination, figure-ground, visual closure, and visual memory.

Scores: Perceptual ages and perceptual quotients

Other Considerations: To perform on this test, the child must understand the concepts of "same" and "different." It is useful to assess visual and perceptual abilities without involving significant motor responses.

Peabody Picture Vocabulary Test-Revised (PPVT-R)

Authors: L. M. Dunn and L. M. Dunn

Publisher: American Guidance Service, Publishers' Building, Circle Pines, MN 55014-1796

Ages: 2 years to adult

Required Responses: Nonverbal

Administration: Individually by teachers in 10 to 20 minutes.

Scoring: Easy

Description: This test requires the child to hear a cue word and to point to the one picture out of four that corresponds best to the perceived word. It is a test of hearing vocabulary and receptive language.

Scores: Percentile ranks, age equivalents, and stanines

Other Considerations: A child must have adequate hearing, sight, some degree of motor coordination, and understanding of standard English to respond appropriately. Caution is urged in using this test to measure more than receptive language.

The Portage Guide to Early Education

Authors: Portage Preschool Project

Publisher: CESA 12, Box 564, Portage, WI 53901

Ages: Up to 6 years

Required Responses: Nonverbal and verbal

Administration: Individually by teacher or trained paraprofessional in approximately 30 minutes

Scoring: Easy

Description: This criterion-referenced checklist assesses behaviors in five developmental areas: cognitive, self-help, motor, language, and socialization.

Scores: Developmental levels in years

Other Considerations: This checklist combines items from a number of developmental scales and originated as part of the Portage Project, a home-based early intervention program. Each skill is referenced to a card that describes how to teach the skill assessed.

Psychoeducational Evaluation of the Preschool Child

Authors: E. Jedrysek, Z. Klapper, L. Pope, and J. Wortis

Publisher: Grune and Stratton, 111 Fifth Avenue, New York, NY 10003

Ages: 3 years to 6 years

Required Responses: Verbal and nonverbal

Administration: Individually by teacher in one setting or a number of settings

Scoring: Easy

Description: The five skill areas that include physical functioning and sensory status, perceptual functioning, competence in short-term retention, language skills, and cognitive functioning are arranged in developmental sequence. Emphasis is placed on how a child functions.

Scores: Age and grade norms

Other Considerations: This instrument is intended to supplement more formal test results. The purpose of this technique is to provide information to be used in formulating teaching goals. Probes are allowed to encourage modification of test items to obtain the most data possible.

Screening Children for Related Early Educational Needs (SCREEN)

Authors: W. Hresko, D. K. Reid, D. Hammill, H. Ginsburg, and A. Baroody

Publisher: Pro-Ed, 8700 Shoal Creek Boulevard, Austin, TX 78758-6897

Ages: 3 to 7 years

Required Responses: Verbal and nonverbal

Administration: Individually by or under the supervision of an experienced test administrator

Scoring: Relatively easy

Description: The SCREEN is comprised of highly discriminating items from the Test of Early Language Development (TELD), Test of Early Reading Ability (TERA), Test of Early Written Language (TEWL), and the Test of Early Mathematics Ability (TEMA).

Scores: Percentiles, Overall Early Achievement Quotient, and Component Quotients in language, reading, writing, and math

Other Considerations: SCREEN was standardized on 1,355 children from 20 states. Suggestions are given for "testing the limits" on some items.

Uzgiris-Hunt Ordinal Scales of Psychological Development

Authors: I. Uzgiris and J. M. Hunt

Publisher: University of Illinois Press, 54 East Gregory Drive, Urbana, IL 61820

Ages: 2 weeks to 2 years

Required Responses: Verbal and nonverbal

Administration: Individually by trained examiner in several sessions

Description: These criterion-referenced scales cover tasks equivalent to Piaget's sensorimotor stage. They relate to the following six areas: visual pursuit and performance, eliciting desired environmental events, vocal and gestural imitation, operational causality, object relations in space, and schemes for relating to objects.

Other Considerations: Assistance in interpretation may be obtained from C. J. Dunst. (1980). *A clinical and educational manual for use with the Uzgiris and Hunt scales of infant psychological development.* Baltimore, MD: University Park Press.

Vineland Adaptive Behavior Scales

Authors: S. Sparrow, D. Balla, and D. Cicchetti

Publisher: American Guidance Service, Publishers' Building, Circle Pines, MN 55014-1796

Ages: Birth to 18 years

Required Responses: Rater responses

Administration: Individually rated through interview with caregivers in 20 to 60 minutes

Scoring: Moderately difficult

Description: Factual information assessing an individual's level of maturity in communication, daily living skills, socialization, and motor skills is sought by individuals trained in interviewing techniques.

Scores: Standard scores, percentile ranks, stanines, age equivalents, and adaptive levels

Other Considerations: Booklets and report forms are available in Spanish.

Individual Materials for Use with Young Children: A Sampling

Authors' Note: The following chart lists a sampling of individual instructional materials that are useful in early childhood classrooms. The methods of using these materials are dependent on the philosophy and goals of each program and on the individual characteristics of children who are enrolled. The skills listed represent target behaviors within many programs, although they may not merit universal agreement. We have made no attempt to provide an exhaustive list of either skills or materials; we simply list resource ideas. They are provided to stimulate imagination and further analysis of available materials.

	Sensorimotor Development									Perceptual Efficiency					
	Balance	Body Awareness	Coordination	Controlled Movement	Fine Motor Dexterity	Laterality	Sensory Awareness	Self-Help Skills	Visual-Motor Integration	Attention and Concentration	Directionality	Visual Discrimination	Visual Memory	Visualization	Spatial Relationships
Abacus					X	X			X				X		X
Association picture cards															
Attribute blocks									X			X	X		X
Balls			X	X					X						
Beads			X		X	X			X			X	X		X
Bean bags		X	X	X		X			X	X	X				X
Blocks			X	X	X				X		X		X		X
Books		X			X	X	X			X		X	X	X	
Bowling set			X	X					X	X	X				X
Cars and trucks			X	X					X		X				X
Chalkboard			X	X	X	X			X	X	X		X	X	X
Clay (Playdoh)		X	X	X	X		X	X	X						X
Climbing equipment	X	X	X	X		X	X		X		X				X
Color cubes			X	X	X	X			X		X	X	X	X	X
Crayons			X	X	X	X			X		X				
Dolls		X				X	X	X	X					X	
Dominoes			X	X	X	X			X		X				X
Dressing frames		X	X	X	X	X		X	X	X	X				X
Dress-up clothes		X	X		X	X	X	X	X					X	
Easel and paints			X	X	X	X	X		X			X		X	X

	Communication					Cognition and Academic Readiness								Social and Emotional Development					
	Auditory Memory	Comprehension	Nonverbal Expression	Verbal Facility	Vocabulary	Academic Readiness	Association	Classification	Creativity	Part-to-Whole Relationships	Problem Solving	Serialization	Quantitative Skills	Cooperation	Imitation	Self-Control	Self-Expression	Self-Esteem	Understanding Feelings
													X						
		X			X		X	X		X			X						
		X			X	X	X	X			X		X	X					
														X	X	X			
	X					X		X			X	X	X						
														X		X			
			X			X			X	X	X	X	X	X	X	X	X		
		X			X		X	X					X						X
			X	X			X	X	X			X	X	X	X	X	X		
			X			X				X			X	X	X	X	X	X	
			X							X			X	X	X	X	X		
			X	X		X								X	X	X			X
	X	X				X		X				X	X	X	X	X	X		
		X		X		X			X				X	X	X		X	X	X
		X		X									X	X	X		X	X	X
						X			X		X	X	X	X				X	
			X				X	X						X	X		X	X	X
			X				X	X								X	X	X	X

	Sensorimotor Development									Perceptual Efficiency					
	Balance	Body Awareness	Coordination	Controlled Movement	Fine Motor Dexterity	Laterality	Sensory Awareness	Self-Help Skills	Visual-Motor Integration	Attention and Concentration	Directionality	Visual Discrimination	Visual Memory	Visualization	Spatial Relationships
Etch-a-Sketch			X	X	X	X			X	X	X			X	X
Farm animals												X			
Flannel and felt board				X		X			X	X	X	X	X	X	X
Form board						X			X		X		X		X
Geo boards			X	X	X	X			X		X			X	X
Housekeeping equipment		X			X		X	X	X					X	
Hula Hoops	X	X	X	X		X	X		X		X				
Knob boards					X				X				X		
Lacing boards			X	X	X	X		X	X		X			X	X
Legos			X	X	X				X					X	X
Lotto						X			X	X			X	X	
Magic Markers			X	X	X	X			X		X			X	X
Magnetic board				X	X	X			X		X	X	X	X	X
Match-ups					X				X	X		X		X	
Mirrors		X				X	X	X			X	X	X		X
Musical instruments		X	X	X			X		X	X					
Nesting toys			X	X	X				X			X		X	
Parquetry			X	X	X				X			X	X	X	X
Peg boards			X	X	X	X			X		X		X	X	X
Photographs		X						X					X	X	
Pictures		X								X		X	X	X	
Play store					X			X	X			X	X		
Punching clown				X					X		X				X
Puppets															
Puzzles		X							X	X		X	X	X	X
Records		X		X			X			X	X				
Sandbox				X	X		X	X	X						
Science equipment					X		X		X	X		X	X	X	X
Scissors			X	X	X	X		X	X	X					
Sequence cards					X	X			X			X	X	X	
Shape sorting toys			X	X	X				X			X			X
Sound boxes							X								
Tactile surfaces							X					X	X		
Telephones		X					X	X		X					
Tunnel	X	X		X		X	X		X		X				X
Unifix cubes				X	X	X			X			X	X		X
Water play toys		X			X		X	X	X						
Wheeled toys	X	X	X	X					X						
Work bench		X	X	X	X	X		X	X	X				X	X
Zoo animals									X					X	

	Communication					Cognition and Academic Readiness								Social and Emotional Development					
	Auditory Memory	Comprehension	Nonverbal Expression	Verbal Facility	Vocabulary	Academic Readiness	Association	Classification	Creativity	Part-to-Whole Relationships	Problem Solving	Serialization	Quantitative Skills	Cooperation	Imitation	Self-Control	Self-Expression	Self-Esteem	Understanding Feelings
			X						X	X				X		X			
			X	X			X	X	X			X					X		
			X	X	X	X	X	X	X	X		X	X				X		
							X	X			X	X							
						X				X			X						
			X	X			X	X	X			X	X	X	X	X	X	X	
														X			X	X	
												X	X						
									X					X		X			
									X					X					
	X	X			X	X	X	X											
			X						X	X				X	X	X	X	X	
			X				X	X	X	X		X	X	X			X		
				X		X	X	X		X	X		X						
							X								X		X	X	X
	X	X	X	X			X		X			X		X	X	X	X		
						X				X	X	X							
						X	X			X	X								
						X	X		X	X		X	X	X	X				
				X	X		X					X	X	X	X		X	X	X
		X		X	X	X	X	X		X		X							X
			X						X				X		X	X	X		X
				X					X					X	X	X	X		X
	X	X			X		X					X							
			X	X			X	X	X								X		
	X	X			X	X	X	X		X	X	X	X						
		X				X	X	X		X	X	X	X						
				X			X	X				X	X						
	X	X		X			X	X				X							
					X		X	X	X			X					X		X
				X	X									X	X		X		
	X	X				X	X	X					X	X		X			
			X	X					X					X	X	X			
														X		X	X		
									X		X			X	X	X	X		
		X	X	X			X	X	X					X		X	X		

Appendix G

Periodicals Relevant to Early Intervention

Beginnings
P.O. Box 2890
Redmond, WA 98073

Child Care Quarterly
Behavioral Publications
72 Fifth Avenue
New York, NY 10011

Child Development
Society for Research in Child Development
5801 Ellis Avenue
Chicago, IL 60637

Child Education
Evans Brothers Limited
Montague House
Russell Square
London, WCIB 5BX
England

Child Welfare
Child Welfare League of America, Inc.
67 Irving Place
New York, NY 10010

Childhood Education
Association for Childhood Education International
11141 Georgia Avenue, Suite 200
Wheaton, MD 20902

Children in Contemporary Society
Pittsburgh Association for the Education of Young
    Children
P.O. Box 11173
Pittsburgh, PA 15237

Children Today
Department of Health and Human Services
Office of Human Development Services
Washington, DC 20201

Cycles
TADS (Technical Assistance Development System)

625 West Cameron Avenue
Chapel Hill, NC 27514
(Administered by the Bureau of Education for the
    Handicapped)

Day Care and Early Education
Behavioral Publications
72 Fifth Avenue
New York, NY 10011

Early Child Development and Care
Gordon and Breach Science Publishers, Inc.
One Park Avenue
New York, NY 10016

Early Years
Allen Raymond, Inc.
11 Hale Lane, Box 1266
Darien, CT 06820

Educating Children, Early and Middle Years
American Association of
    Elementary-Kindergarten-
    Nursery Educators
1201 16th Street, N.W.
Washington, DC 20036

ERIC-ECE Newsletter
ERIC Clearinghouse on Early Childhood Education
805 West Pennsylvania
Urbana, IL 61801

Exceptional Children
The Council for Exceptional Children
1920 Association Drive
Reston, VA 22091

Infant Mental Health Journal
International Association for Infant Mental Health
4 Conant Square
Brandon, VT 05733

Infants and Young Children
Aspen Publishers, Inc.

7201 McKinney Circle
Frederick, MD 21701

Journal of Child Language
Cambridge University Press
110 Midland Avenue
Port Chester, NY 10573

Journal of Early Intervention
Division for Early Childhood
The Council for Exceptional Children
1920 Association Drive
Reston, VA 22091

Journal of Speech and Hearing Disorders
American Speech-Language, Hearing Association
10801 Rockville Pike
Rockville, MD 20852-6897

Journal of Speech and Hearing Research
American Speech-Language, Hearing Association
10801 Rockville Pike
Rockville, MD 20852-3279

Merrill-Palmer Quarterly
Wayne State University Press
5959 Woodward Avenue
Detroit, MI 48202

Parent Cooperative Preschools International
Journal Editorial and Publication Office
9111 Alton Parkway
Silver Spring, MD 20910

P.E.N. Preschool Education Newsletter
Multi Media Education, Inc.
11 West 42nd Street
New York, NY 10036

Report of Pre-school Education
Capitol Publications, Inc.
2430 Pennsylvania Avenue, N.W.
Washington, DC 20037

Teaching Exceptional Children
The Council for Exceptional Children
1920 Association Drive
Reston, VA 22091

The Exceptional Parent
296 Boylston Street, 3rd floor
Boston, MA 02116

The Volta Review
The Alexander Graham Bell Association for the
   Deaf, Inc.
2000 14th Street North, Suite 380
Arlington, VA 22201-2500

Topics in Early Childhood Special Education
Pro-Ed
8700 Shoal Creek Boulevard
Austin, TX 78758-6897

Topics in Language Disorders
Pro-Ed
8700 Shoal Creek Boulevard
Austin, TX 78758-6897

Young Children
National Association for the Education of Young
   Children
1834 Connecticut Avenue, N.W.
Washington, DC 20009-5786

Zero to Three
National Center for Clinical Infant Programs
733 15th Street., N.W., Suite 912
Washington, DC 20005

Glossary

abduction: Movement of a limb outward (away) from the body.

acquired immune deficiency syndrome (AIDS): A communicable disease that reduces the body's ability to fight some types of infection.

acuity: Degree to which one is able to hear sounds and see visual images.

adapt: To change or modify while retaining the basic model.

adaptive equipment: Any device that is modified to enhance the independence of the user.

adduction: Movement of a limb inward (toward) the body.

advocate: One who acts on behalf of another.

affective: Pertaining to emotion, feeling, or attitude.

anecdotal record: A factual account of a child's behavior.

anomaly: Abnormality.

anoxia: The lack of oxygen.

arena assessment: The process of one professional conducting assessment while other team members, including the family, observe and contribute.

arthritis: Inflammation of a joint or joints.

articulation: The manner in which speech sounds are produced.

assessment: Either a test or an observation that determines a child's strengths or weaknesses in a particular area of development.

association: The process of relating one concept to another.

asthma: A complicated pulmonary symptom characterized by obstruction, labored breathing, and wheezing.

asymmetrical: Unequal; lack of similarity in form between two sides of the body.

ataxic: Unbalanced and jerky.

athetoid: Moving uncontrollably and continuously.

atrophy: Wasting away or diminution in size.

atypical: Not typical. Different from the norm or average.

audiologist: A trained professional who measures hearing acuity, diagnoses hearing impairments, and assists in planning for remediation, including hearing aids and educational adaptations.

auditory discrimination: The ability to distinguish one sound from another.

auditory memory: The ability to retain and recall what has been heard.

behavior modification: Systematic, consistent efforts to change an individual's behavior. Carefully planned consequences for specific behaviors are designed to help a learner develop new and more appropriate responses to situations and experiences.

behavioral objective (also referred to as performance objective): Identifies exactly what the teacher will do, provide, or restrict; describes the learner's observable behavior; and defines how well the learner must perform.

bilateral: Both sides.

biological risk: Insult to bodily systems that makes normal development problematic.

body awareness (image): Awareness of one's own body and its position in time and space.

case management: Assumption of responsibility for coordinating services for a family and ensuring that individual family service plans are written and carried out.

categorical placement: Placement of children according to classification of their suspected disabilities. Classrooms that are categorical usually group children according to disability labels, for example, classes for children who have learning disabilities or emotional disturbance.

catheter: Small, flexible tube inserted into a body channel to distend or maintain an opening to an internal cavity.

cerebral palsy: Disorder of posture, muscle tone, and movement resulting from brain damage.

child-find: The process of finding and identifying children with special needs.

choreoathetosis: Type of cerebral palsy in which there are uncontrolled muscle movements in all four limbs of the body and sometimes in the face.

chronological age (CA): A child's actual age in years and months.

classification: Distinguishing characteristics of things, then sorting, matching, or otherwise grouping them.

cognition: Analytical, logical acts of mental behavior that result in the act of knowing.

collaboration: Laboring together. Working side by side with mutual respect and cooperation to complete a task.

concepts: Mental images or ideas.

confidentiality: Records and other information about children must not be shown to anyone other than those who have been approved to have the information. Parental consent in writing must be obtained before information can be released to other individuals or facilities.

congenital: Presumed to be present at birth.

contracture: Permanently tight muscles and joints.

coordination: Harmonious functioning of muscles or groups of muscles in movement.

corrected age (of infants): Calculated by subtracting the number of weeks of prematurity from the chronological age.

correlation: The relationship between factors.

The Council for Exceptional Children (CEC): A national professional organization for anyone working for and with gifted children and children with disabilities.

criterion: A norm or standard for a behavior or item.

criterion-referenced tests: Tests or observations that compare a child's performance on a particular task to a standard established for that specific task. Such tests identify what a child can and cannot do.

cross-categorical program: A program designed to serve children who have differing disabling conditions.

curriculum: All of the specific features of a master teaching plan that have been chosen by a particular teacher for his or her classroom. Curricula may vary widely from school to school, but each curriculum reflects the skills, tasks, and behaviors that a school has decided are important for children to acquire.

custodial care: Usually refers to the constant supervision and care of bodily needs provided in institutional settings.

cystic fibrosis: A chronic disorder often causing respiratory and digestive problems.

decibel: Unit used to measure hearing intensity or loudness.

decoding: The act of deciphering or obtaining meaning from what is seen or heard.

developmental curriculum checklist: A checklist of behavior often prepared by choosing items from standardized tests or scales. Duplicate items are deleted and those remaining are arranged in a developmental sequence. The checklist is then used as a guide in designing curriculum and in providing a record of individual children's progress through the curriculum.

developmental delay: Classification for children with or without established diagnosis who perform significantly behind developmental norms.

developmentally disabled (delayed): Persons who have an identifiable delay in mental or physical development compared with established norms are referred to in this way, rather than as "impaired" or "retarded."

diabetes mellitus: A metabolic disorder related to insufficient insulin.

diagnosis: A diagnosis is an effort to find the cause of a problem by observing the child and considering the results of tests.

diplegia: Condition of cerebral palsy with major involvement of the legs and minor involvement of the arms.

directionality: The ability to know right from left, up from down, forward from backward, and other directional orientation.

discrimination: The ability to differentiate among similar stimuli.

divergent thinking: Thinking that is unusual, different, and searching.

dystrophy: Weakness and degeneration of muscle.

early intervention: Services for children (and families) from birth to school age.

echolalia: A habit of repeating (without meaning), or "echoing," what is said by others.

eclecticism: Method or practice of selecting what seems best from various systems or programs.

efficacy: Positive effects or impact of a program, strategy, or procedure.

emerging skills: As children learn, they may use a new skill some, but not all of the time. A skill observed at least some of the time is said to be emerging.

encoding: The act of expressing oneself in words or gestures.

en-route behaviors: Tasks to be mastered or behaviors to be demonstrated as the child moves from one level of functioning (entry behavior) to a designated goal or objective (terminal behavior).

entry behavior: The level of functioning or behavior already acquired before beginning a series of tasks.

environment: Everything the child encounters. The rooms, furniture, toys, the opportunity to experience new and different places, and the behaviors of those around the child constitute the environment.

environmental risk conditions: The presence of factors in the family or community that lead to experiences that may result in developmental delay.

epilepsy: A brain disorder frequently resulting in seizure activity that may be very mild or severe enough to cause loss of consciousness.

equivalent practice: To prevent boredom in repetition, the teacher provides equivalent practice by offering a variety of materials and activities that are designed to develop the same skill. The task must also be at the same level of difficulty and provide the same kind of practice to be equivalent.

established risk condition: The presence of a diagnosed physical or medical condition that is likely to lead to developmental delay.

etiology: The study of the causes of diseases or disabilities.

evaluation: The process of making value judgments based on behavioral information about the effectiveness of a program in meeting the needs of children enrolled.

eversion: Turning out.

expansion: Adults expand a child's utterance by stating the child's idea in a longer phrase or sentence.

expressive language: What is said or written to communicate an idea or a question.

extension: Straightening of trunk and limbs of body.

family-focused early intervention: Concentrating intervention equally on the child's family and on the child.

family systems perspective: The family is viewed as an interactive unit; what affects one member affects all.

feedback: The receipt of knowledge of results (the effect) of one's own behavior.

figure-ground discrimination: The ability to attend to one aspect of a visual or auditory field while relegating other aspects of the environment to the background.

fine motor skills: Activities with the fingers and hands.

First Chance programs: Preschool programs for children with disabilities funded by the Bureau of Education for the Handicapped.

flexion: Bending of elbows, hips, knees, etc.

floppy: Loose or weak posture and movements.

Free appropriate public education (FAPE): Designed by Public Law 94-142 to mean special education and related services provided at public expense. Such services are to be described in the individualized education program, appropriate to the child's individual needs, and meet requirements of the state agency.

functional skills: Skills that will be immediately useful to the child and that will be used relatively frequently in the child's typical environment.

genetic: Having to do with the principles of heredity.

goals: The general statement on the individualized education program that states what teaching is expected to accomplish, for example, "To improve Johnny's fine motor skills."

grammar: The linguistic rules of language.

gross motor skills: Activities such as running, climbing, throwing, and jumping that use large muscles.

hemiplegia: Condition of cerebral palsy with major involvement of one side of the body.

high risk signals: Those signs that when observed in very young children have been known to be predictive of more than normal likelihood of future disabilities or developmental delays.

hydrocephalus: Congenital condition in which the accumulation of the fluid in the brain causes enlargement of the skull.

hyperactivity: Exceedingly active behavior not typical of most children.

hypertonicity: Condition in which muscles are stretched and constantly excited.

hypoactivity: Opposite of hyperactivity; lethargy.

hypotonicity: Condition in which muscles are limp and do not exhibit resistance to stretching.

identification: The process of finding and screening individuals to determine whether they might benefit from specialized services.

individualize: Match a teaching task to the capacity of the particular individual being taught.

Individualized education program (IEP): A written plan that states a child's present level of functioning; specific areas that need special services; annual goals; short-term objectives; services to be provided; and the method of evaluation to be implemented. An individualized education program is required for every child receiving services while Public Law 94-142 is in effect.

innate: Inherent within an individual.

inner language: The language in which thinking occurs. The process of internalizing and organizing experiences that can be expressed by symbols.

instructional objectives: These define specific accomplishments to be achieved. See "Behavioral objectives."

integration: Education of children with disabilities together with their nondisabled classmates to the maximum extent appropriate.

interdisciplinary approach: Professionals from different disciplines work together to assess and provide intervention based on mutual decision making.

interindividual differences: Differences between individuals.

intraindividual differences: Differences in performance within one child on different factors or on the same factor at different times.

inversion: Turning in.

involuntary movements: Unintended movements.

labeling: Giving a categorical term (label) to a disabling condition and to those who exhibit such a condition; for example, "emotionally disturbed" or "mentally retarded."

laterality: Awareness of sidedness; left and right of the body.

least restrictive environment: This is a concept inherent in Public Law 94-142 that requires children with disabilities to be educated with nondisabled peers in regular educational settings to the maximum extent appropriate.

litigation: The act or process of contesting by law through lawsuits.

locomotor: Pertaining to movement from one location to another.

mainstreaming: The practice of placing children with special needs in regular classrooms whenever appropriate.

mental age: Level of mental functioning. A child with a mental age (MA) of 4-0 is thought to be mentally functioning like a 4 year old.

modality: The pathways through which an individual receives information and thereby learns. Some individuals are thought to learn more quickly through one modality than another; for example, some process auditory information more efficiently than visual information and would thus be classified as auditory learners.

modeling: Providing a demonstration of an expected behavior.

multidisciplinary approach: Individuals from different disciplines carry out evaluations, and intervention may be offered with little opportunity for professional interaction or integrated planning.

multiple sclerosis: A progressive central nervous system disease affecting motor control.

multisensory learning: A technique to facilitate learning that employs a combination of sense modalities at the same time.

muscular dystrophy: A central nervous system disease that affects skeletal and respiratory functions.

neurological examination: An examination of sensory or motor responses to determine whether there are impairments of the nervous system.

noncategorical: Grouping children together without labeling or categorizing according to suspected disabilities.

nonlocomotor: Lack of movement from one place to another.

nonverbal ability: Having skill to perform a task that does not involve using words.

norm-referenced tests: These are tests that report a particular child's performance in relation to other children of the same chronological age. Such tests are highly standardized and usually do not include individuals with disabling conditions in the normative sample against which behavior is being compared.

norms: A sample of a large number of people's behavior against which a particular behavior can be compared.

observable behavior: Behavior that can be seen, heard, or felt.

occupational therapy: Treatment given to improve movement for daily living.

ocular pursuit: Following an object with the eye.

olfactory: Pertaining to the sense of smell.

opthalmologist: A physician trained in the diagnosis and treatment of diseases of the eyes.

optometrist: A vision specialist trained to measure refraction and prescribe glasses but not licensed to treat eye diseases.

otitis media: Inflammation of the middle ear; a common infection.

otologist: A physician trained to treat problems of the ear.

parallel talk: Parents of young children often talk about what their children are doing as it is happening. Their "talk" occurs parallel to what the child is doing. This practice appears to help young children learn language.

paraplegia: Paralysis of both legs.

paraprofessional: A trained assistant to a professional teacher, often referred to as a teacher aide.

pediatrician: A physician whose specialty is working with and treating infants and young children.

percentile rank: The percentage of persons in a normal distribution who score below a particular point.

perception: The process of interpreting what is received by the five senses.

perceptual-motor: The interaction of various channels of perception with motor activity, for example, the act of kicking is a perceptual-motor interaction between sight and gross motor responses.

performance objectives: See "Behavioral objectives."

perinatal: Around the time of birth.

perseveration: Continuous repetition of the same action characterized by the inability to shift readily from one activity to another.

physiotherapy: Treatment of disorders of movement.

pincer grasp: Coordination of index finger and thumb.

positioning: Placing a child in certain postures in order to promote symmetrical body alignment, normalize muscle tone, and promote functional skills.

post-ictal sleep: The sleep that occurs naturally after seizures.

pragmatics: The use of language in social contexts, including how language is used for communication.

prognosis: A forecast of the probable course of disease or illness.

prompting: Using cues and partial cues to build desired behavior. Verbal prompting often involves saying a single sound or word to help a child remember what to say or do. Physical prompting that involves physical assistance or touch can be helpful to initiate a motor or self-help skill. Prompts should be reduced gradually (faded) until they can be eliminated.

pronation: Turning of the palm downward or backward.

prone: Lying on the stomach.

prosthesis: Artificial device used to replace a missing body part.

psycholinguistics: The field of study that combines psychology and linguistics to create an understanding of the total language process.

quadraplegia: Condition of cerebral palsy with major involvement of arms and legs.

rapport: A harmonious relationship. When working with a child, establishing rapport involves developing a climate or atmosphere in which the child feels comfortable enough to perform as well as possible.

receptive language: The ability to understand the intent and meaning of someone's effort to communicate.

reflexes: Postures and movements completely out of the child's control.

reinforcer: An event or consequence (reward) that increases the likelihood of a behavior being repeated. May be concrete or social.

reliability: Extent to which a test measures a given performance consistently. The degree to which it is dependable, stable, and relatively free from errors of measurement.

remission: Period during which the symptoms of a condition disappear for an unpredictable period of time.

residual hearing: Auditory acuity of an individual after an impairment without amplification.

respite care: Child care arrangements that permit parents and/or families to have time out from caring for a child with disabilities.

retarded: Traditionally this term was used to describe any individual who was slow to learn or difficult to teach. The term is not precise and is less often used today. Laws specify that one must correlate test scores, adaptive behavior, and other factors before this term can be used appropriately.

reversal: A transposition of letters.

reverse chaining: To begin teaching with the last step of a task and work backward. Particularly useful with self-help skills.

reverse mainstreaming: Nondisabled children are integrated into classes composed primarily of children with identifiable special needs.

righting: Ability to put in or restore the head and body to a proper position when in an abnormal or uncomfortable position.

rigidity: A type of cerebral palsy characterized by widespread continuous muscle tension. Muscles of the body become very stiff.

role release: The systematic training of other professionals in one's own discipline-specific skills.

schemata: Patterns.

scissor pattern: Body movement in which one leg crosses over the other.

screening: The process of sorting out from a total group children who may have problems. It is often a part of a total program called Child-Find, or Child-Check. The intent is to test all children with specially designed screening instruments to determine those who need further diagnostic testing and to determine if a problem really does exist.

self-fulfilling prophecy: The tendency for individuals to behave in accordance with views they perceive others to have of them.

sensorimotor: The combination of input of sense organs and output of motor activity.

seriation: Ordering according to relative differences.

shaping: A technique of behavior modification in which behaviors that are successive approximations of the target behavior are reinforced until target behavior is acquired.

sickle cell anemia: A hereditary condition in which misshapen blood cells clump together in the blood vessels causing varied symptoms: painful joints, chronic ulcers of the ankles, episodes of abdominal pain, and neurological disturbances.

sorting: Discrimination and separation according to differences.

spasm: Sudden tightening of the muscles.

spasticity: Muscular incoordination resulting from sudden, involuntary contractions of the muscles; a type of cerebral palsy.

spatial relationships: The ability to perceive the position of two or more objects in relation to oneself and in relation to each other.

spina bifida: A disorder of the spinal column that may affect motor coordination and body functions.

standardization: The procedure of having standard directions and scoring so that normative data about others who have taken the test can be used.

standardized tests: Tests that are administered in a

specifically described standard way, scored in a particular way, and then compared with the performance of a standard group.

stanine: A single digit derived score based on the normal curve. It ranges in value from 1 to 9 with a mean of 5.

status epilepticus: Refers to a situation in which a person has two major seizures, one right after the other; signals that an ambulance should be called immediately.

stimuli: Information that can be received by the senses.

stoma: Opening in the abdominal wall, created through surgery, to allow the urine from the kidneys to drain into a collecting bag.

stuttering: A speech impairment evidenced by hesitations, repetitions, or spasms of breathing.

successive approximation: The process of gradually increasing expectations for a child to display behaviors that are more like the desired target behavior; used in shaping behaviors not previously a part of the child's behavior pattern.

supine: Lying on back.

symmetrical: Similarity in form between two sides of the body.

systematic fading: The gradual removal of any support that assists a child's learning.

systemic: Refers to a disease that can exist throughout the body, e.g., arthritis.

tactile: Refers to the sense of touch.

target behavior: The terminal objective or final desired behavior that is the goal of shaping when using behavioral (performance) objectives. This same term, when used in relation to behavior modification, refers to the negative behavior to be changed.

task analysis: Breaking down a difficult task into small steps that lead to doing the difficult task. En-route behaviors are behavioral objectives that state the individual subskills leading toward the terminal objective or the difficult task.

terminal objective: The behavioral objective that a particular teacher has chosen as the highest level of skill he or she intends to strive toward to help a child or children achieve.

tone: Firmness of muscles.

tonic neck reflex: Uncontrollable movement in which turning of the head causes one arm to straighten and stiffen and the other to bend.

total communication: A philosophy involved in teaching individuals with hearing impairments that includes using aural, manual, and oral methods to ensure effective communication.

tracking: Following an object with one's eyes.

transdisciplinary approach: The use of a team approach to services in which team members work across disciplinary boundaries to plan and provide integrated services.

trauma: The condition, physical or mental, that results from shock or a violently produced wound or injury.

tremor: Involuntary vibration in large muscles.

utterance: Something that is said or produced orally. It is not necessary that an utterance be spoken correctly to be counted in the child's mean length of utterance (MLU).

validity: The extent to which an instrument measures what it is supposed to measure or what the test giver needs it to measure.

verbal expression: The ability to express one's ideas verbally.

visual association: The process of relating concepts that have been presented visually.

visual discrimination: The ability to differentiate between and among various shapes, sizes, colors, numbers, and/or letters.

visualization: Imagery; the ability to retrieve a mental image or to produce a mental image.

voluntary muscles: The muscles in the body over which there is conscious control of contraction.

Author Index

Subject Index

About the Authors

Ruth E. Cook is director of the early intervention specialist personnel preparation program at Santa Clara University, California. Dr. Cook received her Ph.D. with an emphasis in developmental psychology and two related M.A. degrees from the University of California at Los Angeles. Her interest in integration of young children with special needs focused while serving as director of the Early Childhood Center at Southern Illinois University at Edwardsville and the Child Development Center at Mount Saint Mary's College in Los Angeles.

Annette Tessier is professor emeritus of special education and director of Centro de Niños y Padres, a model early intervention program on the campus of California State University, Los Angeles. Dr. Tessier received her graduate degrees from the University of California at Los Angeles and has a background in physical therapy and early childhood education.

M. Diane Klein is currently professor of special education at California State University, Los Angeles, and coordinator of training programs in early childhood special education. Dr. Klein received her M.A. in speech-language pathology and audiology from Western Michigan University and her Ph.D. in developmental psychology from Michigan State University. She has worked with young children who have severe disabilities as well as high-risk infants and their families.